The Arrow Closest To The Acorn

An American Woman's Walking Adventure On England's 630-Mile South West Coast Path

Debby Lee Jagerman-Dungan

Dedicated to my husband for his full support, love, and companionship. Dedicated to my mom for her full support, love, and listening to my book. Dedicated to the rest of my family (my dad, my step-mom, my two sisters, my brother-in-law, my niece, and my uncle and aunt) for their full support and love. To my inspirations and friends, Sasha and Simone. To all my friends, as well as people I don't know, who follow my travels. To anyone who may be inspired, even in some small way, by my travels.

The Arrow Closest To The Acorn: An American Woman's Walking Adventure
On England's 630-Mile South West Coast Path

© Copyright 2018 by Debby Lee Jagerman-Dungan

Published by: Windows and Doors Publishing, 2018, Renton, WA
WindowsAndDoorsPublishing@yahoo.com

All rights reserved. This book may not be reproduced in whole or in part, including all photographs, without prior express written permission from the publisher, except for the quotation of brief passages in review; nor may any part of this book be reproduced, stored in a retrieval system, or transmitted in any form or by any means, electronic, mechanical, photocopying, recording, or otherwise, without prior express written permission from the publisher.

ISBN-13: 978-0-9960830-8-9
ISBN-10: 0-9960830-8-1
Library of Congress Control Number: 2018913922

In addition to walking the South West Coast Path, I am an avid traveler who loves walking in the places I visit, as well as taking lots of pictures and writing about my travels. Sauntering the 482-mile Camino de Santiago across northern Spain led to my meandering an additional twenty miles along Spain's Atlantic Coast, the inspiration behind me wandering along England's coast. I have trekked to Laya in Bhutan at 12,500 feet, backpacked the 93-mile Wonderland Trail around Mount Rainier in the state of Washington, ambled 100 miles of the Cotswolds in England, and I am one of the few who has strolled around the perimeter of Île d'Orléans on its 42-mile Chemin Royal near Québec City, Canada. I have journeyed from the Galapagos Islands to Punxsutawney, PA; from Cambodia and Vietnam to at least 25 countries in Europe; from at least 35 states in the United States to Belize, New Zealand, and Australia. Many of my travels have been solo. I enjoy exploring lighthouses anywhere I travel that has a coastline, and I have also created my favorite subject to photograph when I travel - windows and doors - into six travel photography books, which are listed in the bibliography at the end of this book. In addition to all this, I blog about my travels under the name Debby's Departures. This is my first full written book!

General travel blogs by Debby Lee Jagerman-Dungan, as Debby's Departures: DebbysDepartures.com
Specific travel blogs on the South West Coast Path: DebbysDepartures.com/category/south-west-coast-path
Debby's Departures on Facebook: Facebook.com/DebbysDepartures
Contact: DebbysDepartures@yahoo.com
Six travel photography books with the theme of "windows and doors" by Debby Lee Jagerman-Dungan available on Amazon (see bibliography for titles)

As I say at the end of all my blogs, Sweet Travels!

I shall donate a percentage from the net profits during the first year of the sale of this book to the South West Coast Path Association.

Front Cover Photos: Main photo taken on way to Polperro July 24. I chose this photo because it shows an example of rocky coastline, green farmland, hillsides and headlands, the SWCP itself is visible, the skies and seas are blue, and it has an example of an arrow and acorn waymark sign, all considered my "ideal elements" of the SWCP. The two photos in the middle were taken July 23 on the way to Porthpean Beach showing the spectacular views that day. The row of beach huts was taken at Saunton Sands on June 13.

Back Cover Photos: Mevagissey harbour, breakwater, town and headlands beyond July 21. My purple shoes at Worbarrow Bay May 5. Wembury Church with Great Mew Stone and great scenery July 30. Two examples of The Arrow(s) Closest To The Acorn. Walking in the Lulworth Range area August 25. Waymark sign at Wembury Beach showing 424 miles from/to Minehead and 206 miles from/to Poole July 30.

Map of the South West Coast Path
Inset Map showing SWCP location in England

Notes: Not drawn exactly, nor to scale; county borders, and locations of towns and lighthouses are approximate; LH = Lighthouse. Lighthouses mostly used as reference points, rather than names of towns.

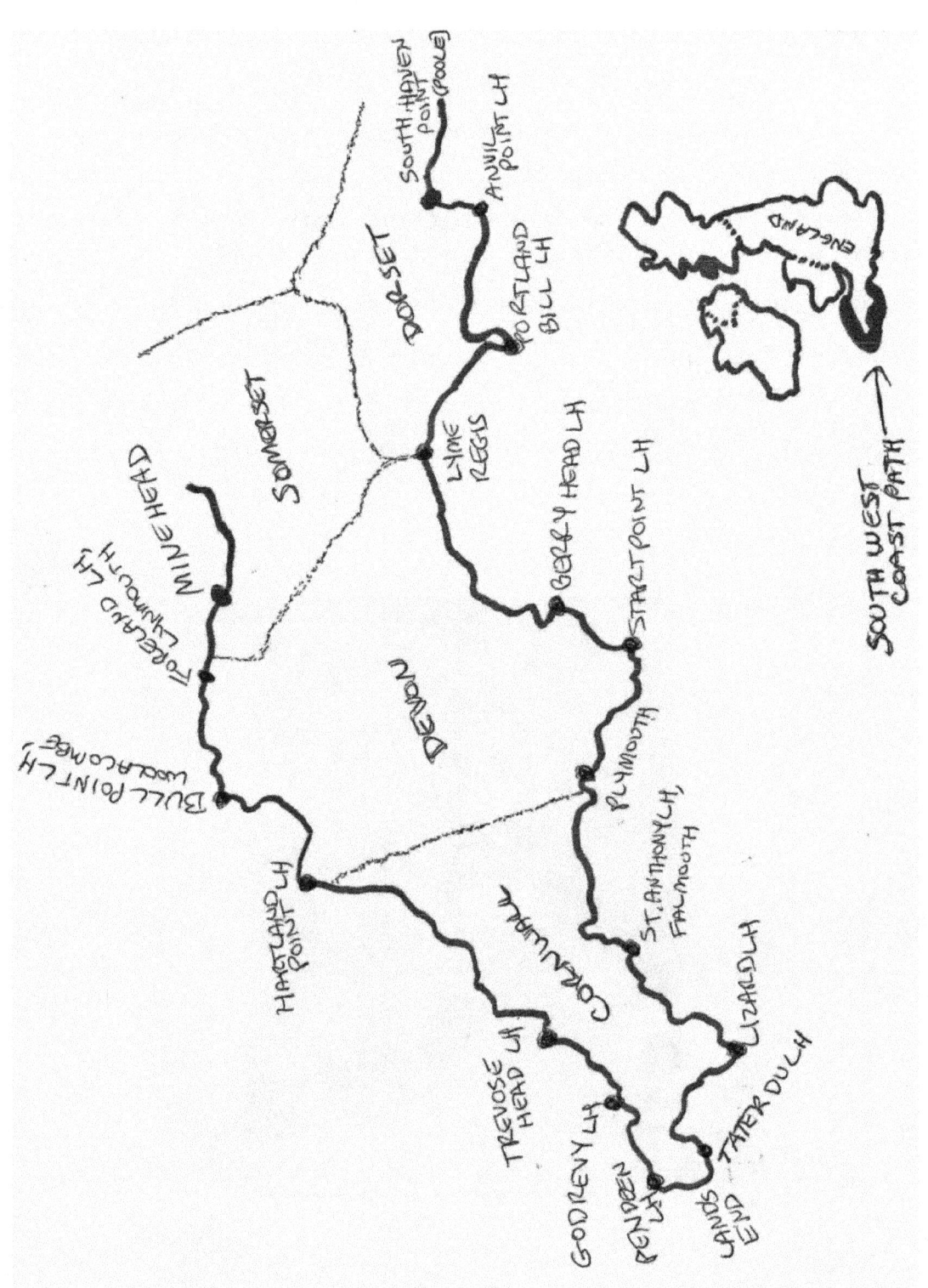

Table of Contents

BESIDE THE SEASIDE 5

SUMMER 2017 (3 JUNE TO 29 AUGUST) 7

IN THE MEANTIME (29 AUGUST 2017 TO 26 MARCH 2018) 282

SPRING 2018 (27 MARCH TO 6 MAY) 289

THE FINAL HOURS, BACK HOME, EPILOGUE/REFLECTIONS, AND WHAT'S NEXT (7 MAY 2018 TO BOOK COMPLETION) 373

List of Lighthouses/Aids to Navigation along the South West Coast Path 377

List of Disclaimers 378

Bibliography of Books 379

Websites of Important Organizations 380

Lighthouse painted by my Niece for my 50th Birthday!
"Not all who wander are lost." – J.R.R. Tolkein

BESIDE THE SEASIDE

> Oh! I do like to be beside the seaside!
> I do like to be beside the sea!
> I do like to stroll along the Prom, Prom, Prom!
> Where the brass bands play, "Tiddely-om-pom-pom!"
> So just let me be beside the seaside!
> I'll be beside myself with glee
> and there's lots of girls beside,
> I should like to be beside, beside the seaside,
> beside the sea!

    As I walked towards a restaurant to get something to eat, I walked past a very nicely-dressed grandfatherly-aged gentleman, strutting along, almost dancing. I heard him happily singing out loud, sharing his joy with anyone who was listening on this sunny warm glorious day. Something like, "Oh, I do like to be beside the seaside..."

    I really don't think this gentleman was actually singing to anyone in particular, other than to himself, and he probably didn't care if anyone was listening or not, but I was listening, and I began to form a smile across my face. I was passing by him as I was just coming off walking a half-mile meditative stretch on a pebbly beach after walking several more prior miles on this glorious day with its blue skies, white clouds, and turquoise seas. I was in my hiking clothes, carrying my rucksack, and just removed my proper British sun hat. He continued, "I do like to be beside the sea..."

    Those were the only words I heard, but it was enough to make my smile widen. I smiled not only because here was this happy gentleman enjoying his day so much that he felt compelled to sing out loud, but also because the words for some reason immediately grabbed my attention. I had never heard these British lyrics before, being from the U.S.A. The grandfatherly gentleman noticed my smile and commented, "Glad I could make you smile." I didn't say anything in response other than make eye contact and keep smiling, as I wanted to keep hearing what he was singing. Since we were walking in opposite directions, alas I did not hear any more. I didn't want it to seem like I was eavesdropping so I didn't stop, and I kept walking. Fortunately, I had heard enough though. Enough to know that even in these few words I heard, in these two little sentences, what he sang spoke to me, and rang true to my heart. I knew that the seaside is definitely where I like to be beside.

    I felt immediately that these lyrics represented my walk on the South West Coast Path in many ways, after 77 days thus far of walking and being beside extensions of the Atlantic Ocean in the forms of channels and seas. The words made me realize my love for my being beside the seaside, and how I fell in love with the South West Coast Path. The lyrics represented my love for hearing the ocean waves crash on the beaches. For seeing the rocky coastlines and the beaches and the coves and the bays that the waves touch. For seeing the greens of the hillsides and valleys and headlands, and the blues and turquoises of the waters. For being with nature, the various plants and grasses and shrubbery and trees and wildflowers. For the birds and the sea life and the animals. For smelling the salty and fishy sea air. For feeling the sea breezes and winds. For walking near mountain goats and sheep and horses. For getting my beneficial and positive supply of negative ions. For appreciating the timeless fishing villages, and the people who fish on the seas. For walking in my bare feet on the sand and paddling in the waters. For all the harbours and the many types of boats floating or resting in them. For appreciating the mining and farming industries, and learning about smuggling of the past. For all the people I had met along the way, and the friends I have made, whether for a brief moment in time, or for a few hours, or for a lifetime. For the Trinity House and the HM Coastguard and the National Coastwatch Institution and the Royal National Lifeboat Institution. For all the churches and chapels and lighthouses. For deciding which beach would be my ultimate location for a beach hut. For celebrating my 50th birthday in an epic way. For meeting local people and delving into local culture and local ways of life. For the food and the desserts and the cream teas. For walking and walking and walking. For filling my heart and soul and spirit with everything that I have experienced along my nearly three months on the South West Coast Path thus far. Even on my days off, even with the uncooperative weather, and even with the cows and the golf courses. I had fallen in love with being beside the seaside on the South West Coast Path.

> Now everybody likes to spend their summer holiday
> down beside the side of the silvery sea.
> I'm no exception to the rule, in fact, if I'd me way,
> I'd reside by the side of the silvery sea.

But when you're just the common or garden Smith or Jones or Brown
at business up in town, you're got to settle down.
You save your money all the year 'til summer comes around.
Then away you go to a place you know, where the cockle shells are found.

Oh! I do like to be beside the seaside!
I do like to be beside the sea!
I do like to stroll along the Prom, Prom, Prom!
Where the brass bands play, "Tiddely-om-pom-pom!"

So just let me be beside the seaside!
I'll be beside myself with glee
and there's lots of girls beside,
I should like to be beside, beside the seaside, beside the sea!

Now while not all words are entirely appropriate for me (I would change the word "girls" to "boys"), I decided that day that the wisdom that came from this joyful happy nicely-dressed grandfatherly-aged gentleman singing would become my theme song for my mostly solo walking adventure on England's 630-mile South West Coast Path.

SUMMER 2017 (3 JUNE TO 29 AUGUST)

INTRODUCTION: AT THE AIRPORT ON MY WAY TO ENGLAND – THE BACKGROUND, THE PLANNING, MY 50TH BIRTHDAY, THE DEBATE, THE SOUTH WEST COAST PATH, AND ALL KINDS OF OTHER INFORMATION - Saturday, 3 June 2017

"Not all who wander are lost." – J.R.R. Tolkien

The Background

I was in my element. I had my daypack next to me. I had my hiking boots on. My new camera was in hand ready to go. My hiking poles, hiking pants, many pairs of socks, a few various shirts and jackets and rain gear, and my purple sneakers were in my checked luggage. My passport was ready to be stamped. I had my inner sense of travel and adventure turned on. I was off to walk a long-distance walking trail. In another country. The longest walking trail in the United Kingdom. The sixteenth longest hiking trail in the world (not including any in the United States). And I was about to walk this by myself, on my own, solo, alone. I had that feeling of strength and confidence and freedom and enjoyment and sense of adventure and learning and growing and exploring that I get from travelling. I also felt deep down that everything would be all right. That I would be taken care of - by myself, by others if I need to ask for assistance, and by what I call "guardian angels" - amazing people, both strangers and friends, who one way or another show up just at the exact right moment in time that I need something, anything, whether big or small, usually when I have not even asked specifically for assistance at the moment, but have needed it anyway. I have experienced being in my element and being taken care of in my past travels and adventures, and I was sure it would happen again. 630 miles. Of walking. I was ready. I was in my element.

I arrived at the airport, SeaTac in Seattle. Way too early. But that is my way. I always leave early to get to the airport in case of traffic, or long lines, or some other unforeseen circumstance. Leaving the house at 9:30am, my husband, Scott, kindly driving to drop me off, we arrived at the airport exactly at 10:00am, and after saying our "I love yous," by 10:30 I was at the gate, having checked my luggage, gone through security, and taken the tram to gate S10. Three hours before my flight departed. I walked around, got some food, and I started my new thing - typing my experiences and thoughts on my new laptop.

It took a year to get to this point. Technically it took 50 years and a few months, but who was counting. A year ago with my husband Scott, we walked 100 miles of this long-distance walking trail together, the 630-mile South West Coast Path, that I was about to walk now on my own. This long-distance trail is located on the south west coast of England. The scenery, and so much more, that we experienced in May of 2016 were spectacular, as we walked from Carbis Bay to Falmouth. When we could see it. We had some fog now and then. But it was the scenery. The ocean, the waves, the beaches, the never-ending sky. The farmland, the hillsides, the coastlines. The wildflowers, the grasses, the cows and sheep grazing. The quaint fishing villages, the lighthouses, the food, the beds-and-breakfasts. The people. And the plethora of negative ions, those positive beneficial invisible molecules found in certain environments like mountains and forests, waterfalls, oceans, and beaches that have positive effects on you, thought to uplift your mood, release tension and stress, increase your levels of serotonin, making you feel more alert and energized. These are just some of the many reasons why I decided to return to the South West Coast Path.

Last year when my husband and I walked our 100 miles, we got lost a few times. We also had some uncooperative weather, complete with a mix of rain, wind, and fog. Sometimes on the same day, and at the same time. I wanted to enjoy the entire walk, but at times I did not when things did not go right. Since then though, I had this desire to walk the entire path, by myself, but also seriously questioned the thought based on some of these experiences my husband and I had. I even cried few times when things did not go right in May of 2016. Still I thought, wouldn't it be something epic to walk the entire path? All in one go. Especially to celebrate my 50th birthday. By myself.

Therefore one day I decided to commit. I will thank my girlfriend Simone. We were on one of our girl-bonding-chit-chatting-giggling walks, and I was telling her of my plans to perhaps walk this long-distance path in three chunks, 210 miles each, over the course of three years. However I kept struggling with that thought, feeling like I was making excuses for not trying to walk it all at once. "Why can't I walk it all at once?" I asked myself as I talked to her. What was stopping me? Yes there were the possibilities of getting lost, or of having uncooperative weather, or of getting lost in uncooperative weather, but putting those aside, what was really stopping me from doing the entire path all at once?

Time and money…But those are just things. Things that can be worked through when absolutely needed and wanted. During the course of the conversation with Simone, I thought it all through. Time…I didn't want to rush the walk. I wanted to enjoy it. I wanted to treat my feet and body well, allow for rest days, allow for the possibility of uncooperative weather days, and the possibility of getting lost. Most people walk the South West Coast Path (which from here on out I shall mostly refer to as "SWCP" throughout the book, or might also be mentioned as "Coast Path" or "Coastal Path" or still "South West Coast Path") in seven to eight weeks if they are going to do it all in one go. At least in the few books I have read, and according to what some guidebooks recommend. However, I wanted to take longer. To have time each day to not only walk, but to also explore and see and experience and feel as much as I could. I also wanted to go during the summer to assure that perhaps I could have the best weather possible. Three months. June, July, August. Of 2017. So what was stopping me from taking that much time? Perhaps my husband…I asked him as soon as I got home from my walk with Simone, and he was agreeable and supportive with my idea right away. Perhaps my accounting job…I had taken chunks of time off before. I had a very understanding boss. With some courage, I asked him a few days later, and he said yes. Other family… they were all alright with my idea of taking three months to walk the SWCP, including my loving and supportive mother. So with that the matter of time was settled.

Now money. Time off without pay for nearly three months (although there were a few weeks of paid vacation included in that) is a lot. But that is what a credit card is for, and a savings account. And a very generous mother. Thanks Mom, for some money.

So here I was at 11:37am, at the airport in Seattle. Typing on my new laptop. On the 3rd of June 2017. Getting ready to board a plane bound for London. On my way to the south west coast of England.

However that decision to commit after my conversation with Simone was actually back in August of 2016. What about between August and now, ten months later? What did I do to plan and get ready for my long-distance adventure? In a nutshell, I was busy. Quite busy preparing myself, my husband, my home, and my job. Before I start typing more detail about the planning, I think I will get up and stretch my legs and take a walk around the terminal to get some exercise. And to practice walking.

I'd been practicing walking a lot actually. I'd been taking two-and-a-half to three mile flat walks during my lunch hours at work; I'd been going on "training hikes" during the evenings when the days are longer in the "Issaquah Alps" near where I live, one of which is about a 1,600 foot elevation gain in two miles, and another about 2,500 feet of elevation gain in 1.5 miles; on the weekends, Scott and I took longer hikes at Mount Rainier or elsewhere that we conveniently have in the state of Washington where we live. I walked around my neighborhood. I had also been working out and doing other forms of cross-training. But now the planning…

The Planning: How Many Days, How Many Miles per Day, Utilizing Websites and Creating a Spreadsheet

Creating a large spreadsheet to organize, and utilizing three websites to plan my itinerary, took up the first week of my planning. Booking 50 (yes 50!) accommodations including beds-and-breakfasts (to be mostly referred to as "B&Bs" from now on), small hotels, one fancy hotel, inns, pubs, guest houses, even a caravan, and a friend's house, took another week of planning. Making packing lists and shopping lists, shopping and packing, took up more of my planning over the coming months.

How does one plan a walking itinerary of 630 miles for three months? How does one know how many miles per day they want to, or would like to, walk? Especially when one also needs to book their accommodations so as not to chance showing up in a town in the middle of the busy summer season only to find everything full. One starts out by first figuring out how many miles a day to walk that seem reasonable and hopefully doable. One gets on the internet. So that's what I did.

First a bit of math. I had three months. That's about 90 days. Divide 630 miles by 90 days, and you get an average of seven miles of walking per day. Well that is feasible. I did more than that some days in Spain on my Camino de Santiago walk. I wondered though what the Visa requirements for England were. I needed a few days at the beginning and at the end to fly and take trains there and back. I wanted rest days too in between walking days, as that is good for the feet and body. Upon researching the Visa requirements, I found conflicting information. Some websites said six months on a Travel Visa, others said 90 days. To be on the safe side, I chose the 90 days rule as my maximum.

I started factoring in about four days for travel time to and from England, and a rest day about every 100 miles of walking, which would give me about six rest days. It would turn out to be nine rest days actually that I chose as the planning went on. Finally just to be sure, I decided to spend 89 days in England total, one day less than the 90 days. Updated math – 89 days, less the four for travel, and less the nine for rest days is 76 walking days. Divide 630 miles by 76 days, and now I was at about an average of eight miles per day. Still feasible. I went with that. The next step was to get on the internet and create my itinerary.

There are three fantastic very helpful websites of organizations that helped with my planning. Without either one of them, my planning may not have gone as smoothly as it did, for each of them had their own valuable nuances. The first website is the South West Coast Path Association, "a registered charity working to protect and conserve the Coast Path to give us all the opportunity to improve our health in the great outdoors. [They] work to ensure the path is one of the best walks in the world and protect it for all to enjoy. [They] try to ensure as many people as possible know about, and have information to enjoy, the Coast Path. [They] fund vital improvement projects to protect the Path for future generations." I am a member of this great organization, and have been for several years.

The SWCP Association website has great maps with trail information, as well as very useful gain and loss "Interactive Elevation" maps. That helped me in my planning that if in any of my given approximate eight miles, there were a lot of ascents and descents, I could reduce the mileage. Alternatively if the eight miles was relatively flat, I could increase the mileage. I continued to use the SWCP Association interactive elevation gain and loss maps during my walk as well, checking each night before I went to sleep to look up the next day's elevation gains and losses to remind me of what I had coming up for the next day. How this website shows the elevation gain and loss is by a map of the SWCP in sections, and as you follow the dot moving along the path, a chart shows you the elevation by little lines going up and down to as far as the path is going in elevation at the moment. For example, the line for a particular climb might start near the zero marker, indicating sea level, then the next line is longer, and the next line is even longer, until the highest line is at the 675 mark, thus showing that the elevation gain for at least that particular ascent is 675 feet. Then the lines might go down for a descent, and may go back up for another ascent, etc. I used the tab "Walk the Path - Trip Planning - Day by Day Guide" on the SWCP Association website a lot, clicking on individual sections of the SWCP, to help with this phase of the planning.

Under the "Walk the Path" tab, there is also a very useful page called "Distance Calculator." Here you can choose your start location and your finish location of any two places and it will calculate not only the mileage distance between the two places, but also tell you intermediate places and their mileage in between the two places selected. This is helpful to choose shorter or longer walking options.

The second fantastic website is National Trails UK, a website for sixteen managed long-distance walking, cycling, and horse-riding trails in England and Wales, totaling nearly 2,500 miles of trails for walkers (soon to be a lot more as they are in the midst of creating the England Coast Path which will add about 2,800 more miles). National Trails "pass through some of the most stunning and diverse landscapes in Britain. There is something to suit everyone, from short walks to a 630-mile adventure." Yes, I was about to partake on that adventure. Funding for National Trails UK is "provided by national government through Natural England and Natural Resource Wales and also by local highway authorities and other funding partners." I made a donation.

The National Trails UK website is useful for finding accommodations close to the SWCP with their interactive maps, so that I wouldn't have to walk too many extra miles on getting to and from the path and the accommodations. The SWCP Association website also has accommodation information, but I used the National Trails UK website mostly for this task. While on the SWCP page on the National Trails UK website, I clicked on the "Plan Your Visit" map, which took me to a "Plan your personalized visit to the Trail" page. On this page, I chose the "Accommodation-B&Bs/Hotels/Pubs" option, although there are other options as well for self-catering, camping, hostels, and other information to choose from. Once I clicked on my option, blue circles appeared on a map which when clicked on would show the specific accommodations located at that spot.

The third fantastic website is Luggage Transfers, LTD. (Note that none of these three websites asked me to mention them. I am doing so on my own accord, and have received nothing in return from them.) Luggage Transfers, LTD is mostly a service for "baggage transfers on Britain's walking routes." I used them for this service so that I would only need to carry a daypack (which from here on out I shall refer to as a "rucksack," since that is the proper British term for a backpack or daypack) on my walk without much weight. The service would take my new wheeled suitcase from accommodation to accommodation (more on my wheeled suitcase later). At one point on my walk I picked up a Luggage Transfers, LTD flyer which stated, "Enjoy the beautiful South West Coast Path without the hassle of having to carry your heavy luggage." "Heavy" being the key word in my case, as I shall describe.

For planning purposes however, Luggage Transfers, LTD had some written detail and description on accommodations, plus contact information for the accommodations. I was even able to contact some accommodations directly from the Luggage Transfers, LTD website. Therefore, along with the National Trails UK website, I used both of these websites to choose the majority of my accommodations.

In addition to those three very helpful websites for my planning, I also checked out each accommodation's website once I chose a few options to get a feel for its atmosphere, to look at photos of the homes and the rooms, to verify its location, and get more information about the hosts, the price, meals, and availability. Sometimes I would contact them from their own website, either via email or online enquiry, or even just booked directly through an online system.

Before I get too much more into explaining about how I booked accommodations, I was still in the mileage-figuring-out stage however. Knowing where there were existing accommodations though helped with the mileage planning because occasionally the eight-mile average proved to be in a place where there happened to be no accommodations around. Many people do carry a tent and camp along the SWCP, but that wasn't for me. Don't get me wrong, I have done plenty of backpacking and camping in my life, and would do more, but not for this adventure. I wanted really comfortable evenings, with a bed and a shower, and shelter. A place that I could call home for a night or two or three. Not that a tent couldn't be home, but I just wanted my home-away-from-home for 88 nights to be a home, usually literally.

Taking about a week, I sat in front of my computer, first with a pen and paper in hand, and then eventually created a spreadsheet, which if I might say so I am quite proficient with as that is part of my accounting job, I started jotting down towns and their mileage in distance from one town to the next.

I started at the beginning - a town called Minehead. (Alternatively, that town could also be the ending if you were walking the SWCP in the opposite direction, but for me Minehead was my beginning.) Most people do nine miles the first day to Porlock Weir. There is one big ascent, one decent, and then some flat walking. I wanted to take it easier though on my first day of walking, even though nine miles is close to my eight-mile average. Where should I stop instead? There were no other accommodations within those first nine miles. Then it dawned on me, well this idea dawned on me during the 100-mile walk Scott and I did in 2016, that instead of staying only one night in each accommodation and moving each and every day as Scott and I did, I could plan this walk in such a way that I could stay in an accommodation two, three, or even four nights in a row. But how? By utilizing public transportation, buses, taxis, or even the owners of the B&Bs, to transport me to and from the start and end of my walks, to and from my accommodations. In addition, in the busy summer months, accommodations may also have a minimum requirement of two nights anyway. Finally this way I would not need to unpack and pack on a daily basis, and I wouldn't have to use Luggage Transfers LTD every single day either. I could settle in to certain places for two, three, or four nights in a row, in my home-away-from-home. I thought it was a brilliant idea!

Therefore, for my first day of walking from Minehead, it looked like there was a good intermediate stopping point in Bossington. Bossington was about six miles from Minehead, but had no accommodations itself. Shorter than the eight-mile average, and that was perfect for my first day. It was settled. I had planned my first day of walking. From Minehead to Bossington. Six miles. Unless of course I take the alternate route that day which would make it a bit longer, of six and a half or seven miles. In either case, day one figured out.

Where to next? Counting miles, I ended up in Culbone at what would be "the smallest complete parish church," St. Bueno's Church in Culbone. However that wasn't far enough, so I added another few miles to get me to Silcombe Farm, at five and a half miles. Not quite the eight again, but using the Interactive Elevation maps there seemed to be no logical place eight miles from Bossington. Therefore Silcombe Farm would be the end of my second day. With all that, I decided I would stay in Minehead my first three nights. Night one would be my arrival in England, night two would be after walking from Minehead to Bossington, and night three would be after walking from Bossington to Silcombe Farm.

And so it went, counting miles, looking at elevation gain and loss, seeing if accommodations were nearby. Perhaps adjusting every now and then, until my spreadsheet grew and grew into my 89-day and 88-night itinerary that was complete and perfect. Or what I hoped would be perfect.

I ended up overall with a few days that were longer than my eight-mile average, and a few days shorter. That was alright. I had to adjust some days for other circumstances, such as one day would be eleven miles, which I originally wanted to split up, but with no accommodations or convenient transportation options or intermediate stops, instead I gave myself a rest day both before and after this eleven-mile day. I did plan on one day as short as four-and-a-half miles, and one as long as thirteen mostly flat miles. By and large though, most of my days were an average of eight miles. It was a big task to figure out all of this, but I really enjoyed doing this complex planning, and if it would be successful, then I would be quite proud of myself.

I will say that many people walk a lot more miles each and every day in order to complete the 630 miles of the SWCP in seven or eight weeks' time, perhaps always averaging eleven to thirteen miles or more each day, but since I had my three months, I could take my time with my shorter days. To explore and see and experience and feel as much as I could.

The next planning step was to decide on my exact day of departure which would thus set the rest of the days of my walk. I could not do my following steps of planning the flights, the beginning trains, and reserving the accommodations, without my exact dates. Since I had decided on June, July, and August, in order to maximize my time there, keeping within my 89-day parameter, and completing a week of work on a Friday with closing out the previous month's end accounting cycle, I chose Saturday, the 3rd of June 2017 as my departure day.

After I figured out the mileage, and my departure day, with thus my return day being Thursday, the 31st of August, the next steps would be arranging the flights, the beginning trains, and reserving the accommodations.

The Flights, The Beginning Trains, and The Accommodations

For the flights for this trip, I utilized a travel agent. Most of the time, I book my own flights, but sometimes when precision and hopefully the lowest prices are needed, I use a travel agent. Although sometimes I find a lower price, it just all depends. I also preferred a direct flight to London Heathrow from Seattle. With a departure date of the 3rd of June, leaving in the early afternoon Seattle time, I would arrive in London in the early morning hours the next day, the 4th of June, a similar flight Scott and I used during our 100-mile walk, which gave us the rest of the day to travel from Heathrow to Carbis Bay last year, and would give me the rest of the day to travel to Minehead.

Trains and buses to Minehead were thus the next planning from London Heathrow. I utilized National Rail UK to help with this phase of the planning. The plan was to take the Heathrow Express train to the Paddington train station in London, and then take a train to Taunton that would leave about three hours after my flight arrived. Two hours on this train, and I would take a bus to Minehead that would be just over an hour. Therefore by 1:18pm on the 4th of June 2017, I would be in Minehead. Once I decided on my first B&B, I also prearranged with them that they would pick me up at the bus stop in Minehead and take me to their home.

Speaking of accommodations and B&Bs, it was finally time to hit the internet once again in full force to look in more detail for all the specific places I wanted to stay. I started in Minehead, looked on all three of the above websites to find accommodations, but especially the two that I already mentioned that I used the most. I read descriptions, figured out their exact location in relation to the SWCP, and looked at the websites in more detail of the accommodations, including getting a feel for the atmosphere and other information. I chose my favorite B&B and contacted them to book my specific days. As mentioned, sometimes the contact was by an online enquiry, sometimes by email, and other times I just booked directly.

When I planned the mileage in my first planning step of creating my excel spreadsheet itinerary, I also figured out how many nights I wanted at each accommodation, anywhere from one to four nights. Most times I was able to reserve my first favorite choice that I wanted on the first try. After all, I was planning eight to ten months in advance. A few times however I was unable to get my first choice, so I would move on to my second choice, and usually was able to reserve that one.

The net result of all this planning was a six page spreadsheet that I called "SWCP 630 Full Itinerary." Columns included the number of days, the exact dates, the places I was walking from and to each day, along with some notes of important information I might need to know on any given day, how many miles of walking each day, and the B&Bs themselves including their name, the name of their owners, their phone numbers, and booking information such as if I paid a deposit or not, and how much I still owed.

In total, after about another week of spending my time planning, I had booked 50 accommodations in all! I think that might be a world's record of an individual reserving that many places to sleep. I was amazed that I was able to accomplish this big task. Ironically, I booked 50 accommodations for my epic 50th birthday celebration!

My 50th Birthday!

Speaking of my 50th birthday, as I have mentioned a few times already this epic event, somewhere in between the 100-mile walk Scott and I did in May of 2016, the planning that started in August of 2016, and this new adventure I was about to partake in the summer of 2017, was my 50th birthday. On the 2nd of February 2017 to be exact. Groundhog's Day. Instead of having a mid-life crisis however, I decided that I wanted to celebrate. To do something epic, or "monumental" as my Mom would say, to celebrate my 50th birthday. Thus, walking the 630-mile SWCP would be it!

For my birthday, one of the best gifts I received was from my seven-year-old niece. She knew of my love for lighthouses (of which I will be seeing many on the SWCP and talking about in more detail), and so my niece painted a lighthouse on canvas for me for my birthday. My sister helped, and added the quote, knowing about my love for travel, and my upcoming walk, "Not all who wander are lost." Appropriate and perfect! Reminding me that if I do happen to get lost while walking the SWCP, it really doesn't mean that I am truly lost.

My Debate of Walking Alone or with My Husband

As already mentioned, the previous year I walked 100 miles with my husband Scott. He and I do a lot of walking, hiking, backpacking, camping, and some traveling, together. There was something in me though that wondered if I could do this epic walking adventure on my own. Or if I should walk with my husband. I grappled over this debate of walking alone or with my husband for months during my planning. By myself or with my husband? With my husband or by myself? Will I miss him enough to want him to join me at some point if I walk alone? Will I feel like I should have tried to walk alone if he joined me from the beginning? How would he feel if I went alone? How would I feel if I went alone? These questions were difficult to answer, we discussed the options, and inside me, the debate went on for a while.

But in the end, the thought of what an epic walking adventure it would be to say that I attempted to walk the entire 630 miles on my own, won the debate. It just felt like it was something I wanted to try to accomplish. So I started out walking on my own.

It also would be something to say that not only would I attempt to walk the entire 630 miles as a solo female, which others have done, but as an American solo female, which in my research, I could not find that another American solo female has walked the entire path in one go. Although maybe one has, but has not written a book about it. Therefore, I thought that I could write a book about my walking adventure. About an American woman's walking adventure on England's 630-mile South West Coast Path. Perhaps it would even become a best seller, I could make my millions of dollars and be able to retire, and maybe they would even make a movie out of it…

Anyway, I still had some shopping and packing to do.

The Packing and The Shopping

After all the miles and accommodations were planned, I started to create a list of things to pack. I used a list that I had from our previous 100-mile walk as a base, plus I took ideas from various other packing lists I had from some of my other travels, just to make sure I wasn't forgetting anything. My list was several pages long, double-lined, and included sections for clothes, shoes, socks, raingear, hats, toiletries, first aid items, paperwork, electronics, other miscellaneous items, and of course don't forget the passport and credit cards. The packing list would change, evolve, and be modified several times over the coming months until I thought I had it perfect.

I had to do a bit of shopping to get some things from my list that I was missing. Anything from a few of my clothing items and new socks, to guidebooks, and even my new camera.

For me, about 15% of the fun of traveling is all this planning and shopping and packing. Seventy-five percent is the travels itself, and the other 15% is everything that happens when I get back – scrapbooks, telling people stories, looking at photos, writing my travel blogs, and in this case, writing this book – all reliving the memories. Yes, I know that is 105%!

The Wheeled Suitcase

My husband. My loving husband, Scott. Sometimes he does things at the last minute, or may run a bit late. I am the type of person who likes to do things in advance and likes being on time or early, such as how early I arrived at the airport. When we do run late though or something happens at the last minute, what I realize is that things usually all work out anyway, and running late, or doing something at the last minute, does not matter.

Here is a case in point. This is something he did for me at the last minute which completely worked out. He got me a suitcase, with wheels. I never thought I would ever use or own a wheeled suitcase actually. They always seemed so awkward to me. I've seen people struggle with them, lugging them up a curb, or the suitcase tipping over. I thought, never me. I'm a daypack/backpack, I mean rucksack, kind-of-girl. In fact, I was planning on taking my big hiking rucksack with me for the majority of my packing. I would really only have to have it on my back for the travels to Minehead. After that, Luggage Transfers, LTD would take it from there. I also had two smaller rucksacks for the plane at this point. How would I manage with three rucksacks and only one back? I was really not sure, but I figured that I would figure it all out.

Then my husband said three days, yes three days, before my departure, "I got you something for your trip. I wanted to get you something that would make it easier…a wheeled suitcase." At first my usual reaction was no please don't meddle with my ways, and what I had planned. I would be fine with all my rucksacks. However that thought fleeted after a few seconds, and I said to myself, "What if he is right? What if his last-minute-loving purchase was perfect?" I waited two more days. The day before I was going to be leaving. Yes, the day before. For the wheeled luggage to arrive at the store he ordered it from online, hoping that it would arrive on Friday, the day before I would leave, not Saturday the day I had to leave, so that Friday night I could try it out and make sure I liked it. It arrived just in time. I will admit that it was a bit unsettling to me to think of doing my final packing and switching to a different plan of packing at the last minute, the night before I was about to leave, but like I said, sometimes doing something at the last minute all works out anyway.

I picked up the wheeled suitcase up after my usual grocery shopping on Friday night, where I bought a lot of extra groceries for Scott to have for several days so that he did not have to go shopping soon, and took the suitcase home. After putting away the groceries, and doing to do a few other items on my own last-minute to-do list, I tried out my new wheels. I couldn't wait any longer. I lugged out my heavy backpack, which wasn't even full of all my stuff yet, and neatly organized all my stuff sacks and miscellaneous bags of stuff in the suitcase. It fit. It all fit, and it all fit quite well. I zipped the suitcase up, pulled out the handle, and wheeled it around the house. Yes it was still heavy, as I lifted it a bit (forty pounds once I got to the airport and had it weighed, including the weight of the luggage itself), but it would not have to reside on my back even for a moment. Forty pounds would have been quite heavy on my back actually, after I thought about it. What a loving thing my husband did! It was easy to wheel around too even though it was big in size. It didn't seem like it would tip over awkwardly. It was also easier to get items in and out of rather than a top-loading rucksack. I hoped that it would be easier for Luggage Transfers, LTD to transport than my rucksack as well.

I called my husband to thank him, as he was not home yet. He comes through for me a lot. He cares about me a lot. And I appreciate that. I will miss him during my adventure. And yes, as I will find out as I walk along the SWCP, I over-packed, even with my so-called perfect packing list.

Aboard The Plane

It was now time to board the plane. I seem to like the British accent, listening to it as I boarded. It was warm and welcoming. I am not good at mimicking other accents. I wondered if after three months in England, if I would pick up any of the accent at all. I did not. I picked up a few different words and expressions though, but said them in my accent.

As I sat in my seat, for a few moments, I actually got a bit nervous about my walking adventure as I had some nervous thoughts. What if I do get lost? What if the weather becomes really uncooperative? What if I get lost in uncooperative weather? I guess I have control over some things though and I tried to rationalize my thoughts. If the weather forecast is that uncooperative, I just don't walk. I can combine days to make up the mileage, or switch a scheduled rest day if needed. If I get lost on a good weather day then hopefully I can figure out sooner rather than later that I am lost, go back, retrace my steps to where I got lost, and embrace the extra mileage. And remember, not all who wander are lost.

Perhaps however in reality my nervousness was really excitement!

One more final very important item to discuss, the South West Coast Path itself…

The South West Coast Path

They do say on the SWCP Association's website that walking the entire 630 miles of the South West Coast Path is the equivalent elevation gain and loss as climbing the world's tallest mountain, Mount Everest, four times. Four times! That's 115,000 feet of ascent and descent! Now I can't say that I have ever climbed Mount Everest. In fact I have no desire to climb that mountain at all. While I respect those that do, with utmost respect for those that summit, I myself prefer not to be exposed to that many elements of snow, ice, crevasses, glaciers, bitter cold, altitude, oxygen tanks, climbing ropes, and ice axes. That is why I appreciate that the SWCP is mostly at or near sea level. As far as I know I am guessing that it doesn't snow there that much either, at least not in the summer.

As described on the website, "The South West Coast Path itself is 630 miles long and is the longest National Trail in the country [of England]. Starting at Minehead in Somerset it runs along the coastline of Exmoor, continuing along the coast of North Devon into Cornwall. It follows the entire coastline of Cornwall, goes across the mouth of the River Tamar and continues into Devon. After running along the south coast of Devon it then follows the Dorset coastline before finally ending at Poole Harbour." (Note that Somerset, Devon, Cornwall, and Dorset are counties in the south west of England, which I shall write about more on those later.)

Historically, according to the SWCP Association website, "The South West Coast Path was originally created by coastguards, patrolling the south west peninsula looking out for smugglers. They literally had to check in every inlet so their cliff top walk was well used and gives us the amazing Path we use today." Coastguards would patrol the whole coast on foot, every day. A series of coastguard cottages were built at convenient intervals, and some still stand today. In addition, "The coastguard's children used these paths to go to school, while their wives used them to get from one fishing hamlet to the next."

I found out from another website that the SWCP's "origins date back to Tudor time (1588) when men were posted to the headlands all over the south west to look out for the approaching Spanish armada. Import duties on traded goods (particularly brandy) caused a lot of smuggling to occur in the 18th and 19th century. To combat this, in January 1822 a national force of 'Coastguards' was created. Cottages were built around the coast and paths were necessary so Coastguards could move along the coast checking on all the small coves and inlets. Smuggling in Devon and Cornwall was particularly strong so the coastguards were particularly numerous in these counties. Gradually as smuggling was reduced the duties of the coastguard expanded to cover assistance to shipwrecked sailors and in 1856 the service was taken over by the admiralty and it no longer had any anti-smuggling duties. All the parts of the coastal path were finally linked together in 1978."

Furthermore, back to the SWCP Association's website, "The Path has also been used by fishermen looking for shoals of fish and checking sea conditions."

Some statistics, also according to the SWCP Association, are that in the 630 miles, "you will cross 230 bridges, catch 13 ferries, open (and close!) 880 gates, climb over 436 stiles, pass more than 4,000 Coast Path signs, and go up or down over 30,000 steps." And "that's not counting the many climbs and descents where no steps are found." Finally, "approximately 71% of the Path is either a National Park or an Area of Outstanding Natural Beauty."

The SWCP can be walked in any direction. One can walk just a day at a time, or a few days at a time, in any location, in any direction. Alternatively, one can walk a few weeks, or months at a time, in any location, in any direction. One can walk only a part of it over a lifetime, or take a lifetime to complete it. However one chooses to walk the SWCP is entirely up to you.

The SWCP Association itself held its first public meeting in May of 1973 and was originally called the South West Way Association. From 1973 to 1978 the South West Coast Path itself was linked together in stages, with Cornwall in 1973, South Devon and Dorset in 1974, the Exmoor Coast in 1975, and "the final section through Somerset and North Devon in 1978." Over the decades, a lot of activities occurred including, but not limited to, alternate routes and other improvements were made, the number of members increased, path markers were installed on either end of the path as well as mid-way, trustees established local representatives to assist with the reporting of the condition of the path, and they changed from a charity to a Charitable Incorporated Organization. As I mentioned, I am a member of this great organization.

As I sat in my seat as my flight took off, I was still in my element and the excitement increased. I was really looking forward to learning more about the coastguard, about the history of smuggling, the important industry of fishing, and everything and anything else that the South West Coast Path would offer me. I was looking forward to exploring, and to see what growing I would do on this adventure. I was looking forward to crossing those bridges, catching those ferries, opening (and closing) those gates, climbing over those stiles, following the signs, and even going up and down all those steps, and climbs and descents where no steps are found. I was really looking forward to seeing all of the natural beauty of the entire South West Coast Path. And looking forward to whatever other experiences were ahead of me for the next 89 days on my walking adventure on England's 630-mile South West Coast Path!

Information on the South West Coast Path from
bbc.co.uk/somerset/content/articles/2005/06/30/coast05walks_stage8;
nearwaterwalkingholidays.co.uk/south-west-coast-path;
and southwestcoastpath.org.uk/love-the-coast-path/about-us/our-history.
Information on the Longest Hiking Trails in the World from
adventurestrong.com/hiking/top-10-longest-hiking-trails-in-the-world.

GETTING TO MINEHEAD: THE TRANSPORTATION, THE INDECISION, THE DECISION, THE OFFICIAL SWCP MONUMENT, A GROUNDHOG, THE ARROW AND THE ACORN, AND THE WALKING ADVENTURE BEGINS – Sunday, 4 June 2017

"The journey of a thousand miles begins with one step." Lao Tzu

The Transportation

It was 5:30pm England time on the 5th of June, and the winds were blowing something fierce outside. The trees were rustling almost doing a dance with much vigor and intention, pushing the rain into the windows. The sounds of the rain felt like someone was throwing tiny pebbles up at me to call my attention. Perhaps telling me that it was good that I was inside at the moment. The forecast had called for the possibility of gale force winds today, and it sure seemed like they were pretty accurate. When I saw the forecast for gale force winds in June, I couldn't believe it. It was supposed to be summer, the months that I planned on walking. The months when the weather should be warm and sunny. As I sat in my nice cozy B&B in Minehead, England though I felt warm and grateful that I had already walked two of my planned walks the last two days, a total of twelve miles, so that I could be inside during these winds. My first walking days on the 630-mile South West Coast Path. Let me catch up to this moment.

The nine-and-a-half-hour flight from Seattle's SeaTac airport to London Heathrow was like a typical long-distance flight for me. I watched a few movies on the airplane after taking a short nap. I probably slept about an hour just as soon as we departed. I tried to sleep again in order to reset my body clock to adjust to London time, to fend off jetlag, but alas that was not successful.

We landed on time, but it took a while to get through Passport Control. When my turn came up, for the first time in all my worldwide travels, I was actually asked quite a few questions. Not because of who I am or anything like that, but because when the Border Agent saw that I was staying in the country for 89 days she wanted to know more about why I was here so long. It was a good thing I decided on that number, and didn't stay longer.

I explained that I was walking the South West Coast Path. I should have said that it was 630 miles, but I didn't because I figured she must know all about it, right, since she lives here in England? Probably not based on her continued questioning. She asked about my job. I told her I was taking a Leave of Absence. She wanted to see my return flight information, and to see a letter about my leave from work. The return flight was easy to show. Fortunately, I had a feeling about a week before I left to get my boss to sign a letter that I wrote up explaining my employment with the company, my unpaid leave, and that pending any unforeseen circumstances, I would have a job when I returned. I did not anticipate any unforeseen circumstances. The letter also explained I had been with the company for over twenty years.

"Unpaid?" She asked, "How do you intend to fund your 89 days?" I explained that I had two credit cards, and a couple of large savings accounts. "What is the credit limit on your credit cards?" she inquired. One credit card was about $10,000 (about £7,500) (for this I took a guess actually as I could not quite remember), and the other card was actually more of a debit card which would automatically take money out of one of my savings accounts. "Do you have any cash on you now?" Yes. "How much?" About £1,000 (about $1,360), not quite remembering exactly how much I actually did exchange before I left as I did that several weeks ago, but that seemed about right. (Note that from here on out, I will be using the symbol "£" for any monies for Gross British Pounds, and "$" for US Dollars. I will put both amounts in whenever I mention any money. Also note that in both instances, one amount may be approximate to the time of the writing of my book, since currency rates fluctuate.)

The Border Agent finally seemed satisfied with my answers, to which I didn't feel worried or offended about, but relieved. She stamped my Passport, I thanked her, and I was on to getting my checked wheeled suitcase. I usually don't check luggage, but this time I did mostly because of wanting to take hiking poles that cannot be in a carryon, but also because for once in all my worldwide travels, I had a lot of stuff, too much stuff actually, to take with me than other trips. In addition, last time my husband and I went to England together, we tried to carry on large rucksacks, but they made us check them anyway. Finally the new wheeled suitcase that my loving husband bought for me would not qualify as a carryon.

With my wheeled suitcase, and the two smaller rucksacks, I set off for the next portion of my day. Getting to my first town, the official start of the SWCP, or the official end if you walked from the other direction, Minehead. I took the Heathrow Express train to the London Paddington train station as I planned, picked up my tickets that I previously reserved, and had a small but healthier bite to eat to try to make up for what was served on the flight. I had an hour to wait for my train.

The scenic train ride through the country side of England took about two hours to the town of Taunton. I tried to sleep on the train to fend off the jetlag and lack of sleep, setting the alarm clock on my cell phone (or "mobile phone" as from here on out I shall refer to them because that is what they call them in England) so I wouldn't miss my stop. My first attempt at sleeping failed. Finally, later I dozed off for about a half hour. That was much needed.

One of the previous times my husband and I came to England, to walk 100 miles in the Cotswolds, we did not know that sometimes you have to open train doors by reaching through the window and turning the handle that was located on the outside of the train. We missed our stop because of this, and I had a bit of a panic attack at that time. Fortunately someone on that train explained it to us, so we got off at the next stop, and got a taxi to our destination. Needless to say, ever since then, I have this fear of not being able to get off trains in England.

As I boarded the train to Taunton, I looked to see if this train had the same handle situation. Sure enough it did. I knew that my fear of not being able to get off would not come true this time, as I knew to check it out beforehand. Actually not only would I have known what to do once my stop at Taunton arrived, the gentleman working the train ended up opening the door anyway.

With getting off the train a success, I did not know though how to get out of the train station. Now my fear of not being able to get off trains had turned into being forever stuck inside a train station. I watched as others ran their ticket through the machine at the turnstile and got out. I thought, sure that seemed easy. I have done that before. For some strange reason, my turnstile would not open when I put my ticket through. I tried again. Still no. And again. Still no. Hmmm. Strange. Panic set in knowing I had a bus to catch soon.

I was about to go ask someone for help, when somehow out of the blue, the turnstile opened. I do not know why or how or who opened it. Even a gentleman on the other side noticed this, and we gave each other a puzzled look. I was free. That was what mattered.

I had about ten minutes before my bus appeared at this point. As I boarded, I asked the driver if he would be so kind as to tell me where to get off the bus in Minehead. He said he would when we got to this place in Minehead called "The Parade." I had this fear that he wouldn't tell me and I would be forever stuck inside the bus. I sat as close to the front of the bus as possible so that he could perhaps still see me and remember to tell me where to get off the bus.

I wanted to sleep on the bus because by this time my internal time clock was way off telling me it was about 4:00 in the morning and I should have been asleep long ago, but I was afraid that I would miss my stop, on top of the fear of not being told when my stop arrived and staying on this bus forever. I stayed awake for the over an hour bus ride through the picturesque English countryside.

I figured we were getting close to my bus stop since I starting seeing signs for Minehead. I really became excited now that after months and months of planning and making my decision to walk the SWCP, I was finally arriving in Minehead. The slight nervousness that I felt earlier on the plane disappeared. On this street near a roundabout several people got off, and the bus driver kindly turned around and told me this was where I should get off. "Thank you so very much," I thanked him. I was on time arriving in Minehead after all the planes, trains, and buses. It was 1:18pm and I was glad all that planning I had done to get me to this moment went according to plan. And that none of my fears happened.

Now it was time to see if my mobile phone worked. I knew at least the texting part worked because I texted Scott when I was in line for Passport Control to tell him that I had landed safely. Apparently they are alright with you texting in this line because many people were. Now I had to see if the phone part of my mobile phone worked. I was to call Janna from the B&B I would be staying at for three nights. She had agreed to pick me up at the bus stop as we pre-arranged via email when I was making my reservations.

I dialed her number, and got an answer. I told her I was at a place called "The Parade." She asked me what stores I was near, I told her, and she said she would be there in about five minutes. Janna picked me up in her little Toyota. I easily put my two rucksacks in the boot of her car. In England they call the trunk, "the boot." I struggled to lift the large wheeled suitcase up however because it was that forty pounds they told me at the airport when I checked it in. Yes, I packed too much.

The Indecision

Now for a moment of brief indecision. I was hungry. Really hungry. I also wanted to settle in after my long travels to arrive here. I was also wondering if I should do my first planned walk of six miles today, which might take about three hours. Especially based on the forecast for tomorrow, that I recently had checked on BBC Weather, which much to my surprise, and disappointment, was calling for gale force winds. Ironically I did not want to sleep now, as tired as I was, since now that I forced myself to stay awake for this long, I didn't want to ruin the good thing I had going on and put my body clock in further disarray. I asked Janna where there was food. There was some food right here where she was picking me up if she wanted to take my bags up to her place, and I could walk to the B&B after eating. I figured I might not be able to find her place easily though, and I wasn't prepared to walk quite just yet. After thinking about what to do, unable to make a decision, I decided to go with her to the B&B, and then figure it all out.

Good thing I didn't stay down at the bottom of this hill and try to find my way back to Janna's because the roads twisted and turned, turned and twisted, uphill. Yes, I was planning on walking lots of uphills, but I guess just not quite yet, and at least not now on the roads. When we pulled into her driveway, I grabbed my two rucksacks out, and she told me that her husband could carry by heavy suitcase up the stairs for me. Thank goodness. I thought I would at least give him a hand by taking the suitcase out of the boot and leaving it by the car.

We walked through her gate, down some steps, through the front door, and she showed me the common area of the B&B, which is a common thing for B&Bs to have. An area we all have in common, for me and any other guests that we can share. Usually the living room with couches, chairs, and a television, and the dining room where we would be dining for breakfast. Janna then showed me up the stairs. Good thing I didn't have to take my forty-pound luggage up those. I wondered if I would have to lug the luggage upstairs in future B&Bs.

She showed me my room. Adorable and comfortable. Good choice for my first B&B. A nice spacious, well-decorated room, with my own private bathroom. This is why I love to stay in B&Bs. Yes, I used to be a hostel girl in my younger years, and I have stayed in plenty of hotels. As mentioned, I do like to backpack and camp. However my favorite places to stay these days are B&Bs. After all, they are like home. Because they are in a home. Someone's home. Someone who graciously welcomes you to their home, trusts you with their belongings, and makes you feel at home.

Janna pointed out a pot to make tea, and mentioned a few other bits about the room that I can't remember now as the lack of sleep made for some low thinking capacity. However I did think to ask Janna where the official monument and start of the South West Coast Path was, and if there was food nearby the monument, as perhaps I should at least go get some food and prepare myself for walking either today or tomorrow by knowing where my first steps would be. Yes, indeed there was a pub with food near the monument. Good proper British food. It was a brief walk down the hill. Oh, yes, that hill.

The Decision

Janna left me to myself. I freshened up a bit, made some tea, and decided what to do. Sometimes when I think too hard about what to do, like I was doing earlier at the car, I can't figure out what to do. Then when I just take my mind off the subject for a while, then my decision comes to me without much thought. I would walk the SWCP! The entire six miles I was planning on doing tomorrow. I would make my day today my first official walking day, instead of tomorrow. The weather for the afternoon looked really good, and tomorrow's weather forecast wasn't looking so great as mentioned. Besides, taking a walk is a good way to not sleep, to stay awake, adjust to this time zone, get some fresh air, move the body, and help with the jetlag. Scott and I did something similar last year to help with jetlag by walking after we arrived a few miles in the opposite direction of our first planned walk in order to get fresh air and to move our bodies.

I immediately got out one of my rucksacks, and organized it with my version of the "Ten Essentials" that are recommended for hiking and walking. Extra food – some nuts, a protein bar, and some dried fruit that I brought with me from home. Extra clothing – rain gear, an extra pair of socks, a couple hats (sun hat, rain hat, and a warm beanie), and a warm jacket. A first aid kit that I already put together at home, with various items like ointments, an ace bandage, safety pins, duct tape, band-aids (aka "plasters" in England), and blister prevention and protection items. A guidebook and the little booklet for today's walk (more on those later). Sunscreen and sunglasses. Headlamp just in case, with extra batteries. Emergency blanket and a whistle just in case. Water in a water bladder. New camera, mobile phone, and my new small video camera (yes, I had all three electronics). Extra batteries for the electronics and extra mobile phone charger. Chapstick, two kinds, one a zinc sunscreen, the other my favorite regular chapstick. Toilet paper. I also made sure I had my credit cards, cash, and even my Passport. A few other miscellaneous items also went into my rucksack. Eventually all these items in my rucksack would evolve over time, might include more or less clothes, and more or less items, depending on the day and the weather, but by and large I took these items with me every day. For now, I put on my hiking clothes, socks, a pair of hiking boots, grabbed my rucksack, and I was ready to walk!

I was still hungry though. I didn't want to take the time for a sit-down meal, so I hoped that perhaps the pub would make something for me "to go," or as they say in England, "take away." I went downstairs to ask Janna how to get to the official SWCP monument down that hill, the monument that I had seen only in pictures, but was about to make my way towards after months of planning to actually start walking the SWCP. Janna explained. "Go down the path of stone steps by the side of the house, take a left at the next path of stone steps by the garden, and out the front gate. You will end up on a street. Turn left. Go to the hairpin turn. You remember that hairpin turn, right?" I said "yes" out loud, but inside I wasn't so sure. Apparently we drove around the hairpin turn earlier in all that twisting and turning. Remember, I was on lack of sleep and jetlag and the thinking capacity was on the low side. "When you get to the hairpin turn, there is a sign for a footpath, so you don't have to take the road down, that will take you down the hill to the quay (which is pronounced "key," not "kway," and is a wharf, pier, or jetty), the official SWCP monument, and the pub." Great, I thought! Sounds pretty easy and straightforward. Apparently not for me though in my condition.

First, a word of warning. Stone steps when wet can be slippery. It had been raining earlier and the ground was still wet. Even in hiking boots stone steps can be slippery. I hadn't walked maybe a few yards still on the B&B property when suddenly my foot slipped out from under me. Great, I'm not even on the SWCP yet, and I already slipped. Of course, I don't want to slip at all on the path. Fortunately, I caught myself before falling on my rear and on my rucksack. Fortunately, I did not twist an ankle or anything like that. So fortunate! I would definitely not liked to have ruined my 630 mile walk in the first few feet of my adventure, and I wasn't even on the SWCP itself yet. I did feel a bit of a pull though in the thigh of my right leg. That did concern me actually. I felt my breathing get a bit erratic and I actually nearly cried.

After looking around to make sure no one saw my embarrassing slip, I took a deep breath, and walked slowly and carefully down the rest of the stone steps and off the B&B property, testing out the thigh and seeing how it would react to walking. So far so good. I breathed a bit easier.

Another word of warning. If you stay at this B&B, it turns out there are two hairpin turns. I'm not sure why Janna didn't mention that. Maybe she did, and I was just not in a clear state of mind to comprehend clearly. I walked to the first hairpin turn as instructed, but was unable to find the sign for the footpath. I paced up and down the street a couple of times looking my hardest. Even searching to see if I could see the monument below in the distance. Great, I'm not even on the SWCP yet and I'm already lost. Of course I don't want to get lost at all on the path. Fortunately I have a keen sense of direction. Sometimes, I can actually figure out the way. Or so I thought.

I started heading down the street in one direction based on the fact that I actually could see in the distance the shoreline of the water and the quay. I figured if I follow the streets in that general direction, I would find where I was going. However not walking too much down the road, I had options, the street on the left, or the street on the right, that both seemed to head downhill. Hmmm.

Fortunately two people were sitting romantically on a little park bench. My guardian angels of the moment, the first guardian angels of my walk. The first in a long list of upcoming guardian angels. I asked them if they knew the way down to the SWCP monument. Sure enough, head down the first option, the street on the left, past the red mail box and soon I would come to a sign for the footpath down to the quay. Ok, that sounded familiar. It must be the same path as above, but a lower entrance. I thanked them, and sure enough, I found the footpath. Down to the quay. And down to the official SWCP monument.

The Official SWCP Monument

Actually, the footpath led right down to the official SWCP monument! It stunned me a bit when I first saw it. Not because of what it looked like, but because I wasn't expecting it to be there at that exact moment. It also stunned me because it was now official. I was there! I was really there! Months and months of planning. Weeks and weeks of looking forward to this day. Days and days of anticipation. Hours and hours of traveling to get here. I was here! I was really here! At the large bronze monument of large hands holding a map, marking the beginning of the SWCP. Or the ending of the SWCP if you walk in the opposite direction. In Minehead, England. My epic walking adventure was about to begin.

I carefully crossed the street. Careful is the key word here. This is the one thing I must be aware of the most I told myself before I left for England. Traffic moves in the opposite direction in England than I am used to in the US. We drive on the right hand side of the street; they drive on the left hand side. If I looked in the direction I was used to, I would not see cars coming in my direction. My rule of thumb I told myself would be to cross the street when there were absolutely no cars visible or audible whatsoever. Look both ways about ten times, and wait till there were absolutely no cars coming whatsoever. Only then can I cross the street. Run. Fast. As fast as I can. Yes, I am exaggerating a bit, but if I had someone to hold hands with, I would. The point is I need to be very careful about crossing the street for the next three months because the direction of traffic moving is not what I am used to.

After carefully crossing the street, I was standing in front of the official SWCP monument. This monument was "based on a design by local art student Sarah Ward," according to the SWCP Association website. Looking at the monument from one side, where the two large hands are holding a map, I could not quite tell what the map the hands were holding was of exactly. I was not familiar enough with the geography of England, but perhaps it was the coast around Minehead, or some other segment of the SWCP. A plaque told me that the sculptor of this monument was Owen Cunningham. On the other side of the monument, there was a smaller etching of the full map of the SWCP with specific dots for Minehead and Poole, along with the words, "WALK: 630 miles – 1014 Km."

I grabbed out my camera, as well as my mobile phone, for some photos of the monument. Note that whenever I grab out my camera from here on out, I would also grab my mobile for photos. Actually, I would always have those two objects handy, one hanging around my neck, the other in a pocket. For most photos, I would take the picture twice. The camera photos would be most likely for blogs if I do some when I get back, this book, and "official" pictures. The mobile photos will be for Facebook posts. Unless of course, some of the mobile pictures turn out great, then they can also be for blogs, this book, and "official" pictures too.

I took some pictures of this monument from a few angles as it was still sinking in to me that I was actually here. Close up photos of the maps on the monument, and a few further away pictures with a seawall separating the sidewalk and the water on the other side, and the blue sky with its white clouds. I asked some people walking by if they would be so kind as to take my picture with the monument because after all, I was about to start walking the 630-mile South West Coast Path, and I should have a picture of myself, don't you think. I don't like taking selfies or setting up the timer on my camera, and since I was walking by myself, asking someone else to take the pictures was a great option. The gentleman of this couple actually took several pictures of me using my mobile. I liked them. The pictures, that is, not the couple. Well, I liked this couple, too, because they took pictures of me, but really I usually don't like pictures of myself no matter who takes them. Ask my husband. He will tell you. I tell him to delete many pictures of me. Anyway, I posed in front of the official SWCP monument with my rucksack on my back, holding my camera and my first guidebook in my hand. I thanked the gentleman a few times for taking my picture, and if he happens to be reading this book and remembers this moment, thank you again.

Punxsutawney Phil

I then took out my picture of Punxsutawney Phil. To photograph him. You know, the Groundhog. February 2nd. The Seer of Seers. The Sage of Sages. The Prognosticator of Prognosticators. The Weather Prophet Extraordinaire. The movie with Bill Murray and Addie McDowell. The movie with Bill Murray and Andie McDowell. Over and over and over again. And my birthday. My 50th. Remember, my birthday is February 2nd. You might be wondering why I have a photo of Punxsutawney Phil and why am I taking pictures of him at the SWCP monument. Well let me explain a bit more…about my birthday, and about Phil.

My 50th birthday, which I have mentioned, is on Groundhog's Day, as it has been for the past 49 previous birthdays as my parents somehow planned me being born on February 2nd. Honestly, I'm not sure if they actually planned this, and I have never asked, but that is how it happened. One thing all Groundhog's Day babies should do at least once in their life is make the trip to Punxsutawney, Pennsylvania. The place where Punxsutawney Phil, the groundhog himself, makes his infamous weather prediction. I was actually hoping that maybe he could predict perfect weather of warmth and sun for the summer of 2017 in the south west of England just for me.

My husband's birthday happens to be on January 31st. Yes, two Aquarians. I'm not sure astrologically what that means and if our relationship would have been advised, but we got married anyway. We really actually should have gotten married on a February 1st, so we could celebrate birthday-anniversary-birthday all in a row, but got married on August 18th instead. Probably to ensure better weather in the summer. (See how this is all tying together somehow.)

I once thought that I should go to Punxsutawney, PA for my 50th, but my 47th birthday beat my 50th to the punch. You might be asking why I am rambling on about a groundhog, when this book is about the SWCP. Nothing really, other than a hopeful weather prediction, and that I am talking about my birthday, my 50th. Again. And a photography contest which I will get to momentarily.

We had a beautiful outdoor wedding at a lighthouse. My husband and I. Not Phil and I. At a lighthouse. Now where am I going with that tangent? I love lighthouses. I am fascinated with them, love visiting them, enjoy reading about people who were once lighthouse keepers or grew up in some seemingly romantic, yet many times harsh, conditions. So my husband and I got married at one. At a lighthouse. As mentioned, my niece painted one for me for my 50th birthday, and I will see many along the SWCP.

Three years ago, my husband and I made the trip across the country from our home in Washington state (where I have actually seen all the lighthouses that can be visited) to Punxsutawney, PA, and had a great four-day celebration of our birthdays. Especially mine. We got up at the wee hours of the morning to see the prediction of that year (six more weeks of winter). We toured the quirky town. We even got our names and a picture in the local small-town paper, where it was declared that I was born on Groundhog's Day, and my husband was born on February 31st!

Now back to the SWCP. Needless to say, the epic adventure I will not be doing for my 50th is Punxsutawney, PA since that has already been done. Instead, the SWCP is the epic birthday plan. Who knows, maybe I will see gophers, marmots, hedgehogs or other cousins of the groundhog on the SWCP.

With all this, the point I am really trying to get at is there actually a photography contest each year put on by the official Groundhog Club in Punxsutawney, PA. I have participated in this contest a couple of times already. The premise is that they give you a picture of Phil, and you take him with you on your travels, take photos of him on the travels, and you enter the contest. I have won! First place. In the International Category of the "Worldwide Adventures of Phil" contest. When I took him to the Cotswolds here in England a few years ago. I sat Phil on a bench in front of Saint Michael's Church in Buckland, possibly one of the oldest churches in England with some parts still existing from around the year 1200. This photo won first place. I also was an Honorable Mention the following year when Phil walked with me in Spain, on the Camino de Santiago Camino Francés 482-mile walk I did. In fact, my idea for this year is to take several pictures of Phil along the SWCP and create a collage. From beginning (Minehead) to end (Poole/South Haven Point). Who knows, maybe I will win something again this year!

Therefore, I took out my picture of Punxsutawney Phil from my rucksack, leaned my rucksack against the monument, placed Phil's picture on top of the rucksack, and placed the guidebook I was holding in front of the rucksack. Sort of like a "still life" photo. I took my first pictures of Phil for my collage.

The Arrow and the Acorn Symbols

I also took photos of the fading writing on the ground near the SWCP monument saying "South West Coast Path National Trail," complete with an arrow pointing me in the right direction, and an acorn, the important directional symbol of the 16 National Trails in England, including the SWCP. I took photos of one other sign, one that showed me that I was also about to walk "part of the England Coast Path" too.

Before I walk on, please let me mention more about this "acorn" symbol. According to the SWCP Association, "The acorn symbol is used on waymarks on all the National Trails…in England and Wales." It is the directional symbol. So you know which direction to walk. You follow one waymark, a signpost marking the route of a path, with an acorn on it to the next signpost and acorn, to the next signpost and acorn so you can find your way. So that you don't get lost! On the Camino de Santiago in Spain, the important directional symbol was the scallop shell. Here in England and Wales, on the National Trails, including the SWCP, the important directional symbol is the acorn. "Follow the acorn" is the rule of thumb for directions and finding your way on the SWCP and the other 15 National Trails.

Interestingly, both long-distance walks also use the yellow arrow as another important directional symbol! The acorn and the arrow. The arrow and the acorn. At some point, I shall describe all this in more detail as well as the significance of "The Arrow Closest To The Acorn."

Minehead, South West Coast Path – June 4
Me at the Official SWCP Monument (one side of monument)
My Purple Shoes at the Official SWCP Monument (other side of monument, photo take two days later)
Official SWCP Monument (one side of monument with full hand)
Sign pointing a quarter mile to Minehead and 629 3/4 to Poole

Time to Walk

Now that the photography was complete, it was time. Time to walk. Time to start this path. This adventure. This epic 50th birthday celebration. Was I nervous? Was I excited? Was my right thigh doing alright? A bit of both actually at the moment for the first two questions, but definitely more excited than nervous. Fortunately, it seemed that for the third question that my right thigh was doing alright. I still told myself at this moment as I started walking away from the official SWCP monument, "Take a deep breath, just put one foot in front of the other. And walk. Don't think." That's what I told myself. One step at a time. After all, the journey of 630 miles begins with one step.

I was off. At exactly 3:00pm on Sunday the 4th of June 2017, England time, I started my walking adventure on England's 630- mile South West Coast Path!

But I was still hungry…

MINEHEAD TO BOSSINGTON – Sunday, 4 June 2017

"If you're walking down the right path and you're willing to keep walking, eventually you'll make progress." Barack Obama

The pavement of the Esplanade just beyond the fading writing on the ground as I walked my first steps after the official SWCP monument took me along a seawall with some large rocks just on the other side. On my right hand side. And along the waters. The seas. The ocean. The channels. The Bristol Channel to be exact at this moment. An extension of the Atlantic Ocean. These various waters, seas, oceans, and channels would remain on my right hand side for the next 88 days. Unless of course I walked on any given day in the opposite direction. Then they would be on my left hand side. The waters, seas, oceans, and channels that I would fall in love with!

Today my left hand side took me past a small tea shop and café. I walked passed it. Even though I was hungry. I saw the pub a bit beyond that Janna told me about where I planned on getting some food. I stopped to take pictures of the boats in the harbour first however. Sailboats, motorboats, fishing boats. The first of many, many boats in many, many harbours that I would fall in love with!

The pub was closed. As many pubs and restaurants are between 3:00pm and 6:00pm. That time frame is in between their lunch and dinner menus. Just a note that if you are going to walk the SWCP, it is very possible that some places you might be planning on eating at might be closed during this time frame.

I went back to the tea shop and café. They were open. They had some quick items in their display case that I could take away with me on my first walk and eat along the way. "Pasties" were what they had. Oh yes, I remember those from the time I walked the SWCP with my husband last year. Pasties are pastry dough filled with something inside, like meat and/or vegetables. They are basically ready to eat and I could take one with me and eat it as I walked so as to not waste any more time and walk more than the few feet on the SWCP that I have just walked.

They didn't have any more of their "veggie" version of the pasties left though, which would have been filled with cheese and potato. I got one of the ones filled with meat instead. I am not much of a meat eater. In fact, I am mostly a vegetarian. But it was food. And I was hungry. And I really wanted to walk. They also had a large cheese scone. That's better. I bought both. The cheese scone for now, the pastie for later, and the other snacks I had already packed just in case. I was set with food for my six mile walk to Bossington.

Pasties have a "long and fascinating history." According to an information sign that I saw about a month later as I walked along the SWCP in the Land's End area, "Cornwall's main industry back in the 1800's was tin and the Cornish pasty was lunch for every miner. Tin mining was hard and dangerous work and the pasty provided the perfect portable combination of meat, vegetables and carbohydrate with everything they needed for the grueling day down the mines and the long walk home afterwards. Meat and vegetables were cooked together and enclosed in a thick layer of pastry which acted as a thermos keeping their delicious contents warm, while being easy to carry." (Note that I shall be learning about tin mining later, and I shall be in Cornwall later too.)

I started eating the cheese scone as I set off again. For real, this time. No more stopping. Unless I wanted to stop to take photos. Or stop to rest. But I better not rest now, after not even walking a quarter of a mile yet. The pavement continued on for a bit, turned into a parking lot, which I shall refer to as a "car park" from here on out as that is the English term for parking lot, or maybe it was actually a turning circle for cars to turn around in and not an actual car park.

Smaller rocks were now to my right. Then I saw my first wooden signpost. The first of many, many wooden signposts I would be seeing, about 4,000 to be exact. This one told me that now I had walked a quarter of a mile! How did I know I only went a quarter of a mile? Because this first sign post I saw with mileage printed on the sign said "Coast Path - Poole 629 3/4. Porlock 7," in the direction I was headed, and "Coast Path - Minehead 1/4," pointing in the direction I had just come from. A quarter of a mile done! I was well on my way now. Any nervousness I had completely shed. The excitement grew even more. I overheard two women looking at the same sign I did, who clearly were not walking the SWCP, say excitedly, "Look, we've walked a quarter of a mile on the SWCP!" They turned around and went back towards Minehead.

I walked on, eating the cheese scone as I went. The path was flat so far. I passed a grassy field on my left and a rocky beach on my right just beyond some shrubbery. The waters were beyond that. On a clear day there are views of the country of Wales from here. On this day for me however, unfortunately there was some cloud coverage obstructing my views of Wales.

I stopped at a bench to tighten up the laces on my hiking boots. I also tucked the legs of my pants into my socks. At the last minute, my friend Sasha (much more on her later) warned me of ticks in this area of the SWCP, which I already knew of the possibility actually. She suggested tucking the legs of my pants into my socks for the first few days to hopefully avoid getting bitten by any ticks, as I would be walking along the edge of the Exmoor National Park area of the SWCP. An area of about 270 square miles, Exmoor National Park "is a hilly and moorland area of Somerset and North Devon" which also includes some managed farmland, of which the SWCP runs along the National Park's edge from Minehead to Combe Martin, about my next five or six days of walking. I was in the county of Somerset at the moment.

I may have looked a bit silly with my pant legs tuck into my socks, but better safe than sorry. As I continued to walk, I passed by a farm. The path soon turned into some woods. Trees surrounded me, and a leaf-covered trail was below my feet. Ferns and other green foliage added to the greenery of my surroundings. It was a climb up. My first of many, many, many climbs up on the SWCP. For me, not to sound too sure of myself, this climb was not that difficult. My love of hiking in the area in which I live, and the many years of hiking that I have done, and the training hikes I did leading up to this walk, have hopefully prepared me for all of the climbs I will encounter in the next 629 miles. Yes, I have walked a mile thus far! The cheese scone had been eaten. Views of the water appeared every now and again through the trees and foliage, with one distinct ship off in the distance. A freighter perhaps, with a white top half and a red bottom half. This freighter appeared in my photos several times today.

Not too far into the walk, I was now out of the woods. Out in the open landscape. With views of the water constant now, with grassy areas, and blooming bright dark pink foxglove wildflowers. The skies were a different shade of blue than the water's blue, I noticed. Light blue sky, and turquoise and deep blue patches of the water. White clouds covered the sun now and again. It was nice warm afternoon. Not overly warm or hot, but by no means cool. Perfect weather actually for my first day's walk. I passed a sign that said I had now walked two miles.

About two and a half miles into the walk, I had a decision to make. There were two possible paths. The official Coast Path was the "gentler" inland route. The alternate Coast Path was the lower more seaward "rugged" route. Originally, I decided to do the inland path. After all, I was going to walk 630 miles, why not take it easy on my first day and walk the gentler route. A few weeks ago however, some folks who were chatting on a "SWCP Facebook Group" page I belong to (much more on that later) were saying that the rugged path was not that rugged, and would just take about an hour longer as it was about a mile longer. I had changed my mind at that point then to do the rugged path. However, at this moment, on this day, considering I started my walk much later in the day than my normal walk would have started if I walked tomorrow, and since I was still on lack of sleep and jetlagged, I did not want to take any chances. I took the official inland gentler Coast Path, and became quite happy with my decision right away.

Fields of sheep appeared. I was surprised. It was so cute to see these animals. I loved seeing the sheep daily during our previous trip in the Cotswolds, and hearing their "baaaaaas," remembering that when I got home from that trip, I said to my husband, "I miss the sheep." Now I could see them again!

A few horses appeared as well. My husband loves horses. I took photos for him, and texted him the photos later that day. I was later corrected by Janna telling me that actually I saw "Exmoor Ponies." According to the Exmoor National Park website, "For many people, seeing Exmoor Ponies on the open moors is one of the highlights of a trip to Exmoor. The Exmoor is one of a number of native British ponies. They are a common sight on the moorlands of the National Park where a number of managed herds graze the rough pasture." And I saw some on my first day of walking!

It was nice flat walking on stone tracks and trails on this inland path, with views of the sheep pastures, more bright dark pink foxglove, green ferns and other green shrubbery, and the blue waters beyond. I occasionally caught a glimpse of the rugged path as I saw it winding its way along the terrain below. I was still glad I chose the inland path for today. The views were breathtaking from up here to me, and it was actually finally sinking in that I was actually walking the SWCP! That I would be seeing similar, but different, views day after day after day for the next 88 days.

Soon I passed a sign that said I had now walked four miles! The path so far had been nicely signed so that I did not get lost once today. Other than the time leaving the B&B, but that doesn't count. It was a good feeling to not get lost on my first day. A good feeling to have good weather on my first day, too. Let's hope that continues.

The views of the water that had been on my right hand side, I now had a view of in front of me, and of a headland ahead of me, which is a peninsula of land that juts out into the water. I bet that I would be walking on and around that headland in the next couple of days, I thought to myself. The headland consisted of small hills of light green grass and darker green trees. I could see square and checkered pastures of farmland, and what was probably a village or town below the hills. The sun was shining on the water from this direction in such as a way as to create a shimmering glow. A beach was below me as well, with a few people walking along its shore. It was all quite picturesque.

Just after that view, the rugged path met up with the official path, and the combined path now began to descend. Quite steeply. The first of many, many, many climbs down. I realized that I forgot to take my hiking poles with me today. I brought them for the purpose of helping my knees during these many descents. I made a note to myself to remember them in the future. One other item that I forgot to take with me today that I will remember for the future was the waterproof map case that I had bought specifically for maps, but which I will use for my guidebook and booklets to keep them dry in case of rain, which of course I hope I don't encounter. Fortunately, since there was no rain today the waterproof map case was not needed anyway.

I made my way very slowly down the steep rocky, then grassy, hillside. At the bottom was that beach I saw from above, which I didn't walk on, but continued on the path towards Bossington. As I stopped to take a picture with my mobile I noticed that my sister had just called me. I could not listen to her voice message, so I called her back. I told her that at that moment I just happened to be finishing up my first walk of the SWCP as we were speaking. It was great to hear her voice, and talk to her for a couple minutes. Good mobile reception too at this spot. I was surprised, and pleased.

I crossed a small bridge over a stream, and emerged at a car park in Bossington. Complete with a quintessential English red telephone box. I had done it! My first official walk on the SWCP! The time was about 6:00pm. (Note that I won't be telling you all the exact times from now on for the majority of my days unless it has significance, but I thought it might be significant for my first day.) I was feeling rather triumphant. I was feeling that I was definitely in my element.

Three hours of walking. Six miles down. 624 miles to go! I was walking down the right path, I am willing to keep walking, and I had made progress.

There was a bit more to the rest of my first day on the SWCP. I wanted to explore this little village of Bossington. I love the quaint quiet quintessential English villages with stone homes, thatched roofs, and tall chimneys, which make me think of Mary Poppins. I was also hungry again, and I wanted to see if any cafés were open. I walked down the one quiet street of Bossington, passing by about ten buildings, which were mostly homes. The only café and tea shop had already closed. I think the general rule of thumb is pubs close from 3:00 to 6:00 as I previously mentioned, and small cafés close around 5:00 or 6:00 for the evening.

Since there seemed to be no food options, I walked back down the quaint quiet quintessential English street, back to the car park. I got out my mobile phone and gave Janna a "tinkle." That is what she referred to it when she wanted me to call her. We had pre-arranged that I would call her when I arrived in Bossington, and she would very kindly pick me up and bring me back to her B&B in Minehead. I let her know I had made it to Bossington, and that I was at the National Trust car park. She knew where that was, and would be there in about fifteen minutes to pick me up. In the meantime, I still had that meat pastie I bought earlier, which since I never did eat it during my walk as I was so busy enjoying the scenery, was now unfortunately a bit old in my opinion to eat since it had been sitting in my rucksack for three hours by now in the warmth, so I never ate it. I munched on a few nuts and dried fruit instead.

Janna arrived on time, and we chatted about my walk and a few other topics on the way back to Minehead. I kindly let Janna know that I was hungry once again, and asked as we drove back if there would be a place to get a fresh salad or something for take away that I could bring back to the B&B and eat there. She told me that since it was Sunday that many places would be closed already. Sure enough as we drove back through The Parade, it was deserted. We even tried to see if the small grocery store was open, but it was not. She asked if I would eat fish and chips. "Sure," I said, thinking, "Yes, that would be fine, as I am in England after all." Around the corner was an open fish and chips place so I got some fish and chips. Beer battered cod and "fries," which is what I would call them. Complete with tartar sauce for the fish, and malt vinegar and salt for the chips. Proper British style. That's what the gentleman working there told me was the way people ate their fish and chips. I thought I would give it a go, and try it their way. Besides, I don't like ketchup anyway.

Back at the B&B, the first thing I did after settling in was eat my fish and chips, complete with tartar sauce, malt vinegar, and salt. Yes, it was tasty that way. In some ways, I really would have preferred a fresh salad for dinner, but this was a very nice meal anyway after my first day's walk, and a nice introduction to English food.

I called my Mom and Scott, which I have done actually several times in the last couple days, and I will do again daily. I couldn't do much else this evening. I was really tired. Feeling successful for my getting to Minehead and walking from Minehead to Bossington, I turned off the lights at 9:00pm, and was asleep within minutes.

DAY ONE STATS: 6 MILES. 3 HOURS. EXTRA HALF MILE FROM B&B TO SWCP MONUMENT. HIKING BOOTS. PUB IN MINEHEAD IS CALLED "THE OLD SHIP AGROUND." NO PUB THAT I COULD FIND IN BOSSINGTON. Quote about Exmoor Ponies from Exmoor-nationalpark.gov.uk/Whats-Special/wildlife/Exmoor-Ponies.

BOSSINGTON TO SILCOMBE FARM – Monday, 5 June 2017

"My grandmother started walking five miles a day when she was sixty. She's ninety-seven now, and we don't know where the heck she is." – Ellen DeGeneres

I woke this morning to the sound of my alarm two hours before breakfast was to be served, as I wanted a few hours to regroup myself and get a few things done. Nothing like sleeping nine hours though. I felt refreshed. Perhaps in just one night's sleep my internal body clock was reset to England time, and the jetlag was gone.

The weather for today was supposed to be a bit tricky. As mentioned, BBC Weather, the app on my mobile phone that I would rely on heavily for the next several months, called for a revised forecast of heavy rain and wind gusts, sometime later in the afternoon that might be as high as "gale force winds." I read before I even left home for the SWCP that it is not advisable to walk in gale force winds. Today's forecast would be dry till around 3:00pm when the rain and winds would start. Therefore, I wanted to get my walk for today done by that time.

When I travel, especially during my walking travels, I shower at night. I do this for a few reasons. First, after a long day's walk, perhaps getting sweaty or wet or dirty, it feels nice. Second, I am one who believes in that having as dry as feet as possible in the morning can help prevent blisters. I have other blister theories, which I shall explain at some point, but this is one of them. At home I have a different routine, where I shower in the morning because I feel fresher. However, when I shower at night during my travels, I somehow feel just as fresh in the morning, and I hope that my completely dry feet will prevent blisters. An important goal for walking 630 miles.

Therefore this morning I didn't need to shower as I took one last night. I do however like to wash my face in the morning. It confuses me however how to wash my face properly with warm water using sinks in England. Many sinks in England have two separate faucets, one for hot and one for cold. Not one faucet with handles for both temperatures where it is easy to adjust the temperature to warm, but two separate faucets with two separate temperatures. I can never figure out a way to combine them to get warm water. The only thing I have come up with is moving my hands quickly back and forth between the two faucets to combine the water in the cup of my hands and try to make it warm. I need to do that though before the hot water faucet gets too hot to touch. I suppose though that I could put a stopper in the sink drain and fill up the basin with both temperatures to create warm water, but for some reason I do not.

Anyway, since my rucksack was about ready to go from yesterday's walk, I just needed to add the waterproof map case for my guidebook and booklet. I also thought about the hiking poles that I had forgotten yesterday, but knowing that today's walk would be mostly flat, I chose to leave those behind. Now I just had to decide on which shoes to wear today. Yesterday I wore my hiking boots, but with the dry weather yesterday, and the terrain being pretty gentle yesterday, I wished I had worn my "purple shoes." Let me introduce you to my "purple shoes."

They make my feet feel more comfortable. I originally bought them in Spain, during my Camino de Santiago walk, after I had some blister problems there with my hiking boots of the time. Long story short, as much as I could do to prevent blisters on that walk, even with showering at night, I had nearly two weeks of very hot weather, which along with some hiking boots that didn't fit very well, I developed two bad blisters, one on the back of each heal. Those actually forced me to take a few days off from walking, and then walk in Teva-type sandals that had no heal for a few days, which was then followed by my very great purchase of my shoes - some Adidas sneakers, or "trainers" as they are called in England – which happened to be the color of purple. These purple shoes aka purple sneakers aka purple trainers got me through the rest of my Camino walk blister-free!

The purple shoes I brought with me to England however were not those exact original pair, but two more pairs I bought on the internet when I got home from that walk. Yes, two new pairs. Just in case either one of the pairs wore out or got wet, as they are not waterproof, or anything happened to one of the pairs on this walk. They are that comfortable. (Note that while I could refer to these shoes in this book as either my "purple sneakers," or "purple trainers," or "purple shoes," most of the time I refer to them as my "purple shoes.")

The hiking boots I brought with me to England this time, which are waterproof, are comfortable also and not the pair I had in Spain. In general though, my purple shoes for me are the most comfortable, and are my shoe of preference. Therefore, today I would wear the purple shoes, but bring the pair of hiking boots in my rucksack just in case. In case of terrain that might have called for boots, such as hills to climb up and down, larger rocky or smaller loose pebble conditions, or puddles or mud. Or in case the weather might be rainy and I need the waterproof material of my boots. This will be the way I walk many days of my SWCP walk, wearing purple shoes but bringing my hiking boots as backup. Unless I already know that the terrain or weather will be such that I know the hiking boots are necessary. I know that carrying boots in my rucksack adds extra weight and bulk, but it is not that much extra, and I think worth it to keep my feet extra happy in any condition.

Back to today. Breakfast was the "Half English" for me. Scrambled eggs, warmed grilled tomatoes, warmed fried mushrooms, toast aka fried bread, orange juice, tea, and a bowl of fruit. I rather like this breakfast. Protein, carbs, and nutrients. I skipped the baked beans, but that is an option for future breakfasts for me. I will always skip the bacon and sausage, due to my vegetarianism. With the meat and everything, they call it the "Full English" breakfast, and it is the quintessential English breakfast. It can also be called "The Full Monty" or "the fry-up." The Full English may also include potatoes or hash browns, kippers which are smoked herring, black pudding, which I prefer not to describe its ingredients, and coffee. The eggs can be fried, poached, or scrambled. The tradition of the Full English can actually be traced back to the early 1300's.

I brushed my teeth, put on my purple shoes, grabbed my rucksack with hiking boots inside, and I was off for my second walk of the SWCP. Today would be another six miles. I actually felt my right thigh ache a bit last night from yesterday's slip, and thought that it might again ache today, and it did a bit, but all in all fortunately it was not too bad.

Janna kindly drove me back to Bossington to the same car park as she picked me up in yesterday. I already had my rain pants and rain jacket on, as it was just lightly raining, which I kept on all day, put my rain hat on, which I occasionally took on and off, and I took a photo of the arrow and acorn signpost that said "Coast Path" as well as "Bossington Beach, Porlock, Porlock Weir" and pointed me in the right direction. I was off for my second walk. I took a picture of my purple shoes to commemorate the use of my purple shoes for walking next to another directional arrow signpost a few feet later that said "Coast Path" with an acorn.

A few other quintessential English buildings decorated the paved road as I headed out of Bossington, including a farm selling homemade pure apple juice made with "locally grown apples without the use of fertilizers or pesticides" which was all "processed and bottled on the farm." Too bad they were selling the apple juice in big heavy bottles, otherwise I would have liked to try some.

The paved road turned into a path. A couple people with a dog passed me by. They continued on towards the sign that led them to a beach while I followed the Coast Path signs. The path took me around the outskirts of a marsh. The path itself was wet, but not overly muddy or puddly at all so my purple shoes did just fine. I noticed another walker in front of me and another behind me once in a while. They had rucksacks on like me. An old abandoned building that looked like a horse stable would have made for good shelter if needed, but made for a couple of good photos with a leafless tree and gray skies (or in the UK, "grey" skies).

It was in this marshy area that I saw my first of many World War 2 reminders. This one was a memorial to a US plane that unfortunately crashed into the marsh in October of 1942, with only one of its crew of twelve surviving.

I saw some sheep again as the flat terrain continued around the marsh. Only light rain, which alternated between raining and not raining, and an occasional light gust of wind, kept me company. Soon I made it to a rocky beach, with rocks about the size of my fist. The rain on the rocks made them glisten with shades of red and brown and green against my purple shoes. I took it slow as to not twist an ankle because the rocks could have been quite slippery, learning that from my slip on the stone steps yesterday, although a path used by many others had made the walking fairly easy and flat, and you could even see the path of rocks as you looked forward. My first of many, many beach walks!

A short distance down the rocky beach there was a set of stone steps (yes, I was careful) leading up to the street that took me into the next village of the SWCP, Porlock Weir. More quaint quintessential English homes lined the street greeting me as I walked along. Thatched rooftops, old stonework, and decorative flowers and plants adorned the homes. Note that many people actually walk from Minehead to Porlock Weir on their first day, since guidebooks and websites break up the walk that way, but as explained, I am walking shorter days, and am doing this entire walk a bit different than many people.

One of my favorite types of buildings to go into whenever and wherever I travel is churches. Especially those when I have travelled around in Europe and in England. Filled with long history, detailed stories, decorative art and stained glass, architecture built without modern machinery, religion and spirituality. I have always found churches to be inspiring, heartwarming, admirable, humbling, calming, peaceful, and grand. From the very small churches and chapels (as I was about to see) to the very large abbeys and cathedrals, I have always made it a point to visit as many as I possibly can. I had a five-month, seventeen-country travels around Europe once, visiting countless churches.

I also love hearing the bells of the churches ring. I love hearing their chimes whether for telling the time, or for playing songs, for a call to a church service or a call to prayer, or for a special occasion such as a wedding or a funeral. In the US, at least where I live, I just don't hear church bells ringing at all. During my Europe travels, I never got tired of hearing the church bells ring, any time of day, even in the late night or early morning hours.

Therefore when I saw the sign pointing me to the "top of the steep then 50 yards on the right" to St. Nicholas Church in Porlock Weir, I walked right up that steep and into the church. Before I entered, I took off my wet rain hat out of respect, and rain jacket to not dribble water in the church. A small church, but yet powerful as I always feel them to be when inside. My first of many, many churches on my SWCP walk!

I am not a praying type of person, but when I am in these churches, I do say a prayer. I first ask please for my safety during my walk, to be healthy, injury free, blister free, to have good weather, and all things to happen positively for myself during my 630-mile adventure. I then pray for my family and friends, for their safety and health. Finally I pray for the world, for peace, love, compassion, and understanding.

Once I was done with my usual prayers, I walked around the church looking at its intricate details, and took a few photos. I noticed papers near the entrance of this church explaining "the true story of Santa Claus," and St. Nicholas, who "became known throughout the land for his generosity to those in need, his love for children, and his concern for sailors and ships." I also noticed a sign saying "Refugees Welcome Here." I also made a small donation, which I always do in churches, and thanked the church for its time. I put my rain hat and jacket back on, took a picture of the exterior of the church, and went back down the steep.

In Porlock Weir I took few pictures of the boats in the harbour. The tide was out so the sailboats and rowboats and fishing boats were resting on the mud and rocks. An old anchor, possibly dating from 1805, was displayed along the seawall. I needed a restroom so I went into a little shop and asked if he had one. He told me there was one in the car park. I bought a small scoop of chocolate ice cream in the little shop though first. I told myself I would have very little to almost no sugar this trip. So just a little bit for now, that's all.

After using the car park toilets, I continued on the path which started in between the two buildings of The Ship Inn. There was a bit of a climb through the woods of Exmoor National Park again, with lush trees and green ferns and other types of shrubbery. I had occasional views of the waters, but the cloudy misty day made the waters seem muddled and not as blue today as they were yesterday.

As I walked I had these thoughts sneak up on me: It felt surreal today. That I was walking. Here. On this path. On the SWCP. That I had planned for so many, many months. That I was walking on my own. It felt surreal that it was me, actually me, walking. In all my 50 years, except for the last year or so, I never thought that I would be walking a long-distance path such as this, and yet here I was. It actually did feel epic for me, even though I had only just begun the long walk.

I passed by an old stone wall and the remains of a couple of some old tunnels. I had more climbing through the woods with that occasional misty muddled view of the waters until I reached "the smallest complete parish church" in England, the total length of which is 35 feet long, 12 feet wide, with seating for only 33 people, St. Bueno's Church in Culbone. I started with taking photos of the outside on my way down the small road towards the church, and a few other exterior photos once I was on the church's grounds. Nestled between some trees, the church looked like it was made of stone, with some parts perhaps as old as the 13th and 15th centuries, with some restoration work and additions done in the 1800s.

I went inside. Even though I had just said my usual prayers about an hour earlier in St. Nicholas Church, I said them again in St. Bueno's Church. The exact wording of my usual prayers is usually different each time, but the gist is the same. Even though the church was small in size it still felt grand as they all do with its history and spirituality.

A few photos later, I donated some money and bought their brochure about the church, from which I obtained some of the information I mentioned above. In addition, this brochure told me that, "The ancient name of the place was Kitnor, said to be from Anglo Saxon words "cyta" – a cave, and "ore" – sea shore." Perhaps a cave by the sea shore.

I took a few more photos of the outside from various angles of the church. I also glanced at the tombstones. My husband likes this part. I find it fascinating too, but he really takes his time looking at the graveyard and tombstones, sometimes looking at each and every one. It is interesting to me that these tombstones can date as old as the 1700s or 1800s, or even earlier, and people have been buried for 100, 200 years, or more. Names and dates can still be read on some tombstones, but not on others. Some tombstones are deteriorating or covered with moss or lichen or something, and have become illegible. On the ones you can read, the years of birth dates and death dates are given. Some tombstones tell stories of who is buried there. Some tragic - war stories, or children or people that have died too young. I read a few stones in contemplation about the shortness of life, compared to how long people have been buried here. For example, my life has thus far been its 50 years, whereas people had been born, lived, died, and have been buried here long before my own birth. This surely makes one appreciate life!

I walked back into the woods again. Soon there was a second time where I needed to choose from two optional paths. This one was easy to decide. I prearranged with Janna that she would pick me up at Silcombe Farm when I arrived there. To get there I needed to take the inland "Alternative Coast Path," which was actually slightly longer than the "Coast Path/Permitted Path route," but both meet up within a few miles and would eventually take me onwards to Lynmouth.

I emerged out of the woods back into the openness. The wind blew some, but at the moment there was no rain. I wasn't far from the farm at this point, and within a half hour of leaving St. Bueno's Church I was at the farm. Three and a half hours of walking, including time in two churches, and another six miles done on the SWCP! I was feeling triumphant once again.

I tried to call Janna as we had arranged from the road near the farm, but I was unable to get mobile reception this time. Oh no, what was I going to do? I tried several times in various locations to see if I could make the call. I couldn't. I panicked for a moment. I thought of two options. One was to knock on the door of Silcombe Farm to see if I could use their landline phone. Alas no one was around. Option two, walk down the road back towards another farm or the highway until I was able to get reception, but that would add who knows how many more miles to my walk as I had no idea when I might be able to get reception. It was also getting closer to the 3:00 time when the wind and the rain would really start. I thought I would start to panic now, but then my guardian angels appeared.

I had actually noticed this car driving around the farm a few moments earlier as I was making my way to knock on the door of the farm. They had stopped to read a map or book. After no answer to my knock I thought well I could ask the people in the car to use their phone. By the time I walked back to where they had parked though, they had driven away. Oh no, now I did start to panic slightly.

Fortunately I noticed that the people in the car had stopped once again just up the road. I picked up my pace hoping that they would not drive away, and reached them with a sigh of relief. I knocked on their window and asked if I could please borrow their phone and explained my story. They said yes, even though I don't know if they completely understood my story. While it seemed they spoke English, turned out they were from Holland. I thought they were German by the words on their phone.

The first time I dialed Janna using their phone it did not work. Uh oh. I decided to try it again and it worked! Janna answered and I told her I made it to Silcombe Farm and could she please come get me. She explained she was taking her dog for a walk, but would return home and come get me soon. She then asked me some question that I did not understand, and when I tried to answer her, the mobile service cut out. I tried to call back, but no luck. Oh well, that was ok. I was sure that we figured it all out, and she would be there soon. I thanked the couple in the car, who then parked just up the road so that they could go walk down to the smallest complete parish church in England.

As I waited for Janna I sat and ate some dried fruit as a snack that I had in my rucksack, and glanced at my guidebook and booklet for the next day's walk, which actually wouldn't be for two days due to the weather (more on that later). Soon a man with a dog came through the last gate that I had come from, and started talking to me. He was local. Of course as soon as I talk out loud people can tell that I am not from around here, so he asked me what I was doing in England, and I told him of my walk. He seemed impressed. Off he and his dog went into the sunset.

Well ok not the sunset as it was only the afternoon, and the sun was not shining at the moment. In fact, the wind was beginning to pick up, and it was beginning to rain more as well. I took shelter at the edge of a shrub-covered wall which blocked some of the wind and rain. Time passed and I started to wonder if in my conversation with Janna she understood to pick me up. But then again I told myself that she had to take her dog home, and drive twelve miles. A39 is the main road, and is faster, but she told me that she had picked up another couple at the farm a couple months ago, and once you get off A39, the road is narrow for only one car and slow-going. I waited for Janna. About an hour.

Just then the couple that allowed me to use their mobile phone arrived up the path and through the gate. "Hello Debby," the woman said. Surprised that she knew my name, I asked her, how did she know my name? She reminded me that when I made the call to Janna from her phone earlier, the first thing I said was, "Hi, Janna, this is Debby." This woman from Holland was listening well and remembered.

They walked up to their parked car, and just then who arrived? Janna! This is where the term "it's a small world" comes into play. As Janna drove up she noticed the license plates on the couple's car. From Holland. Janna was originally from Holland. She told me so the other day. Janna stopped to chat with the couple, which I could not hear as I was down the road. I guess they confirmed that they were all from Holland. The woman then told Janna that it was her phone that I used. When Janna drove a bit down the road to get me she said, "Did you know that couple was from Holland when you used their phone?" I did not as I thought maybe they were German, but what a coincidence. See it is a small world after all. With the rain and wind picking up even more, I was glad to be inside Janna's car.

It was a narrow single-lane slow country road going back until we got to the A39 main road. Janna said if a car meets a tractor on a narrow single-lane road like this, and there are no places to pull over, it is a long ride "backwards." Janna actually had the couple from Holland tag along behind us as we drove back. I guess two cars beats out one tractor. How would the tractor back up, I wondered? I didn't know, and fortunately we didn't have to find out. I would come to learn that these narrow single-lane country roads are very, very common in this part of England. I had many future encounters in cars where someone did need to backup, but with consideration and cooperation, it all worked out well.

It was a long ride back to Minehead, about forty minutes. No wonder it took Janna an hour to reach me. As we drove up the road to her home, I confirmed where the path was down to the quay. She showed me. The second hairpin turn. Ah ha! There was the sign. It said, "Zig-Zag Footpath Leading to Webbers Garden, Marina Garden & Sea Front." They weren't kidding either about either the zig or the zag, as after I got dropped off at the B&B, I later walked down this path to the quay to get a bite to eat, taking the correct route this time. It was raining.

There it was again, the SWCP monument! I turned left and walked towards the Tea at the Quay café, the same place I picked up food yesterday. When you pronounce "quay" correctly as "key," it makes for a cute name for this café. As I was walking one of those things you see in a movie happened to me. I car drove right by me through a puddle, and the water from the puddle splashed up all over my lower legs. Great! Well better that I got soaking wet now than on the SWCP, I thought to myself.

I ate a veggie burger for now, and I ordered a "rocket potato" with beans for take away for dinner later. A rocket potato is a baked potato. I walked back up the zig zag path. Must be at least a half a mile from the B&B down to the quay. Thus I added an extra mile of walking to my six miles for the day. I decided that I needed to keep track of all the "extra mileage" I walk during this walking adventure.

I got back to the B&B just in time. As I mentioned at the beginning of the 4th of June in the "Getting to Minehead" part of my day yesterday, which is now the early evening today, the winds were blowing something fierce outside now. Trees were rustling, and winds were pushing the rain into the windows of my room, sounding like tiny pebbles. It was good that I was inside at the moment. It was supposed to be summer. I had at least walked two days, and a total of twelve miles, with good weather. The winds were supposed to continue tomorrow.

By the way, if someone walks five miles a day, every day, for 37 years, like Ellen DeGeneres' grandmother, they will have walked approximately 67,525 miles. That's like walking the SWCP 107 times!

DAY TWO STATS: 6 MILES. 3.5 HOURS. EXTRA ONE MILE FROM B&B TO SWCP MONUMENT/QUAY AND BACK. PURPLE SHOES. PUB IN PORLOCK WEIR IS ACTUALLY REFERRED TO AS "THE BOTTOM SHIP INN," AND "THE TOP SHIP INN" IS IN THE VILLAGE OF PORLOCK ITSELF.

"REST DAY" / DUNSTER – Tuesday, 6 June 2017

"On the water – Moderately high (18-25 ft) waves of greater length, edges of crests begin to break into spindrift, foam blown in streaks. On land – Twigs breaking off trees, generally impeded progress." – Beaufort Wind Scale

The wind and the rain last night stopped at one point, and all was quiet. The trees stopped rustling intently in the wind, and the rain stopped pushing against the windows. I don't exactly know when that happened, but it wasn't quiet for long. By the time I laid down to go to sleep the wind and rain was at it again. I still shut the lights and drifted off to sleep through all the noise.

I took a "rest day" today. Not one of my planned rest days. A rest day due to the weather. The winds of last night were to continue today. The forecast called for gale force winds on the coast. No rain, but very strong winds. There was a man named Sir Francis Beaufort of the U.K. Royal Navy who in 1805 created the "Beaufort Wind Scale." He had twelve classifications of weather from calm (less than one knot), to light air (one to three knots), to various stages of breezes (between four and 27 knots), to "near gale" (28-33 knots), to "gale" (34-40 knots), to "strong gale" (41-47 knots), to storms, violent storms, and finally hurricanes. For my forecast of "gale," it sounded like it could be 39 to 46 miles per hour, and is described in the above quote. I was not about to walk in that. Seemed too dangerous, and not advisable.

What I still didn't understand was it was June. I thought it was supposed to be summer. As far as I am concerned, summer should not include gale winds.

Since I had done Monday's scheduled walk on Sunday after I arrived in Minehead, and since I did today's, Tuesday's walk, yesterday on Monday, I decided to thus take today, Tuesday, off from walking and not walk where twigs might be breaking off the trees. This actually gave me some time to do a few things anyway. It gave me some time to reorganize myself and my belongings. It also gave me time to catch up on writing because otherwise as the days went on, I would forget what I did each day, and it would all become a blur. It was a good thing overall to take a day off already. I would still be on schedule as originally planned for tomorrow's walk.

I still went down for my "Half English" breakfast at the same time as I did yesterday. Yesterday I had dined alone, but today there were four other people staying at this B&B, two couples traveling together who also knew Janna. The conversation was about my walk, and what they were doing on their holiday. They seemed quite intrigued with my 630-mile three-month walk. I loved describing it to them. It felt exciting explaining to total strangers what I had just embarked on. Sure, I told family and friends back home, but there was a different vibe when telling people I didn't know. I appreciated their interest in me.

I then took over two hours to organize my belongings, going through each bag, each nook and cranny, and putting things either into my rucksack, or back in the wheeled suitcase more organized than before. It felt good to get that done. I actually had felt a bit off balance for the past few days because of the organized person that I am, and up until then I didn't feel organized. Perhaps it was because I walked basically right after getting off the airplane, train, and bus without time to completely settle in. I still realized though that I packed too much, as taking two hours to organize seemed like a really long time.

Yesterday Janna told me of a cute village, Dunster, just a five-minute drive as a suggestion for something for me to do today in addition to what I wanted to accomplish. It was just a bit inland rather than being on the coast, so perhaps the winds wouldn't be as strong, and it would get me outdoors. Janna's husband drove me there. It was quite a busy place with lots of people, but it was something to do for a few hours. I ate a good lunch there, a brie and caramelized onion "toastie" (a toastie is a sandwich which has been toasted or grilled). I went into a few shops to look around, I went into the Priory Church of St. George, and I looked at a very cute and interesting doll museum. It was a good couple hours spent, even with its busy feel.

I would have liked to have been driven back to the B&B but Janna's husband was out with the car for several hours, and they only had one car between the two of them. I could have waited for him, but that would have taken too long. I was going to take a bus back to Minehead, but in the 25 minutes waiting for it, I could be half way back to Minehead if I walked. So I walked. Two and a half miles. Near busy roads. To the water's edge and to the quay in Minehead once again. It took nearly an hour. It was windy, but it did not feel like it was dangerous and gale force. Sir Beaufort might have classified the winds at the moment as some kind of "fresh or strong breeze."

I ended up at the official SWCP monument again and decided to take a few pictures of my purple shoes posing at the SWCP marker this time for fun. Since I already had a good lunch, I went back to the Tea on the Quay (did you pronounce it correctly?) to get some food to take back to the B&B later for dinner. I had that half mile uphill zigzag footpath once again. Apparently maybe this actually used to be the official SWCP, but then they changed it. Today's zigzag up reminded me of Lombard Street in San Francisco. With no cars.

I spent the rest of my rest day eating, writing, backing up all the photos I have already taken onto several places including my laptop, a flash drive, and a cloud storage, checking my bank accounts, talking to Scott and Mom, charging the camera and mobile phone batteries, making sure the extra battery backup for my mobile I will keep in my rucksack was fully charged, making sure my alarm was set on my mobile, filling my water bladder with water for the next day's walk, getting the rucksack ready for the next day, washing socks and underwear in the sink just using running water from both faucets, figuring out what clothes to wear tomorrow, figuring out which shoes to wear tomorrow, showering, taking care of my teeth, seeing where food stops might be on the walk for tomorrow, and figuring out if the snacks I would carry in my rucksack would be enough, or if I would need to get a few more snacks or something more substantial, or if the food stops would be sufficient, looking at the SWCP Association's website at their useful elevation gain and loss interactive maps, getting some extra toilet paper to take with me just in case, doing my first Facebook post with photos, checking the news on the couple of news apps on my phone, including BBC News and NPR news, and checking the weather forecast! Whew. Not necessary in that order. These are things that I would be doing every evening from now on, although some items on this long list I might be doing every two or three or four days instead of every day, depending.

I also read about my next day's walk in both the guidebook and booklets I brought, and made sure I had the appropriate ones to take with me. Speaking of guidebooks and booklets, there are several out there to choose from. Many people use the single guidebook covering the entire SWCP from the SWCP Association called, "The Complete Guide to the South West Coast Path." Along with lots of great general and useful information, such as safety advice, packing tips, and accommodations, transportation, and tide information, this guidebook breaks up the entire walk into a suggested itinerary of eight weeks. I am obviously not following this suggestion. This book is similar to all the information on their website.

National Trails publishes a series of four guidebooks, each covering approximately a quarter of the SWCP, including descriptions of the walking. For me, I like these books because they include the important topographic Ordinance Survey Explorer maps, which show contour lines and other great navigational detail. I brought these four guidebooks with me to carry the appropriate one in my rucksack on a daily basis. These guidebooks also include background information "on everything from archaeology to wildlife."

Finally, also from the SWCP Association, are their booklets, which I bought before I left for my walk to take them all with me. They are a series of 71 small booklets of about fifteen to twenty pages each, covering short distances each ranging from five miles to fifteen miles, give or take. They have helpful hand-drawn maps which I will find very useful, and quite detailed written description and directions about the walk itself, which I will find the most useful for me for my walk. The booklets include photos that also help in locating where you are or where you need to go. They have good tidbits of factual information as well, such as about the towns, sites, and history, and the booklets even put the directions about the walk itself in "backwards" order in case you are walking the SWCP from Poole to Minehead. I will take the appropriate booklet(s) each day with me on my walk, and along with the appropriate guidebook, they are both protected by the waterproof map case I have and both fit well inside. Both to me are invaluable, and between the booklets, guidebooks, and all the signs, arrows, and acorns along the SWCP, I really should never get lost.

Important Note: Throughout this book, I will be quoting some factual information about various things, like about places and history, from these SWCP Association booklets, "Exploring the South West Coast Path: 71 Booklets." I won't be mentioning exactly which booklet number the quotes are from, and occasionally, instead of saying, "according to the booklet," each time I quote them, please note that when I do not reference any other source for my quotes, the quotes will have come from these very invaluable booklets. Therefore I thank very much the SWCP Association, and Dave Westcott, the writer of all the booklets, for their use of me quoting from the booklets!

DAY THREE STATS: NO SWCP MILES. EXTRA THREE MILES FROM DUNSTER BACK TO SWCP MONUMENT AND BACK TO B&B. PURPLE SHOES. SINCE DUNSTER IS NOT ON THE SWCP, I SHALL SKIP MENTIONING ITS PUBS. Information about Beaufort Wind Scale from spc.noaa.gov/faq/tornado/Beaufort.

One final comment for today. My Daily Stats. You may have noticed these at the end of each of my days thus far, and you will notice these each and every day. They will include the following items:
1. How many miles I walked on the actual SWCP that day.
2. How many hours it took me to walk those miles. Note that most of the time, I will have included any stopping time in those hours, such as if I stopped for a snack or lunch or to enjoy the scenery. Occasionally, I will be excluding my stopping time in the stats and will most likely mention that.
3. How many "extra miles" I walked that are not on the actual SWCP. Such as walking to and from the SWCP from the accommodations if the places are not right on the SWCP, walking back and forth from accommodations to dinner, side trips I may have made, etc.
4. Whatever shoes I wore that day, whether it be purple shoes, hiking boots, flip flops, or some combination.
5. Pubs. While I did not go into every pub in every village or town, and while in some villages or towns, there are more than one pub, I thought it would be fun to include their names in my book for informational

purposes, because pubs are quintessentially British, and because I like some of their creative names, such as how they may relate to the SWCP, including nautical themes. Note that there are a lot of pubs I did not mention, as I tried to include just the ones either right on the SWCP, or very close by, rather than a bit further away. Although, however in some cases, I did include those a bit further away. Note that no pub has asked me to mention them, and I have not received anything from any pub for mentioning them. I just thought this would be fun to include in my daily stats.
6. Finally, if I obtain a quote or other information from another source other than the SWCP Association booklets, such as mostly from websites from my online research, I will mention it in the particular day, rather than have a long reference section at the end of my book just for quotes or other information mentioned only on a particular day.
7. I realized much later that I should have included lists of "Tea Rooms," due to the importance of tea and cream tea in England (more on both of those subjects as time goes on), but since I realized this much later, unless I end up finding a big chunk of time to research them all along the SWCP, they won't be included in the book. However, note that their importance and significance is still recognized by me, not to mention the delicious flavor of the cream tea.

SILCOMBE FARM TO LYNMOUTH – Wednesday, 7 June 2017

"This church is never locked. It is open for shelter or quiet meditation. Would you please wipe your feet before entering and close the door behind you. Thank you." – Door of the Church in Countisbury.

After a good night's sleep, I got ready for the day, talked to Scott, and went down to breakfast. The same two couples were at breakfast this morning, and for today's conversation we discussed the difference between "ham" and "bacon" in America vs. England. I think what England refers to as "bacon" looks more like America's "ham." What America thinks as "bacon," England refers to as "streaky bacon." We agreed that in any case, either version still comes from the pig. One of the gentleman also commented that we have so much space in the US, meaning how large the country is. "UK is a tiny island in comparison," he said. I guess I never thought of it that way. Also that we are "across the pond" from each other, meaning across the Atlantic Ocean from each other.

I said a big thank you to Janna for her hospitality and gave her a hug, as it was my last morning at this B&B. She wanted to know in three month's time that I had completed my walk. She also informed me that Luggage Transfers, LTD would pick up my heavy luggage a bit later this morning. I'm glad that they remembered. I love this service, and that is one of the reasons I love walking the SWCP – all the great home-style beds-and-breakfasts, and that someone else will carry my heavy luggage.

Janna's husband drove me back to Silcombe Farm where I ended my walk two days ago. I had recalled that when Janna and I were driving back, we drove through the village of Porlock (not Porlock Weir) and there was a "traffic jam" as the road was narrow and with cars parked on the side and a big truck going through, it took a couple minutes to get through. Janna was complaining about the traffic. I thought to myself, this is not traffic especially in comparison to traffic in the Seattle area! I paid Janna extra for all the kind chauffeuring they did for me.

I should mention that in addition to cars driving on the different side of the road than I am used to that I have to be careful of when crossing the street, the drivers and passengers sides in the car is also opposite. I have to think very hard which side to enter a car on. Otherwise I might be driving, which I definitely do not want to do.

As I started walking from Silcombe Farm on the Alternative Coast Path, the terrain started out as a gravel country backroad, overlooking fields of sheep, with a row of trees. The hills were squared and checkered off in fields and pastures and farmland of light green grass separated by dark green trees. Looking out further was the blue water. Lovely, just lovely.

As a little bunny rabbit hopped out onto the road, the road began to narrow down. After about 25 minutes of walking, I followed the acorn symbol leading through a heavy gate. For a while it became very quiet along the small thin gravel road except for the sounds of the sheep baaaaing, and the breeze wrestling the leaves of the trees. The weather for today was much, much calmer than yesterday. In fact, the weather was great today, as the sun was getting warmer as I walked along with some white clouds above. No rain or strong winds forecasted for today. At the moment however, my views of the water were blocked by a row of tall shrubbery on either side of me.

The gravel road turned into a paved road, and then as I passed by a farm house, the paved road turned into a grassy narrow path. My views were obstructed once again by tall shrubs, but every so often a gate leading to a sheep field allowed for me to see the views of the water of the seas beyond.

As mentioned, there are a lot of gates to walk through on the SWCP, apparently 880 of them. They open different ways, and are usually quite easy to open and close. For some reason, I had trouble opening one gate at the moment, so to rectify the situation quickly I just climbed over it. I emerged onto a field of sheep and walked downhill. I love walking through fields of sheep. I do so carefully though so as to not step in something, and to not disturb them too much. They seemed oblivious to me, except a bit further down when a mama sheep and her babies trotted away because I was getting a bit closer to them as I followed the path. I saw one black sheep amongst this flock of white sheep. I wondered if it had any wool. Perhaps three bags full.

As I opened another gate, I shut the gate behind me as you are always instructed to do so when walking the SWCP. This is to prevent animals from wandering to a place they should not be. At this moment, I actually did not know about the 880 gate statistic, so I wondered how many gates opening and closing I would be doing in 630 miles. I didn't dare start counting though, although I do like to count things. I do math and accounting for a living. But no, I won't count how many gates. Steps perhaps, when I encounter those perhaps I will count, but not gates.

The path zigzagged its way through a forest of shrubbery and bushes, and emerged out of the woods to a complete open view of the ocean and of the clouds. Ahh this was brilliant! And beautiful. The clouds in the sky created darker patches on the water, giving the water a two-toned blue look. Looking behind me I could see where I walked days a few ago. Wow, I have come that far already! (Note that throughout my descriptions of the waters I look at in this book, sometimes I use the word "water" or "waters", a few times "channels", other times "seas", other times "ocean" or "oceans". To me they are all describing the same thing and I just use whatever word I decide to use at the moment.)

I passed by a sign that said "County Gate" indicating that I think that I had passed from one county of England and the SWCP to another. From Somerset to Devon. I will be going from one county to another along this path. Four counties in total, but one you get its "north end" first, and later you get its "south end." In order, I started in Somerset, just crossed into North Devon, and then I will walk around the entire county of Cornwall, followed by South Devon, and finally Dorset. In summary, four counties total, in five parts, and one county in its entirety.

The Alternative Coast Path route I was on met up with the other Coast Path route after about two miles of walking, and a sign told me that I had seven miles to go till my destination for the day, Lynmouth. Walking once again through the forest, this part of the path was now called the County Line Nature Trail, so if I hadn't exactly crossed the county line a bit earlier, I think I would be very soon, if not at this moment. I had a very gentle climb uphill through this forest. The Nature Trail soon ended, and then the SWCP entered into a darker eerie looking forest with an eerie cool breeze against my face. It almost felt ghost-like to me for some reason. Not that I know what ghost-like feels like really, but this could be close.

I realized that I was still in Exmoor National Park at this moment, and I remembered Sasha's advice about tucking my pants into my socks in case of ticks, so I stopped to do that. Whenever I stop to do something, whether tuck my socks in my pants, or eat, or just sit and enjoy nature, if I take my rucksack off and start to take things out of the rucksack, when I am ready to leave the area and have my rucksack back on, it is my rule of thumb to always look behind me as I walk off to make sure that I have not left anything behind.

I noticed the sounds at the moment as I started walking again - various birds chirping including a dove, my footprints on the ground, and the sound of my own voice recording notes on my mobile phone. This was now how I would know about my day and what to write. A dictation app on my mobile. That I have had since I arrived but finally decided to utilize it more often than I had been. I would either record by voice or by typing on this dictation app as I walk. Well, not actually as I walk, for I need to stop, pay attention, so that I won't trip and fall. I would stop to either talk or type my thoughts, feelings, sights, sounds, smells, tastes, etc. At the end of the day, this handy app allows me to email myself all the notes I recorded when I have reception, copy and paste the contents of the email to a Word document on my laptop, and then I can spend time in the evenings typing up the notes in more detail. No pen and paper. As I type up more detail in the evenings I would save my editing and writing process constantly, and even email each day of writing to myself every so often as backup, especially when done for the day. This process ultimately would lead to this book.

I emerged from the uphill climb out of the woods. Then I had my first experience of "getting lost." Well it was more like a matter of me not paying attention and missing an important directional sign to take a right turn. I spent about fifteen minutes trying to figure out where I had gone wrong after not seeing any acorn or arrow signs for a short while. Apparently I did not see the sign pointing me off the straight stretch I was on, pointing down some steps to the right. I figure I ended up about a quarter mile up the path I was on when I came to a couple of gates and a winding gravel road. I thought I should go from gate to gate, but I did not see any acorns or arrows. At this point, I should have just turned around to go back. But did I? No. First I thought I would try to figure out where I was by reading my guidebook and booklet and looking at the maps too. That didn't help. I couldn't figure anything out. I thought I had pretty good map skills, but this one stumped me. I had no idea where I was. Except that I don't think I saw the landmark called "Sister's Fountain." That should have been my first clue to just turn around and go back.

But did I go back? No. Why not? I don't know. I thought I would take a guess as to which direction to walk. I went through the double gates, but after about one minute up that path, it just didn't seem right. It was too narrow of a path and too overgrown with ferns, and led up a grassy hill. I turned back around and went back out the gates. Then I thought I would walk up the gravel road. Why? I don't know. But I did for a couple minutes to which it finally dawned on me that since I hadn't seen any acorns or arrow signs, and the guidebook or booklet didn't tell me to go up any gravel roads, I knew that I needed to go back from where I came to see what I missed, including trying to find Sister's Fountain.

Finally, I went back down the gravel road, back down the path I originally came from, and passed a sign that clearly said that the direction I was going was some footpath and that the Coastal Path was back a bit further ahead. I continued on, and within another couple minutes, voila, there was the sign, clear as day, pointing me off this straight stretch I was on, and down some steps. This time it was a left turn down, which should have been the right turn a bit ago.

I don't know how I missed this sign. Perhaps I was talking on the dictation app and not paying attention. Maybe I was daydreaming. Perhaps though it could have been that since I was walking in the shade of the trees it was a bit darker, and the sign pointing down was a bit smaller than what I had been used to, so perhaps I just did not see it. I'd be happy if that was the last time I "got lost." Get it out of the way now I say, and never do that again. And let that also be a lesson that if it does happen again, just go back first, and don't start wandering around.

After passing by Sister's Fountain, which is actually a spring and a pool, and apparently really crossing the border from Somerset into Devon, I walked on a trail lined with bright dark pink foxglove wildflowers like I saw a few days ago, and emerged out onto an open area overlooking the water constantly out in the open. The views were amazing. Simply amazing. On the ground there were pink pedals of rhododendrons flowers that had fallen. There were bushes of bright pink rhododendrons in bloom, and more pink foxglove in bloom. Green ferns lined the path. I could see the headland in front of me where soon I would be walking. It was all very, very pretty. My purple shoes aka purple sneakers aka purple trainers made a nice contrast in color to the pink rhododendron pedals on the ground.

I stopped for a small snack, munching on some dried apples and dried cherries that I had brought with me from home. The path continued to have a lot of pink rhododendron bushes, and I passed a sign that said I had four and a half miles to Lynmouth. The only sounds I heard now were chirping birds and a babbling brook flowing by, which I gently needed to step over.

Looking behind me I saw where I had been in the distance, and below was a rocky beach where I could see some small white waves hitting the coastline. That was just a stunning view, and would become one of my favorite parts about walking the SWCP – seeing and hearing the coastline with its beaches and waves crashing. On the edge of the hillside I was standing on, I could see the line of the path I just walked through surrounded by bushes on either side, and on top of the hills was some farmland. So picturesque.

I passed by a sign that pointed inland two miles to a village called Countisbury, and onwards towards Lynmouth in four miles. I was originally just going to walk to Countisbury today (this would have been the inland option way to go there if one wanted to) by taking the SWCP way, but because the weather forecast for tomorrow called for rain, I thought I would add on a couple of miles to today's seven mile walk and walk to Lynmouth so that tomorrow's walk in the rain could be shorter. I could take a taxi back from Lynmouth to Countisbury where my accommodations were for the evening.

The terrain of the path leveled out. This path today went around several "combes," pronounced "koom," which by definition means a short valley, a deep hollow, a deep narrow valley, or a ravine, mainly in Southern England. For example, Silcombe as I have been to, and Combe Martin, Ilfracombe, and Woolacombe as places I will be going to.

Ahead of me were more views of the path cutting though the bushes, and there was another rocky beach below. Although, I don't know if any of the beaches I had been seeing could actually be accessed by land, or at least I didn't know the way to them, so I did not go visit these beaches to sit on them and enjoy the crashing waves.

I realized that a bit ago I must have lost one of my favorite chapsticks out from the little pocket in my rucksack. In this little pocket I was keeping my sunscreen tube, my zinc lip sunscreen, and my favorite chapstick. My favorite chapstick was not there when I went to use it just now. It must have fallen out perhaps when I stopped for my snack. I was disappointed. Good thing I have three more with me! Really! That is how much it is my favorite chapstick. Although they were all currently in my wheeled luggage. As I mentioned, it is always a good idea to look back after you stop before you walk off to see if you left anything behind. I was not sure why I didn't look back after my snack stop. Perhaps I did, but my chapstick was too small to see amongst the pink rhody pedals on the ground.

Another good reason to look back and behind is for those views of where you have come from. To see the headlands and waters and farmland, and any other scenery, for its beauty. To take some photos. And to be in awe of how many miles you have already walked. This was advice from a great friend of mine, Sasha, the same friend who warned me of ticks – to "always look behind you."

I've been through many gates already, but I just stepped up and over and down my first "stile." A stile is some steps that allows you to climb over a wall, and similar to gates, does not allow the animals to go through. Perhaps there are two or three or four steps on one side of the wall, then after you pass over the wall itself, there are another two or three or four steps back down. I guess I will be climbing up and over and down 435 more stiles.

I passed by a sign pointing to the first of many, many lighthouses I will see along the SWCP, Foreland Lighthouse. I stop here to mention once again, my love for lighthouses. Remember that I mentioned that my niece painted a lighthouse for me for my 50th birthday? It is because I am quite fascinated with them, their history, and mostly by the way people used to be responsible for lighting the lights each night to keep all those people safe at sea. Today these aids to navigation are automated so the need for Lighthouse Keepers is no longer. But reading about people who did care for the lighthouses back in the day when one had to climb stairs, and light the wicks and lights by hand with oils and such, and make sure the lights stayed on all night, especially in bad weather and storms, just fascinates me. I make it a point to visit lighthouses when I travel, and even at home. I have been to all the lighthouses in Washington State, most along the coast in Oregon, and some in the state of Michigan. I have seen lighthouses in Spain, and one summer I spend a few weekends helping to restore a lighthouse. Scott and I even got married at a lighthouse! Knowing that I would see lighthouses along the SWCP was another reason I wanted to do this walk. However, as much as I love lighthouses, I did not go see the Foreland Lighthouse up close as it is not recommended to go because it is located on a very steep and narrow loose scree and rocky slope and exposed path.

This lighthouse "was built in 1900 to aid navigation along the Bristol Channel. The keeper's cottages are now holiday cottages," according to the booklet for today.

In addition to the many, many pictures I have already taken today and the past several days, I noticed a bench and took a picture with the bench in the foreground, and the scenery of the SWCP as the background. This would become one of many, many "bench" photos I would be taking along my walk, and I may even do a photography book called "Benches of the South West Coast Path."

Soon I arrived at the church in Countisbury, a church that dates from the 18th and 19th centuries. The door of the church welcomed me with the greeting quoted above. I went inside the church, looked around, and did my usual prayers. I also texted Scott from the church and he texted back too, as I was able to get phone reception from here. I was not able to get much phone reception on my walk today until now. I could also see The Blue Ball Inn across the street where I would be staying tonight.

I saw the town of Lynmouth in the distance, and began my walk on to Lynmouth. The path to Lynmouth was a downhill and a bit steep at times. I munched on a snack of nuts that I also brought with me from home. Needless to say I was a bit hungry, and probably should have stopped to get food in Countisbury before going on to Lynmouth, but as I thought I was close, with only two miles to go, I opted to wait till I got to Lynmouth to eat lunch.

It was the "longest" two miles I have ever walked, or so it seemed, with the steepness. Somehow, as I shall come to notice, the last mile or two always feels the longest. Sometimes it is the terrain, sometimes it is just a feeling. My great friend Sasha, whom I have mentioned a few times, told me of this phenomenon – that the last mile always seems to take the longest. Sasha has also walked the SWCP in one go, and I shall definitely be discussing more about her later.

The weather had remained dry all day, with an occasional light wind, and just as I arrived in Lynmouth, I felt a few rain drops. Good timing. Down by the rocky sandy beach in Lynmouth, where a few people were, a sign told me that I had come twenty miles since Minehead! Like I said, it is a good idea to look back to see where I have been and how far I have come. Although, according to the booklet, I have actually walked 21.4 miles since Minehead!

The tide was low at the harbour in Lynmouth so the boats were resting on the sandy ground covered with seaweed. It was now time to find some food. I peeked at a couple menus, and asked one place what their soup of the day was. Tomato basil. That sounded good, and it tasted good too.

Since it was early afternoon, I did some window shopping along the busy roads of Lynmouth. I found a great little museum called the "Lyn Model Railway," showing small model trains moving around on small tracks with lots of small village buildings and other objects. Per the museum's brochure, it is modeling the 1935-40 period and "The exhibition has been designed and built by a local resident for the interest and enjoyment of visitors to Lynmouth." It reminded me of my childhood, as my Dad had a large intricate model train setup in our garage when I was growing up, so this museum reminded me of that!

I visited the church in Lynmouth as well, which I think was called St. John the Baptist. By the way, many towns end in the word "mouth," which means "the mouth of a river." For example, Lynmouth. I will also be walking to Falmouth, Plymouth, Weymouth, Dartmouth, Teignmouth, and Widemouth Bay for example. Note that "mouth" is actually pronounced "muth." I suppose if you have something called "mouthcombe" or "combemouth," combining "mouth" and "combe," it could mean "a river valley" or "a short valley at the mouth of a river." Actually, there is a town along the SWCP called Mothecombe.

The few drops of rain turned into a drizzle. At this time I was actually ready to go to my B&B for the evening, so I walked back to the tomato basil soup restaurant and asked if they could please call a taxi for me. They said that the pub next door had taxi number, and within five minutes I took a taxi back to The Blue Ball Inn in Countisbury and checked in. I had a cute little room where the view from my window was of the roof of the church across the street that I had been inside earlier.

I placed my purple shoes in a tray that I would be seeing in many of the accommodations I will be staying at which says, "Please place your footwear here" with images of some shoe prints. I did a few quick things from my evening "to-do" list, went down for dinner, came back up, did a few more things, stared editing today's notes on my laptop, did yet a few more things, and then caught up on typing the rest of the day up to this very moment.

The Blue Ball Inn, according to their business card, is a "traditional country pub…with low ceilings, blackened beams, stone fireplaces including a 13th century inglenook fireplace, and an atmosphere of unspoilt old world charm [with] real ales, fine wines and locally brewed beers." In addition, I haven't mentioned yet, but they allow dogs in pubs and restaurants in England. It is very common here. Something not allowed in the United States. I almost stepped on a dog in the pub when I was ordering my food.

I will also mention that the sinks in some public restrooms I have found are all automatic. You put your hand underneath to trigger it to start, and it spits down soap, followed by water allowing you to soap up and rinse off, finally followed by air to dry your hands. No need to touch anything. It senses your hands from the beginning. Brilliant! I still wondered why many sinks have two faucets.

DAY FOUR STATS: 9 MILES. 5.5 HOURS. AN EXTRA HALF MILE ABOUT WHEN I "GOT LOST." PURPLE SHOES. PUB IN COUNTISBURY CALLED "THE BLUE BALL INN." PUB IN LYNMOUTH CALLED "THE VILLAGE INN."

LYNMOUTH TO HEDDON'S MOUTH – Thursday, 8 June 2017

"Here comes the sun
Here comes the sun, and I say
It's all right" – The Beatles

"Here comes the rain again." - Eurythmics

You may have noticed that I am writing the dates "8 June 2017" instead of "June 8, 2017." That's the way they write them in England, so I decided to write them that way at the beginning of each of my days. I also decided to research why the two-faucet sinks, to which there are plausible explanations if you look online, which I could not entirely understand, but it has something to do with the historical construction of houses, the plumbing, and safety of the water. In addition, you may have noticed that I am putting in a quote at the beginning of each of my chapters, where each chapter itself equates to each of one of my walking/rest/traveling days. Each quote itself is appropriate, relevant, and has significance to that particular day!

Breakfast at my new B&B, The Blue Ball Inn, was a half hour later than I have been doing, as some places have their own set hours for breakfast, while others ask what time you would like to eat. In either case, they are usually within a window of an hour or two. I made my way downstairs a few minutes before breakfast because I figured that if I am the first one there, I can get served first and I don't have to wait too long so that I can get on with my walk for the day. The forecast for today called for heavy rain at first, followed by light rain. I needed to drum up a bit of bravery and courage for this, especially for walking in the heavy rain, but I didn't feel that nervous since at least no gale force winds were called for. I figured I could always turn back or bail out at any point if I was not comfortable or not having a good time. As it turned out, the forecast was a bit incorrect anyway. The heavy rain came towards the end of my walk in the form of a downpour...

My breakfast today consisted of a few bowls of porridge, scrambled eggs, toast, and tomatoes, a bit different than the Half English, to which when I ordered my food, I pronounced the English way tomAtoes, rather than tomaatoes. I was impressed with my try at the British accent. Perhaps by the end of my trip, I will have the accent down pat. Jolly good. Brilliant. Lovely. Cheers. As I said, no I did not have the accent down pat and did not try again so as to not embarrass myself.

I had someone at The Blue Ball Inn kindly call a taxi for me to take back to Lynmouth. I felt glad that I walked the extra two miles yesterday, so today's walk was shorter, with the weather forecast and all.

There's nothing like an uphill climb on a paved path to start today's walk out of Lynmouth first thing in the morning. Makes for great exercise, and wakes up the heart and lungs. Most of today's walk would be on paved paths or paved roads. This first climb though was a zigzag path (not the one in Minehead) near the Cliff Railway that takes you up and down the hillside of Lynmouth with the adjoining town above of Lynton. Apparently you can take this railway as an alternate way of getting up the hill instead of the walk, but not for me today. I wanted to walk. I did watch the Cliff Railway as it took someone downhill as I was walking up. "The Cliff Railway was opened in 1890 and was described at the time as 'the steepest in the world' [with a track that] is 862 feet long rising to a vertical height of 500 feet."

I timed myself. It took me about eight minutes to go up this zigzag path. Just as I was about to depart from the paved path, which was now a flat road and emerged onto a paved path which would take me on a wild ride complete with wind, a cliff ledge, and mountain goats, I first ran into an entire group of people walking a part of the SWCP. I started chatting with them, and from their accents I could tell they were from the same country as me. I confirmed this by asking where they were from, which turned out to be from various parts of the US, and they were part of a Sierra Club group. They asked me if I was doing the entire SWCP at once. I said, "Yes. At least trying to. And trying to by myself." They seemed impressed.

I didn't want to join the group and walk with them, but it was good to know that a group of others would be on this walk today in the predicted rainy day. Turns out after a few moments of walking, they turned off a side path and I never saw them again, and I was wondering where they went. It wasn't until I arrived at my accommodations for the evening that I saw them again as that was where they also ended their walk for the day.

As I started walking along the paved path ledge that felt quite close to the edge of the hillside I was on, I looked back behind me and saw a flash of light. Not lightening though. It was the light of the Foreland Lighthouse that I could not see yesterday. It was far off in the distance so that in any photos I took it was a small white dot. Still, I officially saw my first lighthouse!

It was lightly raining, and it was windy walking on this ledge. The ledge was wide enough that I didn't feel unsafe, but narrow enough that when I saw a mountain goat, yes a mountain goat, on the path, directly in front of me, coming in my direction, I wasn't quite sure who was going to have had the right of way if we met on the path at the same time. While the winds were not gale force, to help with the wind, I stayed close and hugged the left uphill side (as opposed to the right downhill side), and was determined to stay on that side should the goat and I need to choose sides. I didn't want to put the goat in danger, but I really didn't want to put myself in danger either. It didn't seem like the goat was going to charge me, which would have been an interesting concern. I looked behind me to see if the Sierra Club group was there just in case I needed to join them, thinking that about ten people could take on a single goat. They were there for the moment, but that was when they disappeared. I also had my hiking poles out, which I took with me today, ready just in case as I was using them to steady myself in the wind.

Less than thirty seconds later as all this was going through my head, the goat happily galloped up the rocky grassy hillside as mountain goats easily do, leaving me in the path by myself. A bit higher up I noticed a second goat, perhaps his or her mate. Safely out of my way, I took a few pictures of the goats. After turning a corner on this paved path, the wind decreased to almost none, and I continued walking on. I looked back at one moment and saw an entire herd of mountain goats on a trail below. I was in an area called the "Valley of Rocks," and my guidebook even told me that I may be fortunate enough to see mountain goats in this rocky area. Including my close encounter, I was fortunate enough. There might even been about 100 goats in this area.

The paved path turned into a grass track along a grass and fern covered hill for a while, then made a bit of a climb up a rocky path and emerged out onto a paved road still surrounded by the grass and fern covered hills, which would be my road for the next several miles. Another few gusts of wind occurred, but fortunately that was about all the wind I had the rest of the day. Well until my last mile. More on that later.

By the late morning, the sun was actually trying it's best to come out and there were even patches of blue skies. The rain had stopped as well as the wind. I passed a field of cows behind a fence and I politely asked them to smile and say "cheese" for the camera. One of them just stared me down. I'm not sure they got the joke. I passed by a field with some cute sheep behind a fence and I asked them to smile and say "cheese" for the camera. A cute little guy just stared me down. Not sure they got the joke either. Well, you can make cheese out of sheep's milk, too.

Apparently it was "Chocolate Day" at the Lee Abbey Estate Tea Cottage. A cutely decorated sign told me so as it said, "Chef's Recommendation – Chocolate Day." The sign was decorated with drawings of chocolate cake and hot chocolate and flowers. I would bet though that every day is chocolate day at this place! I wandered inside and looked around noticing the nice display of sweets and chocolates. I apparently didn't read the sign though that said to order outside as I walked right into the kitchen to look at the display. The woman politely said that I was not allowed in the kitchen due to health reasons, and that I could order outside. Oh my, I apologized and said that I understood and did not read the sign. I went outside.

There was a very nice display of sweets and chocolates. Fruit cake, spicy rock cakes (not sure what those were), chocolate cake, chocolate flapjack, lemon drizzle, chocolate brownie, cheese scones, chocolate truffle cake, even vegan cakes and gluten free sweets. My first reaction when I saw the scones mixed in with all the chocolaty sweets was that the scones seemed out of place. I will soon come to learn however that scones are never out of place! Rather, scones are very much in place.

I told myself I wasn't going to have any sugar this trip, but this was a special occasion. What occasion, I really didn't know, but it was special anyway. Well, it was Chocolate Day, so that is a special occasion. Even though I had that ice cream in Porlock Weir, oh and I forgot to mention a chocolate mocha cake one of my nights in Minehead, I promise really that this will be my last sweets I have for a long time. While they taste really good, my body does not feel great with sugar in its system, and I know that sugar is not healthy to eat. I got a piece of the chocolate truffle cake, and a piece of the chocolate flapjack.

I wanted to try the flapjack, as I had never had one before, and it is a traditional British baked item. Made from just a few basic ingredients of porridge oats, golden syrup (a "thick golden sweet syrup used in British cooking since the mid-1800s"), butter, sugar, and perhaps a pinch of salt. They are not "pancakes" like in the US, as thick pancakes in the US are sometimes referred to as flapjacks. British flapjacks can be "served as a sweet treat with tea or coffee, can be part of a lunch box, or simply a delicious snack." The oats make the flapjack "healthy," since oats are full of "iron, zinc and vitamin B." You can add all kinds of things to the basic ingredients, such as "nuts, seeds, dried fruits, coconut," etc. At least when I choose to eat sweets and chocolate, I chose only the best!

As I walked on, along a road lined with lots of small green trees, my clothing situation seemed to change at each minute. It was warm most of the time now, but sometimes it would drizzle or mist again, and other times the sun would try to appear. I originally had two shirts on, and finally opted for keeping one shirt on as well as rain gear on, and this combination worked well.

Then another situation occurred a bit like yesterday's fifteen minute "getting lost" story. This one only took four minutes though. The sign for the Coast Path pointed at a slight angle, so I thought that I was meant to get off the road. I walked down this slightly muddy dirt road, which felt much like a driveway actually, and I happily started taking pictures of the little sheep in the field and a yellow and white colored fishing boat in the distance on the water. I was quite thrilled with the scenery, especially the fishing boat. Well no sooner was I on my way that I ended up at a covered shack where a few tractors were parked and a couple of closed gates and no acorn signs. I knew at this moment, that the angled sign above was really telling me to stay on the road. So I turned around, passed by the sheep again, telling them that it was a pleasure to see them once more and to have a great day, (yes, I was talking to the animals today), went back up the muddy dirt road that I now realized was a driveway, and then I noticed the other sign on a gate: "Private No Access." Boy was I day dreaming or what? I really need to pay attention and read the signs. Between this one and the one at the Tea Cottage, I have walked down a private driveway and into a kitchen.

Today I put my hiking boots on because of the weather forecast of the rain, but so far with all the pavement I've been walking on (other than the slightly muddy dirt driveway), the purple shoes would have been just fine, even in the light rain. I did have them in my rucksack, but opted to keep the boots on anyway. I also brought hiking polls with me today as mentioned because the terrain looked like there would be some ascents and descents. I haven't used them so far other than on the windy ledge with the goats, and I have been carrying them in my hand ever since. I suppose I could have hooked the poles to my rucksack, but at the moment I opted to carry them. As I continued down the road, the sounds at the moment were of the birds chirping and the fishing boat putting on the water. The sun came out and started shining. Just lovely!

I picked up some trash or garbage, or rubbish as it is called in England, on the side of the road and put it in my pocket. When I walked the Camino de Santiago in Spain, as part of my contribution and way of giving back to the walk, I picked up little bit of rubbish here and there when I saw it, unless it was something really gross like toilet paper, or it was too big to fit in my pocket. I decided to do this as well on the SWCP. It is my way of contributing back to this path as I walk.

Speaking of the Camino de Santiago walk that was the first really long-distance walk I have done. Yes, I have walked and hiked and trekked and backpacked plenty of other times, some shorter distances, and some one-day or a few days at a time only. Others longer, such as splitting the backpacking hike of the 93-mile Wonderland Trail around Mount Rainier into two summers of about one-third one summer and the other two-thirds the following summer with a great friend of mine, Melissa. There was also the seven day (one of the days was a "rest day"), 66-mile round trip trek to the village of Laya in Bhutan at an altitude of 12,500 feet. There was also the time I trekked in New Zealand, and I am one of the few to walk around the 42-mile Île d'Orléans near Québec City. I have already mentioned the 100-mile walk in the Cotswolds with my husband, and the time about a year ago that we walked 100 miles of the SWCP. However, by and large, the Camino de Santiago walk, specifically the 482-mile Camino Francés, has been the longest walk I have done (even though I had to miss a few miles due to those blisters that I so carefully tried to avoid with my blister theories). At least until now on the SWCP, the Camino de Santiago walk has been the longest walk.

I passed a sign that said two and a half miles to Heddon's Mouth, and then there would be another half mile more to The Hunters Inn, my accommodations and my destination for the day. I was more than halfway at this point for the day, and I was off the paved road back onto a path. With two more miles to go to Heddon's Mouth, I decided to change into my purple shoes so my feet would be more comfortable at this point. The path was just gravel and then turned back to pavement. I also finally decided to put my hiking polls away on my rucksack. I passed by an "International Finger Post" directional sign pointing to Iceland and New Zealand, America and Russia. I suppose if I didn't want to continue the SWCP and I wanted to go back home, I could have followed the direction for America.

Then of course, it started slightly raining but in the horizon above the seas, I could see blue skies, so it did not bother me much. Looking back, I could see where I just came from including the Foreland Lighthouse again way off in the distance flashing its light. The trail started going uphill, began to narrow and run through some trees. I passed by two people who were out for a walk. An opening through the trees offered me a view of the waters below, a rocky beach, and the rolling green hills I had come from. The view was a bit misty, but it was still refreshing. A wet bench in front of this background made for a nice photo.

When I emerged from the trees and saw the water below once again, I stopped. To listen. I haven't stopped much just for the sake of listening. Yes, I hear sounds as I walk, but I wanted to just stop and listen this time. I could hear the light rain that had started hitting the hood of my jacket. I heard the light rain hitting the leaves of the trees above me. I listened to the small waves subtly crashing against the rocks below. That moment I stood there I was in a peaceful state of mind, listing to some soothing sounds of nature.

I continued on through the fern lined narrow path, past the Hollow Brook Waterfall, which "falls a distance of over 780 feet making it one of the highest coastal waterfalls in Britain," according to the booklet for today. I paused to let four gentlemen who were out for a walk pass by me as the light rain started falling just a bit more.

And then the fun began! The rocky path began to climb, not steeply, but a gentle climb. As I climbed up, it seemed as if the rain climbed as well. It wasn't too bad at first, so I continued on. Well I had no choice but to continue on at this point. The path leveled out, and for the moment, so did the rain. I turned around to see the views behind me and take a few photos – the green covered hillside with its rocky edge leading down to a rocky beach below and the water. I saw two people coming up the path behind me as well. I wondered if they were part of the Sierra Club group. The views in front of me were my path ahead along the fern covered hillside also leading down to rocky beaches below and a small line of white frothy waves. The turquoise waters and the gray skies were in the last few photos I took of the day.

Because then the rain started to get heavier. And a slight breeze started. I continued on. As the rain increased again, I decided to pick up my pace a bit. Not that I was worried or anything, but I was getting closer to my destination for the day and thought it would be nice to stay as dry as possible. Ha, good thought only! I could see in the very near distance the bend in the path that would take me left downhill to Heddon's Mouth. I knew I didn't have far to go. Remember, I still had my purple shoes on at this point.

The rain continued to pick up but for some reason I refused to change back to my hiking boots. I reached the bend in the path. Where I was to turn left. And then all heck broke loose. Well at least skies broke loose. The winds and the rain just started dumping in a downpour. Very heavy rain and quite windy as I turned the corner in fact. With only a mile left to go, I trod on in my purple shoes. The rains got only heavier and the winds whipped around. I did not dare take out my camera or mobile at this time to take any pictures, as I did not want them to get

Benches of the South West Coast Path
Between Lynmouth and Heddons Mouth (wet bench from rain) June 8
Between Ilfracombe and Woolacombe (Bull Point Lighthouse in the distance) June 11
Overlooking Woolacombe Sands Beach June 12

Benches of the South West Coast Path
Between Westward Ho! and Bucks Mills June 17
Between Perranporth and Porthtowan (looking out towards nothing but blue skies and blue water) July 2
Looking towards Scabbacombe Sands area April 25

Benches of the South West Coast Path
Two from between Sidmouth and Branscombe Mouth August 15
Between Stonebarrow and West Bay August 18

water damaged. My non-waterproof purple shoes were just getting wetter and wetter, but I didn't really want to stop to change back to my waterproof hiking boots.

Finally I caved in. There was a bench. I took it as a sign. A sign to change back to my waterproof hiking boots. The purple shoes were soaked. As fast as I possibly could, which was probably a "Guinness Book of World Records" breaker if someone was around to see it, not only did I change out of my purple shoes and into my boots and tied the laces, as the rain kept dumping down, I also did my best to keep all my belongings as dry as possible which was impossible in my rucksack since I had to take every stuff sack out because the boots were at the bottom. Of course. Just as my rucksack was back together and I was tightening up the laces the two people that I had seen earlier behind me walked by. I thought to myself, I thought this was supposed to be summer!

I started followed the two people. Not that I really needed to, but it seemed like a good idea at the time. It was still quite rainy and windy. Not gale force winds that I know of, but possibly good "strong breeze" or "near gale" according to the Beaufort scale. The path leading downhill at this point was like a small stream of watery mud. It was like walking through a miniature brown river. Boy was I glad I put my waterproof boots on. My purple shoes would have been dyed brown.

I then had a slight panic attack. My rule of thumb, as I have mentioned, was to look back and make sure I had everything. I was quite sure that I did put everything back in my rucksack at that bench, but I thought, oh no, what if I really didn't. I know I looked as I usually do, but with the heavy rains and wind, and being rushed to get everything back in my rucksack before it all got soaked, what if I left something behind? Still going downhill, with the rain and wind, I did not want to go back up to the bench to look. I tried to think about all the items I had with me, trying to visualize that I put them back in my rucksack just hoping, praying, that I remembered that everything was back in my rucksack during my record-breaking shoe change. I just trusted that I did.

For about a half mile and maybe fifteen minutes total since I turned that corner above, in the downpour with the wind and the rain and the muddy miniature river under my feet, I marched on. I finally reached some woods where the trees provided some much wanted shelter. Of course just as I was under the shelter, the rain and wind finally let up. I was still kind of "tagging" along behind the two people when we all had reached the trees, which I will admit that it was nice to have some "company" in the downpour. I did consider them as some guardian angels for these moments as I kind of had someone to walk with during what has so far been the most rain I have had on the path all at once in my first five days on the SWCP.

I came to a trail junction. The Hunters Inn, my accommodations, was in a half mile, the SWCP to Combe Martin (tomorrow's destination) was eight miles in one direction, a "Bridleway to Beach Only" in another direction, and of course the SWCP from where I just came behind me. I decided to stop and check my rucksack at this point to make sure everything was there so I wouldn't worry anymore. I suppose if something was missing, I could go back up to the bench tomorrow to get it, but fortunately it seemed like everything was there. A bit wet, but at least it was all there. I realized that my rain gear that I was wearing was dripping wet on the outside. My rain gear worked great though, and kept me feeling dry inside.

As I walked towards my accommodations, still in the woods, another sign pointed off to continue the Coast Path, where I will need to go tomorrow, and another sign pointing to The Hunters Inn. However, there was an upper path and a lower path at this point. It really looked like the sign was pointing towards the upper one, but knowing how signs can point not exactly correct, as I have already found out, or really as sometimes signs can be confusing-looking to me, I took out my guidebook to make the right choice. Brilliant! Fortunately, it said, "the path now turns inland and downwards (yup I can confirm this) until it joins the Riverside Walk towards the Hunters Inn." Ah ha! Riverside. That is the key word. Boy am I smart. There was a river right next to the lower path, so I took that one. Flat and easy walking along the river. As I was getting closer to The Hunters Inn, it appeared that the upper path joined the lower path anyway.

This was followed by another choice of paths. Hmmm. Just then though, a couple came through a gate with their dog, and I figured that was right the choice, so I took that one. No sooner as the peacock flies did I all of a sudden emerge from the woods to be in front of this large yellowish building with green trim. If that wasn't The Hunters Inn, I didn't know what was. Through the windows I could see people eating. I was also greeted literally by two peacocks sitting on the railing, and a third peacock wandering around the garden. I was still dripping wet.

I walked around to the front of the building and thought I would be ever so kind as to take of my wet boots before entering the fancy-looking Inn. With only wet socks on and my wet dripping clothing, I gracefully entered the building and walked to the bar. I should have taken off my rain gear. I told the gentleman there that I had a reservation. He looked at me without smiling noticing the state I was in. I don't think he was that thrilled with me. Two of the women from the Sierra Club yelled out, "Oh good, it looks like you made it!" I said, "Yes, but I'm a bit wet." (No kidding). They said they were wet also when they arrived, so that made me feel better. I still don't think the gentleman was thrilled with me though.

Still, he led me back to the entrance area to go up the stairs to my room. My heavy wheeled luggage was waiting there below the stairs so I asked the gentleman if he could so kindly take my luggage up. I warned him that it was heavy. I think I heard him grumbling and struggling as he went up the stairs. Now I really, really didn't think he was thrilled with me. He showed me to my room, and I thanked him so very much for carrying the bag. He left me after showing me the remote control for the TV.

First thing I did. Take off the wet rain jacket and rain pants ever so carefully and hung them up to dry. Second thing I did. Open the door to the balcony. Just then the sun shone and blue skies appeared. Great, I thought, where was that a half hour ago? But no matter. I was there and that's all that mattered. I think tomorrow's forecast looked nice. I heard a peacock cawing.

I took out everything from my rucksack, which was all still there thankfully, and hung things up in various places around my room to dry. Including the purple shoes that were still purple. They were not brown. But they were wet. Some items I hung on the nice warm metallic heaters/drying rack in the bathroom. These metallic heaters/drying racks in the bathrooms of accommodations get warm and conveniently dry your wet clothes completely, and are very helpful for rainy situations or to dry wet clothes after they have been washed. When we walked the SWCP before, and perhaps even in the Cotswolds, we were introduced to these metallic items which we don't seem to have in the US. They are brilliant. Turn the knob on or flip a switch to turn them on, and they heat up. I would use these as often as I had them to dry any socks, underwear, or any other clothes that I washed. Before I would go to sleep each night, I might turn the washed items over to dry the other side, and by the time I woke up the next morning, my clothes were dry. Brilliant!

Anyway, eventually my purple shoes also dried out and were not ruined, and I had that second pair with me anyway just in case. I was hungry for some lunch and went down to the restaurant to one of the best lunches I have had so far. A refreshing Vegan Super Salad with pine kernels, mixed seeds, and roasted vegetables. Later on I would go back down for dinner and have a good cheese platter. Even including the close call with the mountain goat on the ledge, and my experience with the downpour, it was a good day. The quotes above seem to reflect the weather well for today.

DAY FIVE STATS: 6 MILES. 3.5 HOURS. EXTRA HALF MILE TO "THE HUNTERS INN." EXTRA TINY BIT FOR THE "DRIVEWAY," WHICH I WON'T COUNT AS EXTRA. BOOTS FOR ABOUT 3.5 MILES, THEN PURPLE SHOES FOR ABOUT 2 MILES, THEN BOOTS FOR LAST MILE. PUB IN HEDDON'S MOUTH IS "THE HUNTERS INN." Information about Flapjacks obtained from thespruce.com/what-is-a-British-flapjack.

HEDDON'S MOUTH TO COMBE MARTIN – Friday, 9 June 2017

"What adventure am I going to have today?" – My seven year old niece upon waking up one morning.

After a good night's sleep with both falling asleep and waking up to the strange cawing sounds of the peacocks, I had some time before breakfast. Scott and I finally realized that instead of just calling each other, we could do a video call instead and therefore see each other in addition to hear each other, so we tried that out this morning successfully. Eventually I even realized that instead of using my mobile for this, it would work on my laptop. Eventually we realized that using Facebook Messenger gave us a better connection than the other video call app we were using. I also spent some time this morning repacking all my stuff after it all dried out overnight. My purple shoes, and believe it or not my hiking boots, were both still a bit damp, so I will need to continue drying those out tonight. See, good thing I brought two pairs of purple shoes, and two pairs of hiking boots. Did I mention yet that I brought two pairs of hiking boots? Yes, I came to the SWCP quite prepared! One pair of Merrells, in a brownish color, and one pair of Keens, in a black color. They both seemed to work well during my training hikes, and it gives my feet options. Thus far I have been wearing the Merrells.

After my Half English breakfast with porridge, as porridge is not really part of the Half or Full English, I set off for today's eight mile walk to Combe Martin. I left the Hunter's Inn Riverside path and walked ten minutes to get to a junction where I crossed the river, turned back a quarter mile, and began an uphill climb which equates the downhill slog in the muddy stream I did yesterday in the pouring rain. Fortunately the weather forecast called for about 60F/15.5C today with some sun and some clouds. Yesterday I still wondered where the summer season was, so maybe today I would have some glimpse of it. Two gentlemen passed me by with daypacks, to which I saw them off and on for a couple miles and then lost sight of them for the rest of the day.

It was just before the start of the uphill where I realized that if I had crossed the river at The Hunter's Inn itself, I only would have needed to walk a quarter mile to this point, rather than the half mile to the other bridge and a quarter mile back. Oh well, it means that at least this way I did not miss the official SWCP. I will count the half mile towards my "extra mileage" for today. The uphill climb at this point took me twelve minutes. Yes, I looked at the clock on my mobile phone to time myself, as I did yesterday with the uphill climb out of Lynmouth. It is fun to time myself. Not that I have any comparison to anyone else's stats up a hill, but more for my own sake of exercise, challenge, and because of my accounting background, as I have kind of mentioned, I like numbers.

I saw views across the valley to the path I walked down yesterday in the downpour of rain. I squinted to see if I could see the bench I had that record-breaking shoe change on, but I could spot it. I could see however the beauty of where I walked – the hillside was covered with green grasses, shrubbery and small trees. There were green ferns lining the path I was currently on and a few bright dark pink foxglove wildflowers. I turned a corner to go left as the sun came out briefly, but clouded over again once I got moving. It was quite windy out, too, but not cold, and for the majority of the day, this was the weather pattern.

After I turned the corner to the left, I realized that one cannot have a fear of heights on this part of the path, for on this short stretch, it felt like I was quite close to the edge of some steep drop-offs. I knew I was not in danger, and it was my perception, but since the wind was blowing, it made this part a bit nerve-wracking actually for me, similar to yesterday with the mountain goats. I opened up the hiking poles I brought with me today to help stabilize myself as I got through this part fairly quickly. These were the kinds of places I would definitely not want to be in gale force winds. The booklet described this short section as, "narrow cliff-edge section covered with heather. A spectacular walk." Nerve-wracking, but spectacular.

I stopped at a sign that said it was six miles now to Combe Martin. I saw a freighter ship in the distance mostly red with a white hull. It was sitting on turquoise and blue waters, and I also had views of the headlands beyond, and farmland on the other side of a fence inland. The grassy path had widened out now, no more steep drop offs seeming quite close to the edge, and it was grassy all around.

I wore my second pair of purple shoes today mostly because the ones from yesterday were still a bit damp as mentioned. With the dry forecast, I thought they would be the shoes of the day. I wore them all day, even though there were a couple of rain sprinkles. The forecast was a bit off. I passed a sign that requested, "This is Exmoor National Park. Please Donate to Preserve the Endangered Exmoor Pony and help Preserve these Paths and Lands. Thank you." So I did. I was still in the Exmoor National Park area until I reached Combe Martin today, but now that I think about it, I forgot to tuck my pant legs into my socks in case of ticks. (No worries, I did not have any ticks.)

Now don't tell anyone this, but I did it again just after the donation sign. I went the wrong way for a small bit. The next sign that pointed in the direction I should have gone said "Footpath" not "Coast Path." Now you would think that that would be the sign I should not follow. I mean no other signs so far that I have followed said "Footpath," only "Coast Path." With some hesitation and uncertainty I started walking across a field of sheep instead. The grass was flattened in such a way as to make it feel like it should be the correct path. There were gates at the other end too, to which I had gone through many gates already. I figured it must be right. As the sheep kept baaaaaing at me though and trotting off in all different directions, I now felt like I had made the incorrect choice.

I tried to look in the distance if there were acorn signs at the gates ahead but could quite see yet. Within a few minutes I arrived at the gates, and nope, no signs. This was not the right way. Extra mileage for the day. I turned around and as the sheep continued to baaaaaaa at me, trotting off in all different directions, I apologized to them profusely, and I made my way back to the Footpath sign. Sure enough I walked only a few more yards and there was an acorn leading me through a different gate. Note to self: Look ahead if you are not sure where to go to see if you can spot any signs or acorns, or even arrows. I need to also call that about a quarter of a mile extra for today.

Not too much longer after this incident, it started to drizzle. So much for the sun and clouds only and dry day. The drizzle felt so light that for a while I didn't even put my rain gear on (note that the British refer to rain gear as "waterproofs," but I shall refer to as rain gear), as it was warm out as well. I decided to put on my waterproofs just in case. Of course by the time I put it all on, rain jacket, rain pants, and rain pack cover for my rucksack, the drizzle stopped. I kept my rain gear on just in case as I spotted a few dark clouds hovering over the waters.

As I looked out into the waters it was something else, something breathtaking. It was so vast. If you look way out there you see nothing, nothing but waters and skies. Nothing. I could see cloud patterns closer in, wondering what direction they were blowing. There were darker rain type clouds but not super dark, there were some white wispy clouds, and some patches of blue skies. The waters were a different shade of blue than the skies. Back on land there was a lot of various shades of green. Trees, bushes, plants, grass. There were colorful wildflowers in bloom every now and then - bright dark pink foxglove, and some white wildflowers that I don't know the name of. The yellow, I think called Scotch Broom (which I later found out was called gorse and is quite plentiful along the SWCP), was not in bloom, but I could tell it had been earlier, perhaps a month or so ago. White sheep speckled the green grasses. Occasionally a home or other building appeared and offered a subject in the natural scene. The landscape was breathtaking and colourful. (Note that the British spell colorful as colourful.)

The mileage signs along the SWCP seemed a bit off today. One sign about a half mile back said "five and a half miles to Combe Martin." Very soon thereafter, I passed a sign that said "four miles to Combe Martin," but I certainly had not gone a mile and a half. Soon after that, I saw another sign saying "four miles to Combe Martin," but I know I have walked a bit since that second sign. I guess some mileage signs on the SWCP are a bit off, as I will notice that that happens every now and then over the next few months.

The path had been quite flat for a while with a few puddles, but I was negotiating well so as to not get my purple shoes wet. When I stopped to take a picture at the second four-mile sign, I of course stepped in a small puddle. I decided to continue to keep my rain gear on because it was a bit windy still and there were a few darker clouds around me, but it fortunately continued to stay dry. I debated taking the rain gear off, but currently left them on. Just then a local woman passed me by jogging. Wearing shorts and a t-shirt. All of a sudden I felt quite overdressed for the occasion. We smiled as she went by. I wonder what she thought of me in all my rain gear. Perhaps she thought that I was overdressed for the occasion.

A bit of a ways on, I passed by four men who just came up a hill. One said to me something like, "It is just as hard to go up as it is to go down." The Great Hangman, he was talking about. The highest point on all of the South West Coast Path! A few feet later, I passed through a gate that said "The National Trust - Great Hangman." I went down the valley. Slowly, carefully, as it was quite steep. I'm really glad I brought my hiking poles with me today. They help with these steeper descents, especially for protecting the knees. I didn't think that the descent was that hard though as the man was implying. As I descended, I could actually see the path I would be ascending out of the valley leading to the Great Hangman, etched in the green hillside just beyond.

I stopped at the bottom of the valley before it ascended to take a "rest." I haven't "rested" all morning. I was hungry, too. The scenery I stopped at was a quaint babbling stream going under a footbridge covered with trees. It was quite peaceful in this spot called Sherrycombe. Very meditative and centering. I stopped to sit and eat something to gain my energy and strength for the "hard" climb up. The Great Hangman is also the highest sea cliff in England at 1,044 feet high. The ascent would not be from exact sea level of zero feet though. From this part of the valley, there will be about a 500 foot elevation gain. I decided to shed the rain gear at this point.

After about a fifteen minute rest, I put my rucksack back on, fixed my hair under my hat, put my camera and mobile phone around my neck (I have my mobile hanging from a lanyard since I have not mentioned that yet), grabbed my hiking polls, checked my surroundings to make sure I had everything (good for me!), and geared up for conquering the Great Hangman. I nearly bumped my head on a tree above me.

The path started climbing steeply right away through some other trees, and then it was out into the open. I got hot. I took my hat off and fixed my hair again. The weather got warmer and the winds were non-existent as I made my way up. I spotted the red and white freighter ship in the distance that I had been seeing on and off all day. The climbing then was not so steep any more, but more gradual. Then it pretty much flattened out to a grassy path. The wind picked up again though so I put my hat back on. The flat grassy path took me the summit of the Great Hangman, twenty-five minutes later from the valley. That was it? That was the ascent to the Great Hangman? Not to sound overconfident, but my training hikes were longer and steeper than that back at home. But then again, I guess that is why I trained. So that these ascents would not be so difficult.

I was at the highest point in all of the SWCP, the highest sea cliff in England, though! It was a "great" feeling to be there, at the Great Hangman! There was a huge pile of rocks to mark the summit. I was really not sure why the huge pile of rocks was here, but perhaps they had to do with the iron, copper, lead, and silver mining that was done in this area in past centuries, which I read about in today's booklet. The pile of rocks reminded me of the Cruz de Ferro rock pile on my Camino de Santiago walk. That was a place that had a pile of rocks, and a cross on top of a long pole stuck in the pile of rocks. People bring things from their home from all over the world, such as rocks or some other significant object, to the Cruz de Ferro in order to remember someone, or to say a prayer for anything. It is a very significant place on the Camino. I had brought a couple of Native American "Pocket Spirits," small pewter "coins" that I bought at store near Seattle, that are engraved on one side with a Northwest Coast Indian symbol, such as a butterfly or bear or dancing bear or eagle or raven or whale or heart on one side, and an inspirational word on the other side, such as grace, strength, protection, intention, creativity, dedication, or love.

I decided to start a new tradition on the SWCP. Since I did not bring any Pocket Spirits with me, I found a small rock around the huge pile of larger rocks to place on this pile, and said a prayer.

More on the silver mining from information I read in the booklet. "The silver mines were first worked during the reign of Edward I in the 13th century and finally closed in the 1890s...Combe Martin silver is present in the Crown Jewels and Queen Victoria had several items of jewelry made from Combe Martin silver."

As I continued my way down towards the Little Hangman, there was a breeze as I walked across the grassy path still lined with ferns and shrubbery. A few raindrops happened but not many so I opted to keep my rain gear off. A couple was taking shelter under a tree, putting their rain gear on. We discussed how many times we take off and put on rain gear on this path and had a good chuckle. I continued to walk across the flat grassy path, and saw a rocky beach area below me. I came to the sign that pointed uphill to the summit of Little Hangman. It was an optional path. I chose to not take this option. I descended steeply towards Combe Martin.

I passed by another jogger carrying nothing, and this time I laughed at myself for carrying so much in my rucksack, including my hiking boots. I guess I have to think of these as just "day walks." But then again they always say to take the "Ten Essentials," most of which I mentioned on 4th June in the "Getting to Minehead" chapter. Better safe than sorry. I shall continue to carry all my essentials.

It was a steep descent from the junction with Little Hangman at first, but then it flattened out. I noticed a couple with their baby on his back making their way down a permitted footpath to Wild Pear Beach. As cute as the name sounded of this beach, I did not go to this beach.

I came to a sign pointing to Combe Martin via the Coast Path, and another sign pointing to Combe Martin via a Footpath. For this one, I definitely took the Coast Path. I passed by field of sheep and started singing "Baa Baa Black Sheep, have you any wool. Yes sir. Yes sir. Three bags full." Then it occurred to me that I actually do have three bags of wool. From New Zealand. Before I left home for the SWCP, I read that the oils in sheeps' wool help prevent blisters. You put this on any area that you start to feel a hot spot where a blister might be forming. I bought three small bags from a company in the US that sells this New Zealand wool, in case any of my blister theories don't work. I hope to never use it.

As I continued walking I saw Combe Martin from across another field of sheep. Combe Martin was one of the bigger towns I've seen since Minehead. Exactly five hours and one minute since I left this morning, I arrived at Combe Martin. A sign told me that I have 595 miles to go till Poole, and I have come 35 miles from Minehead thus far, and eight miles from The Hunter's Inn!

I sat on a bench in a car park overlooking a small beach. I emailed Scott to let him know I arrived. It would have been about 6:30am for him, and I didn't think he would be awake yet, so I didn't want to text or call or video call, as those sounds would wake him. The time difference between us is that I am eight hours ahead. I got good mobile reception here. I also needed to take out the directions I wrote and a little map I drew for myself months ago to find the Guest House I was staying in tonight. As I stared at my little map and directions, I couldn't figure out what I wrote.

I was hungry anyway first, so I walked down to the main street of Combe Martin where there were several beachy-themed stores and a few places to eat. I chose a cute café and had a well-deserved "tuna mayonnaise" sandwich. Yes, I know, not vegetarian. While I was sitting there, I had a brilliant idea though. I turned on the map app on my mobile phone with GPS to see if I could find the Guest House without having to ask anyone. Sure enough it worked, and less than five minutes later I arrived at the Guest House. I make a note to self to remember to use the map app again to find my accommodations, as it was a brilliant idea.

Denise greeted me very warmly. She had recalled that I made this reservation back in October, thinking that I planned very far in advance. I explained that yes, since I was walking in the "summer" months, I did not want to risk not having accommodations on any given night on the SWCP. She asked if I planned it all myself and booked it all myself. I said yes! Her husband Steve also joined us, and he greeted me very warmly as well. We chatted about all kinds of things, from rides over the next few days (I will be staying here three nights), to the weather, to places to eat dinner in town, to some of the other longer distance walks I have done. They have had this Guest House since 2011. After about twenty minutes of talking, Denise showed me to my room, and I started typing away on my laptop for today's walk from the dictation app on my phone. I must say that the modern technology of apps on my mobile phone is quite convenient for this walk – dictation apps, map apps, weather apps.

Eventually I got hungry and made my way back down to the beachfront area of Combe Martin. I ordered a squash chickpea spinach curry served on a bed of rice. In a pub. I forgot to mention that last night for dinner I had a soup as an appetizer, although I can't recall what it was at the moment, and I also ordered a cheese plate from the dessert menu as my dinner. No sugary desserts both nights though!

I did some Facebook posts tonight. I have been doing them every couple of nights. I picked some of my best photos from the past few days and put it on not only my personal page for my friends and family to see, but also on a SWCP Facebook Group page that I belong to so that the locals and others who love this path can see my progress. Let me explain a bit more about this "SWCP Facebook Group" page. I can't remember exactly how I found them on Facebook, but I do know that at one point I had "liked" the SWCP Association's page, "The South West Coast Path," but I don't think that was how I found this group page. I also "liked" at one point the "National Trails" Facebook page, but again, I don't think that was how I found this group page. However, both of these pages have been great resources for me as well.

I think perhaps one day I was just doing a search on Facebook for "South West Coast Path" in general to see what else I could find, and I came across this group, and just asked if I could join. They accepted, and I have been able to following other's walks on there, reading other's posts, and posting my own posts on there ever since. People post good helpful and useful information on there as well. People post photos and experiences of their own walks, whether a day-walk, or several weeks, or the entire path. People ask for, and receive, advice. I will become attached to this group in more ways than one as my time goes on during the next several months. They are officially called, "South West Coast Path (England, UK) Minehead to Poole 630 miles."

I video called my husband, finished typing, and will be going to sleep soon. I think today had actually been the longest day so far for me, and quite a spectacular adventure, answering my niece's question from above. I was grateful for the weather, for my feet and shoes, for the breathtaking scenery, and for the people of the accommodations who have been warm and welcoming.

DAY SIX STATS: 8 MILES. 5 HOURS AND ONE MINUTE. THREE-QUARTERS EXTRA MILES FOR WALKING FROM ACOMMODATIONS AND ACROSS A FIELD OF SHEEP. PURPLE SHOES. THE PUB I ATE AT IN COMBE MARTIN IS "THE FO'C'S'LE INN." UP THE ROAD IN COMBE MARTIN IS THE "PACK O'CARDS INN" PUB.

A couple interesting tidbits is that Combe Martin "is thought by some to be the longest village in England – just over 1.5 miles. About half way along the village is a well-known pub called the Pack of Cards. It was built in 1690, has 4 floors (one for each suit), 13 doors on each floor (one for each card in a suit) and 52 windows and 52 stairs (one for each card in the pack)." I should have gone there for dinner one evening.

COMBE MARTIN TO ILFRACOMBE – Saturday, 10 June 2017

"The Little Chapel on the Hill, looks so bleak and bare,
But oh! The tales that it could tell of history made there.

The ray of light that shines from the tiny window gay,
Gives safety to each passing ship and guides them on their way.

O Little Chapel on the Hill I sit and listen and pray,
That God will always keep you safe for many and many a day."
    L. Vickers - Part of poem from "The Little Chapel on the Hill."

After hearing the rain all night long out the window from my Guest House, I was lucky to have a mostly dry and somewhat humid day today. Yeah, summer! I also met a wonderful woman whom I connected with via the SWCP Facebook Group, and who took me out for my first cream tea!

I left the Guest House after my Half English, and talking with Denise about my pickup this afternoon. I followed the street down for about two minutes as part of my walk for today. When you are in a town you still follow the acorns, but the signage is a bit different. For example, they might appear on electric poles, and the ones here say "Combe Martin" with a shield symbol of some sort, as well as a yellow arrow and the acorn.

Like I have had before, there is nothing like a good uphill climb to start the morning! When I say that, I really mean that it is lovely to start that way to get the muscles and heart and lungs moving and ready for the day. The path started out actually on a road going uphill. I had to wait at the bottom for a moment to let two people and a car pass by before my ascent, followed by a flat sidewalk parallel to a road for a bit, followed by a bit more uphill road climbing, and again paralleling a flat road again on a sidewalk for a bit. Today's walk had been pretty much paved for the first half hour. That will soon change. The next SWCP sign told me to follow the Old Coast Road.

The Old Coast Road soon became an eerie stone paved road, lined with trees that obstructed my views of the water. I'm not sure why a couple of bits and pieces of this path have felt eerie to me. I don't feel unsafe; they just seemed odd to me, perhaps because I had no views of the water. I guess I just prefer to be either right by the water, or at least have good views of the water.

Soon though there was a descent into a campground with tents and camper vans overlooking Watermouth Cove and Watermouth Harbour. I spotted fishing boats and a freighter in the water out at sea, and more boats parked in the harbour. Below was the small quiet cove with a small sandy beach surrounded by the green covered hillsides. It looked peaceful down there.

I stopped to put rain gear on at a picnic bench as is started to sprinkle, only for the rain to stop once I had the rain gear on, of course. I did that a couple more times today, but never did get more than a few minutes of sprinkles all day. Until I arrived in Ilfracombe, but more on that later.

I was about to leave the campground after my rain gear stop when I spotted a couple next to a large tent as the man was waving to me. I think he was pointing as if to offer me some tea. They were too far away to talk, so I walked over there. I politely declined the tea as I just drank a few cups with breakfast and I had plenty of water. The woman then said, "Oh you must then be a coffee drinker based on your accent." I explained that while I happen to live in the Seattle area of the US, one of the places known for its coffee, I may be one of the few who is actually not a coffee drinker. I prefer tea actually. We continued to chat. They asked if I was doing the entire walk of the SWCP. The gentleman told me he did part of the SWCP a few years ago. We chatted about the weather, and I remarked on the large tent they have, as it seemed to have two rooms and enough room to stand up in. I don't think I have seen a "luxury" tent that large before. The woman asked me, "Don't you have coastal walking the US? Why come to England?" I told her that there is some coastal walking in the states of Washington and Oregon, but they are for backpacking and carrying tents, not with "luxury" beds-and-breakfasts. I said that it was nice to meet them, thanks for the offer of the tea, and to enjoy their summer.

I enjoyed some more parallel flat road walking on a sidewalk that was tree-lined and Watermouth Harbour next to me to which I took photos of the boats sitting on the sand, as it was low tide. I always find it surreal that in my more than 50 years, and the couple's however many years, that we meet up together at that moment in time for a brief moment of time to connect on some level, not planning it, never ever imagining that it would happen. Does that make sense? I think I just have to call it "randomness."

The path opened up and I walked along the water's edge, which I love, to which I saw nine jet skiers on the water and watched for a moment. I then climbed 78 steps up the path. I counted. I looked back at a few of the headlands that I have walked on the past several days. I looked ahead to see the headlands I will be walking on in the next few days. So amazing! I also saw Watermouth Harbour with the boats I just walked past. I descended 65 steps down the path. I counted again. The path was lined with a few bright dark pink foxglove and some yellow dandelions.

I looked back to see the small hill with the steps I just climbed up and down. I could see the narrow path itself surrounded by the greenery of the hillside. My breath was just taken away at how even the smallest of green hillsides can be so beautiful against the blue waters. My favorite colors are becoming green and blue! (Just as the British spell "color" as "colour," they also spell "harbor" as "harbour," so I shall continue to write harbour.)

I walked another brief uphill climb and then turned left over a stile. I needed to negotiate my way through a path filled with brush, wildflowers, and thorny plants. At this moment I was glad that I was wearing long pants and a long sleeved shirt (I had taken off the rain gear at one point) which protected my arms and legs from getting scratched by the thorns. I spotted Ilfracombe in the distance, my destination for the day, which from this perspective did not look that far away. The weather thus far had been warm and muggy. The sun tried to appear through the clouds but didn't make it for very long. I appreciated today's weather very much. Summer!

I stopped on a small patch of grass to sit for a while. I listened to the waves crashing against the brown rocks below. If I have not mentioned this yet, this is one of the most soothing sounds for me to listen to. The waters were various shades of blue, perhaps because of the different depths of water and/or from the shadows of the white clouds above. Ilfracombe was just off in the distance, some small rocky brown and sandy beaches below, and green headlands beyond. Another jet ski went by. I watched a seagull playing with the wind currents above me. I had some meditative and peaceful moments sitting here.

Just before I got up from sitting I had briefly looked in my guidebook, and happened to read that there is a lighthouse in Ilfracombe. I did not know that and was very glad I just read that. I love lighthouses and have a fascination with them, which I have mentioned before.

After some more bushwhacking through those overgrown thorny plants, which I think was gorse, there was a Coast Path sign that said, "Ilfracombe 2.5 miles." I came to a small town called Hele Beach. Here was where I had to keep my eyes open for Coast Path signs as I was in a town again. As I entered Hele Bay I was greeted by a very small sign on a decorated pole that said, "Hele Bay is a Place to Swim, A Place to Play, A Place to Relax, A Place to Stay, Joy as We Do our Hele Bay." There was a scallop shell above the sign, and also decorating the wall outside a house, that important directional symbol of the Camino de Santiago. I wondered why it was here. Perhaps Hele Beach has a connection with the Camino? Perhaps it was just because Hele Beach was near the sea? I stopped in a cute café to get some lunch, and didn't contemplate the scallop shell any longer. I ordered a very tasty "beetroot, butternut squash, and goats cheese burger."

Then the confusing part of the day happened. Negotiating my way through Hillsboro Hill. Even though the booklet told me that "there are many paths around Hillsborough" and that "the Coast Path is clearly marked and is the most obvious path," to me with all the paths going in various directions, I found it somewhat confusing. Fortunately, I did not get too lost in this maze of trails on Hillsboro Hill, but I did go on an incorrect path every now and then which I soon realized was incorrect and back-tracked to get back on the correct path.

After the hill, the views ahead to Ilfracombe were fantastic. One of my favorite scenes I realized is the approach to a village or town from above where you get the hillsides, spotted with the homes and buildings, leading down to the harbour area with boats and perhaps a beach. Stunning!

A sign greeted me as I got very close to Ilfracombe that said, "For Coast Path (acorn symbol) & Tarka Trail (walking route) follow the Footprints." There were a few footprints on the sign and some examples below my feet on the ground. Engraved on the footprints on the ground they said, "Ilfracombe, curious coastal charm." A bit further up I took pictures of my purple shoes next to some footprints, which I would follow for directions. The Tarka Trail is 180 miles of paths both for walking and for bicycling around North Devon. Parts of the SWCP are actually on the Tarka Trail. Tarka is an otter from a children's book written by Henry Williamson. "In 1927, novelist Henry Williamson wrote about the area in North Devon which he loved so much. The Taw-Torridge Rivers were the inspiration behind his classic book, Tarka the Otter, and the work has left a lasting legacy. Several decades later, the Tarka Trail is giving cyclists and walkers the chance to take in the scenery described by Williamson." Perhaps I should read the book, or see the film!

I arrived at the start of the harbour area of Ilfracombe. Immediately I realized that I love seeing these fishing villages with all the boats right there, the breakwaters and seawalls for protection, and the buildings and shops and restaurants that surround the harbour. Small rolling green hills surrounding all that. It was low tide and there were even cars parked on the sandy area with the boats. The colors of the buildings surrounding the harbour were blues and pinks and yellows and peaches and beiges and browns and whites. The boats were mostly white with blue coverings, but a few orange and yellow and green boats all made for a very colorful harbour. Even with the current gray skies.

I looked at a sign outside a restaurant of all the "locally caught fish and shellfish landed in Ilfracombe Harbour" – mackerel, turbot, sea bass, monkfish, brill, lemon sole, Dover sole, Pollock, cod, hake, haddock, huss, ray wing, megrim, skate cheeks, sand sole, plaice, and John Dory. I have never heard of most of these fish. It is what those fishing boats are doing out in the seas. I feel comfortable in these places for some reason, and I appreciate the life of the fisherman at the moment. I took more photos of the harbour as I walked around it.

I mentioned breakwaters and seawalls. I had to do a bit of research on what these are, as I have seen some of them thus far on my walk, and will see a lot more. A breakwater, aka breakwall, is a structure that juts out into the water, a stone wall that protects the harbour, the boats, and the town inland from the seas during storms and large waves. A seawall is also a stone wall, but this one is built on land, paralleling a beach, and also used for protection.

I sent a message to Jo, a woman I met via the SWCP Facebook Group, and we agreed to meet in about an hour so that I could have a chance to go to the lighthouse first that I read about earlier. She had connected with me originally when I posted on the group page that I was on my way from the US to walk the path. She invited me that when I pass through Ilfracombe, where she lives, to message her, and she would treat me to a "cream tea" as a celebration of my 50th birthday. She will be turning 50 in three years. I had let Jo know the date I would be arriving in Ilfracombe, which turned out to be a Saturday and she would not be working. Yesterday, I contacted her again to make sure we were still going to get together for birthday celebrations and my first ever cream tea. We were.

It turned out that the lighthouse was also a chapel, a small museum, and a gift shop on top of Lantern Hill, a small hill that overlooks the harbour of Ilfracombe. "The Little Chapel on the Hill," the 14th century St. Nicholas Chapel, which "from the middle ages the chapel maintained a light to guide shipping into the harbour. It is still a working lighthouse today and is said to be the oldest in the country," according to the brochure that I picked up here. The brochure I picked up further remarked, "For centuries its beacon light has been a landmark to ships at sea and the little building has been a shelter for those watching and waiting for the return of a vessel caught in a storm." As far as the chapel part goes, "St. Nicholas being the patron saint of sailors, his Chapel would have served the mariners and their families in the little houses around the harbour." So very interesting and historical. I love that this place has so much meaning for those out at sea, and for those on land thinking of those out at sea.

I met Jo near the interestingly strange statue, the Verity statue, a 66-foot bronze statue that represents truth and justice. Of course Jo recognized me, as I was the only one there with a rucksack and a rain jacket on, as it started drizzling off and on during my two hours in Ilfracombe. I recognized her based on her picture on Facebook, and also because she walked towards me and said my name. We shook hands and hugged like old friends. (Well we are not old, but like we have known each other for a long time.)

We started chatting right away as we walked to The Tea Garden for my first cream tea. We discussed being or approaching 50, my walk, her children (turns out one of her children works at The Tea Garden), her job, my job, losing weight (as I ate the calorie-filled scones, clotted cream, and strawberry jam part of the cream tea), and life. We talked about walking, and about walking alone. At the spur of the moment I thought to invite her to join me on my walk tomorrow from Ilfracombe to Woolacombe. She accepted saying she would cancel some other arrangements. She treated me to the cream tea to which I thanked her kindly. It was nice to have some company and chat with an "old friend."

Let me describe cream tea in more depth. Cream tea is a form of an "afternoon tea," with not only perfectly brewed tea, but with a combination of "crumbly scones, sticky fruit jam, and lashings of clotted cream." Sounds good already! Using loose-leaf tea is best, according to the website of "The Cream Tea Society," brewing the tea in teapots. The tea should be brewed for at least three minutes before pouring, or up to five minutes, if you like stronger tea. After the tea is poured, in a tea cup, never a mug, it is followed with milk and then sugar. After stirring, the spoon should be placed on the saucer, and no outstretched pinkies please. Even just the tea sounds good!

Next is the scone. They should be light and springy, and are best when served fresh and eaten the same day as they are baked. The basic recipe consists of flour, baking powder, butter, salt, and milk, although there are variations on this basic recipe, perhaps adding sugar, egg, lemon juice, or vanilla extract. Further variations might include sultanas (similar to raisins), or cheese (remember the cheese scone I ate about a week ago walking from Minehead to Bossington), or other flavors. Scones are round in shape, not triangular. Once the ingredients are mixed into dough, and baked for ten to twelve minutes, it is best to simply break apart the scone with a simple twist in order to get two halves. Crumbs can be caught by the saucer.

The toppings on the scone include clotted cream and jam. Clotted cream is used, never whipped cream. Clotted cream is made by "heating unpasteurized cow's milk which then is left in a shallow pan for many hours, perhaps even overnight around twelve hours, which causes the cream to rise to the surface and 'clot'." The flavor of jam mostly used is strawberry.

Now is the debate - over these two toppings to put on the scones, clotted cream and jam, jam and clotted cream. Which do you put on first directly on the scone, and which do you put on the top? Depending on the county in the SWCP area of England you are in, you either put the jam on first, or the clotted cream on first. Cornwall vs. Devon. Devon vs. Cornwall. Cornwall says that the jam goes on the scone first, topped with the clotted cream. Devon says that the clotted cream goes on the scone first, topped with the jam.

I was in Devon today, but since this was my first cream tea, and since I am from the US, and since I wanted to be equitable about this debate, but mostly because I wanted my taste buds to experience cream tea both ways, with my two scones, I put on half of my scone halves with cream on top, and on the other half of my scone halves with jam on top. I fell in love with both ways of enjoying the cream tea!

Jo and I then took a short walk together around the stone wall of Capstone Hill as the drizzle continued. We exchanged phone numbers, another hug, and said our goodbyes. Later she sent me a message saying that unfortunately she needed to be around tomorrow for her daughter and could not go on the walk with me. I told her that any day in my entire walk she is welcome. She said she might be able to walk with me later in July or August. Turns out we never walked together, but I still appreciated the friend I made. And that she treated me to my first of many cream teas.

I took a quick walk back to the stone wall area to take a few photos looking back at The Little Chapel on the Hill with some yellow wildflowers in the foreground, some of my favorite photos. I went into the St. Philip and St. James Church briefly, also known as Pip and Jim's Church, and then I called Denise and Steve from the Guest House in Combe Martin to ask if Steve could please pick me up.

I realized as I waited for my ride that today marked my first week on the SWCP. Six days of walking, and one "rest day." I wondered why all of a sudden I asked Jo to join me on a walk. What was that feeling all about, I wondered? Did I just like Jo enough and we got along so I thought it would be nice to walk for a day with her? I thought I wanted to do the entire walk by myself? I also thought of my husband and us walking together. Did I already feel like I wanted some company and someone to talk to as I walked, other than just talking to myself, the sheep, and cows? Although, you know, I do possibly have a day already scheduled to walk with my friend Sasha. And that was all I thought about that at this moment.

Back at the Guest House, I got hungry for dinner and I remembered that Denise told me of a take away fish and chips place, so I decided to get that and bring it back to the Guest House to eat there. I walked a couple minutes to the harbour to "The Black & White" traditional fish and chips shop, and ordered the fish, without the chips though, and a "veg spring roll." It was drizzling when I walked down, but stopped by the time I walked back. "Veg" is short for vegetables.

I ate in the little dining area in this Guest House. Soon Steve heard me and offered me tea. He told me more about the silver mining in this area and that Combe Martin has some spiritual significance. The hill in between Little Hangman and Great Hangman is a place where people come annually as sort of a pilgrimage because of some spiritual event that apparently happened there. There is also a house up the road has some other spiritual significance. I asked him about how the pile of rocks got on the Great Hangman, to which he told me something like they are very old rocks, perhaps from the mining history in the area. I told him of my Camino de Santiago and Cruz de Ferro connection with the pile of rocks.

I decided to do some more research on what Steve and I were talking about, and found out that some believe that "a hill outside Combe Martin, Holdstone Down, is a Holy Mountain imbued with great healing energy," and that people go on Spiritual Pilgrimages there and have gathered there, and have even used a special battery there "to send out energy in the hope of bringing peace and healing to the world" from there.

Tonight I had these thoughts: I don't think that people have really asked me "why" I am doing the SWCP walk. They may ask me "what" I am doing, but not necessarily "why." Perhaps people just guess because it is something that people just do here in England for their holidays and for recreation and for the views and the beauty and walking and nature and outdoors and exercise. Perhaps they don't think of it as some great epic birthday celebration. Perhaps they don't think of it as a way to figure out the meaning of life or learning some life lesson. I decided to do this walk to celebrate my 50th with something epic, as mentioned. I don't think I am doing this walk however in search of the meaning of life in general, or even the meaning of my own life. I don't think I am trying to learn any life lesson. I don't feel that I am on a spiritual journey. I am just walking for the sake of walking, for the adventure, and I would like to do to my best to complete the path largely on my own, but always with the help of booklets, guidebooks, maps, guardian angels, and perhaps even an occasional walk with a new friend.

Other than my epic birthday celebration, so "why" am I walking 630 miles? I suppose I am doing this walk like why I think the English do the walk - holiday, recreation, views, beauty, walking, nature, outdoors, exercise. To just be. Beside the seas. To challenge myself. To do something I consider epic for myself. But I do it humbly, graciously, carefully, slowly.

And you know, I am also doing this walk because I like to be beside the seas and waters and oceans. To get daily supplies of those good-for-me-positive negative ions. I chose the SWCP through a series of events actually. Briefly, after I walked the Camino Francés, which is an inland route across northern Spain from the border with France to the pilgrimage site of the Cathedral of Santiago de Compostela, located in the northwest corner of Spain, but still inland, I decided to do another short walk. Some people walk from the Cathedral to a town on the coast of Spain called Finisterre. I decided to take a bus to Finisterre and walk up the Atlantic coast of Spain about twenty miles from Finisterre to a town called Muxía. It was in this "short" twenty miles that I fell in love with walking by the seas, waters, and oceans! A very significant twenty miles for me actually.

When I got home from Spain, I wanted to experience more of walking beside the seas, so Scott and I took a trip to the Pacific Ocean and walked on the beaches of the Olympic Coast of the state of Washington. We had also done a previous trip a few years earlier along the beaches in the state of Oregon. Then I wanted more, and having also walked in the Cotswolds area of England a few years ago, I already had the guidebook, "Walking in Britain," by Lonely Planet which describes 52 walks that I used to research the Cotswolds walk. Somehow tucked in the back of mind, I remembered reading about several coastal walks in Britain, so I immediately opened that book up and started looking through it again. This book only describes 168 miles of the SWCP, part of the Cornwall section from Padstow to Falmouth, but it was enough to realize that in order to get constant seas and negative ions, the SWCP would be my next long distance walk! I did some more research, bought a few books, and the rest they say is history - My husband and I checked out the waters, literally and figuratively, of the SWCP on those 100 miles we did last year, and now here I am again, a week into my 630-mile adventure!

DAY SEVEN STATS: 5.5 MILES. 4.5 HOURS. NO SIGNIFICANT EXTRA MILES. PURPLE SHOES. FIRST CREAM TEA. AND A NEW FRIEND MADE. A FEW PUBS IN ILFRACOMBE ARE CALLED "GEORGE & DRAGON," "SHIP & PILOT," "THE THATCHED INN," AND "PRINCE OF WALES."

Information about the Tarka Trail and Tarka the Otter from
bbc.co.uk/devon/content/articles/2008/02/08/tarka_trail_feature
Information about Holdstone Down from
news.bbc.co.uk/2/hi/uk_news/england/devon/3097839
Information about Cream Tea from
creamteasociety.co.uk/cream-tea-etiquette; and from
thespruce.com/difference-cornish-vs-devon-cream-tea-435316

ILFRACOMBE TO WOOLACOMBE – Sunday, 11 June 2017

"One day at a time. One mile at a time. One step at a time." – Me, but I wonder if others have thought this quote about walking.

Yesterday I mentioned how I fell in love with walking by the seas and waters and oceans after I walked twenty miles up the Atlantic coast of Spain, after walking the Camino Francés. But my love for walking in general and travelling in general, and walking in the places I travel, did not start there. No, those started long, long ago. To make it brief, I have loved walking, mostly in the form of hiking, and backpacking, for a long time, and mostly in the mountains, as where I have been living was closer to mountains than the ocean. One such long backpack I did in the mountains was the 93-mile Wonderland Trail around Mount Rainier in the state of Washington. I did this backpack, splitting up the mileage into two separate years due to the permit situation, with a great friend of mine Melissa. For this backpack we had to carry quite heavy rucksacks, filled with tents, camping gear, cooking gear, water filters, food for several days, water, clothes for all kinds of possible weather conditions, etc. My rucksack was 40 pounds, just as much as my wheeled suitcase, and Melissa carried quite the impressive 50 pounds on her back. Of course both of our rucksacks got lighter as we ate food, but then filled up again as we were resupplied every few days. The first year when we backpacked about a third of the Wonderland Trail, it rained on us just about the entire time. The second year when we did the other two-thirds, the weather was mostly warm and sunny.

One of the most rewarding walks I did, in the form of trekking, was in the amazing country of Bhutan. Along with another great friend of mine, Beth, and a few other women, and several local Bhutanese guides, we did the seven day, 66-mile walk I already briefly mentioned to the remote village of Laya at an elevation of 12,500 feet. This was not a climb like Mount Everest, but during the season we did the trek, October of 2011, it was several days of hiking. To arrive in a village where there was really no other way to get there other than by walking or animals like horses and yaks, was an experience of a lifetime. For this trek I only needed to carry a daypack as we had horses and the local guides carrying the majority of our supplies. With being at the altitude of 12,500 feet there could have been issues with altitude sickness, but fortunately I never experienced any symptoms. It was an amazing experience the day we stayed in this remote village to meet the people living there and learn about their ways of life.

When I was in Bhutan, as I was there for nearly a month, Beth and I and the other women also had the honor of meeting the newly married King and Queen of Bhutan, His Majesty the Fifth King of Bhutan Jigme Khesar Namgyal Wangchuck, and his beautiful new bride, Her Majesty the Queen of Bhutan Ashi Jetsun Pema Wangchuck. It was the day after their wedding. To make a long story short, the newly married couple was driving along a road on their way from where they got married to the capital city of Bhutan, as we were driving in the opposite direction on the same road on our way to start our Laya trek. Many local people were lined up on the side of the road because as the King and Queen were driving, they would get out of the car and greet and talk to the people. Therefore, we stopped our car and got in line as well. After about two and a half hours of waiting, the King and Queen arrived in the village we were and made their way down the line to us, and we all had a short conversation about where we were from and if we were enjoying Bhutan, which of course we were. We wished the bride and groom "Tashi Delek," for blessings and good luck, and that is how I briefly met the King and Queen of Bhutan. I wonder if I will ever get to meet any royalty in England.

Another place I walked, being one of the few who has done this, is I walked around the 42-mile Île d'Orléans, a small island near Québec City, Canada, of only 76 square miles, but with nearly twenty boutiques and galleries representing over 80 artists and craftspeople, and with over 40 businesses and restaurants representing the agritourism industry on the island. I took four days to walk around this island, stopping at as many of the boutiques and galleries and businesses and restaurants as I could, mostly walking on their roads and sidewalks. I was actually sponsored by Tourisme Québec and Québec City Tourism, and since this was an island located in the middle of the St. Lawrence River, it was another experience of being near the waters.

Back to today…After breakfast, Steve drove me back to Ilfracombe. I picked up a sandwich to take with me today because of the eight and a half miles I was about to undertake. I had snacks with me, but today seemed like a day to have something more substantial, especially with all the ascents and descents of the day, and the lack of food stops.

I started walking just as some church bells were ringing. As I've mentioned, one of my favorite sounds, aside from the crashing waves of the seas, is the church bells in Europe. I probably could listen to church bells next to the crashing waves of the seas all day long.

Today's forecast was for sun breaks through the clouds and about 60F/15.5C. Perhaps summer again! No rain forecasted. What they didn't tell me about though, or what I did not notice, would be the relentless non-gale force winds, but perhaps a strong breeze or a high wind.

I walked around the same place Jo and I did yesterday, Capstone Hill, for fun, as it was part of the SWCP. I suppose I could have skipped it since I walked it already, but I wanted to make sure I didn't miss any of the footprints on the ground that I needed to follow for the SWCP. I caught another view of Lantern Hill and The Chapel on the Hill, sitting proudly on top of a small green grass covered and brown rocky hill. The foreground of this view had rocks jutting out of the blue seas being hit by small waves, and more small hills. Beyond the Lantern Hill was a taller hill and headlands beyond. I've probably described similar scenery of green hills and headlands, and brown rocks, and blue seas, and will continue to describe them, but no two hills or headlands or rocks or seas are alike! And all are quite picturesque. I took a few more photos in today's lighting of Lantern Hill and The Chapel on the Hills, still some of my favorite photos.

An area on the far side of this walk around Capstone Hill, appropriately named "Windy Corner," provided me with a another view, that even though it sounds similar to the view I just described, it was still completely different. The bluish, turquoise, even greenish waters, with white capped waves outlined the brown rocks just below me, and the brown rocks jutting out of the water, the hillsides with the bottom halves of brown and the top halves of green. A headland in the future. Blue skies peeking out behind light gray and white clouds. Even though the corner was appropriately named, I stood in amazement at the beauty I was seeing.

As I made my way through the paved sidewalks and roads of Ilfracombe, the church bells continued to ring. As the road turned into a path, I said good morning to two people coming back from a walk with their dog. I have noticed that people who live near the SWCP use the paths to walk their dogs. If I ever lived near the SWCP, I suppose I would need to get a dog.

A gentle zigzag uphill climb which took me about fifteen minutes to reach the top offered great views. This particular climb actually felt like more elevation gain than the Great Hangman did. This area was called Torrs Walk, leading to Torrs Summit. There was a viewpoint at this summit which gave me amazing views all around of 360 degrees. Looking back to Ilfracombe, from where I came, the green grass and ferns and bushes and small trees was the foreground, the large town of Ilfracombe was the midground, the green hills beyond was the background. There was a bench to sit on just below the summit, and to the left side as I looked back, were the green and blue seas. Above were the blue and white skies. I was just amazed at all the beauty.

When I looked straight out at the seas from the viewpoint in this direction, the seas were a deep bluish-green color, with a thin line of white clouds sandwiched in between the seas and the blue skies above, and nothingness beyond that. Nothing. It seemed like the edge of the world. Just breathtaking.

When I looked beyond from this viewpoint to where I will be going, I was still in awe. Various shades of green between the grasses, shrubs, and trees covering hillside after hillside. Various shades of blue of the seas and the sky. Brown rocks and cliff edges. White waves and clouds. A few speckles of white on the green, which were some sheep. Wow! Words are hard to describe the beauty.

I walked through a gate where a sign told me, "Livestock please secure the gate." That would be a theme for today. The path started out thin, but widened out to almost like an old gravel road in between all that greenery, above the seas.

I spent some time meandering through the paths in and amongst the fields of sheep that I had spotted from above. The cutest must be the babies. I even think I saw a family with a mama sheep, a dada sheep, and two little cute lambs. The wind was relentless here, which made it difficult to decide which hat to wear today. I brought a couple of hats with various lengths of brims for rain and sun protection, and while one of them was the one I used in Spain where I had no trouble with wind, here the wind kept lifting up the brim. Throughout the day, I changed hats a few times before finally deciding on a brown beanie-type hat, which of course was a bit too warm for a warm day like today, but with no brim, it did not flop around in the wind. I need to look at what other people are wearing for hats here and perhaps buy a new hat sometime soon.

It was quiet as I made my way through the rolling hills. The only sounds were the wind and the occasional cry of a seagull. Sometimes I was too far from the seas below to hear the crashing waves.

Ahead of me I spotted a herd of cows. My first herd that was actually close to the path. The path was wide and grassy with lots of grass on either side. These cows though were far enough away to not be any trouble. However, I did recall some of the rules I had read about cows…Appear large and slightly scary to them, but not threatening. They may come close to you but most likely they are just trying to look at you because their vision is not that good. Do not look at them in the eyes. Stay calm. Do not run. Do not walk straight towards them. Stand still or keep walking slowly in the direction you want to go. If the cows are blocking a path, you can try to find a safe alternate route around them. They are used to being herded and moved by farmers. Do not walk in such a way that will separate one cow from the rest of the herd. Do not get in between a mama and her baby. (My disclaimer to you is that please do your own research about walking near cows, because I take no responsibility for your encounters with cows.)

After I passed by this herd of cows without incident, I stopped for one of my hat changes. The path continued to be grassy and wide. I looked up to continue walking, and what was right in the path? A cow, literally right on the path. A second cow was just off to the right a bit. Hmmm. I quickly thought of all the rules again.

Fortunately the area was wide enough for me to just walk around them without incident, following the finding a safe alternate route around them rule. I also found it helpful to talk out loud to them too as I walked by. This tactic probably comforted me more than anything, as the cows most likely had no clue what I was saying. Just then a mountain biker also biked by. I guess these cows must be used to walkers, and bikers.

I emerged from the grassy path onto paved narrow road that led about a mile towards Lee Bay. I liked that name as it reminds me of my middle name, Lee. I arrived at Lee Bay to a row of abandoned houses, and a rocky, stony, seaweed covered beach with a few kayakers braving the wind.

There were some interesting looking tracks in this beach, two parallel concrete tracks. I read this in today's booklet: "At the turn of the 18th century smuggling was widespread around Lee Bay." I did some research on this interesting "business" that I shall see more evidence of as I walk along the SWCP. According to a website about Lee Bay, part of which explains a short walk in Lee to explore some of the places and legends surrounding Lee's smuggling past, "During the 18th and early 19th centuries smuggling was carried out extensively along these coasts and Lee was an ideal location. Smuggled goods were carried into the interior [of Lee], stored in outhouses or cellars. Records from the late 18th and early 19th centuries refer to landings of brandy and gin, red Portugal wine, salt, tea and even playing cards. Many people saw smuggling as a way of making life more comfortable under the extremely harsh laws of the time and often the whole community would be involved, but was often a far more brutal business than today's romantic images suggest." I wondered if the parallel concrete tracks in the water were used to transport the smuggled goods off ships and onto the land using some sort of cart on wheels. Remember, one of the reasons "The South West Coast was originally created by coastguards, [was] patrolling the south west peninsula looking out for smugglers." Interesting.

I stopped to eat half the sandwich I bought this morning. It was a "buttery cheese and tomato baguette," just simple and basic, but when you are hungry and out in nature, simple and basic food can taste quite good.

An ascent up the road out of Lee Bay led to a descent in which I saw a sign about cattle in this area. Oh no, more cows. It said, "In partnership with Natural England, we are grazing this area with cattle. Their grazing habits will help the spread of wild flowers and the control of bracken. Please keep your dog on a short lead at all times. If you come across them, they are friendly and not aggressive, but may take flight if startled. Thank you for your help in this Conservation Project." I did not come across any cows in this area today however, but I could see the descent and ascent ahead of me. Today was filled with several ascents and descents. The views from the tops of each ascent continued to amaze me. I could even see the paths themselves that I have walked on, or will be walking on, making their way through the green covered hills. The descents led to valleys getting me closer to the seas.

Natural England is "the government's adviser for the natural environment in England, helping to protect England's nature and landscapes for people to enjoy and for the services they provide." Natural England is responsible for "promoting nature conservation and protecting biodiversity, conserving and enhancing the landscape, promoting access to the countryside and open spaces and encouraging open-air recreation," amongst other responsibilities for the natural environment. What a great organization.

A couple of today's mileage signs were just as confusing as yesterday's. Not too far back I saw a sign to Bull Point saying a mile and three-quarters. Then another sign said one mile, but I certainly did not walk three-quarters of a mile between these two signs.

A trail runner passed me by at the bottom of a valley. In less than ten minutes, I made it up the next hill to a wide flat grassy path. I wondered if someone comes up here with a lawn mower and mows the lawn to make these paths because they seem so perfectly groomed and quite flat compared to the more natural looking grass on either side of this path.

I arrived at Bull Point Lighthouse, my third lighthouse of the SWCP, in the continuing relentless winds. Per the booklet, "The almost vertical rocks around Bull Point are made of slate seamed with quartz and have been the site of many shipwrecks over the centuries." Thus a lighthouse was originally built on Bull Point in 1879. Lighthouses in general are built for the purposes of emitting a bright light, and sounding a loud fog signal as needed, along important or dangerous coastlines as navigational aids to those out on the seas, and to ultimately try to prevent shipwrecks by warning boats of the dangerous areas. Unfortunately, the south west coast of England has not been immune to shipwrecks. One statistic I came across told me that, "In the 1840's when ships were being lost along the British coast at a rate of two a day, it was estimated that 200 vessels had been wrecked in living memory along this stretch of coast alone." The particular stretch this quote is referring to is between Pentire Point and Hartland Quay, a part of the SWCP that I have not walked on yet, which is less than 50 miles. In fact, remnants of some shipwrecks can actually be seen on various parts of the SWCP. While I did not see any myself, the lighthouses are still a reminder of appreciating those who sail the seas.

The Bull Point Lighthouse entrance gate was open today, and I wanted to go in to visit. A sign at the gate said, "Stand here for attention." So I did. For several minutes. I did not notice anyone around. I felt silly standing there as no one was paying attention to me. I felt like just walking right in as the gate was open. Just then, a couple was walking out of the lighthouse grounds through the gate, so I asked them if someone came to get them and paid attention to them. No, they just walked right in the grounds, so I did too. I spent about ten minutes walking around the Bull Point Lighthouse grounds, including walking around the lighthouse itself, taking photos. In the relentless wind. I tried to open the door of the lighthouse itself to go inside but alas it was closed. The former keeper's cottages are now holiday homes. The lighthouse I was walking around is new construction from 1974 made of brown bricks.

After leaving the lighthouse grounds, I climbed an 89-step climb back on the SWCP, looked back at the lighthouse, and then realized that a lot of people were out walking today, even with the wind. Some seemed like they were just locals out for a stroll, carrying just about nothing. Others had a small rucksack, and a few were like me with a bit larger rucksack.

About a half mile after the lighthouse and after a climb up then back down into a valley, I decided to change my pair of socks. It is a good idea to change into dry clean socks at some point to keep the feet fresh and to help prevent blisters in moist socks. That is another one of my blister theories. This was the first day I did this. I had planned on doing this everyday and brought six pairs of calf length socks with me for the entire SWCP walk, two in black, two in a brownish color, and two in a bluish color. Each day would be a different color. I would have enough to cycle through three days. This would allow for two days of drying time until a color needed to be worn again. I also did the same thing with ankle length socks, but have been wearing the calf length socks so far. So yes, I have 12 pairs of socks with me total! The original intent was that the ankle length socks would be for wearing with my purple shoes, and the calf length socks would be for wearing with hiking boots. One of my other blister theories is that double layer socks also help with blister prevention. The socks I love wearing, are not only double layer, they are also quite thin compared to some thicker bulkier socks out there. I am not saying that these double layer socks are for everyone, and I take no responsibility whatsoever if you get a blister while wearing these socks, but in case you are interested, I use Wrightsock CoolMesh II Quarter or Crew length socks. Needless to say, I put a lot of thought into my sock situation before I left for the SWCP.

The only rain shower of the day occurred as I was down in one valley. It was so light though, and only lasted about a minute, that I did not even stop to put rain gear on. I just covered up my camera and mobile phone with my arm to protect those objects. Then the sun came out. I looked for a rainbow, but did not see one.

I stopped to eat the rest of my "buttery cheese and tomato baguette." It still tasted pretty good. I sat at a bench overlooking the views as I ate in the wind. I could still see the Bull Point Lighthouse way in the distance now, all the hills that I walked since then, the narrow path itself nestled between the green shrubbery, with the brown cliffs of the hills leading down to a long stretch of rocky land leading to the white frothy waves and the blue and turquoise seas. I enjoyed listening to the crashing waves. Even with the wind though, the sun made it feel warm at this stop.

With the sight of the lighthouse fading behind me, I reach Morte Point, a place that yesterday Jo warned me would be windy, and she was right. Even windier than what I had been experiencing most of today. Still at this moment it was exciting to be in that wind. I was at a turning point. Literally. To the left. First it would turn me towards Woolacombe, my destination for the day, similar to that turning point in the heavy downpour that brought me into the Hunter's Inn. Second if I look at a map, Morte Point appears to be a turning point for all on the SWCP. From heading west since Minehead to starting to head south towards Barnstaple, Bude, Padstow, and Land's End. I sat on some rocks to brace myself from the wind, stuck out my legs in front of me pointing to the row of rocks that led into the seas, so my purple shoes could be the subject of a photo at the windy Morte Point.

I also spotted a headland beyond that I expect will be in my future. Now that I think about this turning point thing further, since between Minehead and here I have been walking below the Bristol Channel between England and Wales. Perhaps now I will be near the Celtic Sea. After Land's End it would be the English Channel. And three bodies of water all are extensions of the Atlantic Ocean.

As I walked through a field of sheep toward Woolacombe, I remembered the rule to not get between a mama sheep and her baby sheep. Oh wait, that is a cow rule. Still, I think this is a good rule for sheep also, as one should probably give them the same respect.

It took me another 45 minutes to finally reach the popular and beach-themed, surfing-themed, and ice cream-themed Woolacombe. I skipped the ice cream, changed into the flip flops I brought with me today, searched for something to eat, and settled at eating at the Red Barn Pub which was where Steve would pick me up today. I called Denise and Steve after I started eating, knowing it would take him a half hour to get there. I just realized that I have not yet mentioned my flip-flops. In addition to two pairs of hiking boots, and two pairs of purple shoes, I also brought two pairs of flip flops. One pair that is thick and cushy and oh so comfortable for walking short distances. And one pair of flip flops that I could also walk in, but was more to wear indoors and in the shower as needed. I love flip flops. I was smart today and brought the cushy pair with me in my rucksack to change into after my walk. I realized that yesterday when I was waiting for Steve, even with the drizzle, I thought it would be nice to take my shoes off and let my feet air out. This would not only provide me a bit of extra comfort, but it is another one of my blister theories that, unless totally necessary, to not wear closed shoes in the afternoons and evenings after my walking day ended. Airing my feet out might help prevent blisters.

After I ate my snack, I decided to treat myself to a little something sweet to eat after this windy day. Instead of ice cream, I ended up settling on some fudge. Seemed to be popular in these parts as the last couple towns all had fudge shops. I got a pound of fudge. No, no, no not a pound as in sixteen ounces, but a pound as in a British Pound (£), which is about $1.27. When I tried to tell her how much I wanted and said about an inch, I realized that maybe they use centimeters here in England. I settled on about an inch and a half. Or about four centimeters. But I believe they do use inches anyway. I got a chocolate rum flavored fudge, as that combination reminds me of chocolate rum balls one of my grandmothers used to make. Right on the dot, about a half hour after I called, Steve picked me up to take me back to their Guest House in Combe Martin.

I will admit that even though today was warm and dry, the relentless wind made this day the first day that I have felt the most challenged. There were a lot of ascents and descents today too, but I think it was the wind. I was so glad I did not walk in the gale force winds over a week ago. I could not imagine what that would have been like.

I also had a strange thought today, and I am not sure why. For the first time, the thought of walking 630 miles got a bit overwhelming. I realized though that if I just think of each day individually, as each its own "day hike," it doesn't feel so overwhelming. One day at a time. One mile at a time. One step at a time.

DAY EIGHT STATS: 8.5 MILES. 5.25 HOURS. NO SIGNIFICANT EXTRA MILES. PURPLE SHOES. FLIP FLOPS. PUB IN WOOLACOMBE IS "RED BARN PUB."
Information about smuggling in Lee Bay from leebay.co.uk/smugglers-path.
Information about Natural England from gov.uk/government/organisations/natural-england/about.
Information about shipwrecks from Pentire Point to Hartland Quay from telegraph.co.uk/travel/723860/Cornwall-The-shipwreck-coast.

WOOLACOMBE TO CROYDE BAY TO SAUNTON SANDS AND BACK TO CROYDE BAY – Monday, 12 June 2017

"Chim chiminey, Chim chiminey, Chim chim cher-ee! A sweep is as lucky, As lucky can be. Chim chiminey, Chim chiminey, Chim chim cher-oo! Good luck will rub off when I shakes 'ands with you." – Richard M. Sherman & Robert M. Sherman, Warner Chappell Music, Inc., Walt Disney Movie Company, Mary Poppins.

Ok, I'd like to mention a couple more of my previous significant travels as I mentioned a few yesterday, although I consider all my travels significant in their own way, and just because I haven't mentioned all of my travels doesn't make them any less significant. Anyway, one travels was my successful attempt at circumnavigating the Baltic Sea in fifteen days, visiting the capital cities of seven countries in those fifteen days, Stockholm, Helsinki, Oslo, Copenhagen, Tallinn, Vilnius, Riga, (not in that order) using buses, trains, and ferries. I mention this travel because planning that was kind of along the lines of planning this SWCP walk, with coordinating the transportation for that one, like the B&Bs for this one, and then hoping that everything all works out. In the case of the circumnavigating travels, it all did work out.

One more travel, well progression of travels, I would like to mention is how I became a "solo" traveler. You see, I have actually done a lot of my travels solo. It started because when the "travel bug" in me was biting, I was not able to find people to travel with, so I realized that if I wanted to travel, then I can do it solo. I had to "test the waters" first though, so my first solo trip was just a short weekend in my own state of Washington where I found a hostel to stay in, and a long beach and a lighthouse to walk to, the ten-mile round trip long Dungeness Spit leading out to the New Dungeness Lighthouse. Ah, another walk near water! And solo!

After that weekend was a success, my next solo travels to continue "testing the waters" of solo travel for myself was up to Alaska for two weeks. I took a ferry through the Inside Passage to places like Ketchikan, Juneau, and Skagway, and then travelled inland to Anchorage, Denali, and Seward. Once that trip was a success, I was off for my biggest travels at the time – a five month solo jaunt around Europe doing the "backpacking/hostel" thing, visiting seventeen countries!

The rest is history, as they say. Plenty of other travels occurred since then, some solo, some with friends and family. I would say that each and every one of my travels somehow or other has influenced and contributed to my life and to my decision to walk the SWCP, and they all have brought me to being here now in England.

Oh, and two more significant travels I would like to mention are two of the earliest travels I did in my life when I was in my 20s. When I was about 26, I wanted to travel across the United States, in a motor home. Most people do that sort of travels when they retire, but I said to myself back then, "Why wait till I retire?" Therefore, with a friend of mine, we traveled the country, for nearly three months, in a motor home! But about six years prior to that, between my sophomore and junior years in college, the travel that really started the travel bug in me, and was really that catalyst for my love and passion of travel, was a month-long trip to Europe that I did with my sister. We joined a group of similar-aged people, and toured eight countries, including France, Switzerland, Italy, Austria, Germany, Belgium, the Netherlands, and England. And that was it! I knew I wanted to travel more in my life!

Today I decided to lighten up my rucksack a bit. I wanted to take out the pair of boots because the next few days were forecasted to be dry and the terrain forecasted to be flat. Scott suggested last night that instead what I could do is carry an extra pair of socks in addition to the extra pair I was already bringing. That way if my purple shoes do get wet somehow, I have two dry pairs of socks to change into. Now what he didn't understand is that this plan will mess up my two-same-colored-pair-a-day sock plan. However, I took his advice anyway for safety sake.

I also remembered that I brought with me this multi-purpose/multi-functional scarf/bandana tubular type material called a buff that is very lightweight and is quite versatile. You can wear it twelve different ways according to its packaging - on your head, around your neck, in your hair, etc. It might just solve my "what-to-do-on-windy-but-warm day" hat dilemma. I wore it all day today on my head, and while it might not look like what most people probably wear on the SWCP, it actually worked quite well, as today was warm with a gentle breeze (but not windy like yesterday) so it was a good test of my new theory. In the long run, this scarf/bandana/buff turned out to be perfect, and I wore it often.

To lighten up the pack a bit more, I also took out a pair of prescription glasses, but kept in the prescription sunglasses which worked well with that scarf since the scarf does not have a brim to protect my eyes from the sun. One extra camera battery was also taken out as one battery per day had been enough so far, and I had two extra in my rucksack.

I said my goodbyes to Denise this morning. She and Steve had been so wonderful to me, helpful, interested in me and my walk, and friendly and hospitable. In fact last night when Steve brought me back, he said to me, "welcome home." I was glad to pay them extra for all the rides they gave me. I told her about my writing a book and if I include them in there, I asked if I could I use their real names? She said yes, so I guess I don't have to edit the book to change their names. They didn't ask me to promote their B&B, nor did they give me any special discounts or anything, but they are such lovely people that I will say on my accord that it was the Acorns Guest House.

(Note that my disclaimer here is that anytime I mention an accommodation by its name, or the proprietors of the accommodation by their names, none of them asked me to mention them. None of them gave me any compensation or any special discounts or anything complimentary or asked me to advertise or anything. I decided to choose which people and what accommodations to include entirely on my own choosing. Although, I did get their permission to use their first names when I decided to include those, or once in a while I changed a name. If I mention the specific name of the accommodation, again it is on my own choosing. This also rings true for any restaurants/cafés/pubs/tea rooms I mention in this book. None of these gave me any compensation or any special discount, nor did they give me anything complimentary to eat in order to mention them, nor did they ask me to advertise them, and I have decided to mention them on my own choosing.)

As Steve drove me back to Woolacombe this morning, after my hug with Denise, we chatted during the half hour ride. At one point we were following behind a chimney sweep truck, and I giggled and mentioned that my niece and my Mom, her Grammy, just watched "Mary Poppins" for my niece's first time with that movie. When I talked to my niece yesterday, I even asked her, "Did you know that that movie is set in England where your Auntie is now?" She replied, "I think so."

Steve told me that it is actually considered good luck to have a chimney sweep at your wedding. People will invite a chimney sweep to their wedding even if they don't know the sweep. The sweep will usually wear a top hat. What a great wedding tradition!

Steve also gave me lesson in tipping in England. He said it is only really necessary to tip if you get full sit-down service like in the US. Note that in many pubs, bars, and restaurants, you actually order your food and drinks yourself by walking up to the bar and having the bartender take your order, also giving them your table number so someone can bring you your food. I think I read that 10% is the standard tip when tipping. Steve told me that you can also tip a taxi driver by rounding up. There also may be other various opinions on tipping in England, so please do your own research.

Steve and I also discussed how it is tradition on Sundays for restaurants to have "carverys," where several types of meat are available to eat. Since I don't really eat meat, I will most likely never go to a carvery. I gave Steve a hug as he dropped me off. I set off from Woolacombe for my originally planned six and a half mile walk. I say "originally planned," because sometimes things don't always go according to plan.

Today's walk started along the sand dunes just above Woolacombe Sand Beach. Apparently this beach was voted the best beach around according to Steve, and on a good warm day the entire three miles of it can be packed with people. I looked online and found the article in The Telegraph from 2015 that this beach was named one of the top five beaches in Europe, and in 2016 it was named "the best UK beach." Today it was quite empty even though it was a warm day. Of course I was there in the morning, and it was a Monday.

As I walked through the sand dunes above the beach, it was quite quiet. Other than the sounds of a few chirping birds greeting the day and the gentle crash of the waves on the beach, which I enjoyed listening to this peaceful morning. I was in such a quiet state of mind at the moment that when a barefoot jogger talked to me from behind, she startled me. When she said, "Hello," I jumped. Politely as she jogged by me she said, "I didn't want to startle you." Too late, I thought.

Walking through the sand dunes is good for the calf muscles. Instead of my usual uphill morning climbs, this will do to wake the legs and body up for the day's walk. As I stopped for a clothing change towards the end of the sand dunes, the jogger jogged by me in the other direction and we smiled at each other. The sand dunes were of course sandy to walk on, surrounded by foliage of ferns and other green plants. I had views of the sandy beach, the white frothy waves, and the blue waters. This was the first long beach that I would walk near or on. Some of my favorite sections of the SWCP, being so close to the water, are the beaches. I still love being above the beaches in the hillsides, but being so much closer to the water was fantastic. The constant sound of the waves on the beach and the fresh air of the water supplied me with an ample supply of my negative ions for the day.

After the three miles, the flat walking on the sand dunes turned into flat walking on a gravel road. I had a view from above of the far end of the long beach, and of the green hillsides and headlands I would soon be walking on. It was quite warm out which I was quite glad about. Summer! I wondered if I could have walked on the sand of the beach the entire three miles actually.

An elderly man was walking in the opposite direction and stopped as I walked by. I took this as a signal that he wanted to chat. We started by saying what a beautiful day out it was pointing to the warm blue sky. He asked if I was walking the Coast Path and where was I going to today and tomorrow. I replied, and asked if he has done the Coast Path. He said that back in 2005 he lost his wife. I said, "Oh, I'm sorry." I wanted to give him a hug. He seemed like a kind gentle man. Anyway, he was planning on doing the walk then, but then his back gave out too, so he never did the entire walk. Instead since he lives in Woolacombe, and he walks this section four times a week.

He went on to tell me that he used to be in the Merchant Navy. He had been to New York a few times, but that was back in the 1950's. We chatted about the loveliness of the scenery, and a few other cheery things. He mentioned that he doesn't have much life left, indicating that he is older. He didn't look that old to me. My heart sank. I didn't quite know what to say to a comment like that. The best I could come up with was perhaps some words of shared wisdom between us, "Well, keep on walking. Perhaps the walking will help extend our lives." With that we said our goodbyes. It seemed like a sad conversation as I write about it, but really he didn't seem sad. Just reflective.

I stopped at the café in Putsborough, at the end of the three mile beach, and decided to get hummus and salad "bap." At the moment I didn't know what a bap was, but I figured I would find out soon enough. Turns out it was a sandwich on a hamburger-type bun. I was sure it will be just as good and necessary as yesterday's baguette when I would be ready to eat it.

I climbed a bit to get up from the end of the beach at Putsborough in order to get to the top of the small hillside. The views from here were looking straight down the long three mile beach I just walked near. I can see why it was named "the best." I took a photo of a bench from which one could see this view of the hillside paralleling above the sandy beach, paralleling the white frothy waves, the blue water, and in the distance, Woolacombe.

I stepped over a stile with style and grace, as I made my way out to Baggy Point along the path on the top of the hillside lined with grass and green foliage. I would like to repeat that it was warm out as I have noted before, and I loved it! I appreciated the gentle breeze instead of the relentless winds of yesterday. As I approached Baggy Point, I passed by a flock of sheep, and a bit later, a herd of cows over on the other side of an old stone wall. I thought I read something about this old stone wall, but I can't seem to find the information now. Apparently around here at Baggy Point, you have views out to Lundy Island, an island which has two lighthouses, but even with the great weather, I could not see it. The skies were quite blue today, with thin white clouds.

As I got even closer to Baggy Point, there was a strange white pole, which turned out to be a "Rocket Post." It was used as one of the ways the Coastguard would train their rescue skills, as the post represented the mast of a stranded ship, according to today's little booklet.

What I found great at Baggy Point was the herd of sheep around this area. Not just any sheep, they were all black. What a site to see! I took a few photos trying not to disturb them. Some had horns, so perhaps those were the male rams. There were baby lambs too, and I even saw one lamb feeding on its mama. Now the "Baa Baa Black Sheep" song makes sense. It was quite something seeing an entire herd of black sheep.

I took a picture of my purple shoes near the tip of Baggy Point, just as I did yesterday at the tip of Morte Point. This tip was actually windy at the moment, about the only wind I had all day, stronger than the gentle breezes, but yesterday's Point was certainly much windier.

I passed by a National Trust sign telling me, "Bird nesting season 15 March to 30 June. Please do not climb on the cliffs between white marker posts." Soon another National Trust sign told me, "This pond has been restored to recreate a valuable wildlife habitat." I love nature.

National Trust is another important organization in the UK. They see "the importance of [their] nation's heritage and open spaces and wanted to preserve them for everyone to enjoy. [They] look after coastline, forests, woods, fens, beaches, farmland, moorland, islands, archaeological remains, nature reserves, villages, historic houses, gardens, mills and pubs and one of the world's largest art collections. [They] restore them, and protect them and open them up to everyone. For the Trust, conservation has always gone hand-in-hand with public access. [They] welcome everyone to explore: 775 miles of coastline; over 248,000 hectares of land; over 500 historic houses, castles, ancient monuments, gardens and parks and nature reserves; and close to one million objects and works of art." Wow! I just love all these great organizations in the UK.

I walked a bit down the path towards Croyde Bay, and stopped at a bench to eat my "bap." Yes, it was tasty when needed. I also stopped here because I told myself yesterday that I would stop more often to rest and to listen to my favorite sound of the waves crashing on the sandy beaches or rocky coastline. Today's walking had basically been all flat walking, especially compared to the ascents and descents of yesterday. The view from the bench was of the green foliage, a rocky beach, white frothy waves, the blue seas, the blue and white sky, and then just nothing as far as the eye can see. Ahhhh! Beautiful.

As I made my way into Croyde Bay, I got a bit confused. First, and this was where I added the first half mile extra of my day, I missed a SWCP sign pointing towards the beach. I was not looking up enough. I walked down a sidewalk a bit next to a road and it just didn't seem right to me. I looked at my guidebook and saw that I must have gone too far on the road. To verify, I stopped in a surf shop to ask. He said, well if you actually continue next the road for another twenty minutes, you can get to Croyde Bay, but I did not want to walk next to the road for that long, so I went back and found the sign to the beach.

Then I was supposed to walk on Croyde Beach itself, as a sign clearly stated, "For the Coast Path, follow the beach below the dunes, (to bridge the stream turn inland)," but I got confused because at this point I was looking for my B&B, and I didn't think it would be down at the far end of the beach, which wasn't that far actually compared to the beach at Woolacombe. I started walking on the beach, but at about half way down the beach I decided to get off the beach and walk on some footpaths that were on the map thinking that would bring me closer to the B&B. I had a hand-drawn map of the B&B that I drew before I left, but that wasn't helping me much. I was confused. At least though I passed a colorful sign telling me all about "butterflies and moths" with pictures of about fifteen varieties. Did you know that, "the difference between the two groups is a little blurred but generally, butterflies have club-shaped ends on their antennae, fly by day and fold their wings together vertically when at rest whilst moths fold their wings flat, fly by night and do not have clubbed antennae. However, there are many exceptions to these rules."

Once I got off the footpath, I came to a place where I didn't know where I was on any map. At that moment three women appeared, today's guardian angels. I asked them if they knew where the B&B was. They said, "Oh, yes that is Jenny's place," and gave me directions - go up this small road here and when you get to the main road, turn right and it will be up a bit on your left.

When I got to the main road, I remembered that I had GPS on my mobile phone, so I thought I would verify their directions and sure enough, and they were right. I think walking the rest of the beach would have been about the same distance, which is really what I should have done as I realized later. I arrived at the B&B with four hours of my planned walking including the extra half mile. Thus far. Seven miles total walking at the moment. Remember, things don't always go according to plan.

I knocked on the door of the B&B, and was greeted by a very warm woman, Jenny, who walked 200 miles of the SWCP herself back in February, as she told me she was going to when we wrote via email months ago. I asked her if it was cold to walk at that time of year, winter, and she said it was not really that cold. I was surprised.

During the course of my day, I decided that because it was beautifully warm out today, and the terrain was flat that I wanted to walk an extra two or three miles, so that tomorrow's walk of nine miles could be shorter, and possibly the next day's walk of thirteen miles could be also shorter by adding onto tomorrow's walk. I asked Jenny about where would be a good place to walk to now. She recommended to Saunton Sands, to the hotel there which is two miles, and I can take a bus back from there. Great! I emailed Scott to tell him what I was doing, but before I started walking again, I took some time to drink some tea, rest and relax, change my socks, and take a bit more out of my rucksack for just two miles.

I will interrupt my walk to mention that my room at this B&B was very cute and comfortable. In fact, so far all my rooms have been very cute and comfortable in their own way. This one even had a view of Baggy Point from my window! I have taken one picture of each of my rooms so far to remember them by. I feel that I have done well so far in my bookings and planning of all my B&Bs. Including finding friendly and helpful people that run them. Now note that I am using the term "B&B," which to me encompasses several types of accommodations, all of which supply and a bed and breakfast. Some are in a person's home, which to me is truly a "B&B." Others are Guest Houses, which might also contain the home of the proprietor, but are a bit larger than a home. Then there are "Inns" and "Pubs" which might contain a bar, pub, or restaurant in them as well. I also stayed in a few small hotels, a friend's house, and a caravan, but those are future stories.

Before I continued on with my walk for the day, Jenny offered to do some of my laundry for me if I would like. Of course, I would like. Proper laundry! In a machine, not in a sink. I accepted. She explained that when she walked her 200 miles not a single person offered to do laundry. She decided she would offer that service to walkers. I appreciated that and later on my way to dinner I brought her down a small stuff sack of some laundry.

In the mid-afternoon I started my planned two mile walk. It was easy and flat, starting next to Croyde Beach where I should have walked on earlier to get to the B&B, and I figured out the small footpath that would have taken me right to the B&B.

Soon I had views of another long beach, Saunton Sands. I approached the beach, with views from above looking down, perpendicular to the beach, with its long rows of rolling white waves. I watched the waves rolling in from this perspective, as opposed to watching them from the view point of standing on the beach. Stunning. There were a few surfers and beach-goers on the beach that I was looking at from above. Some of the path I was on towards Saunton Sands was overgrown with sticky bushes, and I decided that from now on I probably should wear long pants every day, even if it was warm or hot out. I do not want to get my lower legs all scratched up if I wore Capri length hiking pants that I also brought.

It took me about 45 minutes to get to the hotel. I decided to listen to some music on my mobile phone during my walk, which I have not done yet. I told myself before I started that I did not want to listen to music because I wanted to enjoy the sounds of nature and the scenery as it was. However, this walk was a bit above the water, and it just seemed like the thing to do today, and since I happened to get regular mobile service as I walked, I was able to listen to some music.

I walked into the pish posh hotel of Saunton Sands looking a bit scruffy to double check and ask about the bus back. A well dressed gentleman said, "You must be walking the Coast Path." "Of course, can you tell by how I look?" "Yes, indeed. How much of it are you walking?" "All of it," I responded. He said that he was impressed. I explained that I needed the bus back to Croyde Bay, he double checked the time, and I had ten minutes to wait. He showed me where to sit by the flower beds, and I should flag down the bus as it went by. I thanked him.

I sat by the flower beds and I waited. Ten minutes passed by. Then 20. Then 25. I was getting a bit unsure. Where was the bus I wondered? Finally after 30 minutes of waiting I said to myself, geez if I walked back the two miles, I could have been mostly back by now. A taxi was out of the question at this point because the guy in the pish posh hotel said it would take a half an hour for a taxi to get here.

Therefore I decided to walk back to Croyde Bay. Add two extra miles to today. It was still warm out, and the walk was flat and easy, and I didn't mind. I even called Scott and talked to him for half the walk back as I had that regular mobile service, as I walked back through the area of sticky bushes. I walked back faster than I walked there, making it back to the B&B in 40 minutes.

That was how my planned six and a half mile day, plus the half mile extra I did trying to find my way getting to my B&B, plus these four miles, turned into an 11 mile day. But wait, there's more.

The last "extra mile" of the day was walking a half mile to dinner from the B&B, and a half mile back from dinner to the B&B, along a sidewalk. By that time I was refreshed and even wore my favorite cushy flip flops. Dinner turned out to be great at a pub called "The Thatch." I had a "Super Serious Salad" – "a mega healthy salad of baby leaves, quinoa, broccoli, spinach, sugar snap peas, soya beans, courgette (zucchini) spaghetti, pumpkin and sunflower seeds finished with a citrus and pomegranate dressing." Very vegan. Like the salad I had at Hunter's Inn. Great way to end my twelve mile day. But wait, there's more.

I did it again. I had to. I deserved it for the extra miles I did today. For dessert, I ate a delicious homemade warm chocolate brownie.

"Or blow me a kiss. And that's lucky too…"

DAY NINE STATS: 8.5 PLANNED MILES (6.5 ORIGINAL, PLUS 2 EXTRA PLANNED). 3.5 UNPLANNED/EXTRA MILES FOR A TOTAL OF 12 MILES. I WILL CALL THE HOURS AS 5.5 (4 FOR THE MAIN PART OF THE DAY, PLUS 1.5 FOR THE FOUR MILES ROUND TRIP). PURPLE SHOES AND A BIT OF FLIP FLOPS. PUBS IN CROYDE BAY INCLUDE, "THE THATCH," "THE MANOR HOUSE INN," AND "BILLY BUDDS." National Trust information from nationaltrust.org.uk/features/about-the-national-trust.

CROYDE BAY TO BRAUNTON – Tuesday, 13 June 2017

"It is your walk, do it your way." – Jenny, the bed-and-breakfast proprietor.

Today was a day of long beaches, one big mistake, and several guardian angels. I went to sleep last night around 11:30, and woke up on my own wide awake at 5:30. You would think that with the twelve mile day I had yesterday, that I would have slept more than that, but nope. I was wide awake.

The start of today's walk had three options. After talking to Jenny about her favorite option, and considering the other options, and the tides, I decided on Jenny's favorite option, the beach route. To walk three and half miles on the compact sand of Saunton Sands beach itself on a perfectly sunny day! Sounded great. The other two options would have taken me along the sand dunes above the beach with no views. Therefore, my choice was the best choice for today. I guess today's beach is longer in length than yesterday's at Woolacombe, and I wondered again if I could have actually walked on Woolacombe Beach itself the entire way.

Jenny was kind enough to drive me back to the pish posh hotel after breakfast so that I could start my beach walk. I double checked on the situation of the tides with someone in a surf shop at the edge of the beach to make sure I would be fine walking the entire beach at low tide. He assured me I would alright, and I certainly was.

The first thing I noticed on the beach, well aside from the sand, the surf, the seas, and the sun, was a row of colorful looking small buildings, looking almost like a row of sheds. There was one with red doors against blue walls, one with purple doors against yellow walls, another with orange doors against blue walls, turquoise doors against orange walls, a yellow door against blue walls, and so on. I knew from previous experience that these are actually "beach huts," small buildings located on beaches used for storage of beach-related items, a place to change clothes, a place to prepare and eat food, a place for shelter from the sun or wind if needed, and most importantly, a place to sit near and relax and enjoy the beach. I will come to see many, many rows of beach huts during my SWCP walk, loving the various colors, trying to peek inside to see what people store in them, and taking lots and lots photos of them. Perhaps I could even do a photography book called, "Beach Huts of the South West Coast Path," to go along with my "Benches of the South West Coast Path" photography book.

Beach huts can also be called "beach cabins" or "bathing boxes." I had read somewhere, or was told by someone, that apparently beach huts were originally Victorian changing huts for women. Some of those huts were on wheels and would go all the way into the water so that ladies could stay inside them and no men could see them in their wet clothes. To try to confirm this I did some research about the history of beach huts and found out the following information: "The noted bathing boxes at Brighton in Australia are known to have existed as far back as 1862. The bathing boxes are thought to have been constructed and used largely as a response to the Victorian morality of the age, and are known to have existed not only in Australia but also on the beaches of England, France and Italy at around the same time. They had evolved from the wheeled bathing machines used by Victorians to preserve their modesty. In the early 20th century, beach huts were regarded as holiday homes for the toiling classes. During World War 2 all UK beaches were closed, [and then with their] reopening in the late 1940s and 1950s, [it] led to [a] resurgence of the British beach holiday and the heyday of the beach hut. Many beach huts were former fisherman's huts, boatsheds or converted bathing machines."

"Depending on the location, beach huts may be owned privately or may be owned by the local council or similar administrative body. On popular beaches, privately owned beach huts can command substantial prices due to their convenient location. There are believed to be around 20,000 beach huts in the UK."

I really liked the concept of these beach huts, as well as the colors and variation to them, and so as I walk the SWCP and see these fun and intriguing beach huts, I decided that I am going to choose which beach would be my "ultimate location" that I would like to perhaps someday have my very own beach hut. (Note that one of my photos of the row of beach huts along Saunton Sands is on the bottom of the front cover of this book!)

As I walked along the beach of Saunton Sands, my goal was to find the perfect and easiest path to walk upon the sand, which would be the hardest compact sand possible. Up closer to the dunes the sand was dry and way too soft to walk on easily. Closer to the water, the extra moisture of the water also made the sand too soft and I would sink in too much. I chose the middle of the beach. It was perfect. The middle path. The middle way. Namaste.

Other than the jellyfish. Which were right on my chosen path. I just needed to avoid stepping on these odd looking clear creatures. Most were a few inches in diameter, but the strangest ones were those that were a foot or more in length. I don't know if when they are up on the beach like this if they are alive or not, and I don't know if they bite, but I was not about to find out by accidently stepping on one. There was a woman walking on the beach with no less than eight dogs. I wondered if she was a professional dog sitter, or just really loved dogs.

The sounds of this walk on the beach were the constant small rolling white waves on this long beach always on my right hand side. My favorite sound. On the left were the birds chirping in the sand dunes. I took pictures of my purples shoes against the tan sand, and the footprints I had made. I took a photo of an abandoned crab and lobster trap. I looked out straight ahead into the water from this spot. The tan colored sand, a few white shells, the edge of the seas glistening in the sun, the white capped waves, the darker blue seas beyond, the blue sky with thin white clouds. This was the brilliant view on my right side for three and a half miles!

I must admit that I did listen to music some of the way down the long beach. I really didn't want to, but it was actually a bit lonely there by myself at the moment, the first time I felt that feeling. I thought that even though the waves and birds might not be listened to as clearly I listened to some music too. I wondered if the lonely feelings were actually that I missed Scott at this moment and that it would have been a very nice walk to experience with my husband together. A long romantic stroll on the beach together. Last night's delicious dinner would have been nice to share with him too. In my planning of this long adventure, there had been a large part of me that wanted to complete the entire 630 miles by myself, as I have mentioned. That would be a great accomplishment! On the other hand, it would be nice to share some of this adventure with Scott as well, like these long romantic beach strolls. He would like it. We had actually discussed the possibility of him joining me towards the end of the entire walk. We agreed that I would decide at some point along the way what I want to do. It would be another bit of extra planning to get him here, but wouldn't be too bad, and I had some ideas thought out anyway. Over the next several weeks, I shall see how I feel. Do I want a completely, or mostly, solo experience, as I do have a day I might be walking with my friend Sasha? Or do I opt for the love story and have him join me? (Don't get me wrong, I love him either way.)

I picked up a small clam shell to hold in my hand as I walked. Even with my contemplations and music, which I actually listened to on the speaker of my mobile phone, not using earbuds, I found it peaceful and relaxing to walk on the beach. There were some small rocks in the sand that I stopped to look at. There was a couple camping with their tent by the sand dunes. Seeing this of course added to missing Scott, as we have done some beach camping together on the coast of Washington.

I saw an abandoned boat up near the sand dunes, and I started to sing "Gilligan's Island." Out loud, as by now I stopped listening to music. "The ship set ground on the shore of this unchartered desert isle…with Gillian, the Skipper too, a millionaire and his wife, a movie star, the professor and Mary Ann, HERE ON GILLIGAN'S ISLE." I hope no one heard me singing.

Eventually I saw the towns of perhaps Barnstaple, Instow, Bideford, and/or Appledore in the distance ahead of me. I wasn't sure which towns they actually were since this was my first time here. I came to a part of the beach where there were a lot more little pebbles, so I slowed my walking pace down to take a look at the pebbles. I picked up a few more small clam shells of the same size as the one I already had, cleaned them, and then clanged them around in my hand. It sounded and felt meditative. Not that I really meditate back home, but certain things to me feel relaxing and calming, so I relate them to how it might feel to meditate.

Every once in awhile I lost the hard compact sand and started to sink a bit, so I zigzagged up and down the beach until I found the hard compact sand again. Every once in a while, I looked back behind me to see where I had come from. The very long sandy beach behind me. Soon I turned a slight corner and those views behind me disappeared. As I approached the ending of the three and a half miles, there was a boat out on the water enjoying the warm weather of the day, and a fisherman standing in the water waiting for his catch of the day.

An hour and a half after I started walking on the beach, I approached the ruins a lighthouse, which was the landmark that I would soon be leaving the beach. The ruins were of some remaining pillars, some brick chunks of perhaps a wall or a chimney, and also some other pillars perhaps from a dock that were used to lead to the water. I took off my purple shoes and enjoyed the sand on my bare feet. I walked the last five minutes or so to the ruins in bare feet. I suppose I could have walked the entire length of the beach in bare feet. These ruins were from the

Braunton Lighthouse. "A lighthouse was built at the far end of Saunton Sands at the beginning of the 19th century. It was a wooden tower built on top of the lighthouse keeper's house. It became unstable during the 1950s and was replaced by the smaller lighthouse at Crow Point," according to the booklet. The SWCP did not go to Crow Point.

I decided that sitting by the ruins of the lighthouse was a good spot to rest, enjoy the warmth of the sun, and eat a sandwich I picked up this morning. I realized that there was not drop of wind today whatsoever. Nor a breath of rain. It had been a peaceful contemplative walk on the beach, with a bit of music and singing and beach huts mixed in. I left the small collection of clam shells I had been clanging around in my hands on the sand where I sat. But soon things changed…

I left the beach and walked through the sand dunes onto a boardwalk and out to a car park to where I made a big mistake. Bigger than any others I have made thus far. This one was entirely my fault. No one else to blame, no signage to blame. I am really not sure why, other than maybe I was so relaxed after my long romantic beach walk, I did not read the obvious big red sign with white letters that clearly said, "No through route. Path closed beyond the fisherman's huts for public safety. Please follow the signed diversion along the toll road flood bank." I "swear" that sign was not there when I started walking along the raised grassy and rocky path along the side of an estuary. Someone must have hung it up while I was walking.

Anyway, about a mile to a mile and a half along this raised path, I finally saw another sign ahead of me, also big and red and white. This one clearly said, "Path Closed. No Access Beyond this Point." What?! I started to have a slight panic attack. What were they talking about? I read the small print of the damage ahead, and obviously knew that I must turn back. I actually spoke a few swear words out loud, and even shed a few tears. For the first time. I didn't shed any yesterday or any other day I went the wrong way, but today, I was upset for some reason about this situation. Maybe I was still thinking about how I was missing Scott. Fortunately, it was not raining or windy, and I had some extra water and extra food. I had no choice but to turn around and go back as there were no other options.

When I got back to where I did not read the sign, sure enough the sign was there. Even another obvious sign that said, "Diversion South West Coast Path Temporary Alternative Route," and pointed me in a different direction. I also should have known because even the normal Coast Path wooden sign pointing down the raised path on the estuary was not there. Geez. In any case, my lesson learned from all this was that if there are any more big red obvious signs in the future, I will know to read them!

When I got back to the red and white sign and took a deep breath, a little dog started barking at me and actually startled me slightly. He was down on the sand below while I was up on the raised path, so I wasn't worried, just in a different state of mind. I had gone from relaxed to not-so-relaxed during my walk back on the raised path. Anyway, the dog's owner began calling the dog's name and apologized to me. I said, "No worries," and for some reason I started telling this man about my woes of not being able to read and walking down the raised path and seeing the other sign and having to walk back. I guess I just needed someone to vent to at that moment. And a shoulder to cry on. Ok, I did not cry on his shoulder.

Instead, I started walking on the temporary alternative diversion route which was a paved road. I figured I had two and a half miles to walk to Braunton, my destination for the day, since that was how long the raised path should have been. I started walking merrily along, accepting that this would be my next hour. I spotted two swans in the little stream by the road. I also went off onto the grass for a moment because two cars wanted to go by each other in opposite directions, and I wanted to get out of their way.

One car passed, and the other car drove up to me slowly. "Would you like a ride to Braunton?" It was the man! And his dog! And his wife! I couldn't believe it. I actually thought as I was walking back on the raised path that if I could ask for a ride or someone offered it, since I did have to double back and walk backwards for a while, I would take the ride. I figured I did my mileage for the day due to the back-tracking. Of course, some might take this as "cheating," that I was not walking the SWCP for this small part, but something inside me just felt like I wanted to take the ride that was so kindly offered to me.

"Of course," I said. "I would love it. Thank you so very much!" My guardian angels, and my guardian dog! As we were driving the short distance towards Braunton, we chatted about a few things that I can't quite recall. I was just somewhat relieved a bit, and a bit stunned actually, that I was actually in a car! The world works in mysterious ways.

I soon spotted a sign that indicated the SWCP, and told them that this would be fine to drop me off there. I asked if they wanted any money for gas, but of course they didn't, but I thought I would offer anyway. I said thank you a million times. I then realized that I didn't actually know where I was, and this SWCP sign didn't make sense to me. I asked a pregnant woman where Braunton was, and she pointed me to go to the traffic circle, then to the right to the main road, and to the left. Another guardian angel, and guardian baby!

I was still not quite sure where I was, but it dawned on me that I have GPS on my mobile phone, that I had reception, and that my guidebook mentioned a key place called "Braunton Countryside Center." I decided that was where I want to go, I set my GPS, and I had about a quarter mile to walk. That would be my destination for the day. Turned out I was dropped off at the traffic circle in an area called Velator.

I had actually originally thought of walking extra today so that tomorrow's thirteen mile walk would be shorter, since I shortened today's walk by walking the extra two miles yesterday. After the estuary incident though, I thought, no not today. In fact, I had a better plan in mind.

The next sixteen miles or so would all be on a paved bike trail. All of tomorrow's walk, and some of the day after my scheduled rest day. I decided to rent a bike and bike the SWCP these sixteen miles instead! Brilliant. That way I would not have to walk on hot and hard pavement for the better part of two days, and I could thus make my day after my rest day a bit shorter still. Would I be "cheating" though if I didn't walk this entire part of the SWCP? Nope, I decided. This is my walk, my adventure, and if I want to bike, then I shall bike. It is still by the power of my own two feet. Besides, when I told Jenny this idea yesterday, she said, "It is your walk, do it your way." Brilliant. I suppose Jenny's comment should have popped into my head when I took the ride in the car, too. "It is your walk, do it your way."

I set about to inquire about a bike rental for tomorrow. At the Countryside Center was a Tourist Information Center which was part of why I decided to use the GPS to get there. I had two questions for the lovely woman inside. One, where was a bike shop to ask about renting a bike please? Two, where was the 13th century church I read about in my guidebook? I felt like I needed a bit of church time.

The bike shop was just up the road, this way she pointed, past the police station and across the street. About a minute's walk. The church was back the other direction either through the park or along the main road, about a five minute's walk. I thanked her for her assistance.

I went to the bike shop first, told them I was walking the SWCP, and was wondering if they had a bike rental one way to Bideford, via Barnstaple and Instow. The woman of the bike shop said that they really only do return rentals, not one way, but that I could call this taxi driver and he could pick the bike up and bring it back. Great. She wrote down the taxi phone number, and just as I was about to call, the man of the bike shop came up and nearly startled us both. He said that a taxi would probably charge 30 quid (that's British Pounds), but that he would charge me 25 quid. I really didn't know the going price of the taxi service, but I felt like that was an easy answer to what I needed, and figured it was the thing to do. I accepted the offer. The bike rental itself would be fourteen quid, and a helmet one quid. Forty quid total. Translation to about $51.00. This was my walk, and I was doing it my way.

Scott, that was the man's name at the bike shop, and I chatted a bit about the strategy for tomorrow. When I get to Instow which is about three miles from Bideford, I would call him. Then we would meet at the car park by the railway station in Bideford where he would get the bike. Done deal. I thanked them both and said I would be back in the morning to pick up the bike.

Now it was onto the church. I sat in the church and said extra prayers today. Thanking for the awesome weather. Thanking for the beautiful and contemplative beach walk. Thanking for the ride in the car with my guardian dog. I asked for some good days ahead. I said thank yous for my health, safety, and feet. This was at St. Brannock's Church, where I also purchased this very cute little artistic print, only about two inches by three inches, of the church, which would eventually get framed and hung on my wall in my living room at home, along with four other paintings, all depicting some of my favorite memories of the SWCP.

The next thing to figure out was where and how to get the bus back to Croyde Bay and my B&B, since I was staying there again tonight. Since my experience yesterday with the no-show bus, I had been a bit hesitant about these buses here. I decided to ask at a magazine store where I might catch the bus. What a nice man. While he himself has never taken the bus, and really didn't know what it was like, he has seen people walk just up the road to the bridge where there was a bus stop. Perfect. Now I asked him if he would know if they take large bills on the bus. The smallest I had was 20 quid. He immediately gave me smaller change.

I walked the minute to the bus stop, and had just turned around to try to decipher the chart of the bus times, when my "knight in shining armor" drove up. Well, not quite. It was a delivery guy in small white van with the words "The Thatch" on the side of the van, the restaurant I ate at last night. "Do you need a ride to Croyde?" He asked. What? Where did this guy come from? How did he know where I needed to go? He startled me a bit actually as I had my back to the road. Twice in one day I was asked if I needed a ride. That never happens.

Of course he knew I needed to go to Croyde because I was at the bus stop which would have taken me to Croyde. Now I know the rule my Mom taught me is to never talk to strangers, let alone get in a car with one. Although, I did just get in that car with the couple and their dog, but they weren't strangers as I had nearly cried on his shoulder. Anyway, sorry, Mom. I chatted with this knight in white van a moment before I got in to test my comfort level. I looked at the "The Thatch" painted on the side of the van again, and when I mentioned which B&B I was staying at and he knew Jenny's name, I figured it was alright. Note that I would never get in a van or car like this back home.

As he chatted and chatted and chatted away about all kinds of things in the ten minute ride, I barely got a word in edgewise. He was kind enough to drop me right near my B&B, and yet again another guardian angel, and a guardian van!

I had one final task for the day, in addition to food. In less than two weeks of walking, I already wanted to mail a small box of stuff back home, as I knew from the beginning that I had packed too much stuff, so I needed to walk to the post office in Croyde. I wanted to ship back things I wasn't using, or wasn't going to use, or didn't need. I thought I was so careful and thorough in my packing that I didn't think this would happen, but I finally made the decision a couple days ago and started making a list of what to send back. Good thing that I got up at 5:30 this morning because that was when I gathered my stuff together. This would also save some weight for the Luggage Transfers, LTD people, and for myself when transporting my large wheeled suitcase up sets of stairs.

One item on the list was the base for the electric toothbrush I brought. It wasn't working so I couldn't use the electric part of the toothbrush at all. It was as if I was brushing with a normal toothbrush. So one thing I did after I got dropped off in Braunton on my way to walking to the Countryside Center was I stopped inside a gas station store to buy a regular toothbrush, so that I could include in the shipment back home my electric toothbrush and the base. Funny thing to do at that moment. Here I walked into a gas station store with my rucksack on, my camera and mobile phone around my neck, and I bought a toothbrush. Just a toothbrush, that was it. I wondered what the folks at the counter thought of me.

Another thing I shipped back home was the SWCP Association's 2017-2018 "The Complete Guide to The South West Coast Path" guidebook. I tore out and kept some of pages of the general information with me, but since I have not been following their suggested eight-week itinerary, and since I was using their booklets anyway, I did not need the guidebook with me.

Another item I shipped back was the new small video camera that I had brought with me. I had only used it three times since my arrival on the SWCP, since I found that the buttons on it were confusing to use. In fact, of the three videos I took, I accidently erased the first two. If I really wanted to take more videos (which I did a few times), I could use my mobile or camera.

I also shipped back some clothes that I was not wearing, a paper journal that I was not using since I was recording everything on the app on my mobile phone and writing on my laptop, an umbrella (aka "brolly") that I was not using, and a few other miscellaneous items. It cost me quite a bit to ship all this back home, but it would be worth it, not only to lighten the load in my luggage, but just to have less stuff for me in general. Which was interesting, because if you think about it, I really did not have that much stuff with me to begin with, compared to all the stuff I have in my house back home.

After the post office in Croyde and dinner, I decided to walk down to the beach in Croyde Bay for a few minutes. Mainly to walk some of the short stretch of beach that I missed yesterday. I also sat for a few moments on a rock in the sand, looked at the seas, listened to the waves, and took in some deep breaths. I thought of contemplating the meaning of life, but I just enjoyed being there at that moment.

As I finished today's writing around 9:30pm, I looked outside my window of this B&B. I spotted a nice light red orange sunset over Baggy Point.

DAY 10 STATS: 7 MILES. 4 HOURS. EXTRA ONE AND A HALF MILES FOR DINNER AND THE BIT OF WALKING AROUND BRAUNTON. PURPLE SHOES. PUBS IN BRAUNTON ARE "THE BRAUNTON INN," AND "WILLIAMS ARMS." Information on Beach Huts from wikipedia.org/wiki/Beach_hut.

BRAUNTON TO APPLEDORE – Wednesday, 14 June 2017

"There are no 'rules' unless you decide to set your own." – A friend from the SWCP Facebook Group.

After waking up bright-eyed and bushy-tailed again at 5:30 this morning, Jenny was kind enough to give me an early breakfast at 7:30, a half hour to an hour before most times I usually eat. I said my thank yous and good byes, and also asked her if I could mention her in my book. She said ok. She also did not ask me to promote her B&B, but Breakers B&B was a comfortable and hospitable place to stay. Jenny had even mailed me a nice handwritten note way back when I booked the B&B months and months ago, "snail-mail" all the way from Croyde to my home in the US, with my confirmation, and a little map-sketch of their general location.

The bus back to Braunton was leaving in either in ten minutes, or not till 10:30. I would not have made the first bus, and did not want to wait that long for the second bus. Therefore, I called a taxi that would pick me up at 9:00, take me directly to the bike shop in Braunton, and cost £12/$15. Done deal. I figured that with the no-show-bus a couple days ago, the bus I didn't have to take yesterday because of the ride from "The Thatch" van, and the bus I wouldn't take this morning, I made up for the expense of the taxi ride today.

There was a part of me that was sad this morning because I realized that I did miss walking a couple of true SWCP miles yesterday, and regretted taking the ride in the car. I thought that maybe I should walk the miles this morning before the bike ride, but I already had the bike to pick up arranged, and a long day ahead of me biking and walking, so I needed to just let it go and walk (and bike) on.

My rental bike was a cross bike with a big cushy seat (or so it seemed at the time), cushy handle bars (that was true), with a lock and a helmet. I set off for my sixteen mile bike ride on the Tarka Trail from Braunton to Bideford, by way of Barnstaple and Instow. I would then walk four more miles into Appledore where my accommodations were for the evening. This plan was brilliant! It would save my feet from walking on hard pavement for that long, and with the weather forecast for the next few days – very warm – the pavement would have been even hotter to walk on. As I cycled, I saw several walkers on the hot hard pavement in the warm sun, and said to myself, "I am so glad I thought of my brilliant plan."

As I biked, I was careful to stay on the left side of the trail, just like the car traffic also flows here in England. I am used to biking on the right, so it was a good lesson in working my brain a bit. I however refuse to drive a car in England. When passing someone as I bike, I am also used to saying, "Passing on your left," but here I needed to say, "Passing on your right." Or easier, I just ring the little bell that I discovered was on the bicycle.

Joining me on the trail today in this brilliant warm sun, were other casual walkers, dog walkers, joggers, cyclists, and as I mentioned what looked like SWCP walkers. I noticed that people were very friendly on the Tarka Trail, and said hello or good morning as I crossed paths with them. The Tarka Trail was tree lined, sometimes on both sides, and much of it was in the open, paralleling the River Taw, which was on my right hand side. On my left hand side was some green colored farmland, and a church tower in the distance as I made my way out of Braunton. I biked between the farmland and the river. Even though biking is faster than walking, I still stopped occasionally to take a good look at the scenery, and take a few photos using my rental bike as a subject in the foreground.

I cycled my way to the town center of Barnstaple. While the Clock Tower in Barnstaple said 8:55 (am or pm), it was really 11:00 when I reached there. I spent about an hour in Barnstable. I locked my bike up outside this café that Scott-the-Bike-Man told me about. I got a bite to eat, window shopped a bit, and went into the Barnstaple Parish Church of St. Peter and St. Mary Magdalene, with its pointed conical-shaped steeple that "has a broached leaded spire," according to the booklet of the church that I bought. "The leaded spire has over the years 'twisted' as the lead has been warped by the head of the sun."

Barnstaple has an indoor "flea market" called the "Pannier Market," which actually first started back in 1855. "The name comes from the baskets or 'panniers' in which produce was brought to the market," per the booklet. I went inside to take a look and see what was selling today. This is a place where you get all sorts of "bric-a-brac" (miscellaneous stuff), from books and music and coins to instruments and dishes and china, from arts and crafts to jewelry, from old stuff to new stuff, and all kinds of bric-a-brac. They had a beautiful dish/china set, white with red, pink, and peach delicate flowers that one vendor was selling individual pieces of. I wanted to buy a small plate or something but I was afraid it might break over the course of the next two and a half months sitting in my wheeled suitcase. Later I kind of thought that I should have at least tried to buy a small piece of the china and very carefully pack it anyway. I did however buy Scott (not the Bike Man, but my husband) a book about horses apparently published in 1968, since Scott likes horses. The book is just about as old as I am.

It took me about forty-five minutes to bike to from Barnstaple to Instow, still along the River Taw but now I was on the other side of the river as Braunton to Barnstaple was eastbound, and Barnstaple to Instow was westbound. I did this just about non-stop, other than to take a few pictures, including of some cows. At one point, I even wanted to get the heart rate up a bit, so I biked faster. When I arrived in Instow, I locked my bike up at the near end of town. I spent over an hour in Instow. First, I wanted to look at the church there, but I kept walking and walking down the main street of Instow and was unable to find it. I gave up and turned back. On my way back, I photographed the beach and the town of Appledore which was across another river from Instow that I would be going around later, the River Torridge. I figured that I would be photographing Instow from that side later, looking across the river. The tide was half and half when I sat on a bench looking across the water, some boats floating in the water and others resting in the sand.

There was a very nice grocery/deli/café called "Johns of Instow" that I got a nice fresh quinoa tomato salad, which I mixed with a nice fresh chickpea, lentil, and beetroot salad. There will be a "Johns of Appledore," too. Then I called Scott-the-Bike-Man to let him know I was on my way to Bideford, as this was our plan. It would take me 15 to 20 minutes to bike to Bideford, and it would take Scott the Bike Man about a half hour to drive there. We were to meet at the car park next to the railway station as planned. I arrived before Scott-the-Bike-Man showed up, and after waiting a few minutes, I thanked him for my brilliant idea. Every now and then an old looking bridge went over the Tarka Trail so I took a series of photos of them as I biked to Bideford.

The last part of my day was walking to Appledore. It started out by walking along a loud busy road in Bideford, following the footprints on the ground. Like Barnstaple being the turning point around River Taw, Bideford was the turning point around River Torridge. The road out of Bideford led me to a path along the quay, then through several housing developments, zigzagging closer to and further away from the river, which was muddy at low tide.

I walked through a tree-lined path after the houses, which was a nice little walk in the woods. At this moment, I somehow remembered that I had a tiny thermometer attached to my rucksack so I looked up what the temperature was. 70F/21C. Very very nice! Today was perfect! As I left the tree lined trail, I started walking closer to the river and noticed these old abandoned broken down boats and ships. I wondered what stories they could tell. I also walked by the current shipyard, as Appledore has been a shipbuilding center since the mid-1800s.

After a few minutes of walking through a bush-lined path, I walked out onto a road, with a sign pointing me to the right, as I was getting closer to Appledore. A half mile on the road took me to the beginning of the quay in Appledore. As I turned right I figured it was time to figure out where my B&B was before I got too far into Appledore. I pulled out my handwritten notes on its location, but decided that since I had my trusty old handy dandy GPS on my phone, I used that instead. It was only four minutes away. A sign greeted me to Appledore saying, "Welcome to Appledore, Ships and the Sea. For the South West Coast Path, Follow the Footprints," those placed in the ground, similar to the footprints in Ilfracombe, and other towns. These footprints included the words engraved in them, "Appledore, Ships and the Sea," like Ilfracombe's "Curious Coastal Charm." There was also a very cute metallic piece of art that greeted me as well, which looked like the artists were probably children, as there were mermaids, fish, crabs, cute little people, starfish, boats, homes, and one cute little person eating an ice cream. I think the name "Appledore" is adorable like sweet apples.

I turned another corner onto the main part of the quay and I saw the many boats lying on the sand at low tide that I saw earlier from Instow. I saw Instow as well beyond this sandy low-tide river. I wondered when high tide was so that I could see the boats properly floating in the water. Tomorrow is my first official scheduled day off, so perhaps I will be around at high tide.

I arrived at my B&B greeted by Penny who I emailed a few times today to let her know of my arrival time. I called my Mom as I usually do on my arrival each day so she knows I am alright. Many times when I call my Mom, I actually wait till 5:00pm though England time, as that would be 9:00am her time, the same day, with the eight hour time difference, to ensure that she is awake. Sometimes if I don't call her at this time, she will call me. Just then I realized that my bottom felt sore from the so-called cushy seat of the bike I rode for hours.

I washed a few pairs of socks in the sink from the last couple days. I had two nights here, and that would be plenty of time for them to dry. Especially when the bathroom included that metal heating rack that I have mentioned. Those are so convenient. Flip the switch on, and the metal heats up. Wrap the socks around the tube-shaped rods, and voila. Drying your clothing without it going through a dryer, and faster than letting it air dry.

I ate a fish cake and cheesy chips made from locally caught fish and locally produced potatoes for dinner. I sometimes need to go back and forth between eating fried bready food, and then finding something lighter and healthier to eat, depending on what I can find.

I did a couple of posts on Facebook, one for each of the last two days, as is part of my usual evening routine, both to my personal page, and then post on the SWCP Facebook Group page. I actually asked the question on Facebook if biking today was considered "cheating," as I was not actually "walking" the SWCP. Not in the least, according to those who commented, whether family, friends, or people in the group. "Being flexible is a super power!" said my sister. "That was a wise decision, not a 'cheat'. Who says it all has to be step-by-step?" said a friend. "Doing what suits you is the way it should be done! Thumbs up." "I wouldn't class that as cheating, this was my worst section by a long way. I did both sides in the same day and it was pretty burning." "I don't consider cycling the Tarka Trail section a cheat at all. You still completed the distance under your own steam." "Genius idea, perfect way to complete that section!" "Great idea, and definitely not cheating. There are no 'rules' unless you decide to set your own. I ran that particular bit." Those are some of my responses from the SWCP Facebook Group.

And one more, "If you want to talk about cheating I have also covered the Braunton-Barnstaple-Bideford section by train! When the lines were still open and the SWCP as an end-to-end route in its infancy." Now how cool is that response.

Speaking of this SWCP Facebook Group as I mentioned, I discovered them months and months ago when I was just searching for information on the SWCP on Facebook in general. As I started following the page before I even left the US for England, there was one man in particular who started walking the entire path a few weeks before me, John, who I am still following his progress from Minehead to Poole. His posts are a way for me to see and read about where I will eventually be walking. Around this time, there is also a couple with their dog currently walking I think the entire SWCP. Others do posts on their walking bits and pieces of the path of a few days or a few weeks, or just day walks. People post photos and commentary on their walks, so now with my posts, my photos and commentary are included, too.

In fact, the first post I did on the group page before I left for England, I asked for some advice about walking the entire SWCP as a woman walking solo. Some advice I received at that time was to carry my mobile just in case of injury, even though you might not get reception all the time. (Doing that.) Take usual precautions for safety. (Doing that.) Perhaps call the B&B you will be staying at that night in the morning with an estimated arrival time, and they can monitor if you have arrived safely. (I have not been following that piece of advice.) One response said that she has been a solo female walker a lot and has had no problems. She has had more issues walking back and forth to work elsewhere in England than walking along the coast. Another solo female walker says she has only ever met friendly helpful people. In general, I had a lot of support and encouragement, especially from other women who walk the SWCP alone, when I asked for some advice.

One person also recommended a book to me called "Walking the English Coast. A Beginner's Guide" by Ruth Livingstone. In 2010, Ms. Livingstone set out to walk all 5,500 miles of the entire British Coast, in sections when she finds the time, by herself! Quite impressive. I bought her book before I left for England which contains loads of information about planning, maps, logistics, clothing, footwear, equipment, transportation, safety, weather, accommodations, even the benefits of walking, etc. While her information in intended to pertain to the entire British Coast, I found some information quite helpful for the SWCP, since part of the British Coast and Ruth's walking is of course the SWCP itself. Ms. Livingstone also has a blog about her actual walk including current experiences and photos, since she is still out there walking. As I was editing this chapter of my book, I looked on Ms. Livingstone's blog, coastalwalker.co.uk, and as of 31 October 2017, she has walked an impressive 3,584 miles!

DAY 11 STATS: BIKE 16 MILES (BRAUNTON TO BARNSTAPLE 5.5, BARNSTAPLE TO INSTOW 7.5, INSTOW TO BIDEFORD 3.0). WALK 4 MILES (BIDEFORD TO APPLEDORE). A BIT OF EXTRA WALKING DURING MY TWO TOWN STOPS. 7 HOURS TOTAL. PURPLE SHOES AND BIKE PEDALS. PUBS IN BARNSTAPLE ARE "WATER GATE" AND "GOLDEN LION TAP." PUBS IN INSTOW ARE "THE WAYFARER INN," "INSTOW ARMS," AND "THE QUAY." PUB IN BIDEFORD IS "KINGS ARMS."

REST DAY IN APPLEDORE – Thursday, 15 June 2017

"When you wake up in the morning, Pooh," said Piglet at last,
"What's the first thing you say to yourself?"
"What's for breakfast?" said Pooh. "What do you say, Piglet?"
"I say, I wonder what's going to happen exciting today?" said Piglet.
Pooh nodded thoughtfully. "It's the same thing," he said.
   - "Winnie the Pooh" by A.A. Milne

Today was my first official scheduled rest day. Yes, I had a rest day after my first two days of walking, but that was due to those gale force winds, and that I walked those two days ahead of schedule. To date, I have done about 85 miles on the SWCP so far, plus about 10 miles extra. 545 miles to go!

I wanted something different for breakfast today rather than the Half English that I have been eating most everyday thus far. The Half English has actually been quite substantial and gets me through many hours of walking. In fact, I do my best each morning to eat enough breakfast to fill me up and last for many hours of walking. However, this being a rest day, I wanted something lighter, and Penny had the perfect solution without me even asking. She had a buffet of granola, yogurt, various seeds, and fresh and dried fruit. Perfect. I had two bowls!

After seven hours sleep I woke up full of energy and ready to walk. Oh, wait I had a rest day in this cute little town of Appledore, and technically didn't need to walk. On a whim I decided to take the little Appledore-Instow ferry (which is actually a little fifteen passenger motorboat) to Instow so that I could see the church, St. John Baptist Church, that I did not see yesterday. I looked it up online to see if it would be worth going to see, and sure enough, it was another historic church, so I knew I must go. I thought it would be fun to take the ferry, too.

I saw a sign yesterday that said the ferry was running only from about 9:30 to noon, due to high tide during that time, so it was a good window of opportunity. I would be able to see the River Torridge at high tide and see the boats floating in the water, as I wanted to see yesterday. For £1.50/$2.00, I took the five minute picturesque ride across the river, along with two families that had four little children between them. The weather was sunny and warm and the water was filled with sailboats, fishing boats, rowboats, and motorboats. Heading towards Instow, I could see the buildings of the little town and the green rolling hills behind them. It was a fun five minutes.

I used my GPS to navigate to get to the church. It was three-quarters of a mile walk one way. That was the spirit – walk on my day off! I set off wearing my favorite cushy flip flops today, to give me feet a rest from closed-toed shoes. They are cushy enough to walk that far in.

The St. John the Baptist Church was in a very picturesque setting. From above a hill top as I walked around the church grounds and its graveyard, I could see the town Appledore in the distance with its buildings and green rolling hills. With the blue skies and white clouds, and the river, it made for a very pretty view. The inside of the church was worth the ferry and walk as well. I said my usual prayers. I spotted a kneeling pillow, as many churches have them, with this particular church sewn on this pillow. I have always loved the various images sewn onto kneeling pillows in churches throughout England. According to the little historical guide booklet I bought about this church, "The church is one of several pre-Norman churches around Bideford Bay founded in the sixth and seventh century by Celtic missionaries from Ireland and Wales later to be known as saints."

On my three-quarters of a mile walk back to the ferry, I stopped to try "Hocking's Dairy Cream Ice," made locally in Appledore since 1936. It was being sold by a truck conveniently parked by the beach. Cream Ice? What is that? I just had to try it. They only had one flavor, vanilla, which is not my usual flavor of choice (chocolate is), but that was ok. It tasted like, well, ice cream, but actually a bit thicker. I guess if you flip the words ice cream to cream ice, then you have something that everyone will enjoy on a summer day. Put some bits of chocolate crumble on top, which I did, and even some clotted cream, which I did not, and you have an ice cream sundae. The chocolate crumble came in a stick form, and I figured out that I had to crumble it myself. I sat on a bench to eat my cream ice by the beach in Instow looking at the turquoise and blue river and across to Appledore. Quite scenic and calming, and the cream ice was tasty.

Then it was back to Appledore from Instow on the ferry while the tide was still high and the ferry was running. Otherwise it would have been a very long walk back around the river. Another picturesque ride across the river. The woman at the dock recommended that I visit a cute little street lined with homes called Irsha Street back in Appledore. The name sounded familiar as I saw it in the booklet, and thought I would actually be walking down it tomorrow, but I decided to check it out today.

On my way to Irsha Street, I had to check out the church in Appledore, St. Mary's Church. This one was also up on a hill top, where I could see Instow from, another picturesque setting, especially as I walked up the path of the church grounds and around the gravestones. Today was turning out to be quite the picturesque day! The church was closed, and I couldn't find another open door, since the main door was being worked on by a restoration service.

I was glad I went to Irsha Street next. It was my first series of "Windows and Doors" photos that I have taken on my walk thus far. You see, one of my favorite subjects to photograph when I travel is windows and doors. In fact, when I travel I make it a point to focus on taking pictures of windows and doors, and so far on the SWCP, while I had been looking, this is the first place that they really caught my attention. I must have walked up the street a mile and back down the street a mile, leisurely taking my time, and taking lots of close-up photos of the windows and doors. I noticed that most of the windows and doors included nautical themes, such as displays and images of lighthouses, boats, various birds, small figures of sailors, and sea shells.

Perhaps I shall create a photography book called "Windows and Doors of the SWCP," starting with these on Irsha Street in Appledore, as I hope to see more that catch my attention. In fact, I have actually already created six photography books with the theme of windows and doors. One of which was from my Camino de Santiago walk, another from the Cotswolds, another from the walk I did around Île d'Orléans, and yet another book is a compilation of windows and doors from ten various countries. (Please see the end of this book in the bibliography for a complete list of all my windows and doors photography books.) Doing these windows and doors photography books actually gave me the idea of also perhaps doing the "benches" and "beach huts" of the SWCP books that I have mentioned.

Ok, self-promotion time over, so with the walking up and down Irsha Street, plus the mile and a half in Instow to and from the church, this means that on my rest day off from walking, I walked three and a half miles. In flip flops. That's the spirit!

On my way back to the rest of Appledore, I walked by a fresh local seafood shop, which happened to be closed, but was advertising selling cooked crab, dressed crab, cooked lobster, crab claws, and spider crab claws. They were also letting you know that you could "Adopt your own or purchase as a gift–Appledore crab and lobster pots. Lovely gift for friends and family-anniversaries-birthdays and any special occasions." A great example of the importance of fishing along the SWCP.

I tried to go into some of the cute little shops in Appledore after my photography session, but by that time they were closed. I'm not sure why they were closed that early, but they were. Even The Appledore Chocolate Shop was closed. I realized I was hungry and went to "Johns of Appledore" grocery/deli/café and got the same salads that I did yesterday. I walked across the street and sat on a park bench along the quay. There was a row of many park benches up and down the quay. They were all just about filled with people, too. It seemed like the thing to do on my day off. To sit and eat on a bench along with everyone else on the quay of Appledore overlooking the lowering tides of the river with the backdrop of Instow, relaxing, resting my feet after their more-than-85-miles of walking, people watching, and just being. It was a beautiful sunny, warm day with blue skies and white clouds, and every once in a while a slight breeze. Ahhhh!

After I ate my food it was only 1:05pm. Frankly I didn't have much else to do today except go back to my B&B and type for my book. However, I wasn't quite ready to do that. But what should I do? You know, I hardly ever just sit. I don't sit much in my life. I'm always going going going doing doing doing. Or here, walking walking walking. So I gave myself a challenge. To just sit here until at least 1:30 doing nothing, or almost nothing. Kind of like some sort of meditation, which I don't do either.

And so I just sat. For 25 minutes. While my body was mostly still, my mind wandered. I don't think that was proper meditation. I thought perhaps if I do the "Windows and Doors" book of Irsha Street in Appledore, they could sell the book here in this town. I saw two men most likely walking the SWCP in heavy boots, taking their feet out of the boots to rest their feet. I wondered if their feet were alright. I observed various birds around, little sparrow size birds, medium size black birds, seagulls. I saw people go by, biking, walking, walking their dogs. I saw people sitting on either side of me, with their dogs. I listened to the sounds of the seagulls and people talking and the motors of boats. When my 25 minutes was up, I sat for five more.

On my way back to my room in my B&B, three small art shops were open on the street of my B&B so I went in for a look. I also took a few more windows and doors pictures on the street of my B&B, Bude Street, walking to its end and back down. Back in my room I started to type on my laptop. I had to catch up on writing about yesterday, and start today. I also called Mom as usual. By 6:00 I was hungry again, so I took a break from writing and went out for dinner. Later, I finished catching up typing to this moment.

Random note: Because of my "accent" when I talk to people, they usually immediately ask where I am from. I respond the Seattle area of the US. They ask me if I am on "holiday" (vacation). I say yes, and that I am walking the SWCP. If they ask where I started, I say Minehead. If they ask were where I am ending, I say Poole, that I am walking the entire Coast Path. Most people seem impressed. A few will ask me if I am camping at all. I say, "Nope. I prefer a proper shower and bed each night."

So yesterday, I brought up the SWCP Facebook Group page again, and I mentioned one man in particular who started walking the entire path a few weeks before me, John. He actually started walking on the first of May. Today he is on his 37th day, walking from Wembury to Bigbury-on-Sea. I won't be there till July 31st and August 1st, splitting his one day of walking into my two days of walking. He is more than 340 miles ahead of me. He is attempting to walk the entire SWCP in eight weeks, maybe even following the SWCP Association's book suggested itinerary, so therefore walking more miles per day than I am. John is a very humorous writer, and I have found myself chuckling out loud as I read his Facebook posts. He always ends each day with a limerick. I believe he is following my walk, too.

I had also written a post on the SWCP Facebook Group page a few days before I left the US for England, saying that I was on my way. I mentioned how I had been planning this walk since August of last year, how I planned my own mileage and itinerary, and booked all my own B&Bs, etc. I even made my own attempts at a couple of limericks that I had posted:

As a 50th birthday celebration
I'm on my way to your nation
To walk the South West Coast Path
630 miles is the math
What a grand summer vacation

(Even though the word for vacation in England is "holiday.")

Soon I walk the Path South West
Hoping for 630 miles of the best
Scenery, people, weather, and food
Me, my boots, and purple shoes
I'll appreciate being your country's guest.

    One other fun thing about the SWCP Facebook Group is the "lanyard" that Lucy, the admin of the group, had kindly made for anyone that would like to purchase one. It is a strap about an inch wide, a green and blue lanyard, with the SWCP Facebook Group name on it, "South West Coast Path (England) 630 miles fb group." The intent of the lanyard is to wear it visibly, perhaps wearing around one's neck like a necklace, or to hook it onto something like our rucksacks, while walking on the SWCP so that we can identify and recognize each other, if we happen to see each other on the path. It would be a form of instant connection and camaraderie. I ordered one a while ago, and since they are now ready, Lucy will be shipping it to one of my B&Bs in a few days. Perhaps I will see someone on the SWCP wearing one, or they will see me!

DAY 12 STATS: ZERO SWCP MILES, WITH NO SWCP WALKING HOURS TO CALCULATE. THREE AND A HALF EXTRA MILES. FLIP FLOPS ALL DAY. PUB IN APPLEDORE IS "THE BEAVER INN." There was also "The Royal George," an 18th century Free House pub once offering home cooked food, live music, and quiz nights, but it looked like it hasn't been open for many, many years. Although I recently checked online and it looks like it might be undergoing major refurbishment.

APPLEDORE TO WESTWARD HO! – Friday, 16 June 2017

"Ho! Ho! Ho!" – Santa Claus

    I left my B&B in Appledore after another different and exciting breakfast, eggs Florentine. I also thoroughly checked around my room for all my belongings, such as if I had hung up any clothes to dry on the metal rack in the bathroom or anyplace else, did I take my electrical/converter adapter that is plugged in to an outlet, did I take all my toiletries, etc. This thorough check is similar to my rule of thumb of looking back when I stop someplace along the path and take my rucksack off to make sure I did not leave anything behind there either.
    As I made my way along the River Torridge, enjoying the boats in the water once again, I walked down Irsha Street once again, this time taking general photos of the street with its colorful row of pastel-colored homes. After leaving the quay part of Appledore, I walked on a few small roads which according to my booklet were designated as the high tide route, instead of the low tide route. I didn't even see signs pointing to the low tide route anyway, but if I did I was still planning on taking the high tide route regardless of the tide level.
    The booklet said I would be crossing the Appledore bridge. I was expecting this large car traffic bridge for some reason. Instead, it was a very tiny bridge, just wide enough for a car or two, taking me probably only ten paces to walk across it. The path then took me on a road to the car park next to and around "The Skern," a mudflats and saltmarshes area, "a haven for overwintering and other birdlife."
    After crossing a grassy area, and the beginning of a beach, a golf course was now to my left for at least a mile, with the crashing waves of the seas on a sandy and rocky beach to my right. This would be the first of several golf courses I would be walking near along the SWCP, and little did I know at this time that I will have some personal connections with some golf courses, some of which will have some quite interesting and surreal stories which I will be telling. Although of course today I had no idea these stories would be happening, so I just walked around this golf course, just being careful to not get hit by any flying golf balls.
    The skies in the distance today looked like potential rain, but fortunately the rains never came. It was overcast my entire walk today, with a breeze, but not cold or windy or wet. After passing by the 8th hole, the 7th hole, and the 6th hole, with par 3, par 4, and par 4, respectively, I left the golf course without incident, and walked on a gravel road for a bit. I was able to hear the sound of the waves crash over a stone piled wall. Groups of school kids were playing games in some grassy fields as I walked by.
    I arrived in Westward Ho! (with an exclamation point) in the late morning, taking "only" two hours to complete today's five-mile walk. I was originally going to walk eleven miles today, but after the brilliant bike idea a couple days ago, I covered most of what I was to walk today previously, so I only had the five miles to go. I sat in a

little community garden of the Happy Café for a few minutes to rest, since I had not stopped walking for two hours straight, and to take a look where my B&B was located. Using GPS once again, I was only a couple minutes away.

I originally told Sally of the B&B I would not arrive till mid-afternoon via email yesterday, but I was definitely off in my estimate. I thought I would go there anyway, but alas no one was home. I tried the door bell and the phone, but no answer. I saw my large wheeled suitcase safely sitting in the locked foyer of the house, which was good to see. I was hungry and wanted to find some food. I used the internet on my mobile to search for restaurants in Westward Ho!, and found a Thai place that looked good. Using GPS to guide me there, I found it and had some Thai food for lunch. I tell you, modern technology of the mobile phone with internet is quite handy and brilliant.

I was then on a quest to get some cash out of a cash machine. I had been using a mix of cash that I brought with me that I got back home, and a credit card to pay for things. Usually when paying with a credit card at a restaurant, or even a B&B, I have had to sign as authorization. I was a bit unsure about getting cash out of a cash machine, as I wasn't sure it was going to work, as this was my first time needing to get cash since I had been here. Turns out, I just needed to use my PIN number and was able to get out £250 pounds, about $330, which I would be using for small purchases like meals and any transportation if needed, and some B&Bs that do not take credit cards. Most B&Bs I try to pay for with the credit card so as to save my cash for smaller purchases.

I still wasn't sure if Sally would be back at the B&B, so I slowly walked around Westward Ho!, including going into a couple of small shops. As I walked around Westward Ho!, the exclamation point in the name Westward Ho! made me want to say "Ho Hum," and sing a few songs: "Hi Ho Hi Ho, It's Off To Work We Go!" from the Snow White and the Seven Dwarfs movie, and Cab Calloway's song, "Hidehidehidehi, Hodehodehodeho, Hedehedehedehe, Hidehidehideho." And then there was also Santa Claus - Ho! Ho! Ho!

After some time passed, I thought I would see if Sally was home yet, and walked back to the B&B. Not yet, so I began to search for a church that I could go visit next whose tower I had seen from the SWCP after the golf course earlier today. I thought it would be in Westward Ho!, but it turns out it was in a town down the road called Northam, St. Margaret's Church. It was about a mile walk. By now I had changed into some flip flops that I had in my rucksack, and was ready to go.

Just as I was about to leave, Sally came home. I dropped off my rucksack, took my wheeled luggage to my room, and took a few moments before walking to the church. It took me about twenty minutes to walk there slowly in my flip flops. Another old historical church which unfortunately was closed. I walked around the entire church and through most of the very large colorful cemetery, with many flowers around the gravesites. It fascinated me reading the tombstones. They must have taken great care back in the 1800s to bury the deceased and give them a tombstone. Perhaps those that made the tombstones had a good business.

I walked the twenty minutes back to the B&B slowly. I did some writing, called Mom as usual, and later went out for an Italian dinner. I guess it was international food day for me on the SWCP in Westward Ho! I went back to my B&B to finish typing, back up photos, do a video call with Scott as usual, although now we actually seem to video call sometimes twice a day. If we call when it is my evening around 9:00pm for example, it would be around 1:00pm the same day for him and he would most likely be at work. If we call when it is my morning around 7:00am for example, for Scott it would be 11:00pm the previous night. He has never been one to go to bed early, so talking at this hour for him was just fine, and I could thus see and talk to him briefly before my walk each day, as well as at the end of my day.

Tonight I even watched a bit of TV, which was the first time I did that, and one of the very few times.

DAY 13 STATS: 5 MILES. 2 HOURS. EXTRA MILES ARE TWO FOR THE CHURCH, AND PROBABLY ANOTHER MILE TO WALK BACK AND FORTH TO RESTAURANTS FOR LUNCH AND DINNER. PURPLE SHOES AND FLIP FLOPS. PUBS IN WESTWARD HO! ARE "THE VILLAGE INN," "FAIRWAY BOUY," AND A BIT FURTHER AWAY, BUT I LIKE THE NAME, "THE PIG ON THE HILL."

WESTWARD HO! TO BUCKS MILLS – Saturday, 17 June 2017

"If you can talk with crowds and keep your virtue,
Or walk with Kings—nor lose the common touch,
If neither foes nor loving friends can hurt you,
If all men count with you, but none too much;
If you can fill the unforgiving minute
With sixty seconds' worth of distance run,
Yours is the Earth and everything that's in it,
And—which is more—you'll be a Man, my son!"
"If" – Poem by Rudyard Kipling

Three interesting things about Westward Ho! First, this is the only town in England which has an exclamation point at the end! Second, it is the only town named after a novel, "Westward Ho!" by Charles Kingsley!

Third, Rudyard Kipling attended United Services College in Westward Ho!, and part of the above poem written by Rudyard Kipling is written on the ground as you make your way out of Westward Ho!

I got an earlier start than usual this morning. It was already sunny and warm out! (Exclamation point intended.) Lovely and beautiful. Yeah, it's summer! I had granola with homemade yogurt and fresh fruit this morning as well as part of a mushroom omelet for breakfast. I wanted to be well nourished for my seven mile walk to Bucks Mills today. Upon my arrival there, I would call Sally to pick me up. I did a long video call with Scott this morning before I started walking.

As I followed the footprints on the ground out of Westward Ho!, I walked by the rocky and sandy beach. I photographed a lone surfer walking as he made his way to the waves. I passed by a couple rows of those beach huts that I started loving walking near, taking photos of the colors, and wondering if this would be the ultimate location that I would love to have one of these huts at. It seems that people in England really love these beach huts, and take great pride in them, for as I walked by one man was out mowing the little grass lawn surrounding his little hut. These huts were also painted with great care, looking like miniature houses, some very detailed in the painting with various colors. Yellow and blue; blue and white; pink and green and white; purple and blue and white; pink and turquoise; green and red; purple and white. Some were painted in stripes; one was decorated with waves and birds; one was decorated with boats and flowers; one was called someone's "palace." Yes, they must really love these beach huts. Some seemed newer construction, while some seem older construction. It was in front of some of these beach huts that part of the Rudyard Kipling poem was written on the ground. It was also to my right along the rows of beach huts that when I looked back to the seas, I was perpendicular to the white rolling waves hitting the beach. It was already a great few minutes of walking to start my day.

As the footprints on the ground faded to acorn signs, and after those days walking and bicycling around the rivers, I was now at back to walking along the seas, listening to the small crashing white waves against the rocks. I walked on a gravel flat path overlooking a flat layer of brown rocks with the small white waves rolling in. This would be the flattest part of the day. I saw a headland front of me which I was sure I would be walking soon, and the headland behind me I already walked on. In between, straight out beyond was just blue - blue water, blue sky. A morning half-moon was also out up to my left above the green fields dotted with a flock of white sheep.

Just then I received a little messenger note from Jo, the woman who introduced me to cream tea in Ilfracombe a week ago, commenting what a lovely day it is for walking, and hoping I have a fabulous day! I wrote back, that it was brilliant out, if I may say so! It was sweet to know that she was thinking of me.

The sheep were chirping, the cows were baaaing, and the birds were moooing on this brilliant day. Ok, the birds were chirping, the cows were moooing, and the sheep were baaaing on this brilliant day.

As I walked along a grassy path, I was being passed by walkers, dog walkers, joggers, and dog joggers. I made that last phrase up. Those are people who are out for a jog and have their dog trotting along beside them. One woman with her dog took a left turn on a footpath which had a huge grassy field by it. The dog happily ran up the field and across and looked like he was having the most fun a dog could have.

Sally asked me this morning at breakfast if I feel like I ever get lonely on the walk or feel alone. I replied that I like my own company and going at my own pace, and don't mind it really. However, sometimes I do miss walking with my husband, such as that day I walked the long beach of Saunton Sands. Today would have been another one of those days - it was such a lovely day that it would have been nice to share it with him. I actually did wonder to myself if I have been feeling alone or getting lonely at times. Oh probably, as it is probably natural to do so when walking alone day after day. I even contemplated a few times today wondering if Scott should join me at some point. We had originally thought the last couple of weeks in August as an idea. I wonder if he should join me after Falmouth, which is where we ended together last year. That would be six weeks of walking together. I wondered though what about leaving the house and the cat and everything for that long, if he would want that. What about me wanting to walk the SWCP solo? Well, this contemplation, and that debate, was still to be determined. In the meantime, I had a brilliant day ahead of me.

The dog joggers went by me in the opposite direction. The last woman said, "Thank you again," because both times I stopped and gave them some room to go by. I replied, "No worries." I say that a lot here, "no worries," because it seems that others do too. I remembered originally learning that phrase in Australia, and I use it often at home as well.

The coastline here was speckled with rocky beaches, where no one was out on these beaches that I was passing by at the moment. They were below the light brown sandy cliffs which were covered with green vegetation.

At least once a day on my walks from now on, I must sit. Just sit. It is my new rule of thumb that I just made up on the spot. Today I must sit on this bench I stopped at for at least five minutes, since there were several benches offering me a view of the rocky beaches and brown rocks leading into the blue waters. Kind of like that sitting meditation I did on my rest day in Appledore. I sat and listened to the waves crash on the rocky beach, heard the birds chirp, and appreciated the warm sun. A fly buzzed around my head as I sat.

My five minutes of sitting turned into fifteen, knowing that I have "only" four miles to go from this point till Bucks Mills, my destination for the day, as I passed a sign telling me so not too far back. I saw a climb up a hillside ahead of me, the first climb that I have had in several days, so I prepared the hiking poles. I looked back at my bench to make sure I had left nothing.

As I gradually climbed, I looked back at the beautiful views behind me. The headland way beyond, the long brown rocky beaches and blue waters below, and inland many green pastures of farmland squared and checkered off with dark green bushes, some pastures containing cows or sheep and a farm. I wondered why no one was on the path that I was on at this moment. Most of the day today I actually didn't see much of anyone after those dog joggers when by. It puzzled me why the path was so empty - it was Saturday after all. Warm and sunny, too. A few purple foxglove wildflowers added a slight splash of color to the greens and blues and browns.

I reached the top of the climb in no time. At the top of some steps, I looked back. I looked forward. I spotted one boat in the water. Occasionally higher growing bushes on the trail offered a bit of shade on what might be an 80F/26.5C degree day according to my thermometer, but according to the forecast should be 65F/18C. I say it felt like 70F/21C. I took my time climbing down a few little rocky and grassy paths of steep steps. My hiking poles were used as support, and to help with the knees.

I heard the waves once again crashing on the rocky beaches below, but this time, as they pulled away, I could hear the tumbling rocks that the waves took away with them on their return to the seas. This was a different sound than just the waves crashing on the small pebbly rocks or on the sand of a beach. It had more of a rumbling sound as the waves took back the larger rocks, and I discovered another sound that I love to listen to!

To my surprise, I ended up descending right onto one of these larger rocks rocky beaches that I had been seeing and hearing today. I double checked my booklet to make sure this was correct and that I hadn't missed a sign, and sure enough this was where I was supposed to be. A very nice surprise. This was Babbacombe Mouth beach. I walked a few yards very carefully on the rocks and found a place to sit. Once again, to just sit. To listen to the rocky tumbling rumbling sound of the crashing waves closer as I was sitting there. I also had something to eat as I sat. The rocks were about the size of my fist. A fly buzzed around my head.

A steep ascent out of the beach, followed by a decent, led me into a rolling path through some high shrubs which somewhat obstructed my views. I still heard the rocky rumbling of the waves below however. I spotted a town in the distance, and I wondered if it was Clovelly, my destination tomorrow. Another bench offered me another place sit. To air out my feet, to have some more food, to add sunscreen on today as it was quite necessary, to change socks, and to sit. Again.

By the way, my color sock plan has been thrown out the window so far. Some shorter days, I don't even change socks. On the days that I do change them, sometimes I use the same color, sometimes a different color. Lately because of the warmth I've been using the lower ankle socks, rather than the higher ones. Knowing that I have twelve pairs of socks doesn't make me worried if I don't have a chance to wash them every day or if they take a longer time to dry.

A bright yellow field appeared ahead of me to my left in and amongst the green fields and trees of the hillsides. I wondered if the yellow was rapeseed as we saw in the Cotswolds. Rapeseed is related to the broccoli, cabbage, and cauliflower family, and the black seeds of this yellow plant can be used to make cooking oils, sometimes labeled as vegetable oil, canola oil, or rapeseed oil. Rapeseed is the third most important crop grown in the UK, after wheat and barley. I hope I saw rapeseed, but I never got close enough to find out for sure.

More rocky beaches dressed the edge of the shoreline ahead of me, in between the blue waters and the green hillsides. I keep describing the scenery in a similar way, using similar words, but it is hard to describe what I am seeing in words actually, and each time I describe the scenery, even though the words might sound the same, the scenery is not the same. Each scene is just a bit different in its terrain as I walk. However, it is all the same in its breathtaking beauty. My favorite colors are still green and blue.

I stopped at another one of those rocky beaches to sit again. Another surprise with the path taking me right to it. This was the beach at Portledge Mouth. I sat again for several minutes. Wow! That's a record. How many "sits" was that now today? Four I think. A couple of people were fishing at this beach as I sat.

As I descended into Peppercombe, there was a sign about cows. It said, "Cattle Grazing at Peppercombe. Whilst passing through, please observe the following points for the safety and welfare of both you and the cattle: Please close the gate behind you. Keep your distance from the cattle. Avoid getting between animals and their young." It listed a few other points if you have a dog. Yes, I know these rules, and I really appreciated the reminder.

Well, sure enough, wouldn't you know it, just my luck, but a cow, even though he was small, was standing right in the path! Hmmm….keep your distance…this is probably a young one, so where were the parents? Hmmm. What to do now? I all of a sudden felt a bit nervous as I still didn't have enough comfort and experience being around cows, and was a bit unsure of what to do actually even with knowing the rules. Perfect timing, though. I knew there were some people walking not too far behind me as I saw them when I turned around at one point to look at the scenery behind me. I paused and waited for a moment for them to show up. Three people showed up. I let them go ahead of me, as I figured safety in numbers. They didn't seem fazed by the cow at all, even though now there were two cows in the path. In fact, the man in the front started talking to them. I couldn't hear what he said, but somehow he made the cows get off the path and they trotted up the hillside. I wondered if he was a farmer and had ever herded cows before, and I made a note to tuck in the back of my mind of his talking-to-the-cows tactic. I actually considered these people my guardian angels of the day at this moment, as I walked past these cows easily after they had trotted up the hillside.

The path entered some tree-covered woods for most of the rest of the way to Bucks Mills. While the trees offered shade, they also blocked the views of the ocean, as well as the sounds of rocky crashing waves. Occasionally however, I did get a view of the seas and the hillsides and headlands from a break in the trees.

At one point, I stopped and chatted with a lovely older lady who was out walking her dog. She walks her dog every day, she told me. Sometimes on this part of the path, sometimes elsewhere. Sometimes she makes a circular walk. She commented though that she was not "walking" like me; instead she was "meandering." I loved that. I think I shall need to meander at times on my walk. She lives in Horns Cross, a mile inland from Peppercombe. This lovely older lady told me she does not like to meander, or walk, across fields with cows, especially because of her dog. It made me feel better to know that I am not the only one who gets nervous around cows.

I descended very steeply into Bucks Mills mostly by many steps, as I got a view of the village from above. In this particular view no more than a dozen white buildings surrounded by green trees sat above the blue waters. My hiking poles had been very handy today with the ascents and descents of the day. I stopped at a little bench once I get down the steps and into Bucks Mills, and put on my cushy flip flops. I know I already mentioned this, but even though the flip flops add a bit of extra weight to my rucksack, I love taking them with me so that at the end of each walk I can put them on while exploring a town, or waiting for a ride, and to just to give my feet some fresh air. Another one of my brilliant ideas. I was hoping there was food in Bucks Mills like a sandwich or something. An old red telephone booth greeted me as I entered the street of Bucks Mills.

The only food here was from a nice woman selling sweets outside her kitchen window. Since I had no choice, I had a chocolate ice cream with a chocolate covered cone. It was her last chocolate covered cone for the day, probably because of the warm day. It was delicious and refreshing. I asked if there was any place that had sandwiches here, and she replied that she would be selling sandwiches once the kids were out of school later this summer. I walked down to the beach at Bucks Mills with my ice cream. The most crowded beach I have seen all day. Quite a few people actually, especially children, on this warm day.

I went inside this little tiny home, "The Cabin," which was once the home of two women artists, Mary Stella Edwards and Judith Ackland. From the 1920s, for 50 years, they would come here to paint or to write poetry. The man who explained this to me said that these women were probably considered "brave" back then for being out here on their own. He actually said that I was "brave" for walking the SWCP alone. I don't think I consider myself brave per se; I am just doing something I wanted to do, and like to do. Probably just like these two women. Doing something we all wanted to do. (Don't get me wrong, I'm not really comparing myself to these two women at all, I am just thinking about what this man was telling me about myself.) He also told me that The Cabin looks pretty much the same as it was when abandoned by one of the women when the other woman passed away. What a great story and historical building. Their art is displayed in a museum in Bideford. If I had known of these brave women and their art and poetry, I might have gone to that museum.

After this, I was ready to be picked up by Sally. However, my mobile was not getting any signal in this tiny village. I went back to the ice cream lady who kindly used her landline to call Sally for me. About one mile down the only road that leads into Bucks Mills was St. Anne's Church that of course wanted to visit. I asked if Sally could pick me up there. It would take me about the same time to walk the mile to the church, as it would take Sally to drive from Westward Ho!

In my flip flops, I walked the mile and went inside the church that was built in the 1860s to look, take a few photos, and make a donation. I always make a donation in the churches. I felt like I had no time for a little prayer as I was inside, as Sally would be here soon and I wanted to be ready for her. Just as I was about to take exterior photos Sally pulled up in her car. I asked her for a moment to take a few more photos, so she went to turn the car around at the car park down the road, and then returned, which gave me time to take a photo, and to say my usual prayers outside the church. (Note that if I don't mention that I said my usual prayers at any church over the coming months, it does not mean that I did not say them. I most always say them each time I visit a church.)

As we drove back, we chatted about her two children and five grandchildren, and that she has had B&Bs for about forty years, this particular one that I am staying in for thirty years. She did this so she could stay home for her children while they got their education. Much like my Mom did. My Mom was a waitress who only worked during school hours so that she could take me and my sister to school, and pick us up each day, giving us a foundation of loving and caring.

We drove near the Thai restaurant I ate at yesterday, so I asked Sally if she could please drop me off here so I could eat just then. She kindly dropped me off. I ate the same tofu veggie cashew rice dish that I had yesterday. It was tasty and hit the spot after my brilliant day.

Since I had good luck with the cash machine yesterday, I went back to get another £250, so that I would be set for quite a while. I went back to the B&B for a while, and a bit later I went to dinner at same Italian place I ate at last night. I had another video call with Scott right after dinner to show him Westward Ho! beach and its surroundings, right then and there, live from my mobile phone. It was a very lovely day, with a lot of beaches and sitting. At the end of my day, it was fun to be able to share some of the scenery with Scott.

In fact, Westward Ho! may be the one of only a few places in the world that ends with an exclamation point! One other might be Hamilton!, in the state of Ohio, but I cannot confirm that this is official. There is also Saint-Louis-du-Ha! Ha! in Québec, Canada, which actually has two exclamation points!!

Brave!!

DAY 14 STATS: 7 MILES. 5 HOURS, WHICH INCLUDES A LOT OF "SITTING." ONE EXTRA MILE TO CHURCH. PURPLE SHOES AND A BIT IN FLIP FLOPS. CLOSEST PUB TO BUCKS MILLS MIGHT BE "COACH AND HORSES" IN HORNS CROSS.
Information about rapeseed from rapeseedoilbenefits.com/guide-rapeseed-oil/what-is-rapeseed-oil.

BUCKS MILLS TO CLOVELLY – Sunday, 18 June 2017

"The best things in life are the people we love, the places we've been, and the memories we've made along the way." – Hanging outside a door in Clovelly.

It's Sunday, Father's Day. Did you know that Father's Day is the same day in the US as it is in England, but Mother's Day in England is in March, whereas it is in the US in May? I wonder why one is the same, the other different.

I started off this morning from Bucks Mills after being chauffeured in the Jaguar from my B&B. I thanked Sally for her hospitality, as I would not be returning to her B&B tonight. I started off walking a half an hour through some woods, which opened onto a long grassy field. But not for long. It was back into the woods, with lots of trees and plants. The woods were well marked with plenty of acorn signs except for a couple of spots where you are directed by a footpath sign to get back in the woods. This made me unsure, so I consulted my booklet, and it did say to get back in the woods after only being "out of the woods" for 250 yards. I will say though that it was reassuring to see an acorn sign again not too far back into the woods.

I popped out of the woods again, walking briefly on some grass next to a field with lots of sheep. The sky was perfectly blue, not a cloud around. The sun was shining brightly. Back in the woods with the trees offering shelter from the day that was growing warmer and warmer. Little did I know that yesterday was the start of a five day heat wave, culminating in one of the hottest June days in 41 years!

An occasional glimpse through the trees I could see the perfectly blue water and the perfectly blue sky. About an hour and a quarter later, I finished the two miles of being mostly in the woods, with the occasional field walking. Next I walked along a flat gravelly road, Hobby Drive, for two and a half miles.

From Hobby Drive I had more occasional glimpses of all the blue. As I got closer to Clovelly, my destination for the day, I had a view of the village from above. Through the trees I could see the white building of the Red Lion Hotel sitting above many boats in the harbour, some of which were sitting on the ground at low tide. A few other boats were floating on the water where it was deep enough. Red brick chimneys popped out of the roofs of the other buildings. A rocky beach just beyond had some cars parked next to it and a few people were enjoying the rocks next to the seas.

"Only" two and a half hours later after leaving Bucks Mills, I reached the top of Clovelly. It was a short walk today, only four and a half miles. That was by design though in my itinerary, as tomorrow I will be walking ten miles, and there are no accommodations along the way to make today a bit longer and tomorrow shorter, and I did not want to plan a 14.5 mile day when I created my itinerary.

I walked down the steep cobblestoned street leading to the village of Clovelly, and turned the corner left to see the village. I took a photo of my purple shoes on the cobblestone. What a cute village! And voila, right there was my hotel, the New Inn Hotel, at the top of a steep cobblestoned street that goes through the village and eventually down to the harbour and the boats of this fishing village. I went inside the hotel to check in and voila my bag arrives also at the same time. I had a view from the deck of my room of the roof tops down the street and some of the seas in the distance.

By this time it was only late morning, with a full hot day ahead of me. Yes, it was hot today, warmer than yesterday, definitely a summer day again! I had the great idea of maybe walking another two or three miles today, in order to make use of the day, and in order to shorten tomorrow's walk. However, after asking around, this was not possible today because there were no ride services to any potential stopping points. A taxi would cost way too much, like £36/$50, and there was no bus service on a Sunday. No one at this hotel was available to do any driving either.

Therefore, I would make the best of my hot day here, making it a leisurely day, in "Lovelly Clovelly." That's my nickname for this village. I am sure I am not the only one who has thought of that nickname. As I started to meander very slowly down the steep cobblestoned street, I immediately noticed the windows and doors. So what do I do, but start to take windows and doors pictures, which I continued to do on and off the rest of the day. Most of the homes were greatly decorated with lots of colorful flowers against the whitewash of the buildings. Now, in addition to the Appledore windows and doors pictures, I also have Lovelly Clovelly to add to my windows and doors photography book.

I stopped at a quaint tea shop for a bite to eat, a tomato and basil quiche. I sat on a bench overlooking the harbor below with boats, the breakwall, and the blue seas beyond speckled with boats. In the distance I could see several headlands that I have walked on the past couple of weeks. Wow! I was amazed that I actually walked from there to here!

Windows and Doors along the South West Coast Path
All from Irsha Street in Appledore June 15
Including window with seagulls, window of the local seafood shop,
window with a sailboat, and door of The Royal George Pub

Windows and Doors along the South West Coast Path
Old Border between Devon and Cornwall in Cawsand/Kingsand July 27 and April 15
Clovelly (two middle photos) June 18
Penberth Cove (windows from home at the harbour) July 9

After my lunch, I continued windows and doors pictures as I meandered my way down to the harbour on the main street, known as High Street. I meandered on a few side streets as well, and took more pictures. As I got closer to the harbour, I had views of the boats on the ground and in the water from above, the breakwall, and the water that faded from turquoise to blue. And those headlands.

Some of my windows and doors photos included lots of the lovely colorful flowers that decorated the village, tables and chairs on porches, bird feeders and heart shaped decorations, and statues of birds, cats, rabbits, fish, and butterflies. Someone had some books for sale next to their door and window. Garden items, such as tools and watering cans, decorated other windows and doors. Shells, buoys, lobster pots, and other nautical items decorated other windows and doors. Sayings such as the touching quote above, and "a fisherman lives here with the best catch of his life," hung near some doors. Someone was selling hand-painted Clovelly stones from their doorstep.

Finally making my way down, I went to the harbour and even meandered along the breakwall as many people were doing. People were also sitting all around, at the Red Lion Hotel, on the beach, and along the breakwall. Crab and lobster pots, and buoys, lined the breakwall. Everyone was enjoying the hot weather, also known as summer! There were quite a lot of people here today. Some people were taking a quick swim in the water. I say "quick" because as people jumped in they all squealed quite loud at how cold the water was, and I bet they didn't stay in for very long.

I sat on one of the rocky beaches watching a boat being pulled up out of the water onto land. Another rocky beach was on the other side of the breakwall. Part of me wished I had brought a bathing suit with me on my entire SWCP walk. I did not even think of it during my packing, which was kind of interesting because I knew that I would be near beaches and waters a lot.

I thought about taking a boat ride from the harbour which would give me a view of Clovelly from out on the sea, but at the moment, I chose not to. From the end of the breakwall I had a view of the town with the buildings layered up the streets, and nestled in the green background of the trees. Later on though, I thought that I should have gone out on the boat, as it might have been nice to be on a boat in the water for a little while in this summer weather.

I meandered (are you noticing how I am incorporating "meandering" into today inspired by the lovely older lady walking her dog yesterday) into a few bric-a-brac shops and art shops. I chatted with an artist in one shop asking her what the weather is like here in winter. Wet and cold. She asked where I am from. Seattle. What is the weather like there in winter, she asked? Wet and cold. A small museum was dedicated to Charles Kingsley, the "Westward Ho!" novelist, which was actually the house where Mr. Kingsley lived from the ages of eleven to sixteen.

My next meandering took me to a few interesting, historical, and educational places in Clovelly, the first being a Fisherman's Cottage. "For centuries, the main occupation at Clovelly was fishing. The village boats sailed out into the waters of Bideford Bay to harvest the vast shoals of herring and mackerel, and returned to unload their catch on the beach into baskets or 'mawns'. These were carried up the steep cobbles by the village donkeys. By 1840 Clovelly was classed as an important North Devon fishing port with 60 to 70 boats engaged in the herring fishery. A Devon guidebook of 1859 stated that in favourable weather 'a Clovelly boat has captured 9,000 herrings at a haul'. Today, fishing continues, but on a limited, sustainable basis. The famous Clovelly crabs and lobsters remain a prize catch and the herring still visit in autumn."

Inside Fisherman's Cottage, "you can see how a fisherman and his family lived in the 1930s. The parlour is decorated with domestic treasures of the period, including simple cottage furniture, colourful pictures and religious engravings, and china and ornaments. The tiny kitchen is plain but full of period charm. Upstairs there are two bedrooms, one small and the other still smaller, a sail loft, and an attic complete with straw mattresses."

I also meandered into St. Peter's Chapel, a "small and intimate place of worship [that] was opened in 1846." There was also John Wesley's Fisherman's Church, which dated from around 1820. "During the late 18th century John Wesley inspired a strong Methodist movement in the West Country. His sermons were aimed at the heart as well as the mind, and made a direct appeal to Clovelly's fisherman, who lived hard, tough lives."

It was fascinating to see this history and learn about the fishing industry and heritage of Clovelly. A start of me seeing so many wonderful, historic, important fishing villages along the SWCP, and a start to me learning and appreciating the livelihood of fishing.

I also learned that here in Clovelly, apparently when you meander, or walk, or wander or saunter or stroll, or amble or ramble or stride, or whatever, down the main cobblestoned street, it is known as "down-a-long." When you go up the cobblestoned street, whether by meandering, walking, wandering, sauntering, strolling, ambling, rambling, or striding, it is known as "up-a-long." The main street actually descends 400 feet in a half mile! Now that is steep. At the top of the cobblestoned street, I saw a donkey that was historically used, but I don't think are used any longer, to transport items up and down the steep street. I think the donkeys were there for picture-taking today. There are however, carts called "sledges," kind of like a sled or sleigh made out of crates that seemed like they slide on the cobbled stones nicely to transport items up and down the street. These sledges even transport items like luggage, as I saw my large suitcase earlier being carried by such a sledge. In other words, I don't think any cars go down-a-long or up-a-long the cobblestoned street.

After I was done meandering through Clovelly, I continued up-a-long back to where I began the down-a-long earlier today when I arrived, to look at the shops at the very top of the cobblestoned street near Hobby Drive. The first shop I went into was a soap shop. It smelled nice in there with all the various scents. There were a lot of different "flavors" of soaps. I bought a small "Chocolate Orange" soap, and a small "Grapefruit and Neroli" soap, "a fresh and fruity smelling bar with White Grapefruit and Neroli Essential Oils." Neroli is an essential oil extracted from orange blossoms. The woman who made the soaps also had a book, "The Natural and Handmade Soap Book." While I may never make soap, or perhaps learn how to make soap in my retirement, I thought the book looked like a very nice coffee table book, so I bought it. Sarah Harper even autographed the book for me. I love buying fun-smelling soaps, especially when they sound like something good to eat, too.

The last stop for me today was to see All Saints Church which was a half mile down a woodland walk in a tree-lined footpath to some gardens and to the church all out of the main part of Clovelly. This church dates from the 12the century. After my usual church visit, it was a half mile walk back to where I needed to go down-a-long again to my hotel.

Tomorrow is going to be another hot day, as was today, so even with filling up my water bladder the full three liters that it can carry, I also bought two extra small water bottles to take with me. Better to be well hydrated, especially with the ten miles I have planned.

I went back to my hotel to call Mom, call my Dad for Father's Day, did some Facebook posts, and a few other things as usual before dinner. After dinner it was video calling with Scott and typing. After my great walk this morning, it also turned out to be a great hot leisurely day in the fishing village of Lovelly Clovelly.

DAY 15 STATS: 4.5 MILES. 2.5 HOURS. EXTRA TWO MILES FOR CHURCH VISIT OUT OF CLOVELLY VILLAGE AND ALL THE MEANDERING IN CLOVELLY. PURPLE SHOES AND FLIP FLOPS. PUBS IN CLOVELLY ARE THE "NEW INN HOTEL" AND THE "RED LION HOTEL." Information on the Fisherman's Cottage from clovelly.co.uk/village/fishermans-cottage, and information on the chapel and two churches from clovelly.co.uk/village/places-of-worship.

CLOVELLY TO HARTLAND QUAY – Monday, 19 June 2017

"Note: This is a shorter section of the walk and the most scenic. However, it is a very strenuous section and takes longer than you think." – SWCP Association Booklet, Walk 12, Clovelly to Hartland Quay.

Today was my toughest day so far. Not because of all the ascents and descents, although there were many, but because of the heat. It was hot! Quite hot! Probably 80F/27C at least according to the weather forecast. I forgot to check my thermometer. I know I said days ago that I wanted summer to arrive when I had all that rain and wind, but today was exceptionally hot. Especially walking ten miles in it!

The good thing was I had plenty of water with me. A completely full three-liter water bladder, plus the two small bottles I bought yesterday. It turned out that up until the seven mile mark for the day where I was able to refill my water bladder, I only drank two liters, even though I was sipping water literally the entire seven miles. After the refill, for the last three miles, I drank a liter and a half. I was still glad I had so much water with me as it was better to be safe than sorry.

Back to the beginning of the day. I left Clovelly at 8:45. A gate with a Coast Path sign led me to a path on a grassy field spotted with what I think were pine trees. By 9:00 I heard some waves crashing, which I really wouldn't hear much of today, just occasionally on and off, probably due to being so far up a hillside far from the coastline down below. Another gate led me to walking in the shade of various types of trees which was a nice start to this already-hot-out-already-this-early-in-the-morning kind of day. In the shade of the trees I heard little critters rustling about in the bushes, which I also heard in yesterday's woods. Most likely birds or squirrels, or according to my booklet, pheasants.

I passed by two covered shelters, one called The Cabin, built in the early 19th century, and the other called "Angel's Wings," also built in the 19th century, with its wooden carvings of angels and angel's wings. While the trees were providing me shelter at the moment, these two shelters could be nice places to sit for a while.

From a viewpoint, I had a glimpse of the great deep blue seas of today, with the great baby-blue sky. I just loved how the several shades of blue connected with each other in the distance on this hot day. From this viewpoint, I saw a rocky shoreline below a cliff, with large rocks, including the Blackchurch Rock, a triangular shaped double arch, apparently about 300 million years old, according to the booklet.

Soon I emerged out of the woods onto a flat grassy area. The walk today was well sign posted (except for two places), not only with acorns and/or yellow arrows, but also with red and yellow ribbon. I don't know if this ribbon is always there though, or if it was for some run or event that occurred on the trail in this section. I literally said "thank you" out loud today each time an acorn, yellow arrow, or ribbon, or any combination thereof, which pointed me in the right direction. I did that when I walked my Camino in Spain as well. It is my way of appreciating not only the directions, but also appreciating the people who made and placed all the signs.

I passed by two beautiful brown colored horses in the grassy area, which Scott would have loved, and after a quick view point to which I saw the all the blue again, I was led back into the woods. This was the first place where it was not well sign posted. In fact, it looked like the post had been broken. Thankfully two guardian angels had just walked up the right hand turn I was thinking I should take, and I confirmed with them that that was the SWCP. Another guardian angel walking her dog also passed by at this moment, and I confirmed with her as well.

I reached Mouth Mill where I was near a small rocky beach, with views of the rocky coastline underneath the brown rocky cliffs covered with green shrubbery and trees. Next to the beach were ruins of an old lime kiln and cottage, grey brick in color with ivy growing along the walls. It so intrigues me to see this old stuff, and I always wonder what stories the walls could tell.

It was near Mouth Mill that was the second place with a downed sign. However, fortunately John of the SWCP Facebook Group, who is walking the entire SWCP, did this walk several days or weeks ago and commented about this downed sign. I had taken note of it when I read his comment, and literally wrote down in my booklet, "Note: At Mouth Mill, do not turn left after crossing the bridge by the old lime kiln. Instead look for a fallen/partially buried sign. The path is almost opposite the end of the bridge." When I got there, I did notice the sign, in some bushes, propped up, so I wondered if someone had since picked it up since John's walk in the area. I was still aware of it however, and therefore I took John as being a guardian angel since I was on the lookout for this sign due to his comments.

The first good little uphill climb of the day in the woods with more shade from the trees took me about ten minutes to complete. It had been relatively flat up until this point so far. I was grateful for this shade at the moment, as the shade would soon disappear for the rest of the day. Need I say again, it was hot! On the other hand, with the shade of the trees gone, a quick view of the blue seas and blue skies were once again breathtaking.

I emerged onto field after field after field where I pretty much followed along the edge of the fields for the next several miles. There were various fields to the left of me and some high shrubbery which blocked my views of the water to my right. Occasionally I could see over the shrubbery, at least to see the breathtaking views. Various wildflowers of white and purple coloring occasionally lined that path.

Because of the sun, today I wore a sun hat I bought in Spain during my Camino walk. It is good for days like today as it has some ventilation holes around the head, and with no wind, the brim doesn't flap around. Along with my purple shoes, I was wearing two items related to my Spain Camino walk today.

I approached a field of cows that were fortunately behind a fence. Unfortunately, as I got closer it turned out that I needed to be on the same side of the fence as they were. Fortunately, they were way out in the field, and with me walking along the edge, they were at a safe distance from me. Still, it got the heart pounding just a bit.

A sign said a half mile to Windbury Point and after a good downhill climb, I reached Windbury Point, to which I then went back uphill to Windbury Hill. I looked back from here and got another view of the triangular Blackchurch Rock at the edge of the green hillsides and cliffs. Looking more inland, amongst a very green covered hillside with shrubs, bushes, ferns and small trees, I could see the path carved out that I had descended moments earlier. With more green shrubbery in the foreground of a photo, and with the blue skies above all this, I soaked up the sun for a moment. It was truly beautiful!

I continued to walk through flat fields with the fields on my left and the tall shrubbery on my right. It was definitely hot out in the exposed terrain. I continued to sip water constantly. I did not want to get sun stroke, heat stroke, dehydrated or anything like that. Once in a while there was a very slight breeze, but it was still hot. I had some more views out in the water, including of Lundy Island, the one with two lighthouses, which was about eleven miles out in the seas. Since I was not able to see Lundy Island back when I was at Baggy Point about a week ago, it was good to see it today. At one point an obvious large white ball was looming in the distance. I suspected this was Hartland Point, and I learned later that it was the Hartland Point Radar Dome.

Still walking on the open grassy fields, I wanted to gauge my time and distance from the signs that pointed to East Titchberry. It was another one of those mismarked mileage situations which didn't make sense however. The first one said three miles to East Titchberry, then more than a half mile of walking later, another sign said two and a half miles to East Titchberry. Then not too long after the second sign, a third sign said one and a half miles to East Titchberry, but I did not feel like I walked another mile. I took the signs with a grain of salt at this point.

Speaking of salt, and electrolytes, to replenish these from my body during the heat, I added some electrolyte tablets that I fortunately brought with me to my water today. A brilliant idea for my body today on such a hot day!

Anyway, around this area some darker grass marked the paths, as well as signs and the red and yellow ribbon. I made a left turn and started to hear some crashing waves. At around 11:45 the signs still said one mile to East Titchberry, and two miles to Hartland Point, with that obvious large white ball getting closer. All day I was guessing what time I would arrive at Hartland Point. My guess was 12:30. At this last sign, I took a break. I had just kept walking and walking in this heat. I stopped to reapply the much needed sunscreen, and have something to eat.

It was odd, but I seemed to be the only one out walking here today. I questioned whether I should even be walking on such a hot day. I mean, I didn't walk in gale force winds, so should I be walking in quite the opposite weather? Especially alone. I was grateful though that I brought so much water and had food with me, but I still wondered if I made a wise choice to walk. At this point though, I had no choice but to keep walking. I didn't feel dehydrated or any symptoms sun stroke or heat stroke or anything, and felt just fine. Although, would I really recognize the symptoms?

Soon after this, I happened to pass by four people walking. The first people I had seen all day, so I guess I wasn't alone. When we passed we said, "Hello," "good morning," and "cheers." They say "cheers" a lot here in England. "Cheers" is a fun term that I quite like a lot which I think has several uses, such as "thank you," "goodbye," "hello," "no problem." Cheers can be used when signing off from a phone call or an email. And, cheers can be used before taking a drink, as a toast. Cheers!

Today I noted down the mileage a lot, and at this moment, a sign said one mile to Hartland Point. It was noon. Will my 12:30 guess be accurate? I liked this little game I was playing of guessing my arrival time. I had views behind me above Shipload Bay, with its curved rocky beach underneath the green covered hills and cliffs.

My hiking poles were coming in very handy today, too. Not just for the ascents and descents, but they also cleared away the brush, some thorny, as I walked through several of these patches today. Even though it was hot, I still wore long pants, originally for sun protection, but also now also so that my legs don't get scraped up from the thorns. Even with the long pants on, my legs didn't feel overly hot.

As I approached the obvious large white ball, I passed by a field of some cute goats. Yes, goats! The last time I saw goats was those mountain goats almost two weeks ago when I was in the Valley of Rocks near Lynmouth, with two goats on that narrow ledge. I arrived and walked around that large white ball that used to be in the distance, and now saw it up close, the Hartland Point Radar Dome. According to today's booklet, "During WW2 there was a large radar station here used to detect low flying aircraft and known as RAF Hartland. However much of the MOD equipment has gone and the present radar dome is used for air traffic control for both civilian and military aircraft."

In the nearby distance from here, I saw the rocky beach below of Barely Bay. A car park at Hartland Point was getting closer, as well as a little café that looked open. Around the cliff ledge, which was Hartland Point, just beyond would be the Hartland Point Lighthouse, which was not visible at this moment as it was on the other side of the cliff ledge. I arrived at the café at 12:25. Not too bad for my predicted time of 12:30! The sign said I had done seven miles from Clovelly, and had three miles to go to Hartland Quay, my destination for the day.

At the café, I ordered a "mezze," a plate with olives, sundried tomatoes, hummus, Mediterranean bread, grilled vegetables, and cucumber. It was so refreshing and tasted really great. It was here that I asked them to completely fill up my water bladder again, even though I had only drunk two liters, and "only" had three miles left.

As I was sitting and eating, several other people came down the trail that I had just come from to this café. I guess I really was not the only one out here today that I thought earlier. First, one couple arrived about 25 minutes after I sat down. I asked them if they had come from Clovelly, and she said, "Yes." Then another couple came about 15 minutes later. Then a solo man. Finally one other couple arrived. Seven others had been behind me! That was good to know. I found comfort in that, and it made my last three miles more comfortable, knowing that other people were out walking today in this heat.

I set off again with a full water bladder, a happy stomach, and the knowledge that there were two people ahead of me as one of the couples already left, and five would be behind me. In addition, I had on a fresh pair of socks! I let my feet air out while I was eating. The booklet for today said that from Hartland Point to Hartland Quay, the next three miles, "Note: This is a shorter section of the walk and the most scenic. However, it is a very strenuous section and takes longer than you think." What the booklet didn't know was how hot it also was! Note that I am not complaining about the heat. Well, I guess I am just a little bit, but I would really rather have this heat over gale force winds any day.

First thing I saw after I started walking again was the sign saying there was a lighthouse, the Hartland Point Lighthouse, but it was closed to the public. When I got to the closed gate of the road leading to the lighthouse, there was actually a man driving in. I was hoping he would say I could see it, but no such luck.

I stopped for a moment to get a good view out to Hartland Point, and took pictures of my purple shoes with the rocky point just beyond. The path took me around for a view of the lighthouse from the other side of Hartland Point. I took many pictures of this white lighthouse, with its bit of turquoise trim under the windows and along its base, sitting proudly on the cliff ledge. I would see the lighthouse once again a bit down the path and would take more photos. Too bad it was closed to the public. Officially opened on 1st July 1874, the Hartland Point Lighthouse, according to the information display near the lighthouse, "Originally there were living quarters for four keepers and their families. The original revolving lens was driven by a clockwork mechanism, which had to be wound up by a keeper every two and a half hours. In 1984, the lighthouse was automated and is now monitored and controlled from the Trinity House Operations Control Centre, in Harwich, Essex. The present light, which has a character of six white flashes every fifteen seconds, has a range of twenty five miles. A fog signal gives a five second blast every sixty seconds that can be heard over a two mile range."

Below the cliff at Hartland Point is also the wreckage of a ship, the Johanna. Per the information display, "In the early hours of 31st December 1982, the Panamanian registered coaster Johanna came ashore less than 400 meters from the lighthouse. The four crew were rescued by helicopter from RAF Chivenor and the three officers were taken off later in the day by the Clovelly lifeboat. The ship was carrying loose wheat from Holland to Barry Island, South Wales. Nearby Hartland Quay Museum has further information about the many wrecks along this section of the coast." While I was not able to see it, the wreckage of Johanna can still be seen below the cliff. Reminders of the powers of the seas.

After leaving the lighthouse, the path started out flat, which was good. Then I was in for a roller coaster ride. Downhill first, although this valley provided me with a welcoming breeze. Then it was uphill. The solo man passed me at this point. Then I think it was downhill again, where a couple was enjoying the sun and heat sitting on the grass. There was a slight breeze here as well.

For the first mile and a half of the last three miles, the views were amazing! Or as the booklet said, "Most scenic." More green hillsides and headlands, brown and green cliffs, turquoise and blue waters, sharp edges of rocks sticking out from the waters, small white frothy waves, rocky beaches and bays and coastline, blue skies with some white clouds. My words cannot do the scenery justice.

At the sign that said Hartland Quay one and a half miles, a lone white house with a brown roof sat amongst the various green shaded farmland of the hillside on the inland side of where I was walking. I could see the path that I was on continue getting closer to the seas.

My original estimate for my arrival time at Hartland Quay was 3:30 because the booklet said that this section would "take you longer than you think." I gave myself over two hours for three miles. But I decided to revise my arrival time to 3:00 because it was 2:10, and it only took me 50 minutes to get the half way mark, so I figured 50 minutes for the other half.

It was another uphill out of the half way point. On several of the uphills and downhills today there were steps to use, but I found it easier to just walk on the edge of the steps on more of a path-like surface so I could go the distance my legs wanted to go, not guided by the steps, as I have done before. The scenery from this last mile and a half was equally amazing. I looked back to see where I had come from – I could see the wiggly path etched on the greenery of the top of the hillside, the cliffs leading down to the rocky beaches, white waves, and blue waters once again. Again, words cannot describe the scenery and do it justice.

Another couple was enjoying the sun and heat at the top of this hill. I think I was able to see the Hartland Quay Hotel from there. Getting closer. Then I heard myself say out loud, "Holy cows" (or something similar), not because there was a herd of cows on the path, but because I saw at least two more downhills and uphills I was about to climb since I was able to see the line of the SWCP clearly etched amongst the greenery. Sure enough, my sight was correct. At the bottom of one descent was another rocky beach. I paused at its beauty.

At 2:40 a sign said one more mile to go. I took my time doing the ups and downs, and still pretty much drank constantly. I actually noticed my teeth and jaws were starting to ache by now, and I realized it was because of me holding the tube to my water bladder in my mouth all day. I wondered to myself if I was "brave" today to do this walk in the heat.

I finally think I climbed my last climb. Off in the distance I saw a church tower. I don't think it was that far away from the hotel, maybe a half mile inland, but there was no way I was going to this church today as much as I like to go visit churches, I thought to myself in this heat. I thought about Scott again. It would have been good to have his company today to help with the heat. Then again, he doesn't like heat that much. The ruins of the "Tower at Warren Cliff," which might have been a summer house at one time according to my booklet, outlined the tower of the church in a photo I stopped to take.

Finally I reached a road and a path that lead to the Hartland Quay Hotel, which is conveniently located on the SWCP and near the waters and a beach. As I approached the hotel, I looked back at this amazing stretch of coastline I had walked. So many brown rocky cliffs leading to large brown rocks seeming to be sitting on top of the blue seas, surrounded by small white waves. I had made it! Ten miles in the heat! At 3:10pm, I was glad to be walking into the reception area of the Hartland Quay Hotel. Ten minutes after my revised estimate, and about six and a half hours after I left Clovelly this morning, including almost an hour break, so about five and a half hours of walking in the heat. The booklet said it would take five hours.

I checked in and went to my little single-bed room with its view out the window of the seas and sky just above the rooftop of the next building. All I wanted to do at this point was to call my Mom and email Scott to tell them of my day. But no, the WiFi wasn't working in my room. My regular mobile reception wasn't working either. I tried to get WiFi in the reception area of the hotel which also didn't work. I tried in the bar/restaurant which also didn't work. I finally asked, and they told me that mobile reception had been spotty ever since they had a lightning strike a while ago.

The woman told me I could get regular reception if I step out to either the car park close to the hotel, or the car park up the road above. I walked to both, but still no reception. I kept walking up the road. Probably a quarter mile up. I finally got reception! I called Mom and left her a message, and emailed Scott from my phone. I walked back down to the hotel a quarter mile.

I arranged for dinner at 6:00, the earliest time possible, because I knew I would be hungry soon. After dinner, I used my laptop with WiFi to video call with Scott, which seemed to work, but still not my mobile phone.

My toughest day thus far due to the heat. Looks like the next two days might be just as hot, and I have eight miles to go each of those days. Cheers!

DAY 16 STATS: 10 MILES. 6.5 HOURS, WITH AN HOUR BREAK. HALF MILE EXTRA TO GET MOBILE RECEPTION. PURPLE SHOES. PUB IN HARTLAND QUAY IS "THE WRECKER'S RETREAT" AT HOTEL.

HARTLAND QUAY TO MORWENSTOW - Tuesday, 20 June 2017

"Hartland is a small, isolated and very picturesque place on the wild north coast of Devon. It is home to a diverse community of creative and interesting people....We love to socialize and especially to cook for, and eat with, friends. Our cooking is as varied as the people who live here and we have some highly accomplished and enthusiastic cooks....Here we offer a selection of our favourite recipes just as we exchange them among ourselves....We hope you enjoy trying out our recipes and agree that 'Hartland Cooks'!" – "Hartland Cooks" cookbook I bought at Parish Church of St. Nectan in Hartland.

Another hot day! I remember having discussions with my physical therapist before I left for England, who was making sure my legs, knees, calves, lower back, and even elbows for the use of hiking poles, were ready for my long walk, about the weather. She asked me what would be my ideal weather for my walk. I responded, "Anything, as long as it is sunny, from 60 to 80F degrees (15.5 to 26.5C). I even tell my husband a lot that I love the heat. Well, after two days of walking in 80F/26.5C degree weather, yesterday and today, I want to modify my response to my physical therapist, as much as I love summer. As long as it is sunny from 60 to 70F (15.5 to 21C), would probably be much better. It has been way too hot for me to walk five to six hours, two days in a row, with many ascents and descents, in 80F/26.5C degree weather. I don't want to sound like I am complaining, but I guess I am just a bit. Still I enjoyed the scenery of the walk again today, however, and would definitely rather have this heat than gale force winds any day.

At breakfast at the Hartland Quay Hotel, I chatted with a lovely couple from Falmouth who walked from Morwenstow to Hartland Quay in yesterday's heat, and today they were going to walk to Clovelly in today's heat, in the opposite direction of what I am doing. In general, they do bits and pieces of the SWCP when they can, not in any particular order, just depending on how much time they have, and the bus schedule back and forth to Falmouth.

Another couple I chatted with this morning was one that was walking in my direction that I saw yesterday. I asked them if they were going to Morwenstow, my destination, today as well. They said, "No, we are going to Bude." Bude! In this heat? That is twice as far as to Morwenstow! They said, yes, but they have no choice, as that was where their accommodations were for the evening as they pre-planned. I took some comfort in knowing that there would be at least two other people on the path with me today going twice as far as I was, and one couple walking "backwards." The couple walking double sounded like they were from Germany.

After breakfast I started off walking at 9:10. It was already hot! I kept track of the time again today as I liked the guessing game I played yesterday as to my arrival times. It was fun. The walk started out gentle enough, first offering me amazing views of yet more different coastline, even though it sounds like I am describing similar coastline – rocky beaches, with parallel looking rocks jutting out into the deep blue waters, larger rocks sticking out above the waters, small green hillsides, larger green hillsides, several headlands beyond. Blue skies, and a single fishing boat making its way up the coast.

A sign told me, "Attention all dog owners - pregnant sheep and lambs in field. Dogs must be kept strictly on a lead at all times or owners may face prosecution." I did not have a dog with me today, but I did pass by a flock of black sheep (again!) and the cutest little baby lambs sitting in the cool of the little shade that they could find. The rocky coastline and the green hillsides and headlands continued to be in my view, slowly getting closer for a better look. A barbed wire fence was to my right reminding me not to get close to the edge.

My theory for coping with today's heat was to not only constantly drink water, but also during the flat stretches walk a bit faster pace, so that on any ascents and descents, I could go slower. That was the theory anyway. In the heat, there is only so fast you can go even on the flat stretches. Today I was carrying a full water bladder of three liters, plus three small water bottles! This made for a heavier rucksack, but quite necessary, as there would be no places to refill water till Morwenstow, about eight miles away, which was my destination anyway. By the end of the day, I would only have one of the small water bottles left.

There actually was a very slight breeze as I started my walk today that would show up every now and then and really helped with the heat. A waterfall, the 50 foot Speke's Mill Waterfall, came into view. By 9:40 I walked about a mile where a sign said I had four and a half miles to Welcombe Mouth. My goal in my guessing game was to be welcomed by Welcombe Mouth by 12:30. A sign on a wooden gate warned me, "Bull - keep out." Fortunately I did not have to go through that gate and gladly kept out!

I saw the German couple ahead of me during that first mile. They said that because of their long distance today, they would be walking slowly. I couldn't blame them. I did pass them up just after the first mile while we were in a flat stretch in a very hot valley. It felt like a desert down there. Not that I really know what it is like to walk in a desert, but I bet this would be similar, hot and dry. Fortunately "the desert" didn't last too long. I was soon back up on the cliff top, which was still hot, but one of those very slight breezes was there welcoming me.

In addition to adding electrolytes tablets yesterday and today to my water to help replenish my electrolytes, I also added some extra salt to my eggs this morning, and added salt to my water later in the evening at the end of my walk. I had also been slathering the sunscreen on. My arms and face my looked quite white as I used a zinc-based sunscreen.

The sound of a flock of seagulls on the cliff top cliff ledge captured my attention for a moment as I continued my walk. More amazing views of beaches of rocks jutting out into the blue waters, a few white frothy waves, the clear blue sky, and all the green hillsides and headlands beyond. Lovely, even on a hot day. At 10:10 I came to a sign that said now I have three miles to Welcombe Mouth, and that a youth hostel was inland from here.

A local man passed me. First, he commented on what a lovely day it was, and I agreed, even with the heat. This man then warned me that just up ahead for about ten or fifteen feet there is a slight gulley next to the path that if I wasn't careful, and I don't see it, I could drop my foot in there and possibly hurt myself by twisting an ankle or worse. I was so glad he warned me about that. A guardian angel.

I walked briefly through a grassy field on top of a hillside. Most of the walking thus far had been either grassy fields or prickly shrubs. I was glad I wore long pants, and used my hiking poles to move the shrubs away. There was a cliff pretty close to my right, with the seas beyond. A barbed wire fence was to my left with various fields beyond. The sun was on my left as well. At 10:30 a sign said two and a half miles to Welcombe Mouth. I took a guess at an 11:30 arrival time, revised an hour earlier from my original guess. First there was a bit of road walking.

Even though I didn't feel very hungry in this heat, I ate some salty nuts anyway to help replenish my body. I came to a picnic bench with views all around. I saw the blue seas and blue skies straight ahead, the headlands that I have walked on behind me, and the headlands I will be walking on ahead of me. Inland was grassy fields and green farmland and the brown brick homes of a small village. A panoramic photo was necessary. As I continued walking, I looked back once again at the farmland with its fields of various shades of green separated by darker green trees, making for a puzzle-like-looking checkered landscape. It was flat from the edge of the cliffs inland, and the grassy path I was walking on looking straight at the scene. A few barrels of hay were laid out in the fields. At 11:15 I had one more mile to Welcombe Mouth. My new revised guess for an arrival time was no later than 11:40.

With a steep, thus slow, descent to Welcombe Mouth I arrived 11:45. From above I saw the path leading me down, a car park with four cars parked, and a beach that was a combination of sand and rocks that led to parallel rows of rocks leading to the seas that I have seen all day today. My arrival time was not too far off my last guess, only by five minutes. I was welcomed into Welcombe Mouth by a few stony steps to cross over a small stream. I wanted to find a shady spot to sit and rest and eat, and of course there were none. Since there was that car park here though, I decided to use the shade that a car was making. I got all comfortable, took my shoes and socks off, and got ready to eat something, sitting next to a car.

I checked my water supply to which I had plenty left. Surprisingly, I had only drunk a liter and a half. I added some of the extra water from the bottles into the bladder, and I still had about three full liters to get me though the last few miles.

Of course, while I had all my stuff spread out, in the middle of eating, the people of the car that I was sitting next to and using the shade of shows up and wants to leave. Of course. Oh my. I need to move all my stuff. I must have looked a bit worn out and ragged as they ask me if I was ok. "Yes, I am, thank you." Thinking to myself that I was also quite comfortable using the shade of your car until you two showed up.

I moved my belongings though so that they could drive away. Then it was time for me to move on anyway. Since I had plenty of water, and my guess and desire was to get to Morwenstow by 2:00, after relocating to a different car with its shade, I packed myself up and started walking again at 12:10, looking behind me to make sure I left nothing behind. I knew I had many ascents and descents ahead of me. I had a clean pair of socks on, and I saw another woman to go ahead of me up the trail. I reached the top of the first hill right out of the car park in ten minutes time. As I passed the woman that had just gone up ahead of me, I asked if I could pass her please. She said, "Sure you are younger and fitter than I am." Younger? I think to myself, well not bad for 50, huh! Fitter? Thanks for the compliment!

I looked back at Welcombe Mouth, seeing its beach, the car park, the line of the SWCP winding its way down the hillside I had descended earlier, the green hillsides going inland, and a few buildings sitting up the valley.

By 12:30 I descended into Marsland Mount. From above as I looked down into this valley, another rocky beach was in view, as was the line of the SWCP going up the hillside that I would be ascending in a short while. This was a much easier descent to Marsland Mount than the one to Welcombe Mouth. The one into Welcombe Mouth was actually the toughest descent I have done thus far on the entire SWCP because it was steep, very small rocks and pebbles made it slippery, and the path was quite close to some ledges. I went very, very, very slow.

I also passed into Cornwall, from Devon, during the Marsland Mount descent, greeted by a sign that read, "Cornwall Kernow," a new county on my SWCP walk! My third county, my 17th day, my 115th mile! Kernow is Cornwall in the Cornish language, which I believe a branch of the Celtic language. I will be walking the SWCP around the entire county of Cornwall, starting today.

Another ascent took me about eleven minutes to Marsland Cliff. I looked back again, seeing where I had come from including the path of the descent, and the amazing coastline. I was sweating. I drank plenty of water. Another descent, which included 135 steps, into yet another valley, Litter Mouth. Then yet another ascent to the top of Cornakey Cliff! It was almost 1:00. On my way up, I stopped and took a couple of breathers. I spotted the woman that I passed coming down the other side of the valley. I was hoping this was my last climb. I saw buildings off in the distance that I was hoping were Morwenstow. It was hot.

I walked on a flat area, but just read in my booklet that there were two more, yes two more, ascents and descents, to which I say out loud, "What! On a hot day like today. What were they thinking?" I think that makes five total ascents and descents since my break in the shade of the car at Welcombe Mouth! They were not small ascents and descents either. Now I'm not really complaining, but honestly if it wasn't for the heat, they would be much more tolerable. It was hot! (I know I have said that countless times yesterday and today, but it was true.)

The next descent was down a grassy field and was at least nice and gentle, however the ascent after that was short, but steep. It took me three minutes to go up that ascent, definitely steep, but short. I looked behind me at the obvious large white ball way in the distance near Hartland Point that I walked by yesterday. Wow, I was there! Amazing.

Then I was pretty sure I spotted the church tower in Morwenstow. However, I had yet one more descent and ascent. The descent was another very steep one with very small rocks which I took super slow and really took my time. I was tired and those very small rocks can be tricky and slippery. With one more ascent to go, it was 1:45. I might just make my 2:00 guess for my arrival time in Morwenstow after all.

After the last climb, I was done. Cooked. Fried. Baked. Done. Enough. Way too hot. I began to think of making tomorrow's walk shorter, as it was still supposed to be a scorcher. I looked back once more to see the steep hillside I had descended, the line of the path again winding its way down nestled in between the greenery, the cliffs leading to the amazingly blue and turquoise waters. I loved how the abundant sun of the day made the waters so rich in color. The sky had some very thin white clouds.

What refreshed me right away though was at the top of my last climb for the day, I was greeted by a nice older gentleman from Yorkshire on holiday for a week with his wife. He was my guardian angel at the moment. I first double checked with him that I was in Morwenstow. Yes. He said I looked quite red and asked if I was ok. I told him I felt fine, other than tired and hot. He was on his way back to the car where his wife was waiting so we walked together the last little bit into my destination for the day. I was actually really glad for the company at the moment and the short chat we had. We talked about my walk, the big businesses in the Seattle area, what I think of English food, and being a vegetarian. There might have been another topic or two, but I can't remember - I was tired and hot.

I was also glad to be walking with him because he knew the exact way into the village, and we had to pass right in between a couple of cows, one with his back to us. I thought one of the rules was that you are not supposed to walk in between them, and even wondered about walking near one with his back towards us. This man just walked right on through without a care in the world, so I stuck close by him. It was exactly 2:00, my guess and desired arrival time when I said goodbye to this nice gentleman from Yorkshire. He told me where that was, but I can't remember. I'll have to look on a map.

I wanted to go into the church first in Morwenstow, the Parish Church of St. Morwenna and St. John the Baptist, eat second, and then go to my taxi waiting area by 3:00. That was partly why I wanted to arrive in Morwenstow by 2:00 – to give me enough church and food time before my ride back to the Hartland Quay Hotel where I would be staying one more night. Although first thing first, change into my cushy flip flops. I was grateful to be in the cool comfort of the church after five hot hours. While in the church I cooled down, quietly regrouped myself, and said my usual prayers, with extra thankfulness for arriving alright.

Restored in the 1850s, "Morwenstow Church is probably best-known for its links with the 19th century cleric, poet and eccentric, the Rev. Robert Stephen Hawker, Vicar from 1834 to 1875. A short stroll out to the cliffs and then south along the Coast Path takes one to 'Hawker's Hut' – the driftwood hut where the Rev. Hawker wrote sermons and poetry and contemplated the sea." I should be walking by Hawker's Hut tomorrow.

After my church time, of course I was hungry and went into the little tea room shop in Morwenstow which I was looking forward to all day having read about it, the Rectory Farm Tea Rooms. Per their brochure, "Built in the 13th century the house is full of character, antique furnishing, slate floors, open fires and original oak beams salvaged from the many shipwrecks along the coastline." I had a bowl of leek and potato soup. I know, why eat something hot when it was hot outside? I sat inside. The soup came with a cheese scone which I saved for later. The soup was really good and hit the spot. I had talked with one man working there who kept calling me "love." I described how far I had come and how hot and tired I was, and he said, "Oh yes, you are "knackered." Ha, I chuckled to myself, a new British word. Yes, I was felt "knackered." (Tired out, worn out.)

The German couple that was walking to Bude all in one day was in the tea room at the same time I was. They said they did a bunch of road walking to get to Morwenstow rather than taking the SWCP. I don't blame them since they have another eight miles to go today. In the heat. I wished them well, and then I walked a short five minute walk to the pub in the village of Morwenstow to meet my pre-arranged taxi at 3:00. The nice woman of the pub, which was also a B&B, and I chatted for a moment as I waited for the taxi. Actually, "Morwenstow is the first (or last) village you reach along the Cornish part of the SWCP," since earlier today I went from the county of Devon into the county of Cornwall.

The taxi arrived exactly on time. During the half-hour ride back to Hartland Quay, I didn't talk much. Although, when the subject of my solo walk came up, he commented that I was a "brave lady." Hmmm, that word again. Well, maybe I am! Especially for walking two days in a row in this heat.

I actually had the taxi driver to drop me off at the church in Hartland, the one I saw yesterday as I approached Hartland Quay, the Parish Church of St. Nectan. It would mean about a twenty minute walk down the road to the Hartland Quay Hotel, as it was a mile up the road, but after rest and food, I was surprisingly alright with that walk. In my cushy flip flops. I also appreciated another church to go into. From this church, I sent an email to Scott, and down the road as I walked to the hotel, I called my Mom and left her a voice message. This was the spot I got mobile reception at yesterday. From this church, I bought a cute little cookbook called "Hartland Cooks," filled with international recipes and adorable little drawings of some of the food. Just like the soap book, I probably will never use it, but they both will make great souvenirs and memories.

It was just after 4:00 when I got back to the hotel. Tonight was one of those nights that I actually watched TV for an extended amount of time as I continued to rest.

By the way, I realized that yesterday, I passed the 105th mile mark at one point, one-sixth of the way done on the SWCP! Five-sixths to go!

In looking ahead for tomorrow since it was forecasted to be yet another hot day, I made a great decision. I just did not feel like I wanted another long walk in this heat again. Therefore, I will have a pre-arranged taxi take me an extra four miles past Morwenstow (thus missing Hawker's Hut). According to the booklet, the first four miles are labeled as "strenuous." The last four are "moderate to easy." I'll just do the last four. It means that I won't quite walk the entire 630 miles, but with the heat, I just did not want to be knackered again for a third day in a row.

I forgot to mention yesterday that I received a package that was delivered to me at the Hartland Quay Hotel. It was the lanyard from the SWCP Facebook Group. I decided to hook its hook onto my waterproof map cover case. I put my guidebook and booklets in there each day, and when not in use, the case sits in the back pocket of my rucksack. Therefore I could hang the lanyard out of that back pocket. I hope that then someone coming from behind me would see it, or once they passed me, if they turned around, they would see the lanyard. Perhaps I should have worn in on my front somehow, like around my neck, but with my camera and the strap for my sunglasses already there, I didn't want the lanyard around my neck as well. The lanyard is a great form of identification, and I appreciated that Lucy shipped it to me so that I would get it when I arrived in Hartland Quay yesterday. I hope I get recognized!

DAY 17 STATS: 8 MILES. 5 HOURS. EXTRA MILE FROM CHURCH. PURPLE SHOES AND FLIP FLOPS. PUB IN MORWENSTOW IS "THE BUSH INN." Information on church in Morwenstow and Rev. Hawker from morwenstowchurch.wordpress.com/caledonia and from the booklet.

MORWENSTOW TO DUCKPOOL VIA TAXI. WALK DUCKPOOL TO BUDE TO WIDEMOUTH BAY – Wednesday, 21 June 2017

"Today will be hot and humid again with widespread warm sunshine. Make the most of it: the longest day of the year will be the last day of hot weather for the moment." 81F/27C for the area of the SWCP I was in! - BBC Weather Forecast.

I also saw a headline from BBC News that said, "Hottest June day since summer of 1976 in heat wave. The UK is basking in its hottest June day in 41 years."

See – Didn't I tell you the past several days it has been HOT!?! And I guess that today will be the hottest! Oh, and I was nine years old during the last heat wave.

My taxi ride today was originally going to be back to Morwenstow this morning, but I decided last night on starting out at "Duckpool" instead which would cut out four miles with several ascents and descents, especially with the continuing heat. This taxi ride would be a bit expensive, but not only would it be worth it, paying for some taxis was all part of my original plan anyway so that I could stay in a bed and breakfast more than one night in a row so that I wouldn't need to unpack and repack daily. I may have already mentioned this tidbit, but I thought I would mention it again as today's taxi would be a pricey £35/$44.

Last night while I ate dinner in the pub of the hotel, a nice couple started chatting with me about my walk. He said they noticed me walking back from the church in Hartland. They kept seeing me last night drinking lots of water, with salt. Not only did I drink water with salt at dinner, I also came back down a bit later to put some water and salt in my water bottles so that I could drink them before I went to sleep. This couple told me that yesterday they swam in the waters by the hotel. That sounded very refreshing on such a hot day. I was wishing I had packed a bathing suit.

This morning as I was waiting for the taxi, the couple actually kindly offered me a ride to Duckpool if the taxi did not show up. That was very kind. The taxi lady did show up fifteen minutes later than originally planned. She said she was stuck in "traffic" in the village of Hartland, which turned out that she was stuck behind a garbage truck. Or maybe they are called rubbish trucks here.

Turns out, getting to Duckpool was a bit of an extra drive, thus the big expense. I was kind of glad that the taxi was taking me, not the couple, as I would have felt bad as we had to zigzag and wind ourselves through several narrow country roads. The taxi lady used her GPS on her mobile phone to help us navigate the way. I laughed out loud when the voice on her GPS had an English accent. As my mobile phone has an American accent, even in England. At one point, we took a wrong turn down the road leading to a farm, but the taxi lady figured it out. It took us 45 minutes to get to Duckpool. I am finding it fun to be driven in those narrow country roads, the ones that are only single lane, so if two cars meet each other face to face, one of them needs to back up to a pull-out spot, as there are convenient pull-out spots along these roads. People seem to cooperate when this happens. Someone kindly backs up to a pull-out spot, and as the other passes by, they thank each other usually with a wave.

There were actually a few moments as I started my walk this morning that I felt sad and felt like crying that I missed four miles today. This means that I will not have walked (or biked) the entire 630 miles. This is on top of the couple of miles I missed back in Braunton. I guess that this is part of the territory though that comes along with walking the entire 630 miles of the SWCP at once – sometimes not walking in order to stay healthy and safe. I hope that I don't have to miss any other sections for any other reason, but if I do, then I will need to accept those missed miles as well, as much as I may still feel my sadness.

It was already quite hot when we arrived in Duckpool, to which I never did see any ducks, even though there is a duck pool there. I looked up at the descent that I would have had to come down probably late morning/early afternoon today to get to Duckpool if I had started my walk in Morwenstow, and yes it was quite long and steep, so that made me feel a bit better about my decision. I started my first uphill climb of today's walk which was actually not too steep. I had views looking back on the beach at Duckpool which already had people swimming and their shade tents and umbrellas up. The tide must have been out, since the rocky and sandy beach was long and leading out to the waters. Once again, the hillsides were green, the seas were turquoise and deep blue, and the skies were blue with a bit of white. I passed by a flock of sheep that were very close to the path.

I immediately started to sip water. Next was a gentle descent down a grassy valley with a great view of a long sandy beach ahead, appropriately named Sandy Mouth Beach. This was followed by walking on some grassy flat areas. The mix of greens of the hills, the blues of the waters and sky, the tans of the sand and the path, and the browns of the rocks were truly breathtaking looking in any and all directions. A few purple foxglove and yellow wildflowers added even more color to the beauty.

I had three liters of water with me today, plus there would be at least one café stop in my four miles to Bude. Turned out there were two café stops. I saw the long sandy beach of Sandy Mouth Beach again with the larger town of Bude in the distance. I ascended a hill. Then I had a gentle downhill slope followed by another gentle grassy uphill slope, and another gentle downhill slope onto a flat grassy area at Sandy Mouth Beach itself. Or something like that. I stopped at the café in Sandy Mouth for a "blueberry super food smoothie" in a bottle. It was very refreshing on this warm day. The beach was busy.

I was kind of in a meditative state of mind as I continued my walk on a flat grassy stretch on top of a hillside overlooking the long Sandy Mouth Beach. I listened to the waves crash on the sand. There were people sitting in all kinds of nooks and crannies on the beach or near rocks. People were enjoying the water, the sand, and the sun. I walked slower today knowing that I only had four miles of walking compared to the eight and ten miles of the previous days, and enjoyed the slow pace. Another stretch of the beach appeared and this time I saw snorkelers in the water, and people bathing in the hot sun. It even looked like there were people out for a Sunday stroll on the SWCP, which was odd because it was Wednesday. Not only was it Wednesday, it was also June 21st, the summer solstice, the longest day of the year, and the hottest June day! I should have brought a bathing suit.

I walked on the flat grassy top of the hillsides continuing with the amazing scenery. Looking out towards the water, rows of brown rocks jutted out onto sandy beaches leading the eyes out to the waters and the horizon beyond. Inland the rolling hills were covered with farmland of various shades of green, each field separated from the other by an outline of darker green trees. The scenery was amazing.

There was just one more short decent via some steps and a short ascent when I approached a sign saying one mile to Bude. I reached the entrance to Crooklets Beach. I smelled the coconut oil of suntan lotion. I stopped at another café to get another smoothie. The heat made it seem like a smoothie kind-of-day. This one seemed a bit fresher served in a glass, although I never heard a blender going, so my bet is it was a frozen mix of some sort. Anyway I got the "green reviver" smoothie with kale, lemongrass, banana, and mango. Oh, and I also got a scoop of "chocolate indulgence" ice cream. The heat made it seem like an ice cream kind-of-day.

The next part of the walk was on a concrete path by the beaches. I passed by a few rows of those colorful beach huts – yellow, red, blue, green, yellow, red, blue, green, the pattern repeated. People on the beach had their colorful umbrellas open as shade from the sun. There was a large outdoor swimming pool right below where I was walking that was literally right by the seas, the Bude Sea Pool, which is under water when tide comes in. At the moment the tide was low so people were swimming in the pool. "Bude Sea Pool was built in the 1930s to provide a safe environment for swimming for the people of Bude. This semi-natural pool, measuring 91m long by 45m wide, was created under the curve of the cliffs in a conservation area. It provides the unique experience of being in or on the sea, close to the ferocity of the Atlantic Ocean, but sheltered from its extreme effects. The water temperature varies from around 11C [52F] in April through to 18C [64F] in August and September. [Not chlorinated], Bude Sea Pool is filled by the tides with the water straight from the Atlantic Ocean, so it's much the same as the salty sea water in the bay." I should have brought a bathing suit.

There was more sandy beach below as I continued walking, more people, more shady tents and umbrellas, and more beach huts. I listened to the sounds of the waves. It was now time to walk the rest of my walk in my flip-flops since I was not very far from my B&B in Bude. I arrived at the Life's A Beach café about three hours after my start for the day. That was a slow four miles. I used my GPS to find my bed and breakfast. I followed the GPS through a busy shopping street in Bude, which I later figured out the area is called The Strand. I passed by two pharmacies and two outdoor stores but at the moment I didn't need anything from either of those places.

I arrived at my Guest House B&B and I found out that the German couple who walked all the way here yesterday stayed here yesterday, as the woman of the B&B told me about people who walked all the way from Hartland Quay. Who else could it be? Therefore, the couple made it all the way in the heat, which was good to know.

The B&B proprietors showed me to the cutest little room ever. It was tiny, but adorable. The bed was in a small alcove under a window, with a TV by your feet. There was a little closet, a little dresser with tea items on it, and a little chair. The toilet and sink were in their own little separate bathroom. The shower/bath tub - well it was not enclosed like showers/bath tubs should be, but part of the main room. You don't stand to take a shower, as you would hit your head on the slanted ceiling. Instead, you sit to shower. An interesting concept I have never seen.

As I was walking the last mile or so, I came up with a brilliant plan for the afternoon. Even though it was still hot out, I had a lot of time, so I decided to walk some more today – about three miles to Widemouth Bay, a relatively flat part of the path, and take a bus back to Bude. That would actually make my walk tomorrow about seven miles instead of ten. The forecast for tomorrow was going to be cooler. Yes, I know that these three miles is about equal to the four miles that I missed this morning, but it would be flatter and a bit shorter than this morning would have been, and the decision from this morning had been made, so now I move on with my new decision.

It took me about fifteen minutes to walk from a café in Bude, where I had lunch of a brie and cranberry sauce panini to walk past a church, a fire station, over a canal, and to find the sign that said three and a half miles to Widemouth Bay, although I would only be walking to the closer end of the Bay at three miles. It was now 3:30 and my goal was to be at the Bay by 4:30.

My plan worked well. It took me an hour to walk to Widemouth Bay. It was quite flat, with many grassy paths and dirt paths along the cliff top. I passed by an octagonal shaped lookout. I passed by large rolls of hay. The views of the seas remained to my right the entire hour. I listened to some music on my mobile just about all the way, as I was able get mobile reception, putting the phone on speaker mode so I didn't need to use earbuds. With the music I actually danced a bit as I walked. If anyone saw me, I didn't care.

When I arrived at the beginning of the beach in Widemouth Bay, I asked an ice cream place on the beach where to get the bus back. "Just pretty much right there up on the road," she told me. I had a small "orange chocolate" ice cream. Ummm, yes, that was two ice creams today. The heat made it seem like an ice cream kind-of-day. I took a photo of my ice cream next to an acorn symbol.

The bus was scheduled to arrive at 5:09. It was 4:55. Good timing. I asked a guy at the surf shop next to the bus area where exactly I should stand, and which side of the road I should stand on. He showed me, and then he warned me that this is "Cornish time" meaning that the bus might run a few minutes late. It showed up only about seven minutes late. Not too bad, and the ride took less than ten minutes back to Bude. By 5:30 I was wandering the streets of Bude looking for some food to take away that I could eat for dinner in my cute adorable little room.

I did a couple of Facebook posts to catch my family, friends, and fellow SWCP Facebook Group up on the progress I have made the last three-out-of-four hot days. I even mentioned my taxi ride skipping the four miles. Some of the encouraging comments I received from the group included, "Good going especially in the heat." "Some stunning pictures, Debby." "Well done, Debby. Hartland Quay to Morwenstow is a very big walk in these conditions." "Respect!" "Well done, Debby. Photos are brilliant." And, "Well done." I guess I should not feel that bad about missing the four miles with the heat.

I did some typing to catch up on writing. During my video call with Scott, we told each other that we miss each other, and he reminded me that "love is the most important" which was part of our wedding vows. Awwww. I did a few other things on my "evening to do" list like backup pictures, and went to bed late actually at 11:00.

DAY 18 STATS: 11 MILES - 4 BY CAR, 7 BY WALKING. 4 HOURS (THREE HOURS FOR FIRST PART, ONE HOUR FOR SECOND PART). ONLY A BIT OF EXTRA MILEAGE TO GET TO THE B&B, SO I WILL SAY A HALF MILE EXTRA. PURPLE SHOES AND A BIT IN FLIP FLOPS. PUBS IN BUDE ARE "THE BRENDON ARMS" AND "KINGS ARMS." PUB IN WIDEMOUTH BAY IS "BAY VIEW INN."Information about the Bude Sea Pool from budeseapool.org.

WIDEMOUTH BAY TO CRACKINGTON HAVEN – WALK AND CAR RIDE – Thursday, 22 June 2017

"Some beautiful paths can't be discovered without getting lost." – Erol Ozan

What a difference a day makes in the weather. Literally almost instantly last night I could feel the temperature drop about twenty degrees down to around 60F/15.5C. It was refreshing with the sky covered in clouds this morning and there was even a cool ocean breeze. I will admit though, that I really do prefer the sun actually, but a 60 to 70 degree sun, rather than an 80 degree sun, to walk in. In any case I was ready to conquer the seven miles for today from Widemouth Bay to Crackington Haven. Or so I thought…

By the way, I found a note that I had written down that it was possible that the temperature on 19 June, when I walked from Clovelly to Hartland Quay, was 77F/25C, and on 20 June, when I walked from Hartland Quay to Morwenstow, it was 86F/30C! Which would make 21 June, when I took a taxi and then walked from Duckpool to

Bude, even hotter! I don't actually remember where I got those temperatures from, and I also don't know if those temperatures were exactly from where I had walked or elsewhere in the UK however. Still, it was hot.

I was going to take a bus back to Widemouth Bay, but as I waited for the bus, seeing that I still had at least a half hour to wait, and based on "Cornish time" that it could be longer, I asked a taxi driver conveniently parked at the bus station how much he would charge for a ride. Only a few pounds/dollars more than the bus, so I took the taxi. What a difference a day, and the weather, makes in the crowds at the beach. It was pretty much deserted this morning at the beach at Widemouth Bay compared to the crowds of people out yesterday. I did a quick video call right there with Scott before starting my walk from near the beach at Widemouth Bay.

The first several miles were beautiful and peaceful. I started walking through sand dunes, up a gentle hill, with views of the beach, down the gentle hill by some steps, and figured that that was my first climb of five potential climbs for the day. Even with the overcast skies today, the tan sandy beach and the brown rocks at the base of the hillsides were refreshing to see, nestled between the tan ledges of the green hillsides and the white waves and blue waters. The waters were a bit lighter blue today probably due to the cloud coverage rather than sun shining upon them. A single person with their dog was on the beach at this end.

The path took me to a road that I walked on for a while. I had a view looking perpendicular over Widemouth Bay and the beach. I wondered if I could have walked on the beach, or at least some of the beach, instead of the sand dunes. I saw the steps that I had climbed down as a line through the greenery. A small soccer field, perhaps from a park or someone's yard, was in the foreground. The walk up the road was actually an uphill climb, so I thought that perhaps this was the second of five potential climbs for the day, and quite possibly the steepest of the five, according to my interpretation of looking at the interactive elevation map on the SWCP Association website. Then it was back to the cliff tops for a short while. Some amazing looking farmland to my left, as the rolling hills were alternating between green patches and brown patches. Perhaps something had just been harvested on the brown patches as those also contained bales of what was possibly hay. On my right, the perpendicular views continued as I looked back on several headlands.

After a somewhat steep descent into Millook Haven, a sign said four and three-quarters miles to my destination for the day, Crackington Haven. I made a guess of my arrival time as 12:30 or 1:00. It was 10:05. That fun guessing game again. Another little bit of walking on the road for a quarter mile, and looking back I could see that steep descent I just did, the tan line of the SWCP through the green hillside, and the buildings of Millook Haven. Apparently, "Millook Haven is one of the most important geological sites on the SWCP. The cliffs are spectacular, with extensive chevron (or zig-zag) folding. Looking north there are some remarkable chevron folds in the bands of sandstone and shale in the cliffs some 300 million years old," according to today's booklet. Even back in Bude, "the rocks and cliffs around Bude are particularly striking. The rocks here are about 300 million years old and made up of the sedimentary rocks sandstone and shale (mud and other minerals)."

The next sign I walked by said four and a half miles to Crackington Haven. I walked on this next path for maybe half mile to a mile, passing by a few horses in a field (I thought of Scott), and some very cute, very fluffy furry brown sheep. That color of sheep was new to me, as I have seen white sheep and black sheep, but not brown sheep! And that was when my day turned around. The good news was I reached my destination an hour ahead of my predicted time. Not because I was fast or anything though. The not-so-good news was that it was because I actually lost the SWCP. And I couldn't find it again. Even though I tried. Heart-breaking. Here's the story.

I really don't know how I lost the SWCP and ended up on a road. I remember walking on a field that turned inland, and I kept walking through this field because I thought it was the SWCP since I did not see any other signs or arrows or acorns pointing me in another direction. I kept walking and walking through the field, and soon I came to a road. A road? That did not seem right. I looked around but I could not find any SWCP signs at all where I was standing. I actually stopped and wondered if missed a sign pointing me in some other direction earlier in the field, but I was really not that sure what happened. All I knew was that I was at a road with no SWCP signs or arrows or acorns. For the first time, I actually felt a bit frazzled at the moment because I felt a bit lost and unsure of where I was and what to do.

What I probably should have done at that moment was go back through the field to see if I could find the point where I somehow got off the SWCP and try to find some sign or arrow or acorn. It was early enough in the day after all. But I didn't want to do that at this point because I did not want to get lost trying to find my way back to where I lost the SWCP, not that I knew where that was exactly anyway. Instead I just kept walking forward. On the road. For a while. For quite a while. However, at least with my "excellent" navigation skills I looked at the map in the booklet and figured out where I probably was at that moment. On the map, I saw a footpath near a farm a bit down the road that could possibly take me back to the SWCP. I found the footpath. The beginning of it anyway. So that was good.

I started on this footpath until all of a sudden it opened up onto a big field with no clear footpath at all in sight. And not just one field, but many fields. I could see the seas way out in the distance, and I said no way am I going to walk through those fields towards the seas with no clear footpath to be seen and risk getting lost in the middle of these big fields. Or risk getting stuck on some field with a herd of cows! I was feeling even more frazzled and lost and unsure, and frustrated. How could this happen to me? Now what should I do? Should I just walk back on the road and go all the way back to that original field to try to find the SWCP?

I walked back to the road from the footpath at least, just as Scott happened to sent me a text message. What?! How did he know to text me just then, at that exact moment? How did he know that I had lost the SWCP? How did he know that I was feeling frazzled, lost, unsure, and frustrated? He has never texted me randomly like this before in the middle of my day. Coincidence or intuition or what, I don't know. Anyway, he was my guardian angel at the moment! He was apparently still awake at 3:00am his time, 11:00am my time, and just thought he would text to say hello, since he obviously really did not know what I was going through.

Instead of texting him back, I called him, a regular phone call, and told him that I had somehow lost the SWCP, and that I didn't want to get lost trying to find it again, and that I didn't want to walk on some footpath on some fields, and that I didn't want to get stuck on some field with a bunch of cows, and that I didn't know if I should walk back on the road to the field to try to find the SWCP again, and that I was feeling frazzled and lost and unsure and frustrated, and what should I do now? Thank goodness I had mobile reception. Thank goodness Scott somehow knew to text me. And thank goodness the weather was not bad so at least my original fear of getting lost in bad weather was not happening.

I kept walking the road while talking to Scott while trying to decide what to do, walking forwards not backwards. I took a deep breath and I realized that I had four options. First option, go back to where I lost the path. I decided that no, it was way too far to backtrack now, and that I might not even remember at this point where the field was that I walked on that led me to the road in the first place. Second option, try a different side footpath to get back to the SWCP. No, I was not going to try that again and risk getting even more lost or possibly coming across a herd of cows. Third option, walk the road all the way to Crackington Haven. That could be a long walk, but it was a good idea since it seemed like the road I had already been walking on would get me there, and it probably would have been similar distance as if I was walking on the SWCP anyway. Fourth option, how about I just hitch a ride into Crackington Haven, which was supposed to be my destination for the day anyway. I was rattling off these options to Scott as I thought of them.

I was actually about to go for the fourth option and knock on a door of a house and ask for a ride when a little red car happened to approach me, with my next guardian angels inside. I waved them down and a nice couple that did not have a British accent rolled down the window. I told them I lost the SWCP and asked them kindly for a ride please to Crackington Haven, if that would be convenient for them. At first he didn't know where that was, but she did. They ate at the pub there last night, she reminded him. I chuckled to myself. They said a ride there would be fine, as they were headed in that direction anyway. I hopped in the car, told Scott what I was doing, got off the phone with Scott, and thanked them for the ride. They were from Spain, on a romantic road trip along the coast of England, going from London to about here. She was originally from the Canary Islands, but now they live in Barcelona. I told them I walked the Camino. I took a deep breath. Another ride in another car?

When we arrived at Crackington Haven I thanked them again very much for the ride. I realized that it would have been a long walk on the road, although it was the correct road that would have taken me there, and although it would have been a similar distance as if I walked the SWCP anyway. I also realized that I missed a few climbs today. It was 11:30. I walked into a café to get something to eat and use their Wi-Fi, since I could not get mobile reception here, to tell Scott that I arrived in Crackington Haven safely. I would not have just jumped in a random car like that back at home. I was glad I had regular mobile reception when he texted me and we talked before. The café did not have Wi-Fi so I went into The Coombe Barton Inn to use their Wi-Fi. Fortunately they had Wi-Fi. I called Scott, who was still awake at 3:30 in the morning his time, to tell him I was alright. I went back to the café to eat something. I took another deep breath and tried to contemplate what just happened to me.

Even at Crackington Haven, "the rocks here are geologically very important. The folded rock strata here was formed some 300 million years ago in the Carboniferous Period. This kind of folded sandstone and shale rock is known as the 'Crackington Formation' and extends along the coast," according to the booklet.

I needed to get a bus or taxi back to Bude since my bed and breakfast was there one more night, which I was going to need to do anyway if I walked here all the way. The woman in the café pointed to the bus stop just across the road. I had about a half hour wait. I took the bus back to Bude. That was easy. It was on time. On my way back to the B&B I saw a "healthy vitamin shop" so I stocked up on fresh nuts and protein-type bars to keep as snacks in my rucksack, since I had eaten most of what I had originally brought with me by now.

I spent some time typing, catching up on yesterday. I went to get something else to eat and to walk a mile to the Bude Haven Church, the Church of St. Michael and All Angels, originally built in 1834, to see the church and do my usual prayers. And to take a deep breath once again. I texted Scott a picture of the church when I was there. The church bells rang 4:00. By this time the skies were blue with a few white clouds. Back at my cute adorable little room, I called Mom, told her about my day, and I spent some more time typing. Later I went out to dinner and back to my room again to finish typing.

I still felt sad and disappointed for missing about four miles today because I lost the SWCP. Maybe I should have gone back through that original field? Maybe I should have tried to walk from Crackington Haven going in the other direction on the SWCP? I had plenty of time and good weather. I don't know what I should have done, or why I did what I did do, or why I didn't do what I didn't do. And now that I also missed the four miles yesterday because of the heat, and the couple of miles in Braunton because I walked on a path that was closed with the obvious big red and white sign and took that car ride instead, I can't say that I have walked the entire SWCP all at once, all in one go. Yes, sad and disappointing. I will admit that I cried to my husband when I was on the phone with him earlier as I was walking the road. My first real cry since I started walking the SWCP.

But now that the day was nearly ended, I have to accept that what happened, happened. At this moment I can't go back, and I must go on. I must walk on. I don't think I have time to try to walk the missed four miles tomorrow because of the walk I already had planned and because of the B&B reservations I have elsewhere. I must accept what happened.

I did discover though that the biggest guardian angel I have had thus far on my adventure is my husband. It was ironic or serendipitous or coincidence or intuition or luck or something that he had no idea what was happening with me at the moment, and yet he texted me out of the blue. Somehow he must have sensed or known that I needed him just at that exact right moment.

DAY 19 STATS: 7 MILES - 3 WALKING AND 4 BY CAR. 2.5 HOURS INCLUDING THE SWCP WALKING, THE ROAD WALKING, AND THE CAR RIDE. ONE EXTRA MILE TO THE CHURCH IN BUDE. PURPLE SHOES. PUB IN CRACKINGTON HAVEN IS "THE COOMBE BARTON INN."

CRACKINGTON HAVEN TO BOSCASTLE – Friday, 23 June 2017

"Please use zig-zag path to prevent erosion." – Sign leading up the hill of Cambeak.

I woke up this morning with a good attitude. I told myself it was going to be a good day - I won't lose the path, I will accept (most) any weather, and I will conquer any hills, both ascents and descents, with grace and ease. I told myself that I would slow down, look, think, read signs, and take my time, after what happened yesterday. At the moment the sun was shining a bit through the clouds when I woke up. I got this!

After breakfast and saying thank you and goodbye to the very nice B&B proprietors at the Guest House in Bude, I walked down to The Strand to catch the bus back to Crackington Haven. I arrived at the bus stop a half hour early, a bit too early, but since this ride was longer I did not want to get a taxi, so I waited for the bus using the time to scroll through Facebook and catch up with family and friends.

With my non-British accent I explained to the bus driver that since I had only been to Crackington Haven once and was not completely familiar with the area, I asked him if he could please let me know when to get off the bus, as I did not want to be forever stuck inside the bus. The bus driver was very nice, and dropped me off without me even needing to ring the bell. I took a few moments to get ready, and I was off. While the booklet said it was 6.8 miles to Boscastle, the SWCP sign said six miles to Boscastle Harbour. I'm going to count it as 6.8. I got this!

As I started walking, there were two people on the beach of Crackington Haven, under the light cloud cover of the moment. With the green rolling hills in front of me, more wonderful rocky beaches below leading out to the blue seas, the cloud cover began to lighten up a bit and some blue skies appeared. The sun peeked out from behind the clouds, casting some light on the green ferns that I walked by.

I knew that there would be several ascents and descents today, one of which would be a large gain in elevation of gradually going from just about sea level to 735 feet. That was about half of one of my training hikes. I would be reaching High Cliff, which at that 735 feet above sea level is "Cornwall's highest coastal point." I got this! However, before that ascent I had a climb up another hill called Cambeak, which was on the easier side because they rerouted the original path that looked like it originally went straight up. Now instead it was a zig-zag path so each zig and each zag was gentler than going straight up. They had a sign saying, "Please use zig-zag path to prevent erosion," so maybe that was the reason for the reroute.

In no time I had reached the top of Cambeak, and after a slight descent, I had more climbing to do to get to the official top of High Cliff. When I reached the top of this second hill, I looked back to see a great view of the zig-zag path going up the hillside I had climbed on Cambeak, the path I had walked on prior to that, including some steps, the green rolling hills, and views back to the beach and buildings of Crackington Haven. The path was definitely scenic, but then there was this wind…

Let me tell you about this wind that lasted on and off, mostly on, throughout the rest of my day. Fortunately, it was not gale force winds, but it wasn't a gentle breeze either. At times it was quite windy, and I actually had to use my poles to steady myself. I didn't feel like the wind would completely blow me over, but it felt better to steady myself with the poles. At least the winds were blowing inwards inland as well, rather than outwards to the seas, so if I did get blown over, I wouldn't get blown over a cliff ledge. I also occasionally walked a bit more inland just to the left of the path when I could so that I was not so close to a ledge just in case. At one point, I did come to a place where I was sheltered from the wind by some tall brush, where I could straighten my hair out. But that didn't last long. I would say that if it wasn't for the wind, it was around 60F/15.5C, partially sunny and partly cloudy today. The winds didn't make it cold, just quite windy. Maybe it was classified as either a "moderate breeze" or a "fresh breeze" or a "strong breeze" according to the Beaufort Wind Scale.

The views thus far have been beautiful. With the light cloud and occasional sun, the ocean waters took on that very deep blue today. There were rocky beaches below, one stretch of which I will see just about most of the day from various angles. First looking ahead to the rocky beaches, then over them from above, and then looking behind on them. Rolling green hill after rolling green hill led to the headlands beyond. The path itself was sometimes a grass path, other times dirt. I spotted today at least two or three people that were ahead of me on the trail today, and at least two behind me.

I walked by a sign that said four miles to Boscastle. Today I actually wore my hiking boots instead of my purple shoes. The guidebook said that there might be some very rocky sections, perhaps shale, or places where it would be quite steep so I figured boots might be better for today. Somehow it seemed like I never found the very rocky sections, the shale, or the quite steep places. Still, boots were actually a good choice for today with all the ascents and descents, including some with steps. I wore the black Keen hiking boots today, the second pair I brought with me to give them a try since I have been wearing the Merrells when wearing boots thus far. I pretty much decided that the Merrells were more comfortable, so I never wore these black Keen boots again. (Note that this is for my feet, and I am not saying anything good or bad about either boot brand, as your feet may differ from mine.)

I took some great photos of all the greens and blues today, my favorite colors. My favorite photo was one was with a few small green trees sitting on the edge of the cliff so that they seemed to be floating. Behind them was a sandy, rocky beach, with some large boulders. White waves led to turquoise and then to deep blue seas, and to a light blue sky. Simply beautiful.

All of the ascents and descents today seemed on the gentler side than some from a few days ago. Perhaps the lack of heat had something to do with this perception as well. I reached the top of the one of the last climbs for the day with a bench on top of the hill overlooking the views below of the deep blue seas, and the last views of the rocky beaches below.

The path then turned into a flat grassy area. I spotted some cows coming up pretty quick, looking like they might be right in my path. So, I started talking to them. Out loud. Like I have done before, and like I remembered the talking-to-the-cows tactic that man did on my way to Bucks Mills several days ago. I told the cows that I was on my way, coming through, and I promised not to get between the mommies and babies, and could they please get back a bit out of my way. Turned out they were behind a wire fence, possibly an electric fence. I guess I didn't need to talk to them after all, but I still enjoyed the conversation. I understood why the electric fence was there. The owner of the cows would not want them wandering off because they might fall off the cliff ledge if they walked further out. I was careful not to touch the electric fence.

As I made a small descent, and then onto some flat walking, the cawing of a flock of seagulls playing on the rock ledges caught my ear. I also tuned into listening to the waves crashing. I saw a couple of people still behind me. Two horses were eating grass on the side of the cliff that was quite close to the ledge. I guess the horses knew not to wander off too far. The horses made me think of Scott again.

Soon I reached Fire Beacon Point and Beeny Cliff. Because of the moderate or fresh or strong breezy wind, I took the optional inland route instead of the main route of about the same distance since I did not want to be that close to the cliff ledge. There were four other horses I saw on this optional route, I believe a different breed than the other two. These four were on the small side for horses, so perhaps they were ponies. I wasn't sure. I thought of Scott again.

The views from this inland route were beautiful – the other path clearly visible beyond in the greenery, the small hillsides and headlands, a few small "rock islands," and a village, probably Boscastle, nestled under a puzzle of farmland. Actually, apparently you could see back to Lundy Island from here as well, but I was not able to today with some of the cloud coverage. I decided, however, that sometime in the future when I come back to England on another trip, one place I would like to visit is Lundy Island. With its three lighthouses, and the island itself being three miles long and a half mile wide, I bet you can do some good walking around Lundy Island. Day trips and overnight trips are possible. I'm going to start a "to-walk" list for some time in the future when I come back to England to include Lundy Island.

Then I had one steeper climb uphill. The booklet said there would be 180, yes 180, steps to climb on this hill. So I counted. As mentioned, counting is something I like to do. They were a bit off in their statistics, however. I counted 181 steps. I actually felt in pretty good shape going up all these steps. I stopped once or twice to check out the views, but was never out of breath. Not bad for 50!

I reached the Boscastle Farm Shop and Café. Three and a half hours from the time I started walking. I probably had a mile left to my destination of Boscastle itself. It was very busy inside the café. I sat outside. In the wind. I ordered a nice spinach and sweet potato frittata. Since I hadn't had any sweets for a few days, I think, I got the double chocolate brownie, which I ate mostly when I got to my B&B later. Note that I also ate a couple of snacks, some nuts and one of my new protein-type bars, during the day today to sustain me till I reached the café.

When I left the café, it was pretty gentle and flat the rest of the way to Boscastle with one more descent into the harbour of Boscastle. What a great harbour! The green hillsides somehow formed their own entrance into the harbour, winding its way inland, arriving at a few manmade built breakwalls. About ten various sized and type boats, mostly fishing boats, motorboats, and a rowboat, were protected by the breakwalls. At this time, the tide was low, so the boats were lying on the ground, but I could tell the tide was coming in. Just beyond the harbour were some buildings of Boscastle, resting in a valley, with farmland above in the distance beyond. Very scenic!

As I walked, I continued to take many photos of the whole harbour scene, including a few with some pink flowers in the foreground, I think an azalea of some sort, and also a photo with artichoke plants, yes artichoke, in the foreground. I stopped at a little blue bench which had the hull of an old row boat around it for decoration, and for shade, to change into my flip flops. It was at this time that I made a note to myself that the Merrell boots I brought were more comfortable than the Keen boots as I took the Keens off. I took a photo of that little blue bench with a blue door next to it, perhaps to include in my windows and doors photography book.

As I made my way to my B&B not far from the harbour at all, only a few minutes, using my GPS and my hand drawn map to get me there, I noticed all kinds of cute little shops. It was a popular place, this village of Boscastle, with many people meandering around. I will say that I think the village of Boscastle itself was cute!

When I arrived at my B&B, I was shown the ins and outs of the B&B, as they all show me, such as where the breakfast area is, the menu, the time for breakfast, up to my room, etc. She asked if it was windy today. Ummm, "Yes," I said. Even though I had my multi-use scarf on my head most of the day, I could tell my hair was quite windblown, and I commented to her that my hair was a mess. She said, "Oh don't worry. Living here my hair is like that all the time. It is 'Cornish Hair' we call it." Hmmm, so I have Cornish Hair. Good to know.

After settling in to my room, including trying to fix my hair, I took a leisurely stroll into the shops and down to the harbour of Boscastle again. In one of the shops I bought a small amethyst stone for myself, costing me only £1.00/$1.35. Amethyst is my birthstone. A bought a heart-shaped polished stone for Scott. In the past, I have bought him heart-shaped polished stones on several of my other travels, so this one will add to the collection. In another shop, I bought a little lighthouse statue that was only about three inches tall and quite cute. In yet another shop, they had some very cute handbags that I thought of getting one for my seven-year old niece, so I texted a picture to my sister of a few choices to ask my niece which one she would like. The one with the little puppy doggie, the one with the elephant, or the one with the owls.

I walked down to near the entrance of the harbour closer to the opening from the seas, and walked along one of the breakwalls. The tide was definitely in now and the boats were floating. It was fun to watch this for a bit - the boats floating on the turquoise waters, with the hillside I walked down behind. It was very picturesque with looking back at the small village from this view point, and the valley it sits in, from the vantage point of the boats. I took a lot of photos from various angles of the boats, the harbour, the village, and the hillsides. I also got a closer look at the entrance to this harbour from the seas itself. Exciting. I had the great idea of video calling with Scott right as I was there so that I could show him this great harbour and great scenery. I got reception very well there on my phone, and was able to share with him where I was at at the moment!

All in all, today was a great day. The only challenge was the wind, but the rest of the weather cooperated. And I did not get lost! I got this!

However, I would like to modify my weather preference from yesterday. Sunny, 60 to 70, and NO wind.

DAY 20 STATS: 6.8 MILES. 4 HOURS OF WALKING, PLUS 45 MINUTE LUNCH BREAK. HALF MILE EXTRA UP AND DOWN THE HARBOUR OF BOSCASTLE A FEW TIMES. BLACK HIKING BOOTS. PUB IN BOSCASTLE IS "COBWEB INN."

TREBARWITH STRAND TO TINTAGEL, THEN BOSCASTLE TO TINTAGEL – Saturday, 24 June 2017

"I tried to catch some fog, but I mist." – Unknown

Today started off on the tough side for me the first forty minutes, but then it turned out quite well, thanks to five guardian angels. I know I keep talking about guardian angels, and I kind of think I made up the term "guardian angels" as I originally defined them as "amazing people, both strangers and friends, who one way or another show up just at the exact right moment that I need something," and I don't know what it all really means, but somehow people do show up for me just at the exactly the right time that I need them. Without even asking. Or text message me just at the right time, like my husband. I am not sure who provides them, or how they get there, but they somehow just show up. Some even literally out of the fog and mist...Here is how it the day unfolded…

It started off with a good breakfast at my B&B in the cute village of Boscastle. I had been eating a lot of eggs again lately, usually scrambled on top of toast. I was getting tired of eating eggs again, and I really wanted something different again. I know the eggs provide good protein, but day after day, they just get to me. Anyway, the people at the B&B in Boscastle made me a "mashed avocado and tomatoes on toast," which mixed with some kind of herbs or something tasted really delicious! I also had a bowl of granola with fresh and dried fruit and yogurt, which is also always lovely. Therefore, my day started off with a great tasty breakfast.

The gentleman of the B&B then kindly drove me to Trebarwith Strand, about seven miles from Boscastle. The plan was to walk "backwards" today back to Boscastle from Trebarwith Strand because I would be staying at this B&B again, and because this morning was a convenient time for the B&B gentleman to drive me there, right after their breakfast serving time ended, rather than pick me up later in the afternoon if I had walked from Boscastle to Trebarwith Strand. The ride was another good start to the day. Walking "backwards" would mean that instead of the seas being on my right side like they have been until today, they would be on my left side. If I could even see the seas today…

There was some light rain on the ride over. The forecast didn't call for heavy rain. In fact, it didn't even call for light rain, so I was a bit surprised, but this is the south west coast of England after all, even in the summer, as

I am learning. I figured rain was bound to happen again, which seems to have not happened for quite a while now actually. In fact, other than perhaps a few odd sprinkles or the bit of rain in Ilfracombe back on the 10th of June, I don't think I have had any major rain since the downpour on the 8th of June as I approached Heddon's Mouth. So wow, over two weeks of relatively dry weather! Sometimes hot, but dry. After I was dropped off, I put on all my rain gear and the pack cover on my rucksack and started walking.

Just as I started walking the rain stopped (of course, as I had put on all the rain gear – see rain gear actually works!), but I noticed right away it was foggy. At least it wasn't raining or windy, but it was foggy. Another type of weather that I had not yet encountered on my walk of twenty days thus far, my approximate 141 miles to this point, my about 82 hours of walking, my extra approximate 24 miles, and only a few days away from being one quarter of the mileage done with the SWCP. To recap the weather, I have had rain and gale force winds, then caught in a downpour, then excessive heat, and then some strong winds. And now fog! I said I out loud to whomever was listening, may I just please, and I would really appreciate, consistently having days with sunshine, about 60 to 70F/15.5 to 21C, no rain, no wind, no excessive heat, and now no fog.

I walked along fine for about 40 minutes. It was only two and a quarter miles to the village of Tintagel on my way to Boscastle. I had some views at first near sea level – a small sandy beach near Trebarwith Strand with white rolling waves, turquoise water, and a large lone island-type rock just off the coast. Ahead I could see more white rolling waves, more turquoise waters, and the bottom half of the rolling green hills. The top half was covered in fog. I was low enough in elevation at the start that I wasn't in the fog yet. The continuing sandy and rocky beach and turquoise waters, and that large lone rock, were in my view to my left side.

But as I climbed a slight uphill, I started becoming surrounded by the fog. At first it was a light fog, and even in the fog, I was able to follow the signs and arrows and acorns. The terrain flattened out. I figured it would take me an hour to get to Tintagel. I passed a sign that said I had one and a quarter miles to Tintagel after about twenty minutes. I could still see below the hilltop that I was on down to the seas, with some white waves and just the immediate cliffs near me. Beyond that I could see nothing. I reached a large grassy area, still clearly marked and I could see the path clearly. I looked back (well that would have been forward if I was walking forward), and saw one more view of the white waves, the immediate cliffs, and then I saw nothing, nothing but fog.

The fog became even thicker, kind of like that pea soup variety, and I started to not like the feeling I was getting. I couldn't see much. I decided right then and there that I would rather have the 80F/26.5C degree weather back, even some wind, over the fog. I have never really walked in fog before in all my hikes and travels that I can recall. I kept walking a little more. Until I got to a point where I couldn't find the next SWCP sign. I ended up on a road (another road?!), but with no sign there and not being able to see out too far in the distance, I did not know if I should go straight forward to a small path ahead, or left on the road, or right on the road. I did not feel like trying to figure it out in the fog and get lost and really turned around and have no idea where I was, again. I didn't quite panic though, but I was definitely a bit upset. Even looking at the booklet and guidebook did not seem to help me at this moment. Being lost in the fog by myself was not my idea of fun. Oh my, that fear – getting lost in the bad weather. One of the first times I was really not having fun on my adventure. Yes, I had rain and downpours and heat, and even lost the path a couple of days ago, and preferred that those scenarios never happened, but this was the first time I said to myself that this fog was not fun.

I decided to "give up," and just to go back to Trebarwith Strand, the place I started, and call it a day. It would be easy enough for me to walk back since I knew it was well sign posted to that point, and I could remember where I had come from. I could get a taxi to Tintagel, so I could at least explore the village that I would have been walking to. I started walking backwards from my backwards walk, which would have been forwards, and by now because of the fog and even some wet mist by now, the ground, which was mostly grass, was wet, and my purple shoes were getting wet. I wore my purple shoes today because the forecast did not tell me about the weather I was currently experiencing. The wet shoes though didn't bother me much because I knew I was carrying extra socks as I always have been, both because of my blister theory of carrying extra socks to change into, and because once my husband suggested I bring extra extra socks to change into in case my purple shoes happen to get wet. He is so wise.

I started walking briskly back, and then they appeared. Out of the fog and wet mist after only about five or ten minutes. My first three guardian angels of the day. Literally out of the fog and wet mist. I immediately felt myself relax. Completely relax. I asked these three people if they were heading to Tintagel, and if so could I please walk with them. They said yes and yes. Wow. Where did they come from? At the right place at the right time. So whoever provided them for me at that moment, I was really appreciative. So I turned back around to walk backwards once again towards Tintagel, this time with my three guardian angels in the fog.

Of course we all began to chat. I explained my fog story of the last 40 minutes. They said they kind of knew the way to Tintagel, as they walked there a couple years ago. They live about an hour north of London, two women, and a man. We arrived at the road where I couldn't find the sign, and sure enough we had to walk on the road for a few yards to the left, and there was a sign. I probably could have figured it out, but I did not want to risk it moments ago by myself. It was so calming for me to walk with these people at this time. It was still foggy and a bit misty, but after this point it was pretty easy to follow the path and see the signs.

As we walked, the four of us chatted more mostly about my SWCP walk, and a few other topics I can't recall. About twenty minutes later we could see Tintagel off to the right. We were in the village moments later. I guess I had walked two-thirds of the way from Trebarwith Strand to Tintagel by myself, I realized. And my guess of about an hour total walking to Tintagel was about right. I offered to buy them tea or cream tea as a thank you, but they were fine without either. I thanked them very much, and went into the first café I saw to dry off, to eat, and to regroup myself. Because of the wet mist while walking, and the ground being wet, and my purple shoes getting wet, and my rain gear getting wet, I just wanted to dry off. I had a good vegetable and goat cheese panini at the café.

After my snack/lunch/brunch, I went next door to the Toy Museum I had read about online last night as I researched things to do in Tintagel. It was cute, and had so many toys to look at. Dolls, toy cars and trucks, doll houses, toys from the 1920s to the 1980s were on display. Vintage and nostalgic. There was also a Post Office Museum in the village of Tintagel, and the big attraction of the Tintagel Castle, but first I needed to decide my next plan of action. There was now a bit of rain, and it still seemed foggy, and I did not want to walk by myself back to Boscastle in the fog. I was hoping the fog would lift, but by over an hour later, it wasn't. It was about 12:15 in the early afternoon.

I decided to just go back to Boscastle, but not by walking. Maybe by then, or soon thereafter, the fog would lift, and I could at least walk in the "forward" direction from Boscastle towards Tintagel. It actually did seem a bit odd to me to walk "backwards" this morning, with the seas on my left side, even though I couldn't quite see them. I realized that I was so used to walking with the seas on my right that I actually prefer to walk in my "forwards" direction.

I wanted to find the bus stop to find a time table to catch a bus back to Boscastle, but wasn't quite sure where it was, so I went to the Visitor Center and asked the ladies there about a bus. The bus stop was right across the street from the Visitor Center, but I just missed the closest bus by about ten minutes. The next one wouldn't be for two hours. The ladies gave me business cards for a couple of taxis, so I called. Tony, the second one I called answered, and in ten minutes he arrived to take me back to Boscastle.

Tony was born in Boscastle, and he said he would probably live there the rest of his life. He used to be a farmer, he remembers the Boscastle flood of 2004, and now he drives his taxi. "Boscastle was propelled into the news in 2004 when a dramatic flash flood destroyed livelihoods and property – miraculously no-one was killed in the devastating summer storm. Boscastle's community rallied [and was rebuilt] after a multi-million pound regeneration project." In the village of Boscastle, I saw a little sign on a wall saying, "Flood Level 16/8/2004." It was higher than the top of a door. (Note that the quote about the Boscastle Flood was from a "Boscastle Village Map, A Short History," an information brochure that I picked up.)

Anyway, I told Tony my fog story, and that I might try to walk from Boscastle to Tintagel, the four and a half miles, and if I needed a ride again later, I would call him, since my B&B was in Boscastle. After I was dropped off in Boscastle, I decided to first buy my niece the handbag I asked my sister about yesterday. At 2:00 in the morning my time, which was 6:00pm my sister's time the day before, I received a text message saying "doggie please." My sister apparently did not remember about the time difference. So I bought my niece the handbag with the little puppy doggie. Cute! I sat on a bench and changed my wet socks. Somehow the purple shoes did not feel wet inside, and they weren't "flooded" or anything, just the top of the toe area was damp.

As I sat there, I decided to give it a go. To walk to Tintagel and see what happens. It seemed like the weather was improving and not foggy and less misty. I could start and always turn around at any point if it became too foggy again. I was closer to "home" now rather than seven miles away. I started out near the Boscastle Harbour. So far so good. I turned a corner to the left and saw several people coming down a hillside, and two people going up the hillside. Two people going up? Really? That means someone else might be on the SWCP going towards Tintagel. I wanted to find out. For some reason, I felt like walking with people today.

I sped up the hill to catch up with them. It wasn't easy, but fortunately they weren't going very fast. Fortunately, it was not a big long steep hill, and they stopped for a moment anyway to take a photo or something. I caught up to them moments later. Before they kept walking again, I called out to them. "Hello. Hello." Fortunately they heard me. Two gentlemen. I just plain out asked them if they were walking to Tintagel. Yes, they were. Then I explained my fog story of the morning and just plain out asked them if they wouldn't mind me tagging along with them to Tintagel in my forwards direction in case the fog appeared again. Well, they said yes! No hesitation. It was great to hear that, and I felt comfortable with them knowing that if the fog appeared again, we could all get "lost" together. Part of me was a bit concerned actually that I may not have been able to walk the four and a half miles to Tintagel and add that to my "not walked" list, but that turned out to not be the case.

When they started talking back to me, guess what? They sounded like me! No British accent. No other "accent." Ironic or what, I don't know. We started walking right away so as to not delay, and not soon thereafter, I asked where they were from. I think they said New Hampshire originally and one now lives in Ohio. Ohio, yeah, I was born there, but I didn't tell them that. They asked where I live, and mentioned the Seattle area. They were Jim and Henry, father and son, and my favorite guardian angels so far on my trip. (Well, except for my husband!) I felt like we immediately bonded.

The weather actually held out for us most of the time. No fog, which was great, with occasional light rain showers. It was even on the warm side. I still had my rain gear on, and at one point took off the rain pants because it did stop raining and I was getting warm, but later had to put the rain pants back on for another light rain shower, and kept them on the rest of the time. And good thing, as there were more occasional light rain showers, even as we entered Tintagel two hours later.

It was 1:15 when I started walking with them. I forgot to mention that I emailed Scott three times what I thought would be my plan, when I started walking, and then again that I found these two men to walk with. I had mobile reception during the first half mile. That way Scott would know that I was alright. Jim and Henry are walking the entire SWCP together. Father and son. I thought that was fantastic. I couldn't quite get Henry's age, but I believe he was still in his later teen years. They were taking eight weeks to walk the SWCP, and mostly camping. They didn't look like they were carrying much, but they had a tent with them.

At one point they asked if I had done any other long distance walks. Why, yes, in fact, I have. The Camino Francés in Spain. Them too! I felt like we bonded again. They did the Camino walk together a couple years before I did mine. We reminisced about that walk, about completing it, and about the "botafumeiro" in the Cathedral of Santiago de Compostela at the end of our walks, where during the noon mass celebrating the completion of the walk, they swing an incense burner from the ceiling of the cathedral across the cathedral filling up the air with smoke and the smell of incense. It is a tradition from days gone by, for purification of the air, and perhaps even the soul, when showers were few, and when pilgrims had just walked hundreds and hundreds of miles. I also mentioned to Jim and Henry the story of my walking from Finisterre to Muxía, and how from that I really fell in love with walking by the coast and the ocean, and thus found the SWCP. We even talked about the movie, "The Way," which I liked and Jim liked, too. I suppose if there was one other guy with us just now, we could be like the characters in the movie "The Way." The South West Coast Path Way! Well, not quite, but the thought was fun for a moment.

But wait, I forgot to mention the cows. At one point we saw them from above and they seemed quite innocent in the grassy field below. But not soon after we started walking together, the big group of them was pretty much right next to the path once we got down to them. Some were on one side of the path, some were on the other side. We had to walk right through them. No choice. No room to go around them on either side. We were breaking one of the cow rules. I am not sure what happened but we caused some of the cows to all start to walking quite briskly, then after we passed them all, one of them started running back seemingly upset. Needless to say, we kept going. I think if I had encountered this group of cows by myself probably only three-quarters of a mile from Boscastle, I would have definitely turned around. Or who knows, maybe a guardian angel would have appeared. But I was with these two guardian angels for this cow encounter, and we were all alright.

The three of us had some views along "the way" to Tintagel. Several small headlands sticking out into the water, some more large island-type rocks out in the water, a couple of beaches, one beach even with a group of surfers, views of other headlands and green grassy hillsides, a view of a camping area filled with camper vans, and eventually Tintagel. The waters now appeared more blue than turquoise. The skies were brighter. There were some low clouds, which I suppose could have been fog, but were "way" out in the distance. There were a few descents and ascents in and out of valleys, but nothing difficult or long or steep at all, even with some having steps. Lots of flat walking actually. Jim's bright green rucksack cover and Henry's red rucksack, added even more color to the scenery, as I walked along behind them.

One valley we walked through had a small river that seemed to feed into or out of the seas. We walked over a wooden bridge to get across the river. We passed by some beautiful bays. One in particular now had the turquoise waters, a sandy beach, and the green rolling hills surrounding the bay. A lone seagull flew by. With the lighter cloud cover, and a bench in the foreground, the landscape made me breathe better without the fog.

Sometimes the three of us didn't talk together, and that was alright. They chatted together at times just the two of them, and that was alright. After about our first hour together, half way, I actually felt alright that I could probably finish the rest of the walk by myself, but I was really appreciating the company today anyway. I did not think I was slowing them down. I felt like I was walking my usual pace and that might have been their usual pace, too. Although I did keep a short distance behind them much of the time on purpose so that they could chat together, have their private family time, and not feel like I was crowding their space.

After four and a half miles and two hours together, we made it to the ruins of the Tintagel Castle on an island. I knew this was where I would be leaving the SWCP for today, walking a half mile inland into Tintagel once again, and getting a bus or taxi back to Boscastle. They would be getting something to eat right there, and I would keep walking into the village. I told them of my writing a book, and asked if I could mention them by name. I thanked them so much for the company, and I was a bit sad to say goodbye. I shook their hands. I felt like hugging them. I should have. Finally I walked off into the sunset. Well at least up the road into Tintagel. I hope Jim and Henry made it alright to Poole, the end of the SWCP. So Jim and Henry, if you are reading this, thank you again so much for walking with me. Well, for allowing me to walk with you. I hope you made it to Poole together.

I didn't want to get anything to eat again in Tintagel or do anything there this time. Instead since I was familiar with where the bus stop was, I checked the time table, but I would have had to wait an hour for the next bus. I called my good man Tony-the-taxi-driver. He was there in ten minutes once again. He was happy that I was able to do the walk today. He asked how long it took. I said two hours. Two hours? "Most people take three or four for that walk," he said. Even the booklet said three hours, and I did not feel like that Jim, Henry, and I had rushed at all. We just kept a good pace, and as I said, it was mostly flat walking. In either case, Tony said that I was a "professional walker." A professional walker? I laughed. I doubt that. If I was, I would be paid to walk. But he meant it as genuine a compliment, so I took the compliment and thanked him. Between Tony and the taxi driver from the other day, I am a "professional walker and a brave lady." Even in the fog.

I ate some leftovers from last night's dinner when I got back to my room as a snack. Later on I went out to get some fish and chips for dinner to bring back to my room to eat there as I typed. As I peeked outside the window of my room around 9:00pm, it looked like there was some sun shining on the hillside next to my B&B. "Please let that sun be out tomorrow," I requested out loud. With the other day being the longest day of the year, it was still light outside this evening.

I will say that it is amazing how things work out for me, and how guardian angels appear for me just at the right time. I thank all my guardian angels today, and I thank whoever it is that provides them for me.

DAY 21 STATS: CLOSE TO 7 MILES. 3 HOURS OF WALKING TIME. NOT GOING TO COUNT THE BITS TO GET INTO TINTAGEL AS EXTRA MILES. PURPLE SHOES. PUBS IN TINTAGEL ARE "PORT WILLIAM INN," "TINTAGEL ARMS," "KING ARTHUR'S ARMS INN," AND "THE CORNISHMAN INN." PUB IN TREBARWITH STRAND IS "THE PORT WILLIAM."

TREBARWITH STRAND TO PORT ISAAC – Sunday, 25 June 2017

**"Do you remember when we used to sing
Sha la la la la la la la la la la te da
Just like that
Sha la la la la la la la la la te da la te da"** – Van Morrison, "Brown Eyed Girl."

This morning I had another "different breakfast" rather than eggs on toast. The couple at the B&B in Boscastle made me couple of "cheese herb tartlets." Along with a bowl of muesli with fresh fruit and yogurt, that all really hit the spot. After breakfast and checking out of the B&B in Boscastle, the gentleman of the B&B kindly drove me once again to Trebarwith Strand where I was to walk seven miles to Port Isaac today. Overall, it was a much, much better day today weather-wise, and I did not get lost once! Furthermore, there were seven, yes seven, valleys to climb down into and up out of again, and while I did feel that in the knees later on, I am not complaining one bit. Hiking poles helped. I got this! Finally, at the end of the day in Port Isaac, I may have seen an actor of the Doc Martin television show fame. Doc Martin? Perhaps you are familiar, perhaps not. I was not…

I started walking at 10:00am. Of course as soon as I started a bit of rain and wind was falling and blowing, but I was prepared. I had my rain gear on from the start. It was a 200-step climb right out of Trebarwith Strand to the top in the light rain and wind, but as soon as I got to the top that all stopped. For the rest of the day, I mostly had dry weather. There was an occasional brief rain shower here and there, but only enough that I needed to keep my rain jacket and rain cover of my rucksack on, but did not wear rain pants. For the rest of my walk, there was a wind now and then, but nothing like it was a few days ago. Mostly cloudy with some sun breaks now and then and around 60F/15.5C, which made for some nice walking weather. And no fog!

The first descent of the seven was not too bad as far as steepness goes, and the weather was dry with even a touch of sun and blue skies. A half hour after I started walking, I was at the top of the first valley. Actually if you count the first 200 steps up out of Trebarwith Strand at the beginning of the day, and the last descent I did at the end of the walk today into Port Isaac, then I would say I actually did eight valleys today. I noticed two people behind me walking, very brightly colored in their clothes. If I recall one was wearing orange and the other bright green. It was easy to see them in the landscape.

In between the ascents and descents of the valleys today, there was usually some nice flat walking. At one point I heard a whistle up ahead and noticed several people in a field and a flock of sheep. I guessed that they were herding in the flock of sheep. It was too far away for me to really watch what was happening, but I could see the flock of sheep moving together in one direction. The people in the brightly orange and bright green colored clothes, who looked like two local women out for some exercise, passed me by. I occasionally spotted them now and again, but eventually lost sight of them entirely.

The second valley for today was pretty short both in the descent and in the ascent. Some of the flat walking for today was through a lot of brush and shrubs, with the prickly plants like thistle and some of that prickly plant called gorse. Again, I was glad I wore long pants. I spotted towns way in the distance, which I am guessing were Port Gaverne and Port Isaac. At about 11:30 I passed a sign that said three and three-quarters miles to Port Isaac. I was down and up my third valley fifteen minutes later. Two couples walking in the opposite direction crossed my path. One of the couples was wearing bigger rucksacks, so I am guessing they were camping.

The scenery for today included not only the green rolling hills and headlands both ahead and behind, but those rocky edges along the coastline leading out to the seas, with the sounds of the white rolling crashing waves. Ahh, my favorite sound. The valleys had small rocky beaches or small coves. Lone large rocks seemed to float on the blue and turquoise seas. As the day progressed and the skies became bluer and bluer, so did the seas, becoming a stunning deep blue. Some yellow and white daisies occasionally gave a splash of color to the greenery next to the path, along with some other white wildflowers that seemed abundant, but I did not know its name. One grassy area was covered with tiny yellow and purple wildflowers. Another grassy area was covered with quite a lot of the tiny yellow wildflowers. (Sorry folks, I am not good at identifying wildflowers, especially because I do not live here.) Each of the valleys today was unique in its own way, and all beautiful.

I passed a sign that said three and a half miles to Port Isaac, when about four trail runners going uphill crossed my path in the opposite direction. I once again felt very overdressed when these trail runners passed me by as I have felt in similar situations before. Even when those two brightly colored ladies passed me by, I also felt overdressed. I suppose, if I lived here and knew these hills better and was out for a run or a brisk walk, then perhaps I would be carrying less and wearing different clothes as well. And I could identify all the wildflowers.

At the bottom of the fourth valley a sign said three miles to Port Isaac. It was just after noon. Many of the posted signs today seemed to be very nice newer looking signs. They must be a recent addition by the SWCP Association, and I thanked them out loud very much for the nice signage.

I needed to walk by a herd of cows at this point, and while three of them stared right at me, I remembered the rule not to stare back at them. Instead, I looked straight ahead to where I was walking, keeping an eye on them with my periphery vision, and using the talking-out-loud tactic to them as I passed. I "mooooved" on without any problems. I congratulated myself for getting a handle on how to handle this cow thing. However, I don't ever want to take it for granted. Just then another trail runner passed me in the opposite direction. I thought you weren't supposed to run when near a herd of cows?

I decided that I was going to stop trying to guess my arrival time at some place any more. As fun as it was for a few days, it also felt like a bit of too much pressure on myself to get there by that time. But, I bet it takes me four hours today to cover seven miles.

The fifth valley of the day was down a gentle grassy slope, but up a steeper rocky slope. The sixth descent was super super steep so I went super super slow. It was on small rock and gravel than can be quite slippery. My knees really felt this one, but bracing with the hiking poles certainly helped. I certainly made sure my hiking poles were tightened up at the spots where they open up or collapse, so that they wouldn't collapse on me as I put some weight on them during the descent. The sixth climb was also somewhat steep, but it was easier to climb up on those small rocks and gravel compared to going down.

Right after this climb though, there was one of those stiles you have to go up and over and down. They are usually two steps up, over a fence-like piece of wood, then a couple steps down. After that super steep descent and the steep ascent, I could really feel the muscles in my legs working overtime to get up and over and down the stile. A good workout!

Then it was time. Time for a test of my true nature and character and bravery! A test of what do I do in this situation when I am alone. It was time to face my fear. My fear of a herd of cows. Right in the way. Standing right on the path. Congregating literally right in front of the next stile I needed to reach. I was walking on some grass, with a wall to my right, so there was no way to go around the cows on my right. There were so many of them in the field to the left that I could not go around them that way either. I looked back first to make sure I was going in the right direction, and I was. The path was clearly marked. So here it was, me and the cows. Face to face. Well, without me staring at them. One on one. Well, one on one herd.

I took everything I have learned so far about dealing with cows and used it. I don't want to get between them, especially a mother and her baby. I want them to move away. I remembered again the gentleman who talked to them and herded two cows out of the path near Bucks Mills. I also remembered reading a post on the SWCP Facebook Group page where someone started saying, "mooooooove." After all, they are herding animals, so I thought I would give that a try. So I said quite loudly, "moooooove," "moooooove," "mooooove," "moooooooooove," as I kept bravely walking in the direction I wanted to go straight ahead. I walked slowly and surely, repeating, "moooooooove." And guess what?! It worked! The cows started mooooooooving away from the path, away from the wall, away from the stile, and into the field. I had done it! I faced my fears, and realized that the taxi driver who said I was brave, was right! I got this! All this only took maybe a less than a minute, but it seemed like an eternity.

Now you are also not supposed to run either when near a herd of cows, but the last several feet as I approached that stile, I didn't care. I wanted to get up and over that stile ASAP, as soon as possible. While I really didn't run, I did pick up the pace quite a lot, and you have never seen anyone climb up and over and down a stile so fast in all your life. Another record-breaking event just like I did when I changed from my purple shoes into my hiking boots in the dumping downpour near Heddon's Mouth weeks ago. With this climb up and over and down the stile, I could feel the muscles in my legs working double overtime. But I was safe! I did it! Heart racing a bit, but I did it! I safely passed by a herd of cows. I hope I never have to do that again though. I don't want to take those cows for granted. I need to respect them, and I appreciate that they mooooooooved aside for me.

I passed by the sign that said one mile to Port Isaac, and by 1:30, I did the final seventh valley descent and ascent. Looking back I saw the hillsides and headlands and valleys I had been walking today. As I continued walking forward I saw the town ahead of me surrounded by the greenery of the hillsides. A flock of seagulls flying and cawing caught my attention as they were playing in the breeze near a cliff ledge. The skies were so blue, with some white clouds, and the seas even bluer. A few purple and yellow and white wildflowers added to this scene. I had calmed down from my cow adventure, and was really appreciating the beauty of my surroundings in a peaceful way, taking in a few good deep breaths.

Animals along the South West Coast Path
Mountain Goat on windy ledge near Valley of Rocks June 8
Sheep between Hartland Quay and Morwenstow June 20
Sheep between Duckpool and Morwenstow looking back towards Bude March 31

Animals along the South West Coast Path
Sitting Cows between Stoke Fleming and Dartmouth August 6
Horses near Scabbacombe Sands August 9 with Scott
Cows near sea stacks at Ladram Bay August 14

I hit the pavement at Port Gaverne, which was just a half mile from Port Isaac. I was hungry, even though I had been snacking on the snacks I had in my rucksack for the last four hours, so I stopped for lunch at the hotel right there. I figured I was going to be eating plenty in Port Isaac, since tomorrow I had a scheduled "rest day" there, so today would be food in Port Gaverne. It was 2:00 when I sat down for lunch, my guessing-game arrival time of taking four hours for today's walk, even though I still had a half mile left to walk. I was greeted with some very nice and warm blue skies.

I was eating a good goat's cheese sandwich, when I heard a band start warming up just below me, behind some shrubbery so I could not quite see them, but I did hear them, and figured that some live music would be starting soon. Since I only had less than a ten minute walk to my destination for the day, I decided to stay for a while and listen. It felt like a nice way to end my walk today, especially after accomplishing seven (well eight) valleys! In four hours. And braving through a herd of cows. The music made me miss Scott because it would have been nice to share the live music with him.

Some of the songs they played, that I sang along with quietly out loud a bit, included:

"Bad Moon Rising" by Credence Clearwater Revival
"Eleanor Rigby" by the Beatles
"Hungry Like a Wolf" by Duran Duran
"All Along the Watchtower" by Jimi Hendrix
"Free Falling" by Tom Petty
"Brown Eyed Girl" by Van Morrison

I listened to the music for about forty-five minutes, and then walked just a few minutes past the few boats in the small Port Gaverne harbour to my B&B, using my GPS to get me there, right at the start of Port Isaac. I was staying in a very nice elegant room on top of a tea shop, the Terrace Tea Rooms. "I must have a cream tea here tomorrow," I thought to myself! A perfect place for it. A cute sign out front said "Cream Tea," then showed a painting of the Devon way–jam on top – and the Cornwall way–cream on top.

After taking my time unwinding and settling in, I headed into Port Isaac to find some dinner. Not before I accidently found a bit of the SWCP that I actually missed because I used the GPS to find my B&B. So I walked "backwards" about a quarter of a mile to where I figured out that I went off the path, then walked the quarter mile in the "forward" direction, taking photos of Port Isaac's harbour and the village. And one very cool picture of this gate that leads to nothing but the ocean. I wondered why the gate was there.

I photographed the harbour of Port Isaac from above, as I walked towards the main part of the village. It was clearly at high tide, with several fishing boats floating in the turquoise waters of the harbour. The harbour was surrounded by green hillsides with some large homes. At the time, I did not know it, but I was seeing one home that is used in the filming of the TV show Doc Martin! I spotted people down by the slipway of the harbour, more buildings, and some brick walls probably used to protect the buildings from the seas. The homes continued back into a valley for a bit, with more green hillsides beyond.

I wandered the streets and side streets of Port Isaac for a while acquainting myself with the town, as I will be spending a full day here tomorrow, while studying the dinner menus as I meandered. I strolled down to the slipway of the harbour, taking photos of some boats that were resting on this slipway, out to the boats that were floating in the waters. Mostly fishing boats and rowboats.

Then I spotted someone interesting. Perhaps famous even. Or at least I thought so. Port Isaac is the location where they film the popular TV series, Doc Martin. I knew of this tidbit already, but honestly, I admit that I have never seen an episode. There was this very nicely dressed man in a brown suit, and a photographer taking pictures of him. Some other people were milling around. I wondered, could this be, might this be, an actor from the TV show? I did not want to totally stare, and I was too shy to take a photo myself, so I just said, well perhaps I was seeing someone famous and I didn't even know it.

Turns out they are actually going to be filming the TV show here tomorrow, and the next day, so more on that tomorrow, but I never did find out, even after asking several people, who this person was that I just saw, as no one seemed to know. He didn't actually seem to match any of the descriptions or photos of the actors in the TV show, so I may never know who he was. But tomorrow, well that is a different story about who I shall actually see!

For now I decided to eat at the "Old School House," no longer used as a school, but as a restaurant and hotel. And used for scenery in the filming of Doc Martin as the village school. I ordered a few small items to comprise a larger meal since the larger meals did not appeal to me. I had a potato leek soup, a fresh salad, some warmed new potatoes, and some warmed vegetables of sweet peas and broccolini. And well a good chocolate cake for dessert, as a congratulations for being brave with those cows, of which I really promised myself I would stop eating sweets for a while after this.

As mentioned, I had quite a nice elegant room in the Terrace Tea Rooms in the floor above the tea shop. It felt quite fun to be in the same building as a tea shop. The view from my window was of some seas and headlands above the roof tops. I love the rooms I get with views like this. I must say that so far I have done well with picking the B&Bs that I picked out months and months ago from just looking at them on my computer back home. Not only the B&Bs themselves, with their rooms and some views, but also the people who run these B&Bs, some very hospitable people.

In looking at my booklet from today, here are a few tidbits of information. "The section of coast between Tintagel and Trebarwith Strand is dominated by slate quarries. Some date from before the 15th century and some were worked until 1937." For Port Gaverne, "for most of the 19th century slate from the inland quarry at Delabole was exported from this tiny port and coal and limestone were also imported. Pilchard fishing was also big business here as well as shipbuilding in Victorian times." And for Port Isaac, "the harbour at Port Isaac was once a large pilchard fishing port and fishing is still important today. Long before that it was involved in the corn trade." Slate, coal, limestone, pilchard fishing, shipbuilding, corn, all within about nine miles of the SWCP!

After video calling with Scott and a couple of other "to-dos," I went to sleep around 10:30pm. I did my writing for today tomorrow, knowing I had the day off to take the time to do that.

DAY 22 STATS: 7 MILES. 4 HOURS. AN EXTRA HALF MILE FOR WALKING BACKWARDS AND FOR EXPLORING PORT ISAAC. PURPLE SHOES. PUB IN PORT GAVERNE IS "PORT GAVERN HOTEL."

REST DAY IN PORT ISAAC - Monday, 26 June 2017

"A great man, a great physician and the greatest thing to happen to Portwenn since the new parking area at the beach." – Doc Martin TV Show about Doc Martin.

Today was a scheduled "rest day" in my planning of this trip. About every tenth day. Unless of course, the weather makes me have an additional rest day, which it has. I was actually considering walking three miles today, which would shorten tomorrow's walk, but it was not possible to get rides to or from the three mile area near Port Quin. A taxi would have been too expensive and difficult to arrange, and for the bus I would have had to walk extra to get to the bus stop and who knows what times the bus came, if at all, and the people at this B&B also run the tea shop, so they wouldn't have time to drive me. However, it didn't matter. I had things to do all day today, and to really rest my feet, which were not hurting at all, but it was good to let them rest after all the walking they have been doing. I will admit it was kind of nice to just chill out today in Port Isaac, also known as Portwenn in the Doc Martin TV show. Of course, the weather would have been perfect for walking today – no fog, no wind, no rain, not hot, just about 60F/15.5C, and mostly blue skies with white wispy clouds. Just what I had been asking for.

After a light breakfast of muesli cereal with fruit and yogurt, cooked mushrooms and tomatoes, a piece of toast, and tea, the first thing I did was go visit St. Peter's Church in Port Isaac. A small church with no graveyard. While this church dates from 1884, on display inside the church was an old church bell dating from 1800, I think from a chapel that was called Wesley Chapel. From information inside the church it appears that this church bell from 1800 was rung when this church was opened in 1884.

I decided that today I would take the guided "walk and talk" tour of Port Isaac to have something to do for a couple hours. First however, it was time to see some of the "action" of the filming of Doc Martin that was filming here today and tomorrow. To see if I could see anyone famous that I would not recognize, since I have never watched the show. The guided walking tour wouldn't be till 11:00 so I had some time. I walked into the little shop that was selling the tour tickets and asked the woman there for some guidance in where to see the filming going on. It was just behind the Old School House where I ate dinner last night. There were already lots of people around, including the actors and actresses (well, I am guessing), the crew, the security, and the many fans looking on. It was filming for the eighth season of filming for Doc Martin, I was told.

I found a spot to stand and watch the action. Not much was going on actually during the time I was there. I took a few pictures of people that I thought might be actors and an actress though. I just used the zoom on my mobile phone and later cropped the photos in to just get close up shots. Turns out that I took a photo of Ian McNeice, who plays Bert Large the father, and Joe Absolom, who plays Al Large the son! The woman I took a photo of might have been an "extra," but no one I asked could confirm this for me. I was really not sure who I saw last night in the nice suit now, since neither of Mr. McNeice nor Mr. Absolom looked like the person in the suit. I wonder if it could have been Martin Clunes, the actor who plays Doc Martin himself, but someone told me that he was not here at all during this filming, so I just don't know. What I do know is that I definitely need to watch some Doc Martin shows now!

The guided tour lasted about an hour and twenty minutes. John, our tour guide, took a small group of us around to many buildings within the small area of Port Isaac, including some historical buildings, an octagonal or round shaped house, and a very narrow road called "Squeeze-a-belly Alley." John also pointed out places of interest related to the fishing and coastguard industries, and told us of some history of the village. Of course, he showed us several locations where Doc Martin has been filmed. I took photos of many of these places, of course never having seen the show. In front of two of them, I even had my photo taken! Well, you know, it is quite rare in my life to be in a town where they film a TV show, let alone be there during filming, let alone me not have a clue yet as to what the TV show is all about, so why not! One of my photos was taken in front of Louisa's house. The other photo I had taken of myself was in front of the large house I saw from across the harbour yesterday, which is the location for Doc Martin's house and surgery center!

I also took a few photos of some "windows and doors" during the guided tour. I went back to my B&B to have lunch there in the very cute tea shop, cutely decorated, which turned out to also be very good food. I had a cheese and onion sandwich, and also to have my second official cream tea of my trip! I opted to only get one scone instead of two because they are quite filling. I ate it the Cornish way, jam first, then cream, and even slices of strawberry on top, since I was in Cornwall after all. I must admit they taste quite good, but oh the calories. (But who am I to talk with all the calories in the chocolate desserts I eat…). The scone was freshly baked here in this cute tea shop. They also were selling other freshly baked items, including but not necessarily limited to Lemon Buttercream cake, Coffee Buttercream cake, and Chocolate Buttercream cake. Believe it or not, I did not have any slices of these.

I went back to my room after eating, as I needed to catch up on my writing about yesterday. It took just over an hour and a half. I spent some time doing a bunch of other things on my "to-do" list. Later on, I was hungry for dinner and went to The Golden Lion Pub.

Speaking of blisters. Well I wasn't really talking about them, but I thought I would mention them on my day off since I haven't talked about them much in a while, other than some of my prevention theories. First I should mention one other blister prevention theory. In addition to double layer socks, changing socks often during walking, even letting the feet air out and dry before putting on the next fresh pair, wearing flip flops in the evenings to air out the feet, and showering at night to keep the feet dry, I also sleep with bare feet, which is to continue to keep the feet dry over night.

However, despite all my theories, honestly, during the first few days of my walking I actually did start to develop two small blisters on the outside edges of my big toes. But they did not hurt and did not seem to bother me and fortunately did not cause me any trouble walking, nor did they prevent me from walking like my experience in Spain. For the most part I left these small blisters on my big toes alone, kind of popping each of them slightly carefully once. Then I left them alone, and now they have just basically calloused up. That is great! I hope that will be the only blisters that I have my entire walk.

Honestly, popping blisters might not be the exact right thing to do as you want to be careful not to get the inside infected. But I was very careful. I disinfected the needle I used to pop them, put band-aids around one of them, used an antibiotic ointment, and used the sheep's wool that I brought to help them from getting any larger. (Note that my disclaimer here is that I am not giving any advice about blisters, and if you try any of these theories or actions or advice on anything I have done, I hold no responsibility whatsoever.) But this is what worked for me at the time. Also, proper fitting shoes and boots help a lot to prevent blisters as well.

Speaking of showers, which I mentioned when talking about blisters, I've wanted to mention that some of the showers in the B&Bs you can't just turn on the water to get hot water. There is sometimes a switch of some sort that must be turned on first, then when the hot water is turned on, the water will get hot.

As I was walking back after dinner near the Doc Martin filming location just before 7:00pm, I heard them say that filming for the day was over and they would start again at 9:00 tomorrow morning. It's a wrap.

Oh, and not only is Port Isaac a location for Doc Martin, it is also the location for another TV show, Poldark, another show that I embarrassingly admit that I have never seen an episode!

DAY 23 STATS: ZERO MILES. ZERO HOURS. ONE EXTRA MILE FOR GUIDED WALKING TOUR AND DINNER. FLIP FLOPS. PUB IN PORT ISAAC IS "THE GOLDEN LION."

PORT ISAAC TO POLZEATH - Tuesday, 27 June 2017

"The Perfect Cup of Tea. Forget tea bags. Loose tea is essential for the perfect brew. And, of course, you should never serve tea in a mug…Add your tea [to the teapot], allowing one spoon per person and one for the pot, and pour over the boiled water. Cover the pot with a cosy and allow to brew for three to five minutes depending on how strong you like your tea. Pour a little cold milk into a cup then add the hot tea, pouring through a strainer." From a book called "Vintage Tea Party" by Carolyn and Chris Caldicott (with my shortened version, see book for longer instructions.)

I watched some TV last night hoping to catch an episode of Doc Martin, but no such luck. This morning though, I think I saw the young actor Joe Absolom talking to John the tour guide from yesterday as I was leaving Port Isaac. Sometimes I can be brave and talk to people like that, but other times, I can be quite shy. This was one of those shy times. Bummer, though as I thought about this later in the day that perhaps I should have tried to get an autograph or even a photo taken with Mr. Absolom. I could have been the fan "who-has-no-idea-who-you-are-and-what-the-show-is-like-but-I-am-a-fan-anyway."

I had breakfast at the Terrace Tea Rooms B&B, including some "proper British" tea here, using fresh loose tea leaves, not from a bag. They gave me a little three-minute sand timer to let it brew. They also gave me a strainer to hold over my cup when pouring the tea. I also had this "proper British" tea yesterday when I had my cream tea here as well. The perfect cup of tea. Teatime began back in 1840. "Little did Anna, Duchess of Bedford, realize that when she succumbed to a late afternoon 'sinking feeling' one day in 1840 and asked for tea, bread, butter and cake to be sent to her private rooms at her stately home, Woburn Abbey, she was starting a new craze. Breakfast at the time was served early and dinner late. Both were lavish affairs but little attention was given to the light midday meal known as luncheon…so by four o'clock it was not surprising that Anna was more than a little hungry."

"Fortified by her tasty repast she soon decided to share the experience with her lady friends by sending out invitations for 'Tea and a walk in the fields.' On returning to London for the Season, Anna continued her afternoon ritual, taking tea in the drawing room with invited friends and, as she was lady-in-waiting to and life-long friend of Queen Victoria, afternoon tea became fashionable." And that is "How Teatime Began," as I read in the "Vintage Tea Party" book by Carolyn and Chris Caldicott.

For today's walk, the gentleman at the B&B made me a cheese and tomato sandwich to take away because there was only one little roadside van café selling food between Port Isaac and Polzeath, my destination of nine miles for today. The van café would be in Port Quin, about three miles away, but I didn't want to risk that they wouldn't be open early in the morning. They actually were open when I got there, but they did not have menu choices that appealed to me, so it was a good thing I had my sandwich with me.

I made my way out of Port Isaac, first passing up the opportunity with Joe, and then doing a short climb which took me to a view point looking back on Port Isaac. One can sit on a bench up this hillside, or just wander the path on the hillside and look down upon the many buildings of Port Isaac, the harbour with its breakwall, and even behind the Old School House. It did not look like they were filming Doc Martin just yet, even though it was past that 9:00 time they said they were going to start.

Today's beautiful scenery along the SWCP was one of several small coves, small little discreet places carved out in the rocks, with small little waves making small little crashes against the rocks. It was a calm day. The first three miles into Port Quin had some rolling ups and downs on the green hillsides, but nothing compared to seven (eight) valleys going into Port Isaac. I don't want to take any ups and downs for granted, but they were much gentler today than a couple days ago. One ascent today though had 148 steps up, shortly followed by 29 more steps. I counted. This time the booklet was correct, 177 steps.

As I walked today it was very quiet out. The only sounds were the small waves crashing in the small coves, the sounds of birds chirping, my footprints crunching on the small rocky ground below my purple shoes, and a couple of "good mornings" when two people passed by me in the opposite direction. It was peaceful. Then suddenly in the distance I heard a car horn honking. So much for the peace and quiet in nature. That was only one time I heard the car honk. The rest of the time it was quiet and peaceful.

As I walked today I saw the green rolling hills and headlands I was walking towards. I was able to see the slithering SWCP as it was clearly etched in the hillsides. I like seeing the path I will be walking on clearly. The seas took on a muted blue color today, almost grayish, due to the cloud cover.

Less than two hours after leaving Port Isaac, I reached the car park in Port Quin, a small village with a few scattered buildings surrounding its own little harbour. No boats were in its harbour today. The little roadside van café in the parking lot with food was open, but with nothing that sounded appealing to me, I ate half the sandwich made for me this morning. It was actually good. Something about those cheese and tomato sandwiches taste good out in nature when walking for miles on end. "At one time there were over twenty cottages here, and Port Quin was a thriving port with pilchard fishing, importing coal and exporting locally mined lead and antimony," per today's booklet. (Antimony is some kind of metallic element.)

During the three miles to Port Quin, I crossed paths with several people going in the opposite direction. One couple kindly waited for me at the top of one of the little rolling hills; a family of four was taking the inland path out of Port Quin; and I also passed ahead of a couple as they were a bit older and slower. They told me they were older and slower and allowed me to kindly pass by them.

There was this one wise-looking colorfully-dressed older man that crossed paths with me as well. You couldn't miss seeing him. We wore red - a red top and red pants - and also had a bright green rucksack cover behind him. He must have been at least in his 70s, and he was moving right along. I really wanted to ask him his words of wisdom, and if he was walking the whole SWCP. As I stopped to let him pass by, this time I wasn't shy, and tried to start a conversation by saying, "Hello, how are you?" He just smiled at me, nodded, kept on walking, and apparently didn't feel like talking. I wondered what his words of wisdom were.

As I ate my sandwich next to the roadside van café, I let my feet breathe, and changed socks just before I was about to leave for the five and a half miles into Polzeath according to the SWCP sign. After leaving Port Quin, I took a short detour to look at Doyden Castle which is actually now used as a holiday cottage. Doyden Castle was built about 1827, and "it was featured in the 1975 version of Poldark and in series five of Doc Martin." There were also a group of kayakers entering the harbour of Port Quin.

As I entered Lundy Bay, another great small cove with its rocks and small sandy beach, some boat also entered Lundy Bay. I couldn't tell though if the boat was a tourist boat or a Coast Guard boat. With some blue and red, my guess was the Coast Guard. The sign in Lundy Bay told me I had two and a half miles to a place called The Rumps. It was mostly flat walking so far since Port Quin, and for the rest of the day. Even flatter than the rolling ups and downs of the first three miles. At one point, I saw in the near distance Polzeath, with New Polzeath appearing closer and Polzeath a bit further on.

Today was also filled with scenery of small rolling green hills. The next several miles into Polzeath it became more "crowded" than any part of the path I had been on so far today. There were many people out today for a Sunday stroll, which was odd because it is Tuesday. (Okay I've used that one before, so that will be the last time I use that one.) Anyway, most people today seem to be possibly people who were staying in Polzeath perhaps doing a walk away from and back to Polzeath.

I reached the place that was called The Rumps, which was an "Iron Age cliff castle," according to the booklet. A small island in the seas, called The Mouls, is where apparently puffins can sometimes be found. I did not see any today. There was a small hill to climb at The Rumps for a view, not really part of the SWCP, but I didn't climb it. Instead I ate the other half of my cheese and tomato sandwich. Soon I went around the corner of Pentire Point, with big views of the two Polzeaths ahead. I had about two miles left. Eventually, a sign said I had three-quarters of a mile left to Polzeath. When I arrived in Polzeath, I circled the paved path around the beach, and changed into my flip flops, about five hours after I started walking this morning.

There were people enjoying the beach, playing games in the sand, playing games in the water, and perhaps even some sort of search and rescue class was going on. Or maybe it was a surfing class, as Polzeath "is one of the premier surfing beaches in Cornwall." I stopped by a café to get something to eat, a salad topped with hummus, before I walked the little bit up the hill to my B&B.

I had some great walking weather today! No rain, no wind, no heat, no fog. Probably 60F/15.5C with cloud cover all day, but that was great! That's nice walking weather, actually. Yes, I like sun, but I will take this weather. In fact, if this would be the weather for the next couple months, that would be great! There were some ominous looking rain clouds behind me today, looking even more ominous by my sunglasses, and fortunately that was where they stayed, behind me. As I went to dinner later on in the evening it was raining very lightly.

A very nice lady greeted me at the door of the B&B. This was the first B&B where I didn't have my own private bathroom, but I knew there would be a few like that. I did have a sink in the room however. I made a couple of outings to get cash and a new toothbrush, to replace the one I had been using since Braunton about two weeks ago. Later, I went out to dinner. It was only a two minute walk to those places.

Summary for today: Great walking. Great weather. No getting lost. No herds of cows. I still wondered what words of wisdom the older man in red would have said.

DAY 24 STATS: 9 MILES. 5 HOURS. NO EXTRA SIGNIFICANT MILES. PURPLE SHOES, AND A BIT OF FLIP FLOPS. PUB IN POLZEATH IS "THE OYSTERCATCHER."

POLZEATH TO TREVONE – Wednesday, 28 June 2017

"Good things come to those who wander." - My sister sent me this quote via a text message.

Sometime during my walk today, I completed the first of the four National Trail guidebooks, "Minehead to Padstow - 160 miles of coastal walking from Exmoor to North Cornwall!"

Today my sister sent me the quote above, which seems to be a derivation of other quotes (like good things come to those who wait), and seems to be true. Today, I was wandering, and wondering, whether I should continue my walk in the rain after my first three miles. Then a good thing showed up, another guardian angel, a really nice man to walk with…Here is the story…

After a nice breakfast of some muesli with yogurt and a tasty homemade gooseberry compote, and a slice of toast with homemade gooseberry jam, I left the B&B in Polzeath in a light rain. The gooseberry was grown in their yard and Pauline makes the compote and jam herself. Gooseberry is a fruit that looks similar to grapes, but are actually a berry filled with tiny seeds that provide nutrients such as vitamin C, fiber, and potassium, and even some vitamin A and calcium.

I knew that today would be mostly flat all day, so the light rain didn't bother me too much at first. The first mile and a half out of Polzeath was mostly paved around a park and some homes and easy to follow. Several locals were out walking their dogs, and a few boats were motoring and sailing in and out of Padstow Bay. The walk was going well, and even with the rain, and it was somewhat warm out, so I was not worried about getting too cold or anything. I was however, wearing my purple shoes, which were already starting to get wet. Using Scott's sock theory of taking extra extra socks to change into, and knowing that the terrain was flat, I really wanted to wear these shoes today regardless.

I had a view looking back to Polzeath and a sandy beach. Even the white crashing waves were nice on this rainy day. As I walked along an area that I would describe as "wild grassland," a few benches near the water's edge gave nice views of headlands, rocks in the water, the muted-colored water, and the gray sky.

I arrived at Daymer Bay, where I started walking along its beach. Still with a light rain, I walked down the beach about half way looking for a stream where just before the stream, a path was to lead me off the beach, to a bridge and over the stream, and the SWCP sign pointing me in the right direction towards "Rock." That is not a rock, but the name of a village, and the location of a ferry that would take me across the River Camel to Padstow.

Before I went on to Rock however, I wanted to go to this great looking church, St. Enodoc Church that was a bit inland off the SWCP. It wasn't too far inland, and I could see it from the path, but how to get there was the question. At the moment where I was standing just after the bridge, there was a Public Footpath sign pointing inland, so I thought I would try it. It kept going uphill a bit, and the church was down the hill, in the middle of some sand dunes, and a golf course. I thought maybe that the uphill path might eventually go downhill, but since it seemed to be leading me in the wrong direction and I couldn't see that far ahead, this did not seem like the correct footpath, so I decided to turn back around and see if I could figure out how to get to the church back down by the bridge. I took a few pictures of the church from above however, as it made for a nice scene, even in the middle of a golf course. I turned around and went back down to the bridge, and crossed back seeing the path clearly on the golf course, but still not sure how to get there. I had to back up even further, back towards the beach, and I finally spotted a sign with an arrow saying conveniently "Church." (See this time when I felt like I was "getting lost," I did backtrack to a familiar place and was able to figure out the correct footpath.)

I followed the footpath which led to and through the golf course where they instructed me to follow the white markers and to watch out for flying golf balls. There was no one playing today. Not in this rain, which was still lightly and consistently falling. So, this golf course I had no incidents on, other than getting a bit turned around trying to figure out how to get to the church.

It was worth the extra effort on my part to get to this church. Apparently, "its origins can be traced back to 1299 but most of the church was built in the 1430s," [Wow!] and was restored in 1864. According to the booklet, "From the 16th century to the early part of the 19th century the church was almost buried by sand. To keep the church open the vicar and church goers had to be lowered through a hole cut in the roof." Interesting. The front door was adorned with beautiful colorful flowers surrounding it. I immediately felt a sense of quiet calmness entering the church. That spirituality and strength that I can tap into when I am inside. That, and I was out of the rain for a bit, drying off, but being careful as to not get the church wet.

After my peaceful church visit, I walked another mile to get to Rock, to catch the ferry into Padstow. This was my first ferry of the SWCP! The first of several. This ferry runs all day, every day, every twenty minutes this time of year, so I wasn't worried about the timing on this one. Others I might need to be more aware of the time they run, including schedules based on tides. The walk to the ferry was through some sand dunes. The path was nice and firm and dry actually considering that it was sand and there was still a light rain falling. As I approached Rock, I saw the River Camel in between with several boats floating on this large-looking river. Actually technically, I did take the Appledore/Instow ferry, but that was not really for getting me to continue on the SWCP itself, which this ferry was. So really this ferry was my second ferry of my walk, by my first official ferry that would be part of the walk taking me from one place, Rock, to another place, Padstow.

I read the sign about the "Rock to Padstow Ferry." It told me how much it costs, known as a tariff, that the first ferry left at 8:00am, and the last ferry leaves at 6:30pm, all day. The sign also says, "To summon the ferry please wave hand flag in the box until the ferry leaves Padstow." Ok, I can do that. I wondered why though I needed to do that though if the ferry runs every twenty minutes. I also didn't know what the ferry looked like, so how would I know when it has left Padstow? Whatever my line of questioning, this was fun. My first ferry! I picked up the bright green flag and started waving. I must have looked silly, in my full on rain gear, but I didn't care. I waved it and waved it and waved it.

"Rock is a small village very popular with the 'upper-class' and affluent holidaymakers with house and restaurant prices to match. The ferry to Padstow has been operating for at least 600 years. The name [Rock] is said to originate from the stone quarries just a little inland including one on the site of the car park." I only hoped that if this was a 600-year-old ferry, at least it has been mechanically serviced after all these years.

A family appeared to take the ferry as well. Two women, a man, and a baby. They were on holiday, have a holiday home in this area, and were going to Padstow for lunch. I wondered if they were affluent. They recommended a fish and chips place to me to eat at in Padstow. They also told me after a couple minutes of waving the flag, that I didn't have to wave it any more. In fact, only in the low season do you really have to wave it. It was high season. See, I did look silly. But it was fun anyway to wave the flag, so I didn't care. I even took a selfie photo waving the flag. I never take selfies.

The family asked me about my walk, and the rain today. I told them that after I had some lunch in Padstow I was to decide if I would keep walking today in this weather. I started to question whether I wanted to walk in this continuing rain or not actually, but I also told myself that I may have more rainy days ahead of me in the next few months, so I can't give up each time. Unless it was quite stormy and gale winds and downpours, but at the moment, it was still a light rain.

The ferry arrived soon thereafter. It was a small boat with seats both outside and inside undercover. We all went for the inside undercover seats. It only took a few minutes for the ferry to reach Padstow. I would have liked to have taken pictures of my arrival, but choose to stay undercover and keep my camera and mobile safe and dry.

Fifteen minutes after I had waved the flag, I was in Padstow. I was hungry, and also wanted some time to try to figure out what to do with the rest of the day. I meandered around the harbour area, window shopping, reading menus, and taking photos. The harbour of Padstow is larger compared to the smaller harbours I have walked by, and this town was larger as well compared to the smaller villages I have been seeing. Padstow's harbour had several rows of various types and sizes of boats, many sailboats, a very large fishing boat, and perhaps even a tour boat, as I walked around the harbour viewing it from all angles, with shops and restaurants surrounding the harbour on most sides. I was carefully trying to keep my camera and mobile phone dry while taking my photos. Padstow "is one of the most popular destinations in Cornwall. Tourists have replaced fishing as the main source of income although a small fishing fleet is still vital to its economy," according to today's booklet.

I did not feel like fish and chips that the family recommended. I chose to eat at a place based on one menu selection: Strawberries and Cream Salad, with "strawberries, avocado cream, cherry tomatoes, feta and toasted almonds with balsamic glaze," and homemade walnut bread. It was delicious!

I was actually dripping wet and the bottom of my rain pants legs and shoes were a bit dirty and sandy from the last several miles of walking, so I actually took off the rain gear before entering the restaurant. Still, I must have looked like a mess when they seated me, but the lady who sat me was kind, and a very nice couple shared their table with me because the restaurant was quite busy. Must be all those tourists. I utilized the bathroom to straighten myself out some more when I arrived, and when I was leaving, I changed into a drier shirt as the one I had on was a bit wet around the neck probably from each time I unzipped my rain jacket to take out my camera to take pictures, which was safely hidden under there from the rain to keep it dry. I also put on a dry pair of socks. My purple shoes were doing alright, surprisingly not overly wet.

As I was eating I studied my booklet and guidebook to see what options I had for the day. I had done about three miles and had six more miles to go, possibly in the rain. Was there a place I could stop that wasn't quite the six more miles if I needed to? Were there any shortcuts? What should I do? I couldn't answer my questions, so I said, ok, Debby, just start walking, and see what happens. You could walk a mile or two, and then if the rain was really annoying, you could just turn back around to Padstow. I geared up putting on the rain gear that had dried out, stepped outside, and walked on.

So far so good. The rain was quite light, the path was paved, which then turned into a rocky paved path, and flat. No sooner than a half mile of this, I saw someone up ahead. Wearing rain gear. And a pack cover. And holding a hiking pole. Immediately I thought to myself that this person must be walking in the direction I am, perhaps even walking to my destination for the day, Trevone. Perhaps this person was even walking the entire SWCP. I decided that it might be nice to have someone to walk with in this rain. I walked a bit faster to try to catch up to them. This person was walking a good pace though, and the distance between us remained the same. Until they stopped. To ask another couple of people a question. I caught up to all of them. The man who I spotted was asking the couple if there was a way to walk on the beach and get back to the SWCP at the other end. There was.

After the couple left, I kind of not-shyly-at-all just asked this man, this guardian angel of the day, where he was going, and what he was doing. He was on his way to Treyarnon, which was past where I was going. And he was walking the entire SWCP, or at least as much of it as he could get done in a month's time, as he told me that he needed to get back home near the end of July to celebrate his son's 40th birthday.

He invited me to join him across the beach. At first I was hesitant because I didn't want to stray from the SWCP. I didn't want to get stuck on the other side of the beach at a high tide with no way out and have to backtrack. I know he just asked the couple, but still my cautious side was working in this rain. For a moment I continued on the SWCP, paralleling the man, but just for a moment until I hit a bunch of wet overgrown shrubbery. That was it! I was heading for the beach. I was headed for this man. Fortunately there was a small pathway down to the beach, and I actually jogged on the beach to catch up to this man.

"I decided to join you, if I still may," I called out to him. My first effort he didn't hear because of the rain and he had the hood of his rain jacket on. He heard the second effort however, and we started walking and talking. There was an instant connection between us. I was glad!

A fortnight ago (that's two weeks ago, or fourteen days ago), Gordon turned 70! He told his wife that for his 70th birthday, he wanted to walk the SWCP. Wow! I was immediately impressed. He had a good walking pace going. I told him I was celebrating my 50th!

Gordon, and his wife Linda, own an organic dairy farm in northern England, where their business is "the home of fresh organic milk, cream, and more." They even do "doorstep and wholesale delivery" and their products are in supermarkets. They have a website which I looked at. The thought of working on a farm has always fascinated me. Gordon and Linda were in the midst of handing down the family farm business to their two children and four grandchildren. Gordon's five year old grandson is keeping track of his grandfathers' walk on a map by using pins to mark where grandpa is each day. Gordon says I am more than welcome to visit their farm anytime. I like Gordon, and was inspired by him.

We walked together for two hours on pretty flat terrain. When we reached Stepper Point, complete with a Daymark Tower, the light rain was now a heavier rain, and windy. We stopped for a short break at the Daymark which "was built during the 1820s as a navigation aid, well before the lighthouse at Trevose Head. The concrete bases by the Daymark are remains of WW2 installations on Stepper Point." In other words, I was seeing another version of a "lighthouse," since daymarks are another aid to navigation like lighthouses, keeping people safe at sea!

Once Gordon and I continued walking, we passed by a flock of sheep. We walked on grassy hilltops with views of headlands. We had a view of a sandy beach with waters shallow enough that they were turquoise. We had a view of a rocky beach, and I seem to recall that we had a descent in this area. It was really great to have someone to walk with.

A couple hours after we originally started together, we walked on a grassy path near another "wild grassland" area, this one with many white wildflowers. The grassy section looked like it had been mowed. In fact, I finally got an explanation that I wondered over two weeks ago on why sometimes it does look like to me that some flat grassy areas I have been walking on look like they have just been mowed with a lawn mower. Gordon told me that yes, the National Trust does bring "weed eater" machines up to the paths that make the grass looks so nicely mowed and flat to create an obvious walking path, and then sheep help to keep it groomed.

Sometimes Gordon and I chatted about other things. He asked about my walk and the planning I put into it, and the B&Bs I was staying at. He was camping most of the time on the SWCP, but currently was staying with friends in this particular area. He hurt his foot or something so will probably take tomorrow off to let it rest so he can continue his walk.

I asked Gordon if he had done other long-distance walking in his life. He replied that his farm life has been his priority over the course of his life, and that he wouldn't change it for the world. So other than the 268-mile Pennine Way and the 26-mile Inca Trail in Peru, the SWCP was his long-distance walking.

Sometimes Gordon and I walked in silence, and that was fine.

Even with the rain, there were the views of headlands and coves. I was taking more photos than he was, and he kindly paused for me when I would take a photo, me also being careful to not get my camera or mobile phone wet in the rain. Gordon took a few photos of me both with my camera and my mobile, and with his mobile, and I took photos of Gordon. Those might be the first photos of me on the SWCP actually (other than my selfie this morning waving the ferry flag). And the few I had taken back at the monument in Minehead.

When we arrived at my destination in Trevone, I felt sad to leave Gordon. Rain (and some wind) continued to fall all day, but it didn't matter since I walked with some great company. As we stood near a beach, we wished each other well on our walks. I hope he makes it all the way to Poole. I will email him on his website so we can stay connected. We first shook hands goodbye, but then just gave each other a big hug! He walked on the beach to continue going to his destination for the day. Gordon was not only my guardian angel of the day, but great company, an inspiration, and also a friend.

I walked to a little café in Trevone, dripping wet. The guy there didn't look too happy with me. I ordered a mango smoothie (yes a smoothie on a wet day), dried off a bit, and then called the "fabulous local taxi" that Kate of SeaVista B&B in Mawgan Porth told me about months ago. Today was an unusual day where I stopped walking about ten or more miles before my B&B. All other times, my day ended by my walking into the town where my B&B was located. I had actually called the fabulous taxi guy yesterday to make sure he was available, as I didn't know exactly what time I would arrive in Trevone, and he said he would be available anytime. Fabulous!

My fabulous taxi guy showed up fifteen minutes later, and it took about a half hour to get to Mawgan Porth, where my B&B was, because we got caught in a school pickup "traffic" slow down in one little town along the way. He dropped me off right at my B&B, and I asked if he would be available tomorrow morning to take me back to Trevone. He would be, and I could call him in the morning. Fabulous! (Ok, enough of that.)

I walked into the reception area of the B&B and there was an adorable little note on the table by the door. I remembered when I was in contact with Kate months ago when I booked the room, she signed her emails "Love" or "Lots of Love" or "kindest regards," and an "X" after her name. I thought that was the sweetest! This note welcomed me and the other guests by saying, "Hello Everyone! If you require any milk for tea and coffee this afternoon, you can help yourself from the jug in the bar fridge…Hope you all have a wonderful day! We will be back a little later for check in at 4pm…We look forward to welcoming you all properly as soon as we return xxx." That was not a typo but kiss, kiss, kiss. The note went on instructing me how to get into my room, and then was signed, "Lots of love Kate xx."

Another note greeted me in my cute little room. This note said, "Dear Debra (that is my legal name), Welcome to Seavista! We are delighted you are staying with us! Please let us know if there is anything we can help you with, whether it be restaurant recommendations, suggestions for things to do in the area or anything to improve the comfort of your stay with us. We remain at your complete disposal and hope that you will enjoy your visit here in Mawgan Porth. Kindest regards." My room had a little twin bed, a couple little tables, and a little bathroom. The room was adorable and comfortable.

I went downstairs to meet Kate a little while later. Right away, she was the sweetest person. I gave her a hug. I briefly told her of my wet day and my walk with Gordon. I asked if she did laundry by chance, proper laundry, and she does. Fabulous. I asked her if there was a good way for me to shorten my walk tomorrow. I had planned a twelve-and-a-half-mile day, all flat, but it might be rainy all day, rainier than today, so I would like to keep the walk around eight miles, which meant I would unfortunately probably voluntarily skip about four and a half miles. She was not quite certain, but I would be able come up with a plan anyway.

Kate also showed me an "airing cupboard." A what? What was that, I wondered? It was the closet where their water heater was located and thus was warm inside. I could hang my wet rain jacket and rain pants, as well as put my wet purple shoes in there to dry. What a great thing! Kate and I chatted about a few other things. She told me of the time she visited the US, working at a camp and doing some hiking herself. She made me some tea and served it in a cute tea set, along with a piece of some sort of sweet cake. I asked her about restaurant suggestions for dinner.

I called Mom, did a few things, and headed down to dinner. In the rain. I had to walk down a hill about a quarter of a mile or a bit more. I put back on my dried-out rain gear and went out to a delicious meal. A brie and mushroom burger (without the meat), along with several other little side dishes. A quarter mile or a bit more walk back to the B&B, in the rain. Waiting for me though in my room was a jug of water, the necessary items to make myself some tea or coffee, and a delicious little homemade piece of chocolate topped with a hazelnut. Kate also lovingly straightened up my room. A video call with Scott, and writing for a few hours wrapped up my day.

Special Moments on the South West Coast Path
My friend and inspiration, Gordon, on our rainy walk together between Padstow and Trevone June 28
Me on the rainy walk with Gordon (photo credit: Gordon)
Me in front of Doc Martin's house and surgery center Port Isaac June 26 (photo credit: John the tour guide)

I thanked whomever provided me with my guardian angel of the day. I wish Gordon well, both on his walk and in life. I will do my best to stay in contact with him. As my sister reminded me, "Good things come to those who wander."

Now I realized today that as much as I wanted to walk the SWCP by myself, solo, alone, on my own, just me and my purple shoes, and hiking boots, as I was kind of originally planning all along, I have now walked part of two days with people. With Jim and Henry between Boscastle and Tintagel a few days ago, and today with Gordon. But I am not disappointed in this in the least. Both days I met some great people and appreciated the company in the weather situations I was experiencing. Besides, when I say "kind of originally planning," it is because in a few days' time, I will be walking part of a day with a great friend of mine who lives near the SWCP, Sasha. So all along, I guess I knew there would be this day planned to walk with my friend, but not any other days to walk with any other people. This one day was always my exception to my rule of wanting to walk the SWCP by myself. Anyway, more on that in a few days…

DAY 25 STATS: 9 MILES. 4 HOURS, WHICH INCLUDES THE CHURCH, BUT NOT TIME IN PADSTOW. A HALF MILE EXTRA FOR DINNER. WET PURPLE SHOES. A PUB IN PADSTOW RIGHT IN THE HARBOUR AREA IS "THE SHIPWRIGHTS INN."

TREVONE TO PORTHCOTHAN BY WALKING; PORTHCOTHAN TO MAWGAN PORTH BY TAXI - Thursday, 29 June 2017

"It takes courage to walk this path alone. It also takes courage to make a decision to not walk from time to time." – Gordon's knowledge and wisdom that he said to me yesterday.

A side note for today: On the SWCP Facebook Group page I saw some photos of an area of the SWCP that had a recent large rock/cliff fall, taking out some of the SWCP itself. The headlines from BBC News from June 29 read, "'Broadchurch Beach: West Bay cliff fall blocks coast path." Fortunately no one was hurt, but "between 1,500 and 2,000 metric tonnes (1650 to 2200 tons) of rock collapsed at Dorset's West Bay overnight. It forced the closure of the cliff-top path between Freshwater and East Beach." In addition, "Dorset Police warned people to stay away from the cliffs amid fears of another collapse." Therefore, the SWCP between West Bay and Freshwater had been closed. The name Broadchurch in the headlines is from a fictional TV show, which like Doc Martin and Poldark, I have also never seen. I won't be walking in that area till August 18 and 19, so I would bet by then they will create a diversion path in place so that I can safely walk that area. And if there are any big red signs about the diversion, I will read them this time. This rock/cliff fall just shows though that the SWCP is fragile and vulnerable, and at all times I should appreciate the path, respect nature, and be aware and careful.

Today started out with the best breakfast ever, made with love from Kate, the "Super Food Porridge," made with coconut milk, coconut oil, nuts, chia seeds, goji berries, with a drizzle of honey, topped with fresh berries. It was a tough choice though what to choose from her fabulous breakfast menu. Should I have the Cornish Breakfast, similar to the Full English? Not my choice, but a good one for those who like this. What about the Veggie Breakfast, with two veggie sausages, two eggs, and slow roasted tomatoes. Or the Homemade Granola; or the Avocado and Poached Egg; or the Maple, Cinnamon and Vanilla French Toast. Perhaps the Homemade Waffles with either bacon and maple syrup, or banana, Greek yogurt, maple syrup and mixed nuts. There was also the Chia Pudding, the Super Seasonal Smoothie, and the Smoked Salmon with buttery scrambled eggs. And with any of these, the Homemade Muesli, with a variety of seeds, berries, and yogurt was always available. I would need to stay here more than a week to try one of each. Fortunately I was staying a total of three nights, so three breakfasts.

Kate kindly called the fabulous taxi guy who picked me up after breakfast and drove me back to Trevone, where he picked me up yesterday, so that I could start my walk from where I left off. Somehow when I originally planned today, to walk from Trevone to Mawgan Porth, I calculated eleven miles. It would be mostly flat, and on a great day, doable for me. However, my calculations were a bit off and the weather was not that great today. It was really twelve and a half miles total. Yes, I am sure I could have done it, but with the on and off rain, and wind, forecasted today, I chose to complete eight of those miles. Which means that I would ultimately be missing another four and a half miles of the entire 630, which made me sad again, knowing I have already missed some other miles previously. However, for my safety, health, comfort, and peace of mind though, I would be happy with eight miles today. Yesterday, Gordon's knowledge and words of wisdom to me were, "It takes courage to walk this path alone. It also takes courage to make a decision to not walk from time to time!" As he shared this with me, it was a bit amazing that he said this to me as "courage" is a synonym for the word "bravery." And the word "brave" has been used before about me. I will remember Gordon's wisdom for future reference.

I started walking in the rain and wind, on the small sandy beach that Gordon and I said our goodbyes on yesterday (sounds like some scene from a movie), and a flat stretch to Harlyn Bay, a bit over a mile. With the wind, the waves crashing on the rocks were a bit stronger today. It made for some nice sounds, with a bit of excitement as if it was really stormy out. I passed by a large field of sheep, which I seem to pass by almost daily now, sometimes more than once a day. Cute little creatures! Even in the rain. The path itself was definitely wet today, but because of the flatness of the day, I wore my dried-out purple shoes again.

At Harlyn Bay I got a bit mixed up about some steps I was supposed to climb. First there was a bit of beach walking and the booklet said to walk in the sand about 300 yards. Well I guess I couldn't count very well. Which is odd, because I love counting. There were two other sets of steps before the one I was supposed to take, one with a shut gate and one that clearly said "private." I couldn't find the third set yet, so I went up the private one thinking those were the steps I was supposed to climb. These steps however, lead right into someone's back yard. I really need to read and pay attention to signs better. But what a nice back yard to have with steps that take you right down to a beach! Fortunately there was a man there getting ready to walk his dog, guardian angel number one for the day, and he was able to tell me that I had to walk a bit more down the beach, past some rocks to find the correct steps. He was correct.

The terrain remained pretty flat and closer to the seas rather than up on a hillside today. The waters changed colors as I walked sometimes appearing deep blue, light blue, turquoise, yet always excitingly beautiful.

Another couple of miles would take me to the Padstow Lifeboat Station and a lighthouse, the Trevose Head Lighthouse! It was not only more flat walking to get there, but more rain and wind. I was a bit hesitant about walking around the headland to get to the lighthouse in this wind. The wind wasn't that strong, not as some other days I have experienced, but with the rain, I just wasn't up to it. I didn't want to potentially be that close to an edge. I saw in my booklet that there was a way to get across the headland without going around it. I asked guardian angel number two of the day, another man and his dog, how I could cut inland to get to the lighthouse to double check what the booklet said.

He directed me to a road just at the end of the field we were near. I would need to take the road up to a house, turn left, continue on that road to the car park and the lighthouse. Easy enough. It would be about the same distance as going around the headland, or a bit less, and definitely less wind. It would mean that I would miss walking next to the Lifeboat Station and around Trevose Head, but I needed to be ok with this due to the weather. Courage. What happened to summer?

Soon I arrived at the Trevose Head Lighthouse however via the roads, and that was what I really wanted to see up close. It was closed to the public however, unless you rent the lighthouse keeper's cottages which are "available to let for holidays." I think I looked into this when planning my SWCP walk, and it would have been an expensive two or three-night minimum, or maybe even a week minimum, to stay there. However, the thought of staying at keeper's cottages intrigues me and seems quite romantic, so I think I shall start an "expensive-places-to-stay-someday" list when I have a lot of extra money to include these keeper's cottages. I have also walked by the Foreland Lighthouse and the Bull Point Lighthouse which also had the former keeper's cottages as holiday lets (rentals), so now my list can start with three expensive places to stay someday…In the meantime, I was seeing another lighthouse!

I spent some time photographing the lighthouse. A "warning fog signal" sign warned me, "The public are advised that a fog signal emitting a very loud noise may be sounded in this vicinity at any time without prior warning." It wasn't foggy today, but I could see off in the near distance in the water, the amazing sight of rain falling on the seas. Per the booklet, "Trevose Head projects further into the sea than most of the Cornish north coast, so the positioning of the lighthouse in 1847 was crucial for shipping. In 1913 the eminent physicist Lord Rayleigh designed a fog horn for Trevose and it was known as Rayleigh's Trumpet. It measured 36 feet long with the trumpet being eighteen feet by two feet. It continued to be used until 1963."

Treyarnon was my next destination, about two miles away. It was more flat walking and at times the rain and wind got lighter. Some of the walking was on that grass that had that freshly mowed look. I passed by one beach, and then at a second beach, I thought that I should like to walk across the beach rather than the sand dunes behind the beach. I started and then asked someone if there was a way out at the other end of the beach leading to the SWCP. The beach wasn't that long, but I wanted to make sure it would be alright with the tides. He said there was. There were plenty of surfers out today, on this beach, and on several others I walked by or on today. Even in this weather. The taxi guy told me that people surf all year here, even in the winter. But this is supposed to be summer!

After walking across Constantine Beach, I stopped at the car park in Constantine to change socks and regroup for a moment. I saw that I was not far from Treyarnon, the place Gordon was walking to yesterday after we departed. I was kind of hoping I would see him there today, as he was most likely taking the day off from walking because of his foot. I unfortunately did not see him. It was almost noon when I took that little rest, and as I left, there was a sign saying two and a quarter miles to Porthcothan, which would be my walking destination for the day.

More flat walking near an area with bench after bench after bench offering seats for great views of mostly just the seas and sky beyond in the distance, sprinkled with a few large rocks in the waters. Views of the next headland and a beach were also offered as the benches continued. Even the benches themselves were interesting, as no two were exactly alike. There could have been a dozen benches in this area, some even old enough that pieces of them were missing. More photos of benches for my "Benches of the South West Coast Path" photography book.

I reached the next beach at Treyarnon, and the booklet said to walk on the beach and cross the little stream to get to the steps to continue the SWCP. Good, another beach walk for the day. Even in the rain, I liked the beach walks. I got to the stream to judge its depth. My purple shoes would get soaked. I had other options. Bare feet, the hiking boots that I did bring with me today in my rucksack in case it was too wet and rainy for my purple shoes today, or the flip flops that I also brought. To cross the stream, I choose the flip flops. It was kind of nice to let my feet feel the cool water.

There were even kite flyers on this beach today, and as usual on most beaches, the RNLI Lifeguards, with their trucks and rescue equipment, flags near the water showing people where they could swim and surf, and even a sign telling me the temperature of the air and water, the wind direction, the high and low tides, and conditions. It was hard to read this sign as the chalk was wiped off, but the air temperature might have been 16C (61F), which seemed on the warm side even with the wind and rain, the water temperature was 16.5C (62F), winds from the west, with a high tide at 21:27 and a low tide at 15:29.

The terrain was still flat as I continued on to Porthcothan, and for a while the rain actually stopped and the sun even tried its best to appear, but no such luck for very long. More benches offered views of the beautiful area. I walked above several small coves, Pepper Cove, Warren Cove, and Fox Cove. These small coves had some amazing deep turquoise color waters, smaller rocks closer to the coastline, and larger rocks just beyond, surrounded by the small hillsides. Stunning. On one bench, a woman was sitting bundled up in her jacket, looking at the seas, while her dog was running around the grassland area.

I also walked around several areas specifically designated as bird sanctuaries. A sign told me, "Private land and rare bird protection area, including corn buntings and skylarks. Please keep to the Coastal Footpath. Thank you." Lots of white wildflowers filled this area and beyond. A second sign told me, "Sanctuary area - The gorse area ahead is a sanctuary for nesting corn buntings during spring and summer. Please help keep their nests and chicks safe by staying on the main outer footpath with your dog on a lead. Thank you for helping these birds to breed successfully." A photo of a corn bunting on this sign told me what to look out for, a small "lowland farmland" bird.

The rain started up again as I started the gentle descent into Porthcothan, with its beach also protected by the RNLI Lifeguards. While it did not look like anyone was on this beach surfing today, the white waves rolling onto the sand, with the rocks and small green hillsides beyond, was stunning. If the weather was better, I would have walked the additional four and a half miles to Mawgan Porth, but the weather was not improving, and as it was, I was glad with my decision to end my walk here for today.

I entered Porthcothan Bay Store, ate a lentil sweet potato salad, and called the fabulous taxi guy to pick me up and take me back to Mawgan Porth. I took a short nap today after I got back to my room, which was the first time I have taken a nap in the entire nearly four weeks I have been here. The four and a half miles that I was missing between Porthcothan and Mawgan Porth would have included supposedly a really nice place called the Bedruthan Steps.

Tonight with the rain, Kate kindly offered to drive me down and pick me up to and from a restaurant so that I could eat dinner without having to walk back and forth in the rain. Very loving!

Do I feel sad for missing some more of the SWCP? Well, part of me of course does indeed. A bit disappointed too with the weather. I wondered if I am not that brave since I chose not to walk in the rain today. Also, my wanting to walk the entire path in one go can no longer happen. But once again, on the other hand, as Gordon said to me yesterday, "It also takes courage to make a decision to not walk from time to time." I contemplated his words of wisdom, and the words courage and bravery, and felt alright with my decision as I listened to the rain pour down outside the window of my room at 9:00 at night.

DAY 26 STATS: 8 MILES. 4 HOURS. NO EXTRA MILES, BUT 4.5 MISSED MILES. PURPLE SHOES, AND FLIP FLOPS TO CROSS A STREAM. PUB IN PORTHCOTHAN IS "TREDREA INN."

CHURCH VISITS IN MAWGAN PORTH AREA – UNPLANNED REST DAY DUE TO WEATHER – Friday, 30 June 2017

"I've walked the SWCP from end to end. Up and down hills, through fields, across beaches, around every bend…" – John Haughton in his book, "Follow the Acorn."

I woke up today and checked BBC Weather as I do every day. I check each evening and each morning. Last night it was predicted that today would be light rain and light winds, much like yesterday was, so I was going to walk the six miles from Mawgan Porth to Newquay as planned. However, this morning the forecast changed – to gale force winds. Can you believe it? From here to there and beyond. Wow, again! Where is a constant summer? I changed my plans just like that within a moment.

I had breakfast at the same designated time, 8:00, since that was already prearranged, I was already awake, and I had developed a plan for my unplanned rest day. I had that super Super Food Porridge again, this time even with edible pansy flowers in the bowl, made with love from Kate. You think that with all those other amazing menu choices, I would have chosen something different, but it was so good yesterday that I wanted it again.

I knew that there were a few churches in this area, having done some research as I do when I am in most places in case I need something to do in the afternoon of any given walking day. The churches in this area though were too far to walk to, at least two-and-a-half miles for the closest one, and given the not-so-great weather, walking was not an option for me today.

I called the fabulous taxi guy, Phil, to see if he would please take me to any or all of the three churches in the area. He agreed. See, Kate was right – he was a fabulous local taxi. All for £28/$37, when all was said and done, and taking several hours, I had a great unplanned rest day. It was like I created my own tour and itinerary of the Mawgan Porth area, and Phil was my tour guide and personal chauffer.

The first church was St. Eval Parish Church, with its 60-foot tower built in 1727, visible for miles around. The original church dates back to the 13th century and was enlarged in the early 16th century. It was located near "the remains of the Coastal Command Airfield of RAF St. Eval where up to 2000 personnel kept a constant vigil against German U-Boats during the Second World War." Phil even pointed out the airfield to me as we drove by. The booklet further expanded on the St. Eval Church and the RAF station saying that the church tower "has been a landmark in this part of Cornwall for centuries. The tower has been used as a daymark for both shipping and aircraft returning to nearby RAF St. Eval. The RAF station opened in 1939 and was an important coastal command airfield during WW2 including the Battle of Britain. It closed in 1959 and is now a communication station."

In other words, I was seeing yet another important aid to navigation, a church that was used similar to a lighthouse because of its tall tower! Fascinating! I think I shall start a list of all the aids to navigation that I shall see, including the actual lighthouses I will see (Foreland, Bull Point, Hartland Point, and Trevose Head so far), daymarks such as the Daymark Tower at Stepper Point that I saw a couple of days ago, and now a church tower! There was The Little Chapel on the Hill and the Braunton Lighthouse Ruins I also saw earlier on that I will even include in this list. There will be more to add as I continue my walk!

I had read in my research that a Flower Festival is held annually at St. Eval Parish Church the last weekend of June, which was last weekend. I didn't know if any remnants of the Flower Festival would still be in the church, but sure enough there were plenty of flowers around. The flowers seemed as fresh as they would have been several days ago. Lucky me!

The Flower Festival was celebrating "The Four Seasons," so on display were flowers representing Spring, Summer, Winter, and Autumn, with various colors and flowers for each season. It certainly seems as if in the last four or so weeks of my walk, I have experienced the weather of all four seasons! It was very pretty inside the church with the various colorful flower displays. Reds, oranges, yellows, purples, whites; daisies, carnations, roses, lilies, hollyhocks, etc. Phil kindly waited in the car as I spent time in this church. I invited him to go in with me, but it was too windy and rainy for him since he didn't bring a rain jacket and preferred to wait. That was so very kind of him! Me, I ran into and out of the church, as it was definitely windy and rainy.

Next on the itinerary was St. Ervan Parish Church. "The present church was built in the 13th and 14th centuries and it has never been enlarged. The original tower, 50 feet high and built in the 14th/15th centuries had the upper part brought down by explosives in the 1880's, but it was not properly capped until 1956 and now stands 24 feet high." In this church, I noticed some interesting old looking plaques on the wall, which were slate memorials, some of which date back to the 1600's. It really amazes me how I am looking at things, churches especially, that have survived hundreds and hundreds, even thousands, of years.

Third stop on today's tour, crafted by Phil and me, since I had not known all about this place except for its church, was the little village of St. Mawgan. Here I had an hour and a half to "spend the day at an idyllic Cornish village with delightful rural scenery, historic architecture and great places to visit, eat, shop & stay," as advertised in "The Little Map of St. Mawgan" that I picked up.

St. Mawgan Parish Church also dates from the 13th century. "St. Mawgan is unusual in that its superb tower, with its stair turret and spirelet, lies to the south of the church. Its lower part dates from the late 13th century; early in the 15th century it was increased to a height of 70 feet. The tower contains eight bells, rehung in 1958, of which seven were recast; the eighth is a priceless medieval bell cast between 1378 and 1407." The church bells rang 12:30 as I was there! One of my favorite sounds.

Next to the St. Mawgan Parish Church was the St. Joseph and St. Anne Roman Catholic Church Carmelite Convent. Not able to go inside the buildings, I was able to walk around the flower-filled peaceful garden. It was still raining and windy, but since I was not on the coast, and was a bit inland, the rain and wind were probably not as strong as they could have been.

Next I browsed in a couple of shops, including a great little vintage shop, the Duchy Vintage Emporium, and a craft and gift boutique store. There were so many things in both shops that I wanted to buy, but didn't, including some dish and tea sets. Finally, I had lunch at the Village Stores & Tea Room. My menu included a homemade mushroom soup and a…cream tea! My third one! I put the jam on first, then the cream, since after all, I was still in Cornwall.

After my hour and a half in St. Mawgan, Phil came back to pick me up as I believe he did another taxi run during that time. He drove me back to my B&B, where I still had some of the afternoon to relax. I realized that I could listen to music on my laptop as I typed today to catch up to this moment. I wondered if I could download a movie onto my laptop for later.

Later…..Just like someone shut off the switch days ago when the 80F/26.5C weather happened, and it went down to 60F/15.5C within a matter of an hour it seemed, someone shut off the same switch today. Within a matter of an hour, it went from windy and rainy, to a breeze and dry calm. It being too late in the day, however, I did not go walking, other than out to dinner later.

Turns out I was able to rent a movie on my laptop however. I rented the movie "Wild" with Reese Witherspoon about Cheryl Strayed and her life and her walking 1,000 miles of the Pacific Crest Trail in three months, with camping and a heavy backpack in adverse conditions. I thought it might be inspiring for me as I do my walk. I hope that my purple shoes will never fall down the cliffs as her boot rolled off a mountain. And I hope all my toe nails will stay intact, as she had a damaged toe nail that she had to pull off. Just the thought of that made me squirm.

Also, John finished his SWCP walk today! He was the one on the SWCP Facebook Group I mentioned who was posting humorous accounts of his walk. It took him 52 days to complete the 630 miles (well there was one day he missed that he will come back soon and finish)! As mentioned, I have been following him daily on Facebook (other than the week he took off in the middle), and he too has had some challenges with the weather. It has been inspirational to follow along with someone in "real time" though, as he was walking at the same time as me. Some days as I was walking, I thought to myself that he is out there too, and I have a "walking partner," just on a different section of the same path.

As mentioned, John has included a limerick in each of his posts. Very clever and they add a nice touch to his descriptions of his day. John's final limerick for today was:

"I've walked the SWCP from end to end
Up and down hills, through fields, across beaches, around every bend
There have been lots of kind wishes that cheered me on
And gave me support and encouragement when things sometimes went wrong
My eternal thanks and good wishes to you all I send"

John also included in today's description of his last walk with Frank Sinatra lyrics, "And now, the end is near and so I face the final curtain." I wrote him the following comment back:

"You've lived a life that's full
You've walked each and every path way
And 630 miles more than this
You did it your way"

About a week later, John went back to the SWCP to do the one day he missed and complete every inch of the SWCP. Congratulations, John! He soon thereafter also wrote a book about his walk. Each day he included his original Facebook post with the limericks, and then wrote a few paragraphs reflecting back on each day as well. Several weeks after I get back to the US, I ordered his book, read it, and thoroughly enjoyed reading about his walk again, "Follow the Acorn – A very Unofficial Guide to The South West Coast Path, Minehead to Poole," written by John Haughton. (And at this point, I still have nearly two months, and somewhere around 445 miles, to go.)

DAY 27 STATS: ZERO WALKING MILES. ZERO WALKING HOURS. NO EXTRA MILEAGE. THREE CHURCHES. FLIP FLOPS, EVEN IN THE WIND AND RAIN. PUB IN VILLAGE OF ST. MAWGAN IS "THE FALCON INN." Information and quotes about the three churches are from the Community Website for the Parishes of St. Mawgan, St. Eval, and St. Ervan: stmawgan.org.uk.

MAWGAN PORTH TO NEWQUAY TO CRANTOCK TO HOLYWELL TO PERRANPORTH/CLIGGA – SOME BY TAXI – AND SOME WALKING WITH A GREAT FRIEND – Saturday, 1 July 2017

"It offered a whole world on my doorstep just waiting for me to walk along it."

"This is what life is all about, and this is what makes this walk such an amazing experience. Here I am...having walked ten miles. I am as chilled as I can be and feel incredibly lucky to be having this experience. I have no worries, no responsibilities, nothing but the now. This is food for the soul and I am a very, very lucky soul."

"After ten days of walking I could really feel the impact of what I was doing. Apart from the daily ups and downs of emotions there was an undercurrent of deep happiness. I felt that this was a natural thing for me to be doing: walking all day, every day. In fact, it felt more natural than sitting at an easel, or driving, or shopping or anything. The walk had become my be-all-and-end-all. My fitness was still questionable, and my big toe was still numb, but my mind had never felt clearer."

All by Sasha Harding, Artist and Author, about her walk on the SWCP, from her book "A Brush with the Coast - An Artist's Search for Inspiration along the South West Coast Path."

Hmmm. "Porth." I wonder what that means. And why is Mawgan Porth two words, but Perranporth one word? I looked up the definition of porth, and it is "a small bay or cove." New words I now know like "mouth" and "combe." I suppose all these words have examples where some towns are one word, and other towns or two words. So if a town was called "Combeporthmouth" that could mean "a short valley with a small bay or cove at the mouth of a river." Enough on the grammar lesson for today.

I woke up this morning to the sun mostly out and blue skies! The forecast called for 60F/15.5C! Perfect! A walk with a friend added to the sun today! What a great day! Not to mention a cute ferry ride, a long walk on a beach, and a music festival! All that in a nineteen mile day, with fifteen miles of walking, and ten hours - my longest walking day yet!

The day started off early though. The earliest I have ever woken up on purpose. I woke up at 5:30, and by 6:00 I had breakfast, and I was out the door walking by 6:45. First I had one more Super Food Porridge breakfast, and had to sadly say goodbye to Kate, with love. Yes, I know, with all those great breakfast choices, I just wanted the porridge once again. I was really appreciative of Kate these last few days with all her help, food, and kindness, and really enjoyed staying at her B&B, SeaVista Guest House.

As I started walking, people were already out jogging and enjoying the sun as I looked back on the sandy beach at Mawgan Porth. What a difference a day makes in the weather. The seas were a deep, deep blue, and the white rolling waves were perfect. Now that I think about it, if I lived near any part of the SWCP, I too would walk (or maybe take up jogging) probably every day (unless the weather was really bad) to get some fresh air before I start the rest of my day. Or I would walk or jog in the middle of my day. Or at the end of my day. Or all three…

There was one small hill to climb out of Mawgan Porth, and all day long there wasn't much else to climb or descend, as it was quite flat. The first part of my walk was to make up for missing walking yesterday, because today I was really combining the walk I was supposed to do yesterday with the walk I had planned for today. It started with views of small rocky coves and long sandy beaches. White frothy waves and deep blue oceans. Blue skies, and the sun creating my shadow in several pictures as I was walking on top of green-covered small hills. Even looking inland at the wheat fields had some nice color with the early morning sun. Maybe I should walk more often this early. Except that most B&Bs don't serve breakfast till around 8:00. I had to ask Kate special if she would get up that early.

As I looked down at a few beaches this morning, it looked like they had no access to them, unless by boat or kayak. It looked like there was no way down the cliffs, so I imagine they remain deserted and have had little or no human contact. The original sign I saw when I started this morning said two and a quarter miles to Watergate Bay. A half hour after starting, I passed by a sign that said one mile. Another jogger passed me by, and I had a view of the large town of Newquay ahead. Soon I started the two-mile walk that would take me above the beach at Watergate Bay for the next half hour of walking. The beach at this end looked deserted mostly, but this beach does have access later on. I passed by somebody sitting on the cliff ledge appearing to be meditating. Or at least just enjoying the early morning sun.

When I arrived at the car park at Watergate Bay, a sign told me two and a quarter miles to Porth Beach (in other words, "a small bay or cove beach") at one end of the car park, and at the other end of the car park, the sign said two and three quarters miles to Porth Beach. Hmmm. I don't think I just walked a half mile across a car park backwards. Soon I reached near the end of Watergate Beach. I had been listening to the soothing sounds of the white waves crashing on the sand for the past half hour. Early in the morning. Ahhh. That is my kind of meditation! Things for me are just so much better when the sun is out. These are the times when I am truly in my element.

Just beyond was yet another sandy beach with more white crashing waves as a person on a mountain bike biked by me. These beaches today were just stunningly beautiful, the blues and turquoises and whites rolling into the sandy color of the sand. While and yellow various wildflowers added more color and made for good foreground subjects in my photos.

Then the shock of the large town hit me as I entered the outskirts of Newquay. Lots and lots of buildings. Seems like the biggest town that I have come across in about 190 miles since Minehead.

I interrupt my walk here to explain that today I am meeting a great friend of mine, Sasha, to walk with. If I have not yet introduced Sasha yet, which I have briefly here and there actually, I have known her for over a year now. I first met her via email after discovering her amazing artistic book, "A Brush with the Coast – An Artist's Search for Inspiration along the South West Coast Path." She is an author second, and an amazing artist first. She walked the SWCP, mostly by herself, and created this wonderful book filled with her paintings of the SWCP and her story of walking the path. She had one of her dogs with her. I bought her book, and was completely inspired by it. If she can walk the entire path in one go, so can I, I thought! She not only found inspiration for herself by walking the SWCP, she inspired me as well. Sasha's book was the only book I found about walking the SWCP in one go written by a woman!

There are actually three books that inspired me to walk the SWCP in one go. Two written by men, and the other by Sasha. The first book I read before Scott and I walked our 100 miles over a year ago was, "500 Mile Walkies," by Mark Wallington. Mark walked the SWCP with his dog. Well, it actually wasn't his dog, but a borrowed one from a friend. Yes, a borrowed dog. Reading Mr. Wallington's book actually inspired Sasha to go on her adventure. But she already had a dog, and thus didn't need to borrow one. She had two dogs at the time actually, but only took one of them with her. Sasha now has three dogs. Anyway, Mark writes his book with much humor. He apparently originally did the walk "to impress a girl [he] met at a party." Well, after he completed the walk, he realized what his true motives really were: "To know the name of the gulls with the black backs, and the flower whose first two syllables were poly…to teach [him]self how to put up a YHA tent…to try all the flavours of Heinz soup except for Lentil…to write a top-ten-best-selling-hit-pop-song." In conclusion, Mr. Wallington concluded, "the walk had been a complete personal success." His book was inspiring to me in its own way.

I actually wondered though why Mark Wallington walked only 500 miles according to the title of his book. My curiosity led me to ask the SWCP Association who told me that he really must have walked the entire 630 miles. It was just that back when he did the walk, sometime in the 1980's, they didn't have modern GPS to really know how long the SWCP actually was, so there was a sign at the beginning of the walk indicated that it was…500 miles. Although at the time he walked, the Isle of Portland (which I will be walking in late August) was not originally added to the official 630 mile count till later. In addition it is possible that if the SWCP were all completely flat, with no ascents and descents, it might be closer to 500 miles, or at least less than 630 miles.

There is a song by The Proclamiers called "I'm Gonna Be (500 Miles)," having nothing to do with the SWCP, yet the lyrics, as some of you may know say, "But I will walk 500 miles, and I will walk 500 more…" I suppose one walking the SWCP could sing, "But I will walk 630 miles, and I will walk 630 more…"

The second inspirational book that I read by another man who walked the SWCP in one go was "The Man Who Hated Walking," by Overend Watts. Even the title is humorous, as well as his book being quite humorous and sarcastic. Mr. Watts is a founding member of the English rock band of the 1970's, Mott the Hoople. As someone who never walked before and was out of shape, Overend basically "complained" just about the entire time. In fact, he had encountered sleepless nights, torrential rains, windstorms, extremely hot days, painful blisters, crowds of people, sheer cliff drops, and getting lost. Some of that sound familiar? You would think that with his "warnings" that I would have decided not to walk the SWCP. Let alone by myself. However, just opposite, as it was another inspirational book to me.

I even tried to rationalize all his experiences: For sleepless nights, he camped in a tent, and I would stay in B&Bs. For those torrential rains and windstorms, I had planned on the summer when he walked mostly in April and May. Ha, was I wrong. For his extremely hot days, I figured what are the chances of that, and I would rather have those anyway than rain and wind. For his painful blisters, I would take as many supplies and footwear and preventative theories as I could, and well, that thus far has been a success. As far as crowds of people, sometimes that can be good, and thus far, I have avoided most of the crowds. As far as sheer cliff drops, I have been close once or twice, but Mr. Watts had taken a wrong turn when he wrote about that. And as far as getting lost, I was hopeful that with all the signage and booklets and guidebooks, that I don't know that Mr. Watts had (although he may have had the Ordinance Survey maps), I would not get lost either. Well…

Even with all that, after Overend's walk, he was transformed. Transformed into someone who had since then completed many other long-distance walks including, but not necessarily limited to, The Pembrokeshire Coast Path (186 miles), Peddars Way and Norfolk Coast Path (90miles), Hadrian's Wall, three times (73 miles each), Wainright's Coast to Coast Path (190 miles), and the 874 mile walk from Land's End to John O'Groats in 63 days, which covers the entire length of Great Britain from its southwest corner in England (which I will be walking to in about a week) to its northeast corner in Scotland. Now if all that is not inspiring, then I don't know what is! Furthermore, Mr. Watts was 51 when he walked the SWCP in 2003.

After I read these two inspiring books, however, I wanted to read a book about walking the SWCP written by a woman, but in searching on the internet, I could not find one. I emailed the SWCP Association to ask them if one such book existed, and that is how I was introduced to Sasha's book and her website, sashaharding.co.uk. (Note that she did not ask me to include either of these mentions in my book.)

Sasha Harding's book became my full inspiration! Not only is her story, as a woman walking mostly solo on the SWCP inspiring to me as a woman, her seven week adventure and experiences are written with heart-felt personal emotions, honesty, and humor. She shares the challenges and the triumphs she faced during her walk. She introduces the people she meets, and expresses her deepening friendship with her dog. She talks about her lifetime love of the ocean, having grown up near the SWCP, and her love of fishing. Her adjective-filled descriptions of the landscape are complimented by the artistry of her drawings, which are playful, adorable, child-like, simple yet elegant. The entire book painted an inspiring picture to me and made me want to walk the SWCP!

Back before Scott and I walked our 100 miles together, I contacted Sasha via email to not only purchase the book, but also to ask more questions about her mostly solo walk after I finished reading her book, which she kindly answered. I asked her about footwear, about if she ever got lost (yes), about the weather (I think she had mostly dry weather), when did she go (September and October), where did she stay (mostly B&Bs, as well as her own home), what are some good villages for rest days, etc. I kept in contact with her after our initial emails, and then last year when my husband and I walked 100 miles of the path, we met Sasha for lunch one day in person! We instantly became friends!

During that 100 mile walk that Scott and I did, I kept feeling like I wanted to come back to England and walk more than the 100 miles, perhaps even attempt to walk the entire SWCP all at once. I've explained already some of that story leading up to my decision to actually do it, but while we met with Sasha for just that hour or so, I told her of my thoughts of maybe walking the entire SWCP in one go. But I was nervous about certain things already like getting lost or bad weather. Or getting lost in bad weather. I will never forget her words of encouragement: "The struggles and challenges are all part of the process. My one piece of advice is to do it!"

After that short, and inspirational, lunch with Sasha, she and I continued to keep in touch via email over the course of the next year. When I was making my plans to do this walk I am currently on now, we decided two promises together. One was that we would walk together at least one, or part of one, of my days. Two was that I could stay with her when I got to Falmouth, as she lives nearest to there.

So here was the day that we would fulfill our first promise, we would walk together for part of my day today. It was also the only planned day that I knew would be the exception to my rule of wanting to walk the SWCP by myself. Our second promise will be filled in about two weeks.

Back to today…The plan for today originally was that Sasha would pick me up at my B&B in Mawgan Porth, and we would drive to Crantock and walk from there together, with me supposedly having finished the Mawgan Porth to Newquay/Crantock section yesterday. However, the revised plan for today became for me to walk from Mawgan Porth to Crantock, meet Sasha in Crantock, and walk with her till Perranporth. But part of that planned changed as well…

After the shock of the large town hit me as I entered the outskirts of Newquay, and as I crossed the sands of Porth Beach having walked about four and a half miles to this point bright and early in the morning from Mawgan Porth, I was supposed to meet Sasha in Crantock, on the other side of Newquay across a river with a ferry, at 9:00. That would be twenty minutes from now, and it seemed like there was still about four miles to walk in order to reach the ferry at the other side of Newquay to get to Crantock. There was no way that I could walk four miles in twenty minutes. I don't even think I could jog or run four miles in twenty minutes.

I called Sasha to ask her about the walk I would have had ahead of me to get to her. She said it was not that exciting, as she already told me it was mostly street walking, and would take at least an hour, or more realistically, probably two hours, of walking through the buildings. I did not want her to wait that long for me as I thought I would originally walk these four miles as I set out early this morning, but as it was, I decided to find a taxi to take me to the Fern Pit Café which would have food and a ferry or footbridge across the River Gannel to take me to the beach at Crantock where I would be meeting Sasha. I would miss another four miles of walking on the SWCP, but while this decision to not walk did not need to take the courage that Gordon wisely said, this time it was just for logistics so that I could meet my friend Sasha in a timely fashion so that she would not have to wait for me any longer. It was the friendly thing to do. Yes, I was disappointed in missing some more miles, but it was more important for me to walk with Sasha today!

I walked just a bit further past Porth Beach and there happened to be a restaurant/hotel there that I went into the lobby of, found a business card for a taxi, called them, and within minutes, I was driven through Newquay to the Fern Pit Café. While looking out the taxi window, the only thing I felt like I missed out on with this taxi ride would have been the harbour at Newquay with all the boats docked, but I was sure I would see plenty more harbours in the next several hundred miles.

I arrived at the café a half hour past the time I was to meet Sasha, and of course they weren't open yet. I called her again, to tell her what was going on. She had a book to read and was enjoying sitting on the beach with her two dogs, including the one who walked the SWCP with her, so she was alright waiting a bit longer. The café wouldn't open till 10:00 and I also wanted to get a take away sandwich before walking down the long steep flight of steps to the ferry or footbridge, depending on the tides. As I waited for the café to open a family with two little children were also waiting, and the father was asking me about my walk. He seemed impressed. A man with a rucksack also came up, so I started talking to him. Lyndon from South Africa was walking whole path. He started two weeks ago, is camping, and expects to finish the first week of August. I never saw Lyndon again after today, and so I hope his walk was successful.

Once the café opened, I looked at the menu. Sasha recommended the crab sandwich, but I spotted a peanut butter sandwich on the kid's menu instead. Peanut butter! I haven't had that since I've been here. Probably one with added sugar, but I didn't care. I asked if they could please make me two peanut butter sandwiches with extra peanut butter than what they would put on kid's sandwich. They would, charged me a bit extra, but I didn't care. I was so excited about peanut butter sandwiches! I skipped the jelly.

I walked down a long flight of steps to get down to the River Gannel. To cross, if the tide is low, they have a footbridge. Today the tide was high, so they had a "ferry," which was really a motorboat, to take me across the river in about a minute's time. The ferryman helped me on board, and there was a cute little dog resting at the bow of the boat. I took pictures of the cute dog and the river on the ride over. Apparently a lot of people photograph that dog. I paid my £1.20/$1.65 for the ride, and Sasha was there on the other side, with her two dogs. It was over an hour for her waiting for me at 10:15, but it didn't seem to matter. We hugged! It was great to see a great friend!

We immediately started chatting with each other and didn't stop chatting for the two hours it took us to get to Holywell Bay. Sasha chose to walk this portion with me because she says it is one of her favorites, and I could see why. It was beautiful, with the deep turquoise-fade-to-blue ocean, the occasional sandy beach, the coves and rocks, the small rock islands in the ocean, and of course the sunshine. Wildflowers were in bloom which made great subjects in the foreground of my pictures like earlier today. Sasha's two dogs, a ridgeback named Jess (the one that walked the SWCP with her), and a little cute guy named Mouse, also made for great foreground picture subjects.

We started by walking on Crantock Beach, as I ate one of my peanut butter sandwiches that was so good, and needed to find our way out through some small sand dunes to the SWCP. Sasha warned me of Adder snakes which could be found in sand dunes. While I knew of them already, and had been aware of them in my previous walking through sand dunes, I really appreciated the reminder. Adders are poisonous, and while biting a human is rare, mostly dogs get bitten since they tend to want to sniff the snake. I believe they have distinctive zigzag markings on them or they can be all black. There are some tips out there on what to do if one does get bitten, including getting medical help. I hoped to never see an Adder. And I never did!

More blue and turquoise waters, green-covered hills, blue skies, sandy beaches, and gray and brown rocks painted the landscape. People were definitely out today enjoying the sun. I definitely saw why Sasha said this area was one of her favorites.

We talked on subjects such as talking about our respective walks on the SWCP. We talked about the "emotional rollercoaster," as she calls it, of the walk, especially when affected by the weather, and in my case also missing Scott at times, losing the path, and missing a few miles here and there. It was comforting for me to know that I was not the only one who experienced disappointment with the weather, although comparatively, Sasha had better weather, less rain, and she even walked during the months of September and October when she did her walk, autumn instead of summer. We also talked about the emotion of sadness after walking with someone and then they depart, as I felt after walking with Jim and Henry, and more with Gordon. We talked about the emotion of appreciating the beauty of nature, and what it feels like to walk day after day after day – calming, in tune with nature, natural, a way of just being!

We touched on the subject of "Public Rights of Way," comparing that in England you can walk on "privately-owned" land, such as farms, whereas in the US, you cannot. That is why I have been able to walk so closely to sheep and cows. Sasha got stopped a couple of times by other people walking today to talk about her ridgeback dog Jess. I guess that breed is rare, but today there was one other ridgeback walking, and another couple said their daughter has one. There were a lot of people on this walk today – the combination of the weather, the flat terrain, and the beautiful scenery made this four mile section popular.

Sasha and I had several other topics of conversation, including about her husband and mine, what jobs they do, etc. Sasha met Scott last year, but we did not get a chance to meet her husband, Jack, a retired fisherman.

Two hours later, Sasha and I arrived at Holywell and its long sandy beach, where she said she would stop walking with me for the day because she needed to walk back to Crantock, as that was where her car was parked, and needed to get home for an art-related event. We stopped on the beach so her dogs could cool down playing in the seas. We also had to walk across a small stream, so we took our shoes and socks off and I learned a new British word – paddling – "the act of walking with bare feet in shallow water." I would call that "wading."

We went to a pub so I could get a bite to eat, and she could have some tea. I would save my other peanut butter sandwich for later. She gave me a little book as a gift. It was a very nice book about the sea and shore of Cornwall. We walked a four wonderful miles together!

Sasha told me that she has most of the rest of the summer off from work, or at least no major deadlines, so asked for my walking schedule so that perhaps she can join me again. That would be lovely! Later in the evening I emailed it to her. I knew I would be staying with her once I get to Falmouth as well, our second promise. She took a photo of me standing next to a large stone which had the acorn engraved on it and two arrows, one pointing to the SWCP, the other to the beach. The stone was as tall as I am, and this is another one of the few photos I have of myself up to this point in my walk.

As we departed, the sad emotion crept up, for both of us. We gave each other a hug, she and Jess and Mouse walked off into the sunset, and so did I. Well, not really, but that was what she said as we walked off. It was so great to walk with someone, especially a friend, and one that can relate to what I am doing and feeling and seeing each and every day!

Not only did I walk alone now, but the scenery, and the weather, changed a bit too. First, the sun started to get covered by a layer of clouds and the blue sky somewhat disappeared. Strange that the weather changed just at that time as I left Sasha. It remained dry and warm however, almost like I had two halves of my day, and perhaps mimicked the emotions at the moment. The scenery of the walk was near a military base after I left Sasha as well, and was not as picturesque as before. To cope with the scenery, the change of weather, and the sadness, I listened to a few songs on my mobile phone. For about three or four songs I was able to get mobile reception, but then lost the reception. It got me through most of the military area though until I neared the very long Perran Beach. A two and a half mile beach, that with the low tide, I was able to walk on its entire length in the sand. Another long beach to walk on like Saunton Sands! (Note that when I have been listening to music, although I may have already mentioned this, I don't use earphones. Instead I listen using the speaker on my mobile phone. This way I can still hear what else is around me. I am, however, aware of the volume of the music so as to not disturb anyone or nature.)

I started with still having my purple shoes on walking in the sand, but then I soon took them off and walked most of the beach in bare feet. It was a nice feeling to be grounded to the earth in this way! I also rolled up my pant legs to my knees. I confirmed with one man walking in the opposite direction that there was a way out of the beach at the other end depending on the tides. He assured me that either there was a staircase if needed, or if the tide was out, I could even continue walking around a small headland to a second beach. About two-thirds of my meditative walk down the beach as I had the constant beach waves to listen to, I came to the headland. It definitely

Beaches and Coves of the South West Coast Path
Crantock Beach with Sasha July 1
Holywell Beach with Sasha July 1
Perran Beach Perranporth with walking its two-and-a-half mile length and "Tunes in the Dunes" July 1

Beaches and Coves of the South West Coast Path
Porthcothan Beach – Happy Place with constant rolling waves and an ultimate location for a beach hut April 5
Sandy beach/cove just past Porthcothan Beach – another ultimate location for a beach hut April 5
Asparagus Island and Kynance Cove July 13

looked like the tide was out as there were many people already walking in between the two beaches, but just to make sure I asked a life guard.

I knew that there would be a music festival here this weekend, on the beach in Perranporth. "Tunes in the Dunes." When I booked my B&B months ago, they told me. Before I left for England, I looked at the lineup of who was playing and considered buying a ticket in advance. I only recognized one name however, Billy Ocean, and the other bands must have been more local British bands and/or music that I was not familiar with. I did not buy tickets in advance because of that, and also because I knew that I would be walking and did not know how I would feel towards the end of a walking day, if I would want to listen to music, and for how long. I also gathered that I would probably be able to hear the music from either the SWCP or the beach, and then I could make a decision then and there if I wanted to buy a ticket.

I started hearing the music as I approached near the end of the beach and then saw the big sign spelling out "Tunes in the Dunes," with colorful festive flags and white tents for the vendors. I decided to sit on the beach and listen to some music since many people were doing that, and I could clearly hear the music from just sitting on the beach. I didn't need to buy a ticket at all. I hadn't recognized any of the songs I had heard so far, but it didn't matter. They had a couple of bands playing at the same time, so I just chose one and sat on the beach. I wondered why some people paid to go in to hear the music, while others didn't pay and just sat on the beach. I ate my other peanut butter sandwich as I listened.

I listened to the music for about 45 minutes. I still was not familiar with what I was hearing, but it was still good. It was also a good way for me to relax a bit, as I had just walked thirteen miles to this point since this morning, and still had two miles to go to my B&B! Therefore, I got up and began the one and a half mile walk to Cligga Head, then about another half mile off-track my B&B. It had been four and a half miles since I stopped walking with Sasha. Just out of Perranporth, I looked back from the hilltop over the long Perran Beach that I had walked all along its length. Turquoise waters with rolling white waves were leading to the long and wide sandy beach which was sitting below some green hills. People were still enjoying the music at the festival, and would be for many more hours. At this view point was an interesting Millennium sundial. "Most sundials are set to tell GMT rather than British Summer time. However, this one tells local time – twelve minutes behind GMT," per the booklet.

The path to Cligga Head was uneventful, and even a bit strange. All of a sudden the terrain changed to a very rocky section. Perhaps this had something to do with the remains of an explosive company that used to be located here, "which had a dynamite works here from 1891 to 1905. Over 700 tons of dynamite were produced annually for the mining industry and for munitions." Or perhaps the terrain changed because of the mining industry. The booklet said that the next several miles "is through lots of mine workings and is often stony and uneven. Keep to the path as there are many spoil heaps and old mine shafts on both sides of the Coast Path." In addition, "in the 17th and 18th centuries Perranporth was a mining village with copper and tin mining being the main sources of income for the locals." Furthermore, "Both tin and tungsten was mined at Cligga Head until 1945." Or perhaps the terrain changed because of the geology since "Cligga Head is a granite outcrop where the near vertical rock strata is layered with black quartz." In any case, purple heather added color to this very rocky section.

Once I got to Cligga Head, I was instructed by my B&B to take a left off the path, walk through some industrial area to the main road, and the B&B would be on the right down the main road just a bit. I remember choosing this B&B because I could not find any B&Bs in Perranporth proper itself most likely due to the music festival. It was not that far from the path, but it was kind of weird to walk through this industrial area. It actually started strangely with two guys sitting outside in big lounge chairs drinking. I felt a bit uncomfortable and picked up my pace, but I am sure they were harmless. Then there were about a half dozen business buildings of sorts till I finally reached the main road, took a right and spotted my B&B.

Later in the evening I had a nice home-cooked dinner at this B&B. They offered dinner to their guests, and I was the only one there eating that evening because all their other guests were down at "Tunes in the Dunes." It seemed like they cooked the meal for themselves as well, as I heard them eating in the other room. They were a nice husband and wife from Finland.

This was my longest walking day of my SWCP adventure thus far, (and will be my longest as far as mileage goes). Nineteen miles total! Four by taxi, so that means I walked fifteen miles! Wow! No wonder I was very tired and my feet actually ached a bit. And that little blister on the inside of my right big toe made another appearance. But it was a wonderful day, from some nice early morning walking, to a walk on a long beach, and especially walking with Sasha.

From my three inspirational books, I really appreciated all of their inspiration, especially Sasha's inspiration, and her friendship! Are you still singing, "But I will walk 500 miles, and I will walk 500 more…"

DAY 28 STATS: 18.5 MILES TOTAL ON SWCP. 14.5 WALKING ON SWCP, INCLUDING 4 MILES WITH SASHA. 4 MILES BY TAXI. EXTRA HALF MILE TO B&B. PURPLE SHOES AND BARE FEET. 10 HOURS. PUB IN HOLLYWELL IS "ST. PIRANS INN." PUBS IN PERRANPORTH ARE "THE WATERING HOLE," AND "THE SEINERS ARMS."

TODAY'S STATS BROKEN DOWN:

Mawgan Porth to Porth Beach: 4.5 miles
Taxi to Fern Pit Café and Ferry: 4 miles
Crantock to Holywell: 4 miles with Sasha
Holywell to Perranporth to "Tunes in the Dunes:" 4.5 miles, with 2.5 miles of beach walking
Perranporth to Cligga: 1.5 miles
Cligga to B&B: .5 mile extra

PERRANPORTH/CLIGGA HEAD TO PORTHTOWAN – Sunday, 2 July 2017

"Kestrel. Jackdaw. Herring gull. Pipit. Black-backed gull. Rabbits. Stonechat. Swallows. Peregrine Falcon. Fulmar. Gannet. Common lizard. Green hairstreak butterfly. Buzzard. Gold ringed dragonfly. Painted lady butterfly. Chaffinch. Adder." - Wildlife listed on a sign at Chapel Porth.

Today the weather was perfect! More than perfect! Sunny, warm, probably 70F/21C. I loved it. That, and three beaches to sit on for a long time each! What a glorious day. May all my days be like today! I woke up at 6:00 for no other reason than to type up my notes about yesterday's day, as I didn't finish last night because I was so tired. After walking fifteen miles to say the least. I got a great night's sleep however, and my feet and body felt rested after about eight hours of sleep. Breakfast was at 8:00, and by 8:35, I started walking through the industrial area to get back to the SWCP. Ten minutes later, I started on the SWCP itself.

Just as I said yesterday, the landscape changed today from the past four weeks. Yes, it has been four weeks since I have started walking the SWCP! It seemed rockier, with what looked more like canyons rather than coves because it seemed steeper looking down, and purple heather covered the cliff tops. I believe that I may have possibly entered more of the historical mining areas along the SWCP. There were several groups of seagulls nesting on the rocks in the water and causing quite a ruckus as they cawed overhead. A mountain biker crossed my path a bit later just as sun peaked out from behind clouds. It was warm out, and I was grateful.

I noticed that my walking pace was not as fast today as some days have been. I am guessing it was because of the weather today, and also perhaps because I feel more comfortable, getting used to walking and all. I am in a groove; I am in a zone; I am in my element. I realized I don't think I have gotten lost or turned around in many, many days. In fact, sometimes it feels like instinct kicks in when it comes to directions now. That, and it was very well signposted. That, and the weather was more than perfect today!

I realized that when one walks for hours and hours and hours about every day, one's mind and body in general slows down. Stresses disappear. Worries go away. Distractions of everyday life don't exist. The world seems like a calmer place. I don't think about work or paying the mortgage. I don't have to drive in traffic. I don't even have to go grocery shopping or cook or do the dishes. Being with nature each day is peaceful and relaxing and good for the spirit and the soul. In fact, even when the weather is not so good. I've always liked walking and hiking and being outdoors, but this experience of walking on the SWCP opened my love up for it even more. Opened my love up even more for the beaches and the boats and the harbours, for the seas and oceans and waters, for the crashing waves and the negative ions. Even just walking alone feels amazing and confidence-boosting and wonderful. I could just be me in my own world.

What was odd though was that at the same time I had those thoughts, my thoughts of having Scott join me at some point got stronger too. I would like his company, the companionship, being able to share my experiences with him. Then I think of the logistics it would take to get him here, and all the things he has going on at home that he couldn't attend to, and I wondered if it was really possible.

An hour after I started walking, I arrived at a small beach, Trevellas Beach, and some old mining ruins, like a mine chimney. The beach was deserted until a family with three kids walked out of the ruins down to the beach. I walked passed "Blue Hills Cornish Tin," which according to their sign is "the only tin producer in Cornwall" with "Cornish Tin and jewelry and giftware for sale." You could even take tours of the working process of Cornish Tin production. In fact, "In the second half of the 19th century Blue Hills was a reasonably sized tin mine producing a few thousand tons of tin in its lifetime."

After a short ascent I was overlooking some of that purple heather, looking down upon the sandy Trevellas Beach and the turquoise and blue waters. I could see the steps of the SWCP carved out of the green hillside that I had descended a bit ago to get down to the beach. Like in other places, there are other paths leading to different places, some here leading closer to the water or an alternate way to get down the hillside. A half hour later, I was overlooking a surfing beach at Trevaunance Cove, of the town of St. Agnes about a mile inland. I could see the beach below, and various buildings up above the beach on the hillside, and other buildings even higher on top of the hillside, including another mining building. From this viewpoint, I could see surfers and swimmers in the water, and a large lone rock in the water in the background beyond the small headland. A few benches offered a seat for this beautiful view, but I was hungry so walked down to Trevaunance Cove at the village of St. Agnes.

I tried to get a bite to eat at one place, but they told me they just stopped serving breakfast at 10:00. I walked down towards the beach to check it out. I took the scenic route, via the "Jubilee Garden" trail, instead of the road. I spotted at a small café which was serving food, and ordered a falafel and hummus toastie, which would take eight minutes to cook. I can't recall if I described a "toastie" yet or not, but it is a toasted sandwich. For example, if the toastie was filled with cheese, the US would call it "grilled cheese." I found some rocks on the beach to sit and wait for my toastie. I took my shoes off. The sun felt so good. It was so warm. I decided to sit. To really sit. For a long time on the beach at Trevaunance Cove. Well, eight minutes later I needed to go back and get my toastie. Then I returned to the rocks. For a long time. To sit. An hour, which may have been one of the longest breaks I have taken in all my walking days. At least in the warm sun. It was 10:20 when I ordered the toastie, and 10:28 when I went back to get it.

I watched the surfers. I witnessed an RNLI crew drive one of their Lifeboats down to the beach, put it in the water, and speed away. I have no idea why they did this, perhaps training, as it did not seem like an emergency. I watched the people sitting on the beach. I heard dogs bark. Little boys and girls were in their wet suits going out for some surfing. A few rowboats were sitting on the rocks of the beach and above on the slipway. Beyond this beach were headlands I walked on, and large rocks jutting out into the deep blue seas. It was pleasant to just sit on the rocks, eat my toastie, and just look and observe. I was just being in my own world.

Many times when I have ordered a sandwich they ask what type of bread I would like, white or granary. I always choose granary because it seems like the better choice for me. I finally looked up exactly what "granary" bread is and it is made of a mix of whole wheat and white flours, and also contains cracked grains of malted barley and wheat. Yes, the better choice for me than white bread. My falafel and hummus toastie was on granary bread.

There was an RNLI Lifeguard truck sitting on this beach, as I have noticed on other beaches before. This one was close enough that I could read some words written on the back in stickers: "Swim Between the Flags." Red and yellow flags are the "bathing flags," meaning that you can only swim between the two flags. "Respect the Water." Indeed! With storms and currents and rocks and other dangers, it is important to respect the waters.

I finally got up from my spot on the rocks. As I left this wonderful place of Trevaunance Cove, which was hard to leave, I stopped inside an RNLI Gift Shop. The ladies in there were sweet. I bought a postcard of the motorboat Lifeboat in action that I saw put in the water a bit ago. Actually, as I was sitting the motorboat came back, and I saw them put it back on the truck and tow it off the beach. I still don't know why they did all that. Perhaps practice for a real rescue. On the back of the postcard I bought, I learned that RNLI is short for Royal National Lifeboat Institution.

Doing further research later I discovered from their website that the organization of RNLI "saves lives by providing a lifeboat service, seasonal lifeguards, flood rescue response, water safety education and our international work. Our volunteer lifeboat crews provide a 24-hour rescue service in the UK and Ireland, and our seasonal lifeguards look after people on busy beaches. Our Flood Rescue Team helps those affected by flooding. RNLI crews and lifeguards have saved over 142,200 lives since 1824 but we're more than a rescue service. We influence, supervise and educate people too. Our Community Safety teams explain the risks and share safety knowledge with anyone going out to sea or to the coast. And our international teams work with like-minded organisations to help tackle drowning in communities at risk all around the world." Lifeboats, Lifestations, Lifeguards. They are a "charity that saves lives at sea." Very important!

After I left the RNLI Gift Shop, I walked by a box of tennis balls for sale. "Used tennis balls (for your child or dog) 50p each. Proceeds to the RNLI. Tennis balls kindly donated by St. Agnes Tennis Club and Heron Tennis Centre at Newquay." I didn't buy a tennis ball, but I did make a donation to RNLI. I have done two and a half miles today so far, and I have four and three-quarters miles to go to Porthtowan, my destination for today. There will be one more beach in between. I started walking again an hour later after I started sitting after I went back to get my toastie. It was still more than perfect weather.

Speaking of realizing that I have not gotten lost or turned around in days, I was so calm from sitting, that I missed a SWCP sign and started walking up a road. I didn't get too far when I realized that it didn't seem right. That instinct was kicking in. I did not even get frazzled that I did this. Instead, I asked a couple walking their two dogs if they knew where the sign was. Back down at the bottom of the road. Of course. I probably could have found it on my own walking back, but they were there at that time, so I asked. Guardian angels. Sure enough the dark color of the sign was blended in and camouflaged with the dark green leaves of the bushes that surround it. That, and I probably wasn't looking high enough being in such a calm state of mind.

I followed a small road out of Trevaunance Cove, which had a row of colorful domestic planted flowers, which made for a great foreground in some photos of the beach and cliffs and water and sky. Reds, pinks, yellows, purples, oranges, whites in front of the turquoise and blue waters, the white waves rolling onto the sandy and rocky beach, the green hillsides and headlands beyond, with views of the SWCP etched in the hillside that led down to Trevellas Beach from earlier. Some of my favorite photos!

As I walked on, I noticed another sound that I love. It was the sound of flies and bees when the sun is out and it is warm. It reminds me of the hiking I do back at home, especially in the summer, and especially at my favorite place to hike, Mount Rainier. It is the sound of a summer day outdoors.

As always when I walk, I look behind me to see where I have been. Soon those headlands I once walked on completely disappeared as I turned some corner, but new headlands always appear ahead of me, which at some point, I will be walking on. The purple heather, and some yellow wildflowers as well, also made for great foreground subjects in some photos today. Even when my photos were just of the purple heather in the front and the endless deep blue seas beyond, and the lighter blue endless sky above. I realized that things are so much better and easier and calmer for me when the sun is out and it is warm. Summer!

More sounds included chirping birds, the small waves crashing on the rocks and beaches that I love, and this time also the sound of lapping ripples a bit further out in the ocean, not crashing on any rocks, just lapping themselves. It was a quieter water sound than the crashing waves. Ahhhh, a new sound. Peaceful.

I spotted a National Coastwatch Institution Station and soon arrived at the station at St. Agnes Head. I chatted with a few people who had large binoculars and cameras right at the tip of the cliff. They were looking for a pod of bottleneck dolphins, which at the moment were about ten miles away. If the pod continued in the direction towards the people, they said it would take about forty minutes for the dolphins to get there. They are volunteers for a wildlife group. My purple shoes made an appearance in the foreground of a few of my photos at St. Agnes Head.

On my way to my second beach of the day, Chapel Porth, I passed by some more mining ruins, which included ruins of the buildings of the Wheal Coates Mine and the Towanroath Engine House. These ruins date from the last quarter of the 19th century, and they used to mine the metallic element of tin. The Engine House "was used to pump water up 600 feet from the Wheal Coates mine." This area was a popular place for people to visit today, with its history and old structures still somewhat intact. In fact, I found out more about tin mining in St. Agnes from their Visitor Guide and Map of St. Agnes published by the St. Agnes Chamber of Commerce. "St. Agnes has an extremely rich mining history due to the unique, high quality tin found in the area, formed by action between the granite and the complex rock around the area's cliffs. Today, St. Agnes remains the last remaining tin production centre in the UK at the Blue Hills mine. The iconic mine shaft at Wheal Coates goes all the way down to the sea, and at high tide you can hear the waves crashing against the rocks through a grate on the floor of the ruin. This mine shaft is accessible through a large cave at the far end of Chapel Porth beach at low tide. The mining that occurred in and around St. Agnes shaped the landscape, economy and society of the parish. This is still evident today in the ruins of the mines themselves, the harbour where ore was shipped and coal received, as well as in the magnificent houses of the mine owners."

I arrived at the beach of Chapel Porth a couple hours after I left Trevaunance Cove and I sat at this beach for an hour as well. For some reason, I was hungry again and got a sandwich at the little café. I found a spot to sit down, take my shoes off again, and ate just part of the sandwich. I guess I wasn't that hungry. I sat at this beach and enjoyed the warm sun again, although here there was a slight breeze. People were surfing and people were sitting on the beach. One couple was collecting rocks of a certain shape and size. I wondered what they will create with them.

A sign back at the café listed "Wildlife at Chapel Porth, Things You Might See This Month." That is the list in the quote above. I am familiar with some of the wildlife mentioned on the sign, but some I am not familiar with. After my sit at the beach of Chapel Porth, I had one and a half miles to go until my destination for the day, Porthtowan. I walked slowly. I was in no rush today. What a glorious day. I looked back and again saw the SWCP etched in the green hillsides leading down from the mining shafts and chimneys down to Chapel Porth. Today has been mostly flat walking. A few minor ups and downs here and there, but other than that just flat. The views were fantastic in the warm sun and blue skies. What an awesome day! (Yes, I am saying this fact again.)

I had one photo with a lot more of that purple heather coloring the green hillsides, with just the various shades of blues of the water and sky. And another similar one, this time with some white wildflowers as well. I arrived at Porthtowan at around 3:00. I immediately put on my flip flops, and then I treated myself to a Zennor ice cream cone, Belgian chocolate, double scoop. I will be walking to Zennor in a few days. I sat on the beach to eat my ice cream, my third beach sit of the day! Many people were out enjoying the beach and the water on this warm summer day.

Then it was time to cool off my feet in the ocean water. I walked down to the water's edge, took the flip flops off, and strolled around the water's edge for a bit, and "paddled" in the water. I was careful though as to where I stepped because there were jellyfish on the surface. Similar to the ones at Saunton Sands, I didn't know if they bite or sting or anything, and I didn't want to take a chance. There were even some purple jellyfish, to match my purple shoes. After my more-than-perfect day, I took a taxi back to my B&B&D (and dinner) back near Perranporth and Cligga. Dinner was served again here. Another home-cooked meal, a pasta dish. Last night's dinner was a fish and potato dish. Both were served with a good homemade bread, but not granary.

By the way, today not only have I been walking for about four weeks, I have covered 210 miles, one-third of the SWCP!

DAY 29 STATS: 7 MILES. 6 HOURS, WHICH INCLUDES A LOT OF SITTING TIME. NO EXTRA MILES. PUPRLE SHOES AND A SOME BARE FEET TIME. PUB IN ST. AGNES/TREVAUNANCE COVE IS "THE DRIFTWOOD SPARS," AND PUB IN PORTHTOWAN IS "THE UNICORN." Info about RNLI from rnli.org.

Random Miscellaneous Photos
Colorful Domestic Planted Flowers Trevaunance Cove July 2
Colorful Rainbow Umbrella Budleigh Salterton August 14
An Old Dry Stone Wall near Abbotsbury May 2

PORTHTOWAN TO PORTREATH VIA TAXI; PORTREATH TO GWITHIAN WALKING – Monday, 3 July 2017

"Please speak only in whispers. Any sudden movement or noise can disturb the seals. Thank you." – Sign at Mutton Cove near Godrevy Island Lighthouse.

It was really disappointing to see the forecast for today - thick cloud and fog - especially after yesterday's more than perfect weather. I was about to give up walking today entirely. Then things changed, and things turned out to be good.

After breakfast of a large bowl of muesli with grapefruit and yogurt, I thanked the woman at this B&B for everything. I was going to have a scheduled taxi to take me to Porthtowan, my original potential starting point for the day. But with the weather forecast, I didn't know what to do. I did not want to walk in the fog, like the experience I had back near Trebarwith Strand to Tintagel. I wrote my next B&B in Carbis Bay to see if they could pick me up in Porthtowan, and I would take a complete rest day and not walk at all. Understandably it was too far of a drive for them. I asked the taxi driver if he could take me all the way to Carbis Bay or St. Ives. Understandably it was too far of a drive for him. I agreed that he would take me to Portreath, a bit further along than Porthtowan, and I could get a second taxi from there, if needed.

Technically, this would mean that I would be skipping another four miles today between Porthtowan and Portreath. I originally planned a twelve mile day for today, but with the impending forecast, that was the decision I made. To either make today an eight mile day, or a zero mile day. The description of the section between Porthtowan and Portreath that I would miss called for walking near a military base anyway with a fence running alongside for much of it. I was saddened by my decision once again because that would now be a total of about twenty-two miles I have not walked to date. But once again, I am reminded of Gordon's advice, "It also takes courage to make a decision to not walk from time to time."

I was dropped off in Portreath, and at the moment, the weather didn't seem too bad actually. It was warm out, and there was actually no fog at the moment. The forecast said it wouldn't be for a few hours that the fog rolled in. I wasn't sure what to do at this point, having not yet called a second taxi. Sometimes in this uncertainty, that is when things just somehow work out alright. Looking at the beach in Portreath, a group of seven surfers looked like they were taking a lesson.

I decided to walk backwards on the path just a bit to start in order to get to the top of a little hill so that I could possibly see in the distance, and see what the weather might be like. Potentially I could see if any fog was rolling in yet. Besides there was a structure up there that looked like a lighthouse, and it was on what was called Lighthouse Hill. Well, I never made it that far, which was the first sign that things would work out alright today. On my way to Lighthouse Hill, I was nearing The Portreath Arms, a "bar, restaurant, and rooms" place. Just outside I saw a woman sitting on a bench. She had on a small rucksack, some hiking poles, and was tying her shoes. Ah ha! I thought. A walker. Perhaps on the SWCP. Perhaps going in the direction I was going. Someone to walk with! I might just go ask her if and where and when she was walking. So I did. I don't know if it is "normal" protocol on the SWCP to randomly ask people to walk with them, but I did it anyway, just like I asked Jim and Henry, and Gordon.

And so she was. Walking. With her family. To Hayle, which was beyond my destination for the day. Perfect. I thought I would just explain my fog story and ask if I could join them please. She said yes. I was happy and thankful. The other three people came of their accommodations and just to be sure I explained to them my fog story and asked if I could join them. They said yes. I mean, of course they kind of had to say yes in some ways. It would probably seem rude if they said no. Although they did seem just fine and alright with me tagging along on their family holiday. So now I have met and walked with Jim and Henry, Gordon, my friend Sasha, and now this family of four.

I first needed to email Scott and the Carbis Bay B&B to inform them of my change of plans, and to put on my purple shoes. I was wearing flip flops at the time. I figured The Portreath Arms would have WiFi. I asked the family if they wouldn't mind waiting for me for about five minutes to take care of this and explained why. They said ok, and I was appreciative of my four guardian angels of the day.

The family that I started walking with happened to be from Belgium, although one of them lived in the US. We introduced ourselves and started talking about our SWCP plans. I explained that I was walking the entire path in one go, although realistically now, I have had to skip some miles here and there. They were walking the path in sections over the years. Today was their last day for this year. They asked why my husband wasn't walking with me, out of curiosity. I explained that I originally wanted to do the entire path on my own, but that was changing too, as I had now walked with a friend, with other people I spontaneously met, and now them.

After our introductions, I actually decided to stay behind them, walking quietly and not talk much with them. I wanted to give them their space and family time. The three younger family members walked ahead chatting and laughing, and the mother was a bit slower behind them, and I stayed behind her.

There were a couple of ascents and descents that started the day, but the rest was quite flat. We passed by some wheat fields inland, and the seas to the right. Fortunately, while there was some light fog it did not obstruct too many views either immediately in front of us, or too far beyond. I could see no thick fog up ahead either that would make it difficult to see and walk in. I decided I would stay with the family as far as Hells' Mouth Café, about four and a half miles, and if the weather continued to be just fine, I would politely excuse myself from them.

The similar yet different rolling green hills, with some more of that purple heather, filled the landscape this morning. Similar yet different cliffs and rocks leading into the waters. Similar yet different beaches of sand and rocks. Similar yet different white waves and turquoise and blue waters. A descent and an ascent. Sheep in a field. Farmland inland with those squared off checkered puzzle like sections. At one point I could see the zigzag of the SWCP carved out of a green hillside that we would ascend. We arrived at the café about an hour and forty-five minutes after we started walking together.

I knew I had about three and a half miles more to go till any sign of food, and with just muesli for breakfast, I figured I would eat at the café. That would also be my polite way of excusing myself from the family so that they could go on and have their family time. The weather was thankfully just fine, with no foreseeable fog. This also seemed like a popular area as a lighthouse was only a couple miles away (not Lighthouse Hill). I thanked the family for letting me walk with them (well, behind them quietly), and I told them I would stay and eat at the café. They had something to drink at the café, and they eventually left the café and we said our goodbyes.

I left the café an hour later, and had about two miles to walk till the Godrevy Lighthouse. I walked slowly. It was warm out actually, just with some high clouds, and fortunately no sign of fog or rain. I wondered about missing the four miles earlier today, and was not sure why the forecast was not quite correct, but chose not to dwell on it too much and just walk on. A sign informed me, "As you walk through the Knavocks you might see our Shetland ponies. Their job is to graze the headland and heathland. They are wild ponies so please take care if you need to walk past them. Keep your dog on a short lead or at your side. For your safety please do not feed them or try to pet them. Please take care when passing close to the electric fence." From the National Trust and the Ranger Team, Godrevy. I never did see any Shetland ponies.

I started to listen to some music however. I was getting good mobile reception, and it seemed like a good time to do that. I listened, even sang out loud, and even danced a bit on the SWCP! It felt good! I recalled and tapped into the fact that I am a woman, and that I am into woman empowerment and our female strength, and realized that maybe this is part of why I am walking the SWCP. Because of my strength, both emotionally, even through the struggles and challenges, and physically, because of my female empowerment, that I can do this. I really can do this. Even if I don't walk every single mile and even if I don't walk by myself all the time. I can still do this, and I am doing this. Walking the SWCP. I felt empowered.

I saw my first views of the lighthouse and heard myself say a little "yippee" out loud because I really like seeing lighthouses! Along with singing and dancing, I waved at some cows safely in a field behind a fence next to the path, and I spotted a few ladybugs on some wildflowers.

I was getting closer to the lighthouse, walking on the flat hilltop, and there were a lot of people around so I shut off the music so as to not disturb anyone. I was also glad I shut the music off because just a bit ahead at Mutton Cove were a couple of signs informing me to: "Please speak only in whispers. Any sudden movement or noise can disturb the seals. Thank you." And another sign: "Shh Whisper for wildlife. Barking dogs, raised voices, shouts and squeals can all scare the seals." Seals! It was a good thing I turned my music completely off, although I did not have it turned up too loudly to begin with anyway.

There were some seals in the cove below, which one woman was kind enough to point out to me. I really am not that good at spotting wildlife sometimes though, and I couldn't really tell if was looking at a seal or at a rock. So I moved on…to the lighthouse.

Godrevy Lighthouse is on a small island, Godrevy Island, not too far from Godrevy Point. Built in 1859, it is run by solar panels today. I picked a spot to sit down for a while on the grass and look at the lighthouse. And to take lots of pictures, including some with my purple shoes, and some with Punxsutawney Phil safety-pinned to my rucksack, and some with both my purple shoes and Phil. Remember Phil? I think these were the first pictures I had taken of Phil since those at the monument in Minehead. Seagulls were flying around.

I have just about made it to the place where Scott and I started our 100-mile walk together last year. I've covered over 210 miles, more than one-third of the SWCP, mostly on foot, mostly on my own, through some emotional and challenging weather conditions. As I sat here in front of the Godrevy Lighthouse, I thanked each and every one of my guardian angels over the past more than four weeks, those amazing people that I am being taken care of by, who one way or another show up just at the exact right moment in time, especially my husband. I also began to wonder about the possibility of the "universe" that also helps take care of me, and possibly a guardian angel above all the other guardian angels who oversees my guardian angels, so I thanked these thoughts and possibilities as well. I still have over 400 miles to go. I will take it one day at a time, one mile at a time, one foot at a time.

Every once in a while I think of the movie "Wild" that I watched the other night, how they started the movie with her biggest struggle and challenge, her hiking boot rolling down the side of a mountain. I think that if this book ever turns into a movie, I would like the movie to start with me dancing and singing on the grassy path just before the lighthouse, with my feelings of empowerment. Of course, they would have to have an actress play me that sings better than I do. I would like to have my movie start out fun, happy moments, rather than moments of struggle and challenge.

On the other hand, with today being such an "emotional rollercoaster" in and of itself, from the disappointments with the weather and the sadness of missing more miles this morning, to the thankfulness of finding people to walk with, to singing and the feelings of empowerment, does one start a movie, or a book, with the ups or the downs of the emotional rollercoaster? There are also the physical ups and downs of the ascents and descents of the SWCP. (Of course, I start this book differently altogether since I had more experiences after today.)

I stayed at the lighthouse area for about forty minutes, taking more pictures from other angles as I walked away, including some with a field of white and yellow wildflowers in the foreground. People were on the rocks below, fishing. More white wildflowers lined one side of the path while purple wildflowers lined the other side of the path. More seagulls were flying around, and many people were out here walking to see the Godrevy Lighthouse.

I walked slowly toward Gwithian. I had less than two miles to go. I was to find the pub in Gwithian and call Anne from my Carbis Bay B&B, and she would come get me, as we previously arranged. I kept looking back at the lighthouse as I walked, and forward to the next beach spotted with surfers. The walking continued to be flat. The Red River cuts through the path and since the tide was high, I had to take a sand dune route, being thoughtful about Adders, rather than a beach route. There were surfers and swimmers though on this beach, Gwithian Beach, with the lighthouse on the island in the background.

The village of Gwithian was a bit inland from the path, and I wasn't quite sure how to get there to find its pub. I ended up walking a bit further than necessary, asked for directions inside a café, walked back some, and then inland. It was a bit confusing to figure this out, and I was sure I added an extra half mile to my walk for today.

I spotted a church tower in Gwithian as my landmark, and to go visit the church, and it turns out the church was right next to the pub. As I walked towards the church, I noticed something very interesting up in the sky as I looked back at the lighthouse. I literally saw the line of clouds that were covering the sky moving inland, and that they would soon pass by me overhead and literally be gone so that the blue skies would follow and appear. It was amazing. The sky was opening up. From cloud cover to blue skies, and I could clearly see this happening. The weather pattern was changing. Over the lighthouse, too. Perhaps it was a good sign from the universe or from the guardian angel above my guardian angels. I took pictures of this phenomenon as I continued walking. I could feel the heat from the sun literally increasing as the clouds were passing by as I walked closer to the church and pub. Soon the sun was no longer hidden, the skies were blue, and by the time I got to the church grounds it was warm and sunny. Amen.

This 15th century church, St. Gothian's Church, had two large pink beautiful flowering hydrangea bushes on either side of the front door. Much like St. Edonoc Church that had the row of flowers surrounding its door on my way to Padstow several days ago. I read in the Gwithian booklet that I bought at the church that Gwithian has a rich history of mining and that "the extraction of tin, copper, lead and silver in the parish, whether by streaming or shaft-mining, goes back many centuries." I am not sure about these two methods of mining, and thus I just find it fascinating to read about and wonder.

After my church visit, and coming back outside to the warm sun, I went into the Red River Inn pub and asked if I could please use their landline phone to call Anne, as I now did not have mobile reception. She said she would be there in about a half an hour. Anne and I chatted like old friends on the ride back to the B&B in Carbis Bay. After all, I did know Anne. Scott and I stayed at the same B&B last year our first night when we did our 100-mile walk of the SWCP. In fact as I already stated, starting in a couple of days, I will be repeating the same 100 mile stretch. It made me miss Scott.

Anne was a very helpful kind person, telling me about my walk tomorrow, even showing me a map, about places to eat, and about offering me rides. I noticed a church near this B&B which Scott and I didn't see last year. There was a view of the Godrevy Lighthouse from my room, like we had last year. Soon I was hungry, but walked to St. Anta Church first, which was closed, but there were a couple of flyers up saying that on Thursdays, starting this Thursday, 6 July through every Thursday till 31 August, from 2:30 till 5:00, they would be serving Strawberry Cream Teas for £3.50/$4.85 at the church in the afternoons. I made a note that hopefully I will be back from my walk that day in time to go. I am staying at this B&B in Carbis Bay for four nights. The proceeds of the Cream Tea will go to the Church Decorating Fund, and the Cream Tea will be served in the St. Anta Church Hall.

I ate dinner at the same Spanish/Mediterranean restaurant that Scott and I ate over a year ago on our first night in Carbis Bay at the beginning of our walk together. I sat outside as it was nice and warm out, having a nice romantic dinner alone. I ate a great vegetable skewer served with some bread, new potatoes, a salad, and some dipping sauces for the vegetables. Eating here also made me miss Scott.

DAY 30 STATS: 12 MILES. 4 BY TAXI. 8 MILES WALKED. 4.5 WITH FAMILY. 5.5 HOURS. EXTRA HALF MILE. PURPLE SHOES. PUB IN PORTREATH IS "THE PORTREATH ARMS." PUB IN GWITHIAN IS THE "RED RIVER INN."

GWITHIAN TO CARBIS BAY – Tuesday, 4 July 2017

"It's the people, the places, the pain, and the trials. It's the joy and the blessings that come with the miles. It's a calling gone out to a fortunate few, to wander the fringes of God's hazy blue." - From Nimblewill Nomad, "The Man Who Went on a Hike, and Never Stopped Walking."

I will start out with a fun statistic from yesterday…I finished my first memory card full of pictures from my camera. To date, I have taken over 1,700 pictures with my camera and over 1,100 with my mobile phone, for a total of over 2,800 pictures so far!

I woke up early this morning, two hours before breakfast, to finish writing about yesterday. This morning's breakfast consisted of muesli with fruit and yogurt again, and I actually had some hard boiled eggs. I was tired of eating eggs, so had I stopped for a while, as I seem to go in cycles like that. Anne drove me back to Gwithian to the car park near the café that I asked for directions from yesterday. That was where I stopped walking the SWCP yesterday going forward, and then backtracked and went inland to the pub. I figured it was the place to start walking today, above the beach and near the sand dunes.

As we were driving towards Gwithian it occurred to me that ever since Minehead on all the roads I have been on, most of them those single lane narrow country roads, I don't think that I have seen that many, if any, stop signs or stop lights! I pointed this out to Anne, and she said I was right, except for maybe a stop light that would allow a pedestrian to cross a street and except for some in larger towns. Although, there are a lot of traffic circles which seem to work well and smoothly. What a concept though – to live in a place where there are roads that are not busy enough to need stop signs and stop lights. This plus the single lane narrow country roads. Ahhh, no traffic. A slower lifestyle. Must be nice to live like that compared to the super busy Seattle area of which I live.

I really wanted to walk on the long sandy beach today, the Gwithian Towans Beach, which itself was three miles long, but for a bit I couldn't find a way down, so walked through the sand dunes at first, being aware of the possibility of Adders. It was somewhat tough walking as the sand was soft. I was looking forward to finding a way down to the beach and be able to walk on more compact sand. I finally found a way down. I also knew there would be a way out the other end of this beach, and I checked the tide tables as well last night seeing that low tide was around this time this morning and high tide would not be till mid-afternoon. I was prepared.

Actually, going through the sand dunes for about twenty minutes was a bit fun in its own way, like finding your way through an easy maze. Whether I was really on the SWCP or not, I didn't know as I didn't see any markers or arrows or acorns, but I stayed on the widest path, the one with lots of footprints, figuring I was alright. If the path split off at any point, I still tried to choose the widest and most used path. The sand dunes in this area are called "Towans," which "comes from the Cornish word "Tewyn' and it means 'sand dunes.' It is used for some place names, for example 'Porthtowan.' Most people think of 'The Towans' as being particularly associated with the sand dunes at Hayle," which was where I was heading towards.

While walking on the beach, I listened to the waves. Being quiet and at one with nature. The beach had a few people on it, but not many. The beach was not only long, but also wide. I enjoyed looking at other foot prints in the sand – from big feet to little feet, from dog feet to my feet. As I looked behind me, I could see the Godrevy Lighthouse standing on its little island in the distance. I had good mobile reception as I walked down the beach, so after my time with nature, I listened to a few rock and roll songs. I really enjoyed my long peaceful and fun walk on this beach.

As I got nearer to Black Cliff, the place I was to exit the beach just after, I confirmed with a lifeguard that I was still alright to walk just past the cliff at this time with the current tides, and that was where the exit would be. I could also obviously see that the tide was still way out, and other people were near the cliff, but I thought I would double check with someone official. She said I would be alright with the tides, but she did not seem too familiar with the SWCP, but did say there was a way up. Just past Black Cliff was the Cove Café and a few steps and a short path up. I figured this was my way out and took it, and sure enough, it was right. I had just spent a great hour walking through the dunes and the sandy beach. It was another three-mile long beach! What a nice way to start today's walk! I could also now see a church with its tower in the near distance, the St. Uny Church in Lelant.

As it turns out, the next section of the walk was a stark contrast to the peaceful and quiet beach. Walking around the Hayle Estuary first started on some pavement through an industrial area, and then continued onto some paved sidewalks by a very loud and busy road. I stopped by for some quiet time in St. Elwyn's Church which was built between 1886 and 1888, just as I started along the road. This church had a unique 88-foot tower, as it was "built in two stages. The lower one is square and the upper one is octagonal with a balcony between the two stages," as quoted from the church brochure that I got while inside.

The SWCP continued to parallel the loud busy road for quite a while, which had their harbour and a few boats sitting on the ground at low tide. At one point the path did get quieter a bit as it went just alongside the Estuary, but not for too long, as I was back again out onto a very, very busy and very loud road. I had to even cross the road twice because of the location of the sidewalks, which I made very carefully made sure no cars were visible or audible in either direction, looking both ways about ten times, waiting till there were absolutely no cars coming whatsoever, because I still needed to be aware of the opposite traffic patterns that I am used to, before I crossed the road. Then I ran as fast as I could across the road, as those were all my rules of carefully crossing roads since day one. Ok, I really didn't run. I also didn't have anyone to hold hands with however. The path through Hayle was posted with black stickers of the acorn symbol and an arrow in white with the words "South West Coast Path," the stickers being stuck onto on poles such as street lights. This was the way to navigate in this area.

The very, very busy and very loud road curved around to a smaller road by a large Inn which probably had food, but I spotted a smaller quieter café just ahead, and stopped there for lunch. Birdies Bistro. I sat there eating a good lunch which I apparently did not write down what I ate as I edit this section of this book months later, and I don't remember what I ate there. After eating, the sticker signs on poles took me into a few housing developments, right then left then right again. I came out onto this quiet country road lined with homes. The roads were getting quieter and quieter which was much nicer to walk through than the busyness of Hayle.

I followed a road to the church I saw earlier, and arrived at the St. Uny Church in Lelant. Originally dating from the 12th century with the present building dating from the 15th century, this church is the start of St. Michael's Way, a 13.5-mile path that leads to St. Michael's Mount. This path is one of the pilgrimage routes leading to the Cathedral in Santiago de Compostela in Spain! Of course you know by now that I walked another pilgrimage route in Spain, the Camino Francés, also leading to the Cathedral in Santiago de Compostela. I felt a connection, a kinship if you will, with St. Michael's Way at this moment even though I technically have not walked it. The booklet informs me that, "Pilgrims travelling by sea from Ireland and even Wales used the land route called St. Michael's Way across Penwith (from here to St. Michael's Mount) to avoid the dangerous waters around Land's End. The route begins at Lelant and leaves the Coast Path on the St. Ives side of Carbis Bay and heads towards Knill's Steeple. It then goes overland to Penzance, Marazion and St. Michael's Mount. It is signed and waymarked by a symbol based on the traditional pilgrim's symbol of a scallop shell."

I knew of this St. Michael's Way actually from when Scott and I came across the scallop shell symbol of this Camino when we were here last year, so I had done some research on it. I even considered that since I had already done the 100 mile stretch I am about to do, I considered doing St. Michael's Way route instead and not repeat the SWCP route. Ultimately I chose to repeat the 100 miles, but I still have the desire and curiosity to do St. Michael's Way at some time in my life, adding it to my future "to-walk" list for some time when I return to England.

Before I went inside St. Uny Church itself, I walked around it. It was next to a golf course, and I had another view of Godrevy Lighthouse from here, further in the distance now. As I walked around, there was a golf ball on the church grounds. I picked it up and tossed it back onto the golf course. Good thing someone didn't hit one of the stained glass windows of the church. Another golf course.

Inside the church I heard the best sound ever. Nothing. Absolutely nothing. It was so quiet in there. Perhaps one or two brief birds outside chirping, but then silence. Complete silence. Not even the hit of a golf ball. It was so peaceful in there. I realized how many sounds that we constantly hear day in and day out. In these moments to hear nothing, well, that was something. I suppose this would be the place where you could literally hear a pin drop. In addition, it was so nice compared to the noise of the traffic of the busy roads earlier.

Inside the church, I also looked at the kneeling pillows, which I like to look at in any church that has them. Today's pillows included embroidery of small birds, an owl, and a cat. In one of the churches I recently visited in the past couple of days, one of the kneeling pillows had the embroidery of the church itself. I said my usual prayers.

Outside the church, a sign told me that I had one and three-quarters miles left till Carbis Bay. I decided to walk slowly. I was feeling emotional, a bit sad and lonely actually, because within a mile or so would be the place that Scott and I walked on the day we arrived in Carbis Bay over a year ago to deal with jet lag. We walked "backwards" on the path our first day since the next day we would be going "forwards." I knew some of what was ahead. I would see a beach sign, there would be a covered bench, the railroad tracks would be nearby. Being here again would make me miss Scott. I even wondered at this moment of spontaneously changing my plans for the next almost-two weeks and walk St. Michael's Way instead of repeating what we had already walked. However, I continued on with the SWCP, as that is what I really set out to do – to walk its entire length (or what I could at this point) in one go! Besides, I had already booked several B&Bs between here and St. Michael's Mount along the SWCP, so cancelling those would have been difficult, and I probably wouldn't have gotten any deposit money back that I had already paid.

As I left the church the path led right through the golf course. I was to keep straight while the golf paths were criss-crossing the SWCP and were for golfers only. Warning signs told me not to go left or right. Just ahead of me all of a sudden I saw three golfers scurrying along quickly crossing the SWCP eager to get to their next hole. It was a funny sight to be seen, with their bag of clubs and all.

I had views across the Hayle Estuary now back to Black Cliff where I was earlier today. Sure enough now the tide clearly was in there and it would not be walkable around Black Cliff, so I was glad I had the opportunity to walk on the beach earlier today. I wondered why they didn't put in a bridge across the Estuary or create a ferry system so one can avoid walking around the busy roads of Hayle.

The walk after the golf course started out in the sand dunes above a beach below. I really wanted to walk on the beach below to my right, but for this one there would be no way out the other end. Railroad tracks, and an occasional train, were paralleling me on my left. I had views looking back of the beach below, then the Hayle Estuary area, then the long beach past Gwithian I walked on, and finally out to Godrevy Lighthouse. The sands were tan colored, the waters that wonderful deep blue and turquoise, with white waves, and the blue sky with white clouds.

The path turned from the sand dunes into a lot of overgrown, sometimes dark, underneath shrubbery. I don't think it was this overgrown last year. At one point I passed the beach sign that Scott and I stopped our "backwards" walk at last year, and then I passed the covered bench where we paused together last year. I took a photo of the bench this year empty. Last year Scott sat on the bench, and I have a photo of him sitting on the bench.

As I walked on, I could see the beach of Carbis Bay approaching. I reached the beach in the mid-afternoon. Scott and I actually did not go down to this beach last year. It may have been too cold. Today was not cold. In fact the weather was great today! Cloudy but warm all day! No rain, no wind, no fog. I went down to the beach, had a forty-five minute sit down, including cooling off my feet in the seas by paddling.

As I walked out of the beach and back onto the SWCP for just a few minutes, I arrived at the sign that points to Lelant Church in one direction and St. Ives in the other direction. From here I took side streets for about a quarter mile back to the B&B, but I could not remember the way to get back which I thought I would from last year, so I used the good old GPS on my mobile phone.

Tonight's dinner was at a fancy hotel in Carbis Bay where I ate a salad with all kinds of veggies and goodies in there, topped with a large chunk of goat's cheese. I contemplated that even with the busy roads today, what a great day with a long beach walk and a long beach sit!

I happened upon this article today probably linked through Facebook somewhere called "The Man Who Went on a Hike, and Never Stopped Walking." Nimblewill Nomad is his nickname, and over the course of fifteen years, Nimblewill Nomad "had hiked 34,000 miles," including the 2,200-mile Appalachian Trail, the 2,650-mile Pacific Crest Trail, and the 3,100-mile Continental Divide Trail, between the ages of 61 to 75. Now at the age of 75, he started "a grueling road-walk from New Mexico to Florida, in order to complete a route he had named the Great American Loop, which connected the four farthest corners of the continental US." That is impressive and inspiring! I was touched by his quote, "It's the people, the places, the pain, and the trials. It's the joy and the blessings that come with the miles. It's a calling gone out to a fortunate few, to wander the fringes of God's hazy blue."

In fact, as I am editing this day in January 2018, it appears as if Nimblewill Nomad, M. J. Eberhart, has now completed walking the Historic Route 66, passing through eight states, about 2,300 miles, in about 124 days. That's an average of 18.5 miles per day.

DAY 31 STATS: 8.5 MILES. 5 HOURS. I WON'T COUNT THE QUARTER MILE TO THE B&B. PURPLE SHOES. PUB IN HAYLE IS "THE CORNISH ARMS." Information on Nimblewill Nomad from theguardian.com/world/2017/jul/03/hiking-walking-nimblewill-nomad-mj-eberhart and from nimblewillnomad.com.

ST. IVES TO ZENNOR – Wednesday, 5 July 2017

"Then one day a Mermaid, sitting on the rocks below Zennor in Pendour Cove, heard his voice drifting down from the church above. She was mesmerized by the sound and every Sunday she would come to the same rock in the Cove to listen to him sing." – Part of "The Mermaid Legend" from the St. Senara's Church in Zennor.

I "slept in" till the alarm went off at 7:00 this morning. However, I woke up to perfect weather! It was already sunny and blue skies, and as the day went on, it stayed like that. Probably a perfect warm 70F/21C day out. I loved it! I got ready, video called with Scott as we usually do about twice a day, and had breakfast an hour after waking. I ate a big bowl of muesli with fruit, and asked if I could take some hard boiled eggs with me for today's walk. Anne agreed, and also suggested I take a "butter sandwich." I wasn't fond of that idea, but took it anyway being appreciative.

Anne's husband John drove me to St. Ives. In fact, yesterday I got a nice handwritten note from Anne saying, "We can drop you in St. Ives in the morning, and we can pick you up at Zennor but not until 3:30 or later. We'll chat in the morning. Love, Anne." Nice note, and we did chat this morning, and after 3:30 would be just fine.

I knew that the more rustic walk started at the end of St. Ives near the "bowling green" area having done this stretch last year, so that was where I had John drop me off. I will walk the mile-and-a-half to two miles from Carbis Bay to the bowling green area of St. Ives tomorrow as part of my "rest day/day off."

I began walking around 10:00. The trail started on a paved path for about ten minutes, where a few benches offered the scenery of a small beach, a small hilltop with St. Nicholas' Chapel on top, and the blue waters and skies. The paved trail then turned into a dirt trail with a rocky beach below and more amazing blue and turquoise waters. It was crowded the first fifteen minutes, and then all but one person disappeared. A couple of nice gentlemen were doing some trail maintenance, using weed whackers to trim the shrubbery that had overgrown on the trail, which I much appreciated.

I made it to Clodgy Point a few moments later. As I walked the two miles between Clodgy Point and Carn Naun Point, part of me could not remember this trail from last year, except for a few spots. I know Scott and I did not have the great weather last year that I had today. The sunshine allowed me to see several shades of blue. The deep turquoise waters where the seas were shallower, the deep blue of the seas beyond, the light blue skies, and even some darker blue waters due to a layer of seaweed underneath. This was colored with the dark green from the shrubbery of the cliffs, splashed with seas of purple heather, and yellow and white wildflowers. Below at the edge of the cliffs transitioning to the seas was the light and dark brown colored rocks, and the white of the small waves. The occasional spot on the water of a fishing boat or motorboat added to the scenery. What a colorful day! As of course most days are, with blue and green still being my favorite colors!

The trail itself was a lot rockier than anything so far in all the miles I had done since Minehead. I kind of remembered this from a year ago, but did not remember how rocky. Later on in the day, I would be scrambling over large boulders, carefully navigating walking on rocks, and gliding through slippery small pebbles. It felt like I was hiking in the mountains near home. I had to watch my footing very carefully as I went along today. Since I knew this, I wore hiking boots today, and used my hiking poles all day long. I arrived at Carn Naun Point at 11:30 with three miles done, three and a half to go for today.

Up until now, I had only seen one person on this stretch of the path today. A man who was not too far in front of me, the only one on the path that I had seen since the dirt trail. Then the crowds appeared. Well, at first it was a large group of people walking together. When I caught up to the group, the one man passed them and I never saw him again. I would see the group of people on and off the rest of the day. They were from Italy. I was behind them at one point and overheard them talking. It sounded Italian, so when I had the chance to say hello, I said "buongiorno" instead and sure enough, they were Italian. I let the Italians get ahead of me as I paused for a break at Carn Naun Point. Then I passed them as they went off trail a bit at one point to sit on a ledge and apparently watch some seals. I once again, could not spot the wildlife.

Soon I stopped for a longer break. I took my boots and socks off to air out the feet, ate a surprisingly good butter sandwich, and the hard boiled eggs. I took a good look at the scenery. Same colors as before just in a different configuration. It is just amazing how from day to day to day to day the landscape changes, I thought to myself. One day I am walking near beaches, and the next day it is more rugged. That's what people love about the SWCP I guess. It never gets boring (well except maybe that part where I biked might have been a bit monotonous if I walked it, and there was that bit yesterday through the town of Hayle), but by and large, the constant change of scenery is incredible! The Italians passed me by as I sat there. I took pictures with my hiking boots in the foreground of the scenery.

It must have been "International Day" on the SWCP today between Carn Naun Point and Zennor. In addition to Italian, it sounded like I heard a few other languages, perhaps German, perhaps Spanish, definitely English. There were various sizes of groups out too walking, some single women, couples, and friends. Everyone was out enjoying the sunshine.

I did have a conversation with a woman from Poland, as we crossed paths going in the opposite direction. She was walking on her own for a week from Penzance to Newquay, about 83 miles, which is the opposite direction as I am going. She was staying only in hostels, a less expensive way to walk the SWCP than the B&Bs, but hostels are not as common and frequent in number. She was carrying all her items with her instead of using a luggage transfer service, but for a week, with an average of twelve miles per day, she did not have many belongings with her.

We got on the subject of how I was walking the entire path. She asked how many miles I had done so far. I answered about 225 so far, less the approximate twenty-three miles that I have missed. In about a month. She seemed impressed. She said to me, "Well if you can do that, then I can certainly do my week." I told her though that I need to remain humble about my walk. But perhaps I influenced her in some way and made her walk a bit easier. The subject of my book came up as well. She said she would be the first to buy it and asked me my name. (Well, I guess really she would be the second to buy it because my Mom already claimed the first copy.) As I walked off, I only hoped that she understood my name and will be able to find my book someday. If the woman from Poland that I talked to briefly today between Zennor and St. Ives is reading this, please contact me and let me know! I hope you had a great walk!

More colorful scenery continued as I walked. Headlands ahead, and headlands behind, covered in green. A few coves with brilliant turquoise waters. Boulders to climb over. I ended up catching up to the Italians, and stayed behind them for the last less-than-mile into almost Zennor. There were too many of them for me to pass, and we were close enough to Zennor that it didn't matter. Since they were walking slower than I was, I would actually get too close to them at times, so I would stop on purpose so as to not interfere with their walk. I would take a look around at the colorful scenery while I waited.

Up ahead I knew there would be a choice of routes to take. The official SWCP would go around Zennor Head, the public footpath would cut the headland inland. I chose the public footpath this time because last year Scott and I did the official route, and I was curious about the footpath. When the two paths joined up again, I backtracked a bit on the SWCP to get to some large boulders which read, "Zennor Headland given to The National Trust December 1953. In proud and happy memory of the friends whose love has sustained me. – A.B."

I sat at the boulders a few moments still taking in the colorful scenery and the headland beyond. I actually remembered the headland I was seeing just beyond from last year. It had the shape of like a dragon or lizard head or something with scales going down the top of its head. I actually remembered questioning why this was not called "Lizard Point" because it really looks like a lizard to me, yet another headland in a few day's or week's time is really called Lizard Point. This headland is called Gurnard's Head.

I walked back down the path as it ran into the road that would take me into the village of Zennor. I remembered walking down this road with Scott last year. It started to rain last year. But not today! I stopped and put my cushy flip flops on.

I went into St. Senara's Church in Zennor, with its famous carved Mermaid Chair and The Mermaid Legend, carved over 500 years ago. The legend from a framed written story hanging on the wall of the Zennor Church goes:

> There was a boy who lived in this village whose name was Matthew Trewhella. He was the son of the churchwarden and came to this Church every Sunday to sing in the choir. He had the most beautiful voice and each Sunday many people would come to hear him sing.
>
> Then one day a Mermaid, sitting on the rocks below Zennor in Pendour Cove, heard his voice drifting down from the church above. She was mesmerized by the sound and every Sunday she would come to the same rock in the Cove to listen to him sing.
>
> She was very beautiful and loved to sing herself. Her voice was hauntingly serene. Then one day she decided to venture up into the village and into the church.
>
> She fell in love with the boy and he with her. She enticed him to come away with her and they were last seen swimming out to sea, down at Pendour Cove. They were never seen again.
>
> It is thought that the Mermaid Chair, created about 400 years ago, was carved in memory of the Choir Boy, Matthew Trewhella.

I enjoyed walking around the inside of the church, which "the earliest record of the building dates from 1150 with the tower being added in 1450," but there were some men doing renovations outside and chatting and had music on, so it was not as quiet inside as it could have been. But it didn't matter.

I was actually an hour early for my prearranged pickup with Anne. I went into the Zennor Chapel, which is now actually a café and accommodations, where Scott and I stayed last year. I called Anne to tell her I was there already, but didn't mind waiting. She said she would be there in forty-five minutes. That was enough time for me to get something to eat. A couple slices of fresh hot pizza with some bell peppers, caramelized onion, and bacon. I think the first time I have eaten any sort of meat, and it was good!

Anne picked me up in their convertible. She used this car yesterday as well to drop me off in Gwithian, and John used it this morning to drop me off in St. Ives. I can tell they love that car, especially on a day like today. With the top down, Anne and I chatted a bit on the way back as she asked me why I chose to do the SWCP. I explained. My 50th birthday. Something epic. The challenge. The constant seas and oceans and waters. The ever-changing beautiful landscape and the colorful scenery.

Anne did my laundry for me today too while I was walking. In a washing machine. Proper laundry! She did the majority of it today, and I will give her a second small batch tomorrow. So nice to have just about everything freshly washed. The last time I had freshly washed clothes was in Croyde Bay with Jenny several weeks ago.

For dinner, I wanted to go to yet a different restaurant in Carbis Bay. I searched online and found "The Bean Inn," a vegetarian/vegan place about a five minute's walk up the road. It was good. I had their "Spanish Paella & Pepperonata – vegetable paella and a Mediterranean sweet pepper stew served with romesco salsa and garlic and basil olives." I also bought their cookbook which was only £6/$8.50 as another souvenir cookbook. Who knows, maybe I will cook something from either of the cookbooks that I have purchased so far!

DAY 32 STATS: 6.5 MILES. 4 HOURS. NOT GOING TO COUNT EXTRA WALK TO DINNER. HIKING BOOTS. PUB IN ZENNOR IS "THE TINNERS ARMS."

CARBIS BAY TO ST. IVES, AND ST. IVES TO CARBIS BAY – "REST DAY" - Thursday, 6 July 2017

"I have nothing to do today, and all day to do it." - I made that quote up today.

After a long nine hours of sleep, I woke up 45 minutes before my scheduled breakfast. Today was a "rest day," although I still ended up walking around four miles and kept quite busy, in contrast to my own quote of having nothing to do today. For breakfast I had just of a big bowl of muesli with strawberries and milk. I got ready for my rest day, packing a few things in a small bag I brought, travelling very light. It would be nice if I could pack this light every day.

I left the B&B in Carbis Bay to walk the mile and a half towards the beginning of St. Ives. Today started out a bit foggy actually, and I decided to walk in it, but it was not too bad as I could see where I was going, and I had walked this area last year, and I could see the Porthminster beach below, and a bit of the edge of the seas, but not much beyond that. As the morning progressed, the fog lifted, and it turned out to be a warm, dry, cloudy day, with an occasional sun break. All around, very good weather. Note that I was actually glad I switched yesterday's walk to

Zennor and my rest day today (they were originally planned the other way around), due to both the weather, and it was nice to have a rest day after the rocky and rolling terrain of yesterday.

As I walked down towards St. Ives, the path started on a road, went in front of a hotel, turned into a paved path, and then a quiet paved road. At one point I passed a sign with the scallop shell symbol on it for St. Michael's Way, one direction pointing towards Lelant in two-and-half miles, to St. Uny Church that I passed by a couple days ago. This sign also had the acorn symbol. Therefore, I have officially walked two-and-a-half miles on St. Michael's Way, from Lelant to this point, and I have eleven miles more to go in order to complete that pilgrimage route someday. I could have continued onto Knills Monument in a mile on St. Michael's Way at this moment, but took the SWCP sign to St. Ives instead.

I passed by Porthminster Beach, and arrived at the beginning of St. Ives just over an hour after I left. It took me a while to walk the one and a half miles because I walked slowly, and also because at one point I missed a sign and ended up walking along a very busy road for a few minutes and had to back track. Yes, I got "lost" on my rest day! At least this time, I backtracked and found the correct way.

When I bought that cookbook yesterday at The Bean Inn where I had dinner, I happened to glance through it last night, and discovered that on Thursdays there is a Farmer's Market in St. Ives. I also saw some flyers for the Farmer's Market, located at the Guildhall, confirming my discovery as I approached the town, so I went there first. I like going to Farmer's Markets when I travel because they give a good sampling of local food and local life. I looked around the market at all the vendors, mostly food vendors, and took a few photos. There were vendors selling scones, brownies, cakes, pies, tarts, and all kinds of sweets. Vendors were selling local jams, jellies, chutneys, marmalades, and relishes. Freshly baked breads and rolls; local free range eggs; fresh fruits and vegetables; and vinegars and oils.

I found one vendor that I shall call "my favorite vendor" because they were selling all sugar-free, gluten-free, and vegan products. Cheesecakes in the flavors of mint chocolate; vanilla, white chocolate and berry; dragon fruit and rosewater; and raw cacao and coconut. They had homemade raw snickers bars. On the savory side, they had spicy bean burgers, beetroot and feta burgers, butternut squash and feta burgers, and lentil and cheddar burgers. For now, I just bought single small delicious raw chocolate almond butter cup. I decided to come back later for lunch.

I wore my purple shoes up till now, but changed into flip flops for a while. I slowly walked down to the harbour of St. Ives and around it, taking many photos from different angles of the boats at low tide, eventually walking all the way down Smeaton's Pier, which was originally built in the 1760s by Joseph Smeaton who also built the Eddystone Lighthouse (more on that later), to see two Harbour Lighthouses. One of the lighthouses, a short one possibly made out of concrete bricks, dates "from 1831 and was where Smeaton's pier ended. The white cast iron lighthouse was built at the end of the pier when it was extended in 1890." This white lighthouse was taller than the brick one, but still relatively short compared to other lighthouses. Thus I added the Godrevy Lighthouse to my list of lighthouses from a few days ago, a lighthouse to help those out at sea, and today I added two "harbour" lighthouses that help those entering a harbour.

There were rowboats, sailboats, and fishing boats sitting on the sand of this harbour at low tide. I could even see the ropes that tied them up creating lines in the sand, some of the ropes covered with seaweed. Some kayaks lined the pier, and a few crab and lobster pots added to the scenery. There was a small chapel, Saint Leonard's Chapel, a "traditional chapel of the fisherman of St. Ives." It may have been built "to commemorate the record breaking passage made by St. Ives lugger Lloyd SS5 Scarborough to St. Ives, 600 miles in 50 hours in 1902," according to a plaque on the side of the small stone chapel. According to a website, "We do not have an exact date for the construction of the Chapel, but records of repairs have been found and these date from 1577. The Chapel was more than likely used for quiet contemplation and prayers before embarking out to sea, as well as being a good source of shelter in inclement weather. In 1971, the Chapel was renovated and opened as a museum and a memorial to the fisherman of St. Ives." Unfortunately, it was closed today, as I would have liked to have visited the museum, and perhaps do some quiet contemplation and prayers myself. In any case, it was just wonderful to learn and know more about the fishing industry, and how prayer, contemplation, shelter, commemorations, and memorials all play a part of the livelihood of fishing.

In fact, "for hundreds of years St. Ives was dependent on fishing and mining but more recently tourism is the main source of income. It was once the most important pilchard fishing port in Cornwall with the harbour crammed with fishing vessels," according to today's booklet. I have mentioned "pilchards" before and needed to research what they are and they are small fish similar to sardines, and are in the herring family.

Some church bells rang 11:30am in the background, as I started my next goal of the day, walking the rest of the SWCP to where I started yesterday at the bowling green so I could complete that section. After the harbour, the path went around a part of St. Ives called The Island, which has a small beach, a National Coastwatch Institution, and St. Nicholas' Chapel, the one I spotted on the hillside yesterday. On the small beach were some beach huts, the first I have seen in a while. These were painted mostly white, with doors of green, red, yellow, blue, green, red, yellow, blue. Per a brochure from St. Nicholas Chapel itself, "St. Nicholas is not only the patron saint of children, but also of sailors and it is natural to assume that the latter is the reason for the dedication of this little chapel, standing as it does on the top of The Island, surrounded on three sides by the sea in this town where our ancestors have for centuries derived their livelihood from the sea." Per the booklet, this Chapel is at least 400 years old, and "It was originally a chapel for fishermen but has been used as a lookout for smugglers and a War Office store at the beginning of the 20th century." I went inside this little chapel for some quiet contemplation and prayers.

I walked along a second beach, Porthmeor Beach to get some of those good for me negative ions, and to arrive at the bowling green area shortly thereafter. Then it was time to walk back to the main part of St. Ives to play "tourist" and to do some errands. First stop was a visit to St. Ives Parish Church. The church bells rang 12:30 as I walked there, the same church bells I heard an hour earlier. "The present building [of this church] was begun in 1410 and consecrated in 1434," according to the brochure of the church I picked up.

Second stop was a cash machine at a bank to get some cash. Third stop was to see if I could find, or find a way to contact the Polish woman I met yesterday who mentioned she was staying in a hostel in St. Ives. I should have got her contact information yesterday, but did not, and realized I was regretting that later. It would have been nice to keep in touch with her. I researched last night that there seemed to be only one hostel in St. Ives, so I went in and talked to the receptionist, but no luck. I described her as best as I could, but even if the receptionist recognized her, which she didn't, due to confidentiality, she wouldn't be able to give me contact information anyway. Oh well, I tried. Again, if you are reading this, Ms. Polish-woman-walking-from-Penzance-to-Newquay-staying-in-hostels, please know that I tried to find you!

Third stop was a pharmacy. To get some joint pain relief cream to rub on the bottom of my feet, especially around the balls of the feet. Yes, after some 225 miles, my feet were actually aching a bit. The aches were nothing that would stop me from walking, but I thought I would take care of my feet and treat them well. Oh, and the blister I had on the outside of my right big toe that developed a few days ago on my very long walking day, also popped yesterday as I was in Zennor after wearing the boots. I actually kind of helped it pop by tugging on the top skin, which at that moment was very soft and easy to pop. And well, gross, but the liquid inside oozed out. It didn't and doesn't hurt, but it was about time I did that. I just have to keep it clean so as to not let anything get inside and cause an infection. I left the skin on, and have put on gobs of triple antibiotic ointment, and wore a band-aid, aka a plaster, on it today. That's my feet and blister update.

By this time, I was hungry and went back to the Farmer's Market to "my favorite vendor." I bought a lentil and cheddar burger, which was edible at the moment, even though she recommended heating it up, but since I had no way of doing that, I ate it as it was. I also bought two "superfood balls." I make these now at home, as I recently bought several cookbooks with various recipes. I bought one "baobab and cacao superfood ball," and one "peanut and maca superfood ball." I also bought the last two raw chocolate almond butter cups that were delicious from earlier. All was delicious, as I sat on a bench over-looking the harbour of St. Ives to eat. I sat for about a half hour, once fighting off a seagull that was staring at me just about the whole time wanting my food.

It was very crowded out today in this part of St. Ives. Proof of the tourism industry. I even noticed several groups of school children around, on field trips I suppose. One group was playing in the sand on one of the beaches. It was higher tide now at the harbour, and the various boats were now floating in the water, so I put my purple shoes back on, and walked part way around again to get some additional photos. People were lying on the sand, or sitting on the edge of the pavement overlooking the sand, or lounging in rented beach chairs overlooking the boats floating on the water, with the two lighthouses, and the town of St. Ives surrounding. Seagulls were flying around harassing people for their food.

I spotted a store selling some hats. Since I mostly have been wearing my multi-purpose scarf/bandana, I wanted to see if I could get a "proper British hat." I actually found a beige-colored one which had a small brim so it won't flop so much around in a wind, and the hat is adjustable. It will hopefully be good on non-windy, non-rainy days, to help with keeping the sun out of my eyes and the top of my head protected from the sun, which I therefore hope to use every day for the rest of my SWCP walk all the way to Poole. It was only £6/$8.50. (Turned out to be a great hat, and I wore it a lot!)

It was getting to be mid-afternoon, so I started my way back to Carbis Bay, on foot. I was originally going to take a bus or taxi back and save the mileage, but it was such an easy flat short walk, the weather was great, and I was in no rush, so I decided to walk back. After a quick stop at the RNLI Lifeboat Station where they had the door open to see a large lifeguard rescue boat, I started my way back. Other than the store selling hats, I did not really go into any other shops today in St. Ives. I thought I would, as there were definitely plenty of shops. I only looked in a few windows, but did not venture inside any.

I passed by Porthminster Beach again, this time not in the fog, and with a lot more people out enjoying the good weather. The tan sand was colored with beach tents of yellows, oranges, greens, blues. A group of people was taking a surfing lesson. Kayakers were out in the turquoise waters. Beyond in the blue waters I could see the tiny Godrevy Island with its lighthouse.

I took my time walking back to my B&B, with a 3:30 arrival. This would give me an hour to plan tomorrow, rub some cream on my feet, and do a few other things before I headed off for cream tea. Remember the flyer I mentioned a few days ago, which said cream tea at the St. Anta Church Hall here in Carbis Bay? That cream tea! I walked to the church around 4:30, and when I entered the little room that had about a dozen people in it, I asked a very lovely older lady about the cream tea. She asked if I would prefer strawberry or black currant jam. I opted for the black currant, as previously I have had strawberry jam. I confirmed that the jam goes on first here in Cornwall, and she said yes, even though I already knew this. The lovely ladies behind the counter in the kitchen actually prepared it anyway for me, and topped three scones with the jam, then the cream, and then with a strawberry. Of course I was also given a pot of tea. I am not sure why I had three scones halves, rather than four halves which would make more sense, but I thoroughly enjoyed them anyway.

I ate my scones, and drank my tea, as a few other people were finishing up theirs, and the lovely ladies were cleaning up. They told me to take my time. A couple who had been sitting at the table next to me approached me to ask where I was from and what I was doing. They must have recognized me as not a local due to my accent, and that they probably didn't recognize me at all in general. I told them and explained my walk. They live locally in a penthouse near the SWCP and can see people walking into Carbis Bay. I thanked the lovely older lady for my tea, and gave them some money to help with the Church Decorating Fund. Going to this little event even for a short time added a lot of meaning to my SWCP walk for me. It was a way for me to connect with a few locals, and to experience and appreciate something that is part of their lives and is important to them!

I also wanted to go into the church itself. The lovely older lady asked the lovely church warden lady if I would be able to go in after I finished my cream tea, since it was locked when I got there. She said that would be fine, but that she would need to take me in herself since they were redecorating, replastering, repainting, and repairing the inside of the church. That was what the proceeds from the cream tea were going towards. She explained this to me, and told me that the church isn't "that old," some parts only about 90 years old. I guess that is "young" for a church in these areas considering many churches are hundreds and hundreds and hundreds of years old. I walked back to my B&B after my lovely day in St. Ives and lovely time with the locals, and called Mom. Overall, I managed to walk four miles on my "rest day."

DAY 33 STATS: 2 SWCP MILES CARBIS BAY TO ST IVES AND AROUND. A VERY SLOW 3 HOURS. EXTRA MILES IS TWO: ONE AND A HALF MILES BACK TO CARBIS BAY FROM ST. IVES REPEAT, AND FOR A HALF MILE BACK AND FORTH TO B&B/CREAM TEA. PURPLE SHOES AND FLIP FLOPS. PUBS IN ST. IVES ARE "SLOOP INN," "THE CASTLE INN" AND THE "LIFEBOAT INN." PUB IN CARBIS BAY IS "THE CORNISH ARMS."
Information on Saint Leonard's Chapel from stivestowncouncil-cornwall.gov.uk/st-leonards-chapel.

ZENNOR TO BOSIGRAN BY TAXI AND BOSIGRAN TO CAPE CORNWALL WALKING – Friday, 7 July 2017

"This is my fight song. Take back my life song. Prove I'm alright song. My power's turned on. Starting right now I'll be strong. I'll play my fight song." – Rachel Platten

I guess the cream tea I had last night was dinner. I never went out again to get a proper dinner. I suppose that having cream tea for dinner once in a while is alright. Anne at the B&B kindly did all my laundry over the last two days, except for a couple things like my jeans, a nice going-out-to-dinner shirt, and a few items I haven't been wearing. Yes, I packed too many clothes. All my walking clothes and socks, etc. though are clean! I arranged yesterday to have a taxi pick me up at 9:00 am after my muesli breakfast, and after saying thank you and goodbye to Anne and John. It had been nice staying in one place for four nights in a row. For their hospitality, I would like to mention their B&B name, The Mustard Tree. While not exactly right on the SWCP, it was close enough and still convenient.

I decided to miss four miles today, from Zennor to just after Bosigran. This included that lizard-looking headland, Gurnard's Head, and a very rocky section that I remembered from when Scott and I walked it last year. Even the booklet reminded me, "From Zennor Head to Wolf Rocks the path is very uneven and walking is much slower – between one and one and a half miles per hour. There are not too many steep climbs, but you have to navigate the large boulders across the path." My average walking pace has been a mile every half hour, so this section is two to three times slower. Since I had already done this section last year with Scott during our 100 mile walk, I had the taxi driver drop me off at the Carn Galver Engine House, about a half mile before Wolf Rocks. I made this decision for my safety because of the difficulty, and the possibility of it taking four to six hours. I did not want to do it alone in case of injury. I did the last half mile of that section alone with no problems, so that was sufficient. Yes, I missed another four miles this year, but it hasn't been completely missed because of last year.

Today was an emotional day for me. I will admit that I have been feeling lonely the past few days, being in the area Scott and I walked together last year, which reminds me of him and of the walk we had together. I miss my husband and his company. I even wonder if it might be easier to face some challenges with him, such as the weather, rather than on my own. On the other hand, I also like my own company, and have been doing the majority of this walk on my own for over a month, by myself, and that feels good and an accomplishment too. I will walk on, not every mile, and I will enjoy the walk, and see what feelings progress over the next few weeks if I would like Scott to join me at some point in my walk. Yes, as Sasha said, an emotional rollercoaster.

The weather was great again today, which always helps. It was cloudy and warm, turning into sunny and warm. About 60F/15.5C, or even up to 70F/21C. Just lovely for the seven miles of walking I did do today.

For the four miles I missed, I do remember Scott and I having a lunch break at Gurnard's Head. Turns out a "Gurnard" is a type of fish often caught in the Cornish waters, per the booklet, so I am not sure why I thought the headland looked like a lizard. I do remember us having to climb over the boulders, and in looking back at my photos, we had at least a blue-sky kind of day, with great blue and turquoise waters, some rocky coves, lots of large rocks decorating the hilltops, even some farmland on top of some hilltops. We had some pink, purple, white, and yellow wildflowers as we were walking at the end of spring. There were a few streams of water trickling downhill, and a sandy and rocky beach just before Gurnard's Head. There were some ruins of something, perhaps mining ruins, along the way as well. We even came across four horses that Scott was thrilled with and we stopped for a while so he could be around them. This is actually a bit about what Scott wrote about our time at Gurnard's Head last year:

"Windy beautiful coast. Rocky outcrops, sturdy grasses, cute snails, gulls, flies, ocean, 60F+ and mostly cloudy. Little trees (two to three feet). Lots of flowers, soft moss or grass rounds, pink flowers. Sharply defined rocks balanced precariously - some for centuries with only gravity holding them in place on top of other rocks."

Back to my day today. I was dropped off at Carn Galver Engine House, some mining ruins with a shaft and chimney dating from the 1850s, a half hour after the taxi picked me up. Between the booklet and map I had, and the taxi driver calling into his dispatcher, we found where I wanted to be dropped off. The booklet indicated there was a footpath which would lead to the SWCP near the Bosigran area. When he dropped me off, there were a lot of other cars in the car park, and just to be sure about the footpath, I asked a few people if it would lead to the SWCP. Most people parked there though were just going to the rocks at the end of the footpath to do some rock climbing, and did not quite know how to answer my question.

I started walking on the footpath anyway, and I could see the beige line of the SWCP as I got closer to the seas. The footpath was maybe a quarter mile from the Engine House, but I had trouble at first connecting to the SWCP. Well, I connected with it at first, but then some cows were in my way, and so to avoid them, I ended up going on the footpath towards the rocks that the rock climbers were at thinking that maybe it would lead me to the SWCP. That was not right though, so I turned around and went back a bit.

I couldn't see the SWCP from that point of view any longer, but I did see the cows again, so I knew that the path had to be in front of me somewhere, so I veered a bit uphill and to my right, and voila, I found the SWCP while also avoiding the cows. Yes! I sighed a big sense of relief actually because with the cows and the footpath towards the rock climbers, I got a bit nervous. All this, from the car park to this moment, took about twenty minutes.

Because of my feelings of missing Scott, and these twenty minutes for me, I started singing a song after this, an inspiring song for me. Singing out loud to myself, as I didn't really care if anyone was listening. This song has actually been one I have listened to some of the times I decided to listen to music on my mobile phone. This time, I just sang it a cappella. The song is "This is My Fight Song" by Rachel Platten, and is a very inspirational and women-empowerment song for me.

Like a small boat on the ocean. Sending big waves into motion.
Like how a single word. Can make a heart open.
I might only have one match. But I can make an explosion.

And all those things I didn't say. Wrecking balls inside my brain.
I will scream them loud tonight. Can you hear my voice this time?

This is my fight song. Take back my life song.
Prove I'm alright song. My power's turned on.
Starting right now I'll be strong. I'll play my fight song.

And I don't really care if nobody else believes.
'Cause I've still got a lot of fight left in me...

I sang this out loud just about all the way to Pendeen Lighthouse and beyond.

The day was easy from there on out after that first twenty minutes. Well, the first half mile was rocky, but it wasn't too bad. Greenery covered the hillsides. I even had a quick view of the Pendeen Lighthouse in the distance at the beginning of the first half mile. The path remained pretty flat for quite a while. There were still some rocks on the path, but it was easy to navigate. There were occasionally some muddy watery sections, but I could move from rock to rock, or once on a piece of wood, to avoid getting my boots wet. I wore hiking boots again today. Coves with turquoise waters, some purple heather, and a few yellow wildflowers colored the greens and blues.

For a long time it seemed like I was the only one out today. In fact until I got much closer to Portheras Cove and the Pendeen Lighthouse, only two other people passed me in the opposite direction. There was some flat grassy path for a while, and I began to have closer views of the top of the lighthouse. I was still singing.

"Like a small boat on the ocean. Sending big waves into motion."

I passed by the sandy beach of Portheras Cove. I did not go down to the beach this time. Scott and I went down there last year, and I remembered that the way down was quite steep and slippery. From above, the turquoise waters today were beautiful, outlined by the blue seas beyond and the brown rocks and tan sand.

Two hours after I started, I arrived at Pendeen Lighthouse. Being here made me miss Scott today since we were here together last year, as we both enjoy visiting lighthouses. In fact the next mile and a half after the lighthouse reminded me of him a lot. I took pictures of the white lighthouse with its greenish-turquoise trim, and black fog horns. Against the blue waters and blue and white sky, and some wildflowers. It was very picturesque. I walked down the driveway to the entrance of the lighthouse, which was open because someone was doing something in there, but I did not go inside since it is not open to the public. I took my photos and walked back up the driveway. This lighthouse was built around 1900. "On a clear day the lighthouse keeper (if there was one) in the lantern could just see the light from Trevose Head Lighthouse some forty miles north, but only at low tide. This is because the earth's curvature between the two places is enough for the rising tide to obscure the view," per today's booklet that also referenced 'Cornwall's Lighthouses' by Michael Tarrant.

I walked up the road, and sat on a bench for a bit to rest and have a snack. It might have been the same bench Scott and I sat on last year. After my snack, I left the bench. I remembered that last time we were here, we had trouble at this point along the road finding the SWCP. There were a few small side paths leading around, and we did not know which one to take. We eventually asked someone who told us where the SWCP was. This time, I looked at the booklet to help remind me where to go: "right off the road about 375 yards inland of the lighthouse by the last white cottage No. 6 Enys." I counted. My paces. To 375. Sure enough there was the white cottage and an unmarked stone marker, and I immediately recognized this location. For some reason the actual sign for the SWCP is down the path about twenty feet. I am not sure why it is hidden. I think someone should move the sign up to the road.

I had views of the lighthouse behind me and took a few more photos. Soon the lighthouse disappeared behind a rock when I descended. I cried. Out loud. With tears. I had a good cry. My first real good cry. (Well, I thinks that's my second real good cry; the first being from my experience near Crackington Haven.) This cry today was for missing Scott.

"Like how a single word. Can make a heart open. I might only have one match. But I can make an explosion."

Five minutes later I entered the Greevor Tin Mine area, which was a "major working mine in Cornwall and finally closed in 1991 ending almost 300 years of continuous mining in the area." Today it is a big tourist attraction offering a lot of information into mining, but both last year and this year, I did not take a tour of the mines.

Ten minutes later, I entered the Levant Mine area. "Mining began here in 1820. Tin, copper and arsenic were mined at Levant." The ruins here are quite intact actually, with some of it being restored, and are another big tourist attraction. In fact, per today's booklet, "Mining in Cornwall has gone on since the Bronze Age, initially simply by digging a hole in the surface or cliff face and removing the ore. However, with the industrial age Cornish mining increased considerably and was at its peak between 1820 and 1870 when there were over 400 active mines in Cornwall."

Ten minutes after the Levant Mine area I was at the Gypsy Caravan, my B&B for the next two nights. It was early in the afternoon. No one was home, so I called the phone numbers I had. Chris would be home in about a half hour, so I went to the pub about a half mile inland up the road to get some lunch.

For the last hour or so I was thinking that since it was so early in the day, and the weather was great, that maybe I could walk some more today, even though I missed some miles this morning. As I was eating lunch, I looked in the booklet. Cape Cornwall was another two and a half miles away, so maybe I could do that today, and make tomorrow shorter. I would need a ride though, back today from Cape Cornwall to the B&B, and forth tomorrow morning back to Cape Cornwall. After lunch, I would go back to the B&B and ask Chris if he would be able to pick me up later today and drop me back there tomorrow.

I went back to the B&B and before I asked about rides, Chris showed me around this quite interesting little B&B I had picked out for myself. I thought it would be fun and interesting to stay somewhere a little different for a few nights than the traditional B&B. The sleeping and living area is literally this tiny little caravan. Think covered wagon. As when people were traveling hundreds of years ago. A little tiny bed. I needed a ladder to get up there. Underneath the bed was a little storage area for my wheeled luggage. There were little tiny sitting areas on either side of the floor in the middle. Two lights, a coffee pot, and some tea supplies. A TV with a full bookshelf of movies to watch. Some complimentary pieces of chocolate, fruit, and muffins. The bathroom was separate. I would have to walk down the five stairs that lead up to the caravan, across my own private little courtyard with lots of colorful flowers in pots and a picnic table, and up a few more steps. It was a nice modern bathroom.

"This is my fight song. Take back my life song. Prove I'm alright song. My power's turned on. Starting right now I'll be strong. I'll play my fight song."

Chris said it would take me a bit over an hour to walk to Cape Cornwall, and that he could pick me up at 4:00 at the car park there unless I called earlier. I was able to get mobile reception at the caravan, but was not sure if I could at Cape Cornwall, so we arranged the pickup time just in case. I started walking at 2:15. I walked by some other area with a lot of mining ruins, some of which were down closer to the water, the Crowns Engine House, with two really intact-looking engine houses that were built in 1835 and 1862.

Eventually I walked down into Kenidjack Valley, complete with more mining ruins. And a donkey. I remembered the donkey from last year, and sure enough, he was there again. Last year, Scott enjoyed the donkey just as much as he did the horses.

I had views of the hilltop of Cape Cornwall with its Chimney Mine Stack sticking up on top of the green hill. The seas were a very deep blue today just beyond. I reached the ruins of the little St. Helen's Chapel at Cape Cornwall an hour and fifteen minutes after I started walking. This little chapel dates from the 4th century however according to the booklet, "the building you see is likely to date from much later although it is thought to include some of the original stone." It is now without its roof.

I walked down to the little fishing area nearby, Priest's Cove, and took a few photos of the several little colorful rowboats outlining the blue seas of the cove. There were rowboats of red, orange, yellow, green, blue, and white. A few people were swimming off the boat launch, which might be a man-made pool area. And way in the distant waters I could see Longships Lighthouse on a rock!

I did not have mobile reception, and had a few minutes before 4:00, so I walked up to the car park where Chris was to pick me up. I was going to just sit there and look at my guidebook, but the parking attendant who works for National Trust and I started talking. It was good to have a conversation with him. He asked me about my walk. I asked him about where he lived and about his working for the National Trust. He gave me a brochure about the important choughs, black birds, "Cornwall's national emblem," according to a sign written by the National Trust hanging on the parking attendant's hut. "Choughs disappeared from this area in the late 1800s and eventually became extinct in Cornwall by 1973. Following their natural return to Cornwall in 2001 when three birds arrived from Ireland and started to breed, immature birds were soon seen in the St. Just area. In 2008, a pair settled and raised young, which they have done every year since. There are now other pairs too finding a home around West Penwith's cliffs. Listen out for choughs as you walk along the cliff tops 'chee-ow chee-ow.' If you see choughs, let us know." I will certainly listen and look for choughs.

Chris picked me up a couple minutes after our designated pickup time, and brought me back to the caravan. On the way, he drove me through the little village of St. Just and pointed out some highlights of the village. I actually remembered it from last year, as Scott and I stayed in St. Just last year, but I did not let Chris know that. I let him play tour guide.

I had to have Scott video call me on my phone, as there was no Wi-Fi in the little caravan for my laptop. At least I could get regular mobile reception. I went to the Trewellard Arms Pub to have dinner, which was where I had also had lunch, and to use their Wi-Fi so I could type on my laptop. They let me sit there for a while as I typed about my day.

"And I don't really care if nobody else believes. 'Cause I've still got a lot of fight left in me."

DAY 34 STATS: 11 MILES. 4 MILES BY TAXI, MISSING ZENNOR TO BOSIGRAN. 7 MILES WALKING. ABOUT 4.5 HOURS, NOT INCLUDING LUNCH. TWO EXTRA MILES AS BACK AND FORTH TO PUB TWICE. HIKING BOOTS. PUB NEAR LEVANT MINE IN TREWELLARD IS "TREWELLARD ARMS PUB." PUB IN ST. JUST NEAR CAPE CORNWALL IS "KINGS ARMS."

CAPE CORNWALL TO LAND'S END – Saturday, 8 July 2017

"What you can see from Land's End." – Information board at Land's End.

"Glamping." That's what I did last night. In this Gypsy Caravan. Probably the closest thing I will get to camping on my SWCP walk. Glamorous camping. One more night here, then back to traditional beds-and-breakfasts. My breakfast here was served picnic-style. In a wicker basket, with a table cloth for eating on the picnic bench outside my caravan. In my little private courtyard. Mostly cereal choices and fruit, and orange juice, but also a warm baguette and other goodies. I could have had my Half English, but chose this instead.

When I booked this Gypsy Caravan, I had kindly received, by air mail mailed from England to the US, information about this B&B. "This 1930s gypsy caravan has been thoughtfully converted to fit modern living needs," said one page. Another page was nicely written walking directions to the B&B, and also their confirmation of my reservation, this being one of the least expensive B&Bs I stayed in. A magazine article on display in the Gypsy Caravan from "Cornwall Today" that talks about the history and restoration of caravans states, "a gypsy caravan which first travelled the highways and byways of rural Britain more than 80 years ago. They are a uniquely English phenomenon and enjoyed their heyday from around 1880 to 1920. The intricate designs – either carved or painted – which became the hallmark of the grandest ones are a reflection of Victorian taste in décor."

This morning, I woke up to some fog and the sound of cows. The cows were in the field next to my B&B safely behind the shrubbery and fencing. As the hour progressed, by the time I had breakfast, the fog burned off. However, it will be back today. Twice. I did a few video calls with Scott, including showing him my breakfast and the caravan. It would have been fun to have shared the picnic breakfast with him. I still missed him this morning, but was doing alright about my walk alone today.

Chris drove me back to Cape Cornwall after breakfast. It was a quiet morning when I started walking. No one else was around. I started listening to some music quietly on my mobile, which I would be able to, on and off, for a few miles, including the song I was singing a cappella yesterday for some inspiration and empowerment. On, when I was up on a cliff top and could get reception, and off, if I was in a valley or behind a cliff where I was not able to get reception.

A half hour after I started walking, I reached Cot Valley. A few moments later a sign said I had four and a half miles till Land's End, my destination for the day. I had already walked one mile, which meant that according to the signs, my total day walking would be five and a half miles. However, according to the booklets, it should be six and a half miles. I'm still not sure why things differ. I'm going with six and a half miles for my stats.

I came across a sign informing me, "We're happy to say that the breeding pair of choughs in this area had three chicks successfully leave the nest. We want to say thank you to all who walk the coast path for your help and support in ensuring their safe fledging and for giving the adults the space to raise their young. Of the nine pairs in West Penwith, five were successful and raised a total of ten chicks. Enjoy looking out for them on your walk, but please do give them space as they are still very vulnerable. For more information on Cornwall's wild choughs, please visit www.cornishchoughs.org. Thank you." In addition to the information I saw yesterday about choughs, I also picked up a brochure about these birds. Choughs are "a type of crow that lives by the sea [and] a cultural symbol of Cornwall. [They were] extinct after 1973 due to habitat loss and persecution [but] in 2001, three wild choughs arrived naturally from Ireland and settled on The Lizard. Numbers are slowly growing as they breed successfully in the wild and return to their former haunts." Aside from their black feathers, their distinctive features are their long red bills and red legs.

As I progressed along the cliff ledge, I could see around me quite well. The fog was nowhere around. I could even start to see Longships Lighthouse on a rock out at Land's End getting closer. I could see Cape Cornwall behind me. Below me were large rocks along the shoreline. White wildflowers colored the green hillsides. The hillsides themselves were rocky and decorated with boulders.

However, the non-existent fog didn't last for long. I walked right into one headland and valley area of fog. However, I was not worried actually, like I was when I ran into fog back near Tintagel. I had this feeling that this fog was only temporary and localized just in this valley, based on the fact that just prior I could see quite well. The fog wasn't too thick either. I could see the trail in front of me, and the trail was wide enough and easy enough to follow. About a half mile later, I walked out of the fog.

An hour after I started walking, I had three miles to Sennen Cove, which was about a mile and a quarter before Land's End. Soon I approached Polpry Cove, a small rocky beach. The sound of the waves were crashing on the rocks, so I stopped to listen for a few moments to one of my favorite sounds. I had stopped listening to music a while ago because I lost reception. I could see Longships Lighthouse way out in the distance once again as well. These were some good moments.

The weather at the moment was actually cloudy today, and quite warm out. Almost humid. I didn't mind. It made for good walking weather, although a bit of sun would have been nice. The terrain was mostly flat today, but there were a few small climbs and a few rocks and boulders to negotiate around as well. I heard more waves crash on another set of brown rocks as I continued walking. I've been seeing some black birds flying today. I could not tell though if they were choughs. Also flying were a few airplanes above me, as the Land's End Airport was nearby, which offers regular scheduled flights to the Isles of Scilly.

I reached Aire Point and I was back to some beaches and surfers. At first I could not recognize the first beach, Gwynver Beach, that Scott and I walked by last year, but then I soon realized why. Last year this beach was fogged in when Scott and I walked near it. I recognized it though when I passed one spot where there was a set of steps going up to probably a car park. Scott and I sat on some rocks near here last year in the fog. Oh, so this is what we missed seeing last year. A beach. With people and surfers. Although I do remember hearing voices on the beach last year. This time, I could also see Longships Lighthouse from here. It was fun to get a different perspective on something we saw together last year from a different weather situation.

I walked on the last part of Gwynver Beach, as per my booklet, if the tide was low, you can walk on the beach. The tide was low. It was somewhat of a busy little beach. I entered the car park at Sennen Cove ten minutes later. I recognized the car park, although I remember that because of the fog, Scott and I took the sand dune way around the beach last year. Then I remembered a good little café in Sennen Cove we ate at last year, Little Bo Café. I went there again and had something to eat.

As I left Sennen Cove I took photos of the little harbour with the little boats. Rowboats, fishing boats, even a sign with one boat offering boat trips. If I haven't said this yet, which I think I have actually, but I will say it again, that seeing the little harbours with the little boats is one of my favorite scenes on the SWCP! I have seen a few so far, and I know I will see plenty more.

As I left Sennen Cove, and for the first time in over a week, I felt a few drops of rain. Wow, I just realized that I have had a great dry spell of just over a week. Summer! The few drops at the moment didn't feel like much fortunately. I was on my way to Land's End, with about a mile to go, and all day it has been nice and clear so I figured it would be nice and clear when I would get to Land's End. I was still able to see Longships Lighthouse. Last year when Scott and I were at Land's End, it was very foggy and cold, and we could not see much at all. In fact, we have a funny picture of Scott standing at Land's End near an information board that tells you "What you can see from Land's End." Scott was pointing out into the distance at just…fog. Here I was, more than a year later, and all day I thought I would be able to finally see Land's End, the rocks and lighthouses, and anything else beyond, especially in July. But, no! Although the rain was light, it picked up as I approached Land's End, and I even needed to stop to put the rain gear on.

When I arrived at Land's End not only was it lightly raining, but it was getting foggy, and I could barely see Longships Lighthouse just offshore in the water. Nor could I see Wolf Rock Lighthouse about nine miles away. Nor could I see the Isles of Scilly about twenty-eight miles away. Nor could I see anything. Wow. On a clear day apparently you can see all of this. I was thinking that since last year I couldn't see any of it as we were here in May, this year I would certainly be able to see most or all of it, since it is July. But, no. All day the weather was nice and clear for me (well except for one short foggy part), and of course just as the moments I arrived here, the weather changed. Oh, well. I still made the best of it. I took some pictures of my purple shoes, Punxsutawney Phil (at this significant place), and even a couple of selfies (I don't like selfies as mentioned but took some anyway) at the "First and Last Gift and Refreshment House in England," with the national flag of the United Kingdom blowing in the wind, rain, and fog. A lone seagull stood on top of the chimney of the building of the refreshment house as I took photos, and I also heard the fog horn of Longships Lighthouse.

I wandered over to the infamous sign that says "Land's End 2017: New York 3147, John O'Groats 874, Isles of Scilly 28, Longships Lighthouse 1.5," and somebody's "30th B'Day Trip 8th July." I took few more photos of my purple shoes, Punxsutawney Phil, and even a couple more selfies at this sign in the wind, rain, and the fog. I guess I wanted to really commemorate the fact that I was at Land's End.

The significance of Land's End is that it is the most westerly point of Cornwall and, well in all of England! The specific spot for this is called Peal Point, which is the place just below the "First and Last House." The Longships Lighthouse was build on some rocks out at sea, and was first lit in December 1873, and "the last lighthouse keepers were taken ashore in 1988; henceforth the light has been operated by an automated programme." Wolf Rock Lighthouse is eight miles beyond Land's End and has a 115 foot granite tower. "The lighthouse was completed and first lit in January 1870. In 1987, the automation programme was completed at Wolf Rock." This information was obtained from the "Land's End–A Brief History" brochure that I picked up.

I also think that I will now change to my third extension of the Atlantic Ocean, from being on the coast of the Celtic Sea to now being along the coast of the English Channel. I had been originally on the coast of the Bristol Channel from Minehead till about 12 June near Woolacombe, then on the coast of the Celtic Sea since then. Now I will be on the coast of the English Channel till Poole.

I have also heard that the Isles of Scilly are a beautiful place to visit, with five inhabited islands, and "countless uninhabited islands to explore." There are lots of activities to do on the islands, including more than thirty miles of nature trails and walks on just one of the islands, with the other islands as well as the uninhabited islands all offering opportunities to walk their length and breadth. I shall add the Isles of Scilly to my future "to-walk" list for some time when I come back to England, in addition to Lundy Island and St. Michael's Way.

I called Chris as we prearranged I would so that he could pick me up here after my walk, and he said it would take about twenty minutes for him to get here to pick me up. He told me to wait for him by the row of columnar pillars, so I made my way through the busy touristy section of Land's End of food, games, and shops to the front of the buildings and waited. Under cover. Out of the wind, rain, and fog.

I got back to my glamping and I spent a few hours with a movie on TV, since I had that full bookshelf of choices, in the background as I called Mom, and did some Facebook posts. I realized that even though I did not have Wi-Fi, I could at least type on my laptop by looking at my notes on my mobile phone and hand-typing them in from scratch, rather than the way I normally did this by emailing my notes to myself, downloading them into Word, and having the notes to type as a base. A bit later, I walked the half mile down the road to the same pub to have dinner and finished typing and using their Wi-Fi to back up my typing as I always do by emailing each day to myself. Of course, now the sun was out as I walked back and forth to and from dinner.

DAY 35 STATS: 6.5 MILES. 4 HOURS. ONE EXTRA MILE WALKING BACK AND FORTH TO PUB FOR DINNER. PURPLE SHOES. PUB AT SENNEN COVE IS "THE OLD SUCCESS IN." THE "LAND'S END RESTAURANT AND BAR/LONGSHIPS BAR" IS PUB AT LAND'S END, AND INLAND IN SENNEN IS THE "FIRST AND LAST INN." Information about Isles of Scilly from visitislesofscilly.com.

Purple Shoes on the South West Coast Path
Morte Point near Woolacombe (windy area) June 11
Croyde Bay Beach (Like Being Back Home) March 28
Land's End (foggy arrival) (two photos) July 8

Purple Shoes on the South West Coast Path
Weston Mouth Beach between Sidmouth and Branscombe Mouth August 15
Chesil Beach May 2 and August 19
Rocky beach with wet rocks from rain near Porlock Weir June 5
Chesil Beach with billions of pebbles May 2 and August 19
With Scott's Shoes between Brixham and Paignton with SWCP acorn symbol August 10
Plymouth, SWCP sign on ground, April 18

LAND'S END TO PORTHGWARRA BY CAR; PORTHGWARRA TO PORTH CHAPEL TO PORTHCURNO TO PENBERTH COVE TO PORTHGUARNON TO LAMORNA COVE WALKING - Sunday, 9 July 2017

"Still…Nothing beats a home-cooked meal." - Unknown

I thought I saw a chough bird in the yard of glamping last night. I took a few photos. It was a black bird with an orange-yellow beak. However, after further inspection, and knowing that choughs have red bills and red legs, alas it was not a chough.

Speaking about birds, last year in the Land's End area, Scott and I experienced an interesting interaction with a few people that resulting in learning about an interesting bird. As we were walking away from Land's End along a road to our B&B, a man in a car driving by stopped us and asked us if we had seen the "Dalmatian pelican." The what? At first I thought he was completely joking with us, perhaps even recognizing that we might have looked like American tourists and was playing some sort of practical joke on us. We said we had never heard of that, and what was he talking about? "The rare bird," he responded. "That has been spotted in this area recently." We still thought he was joking, and said no we haven't seen the bird, and walked on.

Later that night we asked our B&B woman about this, and sure enough, she said that yes, there had been some sightings of this rare bird in the area. Really? Wow. I guess the man in the car was not playing a practical joke on us. The next day Scott and I even saw a few groups of people around bird watching with telescopes and binoculars and cameras with telescopic lenses. We had another conversation with a woman from Canada as we were walking on the SWCP who also mentioned the Dalmatian pelican.

Finally, I saw a newspaper article that explained more about it. "Birdwatchers in West Cornwall have been treated to an 'extraordinary first' this week, as a pelican that has never been sighted in the wild in Britain was spotted. Photographs of a Dalmatian pelican, which is usually native to the Danube Delta in Romania, were captured at Land's End, Sennen, and St. Ives. If this bird is indeed a wild bird it would be the first ever occurrence of the species in Britain in modern times. 900 miles from its breeding grounds, it has also been sighted in Germany and France in recent weeks. West Cornwall residents were not alone in their excitement; scores of bird-lovers from upcountry have arrived since the news broke." Unfortunately, Scott and I did not spot this rare occurrence, but at least we were in the area around the time of it happening last year, which was rare, in-and-of-itself.

Back to today - After my picnic breakfast, this time eating in the caravan, as it was a bit chilly and rainy out, Chris drove me to Porthgwarra, about three and a half miles beyond where I ended yesterday in Land's End. I chose this, for no other reason than to walk less mileage today, to have him drop me off here instead of Land's End. I also figured that since technically Scott and I did all but three of those hundred miles we did last year (those three will be explained in about a week), that if I skip any miles now, at least I had done them already last year, and so I have done them at least once. Chris had never been to Porthgwarra before, so we figured out directions as we went along, but it was easy to find because of signs pointing us there through those very narrow one-lane country roads.

After my drop off, I backtracked on the path about a quarter mile, so that I could see Porthgwarra from above. I remembered this place from last year. A few brown brick buildings, and a café. The Porthgwarra Cove Café was open, but since I had just eaten breakfast, I was not hungry to eat anything else. I took some photos of the two little rowboats in the small fishing cove of this village, one white boat and one blue boat, and a few kayakers who were just coming in and happened to be there. Apparently the TV series Poldark has been filmed here as well as in Port Isaac.

In remembering the mileage last year from Land's End to Porthgwarra, Scott and my walk started out foggy, with occasional clearing, and the weather went back and forth between being warm and windy. It was a relatively "easy" path which I had written in my journal from last year, except for one area where we were a bit closer to the edge of the cliff, but it didn't last for long. There were several interesting rock formations out in the waters, including one with a natural arch, with views of Longships Lighthouse sitting on its rock off in the distance. We had some various purple and white wildflowers along the path, with views of the headlands in front of us. We walked passed a beach with something that looked like caves in the hillside. I wonder if smugglers hid in those. We walked seeing a lot more interesting rock formations that day we walked, with a lot of large rocks and boulders sitting at the bottom of the cliff ledges as they touched the seas. We stopped by a National Coastwatch Institution Station, with its board telling us that is was 11 May 2016, the wind direction was northwest, the weather had fog patches, visibility was one mile, the sea state was calm, the temperature was 9.6C (50F), and the outlook forecast included rain showers. There was a really rocky beach below as we approached Porthgwarra with lots of large boulders. We did eat something at the Porthgwarra Cove Café last year, and at some point along our walk later that day last year we did an inland detour to see St. Levan's Church, a 15th century church, which I did not do this year.

Back to my walk this year. There was a sign indicating a short path diversion due to a collapse of the path. The diversion was easy to follow and did not seem far out of the way at all. As I walked I had views of the green covered rolling hills. Soon I arrived at Porth Chapel, a small sandy beach with large boulders lying on the sand, that I remember Scott and I went down to last year. I remember it was very steep to get down there, and we sat for a while as the tide was coming in. I remember Scott paddling in the water, but I can't remember if I did nor not, as it might have been too cold for me. Turquoise waters fading to blue led out from the sandy beach.

I reached the infamous Minack Theater, an open-air theater built on the side of the cliff. I did not go in because I think you have to pay just to look. Instead, I walked down the very, very steep steps into Porthcurno overlooking the very turquoise waters of the bay, surrounded by a few sandy beaches and cliffs all around the bay. They really need to put some hand rails or some safety barrier here, I thought as I descended what I think was one of the toughest parts of the entire SWCP for me so far. It was a short section, but I used my hiking poles and went very, very slowly. I suppose I could have taken the road down to Porthcurno instead.

I stopped for a snack in Porthcurno since for the next five and a half miles (I had just done one and a half miles) there would be no opportunity for food. I also bought an extra snack, and also had a baguette with butter and jelly that I made this morning out of my picnic basket. Not the most nutritional food, but it was food that would hold me if I needed to eat along the way.

As I walked on, a view of a long sandy beach was in front of me. The tides were such that the beach was actually mostly covered with water, but the water was shallow enough that I could see the sand just below the turquoise waters. The light turquoise faded into a darker turquoise as this lead out to the bluer seas. (I wonder how many different ways I can describe in this book the turquoise and blue waters that I constantly see on the SWCP, so that no two descriptions are exactly the same.)

I passed by a sign saying, "National Trust and the tenant farmer are managing this area by cutting scrub and grazing with Dartmoor ponies. This will help to improve the habitat for wildlife and encourage choughs to feed and breed here. This is a Higher Level Environmental Stewardship scheme supported by Natural England. Please do not feed or pet the ponies. This will encourage them to pester and nip people. Please keep your dogs under strict control. National Trust." While I really enjoy seeing these signs, I did not see any ponies, or choughs, as I walked.

Almost an hour later after leaving Porthcurno, I reached Penberth Cove, another little village with about ten brown stone buildings, five boats in its little cove, and "a population of about twenty-five in the summer." Lots of photo opportunities even with the few boats and the few buildings and the cove, but no food options. "Once lots of fishing boats operated from here but now there are only a handful." A restored capstan, some kind of rotating machine that looks like a turning wheel, that winds ropes or cables, and thus somehow is used for the boats and fishing, was sitting near the few boats at Penberth Cove. One of the homes here was decorated with various sizes and colors of buoys and flower pots, and as I walked by to leave Penberth Cove, a woman was hanging her laundry on the lines out to dry. Last year, I took photos of the "windows and doors" with these colorful buoys and flower pots.

As I ascended out of the cove, I remembered that there was a path junction with no sign here as to which way to go. Last year when Scott and I were here, there happened to be a woman out walking her dogs who told us to go take the right-side path and "follow the coast." Well, that made sense, and throughout this walk so far, there have been times when I have used that mantra. "Follow the coast." I have seen some paths go inland, and I would ask myself, "Why would I go inland?" I need to follow the coast. Now that mantra is not true all of the time, but now and then and quite a bit, it is true. I wondered if I should title my book "Follow the Coast." It kinds of has a cute ring to it, but alas I did not use that as my title.

The path I was walking on was very overgrown with shrubbery and narrow. My long pants were coming in handy. Up until now today's walk had been fairly flat, but there had been some minor ups and downs. I took out my hiking poles at one point to use them as I descended steeply down into a rocky cove, Porthguarnon. In fact the booklet said that the descent into this cove had 112 steps, and the ascent out of the cove had 138 steps. I actually did not count this time to confirm these numbers.

I love all the names of the places today…Porthgwarra, Porth Chapel, Porthcurno, Penberth Cove, Porthguarnon. Today's walk was brought to me by the letter "P." (Not to mention other days brought to me by the letter "P": Porlock Weir, Port Isaac, Polzeath, Padstow, Porthcothan, Perranporth, Porthtowan, Portreath, Pendeen, Penzance, Porthleven, Portscatho, Portloe, Pentwean, Par, Polruan, Polperro, Portwrinkle, Plymouth, and Poole. In that order, and some places yet to occur.)

I started to hear voices along this path, but at first I didn't know where they were coming from. There was no one on the path, and I was quite sure I wasn't hearing things in my head. It turned out that the voices were coming from some kayakers out in the flat calm waters below me. I guess the cliffs bounced their voices up from below.

I walked on a flat grassy path for a bit, when I reached another path junction. This one was marked, but the marker was quite faded. Just then a man came up from one path, and I asked him if this was indeed the SWCP. He confirmed it as he had come from Penzance about eight miles back, which was the direction I was headed, but I was not walking that far today.

I reached the rocky beach at St. Loy and it was time for a sit and a snack. That baguette with butter and jelly tasted delicious. Not nutritious, but delicious. Several people passed by me going in either direction. I could hear them talk about the fifty yards of rocks and boulders that needed to be crossed at this beach, and I also remembered this bit with Scott. When it was my turn to cross, I found it a bit challenging to walk on them because I was afraid of twisting an ankle. I made it through slowly, carefully, and without incident. "There is no sand even at low tide" in St. Loy's Cove.

The next long bit was quite brushy and overgrown, with two and a half more miles left till Lamorna Cove, my destination for today. It seemed that the overgrown brush was common along today's path, with some footing underneath that I had to be aware of because sometimes I couldn't see the ground through the brush. I was glad once again for my long pants. The day was getting much warmer, too. The day was actually warm to begin with, but with cloud coverage. By now the sun was starting to peek out and the clouds were getting thinner.

I had my first brief glimpse of Tater Du Lighthouse, a relatively young lighthouse, built in 1965, built out of the necessity of there being a few shipwrecks in the area. The brush and rocks with twists and turns kept going on, until I finally reached an open flat grassy area. Then I passed by the lighthouse. From the flat grassy area, you look down a very short paved road that leads to the lighthouse. Of course the road is gated off, but once again it was always fun to see a lighthouse. As I continued walking, I paused to listen to the small waves crash on the rocks. There were a few boats and some more kayakers out on the flat calm seas.

I remember last year when Scott and I were at this lighthouse we had a conversation with a lovely couple from possibly Birmingham in the center of England. They told us they had been coming to this location year after year for forty years, at first on their own, then with their children, and now on their own again. How romantic, and this story interestingly shows one the passage of time.

According to the booklet, and my memory, the last mile or so into Lamorna Cove was "very uneven and there are lots of large boulders to scramble over." It was indeed, but I went slowly and carefully and without incident. Down by the shoreline, there were lots of large rocks and boulders. A red and white sailboat went by, and way out in the distance I could see a large freighter ship. As I got closer to Lamorna Cove, there was a Celtic cross sitting on the rocks overlooking the seas. According to today's booklet, "There are over 400 Celtic crosses in Cornwall. Some date from before the 9th century while others are very recent. The one here is inscribed 'DWW March 18 1873.'"

I stopped and talked to a couple who was walking in the opposite direction as I was getting very close to Lamorna Cove. They looked like they were camping by the twin large green rucksacks they were carrying. I asked if they were camping and walking the entire SWCP. I am curious about people who camp. I myself would not do that alone. I like my "luxury" beds-and-breakfasts, as I believe I have said before. Turns out they were walking 1,000 miles! They started someplace before Poole and the SWCP, which I was not familiar with, and will end up in Wales. They average ten miles a day. They started early June. Good for them! And that is inspiring.

After the scrambling over the last of the boulders, I reached the flat pavement leading into Lamorna Cove. I remembered this well from last year. A pile of crab and lobster pots lined the road. A few people were kayaking in the water nearby today. A child was stomping his feet playing in the water's edge today. For food there was the Lamorna Cove Café. I got there just in time too, as they close at 3:00, and it was just about fifteen minutes before that time. I thought about this as my day went on, wondering if I would make it in time before they closed, but that didn't make me rush to get there.

I knew that my B&B for tonight was a mile up the road, probably the furthest B&B I reserved from the SWCP itself. The only option for dinner was a pub half way in between Lamorna Cove and the B&B, but I decided that instead of going out to dinner later, I would pick up two brie and grape toastie sandwiches at the café, one for now, and one for dinner later. I only ate half of one now, so I had one and a half sandwiches for later. That should be a good dinner.

Val gave me directions to their B&B long ago when I booked this one, and printed them out. I followed her instructions. It seemed like a very long mile up the road, but the road was flat. When I arrived, Paul and Val were very warm and welcoming.

Like all B&Bs, they tell you little tidbits. Such as how things work like the shower, and Wi-Fi information, that there is a place to make tea and coffee in the room, and breakfast information of time and choices, etc. Val also told me that on Sundays the pub is closed, and since that is today, they would be making dinner for themselves and for their guests and that if I would like I could eat with them all later at 7:30 I could. Good thing I bought those sandwiches. I told her though that I just bought those sandwiches, so I thanked her for the invitation and said I would consider her offer, but most likely just eat my sandwiches. Her meal sounded good though, as she would make veggies and falafel and salad. And chicken too, which I don't usually eat.

At 6:30 I was hungry, so I went downstairs and ate my sandwich and a half, skipping most of the bread actually, on their deck overlooking their well-maintained large garden. I still felt hungry, so I told Val I would join them at dinner. Not just for the food, but for the company as well.

I went downstairs to dinner, and there were five of us. Me, Val and Paul, and two ladies from Australia. The first topic of conversation was my solo walk on the SWCP. They asked me all sorts of questions about it. Other topics included that the ladies from Australia were walking six days, I think they said forty miles, plus they did some other traveling here and in Europe before and after. We talked about how Val and Paul just opened up this B&B back in May, and how many interesting people they meet as B&B owners. We talked about jobs. They talked about their grown children. There was laughter. And there was a great home-cooked meal. I even ate chicken!

DAY 36 STATS: 10.5 TOTAL MILES. 7 WALKING. 3.5 BY CAR. 5.5 HOURS. ONE EXTRA MILE TO B&B. PURPLE SHOES. PUB IN LAMORNA COVE IS "LAMORNA WINK."

LAMORNA COVE TO MARAZION – Monday, 10 July 2017

"Groceries, homemade bread, cakes, beef, eggs, ham, salads, cheese, sandwiches, wines of the world, afternoon tea, Cornish cider and ales, biscuits, ice cream, olives, chocolate, smoothies, pasties, takeaway tea and coffee, cream teas, lots of gluten free, including ice cream cones! Good doggies welcome." - The color advertising signs outside the Hole Foods Deli and Café in Mousehole.

While I thought the caravan was cute and all, and I had an experience of glamping, I must say that after a restful night in a large comfortable bed in a large room with a bathroom right inside my room en-suite, I much, much prefer a B&B any day. I like being spoiled!

This morning at breakfast, Liz, of Liz and Lynn from Australia, said that I look "fit." I said, "thank you." She said she would like to be fit after walking their six days on the SWCP. I said it takes at least seven days to become fit. Hahaha.

Val and Paul were super nice people. I should have stayed more than one night at this B&B called Bosula House. I had a very nice breakfast with a scrambled egg, granola, fruit, and yogurt, and a slice of homemade bread topped with…peanut butter and jelly! Val gave me not one, but two hugs before I left, and Paul kindly drove me down to Lamorna Cove so that I would not have to walk the extra mile. Lamorna Cove's "harbour wall was built in 1850 largely for the export of granite from the quarries on each side of the cove. Granite from here was used to build the London embankment, the Portland breakwater and the Longships and Wolf Rock Lighthouses," according to today's booklet.

Today was a day of walking from town to town to town, and biking to another town, and back to the third town. As I started walking, looking back on the tiny village of Lamorna Cove, there was a bit of boulder hopping again, and one small climb. The hillsides at the top half were covered with green, the bottom half covered with rocks and boulders as they led out to the seas. A few sailboats were out today. As far as the weather goes, at first there was a slight breeze, but that soon went away and the rest of the day remained cloudy, but warm and dry! I looked behind me and spotted a small view of the Tater Du Lighthouse, as well as the line of the SWCP that I walked on yesterday as I approached Lamorna Cove towards the bottom of the green hillside. Ahead of me, I could see St. Michael's Mount. Below me, I heard the quiet small waves crashing against the rocks.

The path became flat, and included the tree-lined Kemyel Crease Nature Reserve, followed by a few muddy patches in which the hiking poles helped me keep my balance so I wouldn't get my purple shoes muddy, followed by a short but steep climb, followed by some more flat, followed by a tree-lined tunnel, and finally I reached some homes at the outskirts of Mousehole. I walked down a road into the harbour at Mousehole. This so reminded me of Scott. We stayed in this town last year, had dinner here, walked around here, and went into the little deli/café/store called Hole Foods here. And, he likes cats!

I walked around the tiny half-mile harbour of Mousehole (which is actually pronounced closer to "Mowzel") for about 45 minutes, photographing the boats at low tide, rowboats and fishing boats, in their colors of mostly whites and blues with some reds and oranges, and the orange of the buoys. The boats were sitting on the sandy harbour which was covered in green slimly seaweed. A couple of rows of surfboards leaning against the breakwalls around the harbour adding some additional colors of blues, greens, yellows, oranges, and whites. Most of the buildings lining the harbour were brown stone and white, with The Ship Inn adding some bright red flower pots hanging from the windows for even more color. A banner along the harbour wall announced that in July would be the Mousehole Maritime Festival with "Sea, Salt, and Sails." I couldn't figure out what days in July this was though, and it did not seem like it was today when I was there.

As I walked around the harbour, I went into the Hole Foods Deli and Café, where I bought three little delicious "Raw Chocolate" bars that I had actually discovered last year in St. Ives. The flavors I bought this year were Truffle Pie with Raspberry, Peppermint Pie, and Goji & Pumpkin Seed Pie, which were the only three bars they had in the store today. Last year in St. Ives I had the same Goji & Pumpkin Seed Pie, Cacao and Almond with Pink Himalayan Salt, and my favorite a Combo Peanut Pie. I also did some window shopping of the few small shops in town. I finally walked down near some rocks at the tip of the town as I made my way out of Mousehole. It was a nice little 45-minute casual stroll.

There is a legend that is celebrated in an annual festival each 23 December in Mousehole. It is the story of "The herculean efforts of Tom Bawcock, the legendary Mousehole villager who is said to have lifted serious famine out of Mousehole by going out in a severe storm to fish." Tom was thought to have been a fisherman in the 16th century. "Eventually [Tom] caught enough fish to feed the whole of Mousehole, [and] it's then believed that the whole catch was baked into a pie which contained as many as seven different types of fish. The heads were poked through the pastry to prove and celebrate that there was actually fish inside." Known as the Stargazy Pie, it is served on Tom Bawcock's Eve, and in addition, the entire harbour of Mousehole is decorated with lights illuminating the entire harbour.

A book called, "The Mousehole Cat," written by Antonia Barber and illustrated by Nicola Bayley adds a feline theme to the legend, and when I heard about the book I purchased it for Scott since he not only likes horses, he also likes cats. The book ends stating that Mousehole is "lit up with a thousand lights, shining their message of hope and a safe haven to all those who pass in peril of the sea."

The next two miles of walking into Newlyn were all on pavement, some next to a road, some down below the road, then back next to the road. I got good mobile reception here, so I listened to some music all the way. That helped with the loud cars and hard pavement until I reached the beginning of Newlyn.

I passed by Newlyn's Harbour with a Harbour Lighthouse, a small white lighthouse with a red base and red top, which I walked as close as I could get to take a few photos before going on some private part of the pier it was standing on. I walked by the large harbour of Newlyn, probably the largest harbour I have seen on my walk, especially compared to some small harbours with less than a dozen boats. This harbour had many dozen boats. From small rowboats, to sailboats, to fishing boats, and some even larger fishing and other types of boats. The lighthouse was the background for some of my photos of all the boats. In fact, "Newlyn is one of the largest fishing ports in the south west and you pass several fish shops displaying their catches," which I did. I took a short respite near the Fisherman's Memorial. The walking was still on pavement next to a busy street. The Promenade that connects Newlyn to Penzance, the "most westerly coastal town in England," was also pavement. For the first short bit there was some grass, so I walked on that to give my feet a rest from all the pavement walking.

I saw the Jubilee Pool up ahead, as well as St. Michael's Mount. The Jubilee Pool is an Art Deco pool originally opened in 1935 but was damaged by a storm in 2014 and was being fixed when Scott and I were here last year, but was now open this year. It is a large outdoor pool, protected from offshore winds by high walls. I think this pool is fresh water in contrast to the Bude Sea Pool, which is salty sea water, but I don't know for sure. It looked nice to swim in actually, but as I have mentioned I didn't bring a bathing suit. Perhaps I should buy one.

My walking portion for the day ended at the car park just past the harbour in Penzance. Of course I took pictures of boats in the harbour at low tide. The boats here were sitting on the sand also covered with green slimy seaweed like in Mousehole. This harbour was larger as well with several dozen various types of boats. There was also a Harbor Lighthouse here as well, a short white structure with a black base.

My bicycling portion for the day would now begin. My second time renting a bike on the SWCP. To save my feet from walking on more pavement. But first I needed to rent the bike. I searched online for a nearby bike shop on my mobile phone. I knew there was at least one as I researched this idea last year when making my SWCP plans. Sure enough, a couple blocks away was a bike shop. I walked to the store, and while they didn't rent bikes, they gave me the name of someone who did. I called, and within a few minutes, The Bike Guy (I made that name up), met me at the bike shop, picked me up, picked up a bike, and brought me back to the car park next to the harbour in Penzance. I knew the next three miles would be a paved and gravel bike trail into Marazion, so the bike seemed like a better option rather than walking more on pavement.

Forty-five minutes after ending my walk portion of the day, I was on a bike pedaling away. And £10/$14, 25 minutes, and three miles later, I was in Marazion. Home to the infamous St. Michael's Mount, and the destination of the St. Michael's Way pilgrimage route that I considered walking when in the Lelant and Carbis Bay area. Most of the bike path itself is the ending of the pilgrimage route actually, so now I can say that I walked on the beginning of that route from Lelant through Carbis Bay on the way to St. Ives for two and a half miles, and biked on the end of the route today which I would guess be about two miles. Therefore, of the thirteen and a half miles of St. Michael's Way, I have walked/biked four and a half miles, and have nine miles to go! Someday, on my future "to-walk" list.

I took a few photos of my bike with St. Michael's Mount in the background as I made my way into Marazion. I spotted about a half dozen people riding horses at the water's edge, and a kite surfer, as I biked. Once I arrived in Marazion, no shops interested me to go into here since I had been here before. I passed by the hotel Scott and I stayed at last year. However, I did have another cream tea, this one as a snack, before my bike ride "backwards" on the SWCP back to Penzance.

Last year, Scott and I visited St. Michael's Mount, which when the tide is high is an island that you can get to by boat, but when the tide is low, there is a walkable causeway going from Marazion to St. Michael's Mount. Last year, we had low tide so could walk across both ways. This year I did not visit it again. St. Michael's Mount "was granted to the Benedictine monks of Mont St. Michel in France around 1070 and a church and other buildings were built soon after. In 1659 Colonel St. Aubyn bought it and it became his private home. The St. Aubyn family still live on the Mount and it is run in conjunction with the National Trust" for visiting, according to today's booklet.

Once you get to St. Michael's Mount, you climb a pathway to get to the large castle at the top, and a church which dates back to 1135. I noted in my journal from last year that climbing up to the castle was the most climbing in elevation we had done all that day. There were some fancy ornate things in the rooms of the castle. There are also gardens, a small village, a small harbour, and all kinds of history to explore at St. Michael's Mount. What I still cannot figure out, however, is if pilgrims arrived at St. Michael's Mount from Leland, did they then take a boat across the Celtic Sea to get to the northwest corner of Spain and the Cathedral at Santiago de Compostela? Or perhaps St. Michael's Mount was the destination for the pilgrims in-and-of-itself, as "ancient stories tell of fisherman guided to safety by a vision of the archangel St. Michael in 495 AD. It's a legend which has brought pilgrims, monks and people of faith to the island ever since to pray, to praise and to celebrate," according to the "Welcome to St. Michael's Mount" brochure Scott and I picked up there last year.

Since Scott and I stayed in Marazion last year, I have some photos of the castle on St. Michael's Mount lit up with lights at night. For today, I had to bike back the three miles to Penzance for two reasons. One was I needed to return the bike, and two was my Guest House was in Penzance for the evening. I also needed to bike one extra mile to the place where I needed to return the bike, which happened to be only a block away from the Guest House.

Dinner tonight was fish and chips, without the chips, but with an extra fish cake. It was the closest place to my Guest House and I was really hungry. I did take away and ate in my room. For dessert I ate the third raw chocolate bar I bought in Mousehole, as the other two I ate as I walked earlier in the day.

DAY 37 STATS: 9 MILES SPLIT AS 6 MILES WALKING, 3 MILES BIKING. 4 HOURS WALKING, 1.75 HOURS BIKING, WITH TIME IN MARAZION. FOUR EXTRA MILES BY BIKE. PURPLE SHOES FOR BOTH WALKING AND BIKING. PUB IN MOUSEHOLE IS "THE SHIP INN." PUB IN NEWLYN IS "FISHERMAN'S ARMS INN" AND "RED LION INN." PUB IN PENZANCE IS "THE DOLPHIN TAVERN." PUB IN MARAZION IS "THE KINGS ARMS." Information on the legend of Tom Bawcock from cornwalllive.com/whats-on/whats-on-news/story-mouseholes-iconic-tom-bawcocks-933457.

RAINY DAY IN PORTHLEVEN – AN UNPLANNED REST DAY – Tuesday, 11 July 2017

"Porthleven is the most southerly port in the country, originally developed as a harbour of refuge, back in the days of sail. I left here much grimmer than when I'd arrived an hour before. I climbed up through the small streets veering east, studying the guidebook intently. It wasn't long before the inevitable happened: I was lost before getting out of Porthleven." - Overend Watts from his book, "The Man Who Hated Walking, The South West Coast Path."

I dedicate my day today to Overend Watts. His book, "The Man Who Hated Walking," was one of the three inspirational books I had read before my decision to walk the SWCP in its entirety, as I have already mentioned. Today I found out that Mr. Watts unfortunately passed away earlier this year in January. After I read his book over a year ago, I actually wanted to write him to let him know that his quite humorous book inspired me to walk. I was never able to find a way to contact him. So, now I say a big Thank You, Mr. Watts. You inspired at least one person from your book. And, it is good to be reminded that I am not the only one who got lost on the SWCP. Please rest (and walk) in peace.

****

Today was too rainy and windy to walk. Again. I couldn't believe it after I looked at the forecast last night and it called for "heavy rain" all day long today. Nearly mid-July. I was disappointed. I wanted to make sure in the morning when I woke up before I made a final decision today not to walk. That was the final decision as I looked out the window, and double checked the forecast. I did not feel comfortable walking in the rain, and wind, today, and I want to be able to enjoy my walking, not worry about it, not feel soaked, and have good views of the scenery, so I opted to take an unplanned rest day. Courage.

I had breakfast in the Guest House I stayed in Penzance, but since I only had one night there, I took a taxi ahead to my next B&B in Porthleven after breakfast. I was there by about 9:30. Before I had a chance to knock on the door or ring the bell, the door opened. Bridget must have seen me coming, or guessed really well that I would not be walking today due to the weather. She was not surprised by my early arrival and my decision to not walk today, and she greeted me very warmly. Like an old friend. I ran into her home so as to not get soaked by the rain and wind.

My room wasn't ready yet though, which was fine, and I was in no hurry since I wasn't going anywhere today. Bridget offered me some tea, so I sat in her dining room, drank slowly, figured out a game plan for tomorrow to make up some of the missed miles for today, and just hung out until the room was ready. Bridget and I chatted a bit, then she went up to prep the room, and showed me upstairs when it was ready.

I changed clothes, but still put on the rain gear over, and I set off to explore the town of Porthleven. In the wind and rain. I didn't really want to stay inside all day, and wanted to make the best of my day, but literally within five minutes of walking to the first open shop, I was soaked. I slowly walked around the first shop to dry off a bit and look at the items they had for sale.

After a few moments in that shop, I went outside and before I was going to walk to the next store, I tried to take a few pictures of the harbour. Two pictures with my camera were all I could get in, with the wind and rain. I did not want to get my camera wet. One picture started off with a bench in the foreground in front of a grassy area, with two flags, including the British flag, both vigorously blowing in the wind. Several dozen boats were sitting on the sand of the harbour of Porthleven during this low tide time. The harbour itself was surrounded almost completely, in the shape of a square. Three-quarters of the square was surrounded by buildings of shops, restaurants, pubs, and accommodations. The fourth side was the breakwall with a small opening for the boats to go in and out of. Beyond the breakwall in the distance were more buildings, including a row of homes and a very distinctive looking 70-foot tall clock tower built in 1884. Beyond the clock tower were the seas, and there are several photos (not taken by me) of this clock tower being hit by high waves during storms. Quite dramatic. The second picture I took at this time was also of the harbour at a slightly different angle with a few rowboats that were up on a dock as the foreground with the boats, harbour, buildings, and clock tower in the background.

Aside from the still important fishing industry, Porthleven has also historically been involved in "importing mining material and exporting mined tin and copper; china clay was exported; the lime kiln on the harbour produced lime for the local building industry; and shipbuilding was a big employer." (My summary from today's booklet.)

After my few photos, I walked to the grocery store to get cash, which I could not get because the type of cash machines in grocery stores does not accept my US credit card. I really can only get cash at cash machines from banks. I was soaked again just walking a few buildings from the first shop, taking a couple photos, and to the grocery store. I walked to a church, St. Bartholomew, which was consecrated in August 1842. I was still soaked. The church was open but there were people inside having a meeting so I hung out in the foyer. Then I was done getting soaked.

I remembered a great little tea shop here last year when Scott and I stayed in Porthleven, The Twisted Currant Tea Room. I went in. Since I was soaked though, and did not want to walk in all dripping wet, I found a spot outside under cover first, and at least took my rain pants off and rolled them up before I went inside. I stood inside for a moment at the door to carefully take off my soaked rain jacket. The Twisted Currant is a great little place for lunch. And to dry off. I had a brie and cranberry sandwich and sat here for a while. I confirmed what time they closed because this would be my dinner place later, too.

The rain lightened up a bit as I went outside, so I went into a few more shops. I took several photos of the boats in the harbour still at low tide, this time mostly with my mobile phone. Green seaweed covered some of the sand. Someone was walking down close by the boats during this low tide also taking photos. A single swan was floating on a little puddle left over from the previous high tide. I took photos of rows of boats from various angles, with different configurations. Rowboats, sailboats, and fishing boats. Some photos of just the boats themselves, and some photos with buildings in the background.

It was still too windy and rainy however to stay out for long. I was almost soaked again, so I went back to my room in the B&B. But what to do now? It was only about 1:00 in the afternoon.

I know! I will watch the very first episode of the very first season of Doc Martin! On my laptop. So that I would know what and who I saw and learned about in Port Isaac. Brilliant idea. Without commercials. It was about 45 minutes long. It was actually quite funny. I can see why people here really like the show. What is more is I knew exactly where most of the scenes in this episode were filmed! I even recognized some of the actors. Because I was there. In Port Isaac. I saw some of the actors. I saw them getting ready to film. Next to the school, I ate in the school restaurant. At the home of Doc Martin, I had my picture taken in front of that house. At the little harbour, I took pictures of the boats. Even some of the other scenery I recognized. Port Isaac. Or as they refer to it by its other name, Portwenn.

By the time I watched the first episode and did some other things I usually do on my to-do list, like call Mom, I was getting hungry again. I put back on my rain gear to venture out to The Twisted Currant before they closed at 5:00 to get my dinner. This time I got their baked potato with goat's cheese and red onion marmalade. What I did not get, but should have, was their Chocolate Cream Tea, consisting of two chocolate chip scones, with chocolate spread and clotted cream. Sounds delicious!

It wasn't raining as much now so after I got my food to take away, I walked around the harbour again to take pictures of the boats this time at higher tide. I did similar photos as before at low tide, with the various boats at different angles and configurations. I walked around most of the harbour to get my many photos. I even went back to the bench I took earlier, and the flags were no longer blowing in the wind. That swan floated by in a few of my pictures. A row of rowboats really caught my attention, making them the subject of several photos, some with just one rowboat, or two rowboats, or several. Sometimes the town of Porthleven served as a background for my photos, other times it was just the boats.

I ate my baked potato back at my B&B, both meals from The Twisted Currant were tasty, while I video called with Scott. Finally, I watched the second episode of Doc Martin season one! More places I recognized, like the SWCP itself as it leaves Port Isaac above the town looking down. I walked there!

Tomorrow's weather should be better. Calling for clouds and sun and 70F/21C! Oh, I hope so!

DAY 38 STATS: 0 MILES. 0 HOURS. I WON'T COUNT THE COUPLE TIMES I VENTURED OUT TO WALK AROUND THE HARBOR AS EXTRA MILES. I ACTUALLY WORE FLIP FLOPS SO MY PURPLE SHOES WOULD NOT GET WET IN THE RAIN. TOMORROW'S STATS WILL INCLUDE ANY MILEAGE I MISSED TODAY AS I WILL COMBINE BOTH TODAY AND TOMORROW ACCORDING TO MY GAME PLAN. PUBS IN PORTHLEVEN ARE "THE SHIP INN" AND "THE HARBOUR INN."

MARAZION TO PERRANUTHNOE TO PRAA SANDS, TO GUNWALLOE TO MULLION – Wednesday, 12 July 2017

"Weather Forecast: A fine day in store with plenty of sunny spells, the best of these likely to be around the coasts where there will also be a gentle sea breeze. Feeling much warmer than on Tuesday." – BBC Weather

Ummm, no kidding, since Tuesday was rainy and windy. But I was so glad about today's forecast! Since I missed walking yesterday, I needed to pick and choose what to walk today, as I really did not want to walk a total of eighteen miles, which would have been all of yesterday's miles plus all of today's miles. Yesterday was supposed to be walking from Marazion to Porthleven of eleven miles, and today was supposed to be Porthleven to Mullion Cove of seven miles. I figured that since Scott and I did this section last year, then missing some miles today would be alright once again as I have walked the missed sections before. Therefore, I chose the following for today:

Skip Marazion to Perranuthnoe - 2 miles
Walk Perranuthnoe to Praa Sands via Prussia Cove - 4 miles
Skip Praa Sands to Porthleven and Porthleven to Gunwalloe - 7.5 miles
Walk Gunwalloe to Mullion - 4.5 miles

I woke up earlier today because of my chopped-up day. It would require two taxi rides in order to make my connections. I got up at 6:45 so I could eat at 7:00. Scott and I video called after I ate, and I finished getting ready as my first taxi was picking me up at 8:00. I needed to get some more cash, and after I did some research finding a bank with a cash machine in the nearby town of Helston, the taxi driver drove me there first. Otherwise, I would not be able to pay the taxi later, as they only take cash. We arrived in Perranuthnoe a half hour later, and I went to The Parish Church of St. Piran and St. Michael that I remember Scott and I went into last year. Last year, I had picked up a couple of brochures from this church, one being the "details of the registration and history" of its organ, which was built in 1896 and enlarged the following year. It lists the organ's pipes, pedals, and other parts of an organ, which I find interesting. Some parts of the church itself date back to 1160. Also inside this church instead of a Prayer Corner with candles that can be lit, they had a Pebble Prayer Corner. "Hold a pebble in your hand while you pray, then place it in the water, the Pool of Prayers." Unfortunately, this year the church was closed as the interior was being worked on and I was unable to go inside again. However, I said my usual prayers while outside the church.

From my journal and photos from last year, what I missed this year from Marazion to Perranuthnoe included views looking back towards St. Michael's Mount and Marazion itself as the SWCP offered views from various angles as we walked along the flat path. As we were leaving Marazion last year, actually I took a few windows and doors photos first. Then once we were down the path a bit, the views of the "back side" of the castle and church on the Mount were in view, and we could really see much of the castle and church built upon the rocks of the hills of the island. We had a lot of yellow wildflowers lining the rocky coastline. There was one spot with two benches, one facing behind to the Mount, the other facing ahead to where we would be walking.

Today, I left Perranuthnoe and headed for Prussia Cove. There was a bit of road walking, then a bit of a gravel path, then a path which was slightly muddy from the rain yesterday, but not too bad, and not enough to muck up my purple shoes. I walked behind some tall shrubs which blocked my view of the seas for a bit, and I was close to a herd of cows, but not that close to be of any concern, and then I was out in the open once again. I saw the waters, and I had a view back to St. Michael's Mount, the terrain was flat, and the sound of the waters crashing on the rocky coastline below filled my ears with one of my favourite sounds. Those negative ions, and the good weather uplifted my mood, released tensions, and made me feel calm and peaceful.

The terrain continued to be flat as I passed under a building with the name of Acton Castle, but I don't know if it was ever really a castle. I remembered this place from last year because Scott took a picture of me with the building behind me. As I walked under it this year, a bunny rabbit went hopping by me near the path.

It was warm and dry and cloudy out today. That weather was refreshing. I could actually see the ball of the sun behind the clouds when I looked up, and as the day progressed, the clouds vanished and the sun was out and it was warm, and all became good with the world. I know I feel better about things when the sun is out!

I passed through Cudden Point when I saw the first person of the day walking. I passed by the first cove, Piskies Cove, in the series of coves that makes up Prussia Cove. Small waves crashed on the rocks below. I loved these little coves. The sun started to peek out briefly as I walked by the Fisherman's Cottages, which are currently used for storage. I saw a jogger go by, and once again I felt overdressed.

I passed by the second cove, Bessy's Cove, where I remembered from last year that at low tide you can see tracks on the rocks where carts of smuggled goods used to be brought ashore. The tide was too high today to see the tracks. There were also several thatched roof buildings around this second cove. The third cove was King's Cove, and at the fourth cove, Coules Cove, I walked down the small path and spotted one single row boat lying on the sand that was the subject of a few photos. Cute little cove, which might have a small beach when the tide is lower here. The sun was mostly out. I walked on, still on mostly flat ground, and ten minutes later, as I passed above the beach of Kenneggy Sands, the sun was gloriously fully out!

More people were on the path now, including several real serious joggers. I spotted the approximate place that last year Scott and I had to hop over a wire fence to get back on the SWCP after leaving our B&B. You see, we stayed near here last year, about a mile up a road, and in the morning to get back down to the SWCP, they told us to head down through the pastures, and there would be a footpath leading to the SWCP. Not! The pastures ran us quite near a herd of cows, and when we got to the SWCP, there was no way out of the pastures. It was fenced in with either barbed wire or possibly electric wire. Somehow we found a spot where it was easy to hop over the fence only touching the wood posts just in case. It was one of those things I felt like you only see someone do in the movies, and I was grateful neither of us got seriously hurt, by either the cows or the barbed wire or the electric wire.

The sun shimmered on the waters below as I walked by this spot and contemplated what we had done last year, and over the last several miles I realized that I had been enjoying hearing the crashing of the waves on the rocks in each little cove or beach, including the large beach I was approaching. I also enjoyed the views of the green covered hillsides and headlands beyond, the rocky shoreline, the turquoise and blue seas, and the blue skies.

I arrived at the Sandbar Restaurant at the beginning of Praa Sands, a long sandy beach, my first destination of the day. Of course I remember this from last year as well, as Scott and I ate here and our B&B picked us up from here. I ate something here myself today before calling the taxi to pick me up and bring me to the next part of my day.

From my journal and photos from last year, what I missed this year from Praa Sands to Porthleven, after walking on the path behind Praa Sands (I believe Praa is actually pronounced like "pray"), as well as a bit on the beach, was that the path was pretty flat with a few ups and downs, and there were lots and lots of colourful wildflowers, whites, purples, pinks, and yellows. We walked near and above both sandy and rocky beaches and coves, saw some people rock climbing, and walked by some mining ruins called Wheal Prosper at Rinsey Head, and Wheal Trewavas and Trewavas Cliff, used for tin and copper mining, both of which were still well intact with their buildings and chimneys. I remember as I watched the rock climbers I was getting nervous for them, as rock climbing is something I don't do. Well, I tried it a few times, but that was enough.

What I missed this year between Porthleven and Gunwalloe Church Cove, aka Church Cove, was walking by the clock tower in Porthleven, paralleling the sandy beach of Porthleven Sands, and walking on the beach and sand of Loe Bar. Inland from Loe Bar was Loe Pool, "the largest natural freshwater lake in Cornwall," and some farmland. Also in this area was a memorial, a white cross on top a white base, The Anson Memorial, honouring those who lost their lives in a shipwreck. Walking paralleling the long sandy beach continued, passing some old stone building that Scott and I peeked inside of last year, perhaps the "Fish Cellars." Things in there looked like they were from the 1950s, but I didn't know if this building was abandoned or not. Lots and lots more wildflowers lined the path as we walked, passing through Gunwalloe Fishing Cove, aka Gunwalloe Cove, by rocky and sandy beaches until we arrived at the hillside above the 15th century church dedicated to St. Winwaloe at Gunwalloe Church Cove, aka Church Cove, and walked down to the church.

Back to today…The taxi took me to Gunwalloe Church Cove, aka Church Cove. What I realized just now as I was typing this up and looking at my booklet was that unfortunately that I wanted to be dropped off at Gunwalloe Fishing Cove, aka Gunwalloe Cove, which was back further up the path, so my estimate of four and a half miles was too high for this section, so I adjusted it down to three and a half miles in my stats below.

After being dropped off at the church, I went into this church again that is literally right next to a beach. In fact, "it is the only church in Cornwall located on a beach." This 15th century church has a sign above the door saying "The Church of Storms." It is actually built behind a small hillside to protect it from the storms, and "its exposed position has made the church a target for the fierce storms that can sweep this stretch of the Cornish coast and has led over time to the church's popular nickname, "The Church of Storms." I looked through the books people sign when in churches, and I found what Scott wrote last year! "16-5-16. Scott & Debra Dungan, WA, USA, Norway Descendant (Scott)."

I started walking towards Mullion Cove, around and above the beach at Gunwalloe. A few people were enjoying the beach today, sunbathers, swimmers, and surfers. Looking back at the church nestled snuggly in the bushes and protected by the elements from the hillside, this felt like a comforting place for a church. As I walked on just a bit more, I was perpendicular to the white rolling waves moving towards the beach. The seas were a definite turquoise closer to the coastline, and a deep blue further out. The hillsides were covered with those patches of farmland in various shades of green, sectioned and checkered off by rows of bushes or trees. The sun was definitely out, it was warm, and everything was definitely alright with the world. Well, with my world at the moment anyway.

I passed by Poldhu Cove with its sandy beach, and then passed by the Poldhu Marconi Centre/Wireless Station and a monument, the Marconi Monument, commemorating the wireless telegraph. Last year Scott and I visited the visitor centre here, where Guglielmo Marconi invented "the first transatlantic radio station using Morse code. The wireless signal was sent using high frequency radio waves from Poldhu Cove," per today's booklet, all the way to and from St. John's, Newfoundland in 1901. This "first transatlantic radio signal introduced everything from broadcasting to satellite communications, mobile phones, broadband, the Internet and the world wide web and Poldhu was at the forefront of it all," according to The Marconi Center website. Wow! Who knew I would be walking by such an important place? I remembered that Scott really enjoyed visiting this important area. To think that I walked by the place where mobile phones and the internet that I have been using for my walk were introduced.

There were lots of wildflowers out today, some I have not seen before. Purple ones and red ones, as well as the whites and yellows. They made for colorful foreground subjects in many of my photos. Sometimes I wish I knew

Churches of the South West Coast Path
St. Bueno's Church, Culbone, June 5
St. John the Baptist Church, Instow, looking out to Appledore, June 15
St. Mary's Church, Appledore, looking out to Instow, June 15

Churches of the South West Coast Path
Parish Church of St. Morwenna and St. John the Baptist, Morwenstow, June 20 and March 31
Gunwalloe Church, "The Church of Storms," Church by a Beach, July 12
St. Nicholas Church, Abbotsbury, August 19 and May 2

Churches of the South West Coast Path
St. Anthony in Meneage Church, exterior with boats and interior with candles, April 8
Church of All Saints, South Milton (a mile and a half inland), April 22

what they were called, but then again, it is not necessarily the name that is important to know, but that I noticed the wildflowers and that I appreciated them. I passed by "Carrag-Luz" also known as "Love Rock" where last year Scott and I tried to take a romantic picture of us there together, but we could not figure out how the timer on my camera worked. I have a picture of just Scott there instead. Today I just took a picture of just the rocks.

Soon I passed by my hotel for the evening, Mullion Cove Hotel, built back in 1898, to go down the hillside to Mullion Cove just beyond first before I checked in. There was a little café that last year Scott and I did not know about until our next morning, so I wanted to go there for lunch today. I had their specialty, a "crab salad."

After my lunch, I actually spent a good 45 minutes walking around the very tiny harbour of Mullion Cove, taking photos of the few boats there from as many angles as I could, as well as other photos of the scenery. The breakwalls, the cliffs, the rocks below the cliffs, the waters, and Mullion Island just beyond. The tide was mostly out, but the three boats in the harbour were still floating on the remaining waters. The harbour itself was protected by the breakwalls, and just beyond the walls in the cove, white waves were crashing on the shoreline. I watched as one man was preparing his boat to leave the harbour for the seas. I watched him row by as I stood at one end of the breakwall.

A box of scallop shells was sitting on the harbour, and I wondered about why it was there. No signs told me anything. I wondered if it had any connection to the scallop shell symbol of the Camino de Santiago. Or perhaps someone just had a successful time collecting these shells, or they are abundant in these waters. Mullion Cove "was once a thriving pilchard fishing harbour, [and] the harbour itself was built in 1895. It now belongs to the National Trust and still maintains a small fishing fleet."

I walked around to the other side of the harbour to get a closer view of an old house of some sort, and the cove. It was a great time just enjoying this little area and appreciating the scenery and the livelihood of fishing.

I walked back up a very short distance to the fancy shmancy hotel, taking photos looking down over Mullion Cove, and checked in to the hotel. I chose this hotel to stay at for its convenience, because it is right on the SWCP. Literally. The path passes right in front of it. No walking any extra half mile or miles to get to it. It is not a B&B with the home-like atmosphere, but with my fancy shmancy large room, complete with a great view of Mullion Cove below, I wasn't complaining. They served dinner and breakfast here as well. And my room wasn't any more expensive than some of the B&Bs I have been staying in. Sometimes I just love being spoiled. It would have been nice to share this room with a view with Scott.

As the evening hours approached, the view from my room of Mullion Cove changed from the bright blue sunshine to some glowing orange colors on the green hillsides from the setting sun, and that was just brilliant. Everything was definitely alright with my world.

DAY 39 STATS: 18 MILES TOTAL. 7.5 WALKING. 10.5 TAXI. 3.25 HOURS, NOT INCLUDING FOOD AND TAXI IN BETWEEN MY TWO SECTIONS. NO EXTRA MILES. PURPLE SHOES. PUB IN PERRANUTHNOE IS "THE VICTORIA INN." PUB IN PRAA SANDS IS THE "SANDBAR." PUB IN GUNWALLOE IS "THE HALZEPHRON INN." PUB IN MULLION (INLAND) IS "THE OLD INN."
Information on The Marconi Center from marconi-centre-poldhu.org.uk.
Information on Church of Storms from britainexpress.com/counties/cornwall/churches/gunwalloe.

MULLION COVE TO CADGWITH – Thursday, 13 July 2017

"Walkers, Muddy Boots, and Dogs Welcome." – Sign outside The Cadgwith Cove Inn.

Today's BBC weather forecast was brilliantly this: "Thursday will see another generally fine and warm day with plenty of sunshine, although a few showers are also likely, mainly away from the coast from late morning." I did not have a single shower all day, just the fine and warm day with plenty of sunshine!

I left the Mullion Cove Hotel after breakfast, and I started by walking down to Mullion Cove again, taking some more photos of the harbour and the boats floating in the water, as this morning the tide was in. With the tide being in, the beach in the cove was now covered with water. I realized that I really enjoy seeing harbours both at low tide and high tide so that I can see the differences. Such as whether the boats are lying on the ground or floating in the water, and whether I can see beaches or not.

After a small climb uphill out of the cove, with views looking back on the harbour below, the large hotel I stayed at on top of the grassy hill, and the headlands beyond that, I entered a Nature Reserve. The path was flat and grassy. This was a recurring theme for today - flat and grassy. There was a very small ascent and descent, and I could hear the waves crashing against the shore of Mullion Island. Nice to hear that sound this early in the morning.

As the flat walking continued, I listened to the sounds of cute little chirping birds, more small waves crashing, and the crunching on the ground below my purple shoes. I felt a soft breeze at the moment on my face. It was all so peaceful at the moment, and quiet. It was currently warm and cloudy and dry this morning. What a great way to start today!

As I continued walking, I captured a video on my mobile of one of those cute little birds chirping. He was just sitting out on a rock singing away. I was not sure what bird it was, but I guess I don't really need to know the name, just as I don't really need to know the names of wildflowers. It was the beauty of the sound that I enjoyed. I was also seeing new wildflowers today, some purple ones, and more constant bird chirping as I walked along. It was the beauty of the colors of the wildflowers that I enjoyed. I heard more crashing waves, and my purple shoes crunching on the ground below as I walked. It was still so quiet and peaceful.

Then all my meditative-like moments were disturbed at the flash of a moment. My heart started to pound. As I made my way around a corner and down a bit I spotted five cows. Right. On. The. Path. I counted them. I stopped. I took out my hiking poles. Just in case. I'm not sure why. I'm not sure what I would do with the hiking poles and the cows, but somehow just having them in my hands made me feel better. I walked on. One cow at a time.

The first two were easy to get by. They were not exactly on the path, but maybe five feet from it, eating away with their faces not even looking at me. Whew. The third one was also a few feet away. I was able walk by that one too, no problem. Still, I started talking out loud to them anyway. Saying stuff like, "Hello, I'm just walking through. Please keep eating. No worries. All is good. I'm just going to keep on walking. Have a good day."

The fourth and fifth cows however were right on the path. Thankfully there were a few other paths that kind of paralleled each other, so I chose the one that was furthest from the cows as possible, and inland as possible. I was still within feet of the last two cows, but I kept talking and walking and didn't make eye contact, but I still felt my heart beating faster. And then I was past them! All five of them. I breathed a big sigh of relief. I kept walking though at a slightly faster pace, and peeked back briefly to make sure they were not coming my way. They were not. I was safe.

Just then a man was walking, approaching me in the opposite direction. I said to him, "I don't know about you, but my heart beats a bit faster when I walk by cows." He didn't seem too concerned. In fact, he politely told me that there was a herd of them up ahead. A herd! Holy cows!

He and I started to chat for a bit about other things as he recognized that my accent was not from around here. Some of the usual conversation ensued. Where was I from? The Seattle area of the US. What was he doing here? Walking (obviously), but not the whole path. He told me that I should really visit the Isles of Scilly. (Yes, that is on my future "to-walk" list.) Well some of that was not the usual conversation, but then he kindly advised me that when I come to the herd of cows, don't walk between them. Stay to the right of them and I would be fine. "Thanks for the advice," I said as my heart started to beat faster again. Breathe, I told myself, just breathe.

As I walked on, I could see the cows up ahead, and for the next ten minutes or so until I got closer and closer, I was gripping on to my hiking poles, worrying and anticipating my plan of action to get around them. Even just the thought of walking by cows got me all nervous. Breathe.

I passed by a sign. I remembered stopping by this sign last year with Scott for a snack. The sign said, "1.5 miles to Soapy Cove, 2.5 miles to Kynance Cove, 4.5 miles to Lizard Point," in the direction I was heading, and that I had just come two miles from Mullion Cove. I was still worrying about the cows. A jogger went by, and that eased my mind a bit – if he can jog by the cows, I can certainly walk by them. Or maybe…I will jog. I know one of the cow rules is to not run, so I wondered if jogging was alright. Would the cows know the difference between jogging and running, or walking at a slightly faster pace? I tried to think about the Isles of Scilly instead to distract my wondering thoughts.

As I got closer to the cows though, I noticed something. The wide path I was walking on went straight ahead, and another path went to the right. The cows were to the right. Now the man would be correct, if I did go to the right on that path, I would have to walk around the herd on their right. But the wide path I was on went straight ahead and avoided the cows completely. Why don't I just stay here, on this straight wide path, and avoid the cows completely? Don't go to the right at all. Brilliant idea. I figured I wouldn't be too far off the SWCP by doing this. I kind of remembered this area anyway from last year. And I would rather take this wide path ahead of me than have to walk near the cows. I also told myself I wouldn't get lost. In fact, both paths would meet up in a short distance ahead. My booklet said so. I was saved. I completely avoided the herd of cows! (Actually, I think Scott and I walked by the same herd of cows last year.)

As I started to descend the rocky descent into Soapy Cove a couple of people were walking uphill. They seemed local and I was sure they knew more about cows than I did. The cove had a nice sound of the waves crashing against the rocks. Per today's booklet about Soapy Cove, "In the 18th century there was a soapstone quarry here. Soapstone is a metamorphic soft but dense grey/black rock which is very heat resistant. It was once used for making fine porcelain, today it is used for tiles, worktops and ornamental uses although soapstone is no longer quarried at Soapy Cove." Interesting.

There was a pretty good ascent out of the cove that I did, followed by more flat grassy paths, as the sun peeked out from behind the clouds. I walked on more flat grassy paths and heard some more birds chirping, and even saw some butterflies. It was quiet though; there were no crashing waves at the moment. Back to the peace and quiet I was enjoying today.

Soon I saw Lizard Point peninsula about three miles ahead of me. First though, I descended a grassy slope and some steep steps into Kynance Cove. It was a busy little cove. Many people were out enjoying the weather, the beach, the turquoise waters, and the large rocky coast. So much for my peace and quiet. Some people were playing in the water, others were sitting in lounge chairs. This little cove is only 300 yards wide. I was hungry at this point, so I stopped to eat a sandwich I got at the café while overlooking the very picturesque beach. It was so nice out now with the warm sun completely out!

As I left Kynance Cove, I took a lot of pictures from various angles of the cove, especially from above. Apparently some of the rock formations were called Asparagus Island because wild asparagus still grows there. The waters were such deep turquoise and blue, white waves crashing on the sandy beach, the large rocks some covered with green grass (or maybe that was asparagus), and beautiful deep blue seas and light blue skies beyond and above, with the sounds of people laughing with all the fun they were having. For the next two miles to Lizard Point, I would be seeing lots of people on the path.

I passed an area overlooking Pentreath Beach, an empty sandy beach below the cliffs, and then I descended into another cove, Caerthilian Cove, a rocky area with those white waves crashing against the rocks. There were pretty purple and yellow daisy-like wildflowers out, and it was such a beautiful day with the sun and warmth and the blues and greens and colors of the wildflowers. Even though it was crowded with people, some sitting on a patch of grass having a snack and taking their own photos. Once again, the terrain remained flat. More wildflowers decorated the grassy hilltops I walked on, some small white and yellow daisies, so I wondered if the purple ones were a similar kind of wildflower.

Approaching closer to the Lizard Lighthouse, I reached the most crowds at "The Most Southerly Gift Shop" at Lizard Point. I took some photos of Punxsutawney Phil, both at this gift shop, and at the National Trust marker that said "Lizard Point," with the Lizard Lighthouse in the background. The significance of Lizard Point is that it is the most southerly point in all of England. Therefore with me being at Land's End several days ago, the most westerly point in England, I have now been to the most southerly and the most westerly points in all of England. (Well, I had been to both places before with Scott last year, but once again, I have been to these two significant places.)

I didn't want to spend too much time with the crowds at Lizard Point. As I walked on, some cows were safely behind a wall that made for foreground subjects of some photos of the lighthouse. I walked to the Lizard Lighthouse itself off a side footpath, and took a few more photos of Punxsutawney Phil quite near the lighthouse. While this lighthouse offers tours of the inside and up the tower, I opted to not take a tour today because Scott and I really enjoyed the tour last year. They have a lot of information inside the visitor centre, and we were able to walk into the grounds of this white lighthouse with its greenish-turquoise trim. We also were able to climb the steps up the 62-foot tower to the Fresnel Lens area as it rotated around emitting light for those ships out at sea. There were great views from there looking out to the horizon and down on the buildings of the Lizard area. Established in 1619 this lighthouse, while automated now, has a flash character of one white flash every three seconds, with a range of twenty-six nautical miles. One question asked inside the visitor center was, "A person who has an interest in a lighthouse is a…a. Psychologist. b. Pharologist. c. Phrenologist." If you don't know the answer, you might be able to figure it out by process of elimination. But I knew the answer without even reading the options.

Today I continued walking, and as I walked around the lighthouse, I took some more photos from various angles of the lighthouse. I also photographed several beautiful coves and beaches around here. The waters below me were such a deep turquoise in the sun that I wondered if I could even use a different word to describe them, like azure or cobalt or sapphire or blue-green or green-blue or indigo. One small narrow cove I remembered from last year, as my favorite cove, with its small sandy beach, many rocks decorating the beach, and of course the white waves, turquoise, azure, cobalt, sapphire, blue-green, green-blue, or indigo waters leading to the blue seas beyond. Today four people and a dog were on the beach of this tiny narrow cove enjoying the day.

I remembered a great story from around this area from our walk last year. A couple of people were walking in the opposite direction as we were and crossed us on the path. They were carrying quite large rucksacks, and looked a bit rustic looking, so I figured they were walking not only the SWCP, but also camping it as well. I asked them if that was what they were doing. Nope, they said, "We are walking around the entire British Isles." What!?! Wow!?! The entire coastline of the British Isles?! I was in awe and quite impressed. I've never met anyone doing that before. They told us they had already been walking for eighteen months, and have done over 7,000 miles! They still have three more months to go, and yes they are camping and cooking their own food as they walk along. They further told us that after they are done with this walk, which they seemed to be quite casual about, even with its enormous epic grand accomplishment, they will take a month off to decide what to walk next. "Perhaps the 2,650-mile Pacific Crest Trail in the US," they said. All this at the time made me think that our 100 miles of last year, and my 630 miles of this year, seem like a "walk in the park," comparatively, a fraction of a mile, for them. I wish I exchanged emails with them (if they even had one) or something to keep in touch with them so I would know if they finished. I hoped that maybe they would write a book.

I myself did read one other inspirational book recently about a solo woman walking around the coastline of the British Isles, "Midges, Maps & Muesli," by Helen Krasner. Ms. Krasner walked an impressive adventurous 5,000 miles around the coast of Britain! At the time she walked in 1986 and 1987, it was a record-breaking walk, getting herself into the Guinness Book of World Records, and getting herself some attention with the press and becoming a minor celebrity, which were not her original intentions at all. "This trek was simply an idea I'd had for a long time," Helen mentions in an online article I found. As she arrived in Brighton on her last day she was asked all kinds of questions about how she felt, did her feet hurt, how much weight had she lost. Ms. Krasner replied, "I think I annoyed everyone by telling the absolute truth…I felt fine…my feet didn't hurt at all, and I'd put on weight, not lost it." I would share more about this book, but without giving away the great ending, I shall continue on with my adventure…

Back to today. I had a quick stop sitting on a bench at the Housel Bay Hotel to rest my feet for a few minutes and to change socks, the second sock change of the day. Because I was walking ten and a half miles today! Last year, Scott and I ate some lunch at this hotel. From here, there were views of the Lizard Lighthouse with its several black chimneys perched on top of a very green hillside of farmland. And of course, those turquoise, azure, cobalt, sapphire, blue-green, green-blue, indigo and blue seas, and blue skies were surrounding today.

I walked past the Marconi Lizard Wireless Station, Lloyds Signal Station, a National Coastwatch Institution Station, and a pink house. Since Scott and I went in Marconi Lizard Wireless Station and the NCI Station last year, I did not go in them this year. This Marconi Wireless Station, which contains replicas of the equipment used by Marconi, "worked in conjunction with the larger wireless station at Poldhu Cove."

I arrived at the Lizard Lifeboat Station at Kilcobben Cove, and soon thereafter I was in Church Cove. I took some photos of the few rowboats in this tiny cove. One rowboat had plants growing out of it, and some other "junk" sitting inside its worn-out shell, so I wondered how long it had been there and what its story was. This scene also contained some potted plants and a picnic bench which seemed to be part of someone's home. A thin long concrete pier-like track led out to the water. I wondered if this was a way to launch the rowboats into the water, or if it was a remnant from the smuggling days.

I walked up the little road that goes inland in order to visit the St. Wynwallow Church. Scott and I did this last year, too. This church happens to be the most southerly church in England (now that's a cool statistic), and "is thought to have been founded about 600AD, although nothing of the present building can be said with any certainty to date from that time. The earliest dateable part of the church is the twelfth century Norman doorway," per the church's brochure. I have a couple photos from last year of kneeling pillows from this church, one embroidered with an image of the church itself, and one embroidered with a lighthouse! A sign at the door of this church invites one to "go in and be refreshed by the peace of this historic Cornish Church."

After my refreshing and peaceful church visit, including walking around the church's interior and exterior, I walked back to Church Cove. Going to and from St. Wynwallow Church to Church Cove, I passed by several various homes and buildings that I also remembered from last year. An old stone cottage. A whitewashed home with a thatched roof. A pink house. A blue house. I took photos last year of some of the windows and doors.

There was a small ascent out of Church Cove, followed by a bit bigger descent and ascent. For quite a while the path was overgrown with shrubbery because there was some sign that said that due to "glow worms" they don't want to trim the shrubbery, and they apologized for the inconvenience. It wasn't too much of an inconvenience actually, as I was wearing my long pants. But I did wonder what a glow worm was. I went into a Glow Worm Cave in New Zealand once, and wondered if these were the same.

I entered the great fishing village of Cadgwith. I remembered this place well. Not only does it have some great colorful fishing and rowboats in its harbour, but last year when Scott and I entered the village, we had previously gotten lost trying to find some of our B&Bs too many times. So that time I was determined not to get lost. I asked in the first little shop I saw where The Cadgwith Cove Inn was. She said it was just two buildings down the street on the left side. Scott and I had a good laugh.

So today I knew exactly where the Inn was, and it was my accommodations for the night. I was hungry first before I checked in though, so I got a crab sandwich at a little shop, the Cadgwith Cove Crab. Some of the signs outside this little shop informed me, "Fresh fish daily." "Our famous crab sandwich." "Lobster roll coming soon." "Fresh crab and lobster is landed daily from Cadgwith Cove by our boat Kingfisher II." "We sell...fresh crab meat, samphire, scallops, crevettes, crayfish, oysters, mussels." "Fresh Cornish fish: turbot-cod, line caught pollack, plaice-monk, mackerel, hake." "The sweetest crab to take away...yum yum!" "Lobsters Lobsters Lobsters." "Cadgwith Crab with a hint of lime mayo sandwich." "Cold smoked salmon with a hint of lemon/lime mayo." "Cadgwith crab and cold smoked salmon luxury combo." "And...scallops, mussels, oysters, crevettes, samphire, anchovies, teas, coffee, and smiles!"

I figured this would be another place to have some crab, like I did yesterday in Mullion Cove, as I felt like trying some of the local fish. I sat by the harbour of Cadgwith and ate my crab sandwich. Above the Cadgwith Cove Crab shop was the "Crow's Nest Art Gallery" which I went into for a short visit, and next door was "The Cadgwith Fish Seller" selling a "wide variety of fresh local fish." I loved seeing all this local fishing village life!

I checked in to The Cadgwith Cove Inn, being welcomed by a sign that said, "Walkers, Muddy Boots, and Dogs Welcome." I had a different room than Scott and I had last year, but still had a view of a bit of the harbour, a few boats in the harbour, the blue seas, a small hillside above, and several seagulls on the rooftops of the buildings. "Over 300 years old, the Inn has remained unspoilt since the cove's old smuggling days. The bar is full of atmosphere and relics adorn the walls collected from a rich seafaring history," according to their brochure.

Before dinner, I walked back down to the harbour, all of across the small street from the Inn, and took lots of photos of the boats from various angles, including looking out at the water, and looking back in from the water's edge towards the village seeing the backs of a row of fishing boats. I also found a small path that led to the small hillside above the harbour looking down at the beach and harbour, and inland at the village of Cadgwith.

I ate dinner at the Inn, and went back to my room to type. What a beautiful day! Oh, and a person who has an interest in a lighthouse is a "Pharologist." I actually consider myself a pharologist because of my interest over the years in lighthouses.

DAY 40 STATS: 10.5 MILES. ALMOST 7 HOURS. NO EXTRA MILES. PURPLE SHOES. PUB IN CADGWITH IS "THE CADGWITH COVE INN." Quotes from Helen Krasner from her book, and from boomerinas.com/2012/04/10/midges-maps-muesli-my-walk-round-the-coast-of-britain.

UNPLANNED REST DAY IN COVERACK WITH SOME WALKING – Friday, 14 July 2017

"Coverack Harbour – A good example of a Cornish harbour, the main Quay dating from 1724. It is privately owned and run by local boat owners for the benefit of all and is entirely self-supporting. We are anxious to maintain this without further commercialism. Please respect our facilities and help us with your generous support. Thank you. Coverack Harbour Co. Ltd." - Sign at the entrance of Coverack Harbour.

Well another unplanned rest day. This time it was not due to the weather actually, but due to not feeling well, perhaps fortunately the first and only time I felt this way. I woke up in the middle of the night last night with really bad heartburn. Maybe from something ate, I just don't know. It kept me awake for three hours. It is something that happens to me every so often, and it unfortunately happened last night. With lack of sleep and just feeling like I needed to rest, I decided to take a rest day. Thus unfortunately I did not feel like walking the seven miles I had planned from Cadgwith to Coverack today. I guess not feeling well is part of everyday life, even when your current everyday life is walking the SWCP. Fortunately, I did end up walking about three miles later in the day anyway.

Last year Scott and I did the walk from Cadgwith to Coverack, so once again, I was alright with skipping the miles, although needless to say our walk last year was quite adventurous. From my photos and journal from last year, we started out our morning quietly, with no sounds other than birds. Not even the crashing ocean waves. We had views looking back and down at the harbour and village of Cadgwith, walked past an old coastguard watch house, and came across a few Shetland ponies at one point, which Scott loved. We walked towards a place called Carleon Cove, with some abandoned buildings once used for some "large pilchard works," and then later used for polishing local serpentine, I believe to be a dark green mineral stone, the buildings then became used for "serpentine works." It was here that Scott got lost, I mean really lost. I was walking ahead of him, happily following the SWCP signs and arrows, walking across a small bridge. I went out to the remains of the buildings on a beach to wait for Scott, but after several minutes, he did not show up. I figured he must have continued walking on the SWCP without the detour to the remains, so I started walking further. But I did not see him. So I waited once again. And waited. Still, no Scott. I panicked. I actually started calling out his name loudly. I went back down to the building remains. I went back to the bridge. Still looking for him and calling his name. No response.

Now one rule I have learned in all my hiking days is if you are lost you are to stay in one place and not keep wandering around. So I decided to do that, hoping that Scott would not follow the same rule, and he would somehow find me. I took a few deep breaths, hoping he would show up. I even asked a few people who had walked by if anyone had seen him. Finally, he showed up! Thankfully.

I asked him where he went. He apparently did not see the SWCP signs and arrows leading across the bridge, walking inland on another footpath instead. Fortunately, a guardian angel for him, and for me really, told him he was not on the SWCP and directed him back to where he got off the path, and where we found each other once again. Whew!

Anyway, we went back to the building remains so he could look at them and so we could regroup together, and then walked on towards a café at Kennack Sands, and had something to eat there. A light rain started as we ate, and put on our rain gear as we left the café. We started walking again, and the next three miles towards Black Head, things were going fine. The rain continued, but it was not too bad at all. Mostly flat walking, with some domestic looking flowering trees of white, pink and orange that we figured we might be near someone's home, and one descent and ascent into and out of Downas Cove. A couple more photos and I put my camera and mobile away completely because…

That light rain turned into something very windy, rainy, and foggy! Looking back, I wonder if we technically probably should not have been walking. But, we kept walking because we really had no choice at that point. However, I certainly did not like the change in weather, including the fact that we could not see much. Thank goodness I was with Scott at this time last year. Fortunately, we ended up coming across three other people walking in our direction, our guardian angels at this moment. We decided to follow them because they were local and "knew" the area, since Scott and I could not see that well in the thick fog, and since I was nervous.

At one point, we all decided it was best to take an inland path rather than be on the coast for the last bit of the walk due to the weather. We followed them some more and somehow they ended up taking us on a comical adventure because even though they were local and "knew" the area, it was difficult even for them to see in the fog. At one point we had to walk through some very tall wet grass, then through a very wet muddy cornfield as we got closer to Coverack. By this time we were soaked. We all made it nonetheless and re-found the SWCP. Wet and soggy and soaked, but we made it to just near Coverack, and then Scott and I walked the rest of the way by ourselves into Coverack. Needless to say, the hiking boots, and even the socks, I was wearing last year were completely soaked. Looking back on this day, I was very glad that while Scott got lost, we had bad weather, and we kind of got lost together in bad weather by following these people around, at least we were together!

Back to today...I took a taxi to Coverack and checked in at The Paris Hotel. I was given the same room Scott and I had last year, which had a view of the water and a headland. I remembered we had laundry done here in a machine last year, especially after we got soaked. Well, Scott actually had to manage the whole laundry thing. He had to switch it from the washer to the dryer, and he kept going back checking on the dryness several times. Thanks to Scott for not only doing our laundry, but being with me last year in such windy, rainy, and foggy weather! From this room both years, I could hear the waves crash against the rocks at the shoreline below, and could tell the difference by the sound when the tide was in compared to when the tide was out.

Since last year we kind of missed seeing the scenery of the last mile and a half due to the wind and rain and fog, and since it was a blue sky sunny warm day with a slight breeze today, and I was feeling a lot better by mid-afternoon after resting for a bit, I went on a three-mile walk, round trip. I started walking "backwards" from Coverack and walked on what was possibly the same "inland route" as we detoured on last year, a route choice, as opposed to the forty minute outland route, first through some homes, then through some trees, and then out in the open on a hillside covered with ferns and green shrubbery. There were several large freighter ships and sailboats in the distance on those blue waters, and the sky was blue with fluffy white clouds. Some purple heather added more color to the scenery.

After about a mile and a half of walking, thinking it was most likely where Scott and I went inland last year, as I got to the place where there were once again signs for the route choice, I turned around and walked back to Coverack. First out in the open looking at the rocky coastline with those turquoise waters, then through some trees, then through some homes. When I was in the trees this time, I recognized the spot that Scott and I and the people we followed last year emerged soaking wet from the cornfield into nearly Coverack. I guess we didn't walk this "inland route" completely, and followed some other footpaths and somehow ended up here when we were following those other people. Today as I got back to Coverack, I walked by someone's planted vegetable garden, and alongside a row of white homes decorated with colorful potted flowers and benches to sit on. I walked by a child's playground.

As I walked back to my hotel, I happened to have met someone from the SWCP Facebook Group. She posted yesterday that they had walked twenty miles (yes, twenty miles!) from Porthleven to Cadgwith, and I responded that I was in Cadgwith too, but walked from Mullion. I saw them this morning in Cadgwith, but wasn't exactly sure it was her, so I didn't say anything, because I wasn't feeling well. Then when I saw them again here in Coverack, I asked if that was them, and it was! A connection made from the SWCP Facebook Group! And we weren't even wearing our lanyards. I recognized her by her picture on Facebook.

I walked into the only couple of shops in Coverack, and had a smoothie for a snack. I went back to my room, settled in again, video called with Scott, and talked to Mom. Before dinner, I went back out and took several photos of the boats in the harbour from various angles at "half tide." The tide was coming in, but only half the boats were floating at the moment. Rowboats and fishing boats, about three scattered rows of them, with about ten boats per row. I took photos of the boats in the foreground with Coverack in the background from several directions, some being down near the boat launch, some near the breakwall, and some above the harbour looking into the distance with headlands beyond. I took photos of just the boats, too. Once again, I love seeing the local fishing village life, the harbour, and I am just fascinated by these fishing villages along the SWCP. I really appreciated the sign at the entrance to the harbour, especially about how old some of it dates back to 1724, and their desire to maintain the harbour without further commercialism.

I think that The Paris Hotel is probably not named after Paris, France, but rather named after a ship, the US liner 'Paris' that ran aground near here back in 1898 when 750 lives were saved. Just a few months prior to that, the 'SS Mohegan' also was wrecked near here when 123 lives were lost and 44 were saved.

I ate a nice romantic solo dinner at The Lifeboat House Restaurant, which I think used to be a lifeboat station that opened in 1901 after those two shipwrecks. I had a window seat overlooking the water. Eating by myself in general never bothers me. I don't mind eating alone. I have done it a lot not only during this walk, but in all of my other solo travels. I think some people are not comfortable with eating alone, but I am alright with it. Except for once in a while, such as tonight, in such a romantic restaurant. It made me want to share this romantic dinner with Scott

After dinner I took lots more photos of the boats in the harbour from various angles, this time at full tide, and with different lighting from the setting sun. Some people were out sitting on the breakwall enjoying a meal, the blue skies, and each other's company.

DAY 41 STATS: 1.5 MILES IN THE "FORWARDS" DIRECTION. 40 MINUTES. 1.5 MILES EXTRA IN THE "BACKWARDS" DIRECTION. PURPLE SHOES. MISSED 5.5 MILES, BUT WALKED IT LAST YEAR. PUB IN COVERACK IS "THE PARIS HOTEL."

HALFWAY! – COVERACK TO ROSENITHON BY TAXI. WALK ROSENITHON THROUGH PORTHALLOW TO GILLAN CREEK – Saturday, 15 July 2017

"Lizard, dragonflies, damselflies, golden hair lichen, spotted cat's ear, liverwort, quillwort, crystal wort, campion, coral necklace, eyebright, primrose, violet, Jacob's ladder, lichen, moss, sorrel…samphire, squill, buzzard, bunting, butterfly, orchid, chough, curlew, oystercatcher…merlin, peregrine, grey seal…Monk's hood, willow carr, wood sorrel, bramble, furze, foxglove." - A list of some of the flora and wildlife along the SWCP as documented in The Half Way Marker.

After breakfast, I took a short half hour walk through the town of Coverack on the road above the beach. To the other end. Not much open at 9:00, except for the St. Peter's Church that I went inside, and did my usual look around and prayers. This church was consecrated and dedicated in 1885, and its pulpit, font, and lectern "are all made from serpentine from the former serpentine factory a few miles down the coast at Poltesco." Poltesco is another name for Carleon Cove with the abandoned building remains as mentioned yesterday. I also took photos of Coverack's harbour from further away.

I decided to skip three miles today because as I recalled from last year it was walking through trees and a quarry, Dean Quarry, and not very scenic. Not many parts of the SWCP have I considered "not very scenic," but I guess this was one of them. The booklet described part of these three miles as, "The walk between Coverack and Lowland Point is fairly level. However, the path is very uneven and sometimes there are two different routes going in the same direction. Keep to the main path which is usually close to the sea. It takes longer than you think!" Then the quarry part after that was not very scenic. Last year, Scott and I started walking out of Coverack first stopping at a sweet woman's home, Elizabeth, who was selling freshly baked pasties out of her home for take away so we could have some snack food for our walk. We next walked along Coverack's road near its rocky and sandy beach. At one point we came across some more Shetland ponies, which once again Scott was thrilled about. Walking by a rocky beach area there were a couple of fields of pretty yellow iris flowers, and I didn't take any photos in the quarry area.

Back to today…After my short Coverack walk, I had a few minutes before my taxi arrived, so I went down to the harbour one more time to take a few more photos. I happened to have the opportunity to watch for a few minutes something I was fascinated with. It was a fisherman getting ready to go out to sea. Here is what I observed:

He first brought his belongings down to the far end of the breakwall. He climbed down a ladder and got into a small rowboat that was already tied up by the ladder. He rowed the rowboat out to his bigger fishing boat. He got in the fishing boat, tied the row boat to it, and then prepped the fishing boat by starting the motor and putting the back rudder on. He towed the row boat connected to the fishing boat back to the breakwall, and tied the row boat back up to the ladder area. He climbed up the steps of the ladder, hooked his belongings on a wench, lowered them down into the fishing boat, and climbed back down the steps into his fishing boat. Then he motored away out of the harbour into the seas. What a great few minutes to spend. I'm glad I was there to witness this. I respect this man and all those who fish or work out on the seas. A life that I am not familiar with, and probably never will be familiar with. I imagine later the fisherman does the opposite routine when he arrives back at the end of the day.

My taxi picked me up and drove me to Rosenithon. On the way we chatted about the SWCP, and that he would like to walk the Cornwall part of the SWCP. As we drove around, we found a SWCP acorn and arrow sign right on a road in the village of Rosenithon which pointed me in the right direction. He dropped me off, I thanked and paid him, and I started out walking the road. I had the option of walking through a small field, or staying on the road. I stayed on the road. The next place I arrived was Porthoustock. Not much was there, as "a range of rocks is quarried here including gabbro, granite and serpentine," so I continued on. From here the SWCP goes inland towards Porthallow due to another quarry. There was a bit more road walking next to some thatched-roof white homes of Porthoustock, decorated with colorful flowers climbing up the walls. I saw two humorous signs hanging on a door for a "windows and doors" photo, one from the man's point of view, the other from the woman's: "An old fisherman and the catch of his life live here." "Me and my old crab live here."

I walked through a small field where someone was planting rows of daffodil bulbs, then onto more roads and through a tree-lined section. I arrived at a delicious little café I remembered well from last year, the Fat Apples Café. Scott and I had a nice sit-down lunch there last year, and I even bought a t-shirt from there. This t-shirt was decorated with sea-related objects designed together in the shape of a heart, including a whale, an octopus, a starfish, a shell, a ship, a steering wheel of a ship, a crab, a lobster, and an anchor. It is one of my favorite t-shirts. This time at the café, I was not quite hungry yet, but knew I would be at some point, so I bought a goat's cheese, sundried tomato, and walnut sandwich for take away. Being here made me think of Scott as I remembered him petting the chickens that were running around outside.

I walked on more road into the town of Porthallow - the place where the "Half Way Marker" of the SWCP is located! Halfway! 315 miles! 517 kilometers, as the marker tells me. Yes, I have not walked all of them, but I have walked a majority of them, mostly solo, so wow! Halfway! When Scott and I stood here last year, I remember wondering what it would be like to really be halfway from walking the entire SWCP, and how would I feel, to have walked to this point from Minehead. Now I know!

I am amazed, really. That is the best word to describe it, amongst others. Amazed that I decided to do this, that I planned this, that I arrived in England six weeks ago, that I have endured rain and wind and heat and fog, and that I have gotten lost or mixed up a few times. More importantly, that I have seen a lot of breathtaking and ever-changing scenery, that I have walked up and down countless hills. That I have walked, and paddled, on beautiful beaches, and that I have seen beach huts, still trying to decide on my ultimate location for one. I have seen lovely coves, and I have wandered around great fishing villages with their harbours and their various boats. I have looked back to headlands I have walked on, and looked forward to headlands in my future. I have prayed in countless churches, have heard my favorite sounds of crashing waves, birds chirping, church bells, and even complete silence. I have seen a few lighthouses. I have opened countless gates and walked over many stiles, and have encountered mountain goats, horses, gentle sheep, and worrisome cows. I have avoided ticks and adders, and for the most part, blisters. I have had some wonderful warm sunny days, have made connections with some wonderful people, and stayed in some comfortable B&Bs. I have walked with a few people including a wise 70-year old man, and a great friend. I have had good food, a few desserts, and a few cream teas. I have learned some history about the SWCP, and have learned about fishing, mining, World War 2, smuggling, and shipwrecks. I have seen a few famous people, watched a few episodes of Doc Martin, and have had quite a few guardian angels. I have become fitter physically. I have followed signposts, and arrows and acorns. I have reminisced about other travels and walks, including the Camino. I have reminisced about inspiring books that I have read. I have had a lot of positive benefits from the negative ions. I have been brave and courageous. I have felt a wide range of emotions, from happiness, calmness, peacefulness, joy, and that things are alright with the world, to disappointment and some loneliness. I am celebrating my 50th birthday in an epic way, on my walking adventure. I have had 315 miles of amazing experiences. And guess what? I still have 315 miles more to go!

It really is truly something special to experience being able to walk day after day after day (except a few days here and there), to be with nature, with all its beauty and its challenges, to watch and listen to and feel the seas almost daily. The SWCP is truly a special place to be day after day after day.

I am also proud of myself. For not giving up. Especially when the going was tough. Especially when feeling disappointed when the weather was not cooperating, or lonely when I missed Scott, or just not feeling well. Yes, I have given up doing some miles here and there for various reasons, but I have never felt like completely giving up at all! In fact, my stats thus far are that I have walked 246 miles and biked 19 miles, for a total of 265 miles. Of those miles, 245 of them have been by myself, alone, on my own, solo! I have also walked at least 37 "extra miles." Of the 50 miles I have missed, 27 of them I did last year with Scott, so really, I have only missed about 23 miles. All that, and I have taken almost 4,400 photos on both my mobile and my camera to date! Oh, and I have enjoyed five cream teas thus far!

I also felt reflective at this moment that I was here by myself at the Half Way Marker (except for a woman I will write about momentarily). Scott wasn't with me, no friends were with me, there at this moment to share in this accomplishment. But it was my choice to walk the SWCP by myself. Am I glad I made that choice? Yes!

When I arrived at this Half Way Marker there was a woman sitting on a picnic bench next to the marker with her dog. Before she left I thought I would ask her if she would please take my picture with the marker, from both sides. I was hoping someone would be there to do this, as I did not want to take selfies. I guess you could say that she was my guardian angel for the moment. Not because I was lost or anything like that, but because she was the one who in some ways celebrated my arrival there with me. She gladly took my pictures, several of them, first with my mobile phone, and then a bit later with my camera. She asked a few questions about my walk, and as she was leaving she said, "Congratulations!" I really appreciated that she was there.

I also took pictures of my purple shoes with the marker, and of Punxsutawney Phil with the marker. I mean after all, Phil the groundhog has been in my rucksack since day one with me, every day, so what I have experienced, he has experienced right along with me. I guess I really haven't been by myself after all.

The Half Way Marker itself, made out of granite, "was designed by local artist Tom Leaper, in collaboration with local writer Stephen Hall, to celebrate the mental, physical and spiritual benefits of walking the South West Coast Path." (Yes, I agree on all these benefits.) On one side of the marker lists some of the flora and fauna and things of nature seen along the SWCP, as I quoted above, so perhaps I have actually seen some of them, just not knowing their names. On the other side of the Half Way Marker is a poem called "Fading Voices," "things that may have been said by local people" for the village of Pralla, the local name for Porthallow. Next to this rectangular marker is a very large red buoy commemorating the wreck of a ship.

Also in Porthallow is their local pub, which can be traced back to the 1830s, called The Five Pilchards. Porthallow "once had a thriving pilchard fishing industry. Today fishing continues on a much smaller scale. The name [of the pub] comes from the traditional way of counting pilchards in groups of five." Last year Scott and I had dinner at The Five Pilchards. Today at this time it was not open.

I left the half way area feeling quite accomplished. I took a few photos as I started to walk away from the marker, including some of the word "Love" that someone wrote in white rocks on the beach, as well as of the boats on this mostly gray rocky beach. After walking a few yards I said to myself out loud, "Well, now I have less than 315 miles more to go now!"

Soon I had a view of Falmouth off in the distance and then walked through some well-groomed shrubbery and a tree-lined trail. I also walked through a grassy area where the path itself was green grass, but around me the grass was beige as if the grass was all dried up or something. Perhaps it was just the way this variation of grass is normally. I spotted a sailboat with white sails on the waters. Speaking of the weather, which I really wasn't but thought I would mention it as I always do, today was dry and warm and humid and cloudy and a bit of sun as well. I continued to walk across a grassy slope and along a fern-lined trail.

I spotted a man fishing at the edge of some rocks along the shore. I spotted two men in a fishing boat below in the seas and watched as it looked like they were pulling up their crab and lobster pots. Seagulls were flying around them, and the sailboat was still going by. I also spotted the National Coastwatch Institution Station of Nare Point ahead. Now the path was lined with lots of green ferns, with the turquoise, azure, cobalt, sapphire, blue-green, green-blue, indigo, and blue waters in the scenery.

Well, I suppose I could describe all the green I have been seeing as possibly light green, dark green, emerald green, mint green, lime green, sea foam green, verdant, viridescent, forest green, moss green, olive green, cyan, grass green, or seaweed green. Still blue and green, my favorite colors. And purple, my purple shoes.

The Coastwatch people probably spotted me because as I remembered from last year, they write down not only the boats and ships and kayakers and paddle boarders and sail boarders out on the seas, they also record walkers. All for safety-sake. I think they record the colors of clothing walkers are wearing, so hopefully they wrote down that I was wearing my purple shoes. I crossed on the edge of a grassy field where a herd of cows were sitting lazily in the middle of the field at a good distance away. No worries this time!

I arrived at the NCI Station and went inside. The one man was there today and said he was quite busy writing down all the boats and ships and kayakers and paddle boarders and sail boarders that he did not even see me walking down the coast. Oh well, my purple shoes did not get recorded. Last year, the man recorded what Scott and I were wearing. He explained that he is a volunteer, as are all NCI staff, and the Coastwatch helps out the Coastguard by recording the activity, especially if needed if someone gets into trouble and needs help. Scott and I visited here last year as well. I picked up one of their brochures which on the front said, "We are looking out for you…whatever the weather." Good to know! The brochure helped me understand what the NCI does with these five principle roles of the NCI:

"To assist HM Coastguard and rescue services by maintaining a visual watch along the coastline." "To help locate people and vessels in difficulty by visual and/or radar watch and pass on to the coordinating authorities." "To monitor the appropriate channels on the VHF radio." "To monitor and record local weather conditions and provide information to mariners, fisherman, walkers, climbers, etc." "To safeguard the environment, including coastal and marine wildlife."

In addition, according to the brochure, the NCI was formed in 1994 after the loss of two fishermen as "a voluntary organization…to keep a watch along our coastline. Watchkeepers are aware of local conditions even before an accident takes place, providing an accurate picture of events thus helping to speed and secure a rescue."

I would like to thank all NCI volunteers!

Since one of the NCI's principal roles is to assist HM Coastguard, I researched a bit about this important organization. Her Majesty's Coastguard is a section of the Maritime and Coastguard Agency. This agency works "to prevent loss of life on the coast and at sea. They provide a 24-hour maritime search and rescue service around the UK coast, and international search and rescue through HM Coastguard." The responsibilities of the Maritime and Coastguard Agency include: "the safety of everybody in a vessel in UK waters; the safety of all seafarers on UK flagged vessels; making sure all equipment on UK vessels is fit for purpose; making sure all seafarers on UK vessels have correct documentation; the environmental safety of UK coast and waters; the accuracy of hydrographic data on UK charts; and overseeing coastal rescue volunteers, hydrographics, seafarer certification and the port state control inspection regime."

I would also like to thank all those in the HM Coastguard and the Maritime and Coastguard Agency!

I had also read before Scott and I even did our walk last year that if you are in trouble, are hurt, or need help in some way while walking the SWCP, you can dial either 112 or 999 as emergency numbers from your mobile phone. I am guessing that even in places where you can't get regular mobile reception, these numbers might still work. If you dial 999 you ask for the Coastguard. Furthermore, dialing 111 is for lesser medical emergencies, and dialing 101 is for calling non-emergency police. (Now my disclaimer here is that I hope this information is accurate, but do not rely upon this only. Please do your own research on this, and I hold no responsibility for anything related to this.) Fortunately, I never had to call any of these numbers.

I sat outside the Coastwatch building and ate half my sandwich. It was good. After I began walking again, I passed by a tree where last year Scott and I had a brief rest stop. I started to see views of Gillan Creek with its boats and some kayakers and paddle boarders. I arrived at a nice lookout point for Gillan Creek, where I had views of the small green hillsides just beyond this creek, and I could just see the top of a church tower.

I started talking to a couple and their dog that have come here "on holiday" almost every year for the past thirty-five years. He asked me, "Have you walked far?" I answered, "Do you mean today, or in general?" I explained how far I have walked today, and how far I have walked in the last six weeks. He responded, "Now you have less than half way to go." I said, "Yes you are right, I have done about two and a half miles since the Half Way Marker, so I have 312.5 miles to go from this spot." He commented how this area hasn't changed much in the last thirty-five years. Another couple similar to the one near Tater Du lighthouse who has returned to the same place year after year.

I walked by a few areas where I was able to get closer views of all the boats in the creek, taking photos of them as I always like to do. Soon I arrived at the road in Gillan Creek that I would need to walk up for a small bit to get to my B&B. I recognized the road as Scott and I stayed at the same B&B last year. Before I walked to the B&B

though, I thought it might be fun to take the ferry across Gillan Creek to the church in St. Anthony and take the ferry back. I will be missing this ferry tomorrow because I will have the B&B man drive me to the Helford ferry instead. I want to miss the three miles in between the two ferries because it is usually overgrown with lots of shrubbery and not many views. (More on this tomorrow.)

I walked another five or ten minutes to where the ferry would be, but the tide was too low at the moment for the ferry, even though I tried to summon the ferry by opening a board which displayed a bright orange color. The tide was too high for me to walk across the creek, which I guess is possible if the tides are right. Therefore, I couldn't go see the church in St. Anthony. That was alright though because Scott and I saw it last year. This church is powered entirely by candles! No electricity.

The B&B gentleman, Paul, previously told me that my room wouldn't be ready for another hour and a half from this moment, so I walked back to Flushing Cove beach and ate my other half sandwich, while sitting and taking more pictures of boats. I really didn't want to wait any longer though to get to my B&B, so I thought I would walk there anyway a bit early and hoped that Paul would be there, even if my room wasn't quite ready.

I remembered how to walk to the B&B from last year, and found it easily. Last year, Scott and I got lost and had to call Paul who picked us up a bit up the road as we had walked too far beyond it. Today Paul was home, and my room was ready. I also remembered that there was no food within walking distance of this B&B, so Paul agreed to drive me to a pub later so that I could get some food. I hoped that the pub would actually do take away, as I would prefer to sit in this great comfortable B&B. They did, The New Inn in Manaccan a bit inland, and Paul was kind enough to sit and wait in the car while my food was being prepared. Last year, Paul drove us to The Five Pilchards, and picked us up again after we ate. Paul is a nice person.

As I ate, I looked through the guest book and found what Scott wrote last year. "May 20-21, 2016. Paul, thank you for having this wonderfully appointed lodging available to travelers like us. Thank you for your extra help with the weather, ferries, and all. What a beautiful breakfast, too! Do take care! Scott and Debby, WA, USA."

As I ate in the comfort of the B&B I also typed and contemplated my Half Way achievement and accomplishment! I actually wrote this poem a few days ago to commemorate the occasion, but posted it on Facebook today with one of the pictures the woman at the Half Way Marker took of me. Note that I have a couple different rhyming patterns going on here.

I may not have walked every single mile
And the weather didn't always make me smile
But as of today, I am halfway
It's been worth it all the while

I've been in Devon and a lot of Cornwall
I've walked near cows, and had my first cream tea
I've seen lighthouses and coastwatches
And now Doc Martin is my favorite show on TV

I've seen beautiful beaches and lovely coves
And I have heard the crashing ocean waves
There's been fishing boats and harbours at high and low tides
As I've been walking and walking throughout most of the days

Walking on the South West Coast Path
With 315 miles more to go, so cool
I look forward to seeing what's around the next headland
From Minehead to Porthallow and now onto Poole

DAY 42 (HALFWAY) STATS: 8 MILES – 5 MILES WALKING, 3 MILES TAXI. 3 HOURS 45 MINUTES. NO REAL EXTRA MILES AS B&B WAS CLOSE. PURPLE SHOES. PUB IN PORTHALLOW IS "THE FIVE PILCHARDS INN." PUB NEAR GILLAN CREEK IN MANACCAN IS "THE NEW INN."
Information on St. Peter's Church in Coverack from coverack.org.uk/pages/church.
Information on HM Coastguard and the Maritime and Coastguard Agency from gov.uk/government/organisations/maritime-and-coastguard-agency/about.

Me on the South West Coast Path

Me at the Half Way Marker July 15! (photo credit: woman sitting nearby)
Me at SWCP stone marker at Holywell July 1 (photo credit: Sasha Harding)
Me going over a stone wall on way to Abbotsbury May 3 (photo credit: Scott Dungan)

GILLAN CREEK TO HELFORD FERRY TO FALMOUTH – Sunday, 16 July 2017

"The walk along the Helford River is very uneven in places and largely through trees with occasional glimpses of the river and opposite shore. It is best done in the spring before the trees are in full leaf and the bluebells are in flower." – SWCP Booklet.

This was the only three miles that Scott and I missed last year. The official route would be taking the ferry from Gillan Creek/Flushing Cove to St. Anthony-in-Meneage, then walking the three miles to Helford to get the ferry to Helford Passage. We skipped it last year not only due to the above description, but also because Sasha even told us the place was overgrown, there weren't many views, and because it was raining hard the morning we were supposed to walk it. Instead, Paul drove us to Helford so we could just get the ferry to Helford Passage and walk from there.

This year, I decided to skip the same three miles. The weather today was not raining, but with the possibility of it still being overgrown and not many views, I just thought I would skip it. Besides, later today I was meeting up with my great friend Sasha again, and preferred not to keep her waiting too long like I did when I met up with her a couple weeks ago. I was just really looking forward to meeting up with her again. Yesterday I did at least walk to the ferry area for the Gillan Creek/Flushing Cove ferry, but it was not running at the time.

In skipping these three miles today though, while some of the other miles I missed this year, in the 100-mile stretch Scott and I did last year, this is the only one I have now missed twice. I starting thinking about really wanting to make up not only these three miles but all the other ones so far that I have missed this year that I have not done in the past at all. In summary, similar to the stats I wrote about yesterday, I have now missed about 53 miles so far on this walk, including today's three, but have done about 27 of them last year, so at this point I have completely missed 26 miles that I would like to do at some point in time. I am going to start a future "would like to walk at some point" list. When to come back to England, back to the SWCP and do this though, that is the question…

Once I made my decision to skip the three miles, I asked Paul if he would kindly drop me off near the Helford Ferry, just as he did last year. After a nice breakfast and chatting with Paul, a very nice man, he dropped me off as close as he could get to the ferry in Helford, so I needed to walk a few moments to get to the ferry.

To summon the Helford River Boats passenger ferry, I remembered from last year that Scott and I had to open up a circle board from a blue color to a yellow color that the ferryman could see across the water and come with their water taxi. No flag to wave like the ferry from Rock to Padstow. This time when I opened up the circle, I got a good laugh. The yellow circle had a black Batman symbol cut out and attached to the circle over the yellow.

Since I was probably the first customer of the day, the boat took about fifteen minutes to get there as they were just starting up the motor. I made it across the river in five minutes time once the ferry picked me up. On the other side, Helford Passage, I stood near a small beach, and looked across the river at all the boats floating. The earliest ferry going across the Helford River here "was by a Charter of King Canute in 1023," per today's booklet. Wow, that's almost 1,000 year ago!

Shortly after I started walking the SWCP, I guess the SWCP joined a military road. I didn't notice it, but the booklet states this about The Military Road: "This road once led back to the main road and was built during WW2 by the Americans to take tanks and supplies to the landing craft moored on the newly constructed pier at Polgwidden Cove (Trebah Beach). From here the US 29 Infantry Division left in June 1944 for the D-Day landing on Omaha Beach in Normandy. Part of the beach is concrete standing left from the preparations of the embarkation. It was the most westerly embarkation beach for the D-Day landings."

The path towards Falmouth, my destination for the day, started out flat with grassy fields and continued on and off with grassy fields much of the time for a while. At one point there was an inland detour through some trees because the original SWCP was damaged, and the sign telling me of this detour said something like, "This Path Has Foundered No Further Access."

After the trees, there was a bit of road walking through the tiny village of Durgan with its few stone buildings, which was "once a thriving fishing village with a coal yard, donkey sheds, fish cellars and a chapel. In 1876 a schoolroom was built over a fish cellar. Durgan is now owned by the National Trust and is used as holiday accommodations."

A lot of joggers were out today as I walked. The path continued to be flat, with lots of shrubs and trees, with occasional views of the water. Looking inland at one point, I spotted a herd of cows at a good distance away, lazily all sitting down on the green grass, near a lone tree. It was a nice quiet moment seeing them up there.

I arrived at the 13th century Mawnan Church. I needed to take a very short side path to get to the church. Last year Scott and I sat there and had some food, and the church was not open. This year as I approached, I heard some singing. I walked up to the church and looked inside. It was open as there was a Sunday church service going on. I listened for a few minutes but did not want to disturb the service, so I left. "In 1842 Trinity House asked the church to whitewash the tower to aid navigation at sea. It was never done!" Therefore, the church could have been helpful for the safety of those at sea like a lighthouse.

There was some more walking through a little forest of trees, then through some tall shrubbery, then out in the open, and more grassy paths around a headland. It started to mist, but only briefly. I arrived at Maenporth Beach and I remembered this beach from last year. Scott and I stopped here for a respite, and then had to walk inland a half mile to our B&B in Mawnan Smith, to which we went on the incorrect inland path and got lost. This time, I ordered a delicious peanut butter, jam, and banana sandwich at the little café on the beach, sat on a picnic bench, and ate looking at the seas and at the few people enjoying the beach today. Other than that brief mist, the weather for today was cloudy and on the warm side.

After I left the beach, there was more flat walking lined with more shrubbery but where I could still see the seas. I arrived at Swanpool Beach. There were some beach huts! I hadn't seen beach huts in quite a while. I remembered this particular row of beach huts last year because at that moment, I had never seen anything like that before. This row of beach huts was my first sighting of them ever last year. So last year I asked someone what they were and he described that people either own or rent them, and keep their beach supplies in them. Therefore, last year was when I first learned of the beach huts right here at Swanpool Beach. Of course, I described their use and history in more detail back when I saw them for the first time this year in Saunton Sands. These beach huts at Swanpool Beach were mostly gray and white in color with blue, turquoise, and yellow trim and doors. A few people were enjoying this beach today as well. I'm still trying to decide which beach would be my ultimate location to have a beach hut.

In the early afternoon, I arrived at the Gylly Beach Café at Gyllyngvase Beach after a half mile of walking on pavement. This was the same café that I originally met Sasha at last year when we met in person for the first time. Now I will have her pick me up again here today, as I was done walking for the day. There was still three and a half miles left of walking through Falmouth from here, but was all on pavement and some of it was through the busy streets of Falmouth, and once again I had already done this bit last year with Scott, so I was alright missing it today. I was looking forward to seeing Sasha.

The one place I remembered though the most about these three and a half miles I was missing this year was a lookout point, Pendennis Point, the location of the Pendennis Castle, where Scott and I could see across to a lighthouse, the St. Anthony Lighthouse. Last year it was sunny out on our last day of walking, and there were lots of sailboats going by which all made for nice photos with the sailboats in the foreground, and the lighthouse across the waters in the background. Scott and I stopped for a snack stop watching all the sailboats going in and out of Falmouth Harbour. Scott and I continued walking another couple miles all the rest of the way through a few busy streets of Falmouth, which was a shock to the system with all the busyness of people and cars and traffic and so much noise and movement that we had been not used to, all the way to Prince of Wales Pier, the place where you catch the first of two ferries to take you to the next portion of the SWCP, and the place Scott and I officially ended our 100-mile walk. We had a good walk together, great for us to experience together. I wrote this in my journal from last year that evening, "I don't have to check the weather any longer, sad. I will do last Facebook posts, sad. I don't have to organize for another day of walking, sad. But we have memories, photos, videos, journals, and inspiration to walk again!"

Back to today…I called Sasha and she arrived about twenty minutes later. Great to see her again! I needed to get some cash at a bank, and go get a couple items in a pharmacy, so she happily drove me to these errands. Then we went back to her house. For her privacy, I won't describe much, but she cooked us a great dinner, I met her husband, and of course her dogs were excited to see me too. Sasha and I chatted about all sorts of things. Well mostly we chatted about the SWCP. It was great to be around a great friend! Again.

DAY 43 STATS: 10 MILES. 6.5 WALKING, 3.5 MISSED. 3.75 HOURS. NO EXTRA MILES. PURPLE SHOES. PUB IN HELFORD IS "THE SHIPWRIGHTS ARMS." PUB IN HELFORD VILLAGE IS THE "FERRYBOAT INN."

FALMOUTH TO PLACE TO PORTSCATHO – Monday, 17 July 2017

"Dance your cares away, Worry's for another day. Let the music play, Down at Fraggle Rock." – Part of theme song from a children's TV show called "Fraggle Rock."

Today, I had a beautiful walk with a great friend, Sasha, the artist. I stayed at her home last night, and will again tonight. I slept very well here last night. She has a room in her house that is set up very similar to a B&B, with its own en-suite bathroom, but it is more than just a B&B with her, it is our friendship that makes it like home. And this was our second promise to each other, that I could stay with her during my time in Falmouth.

We had decided yesterday to do my walk that I was supposed to do tomorrow today instead. For two reasons, the weather for tomorrow might be a bit rainy, and she was available today to walk with me. Therefore, tomorrow I will have a "rest day" instead, as today was supposed to have been my planned rest day.

After "brecko" at Sasha's house, that is her word for breakfast, and I completely laughed out loud when she said it, we started our way driving to the kind-of starting point for today's walk. On the way, we stopped at a post office shop so that I could mail a second box of things back to Scott that I put together last night which will make my wheeled luggage a ton lighter. Over the last six weeks, not only did I realize I still packed too much, but I've also been collecting things. Little trinkets, the gift purse for my niece, scrapbook paper items, and the two National Trails books I finished. (Oh, yesterday I finished the second of the four National Trails books, "Padstow to

Falmouth – From Golden Beaches to Rugged Coves around Britain's Southernmost Tip"!) I also finished many small booklets, and with the souvenir books I had bought, all that plus some clothes I wasn't wearing and a few other items made my luggage heavy, not only for the Luggage Transfers people, but also for me for the times I have had to lug it up and down stairs. Therefore, I shipped back a box of those things, plus the pair of black Keen hiking boots I wasn't wearing, a warm jacket that I have not needed, and other miscellaneous items. It cost a lot to ship back, but it will be worth it for the sake of ease. I kept a list of the things I brought with me that I didn't need for future use so that I don't bring them again.

Normally to get from Falmouth to a place called Place, which is the start of today's walk, you would take two ferries. One from Falmouth to St. Mawes, and the other from St. Mawes to Place. Since Sasha had a car, she figured out a better way for us to do the walk instead so that at the end we would still have a car to drive back to her home. We drove a bit and then took the King Harry Ferry across the Fal River, which is a car and passenger small ferry so that we could take the car on and continue driving. This bypassed us taking the other two ferries. We drove and parked at St. Anthony Head car park, near the St. Anthony Lighthouse. Now this place was not Place, so after we arrived, since I wanted to start at the place called Place, we needed to walk "backwards" for two miles. This would add two miles to our walk today, and to my "extra miles" stats, but it would be worth doing this. Even though Sasha has walked the SWCP in one go herself, there were a couple of bits she actually missed, and these two miles was one of them, so we did not want to miss it.

With her two dogs that joined us for the walk today, we set off backwards. I chose not to take photos going backwards, and didn't take notes, so that my photos and notes would be going "forwards." At times today, Sasha had to put leashes on her two dogs, which in England they say, putting your dog "on lead." I don't know if I mentioned, but I put a lanyard string on my mobile phone and always wrap the other end around my wrist so I don't accidently drop my phone over a cliff ledge and lose it forever. Perhaps it looks like I have my mobile phone "on lead."

About 45 minutes later we arrived at what we thought was the pier at the place called Place where the ferry goes to and comes from St. Mawes. We stopped here, and that is when I started taking photos all happy that we had made it to our starting point, and we spent a few moments there. Just as we were about to start going forwards again though, we read the sign that said that we still had 200 more meters to walk till the ferry. We laughed at ourselves for this slight error. We walked the 200 meters back and saw the place in Place where the ferry really comes and goes from St. Mawes. It is a people-carrying boat, and one happened to have arrived when we got there so I saw what it looks like at least and took some more photos. I will be adding missing the two ferries to my future "would like to walk at some point" list. Well, in this case it would be ferry rides. I figure I could just make a day of it – taking both ferries back and forth, and spending a bit of time in St. Mawes looking at that village which is supposed to be a nice place to visit (pun intended), and includes a castle.

Finally Sasha and I were really ready to start our "official walk" going forwards. A few minutes from Place was St. Anthony Church, so we stopped for a few moments there. All churches have a book for you to sign your name, the place you come from, and any comments. I am not one who does this, except a couple of times so far. Scott wrote in just about all of them last year, as I have already written that I looked in at least one over a year later. This time Sasha wrote her name "and dogs." I thought that was cute.

Walking the next mile we had views of St. Mawes which appeared closer, along with many boats on the Fal Estuary water in between. Further in the distance and a bit further on were views of Falmouth. The walking here was flat, on a hillside covered with some grass, with a few patches of trees. The views were continuous of boats on the water, and as St. Mawes faded, and as Falmouth faded, we started to get views of the St. Anthony Lighthouse in the near distance. There were a few small beaches as well below, with people fishing and lying out in the sun. The weather for today was perfect all day. Sunny, warm, dry, once in a while a slight breeze. It was bordering hot later on in the day, but I didn't mind. By the end of the day though, Sasha's dogs were tired out. Sasha's dogs, and Sasha herself, were the subjects in many of my photos today.

Sasha's husband, Jack, went out fishing today, and at one point, Sasha called him to see where he was, as she told him where we were. We were actually able to spot him out on the water. She knew what his fishing boat looked like, and he told us about where he was and we could see his boat. As we made our way closer to the lighthouse, we stopped at the "Former Paraffin Store" for the lighthouse and saw him again. We all waved to each other. I think Sasha was thrilled to see him out there in his boat, and I think he was thrilled to be out on the water today in his boat in such great weather.

We arrived back at the car park where we started from, and stopped for a little snack. Four miles so far round trip. Four more miles to go till Portscatho, our destination for the day. Much of the next several miles there were wheat fields to our left, shrubbery and the seas to our right. Sometimes the wheat fields were green, other times they were brown. I realized that I enjoy seeing inland scenery, mostly of farmland, almost as much as I enjoy seeing the scenery out into the waters and seas all along my SWCP walk.

The terrain today was mostly flat, with a few very minor downs and ups. The tops of the hillsides were covered with various shades of green, dark green, forest green, light green, grass green, and verdant. Several boats sprinkled the blue seas. There were a couple of beaches, the empty Porthbeor Beach, and a small rocky beach with a boat parked in the water and two people on the sand. See, I bet that some beaches are only accessible by boat or kayak as I think I thought this thought a while back. We then arrived at the somewhat busy Towan Beach. At Towan

Beach, Sasha wanted to let her dogs cool off a bit and let them go for a quick swim in the water. At this point, we had two more miles to walk.

More wheat fields lined the path to our left. Various wildflowers added color to our right. Soon we arrived in the fishing village Portscatho. A small harbour with four rows of boats made for some photos. Some rowboats and kayaks lined the area above the harbour. A few people were enjoying the nearby beach.

We were originally going to walk another half mile to the other end of Portscatho for lunch at a little café that Sasha knew about, but the dogs were quite "knackered." (Much like the day I was knackered after walking eight miles from Hartland Quay to Morwenstow in the heat.) Sasha let her dogs drink plenty of water and rest up a bit, so that we could possibly still walk to the little café, but after doing some research, they stopped serving lunch at 3:00, and it was now just after that time, so we stayed at the pub where we were at, had some lunch ourselves, and let the dogs rest. I tried my first "ginger beer" which is not an alcohol, but more like ginger ale, a bubbly drink made with ginger. It was tasty.

Sasha had called last night about arranging a taxi to pick us up in Portscatho and take us back to her car at the St. Anthony Head car park. I called as we were finishing eating to let them know we were ready, and within three minutes, our taxi driver was there. Sasha had not quite finished her lunch as we thought we would have more time before he arrived, so she grabbed her sandwich, her rucksack, and her dogs, and we all hopped in the taxi.

Once we got back to the car park, we had actually skipped earlier taking the short side path down to get a closer look at the St. Anthony Lighthouse, another mostly white lighthouse with that greenish-turquoise trim. We walked down there and took a few photos. "The present lighthouse was constructed in 1835 and the lamps were lit by paraffin (from the store) until 1954 when it was connected to mains electricity. The light has a range of about twenty miles," per today's booklet. This lighthouse is another "Trinity House" lighthouse, as most of these lighthouses are, and the keepers' cottages are "available to let for holidays." As I have already started my "expensive-places-to-stay-someday" list, then perhaps someday when I have a lot of money and time, I will make my way along the SWCP again, staying at all the lighthouse keepers' cottages.

Sasha told me about a children's TV show from the 1980s called "Fraggle Rock," using Jim Henson's Muppets. Apparently some of the filming for the show used exterior footage at this lighthouse. I love learning little things like this as I walk the SWCP. Later I looked up the show on the internet and found the theme song, and saw some footage of the outside of the St. Anthony's Lighthouse that then goes inside the lighthouse into the Muppets singing. This is the theme song:

Dance your cares away,
Worry's for another day.
Let the music play,
Down at Fraggle Rock.

Work your cares away,
Dancing's for another day.
Let the Fraggles play,
We're Gobo, Mokey, Wembley, Boober, Red.

Dance your cares away,
Worry's for another day.
Let the music play,
Down at Fraggle Rock.
Down at Fraggle Rock.
Down at Fraggle Rock.

Cute. I may have to add this to the list of TV shows to watch along with Doc Martin and Poldark.

We walked back to Sasha's car and drove, via the King Harry Ferry, and to a store to get some food for dinner, back to Sasha's house. It was probably 5:30 or a bit after when we got back home. Since I usually call Mom at 5:00, I talked to her as we were driving back. Since we did my walk for tomorrow today, then tomorrow I shall have a rest day.

Aside from laughing out loud when Sasha referred to breakfast as "brecko" this morning, I also learned another phrase from Sasha that had me laughing even harder. "Bits and bobs." I suppose it would be similar to the term "bits and pieces" that I would say. The term can be used in a variety of ways I suppose. For example, it could be used to refer to random miscellaneous things, like all the bits and bobs that I had in the box that I shipped back home earlier today.

DAY 44 STATS: 6 MILES. 3.5 HOURS. TWO EXTRA MILES AND ONE EXTRA HOUR. PURPLE SHOES. PUB IN PORTSCATHO IS "PLUME OF FEATHERS."

Lighthouses of the South West Coast Path
Godrevy Lighthouse on Godrevy Island July 3
St. Ives Two Harbour Lights July 6
Lizard Lighthouse July 13

Lighthouses of the South West Coast Path
St. Anthony Lighthouse July 17 (photo taken in 2016)
Portland Bill Lighthouse and Trinity House Obelisk August 21 and 22
Anvil Point Lighthouse August 27 - Photo credit: Scott Dungan

REST DAY AT SASHA'S IN FALMOUTH, DRIVE TO PORTLOE – Tuesday, 18 July 2017

"Portloe Harbour is a working area for fisherman. No vehicles other than those used by the working fishermen are permitted beyond this point. Persons wishing to go on the beach are advised to take suitable care and to beware of working material which may be on the slipway. Visitors are invited to help maintain this little old fishing harbour by placing contributions in the box below. Dues from all craft launching or landing may also be placed in the box." – Various signs on the side of a building in the Portloe Harbour.

I woke up well rested for my scheduled rest day at Sasha's. I still woke up at my regular time of 7:00am. I got my luggage ready for Luggage Transfers after a video call with Scott. I noticed that my bag was much lighter! I hope they noticed it was lighter too when they picked it up later this morning. I took some time to finish writing about my walking day yesterday with Sasha, as I didn't finish typing last night. I also spent some time emailing pictures to Sasha that I took of her, her dogs, and her husband on his boat when we saw him. She was appreciative of all the photos. I did some other to-do's, like checking the checkbook and looking at my increasing credit card balance, backing up photos, updating my stats, etc. I actually started to hear some thunder outside in the early afternoon. I was glad we walked yesterday and I had a rest day today.

Regardless of the weather, I was enjoying my rest day, not doing much, just sitting in Sasha's dining room with my laptop. Sasha asked me earlier today if I wanted to go with her as she walked her dogs. Surprisingly I politely declined, just not even feeling like doing even a short easy walk today. Usually I've been walking on my rest days. I guess I needed this day as a recharging day, with not having to think about where I am going, what the weather will be like, where I will eat, or what will be around the next headland. I wore jeans and flip flops all day. I drank water out of a glass, instead of my water bladder. It was interestingly enjoyable. I didn't even walk a quarter mile. Just back and forth to the kitchen sink to refill my water glass.

Sasha kindly made me some lunch, and I started to feel sad, as soon she would be kindly driving me to my next B&B in Portloe. The same emotion of sadness after walking with someone and then they depart that we talked about and I felt back when we walked together from Crantock Beach to Holywell. Sasha said though that I will be walking through some of her favorite bits (and bobs) along the SWCP. She also said to me that it is really a privilege to be walking on the SWCP. Indeed it definitely is. A privilege, and an honor. And one to which I must remain humble and grateful for. Sasha has truly been my guardian angel and great friend the past 48 hours.

On our way to Portloe, which Jack went along for the ride too, Sasha kindly let me stop by a small store to pick up some snacks (nuts and bars and such), and a bank to get even more cash, and watch that credit card balance increase once again. She then coded in the "post code" (similar to zip codes in the US) for the B&B into her "satnav" (satellite navigation system), and drove an additional twenty minutes to drop me off at my next B&B. I appreciated the ride very much.

When we drove up to the B&B in Portloe in the afternoon, the gentleman who owns this B&B was in his garage, and it turned out that Jack knew him. Somehow there was a relation connection that I was confused on how they knew each other, but they did. Small world, as they say.

After I got to my room, I had a small cry. Feelings of loneliness crept over me. The thunder and lots and lots of rain continued as well. I was warm and safe and dry and not walking in that weather, so that was good. Another type of weather to add to the list of weather I have experienced in the last six weeks – thunder. I distracted myself from the loneliness by watching season one episode three of Doc Martin. It was quite funny and I heard myself chuckling out loud a few times. The sadness lifted.

Then I had an idea! First, I will say that unfortunately Sasha probably won't be able to walk with me at all over the next six weeks. Except that fortunately she can join me the very last few days in the Swanage area, where she grew up. Perhaps even do my last final walk together. I don't know if Scott will join me at all yet, as that is still to be determined. My idea – I sent a message to Lucy who is in charge of the SWCP Facebook Group page. I asked her how I can find people to walk with. She responded right away saying that first, she can walk with me when I get to Fowey, and then she said that I could put a request on the group page, in general terms, to see if anyone wants to walk with me, and then have them private message me in private if they want to walk together. I wrote this:

"Hi, All! So I've been walking this lovely Path mostly on my own now for over six weeks, having passed the half way mark a few days ago, as you may know. And I still have over six weeks to go. Sometimes it has been well, lonely, walking alone. Once in a while I have had an opportunity to walk with someone, and I've really enjoyed the company. I am wondering if there is anyone out there who would like to join me on one of my walks over the next six weeks, anywhere from Falmouth on to Poole. Perhaps if you live in one of the towns along the way, or have a favorite part you like to walk. Please PM me your location, and I will look at my planning calendar to see which day I will be there. I would appreciate the company. Thank you. PS. Just to let you know, when I walk, I stop often to take photos."

Within an hour, I got several responses. They aren't though for areas I will be walking in till mid-August, but that is alright. I will have some company in mid-August.

Actually all that Facebook stuff happened after I went out to dinner tonight at the pub in Portloe. After I ate, I walked down to the harbour, as the rain and thunder had stopped, and it was warm and dry out, and I took photos of the boats in the harbour. Some fishing boats, rowboats, small motorboats, in this quaint little old fishing harbour. Another fishing village that I love to witness. The skies in the background were blue now, with the green hills on either side of the harbour where the water comes in from the seas. The setting sun lit up the scene. The waves coming in were small but rough because there was still a wind. I also went into the small Portloe United Church, a "little building [that] was originally a lifeboat house, built in 1870." Per their brochure, "the church bell was originally a ship's bell." These were the only photos I took all day of the harbour, the boats, and the church.

With all the rain today, I found out through the SWCP Facebook Group page that in the news there was some flooding in Coverack. Yikes. I hope everyone is ok! I was there just a few days ago. I wish the town well and think good thoughts for them. (Glad I wasn't walking today.)

DAY 45 STATS: ZERO MILES. ZERO HOURS. ZERO EXTRA MILES. FLIP FLOPS. PUB IN PORTLOE IS "THE SHIP INN."

PORTSCATHO TO PORTLOE - Wednesday, 19 July 2017

"It's like Boscastle all over again, there is no business or house not been affected." – Newspaper article about the flooding in Coverack (see more at the end of my day today).

At brecko this morning in Portloe, I chatted with a woman from Pennsylvania. She was the first person from the US that I have shared a B&B with thus far. She walked 150 miles of the SWCP last year, and is trying to do 200 miles this year. Speaking of brecko, I may have figured out why cooked tomatoes and mushrooms are part of the Full English, as I usually don't think of those foods as breakfast foods. Now I don't know if this is completely accurate or the real reason why, but I do believe that both tomatoes and mushrooms release more nutrients when cooked, so maybe that is why they are part of the Full English. Anyway, John from the B&B kindly drove me back to Portscatho this morning to the same pub Sasha and I ended at and ate at a couple days ago. I had a 9:30am start for my seven-and-a-half mile walk to Portloe where I was already staying at again tonight, the place Sasha and Jack drove me to yesterday.

I was in and out of the town of Portscatho within minutes. I could already hear the ocean waves crashing, but not see them yet due to the shrubbery after the town. This would be a recurring theme for some of the day today. I passed by the Hidden Hut, which was the original café Sasha wanted us to walk to the other day, but we didn't because of her dogs needing rest and water, and they were closed too when we wanted to go. The café was not quite open yet this morning when I passed by there. It would open in fifteen minutes, but I wasn't hungry to wait, so I walked on. The café was above the large sandy Porthcurnick Beach, which there were two people enjoying the beach early in the morning.

I passed by an NCI Coastwatch Station. The shrubbery, some overgrown, continued, but I could hear the crashing waves which was nice to hear often today. That sound is just so soothing to me, the continuous non-stop rolling motion of the waters going in and back out. It never ends, even if the tide is low, the waves and waters just keep on moving. There is a rhythm to it that resonates with me. The waves could be more powerful if the winds were stronger. Waves may be quieter on sand, compared to over a gentle rumble on rocks. Some places the waves are subtler than others, perhaps depending on the length of the beach, or my distance from the seas, or just the force of the water. The weather and storms can make the waves even more powerful, sometimes devastating. Nature doing her thing, as she has done for a real long time. Sometimes peaceful and meditative, sometime devastating.

Soon I was above Porthbean Beach in some trees, and that descended right onto the beach, where I needed to walk on the sandy beach for a few yards, closer to the waves, and then I walked into an area with some more overgrown shrubbery. I walked down a small grassy field, through another small section of trees, and next to another grassy patch. I could still hear the waves crashing. Ahhh. Meditative. Once again, more shrubbery and another grassy field.

About an hour after I started walking, I passed a sign that said one mile to Pendower Beach. I could still hear those crashing waves. The booklet said it would take about twenty minutes of walking to get to a road, and they were just about right. The small hillside on my left in the section was covered with short growing ferns, and I still had shrubbery to my right. I knew the seas were beyond the shrubs and every once in a while I would get a glimpse.

I arrived at the road above a white building three minutes slower than the booklet said. I passed by a little wooden box where someone was selling eggs. It looked like you could get a half dozen for £1.50, and they asked you to "Please put money in the post box. Thank you for your honesty." I guess they were freshly laid eggs. The sun peaked out from behind the thick clouds for just a moment or two, as a few people were enjoying Pendower Beach.

A couple hours after I started walking this morning, I passed by Nare Hotel. I was originally going to stop there for some food, but they were not open yet for lunch till noon, and since I was curious what was ahead down the road and wanted to peek at the beach, I walked a bit further and instead I happened to find a little food cart called "Tea by the Sea," with a very sweet woman working there. I had a ciabatta sandwich filled with brie and cranberry.

A couple sat down at the picnic bench next to me, and I was curious about the walk around Nare Head, so I asked them if they have ever done the walk. They did it years ago, and will again today. They enjoyed it. They were from Essex, I believe, and they have been coming here often for decades. Yes, yet another couple who go to the same spot, their favorite spot I suppose, year after year after year. How sweet and romantic.

After my food stop, the path started out relatively flat, but then there was a climb up to Nare Point. Below was a cove where today because of the cloud cover, the water was not as turquoise or blue today, but a muted shade of blue. There were two people ahead of me climbing up, a young couple with their little dog, and when I nearly reached the top, two colorfully dressed trail runners passed me by, and then two more people crossed my path in the opposite direction. Nare Point was a busy place.

When I was at the top of Nare Point I walked on some flat grass around a field with some large barrel rolls of hay on my left. My views ahead were of green rolling hills, with various shades of green depending on whether it was darker green trees and shrubs, or lighter green grass. (I'll keep this description simple.) I could see the line of the SWCP I was going to be walking on ahead of me. Below was a rocky beach with small white crashing waves. In addition to the sounds, what a glorious sight to see, even with the cloud cover! This walk is simply surprising at all the beauty day after day.

There was a slight descent above Kiberick Cove, to which the young couple with their dog went down to the beach at the cove. I walked around the edge of a field that had some sheep, and then I had another slight ascent to Blouth Point. Flat once again, then another slight descent. After I got around this area, I looked back and saw the green hillsides I just came from, including the large barrel rolls of hay covering quite a very large area. I had merely walked by just a few barrel rolls of hay. Looking at a photo I took of the rolls, I counted about 150 of them!

As I reached Broom Park the two colorful trail runners passed me going back in the other direction. I heard more crashing waves. There had been one rock island, Gull Rock, in sight out on the water for a while now, which I started seeing back at Nare Head. I walked on a grassy area where other than the path I was on, yellow wildflowers, which I am pretty sure were dandelions, covered the green grass, feeling like a meadow. Such surprising beauty!

I walked on another flat section, with a view of a headland in the distance, which I am sure I will be walking around one of these days. I got my first glimpse of Portloe, and arrived just above the village at 1:30. Most of the buildings were a grayish stone brick, although many were also white. On some of the white buildings, I liked seeing the windows and doors from a distance where they were painted either yellow, light blue, dark blue, or orange. I could see the waters, now a deep turquoise, entering the harbour area. Once I got down to the village, I went down to the harbour, and I took some photos of the fishing boats in the harbour from various angles once again, even though I had done this yesterday, since this is one of my favorite things to do. Although I didn't get photos of the windows and doors up close.

I was hungry so I went into The Lugger Hotel to get some food. I ordered a salad, which I figured was good and healthy for me, and even asked for avocado to be put in it, but unfortunately, while it tasted good, the salad was on the small size in its portion. I took a few more boat harbour photos from the vantage point of where I was sitting outside at the hotel overlooking the harbour. Several seagulls were flying around and sitting in the water of this small harbour. There was one short breakwall. There was one fishing boat in particular which seemed to be the main subject of my photos, a green one with a white interior and red on the underside. It was more like a rowboat in some ways to me, but it seemed very official with several buckets and other objects on a raised platform on the backside of the fishing boat.

I made my way to The Ship Inn, where I had dinner last night, to get something more substantial to eat. As I sat at my table, I was looking around at all the items on display and the old photographs on the walls. A row of various beer bottles became the subject of a couple photos, with various brands, types, and colorful labels. Then an old photo caught my eye – it was of the same green fishing boat I had just taken photos of in the Portloe harbour. Same name and number. This photo also had a man with long water boots on looking like he was getting ready to put the boat in the water and go fishing. I don't know how old the photo was, but it was not a color photo, and looked several decades old, perhaps from the 1950's even, but that is merely a guess on my part. Anyway, I was amazed that this boat has been around for a seemingly long time. I wondered if the man in the photo still takes the same boat out fishing and how old he is now, if he is even still alive. Quite an historical comparison, and just some more of the local fishing life and livelihood that I am so enjoying learning about and seeing on my SWCP walk!

There was also a painting of the Portloe harbour with not only that same green fishing boat again, but also a blue fishing boat, which was in my photos as well, and a rowboat. This painting had two men handing each other a crab and lobster pot, with a dog standing beside one of the men. Seeing this paining and the old photo just gave me the sense that there must be such a feeling of camaraderie amongst the fisherman and the village in which they live and work. It made me appreciate that part of the reason the SWCP exists must be because of these fisherman, and part of why I am walking is to get this sense of this way of life.

I guess it was good that my salad was not substantial and I had to go back to The Ship Inn to notice all this about local fishing. I like how I can turn a 1:30 arrival time into the town into an hour and a half, as I finally walked into my B&B at 3:00. Today's weather had been cloudy and warm, even muggy and humid. Thankfully no rain or wind or fog, or thunder. I also realized that I did not feel the loneliness today that I was feeling yesterday.

In fact, "Portloe is an unspoilt Cornish fishing village, with fishing boats still operating out of the tiny harbour at the centre of the village. In the 17th and 18th century, it was a thriving pilchard fishing port," according to today's booklet. Furthermore, The Lugger was a smugglers inn in the 17th century, and "French Cognac was one of the most smuggles cargoes. The Ship Inn was originally a 17th century fisherman's cottage." Wow, I ate meals at two places with fishing and smuggling history, and are hundreds of years old. I tell you, not only is the beauty of the SWCP full of surprises, but things like this are surprisingly beautiful to me as well.

One other thing I also saw at The Ship Inn was an article in the Western Morning News newspaper dated today entitled, "Flash Flood Terror. Rescue drama as village cut off by deluge." It was about the flooding in Coverack that I had heard about yesterday. The article continued, "Residents of a Cornwall village last night described flash flooding that swept through their homes as an 'apocalypse.' Dozens of people in Coverack had to be rescued from their homes after storm floods saw the entire village totally cut off. Residents said the torrential downpours yesterday caused utter chaos." Wow!

One B&B owner said, "It is utter devastation all along the seafront." "Up to 50 homes in the village on the east of the Lizard peninsula were thought to have been affected. Many were flooded and destroyed, stalls and business were washed away, and several residents hauled out by rescue crews." Wow!

The article continued that the road into the village was impassible. There had been torrential rain for about two hours, with hailstones. One person said, "It's like Boscastle all over again, there is no business or house not been affected." Wow!

While many had to be rescued, fortunately from what I could tell no one was seriously hurt or worse. It was strange to think I was there about five days ago, and I feel fortunate that I was not there during the rain, and fortunate that I also did not walk yesterday when this happened. A definite reason that while it is an honor to be walking on the SWCP, why I need to remain humble about my walk, remain courageous and brave, heed Gordon's words of wisdom, and listen to my instincts and empowerment when I choose that I don't want to walk in the rain or the wind or the fog. Nature doing her thing, as she has done for a real long time. Sometimes peaceful and meditative, sometime devastating.

I send to the people living in Coverack my well wishes and hope everyone and everything returns to as normal as it can as soon as it possibly can.

DAY 46 STATS: 7.5 MILES. 4 HOURS. NO EXTRA MILES. PURPLE SHOES. SINCE I ALREADY LISTED THE PUBS IN PORTSCATHO AND PORTLOE, BUT DID NOT LIST THE PUBS IN FALMOUTH BECAUSE THERE ARE A LOT, I THOUGHT I WOULD RESEARCH THE OLDEST PUB IN FALMOUTH, WHICH IS "THE SEVEN STARS," WHERE THE BUILDING ITSELF DATES BACK TO THE 14TH CENTURY, IT WAS GRANTED ITS LICENSE IN THE 17TH CENTURY, AND HAS SEEN SEVEN GENERATIONS OF THE SAME FAMILY AS LANDLORDS SINCE 1873. falmouth.co.uk/eatanddrink/the-seven-stars.

PORTLOE TO GORRAN HAVEN – Thursday, 20 July 2017

"Wherever life plants you, bloom with grace." – Hanging on a wall of a building in East Portholland.

Do you know the wave-like motion when you stick your hand and arm out a window of a car and move it up and down in the wind? Kind of like a rolling motion, like a roller coaster. Well, over the last several hundred miles when I talk to people about the walk I would be doing each day, they all seem to describe the terrain that way. They use their arm to reflect the roller coaster motion, and say something like, "You will be experiencing a lot of ups and downs today." In some ways, it seems like a "warning" of what is to come, but in other ways perhaps they are impressed of the walk each day that I will be doing. I nod my head in agreement and thank them for the feedback. (Perhaps in some ways they are also referring to the "emotional rollercoaster" as well.)

Last night it was lightly raining, and since I had already eaten "two" meals, I did not go out again for a later dinner. I snacked on some nuts and a protein bar that I bought yesterday, as well as a few "oat and spelt crackers" that I also bought yesterday, which are like rice cakes. All that filled me up quite well while I also watched Doc Martin season one episode four last night. It was another funny episode, hearing myself chuckle out loud. The show also had some romance and mystery.

After breakfast and saying goodbye to John and Barbara, I left the B&B in Portloe. The sun was already peeking through the clouds and it was warm out. It would remain that way all day today till I arrived in Gorran Haven. To leave Portloe, I weaved my way of town. There were some cute little hand painted acorn signs leading the way, and I had a view of harbour of Portloe with its historic fishing boats from above. Then I climbed some steep steps. Today's roller coaster motion started early. The terrain for quite a while actually included some slight rolling ups and downs, and shrubbery including lots of ferns. It would be like this for a while, where sometimes the ferns were overgrown, and with the morning dew on them, they would get the bottom of my pants wet.

The warm sun peeking through the clouds was shimmering on the water and made for some pretty scenery as I walked through the very green ferns and shrubbery of the hillsides. I passed by a rocky beach cove below, and I could hear this time faint quiet ripples of waves lapping against the rocks, rather than crashing waves, the sun casting some great light on the waters creating more shimmering effects. It was rather quite beautiful out! Then I had a good little climb that I tried to power through to see how good shape I had become, which left me a bit breathless. It felt good though, like a really quick short workout.

The overgrown ferns continued to get the bottom of my pants wet, but with the warm air, I was not concerned. The path began to flatten out a bit after the small roller coaster I had been on. Very, very, very small in comparison to some others in the past, like that day with seven or eight quite large ascents and descents back on 25 June from Trebarwith Strand to Port Isaac. And not like those two very hot days in a row, from Clovelly to Hartland Quay, and Hartland Quay to Morwenstow, back nearly a month ago, which were all definitely like those arm-out-the-window-wave-like-motion-roller-coaster days. There were small trees around me, but not overgrowing on the path. I saw East Portholland in the near distance, with its sandy beach and a single row of buildings. Two people and a dog were on the beach, with multi-shaded green hillsides behind this tiny village and beach. It was a lovely view!

There was a small rocky cove with a sandy beach below. No one was on this beach, and I wondered once again if there was even a way down to this cove and beach from the hillsides, or if the only way to reach it was by boat or kayak, and if that was even possible. Or if perhaps no one has ever set foot on this particular beach and cove and coastline. The terrain remained flat and somewhat overgrown, then some trees, more ferns, and another good little uphill climb that once again I powered through, leaving me a bit breathless. Another good short workout. I did feel quite fit and in good shape though! As I looked ahead and behind me today, the headlands and hillside were so beautifully covered in various shades of green, with blue skies, white clouds, and blue waters.

I reached West Portholland just over an hour after I started walking this morning, and since there was not much there, other than a small beach, and taking two photos of windows and a door as my "souvenir" of this village, I walked a road a third of a mile into East Portholland and arrived there ten minutes later. There was the beach I saw from the distance earlier, and I took a few more photos of some windows and doors here. Looking out at the seas from this beach I could see the turquoise-fading-to-blue waters. There was also a cute little "café and crafts" shop, but it was not open yet. It would probably have been cute to go inside if it was open. There was also a little box with eggs inside, selling "free range farm eggs," £1 for a half dozen, and I am guessing that they were probably freshly laid eggs. And the cute little flower sign hanging on the wall of this shop, reminding me that "Wherever life plants you, bloom with grace."

After East Portholland, the trail was flat, then a very slight downhill on a grassy field, then more flat grassy fields, and a very slight uphill out of the grassy fields, and out onto a road. I arrived at Porthluney Cove and had a snack stop sitting near the beach with some of the snacks I bought the other day. Some old castle was nearby, Caerhays Castle, but I did not go in, and I think it may have even been closed anyway. "The present 'castle' was built between 1807 and 1810. The architect was John Nash, who also designed Buckingham Palace and the Royal Pavilion at Brighton."

The path left Porthluney Cove by going around the edge of a field of sheep. I looked back down on the beach at Porthluney Cove, seeing a few people enjoying the waters on this nice warm day. Summer again! Not too far later, I had yet another view of this beach of the rolling white waves perpendicular to where I was standing. Turquoise waters, blue waters, blue sky, white clouds. Yes, again similar description, but never exactly the same, and always surprisingly beautiful.

Then there was another really good short but steep uphill through a thick of trees that once again left me a bit breathless as I powered through it. More good exercise. As I completed that climb and came out into the open, a couple walked by me in the opposite direction, and I think the man chuckled or something because I was breathing heavy. The next bit of path was through some more grassy fields, then onto a hillside of ferns and shrubs and small trees with some more small ups and downs, overlooking a rocky cove. Seems to be a common theme for today. I guess the waving motion of a roller coaster of a person's arm was correct for today.

The path then became flatter once again with more grassy fields. I saw a view of the Dodman Cross on top of Dodman Point, which was small from the distance I was at, but I could still see it. There also looked like there was a big cruise ship in the distance on the seas. Then another grassy field with some cows far enough away. I arrived at Hemmick Beach close to noon, and had another snack stop also of the snacks I bought the other day. Because the café in East Portholland was not yet open, and because the café at Porthluney Cove did not have any good food choices for me, I was glad I brought a bunch of snacks with me today. They were plenty to get me through. While sitting at Hemmick beach, the wind was actually blowing some. The views were still so beautiful of the seas and the hillsides and headlands looking back that I had been walking on.

I decided last night that I wanted to skip a short distance of today's walk, Dodman Point itself. The booklet described it as, "The path to the Dodman is steep and strenuous in places." Even with feeling in good shape and even with all the other ups and downs I was powering through. I am sure I missed some great views since Dodman Point is the highest point of the south coast of Cornwall at 400 feet above sea level. I would therefore be missing about two and a quarter miles. I will add this to my list of miles I would like to walk someday in the future.

The maps showed me that there was a short road, a short track, and a very short footpath that would allow me to cut across Dodman Point rather than go around it. While I was having my snack at Hemmick Beach, I just wanted to verify with the man in a work-truck that I was correct before I went on. He said that yes, that seemed correct and there would be a map of trails at the car park up the short road which would tell me more information.

I set off intending to walk on the road, but just as I started, I saw a sign that said I could take a footpath to the car park instead, a quarter of a mile. It was a bit uphill, but did not leave me breathless this time. At the top, I looked back again at those amazingly beautiful views of the blue waters and green hillsides. I could see the path I had just walked on, and two lone buildings at the beach I just sat at. Once at the Penare car park, sure enough there was a map to compare to my maps in my booklet. I took a photo of it and set off. There happened to be another couple who looked like they just came from Dodman Point, so I confirmed once again that the track I was about to go on would take me back to the SWCP.

"Yes," he said. "Just go up this track for a short bit and you will see a sign to the SWCP." He really suggested that I go to Dodman Point though, for the great views, but I was sure I wanted to stick with my original decision. At least I thought I was sure. Now I was questioning my decision from last night. But I walked on with my plan. A sign said I had one-third of a mile from that point back to the SWCP, and sure enough, after a bit on the track, a sign pointed me to a very short footpath that met up with the SWCP. The sign at this point said I had one and three-quarters miles to Gorran Haven, my destination for the day.

This one and three-quarters miles was quite flat and easy going, except for one little spot as I just got closer to Gorran Haven. The path started out overlooking a long sandy beach, Vault Beach. I had views of Maenease Point until I walked around it, and then had my first view of Gorran Haven. A very slight rain shower started as I walked that last little bit into Gorran Haven, but not enough to get out the rain gear at this point. Gorran Haven had a beach below with lots of buildings surrounding it spread out on the hillside. As I got closer to the town, I could also see their breakwall currently protecting about nine boats floating on the water, but there were several boats out in the seas, one arriving to the breakwall as I was taking photos.

The Coast Path Café was basically the first building I came to as I entered the "picturesque 13th century former fishing village" of Gorran Haven, and since I was hungry, this was where lunch would be. It was a very good choice. My food was good, a nice vegetable quiche with some good side salads. I read the description: It is a co-operative with 27 local members, with four aims. "To promote fresh locally sourced and homemade food. To showcase village arts and crafts. To be an information point for the local area. And to provide a friendly, welcoming and inclusive environment both for local people and visitors to our village." Indeed, I did feel welcome, as the woman who took my order was very sweet, and also found me a seat at a shared table inside, since by now, it was rainier outside. To support the co-op and the village arts and crafts, I bought a local book, "Love on the Beach," by Sue Bunney, and paid a small donation to the school fund and got their laminated recipe for "Chocolate Brownies." I will be reading this book over the next several days as time allows, and perhaps when I get home I will make the brownies, and add the recipe to my cookbook collection.

After spending a bit more time inside the café as the rain passed, I made my way to my B&B for the rest of the day. I stopped in the local church, St. Just, as I walked up the street to say my usual prayers. I walked past the sign pointing me onwards to the SWCP for tomorrow's walk, and into a nice neighborhood. I used GPS on my mobile phone to find the house, rang the doorbell, and a very nice sweet elderly lady greeted me. It was good timing, as she would be leaving soon to do some grocery shopping. I think she might be one of the 27 members of the co-op as she mentioned that she worked at the Coast Path Café earlier today.

My room in her house had a sink in the room, and a circular shower right in the room too, which was an obvious add-in since this was not a bathroom, but the shower was right in the bedroom. What an interesting idea. The toilet was in a separate room, however. I settled in, started writing, video called with Scott, talked to Mom, went out to dinner at the local popular fish and chips place, did a Facebook post, and continued writing back in my room with the circular shower.

DAY 47 STATS: WOULD HAVE WALKED 9 MILES, BUT MISSED 2.25, BUT ADDED ABOUT .5 FOR THE SHORT-CUT, SO A NET OF 7.25. 4.5 HOURS. NO REAL EXTRA MILES AS B&B WAS QUITE CLOSE. PURPLE SHOES. NO PUBS IN GORRAN HAVEN, BUT ABOUT 1.5 MILES INLAND IN GORRAN IS "THE BARLEY SHEAF."

GORRAN HAVEN TO PENTWEAN – Friday, 21 July 2017

"Such is the force of the sea, unrelenting and unpredictable, you have to respect its power." – Sue Bunney in her book, "Love on the Beach."

The weather was bad this morning, really bad, and depressing really. Gale winds and rain, and more rain and more wind. However, with the possibility of the weather clearing up by the afternoon, which the forecast predicted, I had contacted my first person to walk with from the SWCP Facebook Group. Linda and I had been communicating off and on for a few days now, but this morning after breakfast, she said she would come over to my B&B about 1:00pm. What started out as a bad-weather morning, turned into a fairly nice day weather-wise, and it was good to have someone to walk with.

First I had breakfast in my B&B with Wendy, the lovely helpful lady of the place, at my usual breakfast time. I didn't want to throw that part of my day off. I spent the next several hours doing odds and ends, or I should say "bits and bobs," and started to read the little book I bought yesterday, "Love on the Beach." It is sweet. It is about a life that I will never know, having never lived in Cornwall, nor having never married a fisherman. I like reading about other's lives in this way, learning about local life. I also took a short nap. Funny how I take naps on days that I don't walk, and I have only taken one nap I think on all my walking days. Walking must be good for the body to keep it moving and awake.

Reading Sue Bunney's book led me to look at a map of this area to see where Portmellon is, which is mentioned in the book, which I will happen walk through later today. At this moment however, as I was looking at a map online, I started zooming out form Portmellon. I zoomed out far enough to see the south west of England, and discovered Minehead. I looked at how far I have come, mostly walking, since then. Wow! That was a sight to see. It felt like an accomplishment, seeing the big picture like this. It's been about 350 miles now. That's like walking from Seattle to Portland and back to Seattle!

The rain continued to fall hard as I was reading. Then miraculously at about 12:30 it seemed like the rain switch was nearly turned off, similar to like some of the other days where I have had the weather change within a short period of time. At least at this moment the rain was turned down many notches. It was still lightly raining, but the heavy rain and the wind was done and gone.

Wendy had gone out for a few hours, and around this time, the other young woman who was staying here tonight showed up, so I let her in the house. Dianna from Switzerland was walking from Newquay to Weymouth. Linda showed up at 1:15 and by this time Wendy was home as well, so all four of us stood in the hallway and had an international conversation for a few minutes. I asked Linda if she would like to get some lunch before we started walking. She did, so we went back to the Coast Path Café and split their last piece of vegetable quiche.

Just before we started walking it was still lightly raining, so I put on all my rain gear, jacket and pants and rucksack cover, and we started walking. I also chose to wear my hiking boots today because I figured the ground was wet, even muddy possibly, from all the rain, and that was a good decision to have made. We walked through some grassy paths to start, one had some cows a safe distance away, which led Linda and I to share with each other our cow stories. Linda and I chatted about a lot of other things throughout the day, including places we have travelled, and places we have walked.

We continued along several grassy fields with small rolling hills, and then onto flat ground. I was glad I had rain gear on as there were a few passing showers as we walked. We had our first view of Chapel Point, and some sheep in the foreground, about 45 minutes after we started walking. It would have been nice to visit Chapel Point, with some Mediterranean style houses built in the 1930's, but the area seemed to be private property when we got close enough to read a sign later that said something like "beware of dogs." Now cows I have had some interesting experiences walking the SWCP, but not dogs. We decided to avoid any experiences with dogs.

We did a small downhill climb, which led us quite close to the seas and the crashing waves on the rocks. We were closer to Chapel Point, which we passed by at 3:10pm, and saw that dog sign. It was strange to be writing the time as "3:10," as I was usually well near the end of my walk each day, if not done, by that time. But today we got a late start due to the storm this morning.

Linda and I walked along some grass, and then a fern-lined trail. Well, two parallel trails. We weren't sure which one to take as they weren't marked. We started on one a few feet, but thought it might be going too high, so we backtracked not too far back, and started on the lower one. But right away this one did not feel like the main path, so we went back to the first one. Not too far down the path, the two paths met up, of course. So it really didn't matter which one we took.

We started some road walking towards Portmellon, and arrived in Portmellon, the place I read about in Sue Bunney's book. We each took a photo of the buildings there that greeted us as we entered, a row of white homes with various shades of blue shutters and window trim. The homes were quite close to the seas, with just a road in between. Sue Bunney described in her "Love on the Beach" book on pages 66 to 67 a storm that hit Portmellon once many, many years ago: "We decided to walk down to Portmellon to see how the cove had fared. I will never forget the sight that greeted us, the sea had completely washed away a huge chunk of the road beside The Rising Sun pub, leaving a gaping hole. We edged our way past the pub and gazed across towards the line of cottages which faced the sea. The end cottage had taken the worst of the sea….Where there had been windows, there were only gaping holes. Luckily no one had been hurt…Some of the boats which had been parked in the boatyard were picked up and ended two fields up the valley. The scene was one of utter devastation…Such is the force of the sea, unrelenting and unpredictable, you have to respect its power."

Yes, the power of the seas, and the power of the weather. You have to respect them both.

I was wondering if we were looking at the line of cottages that Sue Bunney had described, which I bet we were. Linda and I then walked by The Rising Sun pub as we walked through the small town of Portmellon, continuing on the road to walk one mile into Mevagissey. On our way, we needed to read the booklet to figure out which way to go, which we did a few times today. Also at that point, it started raining, rather than just a passing shower. I think it might have rained lightly all the way to the harbour in Mevagissey the last mile or so.

Looking down on the harbour of Mevagissey from above before we went down a zigzag paved hill, we could see this cute colorful town with many boats in the harbour. The boats were blue, yellow, green, orange, red, white, and some of the homes on the hillside were blue, yellow, orange, and light pastel colors. The boats were arranged into a few rows, with a few other scattered boats. Most of the rows contained fishing boats, and then some rowboats floated nearby. The entire scene was just very picturesque to me, which included some green hillsides and headlands in the background, and the light rain clouds in the sky made the colors more dramatic. (See back cover of this book for a color photo of this scene!)

I didn't know there was a lighthouse in Mevagissey, which is actually a Harbour Light, so we went over to get some photos by walking on the breakwall once we got down to the harbour. Stacks of crab and lobster pots and rope and other fishing supplies, as well as a couple of fishing boats, added to the scenery of the photos of the Harbour Light. There were a lot of boats in this harbour, which made for many more colorful pictures as we walked around the big harbour and were even closer to the boats. Might be the biggest harbour since St. Ives. Down where we were the fishing boats had a lot of reds and blues and yellows. And I had another lighthouse to add to my lighthouse list.

We stopped in a tea shop/café to have a cheese scone, topped with butter. I discovered that the tip to my water bladder was missing, as the floor was quite wet next to our table just before we ate because the water was leaking out of my bladder. At first I could not find the tip, but then went outside and found it at the place where I stopped just feet earlier to put away my hiking poles and booklets. I'm glad I found the tip. I would have had to use water bottles if I could not find it.

I called Mom to leave her a quick message as it was getting closer to the 5:00 time I usually call her to tell her all was good. Just as the sun was coming out! Linda and I started walking again the last couple miles, and we were able to take the rain gear off. I took a few more photos of boats and the Harbour Light as we walked around the rest of the harbour, as well as overlooking the harbour as we walked up and away. The sun now shining on the boats made for different kinds of dramatic photos. "Like many Cornish villages, Mevagissey was a centre for smuggling and pilchard fishing and it still retains a good size fishing fleet," according to today's booklet.

We started ascending some steps which led to a grassy area which was flat which led to a descent and an ascent, or something like that. Looking back we could see views of the harbour, the Harbour Light, the breakwalls, and Chapel Point in the background. At the moment, there were some glimpses of blue skies. We walked on more flat grassy paths and more grassy fields, followed by a footbridge across a boggy area, and one more quick rain shower to which we put back on our rain jackets and rain rucksack covers, only for it to pass quickly by and return to the sun and some heat.

The path was then flat and through some trees, and paralleled a noisy road, and the last bit was walking on the sidewalk that paralleled that noisy road. At 6:00pm we arrived in Pentewan, where "fishing and tin 'streaming' (panning for tin ore in streams) had taken place here for centuries before the harbour was built." Other activities in Pentewan's history included pilchard fishing, exporting china clay, tin mining and exporting, and coal and limestone importing. However, the harbour "gradually fell into disrepair and silted up."

I called Wendy from a phone in the pub since neither Linda nor I could get mobile reception. Within twenty minutes Wendy arrived, and we were back at the B&B about 45 minutes after we arrived in Pentewan. It felt odd to get in so late, but then again we got a late start. It was good to have someone to walk with today, and I thanked Linda before she drove off. I invited Linda to join me anytime on another walk. Thank you, Linda!

For dinner I got fish and onion rings, instead of the fish and chips I had last night, down at the Gorran Haven harbour, and the sun remained out...for now.

DAY 48 STATS: 6 MILES. 4 HOURS. NO EXTRA MILES REALLY JUST TO GET DINNER SINCE CLOSE ENOUGH. HIKING BOOTS. PUB IN PORTMELLON IS "THE RISING SUN." PUB IN PENTEWAN IS "THE SHIP INN." LOTS OF PUBS IN MEVAGISSEY: "THE WHEEL HOUSE," "THE KINGS ARMS," THE "HARBOUR TAVERN," "THE SHIP INN," AND "THE FOUNTAIN INN."

PENTEWAN TO PORTHPEAN BEACH BY CAR; WALK PORTHPEAN BEACH TO CHARLESTOWN TO PAR – Saturday, 22 July 2017

"I hope you have a brolly. You don't have much time." – Some advise I received on a golf course near Par.

I ate breakfast chatting with Wendy and Dianna. Both nice people. Wendy dropped Dianna off in Mevagissey, and then dropped me off one mile before Charlestown. The weather forecast for today was bad once again, calling for thunderstorms in the Pentewan area, where I wanted to start walking. I was not about to risk walking in that kind of weather, so I asked Wendy if she could drop me off in Charlestown instead, a bigger town, where I could hang out for a while and see if the weather improved. As we were driving towards Charlestown, Wendy suggested I walk from Porthpean Beach, then I have the approach into Charlestown at least, and a mile of walking before Charlestown. I carefully checked the skies in all directions before leaving the car, and it looked good for the next twenty to thirty minutes, knowing that is about how long it takes me to walk a mile, so I was dropped off. (Note that I will be making up the Pentewan to Porthpean Beach miles tomorrow.)

After Wendy dropped me off, I walked up a few concrete steps up from the sandy beach. Other than a few seagulls, no one was on this beach this morning. It was flat all the way to Charlestown, on a path that had shrubs on my right, and hedges and gardens of homes on the left. I arrived in Charlestown within twenty minutes of starting. I think that is the fastest mile yet. I seem to average thirty-minute miles just about all of the time, with all the ascents and descents, and taking photos and breaks and such.

As I entered Charlestown, first from above I could see the harbour with its breakwalls. To my surprise, the town was setting up some booths outside near the harbour for something, so I asked someone what was going on. It was the beginning of their Regatta Week, for "having fun and raising funds." I took some photos of the main part of the harbour where there were no boats, as some were a bit inland, including "a famous collection of old ships," which were quite historic looking. Since I needed to hang out in Charlestown to see what the weather would do before I decided if I should walk to Par or get other transportation, I went into a few art shops, and an antique shop to spend some time. Turns out that I believe that the old ships are a small collection of "tall ships" used to make period films and TV shows, possibly even Poldark, but I don't know for sure.

Then the festivities began. First was the Triathlon that opened up Charlestown's Regatta Week. I walked down to the pier, where it seemed that everyone was gathered, and saw the swim part of the triathlon start. There were several dozen people in the water in their wet suits, and when the horn sounded, they swam back in towards the beach. It was a 200 meter swim. The other two parts of the triathlon were a four mile bike, and a two mile run. I could not quite tell if the same person did all three parts, or if they were relay teams. I walked back up the street and watched a few of the runners and cyclists go by. It seemed like the whole town was there cheering everyone on. What was fun was that I was right there watching it all as well. I did not expect this today, so it was a nice to experience this spontaneously as part of my day today, to experience some life with the locals. I would not have experienced this if I had walked starting in Pentewan.

Other events happening during the Charlestown Regatta Week were water polo, raft races, sailing races, rowing races, live music, and activities for children. Per the brochure I picked up for this, "all money raised during the week goes towards the work of the Regatta Committee to support a variety of local good causes."

I was getting hungry so I went into a restaurant for lunch just before noon. I checked the weather forecast, and now it only called for "light rain" or "light rain showers" for the next few hours, no longer thunderstorms, so that was an improvement. I hadn't seen or heard or felt any thunderstorms, nor rain, yet today. In fact, it was just cloudy out. I wondered why the forecast was not accurate.

I wanted to walk to the church in Charlestown, St. Paul's Church, though because photos of it looked like it was a big church. It was almost a half mile up the road inland. It was a big church, but unfortunately it was closed, although I did walk the path around it taking photos of its exterior and looking at the graveyard. I walked back down to the harbour area, looked at the mostly lighter cloudy skies, and figured I would try walking. There was one dark cloud over to the inland skies, but after watching for a few minutes, it was not coming in my direction. However, I did not think to look way far out over the seas to see what was coming from that way…

As I walked around the harbour, a food cart was selling some "peanut butter date energy balls." Of course, I had to buy three of them. I ate them right away, and then put my hiking boots back on to get ready for my walk, as I had taken them off and worn my cushy flip flops while I was walking around Charlestown. I chose boots again today because of the possibility of rain. Good choice, as we shall see…

I left Charlestown to walk three and a half miles to Par. The path started flat and easy, followed by some pavement. I crossed a few grassy park-like patches with several benches. At one point, I passed a sign that said two miles to Par after passing a couple of hotels.

I started walking on a long walk at the edge of a golf course, which was all flat, and for a while, all was dry, and all was good with the world. There was a small beach in my views and the headlands beyond. But that was when it…started…to…rain. And I really don't just mean rain…I mean downpour, dump, come down in buckets. The forecast said light showers, but not a heavy one. This was a heavy one for sure. The biggest downpour I have had to walk in since Heddon's Mouth. Who would have known though that it was a golfer who would save the day for me…Here is the full story…

I was walking along all good and all, looking around at the clouds. I thought they were moving away from me. Well they were, except the one out on the water. The one that I did not think to look way far out over the seas to see what was coming from that way. As I walked by a golfer he said to me, "I hope you have a brolly." (That's slang for an umbrella in England, which I did not have since I shipped that home back in Croyde Bay over a month ago, but I knew that I had rain gear at least, as I carry that around no matter what the weather.) I remarked to the kind golfer that I hope to make it to Par before the rain. He pointed to the cloud over the water and said, "You don't have much time." He was right! Not even a moment later the rain started. As fast as I possibly could, I put all my rain gear on me and on my rucksack, also quickly putting away my mobile phone and my camera. Just like that time I leaped over the stile as fast as I could when passing by the herd of cows on my way to Port Isaac. Or that record-breaking time I changed from my purple shoes into my hiking boots. I think I was even faster at putting on my rain gear and protecting my valuables.

Then it started to downpour, dump, come down in buckets as I started to walk. I still had a mile left to walk, but this was just way too much rain all at once. Did I say the rain was a downpour, dumping, coming down in buckets? I noticed some golfers under some very large brollys on the golf course, so I ran quickly towards one of them, right onto the golf course, hoping no one was hitting a golf ball at the moment, which I highly doubted, and hoped that I could take shelter under their brollys with them, or in a golf cart.

Funny thing was the brolly I chose had that guy under it. That same guy that just moments earlier warned me that I didn't have much time. He was right. He kindly let me take shelter, and kind of chuckled implying, "I told you so." Of course as we were waiting out the downpour under his brolly together, he asked where I was from and about my walk. It was so surreal to be talking about my walk as I huddled under a brolly in the middle of a golf course! I remarked to him that I never imagined I would be huddling under a brolly in the middle of a golf course during my walk! He remarked that this morning he would have never imagined that an American woman would be huddled under his brolly in the middle of a golf course. Guardian angel number one.

Then his friend, who was taking shelter in the golf cart and his brolly next to us, started to remark out loud how some other guy was taking a pee in the middle of the golf course, but of course used a different word. He obviously didn't know I was there. The guy I was sharing the brolly with tells his friend to watch his language, as he has company here and there was a woman nearby. The guy in the golf cart peeks out sees me, and I say, "Hi!" It was a very odd and comical situation if you think about it. And quite surreal. A situation that might only happen in a movie. And remember, little did I know back on 16 June at the golf course between Appledore and Westward Ho! that I would be having some personal, interesting, and surreal connections and stories related to golf courses. Who knows, maybe it is karma because I really don't like to play golf.

Anyway, finally the buckets of downpour dumping of rain lightened up a bit, and the two men were ready to get on with their golf tournament, so I walked on. I first wondered what hole all this happened at, and what the par of the hole was.

No sooner did I start walking again that the rain persisted, even though it was not as heavy. So next I took shelter in a World War 2 observation post. Another surreal moment. I observed out the little window watching the rain cloud passing by. I never thought I would need to take shelter in a WW2 remnant during my walk, and I bet that no one ever would have imagined that decades later, here I would be.

There were two other people under this concrete shelter with me. One of them advised me to take the footpath on the other side of the fence into Par. It would go over a metal bridge and zigzag around and it would seem like I would be lost, but he assured me it would lead me into Par. I wasn't sure if it was the SWCP or not, but I didn't care. It sounded like a good way for me to get to Par, my destination for the day, as I was completely soaked by now. Well my raingear was soaked. Underneath I seemed to remain mostly dry. It turns out his direction was the SWCP, and I was actually really glad he told me because I may have kept walking straight otherwise after the observation post. Guardian angel number two.

I waited a bit longer under the shelter, and finally the rain let up, and I walked on. I looked back at the green grass of the golf course, could still see people out there playing, and the approximate spot where I had taken shelter under a brolly. I wondered how they could continue to play as I imagine the grass must be soaked. But I guess when you love golf, and have an important tournament to play, you keep playing.

The path was all concrete, and sheltered a bit by some trees overhead which were dripping from the rain. I crossed the bridge, zigzagged the path till it met a road. At that moment, someone was driving out of a business that was there, so I asked if I was near The Par Inn, my accommodations for the night. It was just a quarter mile up the road, to the left. Perfect. Guardian angel number three.

As I walked in the door of The Par Inn and pub at 2:00, the rain stopped and it became partially sunny. Of course, great timing! This was one of the few times I was staying in an inn and pub on my walk. I think it was because this one was the only accommodations available in Par, and I will be staying here two nights because I think I had trouble finding accommodations in Fowey, the next town.

Then guardian angel number four...Matt of the Par Inn. He welcomed me happily into his pub, even though I was dripping wet. Not like the gentleman at the inn in Heddon's Mouth who was not thrilled with me. Matt was quite welcoming. My room wasn't quite ready yet though, but he let me use a bathroom to take all my wet rain gear off, and even gave me a clean towel to dry off. I really actually had good cry in the bathroom from this experience of the downpour as surreal as it was. Hopefully Matt didn't hear me cry. I needed to release the frustration from the weather, and it was difficult for me to be in the downpour actually even with the help of some guardian angels. Looking back on this day, I probably could have walked this morning as it did not rain then as predicted, and then I could have skipped this afternoon's downpour.

I went back down to the pub and Matt kindly gave me some hot tea, a snack, and some fruit. He asked if I would like the en-suite room, which might be a bit noisier tonight with the live band, or the other room with a detached bathroom. A classic rock cover band would play till about 11:30 tonight. Cool! I chose the en-suite room (meaning that it has a bathroom in the room, which has always been my preference anyway). I also like that type of music, so I would just go downstairs later and listen anyway, and I definitely prefer en-suite for two nights. Wow, another spontaneous fun unplanned event for today. I guess that made up for the downpour. Matt will also give me rides tomorrow afternoon from Fowey back to Par, and the next morning back to Fowey. He also offered to cook me dinner since this pub doesn't serve food in general. What a nice guy!

I was able to get into my room at 3:15, but for the first time my large wheeled suitcase was not there yet from the Luggage Transfers people. Matt said it might not get there till about 4:30. No worries. I took a shower anyway using their soaps, and using the "emergency clothes" I had in my rucksack to change into. May that be the only time I have to use them. My suitcase arrived at 4:00.

I read a few more chapters in the little book I bought the other day, "Love on the Beach." Sue Bunney mentions that mining, farming, and fishing are the "real things in life." Those are the things here in Cornwall, and the south west part of England. And that is what I am witnessing as I walk along here! Definitely!

I got hungry so I went downstairs and Matt said he could make me a jacket potato (baked potato), some chicken (which I normally don't eat), and a salad. I said that would be great, but if it was too much trouble, I didn't mind walking somewhere else, especially since it was no longer raining. He was fine with cooking, and about a half hour later, it was all done. I went back downstairs to eat, including the chicken, which was tasty.

As I was eating, well who should show up at the pub? Take a guess! The guy taking shelter in the golf cart that was next to the brolly with the other guy that I was taking shelter under on the golf course. Of course. They must live in Par. They must have asked Matt if I was American, because then the entire story came out. Everyone knew of the American-woman-under-the-brolly-in-the-pouring-rain-on-the-golf-course in Par now. It is a small world, I commented. And a small town. And I was famous. We all laughed at what a strange surreal story it really was. It will be a story to tell. I think the golf cart guy texted the brolly guy to tell him that he saw me again. And now I see why Par is called Par, as it is near a golf course.

The classic rock cover band should start playing their music about 9:30.

DAY 49 STATS: 8.5 MILES. 4.5 WALKING, 4 BY CAR. I THINK ABOUT 2.5 HOURS, NOT INCLUDING THE TIME IN CHARLESTOWN, BUT INCLUDING THE TIME UNDER THE BROLLY. ONE EXTRA MILE TO AND FROM THE CHURCH. HIKING BOOTS. PUB IN CHARLESTOWN IS "THE RASHLEIGH ARMS." PUB IN PAR IS "THE PAR INN."

PART 1: PAR TO FOWEY…PART 2: PENTEWAN TO PORTHPEAN BEACH – Sunday, 23 July 2017

"The ocean is calling and I must go. Welcome to our beach house. Happiness is a day at the beach. This is my happy place. Life is better at the beach. Get some vitamin sea." – Sayings on some key chains in a beach-type shop in Polkerris.

Part One: Par to Fowey

Last night I listened to the live classic rock cover band music in the pub for a couple of hours. I mean since I would have heard it through the floor in my room anyway, I may have well listened to it downstairs, so I did. They played cover songs from various decades, as well as some tunes I didn't recognize so I am thinking they must have been British songs. I was around the locals of Par, England all evening. I had a few conversations with a few locals, but it was hard to hear with the loud music, so they were short conversations. I found out that drinking age where they are able to buy alcohol in England is 18, although 16 and 17 year olds "can drink beer, wine and cider with a meal if bought by an adult and they are accompanied by an adult." Compared to the US where the drinking age is 21. And the story of my taking-cover-under-the-brolly-of-a-local-on-the-golf-course-in-the-downpour came up a few times. I felt like a celebrity. (Or the laughing stock.) It was a fun night at a pub in England, to be with the locals, and to hear live music for the third time on my SWCP walk! (Port Gaverne and "Tunes in the Dunes" were the other two times I heard live music.)

After breakfast Matt kindly drove us to the car park near The Ship Inn. I say "us" because he wanted to walk with me to Polkerris. I am not sure why. He might have thought I wasn't sure of the way, or really, I think he just likes the walk himself and wanted to get out of the pub and wanted to enjoy the one-mile walk. He keeps a kayak in Polkerris and likes to walk there and then go on his kayak, so he wanted to show me something important to him. I was kind of all ready to walk from the Par Inn, but the drive to the car park of The Ship Inn was a mile, so I unfortunately missed another mile of walking. I did not want to be rude to Matt and decline the ride and his offer to walk with me. He has been so hospitable and kind to me. Matt said the mile walk was mostly pavement anyway, and then either sand dunes behind the beach or walking the beach itself, so I will just add that to my walk-sometime-in-the-future list.

We started walking at 9:00 and arrived in Polkerris a half hour later. It was pretty much flat all the way, except for a small hill. Looking backwards, I had views of the beach, the industrial part of Par, and the infamous golf course in the distance. I even saw the approximate place where I huddled under the brolly!

There was a small breakwall and about a dozen various boats in the small harbour of Polkerris in the water. About a dozen other boats were lined up on the sand above the water. A row of colorful blue-fading-to-white and red-fading-to-yellow kayaks were also lined up on the sand above the water. The harbour was surrounded by the green foliage of the hillside above. The waters were that turquoise-to-blue color. A small sandy beach and a few buildings completed the scene.

Matt was getting picked up in Polkerris by a friend of his, so I continued on my way. A sign said just under five miles to Fowey, which would be my first of two destinations for today. I peeked into a beach-type shop in Polkerris, where I spotted the above sayings on some key chains that doubled as bottle openers, and then zigzagged my way slightly uphill through some trees to a flat area. The flat continued around grassy fields. There was a small rocky cove below, and I saw a couple people and their dog swimming in the water. It looked like a nice little quiet place to have a swim.

Today was a beautiful warm sunny blue-sky day, all day! Summer! I was so grateful after yesterday's downpour. I am sure there were plenty of golfers out today.

There was a small uphill, then flat, and the sounds of small quiet waves. I noticed that the waves the last few days have been much smaller and quieter than in days past. Someone may have mentioned this to me, that this area is different than other areas of the SWCP in that respect. Either one though, I love, and respect, the sound. As I walked around the Gribbin Headland, it was very flat walking, with grassy fields to my left with a herd of cows, the white of sailboats against the blue of the water, a few rocky shores, and a small beach below on my right. Way back in the distance behind me I believe would be Charlestown.

As I got closer to a red and white striped tower, I had a view of Fowey and Polruan. I arrived at the tower sitting on top of a large grassy area, which was the 84-foot tall Gribbin Daymark, built in 1832 "for the safety of commerce and the preservation of mariners." I couldn't quite tell if it was a lighthouse or not, or just the striped colors were enough to spot from the seas for safety. In either case, it is some sort of aid for navigation and I shall add it to my lighthouse list. According to the flyer at the Daymark there are, "Fantastic views from 316 feet above sea level to Bolt Head in South Devon, the Eddystone Lighthouse, Dodman Head and the high points on Bodmin Moor." While it would be open today to climb up some steps for the views, and I would have really liked to, my timing was off, and I would have had to wait about an hour for it to open.

But I had great views from where I was anyway – inland was the farmland of green fields and brown fields, divided by darker green rows of trees. A few taller trees in the foreground, and the beautiful blue sky with some white fluffy clouds in the background. Even the sky today had several shades of blue, light blue further out and dark blue closer above. What a grand day!

I chatted with a jogger going up a gentle grassy slope as I was going down the slope. He jogs these hills three times a week, six miles each time. What a beautiful place to go jogging! I had a great view of some rocky coves, some farmland, the green grass on the next hillside, the towns ahead, and a few sailboats in the blue water and the blue sky. Lovely! If I was a jogger, I wouldn't mind jogging here three times a week. The view I had ahead of me was more brown and green farmland on top of the hillsides, a herd of cows on one hilltop, the town of Polruan on another hilltop, a few more green covered headlands beyond, the turquoise-blue waters with several boats motoring or sailing by, and that grand blue sky with some white fluffy clouds. What a grand day! As I walked down the grassy slope, I looked back at the Gribbin Daymark, with its red and white stripes against the blue and white sky, standing on the dark and light green hillside. Colorful!

I walked across a boardwalk next to a sandy beach with small quiet waves. Then out of nowhere there was a small lake with two swans. This was Polridmouth Cove and its lake which "was constructed in WW2 as a decoy sight for Fowey harbour. Lights around the water were supposed to draw enemy bombers away from Fowey as it was full of US troops and ships preparing for the D-Day landings," per today's booklet. I found the lake to be a refreshing scene, so I took the opportunity to sit down for a bit and have a snack while looking in one direction at the beach with a few people enjoying the day, and the lake in the other direction inland. After my break, I walked next to another grassy field with some cows, and then a slight incline uphill. A white sailboat floated by. I will say again, because I really appreciated it, that it was a perfect warm sunny blue-sky day.

I waited for a family that was very loving. You see, they were walking through a "kissing gate," which is a certain type of gate that I have passed through many times with kind of a swinging gate that you have to move from one end to the other end and wiggle through. It is meant to keep animals from passing through since they probably could not figure out how to swing the gate. Anyway, this family was giving each other little kisses as they passed through the kissing gate. Awwww. That was so cute. Scott and I did this last year together on our walk whenever we passed through a kissing gate. Although, I didn't tell this family, but what they walked through was actually just a regular gate, not technically a kissing gate. It was adorable anyway. And made me think of Scott.

Speaking of thinking, so what do I think about a lot when I am walking for hours and hours and miles and miles? Aside from thinking about the weather, and the beauty of what I am seeing. Sometimes I think about nothing in particular. Just what the mind does when it wanders from thought to thought to thought. Sometimes I think about the slower pace of life it seems when I walk, about going through life at this slower walking pace. Rather than the rush, rush of traffic and working and the busy, busy of living near a big city. Smaller towns with less traffic have a great appeal to me. A closer-knit community of people, quieter, and perhaps even better for one's health to live life at a walking pace. A walking pace where I can really stop to smell the roses, and to smell the sea air. Sometimes I think about my family, and while I talk to my Mom and Scott everyday and get updates about the rest of them, I think about them. Sometimes I think about what other work I could do in my life. I think about writing this book. I am sure I think so many other thoughts that are just fleeting. But mostly I guess I think about the beauty of what I am seeing at the moment.

More flat walking, then another slight incline uphill, and more flat walking, with views of Polruan getting closer, the rocky shoreline, and a rocky beach with green seaweed. I arrived at St. Catherine's Point which offered great views of the River Fowey and lots of boats in between the two towns of Fowey to the left with buildings going up a hillside, and Polruan to the right with buildings going up another hillside. With boats on the river in between the two towns, and another green hillside in the middle beyond the river, it was a beautiful sight. My purple shoes were in the foreground of one picture.

I took a small detour to visit St. Catherine's Castle at St. Catherine's Point. The castle was built in 1530 to defend the harbour. And I just read this in the booklet as I was typing: "Originally there was a chapel on St. Catherine's point and a candle, burning at a window, that acted as a navigation marker before a lighthouse was built." A lighthouse? What lighthouse? I didn't see a lighthouse? I didn't know to look for a lighthouse? You mean I actually missed seeing a lighthouse? Yes, sure enough, built in 1904, and shining its light for the first time on 7 January 1905, is a red round navigational aid possibly twenty feet tall on red poles with a red ladder near where I was. Whenever I come back to Fowey at some point, I need to go see if I can find this lighthouse to look at. Anyway, I walked a bit more to Readymoney Cove beach. I switched to flip flops at this point since was only a half mile from Fowey proper, and it would be all pavement and road walking.

I arrived at the main part of Fowey, and when I spotted a café that served bagel sandwiches, I stopped in for lunch. I haven't had a bagel since I have been here! I got the sandwich with avocado, spinach, salad leaves, and tomatoes. It was warmed up and delicious. I also decided to splurge and got a warmed chocolate chip and orange scone, with chocolate hazelnut spread on top. It was the first chocolate I had in a long time, and it was delicious too! A sweet variation on the cream tea, without the tea.

I continued walking through the busy streets of Fowey (pronounced "Foy"), with lots of little shops and restaurants, and happened to see a bank so I got some cash. The St. Fimbarrus Church was there as well, so I made a stop in the church. The tower of St. Fimbarrus Church is "the second highest in Cornwall and dates from 1460 when an earlier Norman church was rebuilt after it was severely damaged by the French, it is thought, in revenge for Fowey's sea-faring attacks on the French Coast, [and has had] several rebuilds and restorations." Furthermore, this church "marks the end of The Saints' Way, originally a drovers' route from Padstow to Fowey and taken by merchants and pilgrims travelling from Ireland and Wales to France. This overland route avoided the dangers of the sea route around Land's End." Wow! Another pilgrimage route. I actually did see a different symbol other than the scallop shell and acorn, a Celtic cross marker, as I was walking into Fowey. The 28-mile The Saints' Way is thus similar to St. Michael's Way in that it avoids going around the coast. Perhaps another walk to add to my future "to-walk" list. (Later I looked on the SWCP Association's Distance Calculator on their website that walking from Padstow to Fowey along the SWCP is about 211.5 miles that I would miss if I ever walked The Saints' Way.)

I walked closer to the water of the River Fowey to get a view of the many boats and the river up close, with views across to Polruan, and to take a few more photos on this grand day. Fowey "was once a major pilchard fishing port and is still a major port today, exporting thousands of tons of china clay each year," per today's booklet.

Then I was done with part one of my day. I walked back to the church, and called Matt to have him pick me up as we previously arranged. The church bells rang as I was waiting for him.

Part Two: Pentewan to Porthpean Beach
Now onto part two of my day...to do the four miles I missed yesterday! Since it was early enough in the day, and it was still a warm sunny blue-sky day. And what a great four miles it was, as the views were spectacular. Although many ascents and descents, and one mix up added to part two of my day...

Matt kindly picked me up in Fowey, and dropped me off in Pentewan at The Ship Inn where Linda and I finished the other day. I put my purple shoes back on (this was a brand-new pair of purple shoes by the way that I brought with me since I figured I was more than half way done with the entire walk, and wanted to change purple shoes), and started walking. I stopped in the little All Saints Church in Pentewan, the outside of which looks more like a regular stone building than a church, after walking up a road a short bit.

The path started flat going around a cow field, and then a sheep field, with the first of the great beautiful views of the Black Head area closer to me, and views of the red and white Gibbon Daymark tower way in the distance. Below were some small coves with those quiet waves. The hillsides of the few small headlands in this area were painted with light green grass inland, darker green shrubbery on the edges, the brown of the rocks and coves below, the turquoise waters fading to darker blue waters, spotted with the white of sail boats, with the light blue skies, spotted with a few white clouds. Idyllic. So glad I went back to do these four miles.

I had a small uphill to climb, and walked through some shrubbery. Then the first of several other ascents and descents, with steps. This first one, according to the booklet, which I did not verify by counting, was a descent with 106 steps. Some kayakers were in the waters below. Then 50 steps up, again not verified by counting. It was so beautiful warm and sunny out. The terrain was flat again with some very tall ferns, taller than me, on the path that were blocking some of the views. Then there was a clearing and I overlooked a beach. It did not look like this beach was accessible by land, perhaps only by kayak or boat, as others I have seen that seem like this. The view from here was spectacular of this little deserted beach and cove area just beyond with various shades of brown of the rocks, various shades of green of the hillsides, various shades of the blue skies, and one motorboat speeding by leaving a white line in the various shades of blue waters. I must add this area as a possible ultimate location for a beach hut.

As I walked, the views seemed to get better and better, and they were great to begin with. Sometimes I could see the line of the SWCP ahead of me and the steps I would be climbing. The rolling hillsides, the rocky coastline, and the same colors of turquoises, blues, greens, whites, just all so breathtaking. Then I went up some more steps, which the booklet didn't tell me how many steps though, and I didn't count, followed by a gentle uphill without steps. Then a long descent through a small treed forest with 100 steps, and a zigzag around this area at the bottom still in the trees, followed by another climb with more steps, to which again the booklet did not say how many, and again I did not count. Then I reached the actual Black Head area, to which there was a side trail that went out on the headland, but I don't go out there.

A father and son showed up looking like they had just been fishing. I followed them for a bit as they were walking on the SWCP as well. I got to the Ropehaven Cliff Nature Reserve, to which somehow I got a bit turned around in this area. First, I took a left instead of a little downhill, and ended up on a dirt track, which was not correct. I had to back track a short bit once I figured that mistake out. Then when I got back, I completely didn't see the post at a bench pointing me left. I went downhill to some private house, asked the woman there who said the SWCP was back uphill. Ooops. A short unnecessary uphill for the day, and then I saw the post. All that took about ten to fifteen minutes I would say, so about an extra half mile for today. That was the first time in a long time I have gotten that mixed up it seems. At least I went back each time to correct my losing the SWCP. Then the path went out to a road for a bit, with a sign then saying one and a quarter miles to Porthpean Beach.

It was flat for a while, then another long 170 steps down and 90 steps up out of Silvermine Valley. Wow! A lot of ups and downs today, and nearly ten miles today at that point for both parts of today. I should try to tally up all the steps I did, or at least the ones that the booklet told me…At least 516 steps! Another day with many ups and downs like a few others I have had before. I descended a gentler grassy slope with views of the beach and Charlestown beyond. I could hear the woman speaking on the bullhorn from here, just as she was doing yesterday during the triathlon, for more Regatta Week events.

It was relatively flat all the way to Porthpean Beach. I hoped I would get mobile reception to call Matt again. I did, although he could barely hear me, but it was enough to know that he could pick me up as we once again prearranged. What a nice guy. That was a lot of ups and downs in four miles, after my six miles earlier today, but it was worth it, even getting mixed up at one point, for the spectacular views of both areas! What I did not know during today was that a few of the photos I took today would actually become contenders for the front cover photo of my book. Ultimately I chose another photo for the main front cover photo, and two from today would become the smaller photos on the front cover!

Matt kindly picked me up and we were back at the Par Inn by almost 5:00, just in time to call Mom. I video called with Scott, and Matt kindly made me dinner once again. What a nice guy. Both nights were chicken (which I ate again), potato, and salad.

DAY 50 STATS: 11 MILES TOTAL. 6 MILES PAR TO FOWEY; 3.25 HOURS. 4 MILES PENTEWAN TO PORTHBEAN BEACH SO I DIDN'T MISS ANY YESTERDAY; 2.25 HOURS. 1 MILE MISSED BY CAR IN PAR. HALF MILE EXTRA FOR MIXUP. PURPLE SHOES. ANOTHER PUB IN PAR IS "THE SHIP INN." PUB IN POLKERIS IS "THE RASHLEIGH INN." PUBS IN FOWEY ARE "THE SHIP INN" AND "THE SAFE HARBOUR." Information on drinking age from news.bbc.co.uk/2/hi/uk_news/6598867.
Information on lighthouse at St. Catherine's Point from foweyharbourhistory.com/st-catherines-lighthouse.html.
Information on St. Fimbarrus Church and The Saints' Way from foweyharbourheritage.org.uk/heritage/places/st-fimbarrus-church.

FOWEY TO POLRUAN VIA FERRY THEN WALK TO POLPERRO – Monday, 24 July 2017

"The Arrow Closest To The Acorn."

Before I said my thank yous and goodbyes to Matt for all he did for me over the last two days, I walked across the street to the local little market, Richard's Fruit, Veg & Fish, to look around a bit at their nice displays of fruits and vegetables, eggs, and bags of spices and seeds. Matt kindly dropped me off in Fowey. We arrived just after 9:00 and with my meeting time in an hour to walk today with Lucy from the SWCP Facebook Group, I had time to go into a deli to get a sandwich for today's walk, as there were no food stops till Polperro. Unfortunately, the bagel place I liked yesterday was not making their lunch sandwiches this early in the morning.

I intended to also look in a few shops this morning, but not much was open that early, so I went to the quay and ferry waiting area to wait for Lucy to take the ferry across the River Fowey to Polruan, as we arranged to meet here since she lives in Fowey and responded to my walking request from about a week ago. It was already sunny and warm with blue skies! Again! Two days in a row! I enjoyed just waiting for Lucy in this kind of weather.

Lucy showed up and quite quickly she wanted to catch the 10:00 Polruan Ferry that was already there, so before we really had a chance formally meet and say hello, we boarded the ferry, paid our £2/$2.80 each, and within ten minutes, we started walking. Lucy and I said our hellos and nice to meet yous on the ferry, she already telling me all kinds of tidbits (bits and bobs) about all kinds of things that she would kindly tell me throughout the day, but that I would not remember everything since I don't take as many notes when I walk with someone compared to walking alone. A sign told us it would be six and a half miles to Polperro.

We walked a bit through the streets of Polruan, with views back across the River Fowey, with its many boats, to Fowey and St. Catherine's Castle, and then onto some flat grassy area where the views were already scenic. Blue waters, blue skies, green covered hills, white sailboats, looking back to where I had walked yesterday and days before, including the red and white Gribbin Daymark. There was a slight uphill with views of the green headlands ahead. A warm breeze felt nice. Lucy explained to me about one of the prickly plants that I have been seeing, and occasionally feeling through my pants legs, but avoiding being scratched because I was wearing my long pants, for quite a while on the SWCP. It is "gorse," a plant that is yellow when in bloom, and is a densely branched spiny shrub that makes it have that prickly feeling. At this time, we could hear the clicking of its pods, which may mean that it was seeding. Gorse has a coconut scent to it, and some of its common uses are that "The flowers produce a beautiful yellow dye, can be preserved in vinegar and eaten like capers, or added as a flavouring to spirits."

As Lucy and I walked on the path surrounded by green grass, green trees, green ferns, and the deep blue water with some boats going by, we made our way towards the beautiful Lantic Bay that contained two small beaches, Great Lantic Beach and Little Lantic Beach. They looked like a couple of great spots to spend some time, but not for us today. It would have been a steep climb down and back up. They were quiet beaches without much as far as waves go. In fact, the whole day seemed quiet. I am not complaining, it was quite peaceful. Another sound I like – peace and quiet. Ahead I could see the line of the SWCP making its way in between the greenery.

When we got closer to Lantic Bay, there was a pretty good climb uphill to the place where you would take the path to the beaches. When we reached the top, taking our time, a sign said five miles to Polperro. Looking back down from where we just climbed, the sandy beaches below, and the path we had walked on was clearly defined as a line through the green hillsides. With the blue and turquoise waters, and the blue skies with a few white clouds, it was an amazing view.

As we were at the top, Lucy spotted a Peregrine Falcon soaring against the blue sky. She was very good at spotting things today such as some wildlife, and telling me about wildflowers, as she spotted some wild thyme, and a purple wildflower later on that I cannot remember the name of.

It was around this time that I saw a sign post with arrows and acorns that I have seen hundreds and hundreds of times already that I decided to ask Lucy a question about the signage on the SWCP. Some of these sign posts have multiple arrows, but only one acorn, and while I was somewhat sure of the answer, I thought I would ask her anyway. My question was, "Lucy, how do you know which arrow to follow when there are several arrows on one sign post, and only one acorn?" She responded, "The arrow closest to the acorn is the one for the SWCP!"

Well, she really said, "The arrow nearest to the acorn," but I thought that the words, "The Arrow Closest To The Acorn" had a nice ring to it…

Later, Lucy further went on to describe more of the various sign posts, some called 'waymarks,' and arrows and acorns, along not only the SWCP, but also other National Trails, in a Facebook post. She stated, "The arrows relate to the directions when viewed directly in front of the face of the post. The acorn at the top denotes that the route is a National Trail and the arrow(s) nearest to the acorn are the direction(s) for the Trail. There is then a dividing line. Below that are arrows relating to 'side routes,' i.e. public rights of way which connect with/cross the National Trail at that point, but do not form part of it."

The SWCP Association website describes this in similar form as, "At some path junctions you will find a waymark post with multiple arrows. The arrow at the top nearest the acorn indicates the direction of the Coast Path. Below that, separated by a black line you may find other arrows which indicate the direction of the side routes and their status. Alternatively the side routes may be marked with arrows on the sides of the post that don't have acorns on it. In most cases the direction indicated by the arrow is obvious, but if unsure they are designed to be read when you are standing looking straight at the arrow."

To make this even a bit clearer, Lucy described to me in an email, "Sometimes there are waymark posts with two arrows, both belonging to the SWCP, but they would usually be on different faces of the post and with an acorn on each face. The line below is important if the arrows are both on the same face! If it's the kind of 'just continue along this line in either direction' situation, then there won't be a line and both arrows will refer to the SWCP – There may well be a side route, whose arrow(s) appear on other faces of the post."

Ok to try to make it even clearer, Lucy then gave me these formulas for each face of a waymark:

Acorn plus one arrow = SWCP.

Acorn plus two arrows and no line = SWCP in both directions, one direction towards Poole, and the other towards Minehead.

Acorn plus arrow plus dividing line plus further arrow(s) = SWCP is the direction nearest to the acorn, and the dividing line is for other path(s) in other direction(s)!!

Did you got all that? Really in most cases, it is quite simple to figure out especially once you start walking and use some logical sense. With that being said, though, I have gotten "turned around/lost/off the path" a few times.

Now I would even like to further clarify the situation with colors. You may see yellow arrows, blue arrows, and red or black arrows as you are walking. The SWCP is mostly yellow, which denotes a "Public Footpath," which can only be used by walkers, joggers and runners, and mobility scooters and powered wheelchairs. (And yellow was the color of the arrow on the Camino in Spain as well.) Blue arrows denote a "Public Bridleway," which can be used in addition to walkers, etc., by horse riders and bicyclists. Finally, red or black arrows denote a "Public Byway," which can be used in addition to walkers, etc., horse riders and bicyclists, by carriages/horse-drawn vehicles and motorized vehicles.

Many, many signs along the SWCP can take other shapes and forms as well. Most signs posts are made out of wood and are the arrows themselves, carved with an acorn, and will clearly say "Coast Path," and tell you how many miles you have in either direction towards the next significant place. Signs may also be made out of stone or concrete, stickers on light poles, painted acorns on rocks, or any number of other options.

One other thing you may see on some waymarks is small white plaques at the top which are "Coastguard Grid Reference plates and this is very useful information if you need to call for help or report a problem." For example, I took a photo of a wooden sign post in Porthoustock. This sign post told me that in one direction if I was walking towards the Minehead direction, I would have three and a half miles till Coverack, and in the direction I was walking towards Poole, by taking an Inland route, I had one and a quarter miles to Porthallow. The Grid Reference number at this sign post for Porthoustock was SW 804 216. When I got to Porthallow, the Half Way Marker place, its Grid Ref was SW 797 231.

One final concept to describe is what is a "Public Right of Way." They are places where you have "the right to access some land for walking or certain other leisure activities." I believe this is why when I am walking along the SWCP I am sometimes walking through what could potentially be private land of farms with sheep and cows, for example, but the Public Right of Way allows me to walk through.

So there you have it. All you ever wanted to know about walking the SWCP, or any National Trail. To walk along the SWCP, just follow the arrow closest to the acorn. The title of my book! In reality, the title of my book, and what to follow when walking the SWCP, could have been "The Arrows Closest To The Acorn" or "The Arrow(s) Closest To The Acorn," as in some cases the waymarks have two arrows close to the acorn as mentioned, one arrow going in the direction of Minehead, and the other arrow going in the direction of Poole. (Although, I make a disclaimer here: I have no responsibility whatsoever if you get lost or turned around or off the path or anything following any of this advice.) See photos on the next few pages, and on the back cover, for examples of all this!

After our conversation about arrows and acorns, Lucy took me on a shortcut around the Pencarrow Head headland through some ferny hillside. I don't think we missed very much at all, so I wasn't concerned about missing any mileage or anything. Lucy then spotted a seal in the waters below, and another one she pointed out later on. As I said, I didn't take as many notes today as I usually do, so this next section is a bit of a blur, but from my photos, there was a view of another beach below at one point, and the terrain was somewhat flat for a little while along a fern-lined path. The views were still beautiful of the various shades of green rolling hillsides, with grass and trees and farmland. There was a rocky beach below us as well.

And somewhere within about two miles beyond Lantic Bay on our way towards Polperro, I ended up taking a picture which would eventually become the main photo on the front cover of my book! I did not even know it at the time, but this particular photo had all the elements of what I wanted to show in my front cover photo – the coastline of the SWCP with hillsides and headlands and rocks, the line of the path itself in the front of the photo and continuing on, a SWCP arrow and acorn sign, and lots of my favorite colors of green and blue. So not only today did the title of my book transpire, but eventually so did the main front cover photo of my book! The 24th of July 2017.

Lucy and I had a lunch stop on a bench as we spotted a small herd of horses inland a bit, on a footpath that would lead inland to Lansallos. Our stop was overlooking the rocky Lansallos Cove. At this point the signs said we had two and a quarter miles to go. The path was relatively flat for a bit, and then the fun began. An uphill, which according to the booklet had 136 steps, a slight downhill with 60 steps, then 170 more uphill steps to the top of Raphael Cliff. I think this was where we looked back and on top of the previous hill was a brown barley crop that was being harvested. Then a descent with 158 steps. There were some flat areas in between all this as well. And just the beautiful views, as I shall say again, of the multi-green colored hillsides, the brown rocky beaches and coves, and the multi-blue colored water and sky. I guess all this was a total of 524 steps! Another day of ups and downs, similar count as yesterday, like the hand and arm waving out the window of a car moving up and down in the wind like a roller coaster.

There were still a few more smaller ascents and descents as we made our way into Polperro. I have noticed several times that the last mile feels like the longest mile. We arrived in Polperro overlooking the harbour and all the buildings on the hillsides surrounding. It was still warm out, feeling hot, actually. All in all, it was a beautiful six and a half miles of walking, and it was really great to have the company of Lucy!

We headed towards my B&B to check in as since their restaurant closes at 4:00, and they requested me to check in before that time. I went upstairs really quick to my room decorated with boats and lighthouses, and saw that I had a fabulous view from my room of the harbour, boats, buildings, and even a canal that seemed to feed off the harbour and run through the village. Then I joined Lucy downstairs for a snack together as she still had a few hours to catch her bus. We just missed getting back for the 2:20 bus, so now she needed to wait till about 5:30. I felt bad because she had to wait that long, just barely missing the earlier bus, but she was alright and after we chatted a bit more, we said our goodbyes, she went off to rest and wait, and I went up to my room.

A bit later, I was hungry for dinner, but walked around Polperro a bit first looking to see if any of the many shops in this quite picturesque town interested me to go in, but none did. What did interest me was walking back up the SWCP just a little bit to the place where I started to oversee the harbour as we arrived earlier so that I could take pictures. I took photos of the boats with buildings, the harbour, and the small lighthouse that was just beyond on the other side of the town cliffs. I will be walking closer to the lighthouse tomorrow! I also took a couple pictures of this

The Arrow(s) Closest To The Acorn

The Arrow(s) Closest To The Acorn

Photo credit: Scott Dungan

Wooden Sign Posts/Waymarks along the South West Coast Path
With arrows, acorns, locations, and mileage

Acorn and Arrow Examples

Including black and white stickers, curved-shaped arrows,
acorn painted on a rock from July 20, and Coastguard Grid Reference plates

cute couple sitting on a bench that I couldn't see their faces, but they had hats on, he had his arm around her, and they were enjoying looking at the views out to the waters, and the fresher cooler air out. Romantic!

Polperro felt a bit different to me than some of the other villages and towns I have been in because of its harbour. First there was the waterway leading from the seas towards the town, then the breakwall, then many various types of boats (fishing, row, sail) floating in this area of the harbour behind the breakwall, but then the rest of the harbour took a left turn and continued inland, with more boats, then it seemed to narrow down into the canal, which is what I could see from the window of my room, which seemed to go run through the center of the town. Buildings surrounded all of this on all sides, and up the hillsides. All quite picturesque. "Polperro was a 13th century fishing village…was the centre for smuggling in the late 18th century…and smuggling and fishing featured largely in its history, but now it's mainly fishing and tourism."

I made my way to find someplace to eat, but first I stopped at a little park-type area with a bench and I sat and called Mom. I saw a small church up a short hillside that I would like to find after dinner, and it rang 5:00 as I was talking to Mom. Good timing. After my dinner, I walked the small streets of Polperro a bit more as the crowds had gone away, and I found the church, but it was locked up. For some reason this church looked like to me like a Russian Orthodox type church with a small belfry above the white building which had the date 1838 etched on it. The bells rang 6:00 as I was there. I could never figure out exactly what church this was.

I walked on one more street and then went back to my room with a view. As I typed I took a break every now and then to go to the window to look out at my view. One time a swan and a few birds were floating in the water. Pictures were taken.

I was grateful for this warm sunny beautiful day, including the company. Thank you, Lucy!

DAY 51 STATS: 6.5 MILES. 4.5 HOURS. NO EXTRA MILES. HIKING BOOTS DUE TO THE MANY UPS AND DOWNS. PUBS IN POLRUAN ARE "RUSSELL INN" AND "LUGGER INN." PUBS IN POLPERRO ARE "THE SHIP INN," "THE THREE PILCHARDS," "THE BLUE PETER INN," and "THE CRUMPLEHORN INN."
Information on gorse from edenproject.com/learn/for-everyone/plant-profiles/gorse.
Information on waymarks, signs, Public Rights of Way, etc. from southwestcoastpath.org.uk/walk-coast-path/trip-planning/coast-path-waymarking, and from gov.uk/right-of-way-open-access-land, and from gov.uk/right-of-way-open-access-land/use-public-rights-of-way.

POLPERRO TO WEST LOOE AND SEATON TO EAST LOOE – Tuesday, 25 July 2017

"Slow – chicken crossing." – A sign along a road as I walked.

Today I walked into the same town, twice. Well, into the East and West sides of the same town, twice.

I heard that the House on the Props in Polperro, where I stayed last night, was built in the 1600's. Wow. I find it fascinating to think that this building I was sleeping in is centuries old, and to think of all the people who have stayed here over hundreds of years, and all the stories these walls could tell...smuggling stories, too...it is mind-boggling. I wonder who slept in my room. This rhetorical thought led me to another rhetorical thought…I think of all those people who have walked along the SWCP over the centuries, and now I am adding my footprints to the future history. This is mind-boggling to me as well. It was like the Camino I walked in Spain. For thousands of years, pilgrims walked that, and there I was a few years ago adding my footprints to that path. I wonder if people will be walking either path in centuries or millennium from now. It certainly makes one think about the concept of "time."

After breakfast I checked out of my several hundred-century old B&B, and had a 9:10am start for my first walk today from Polperro to West Looe. As I left Polperro, I walked by an interesting museum, the "Polperro Heritage Museum of Smuggling and Fishing." I would have liked to have gone inside, but their opening hours were a bit later. However, I looked up information online and read about several interesting bits and bobs of information about the history of the thriving smuggling and fishing of Polperro in the 18th and 19th centuries. The Polperro Cornish Gem website told me this about fishing: "Polperro has depended on fishing for generations. In the 19th century, when pilchards were landed in large quantities, the fish were processed and packed in three factories near the harbour. The fishing industry employed many men at sea and many more, with women and children, ashore in salting, pressing, cleaning and washing the fish." Interesting to me, such a close-knit community.

The same website told me this about smuggling: "Contraband goods were smuggled across from Guernsey on a huge scale during the latter half of the 18th century, the Polperro boats often risking seizure by Revenue vessels patrolling the Channel." (Guernsey is an island in the English Channel near France.)

Another website, Cornwall Museums, told me this about something called the Polperro Knitfrock: "The fishing village of Polperro had their very own style of knitted jumpers known as 'knitfrocks'. In the mid-19th century, 28 women and girls were employed in the village as knitters. Each family had their own dedicated pattern so that any man lost at sea could be identified if his body was found." More interesting information about this close-knit (no pun intended) community, and also humbling to read about the possible devastating realities of the fishing industry and livelihood. Reminding me once again to respect nature, the weather and the seas, with their power. And to respect the fisherman and their families.

As I continued walking, I looked back on all the fishing boats floating in the harbour behind the breakwall with the buildings of the town behind going up the hillside. If I needed to rest at this point, a row of benches offered places to sit and enjoy this view, as well as including views of the waters from the seas leading towards the breakwall, which at this moment a sailboat was sailing in.

Within a half mile, I took a mini detour on "Reuben's Walk" to see a mini lighthouse, appropriately named Polperro's Miniature Lighthouse. Located on Spy House Point, this mini lighthouse is only ten feet tall, about twice my height! It was built in 1911, which was painted on the black and white round brick structure. The light of the lighthouse can be seen for twelve miles out to the seas, and is still in use over a century later as it is automated. A navigation aid for those fisherman and others at sea. It was an odd-looking lighthouse in a way, not like most lighthouses you would imagine, it being so short, and black and white. The outside of the top of the lighthouse contained the place where the light was kept. The Reuben's Walk met back up with the SWCP after a few minutes of walking. As I walked on, I occasionally looked back and still saw this lighthouse in the distance below the hillsides covered with lots of various green shrubbery and trees.

I walked next to some tall ferns, and needed to take an inland diversion due to a previous cliff fall to Talland Bay. It took me around a grass field, first on a gravel road and then down a long descending paved road. I arrived in Talland Bay, with its sandy beach half-covered in seaweed, about forty-five minutes after I started my walk this morning.

Before continuing on the SWCP, I decided to take a side trip to see the Talland Church. I saw it from a distance earlier as it was placed on top of a hill and I could see its bell tower. I had to walk up a steep road to get there, and while the church itself was closed, it had beautiful views from the top of the hill to down below of the blue waters, green hillsides, and blue skies. Some of my photos included the gravestones of the church with the scenery in the background. The church dates from the 13th and 15th centuries, and "an unusual feature is that the bell tower, which is partly cut into the hillside, is separate from the church," as I read in the booklet for today. After my church visit, I walked back down the road to rejoin the SWCP. A sign said three and a half miles to the two sides of Looe.

I then walked on a mostly flat path. It was hot out and dry today, and I certainly did not mind at all! There were endless views of the blue skies and blue water, and green hillsides. There was one sailboat with white sails that I saw for the next few hours as it was making its way towards Looe as well. I chatted briefly with a very colorfully dressed woman on holiday with her husband doing the Looe to Polperro walk today, the opposite direction as I was going. I commented how I liked all the colors she was wearing. She was coming down some steps as I was going up this slight uphill.

I caught a view of Looe off in the distance, with the long sandy beach of Portnadler below but closer me, and out in the water I saw Looe Island, aka St. George's Island. This island was in my view as I approached Looe. The path was still flat, but then another short uphill with steps, followed by more flat walking, and a short downhill with steps. I continued to see the beach and the island, but from a different perspective as I kept walking, and that sailboat was still making its way to Looe.

One more flat area, on a stretch of grass, and then I entered the outskirts of Looe at 11:15 with homes and a sidewalk to walk on for a bit. I had a half mile to the center of town. I could smell that ocean smell of tide pools and seaweed, and there were people walking around and looking at the tide pools. I walked along the sidewalk for a few minutes, then walked along a paved seawall, and then needed to walk on the concrete of a road, and then the pavement of a sidewalk as I finally reached the harbour area of West Looe. There was a busy beach on the East side of Looe on the other side of a breakwater, and the East Looe River in between. There was a small red thin metallic like tower on Banjo Pier jetting out into the water which was Looe's Harbour Light, so I saw another lighthouse.

As I walked up the road paralleling the river, I took photos of many boats in many rows. The way to get from East Looe to West Looe is either by ferry or by walking across a bridge. My B&B was near the bridge, so I kept walking towards the bridge, and then arrived at my B&B a half hour later. But this did not end my day of walking. This was the first five miles.

I freshened up a bit, changed clothes, and switched from my purple shoes to my hiking boots because the next part of my day was supposed to have one large uphill and downhill. I was originally going to walk from East Looe to Seaton and take a taxi or bus back, but the nice woman at the B&B said it would be easier if I got a taxi now to Seaton and walked back to East Looe, since later would be when the taxis might be busy transporting school children. I got some lunch, easily found a taxi, and was dropped off at the road where the SWCP met the road above Seaton. It was 1:10 when I started part two of my day, another three and a half miles. Along this stretch of the path, a couple of previous landslips occurred so there were a couple of inland diversions. Because of this, the beauty of this section was not of the seas and coast all the time.

For the next three and a half miles, I am describing this in the "opposite" direction, "backwards," as I have been walking, like the time I walked backwards in the fog from Trebarwith Strand to Tintagel. Therefore, the seas were on my left, when I could see the seas. It was a bit odd at first today to walk in this direction, since I have been used to walking "forwards" with the seas to my right, but it was not confusing.

The first path diversion I walked through was under a tree lined path, but soon I was out of the trees, and I had views of Looe and Looe Island from this direction. Being back on the original SWCP for a bit, this part was flat, followed by a zigzag uphill, which now felt like another diversion, as I walked through a wheat field inland. This was the first wheat field I actually walked right through the middle of, rather than around the edge of and next to. I chatted briefly with a man from Australia who was walking the SWCP, although I was unclear if he was walking all of it, or just the Cornwall section.

After the wheat field, I needed to walk on a narrow road for a bit. One of those narrow country roads that I have been driven on many times before, where if two cars meet, one either needs to move over as far as they could in a little turnout section, or would need to back up until a turnout section was found. At the start of this road-walk, the sign said two and a half miles to Looe. The road became shaded by trees, and there were a few signs: "Slow – chicken crossing." "Real Free-Range Eggs from hens rescued from a battery and now in chicken heaven." "For sale, fruit & veg, chicken & duck eggs" next to a shelf area with such items. I wondered why the chicken crossed the road.

I was back on a path and off the road, this time the path being very flat and through the shade of some trees. It paralleled a road and was refreshing to walk through it being warm out. By the way, all day today it was warm and dry, and I was grateful for that. This tree lined path met up with the original SWCP briefly for some views of the seas, and then descended through more trees and onto a road, which descended to the busy Millendreath Beach. I wondered if this was the "big descent" that I put my hiking boots on for this stretch. If so, I could have worn my purple shoes the entire day, as this descent was not that big.

I climbed some concrete steps, the hardest thing to climb today, and then needed to walk on more pavement and more road walking on concrete through a cluster of homes. More pavement, more road walking, then a flat paved, sometimes tree-shaded, path that led into Looe. More views of Looe Island and views of West Looe and the seawall I had walked on earlier today. I arrived above the busy beach of East Looe from this side. It was a 2:40 arrival time, as I put my flip flops on to wander around the town of East Looe, and stroll through its busy streets as I made my way back to my B&B. Like so many other towns and villages along the SWCP, Looe's history includes fishing, exporting tin, copper, and granite, and smuggling.

I had a very cute tiny single room with view of the bridge that I had walked across that connects East and West Looe, a view of the harbour part on the left side of bridge, and from sitting in bed, I even had a small but nice view of the seas in the distance over the rooftops. I had a separate, but my own private, bathroom at this B&B. After some downtime, I went out for a nice Thai food dinner, walking across the bridge to East Looe, taking photos of the several rows of various boats from that angle. All in all, a nice day!

Oh, and I received an email from my friend and inspiration and words of wisdom provider, Gordon, who I walked with on a rainy day almost a month ago just outside of Padstow to Trevone. Gordon told me that he made it to Poole! After walking 583 miles in 31 days! Wow, that's an average of 19 miles a day! He missed a few miles in the Torquay area, but that didn't matter. He made it back home in time to celebrate his son's 40th birthday. At the age of 70, I say that Gordon is brave and courageous! Congratulations to him!

DAY 52 STATS: 8.5 MILES TOTAL BOTH HALVES OF THE DAY. 4 HOURS BOTH HALVES, NOT INCLUDING TIME IN BETWEEN TWO HALVES. NO EXTRA MILES, WELL THERE WAS A BIT WALKING TO AND FROM DINNER, SO LET'S SAY AN EXTRA HALF MILE. PURPLE SHOES, THEN HIKING BOOTS, WHICH COULD HAVE BEEN PURPLE SHOES ALL DAY. PUB IN WEST LOOE IS "THE JOLLY SAILOR INN." PUBS IN EAST LOOE ARE "THE FISHERMANS ARMS," "YE OLD SALUTATION INN," AND "THE SHIP INN." PUB IN SEATON IS "SMUGGLERS INN."

Information from the Polperro Heritage Museum of Smuggling and Fishing from polperro.org/museum, and from museumsincornwall.org.uk/Polperro-Heritage-Museum-of-Smuggling-and-Fishing/Cornwall-Museums.

SEATON TO CAWSAND, BUT ONLY WALKED SEATON TO DOWNDERRY – Wednesday, 26 July 2017

"In Skagway, ironically that was where I took my very first 'windows and doors' photos." – Me, see below, as part of some of my other solo travels.

Well, I have had a few days in a row of good weather, but of course the forecast for today called for heavy rain till 10:00, then light rain till 1:00, then it should stop. So today was kind of a disappointment as I only walked one mile out of the eight I had planned. The day started out by having breakfast in my B&B. They were very nice people there, and made me a scrambled egg with avocado and tomato. The avocado certainly was refreshing for me. After breakfast, I hung out in my cute little room till 11:00 hoping that the heavy rain would go away and come again another day. Well, just not come back at all really for the rest of the summer. I peeked out the window every so often and confirmed the heavy rain. I made use of my time by finishing yesterday's writing, backing up photos, and watching TV. Not that watching TV was useful time, but I watched some anyway. However, there was no Doc Martin on.

I walked down in the light rain around 11:00 to the same taxi service I used yesterday to take the taxi to Seaton. I was still "early" according to the weather forecast, but I figured I would hang out in Seaton, rather than Looe, since that was where I started my backwards walk from yesterday, and where I would walk forwards today, or at least try to walk forwards. I hung out at Waves Bar Restaurant in Seaton because they had Wi-Fi. I had a small snack of sweet potato fries even though I was not that hungry, but in order to use the Wi-Fi and sit there, I wanted to buy something. I was there from about 11:30 to 12:50 looking out the window at the weather. Still raining. It was supposed to stop in ten minutes.

It did look like the rain was getting lighter, and I was getting bored of sitting, so I decided to walk the mile to the next village of Downderry. The walk was along the beach actually, with sand and shells and seaweed, and since I had not put on my hiking boots yet, I just walked ironically in my flip flops. There was still a bit of lingering mist, but it was warm out, and the walk was refreshing. I passed by a short row of boats sitting on the top of the beach. I was a bit unsure where exactly to turn inland off the beach into Downderry as I walked, but I found a landmark listed in the booklet, and walked into the small village about fifteen to twenty minutes later.

I went into The Blue Plate Café for their Wi-Fi and another small snack of olives, carrots, and hummus. This time I was a bit hungry, and this was good choice for a snack. The gentleman working there was very nice to me, which helped me since I was feeling disappointed today with the weather. At this point, even though the forecast said it should no longer rain, I was unsure as I looked outside at the sky, which still looked like it could rain to me. The booklet described the walk to Portwrinkle "may be strenuous at times." Now I have done plenty of strenuous walks, and I was thinking that maybe I could walk the three miles from Downderry to Portwrinkle at least and call it a day, but with the sky still not looking that great, I just did not want to walk with the way the sky was looking. There was a big hotel in Portwrinkle, and I am sure that if I had done these miles, and decided to not continue walking after that, I could have found a taxi.

As it was, I wanted a taxi from here in Downderry. As time was passing by in the afternoon, and the sky still not looking good, the very nice gentleman working there made a few phone calls, and found me a taxi. It was the nice people like this, a guardian angel, who help make a difference in my life and in my walk, and in my day. The taxi people today and yesterday, the B&B people from this morning, and this nice guy at The Blue Plate Café, all guardian angels. And all the other nice people I have encountered since my arrival in England about eight weeks ago.

The taxi picked me up at 2:45 from Downderry and drove me to my B&B in Cawsand arriving a half hour later. The owners of the B&B were not home yet, but another guest let me in, and I figured out which room was mine by my suitcase being in one of the rooms. The woman of the B&B was back not too long later, and welcomed me warmly. Another nice person.

I felt like crying several times today actually, sad and disappointed, in the weather and its unpredictability, and a bit disappointed in myself actually. I felt like maybe I should be walking when the weather is on the rainy side. Lots of people do it. It wasn't gale force winds or downpours, just rain, and I had rain gear. It wasn't even cold out. But I just did not feel like walking in the rain today. Maybe I was getting tired of the weather changing so often. I love the warm sunny beautiful days. Why can't the weather be warm, sunny, and beautiful every single day? It is summer, supposedly, right? Even in "light rain" sometimes I don't feel like walking. It muddles the views, that's for sure, and it is harder to take photos, and I really want to truly enjoy each day. Not that I couldn't enjoy the days in the rain, but I certainly would enjoy the days much better in the sun.

I also wonder that if I actually had someone to walk with today, like I walked with Linda in the rain a few days ago from Gorran Haven to Pentewan, I probably would have walked in the rain today. In fact, there was a couple in the café in Downderry with big rucksacks, and I asked them where they were walking to, but they were going in the opposite direction as me. I would have asked to walk with them if they were going in the direction I wanted to go.

I started to think of all the times in my life that I have traveled alone. I have traveled alone quite a lot actually. Because there were times in my life that I did not have someone to travel with, and I had a strong travel bug, so I decided that it was time to travel alone. I had to build up to this concept however. The first time I traveled alone I practiced and tested the waters, so to speak, by taking myself on a short, simple weekend trip to a local area close to my home, Dungeness Spit. Dungeness Spit is a five-and-a-half mile sand spit out on the Olympic Peninsula of Washington State. At the end of this sand spit is the New Dungeness Lighthouse (yes, a lighthouse!), and when the tides are right, one can walk to the lighthouse, visit the lighthouse, and walk back in a day. I even stayed the night in my first hostel during this trip. And I ate at a nice restaurant by myself. It was a successful solo walk, proving to myself that I was capable of traveling, eating, sleeping, and even walking, alone! Little did I know back then that this eleven mile walk would eventually lead to a 630-mile adventure.

My solo travels did not stop there. My next longer solo trip to keep testing the waters, so to speak, was a longer two-week trip to Alaska. A bit further from home, but not too far away yet either. I started in Bellingham, Washington and took a ferry up through the Inside Passage, where at the time one could sleep out on the deck of the ferry in a sleeping bag, so that is what I did. I got off the ferry in places like Ketchikan, Juneau, and Skagway, and did some sight-seeing, all in the first week of this solo trip. The second week was flying up to Anchorage, Seward, and Denali National Park, where at the park I joined guided hiking walks. In Skagway, ironically that was where I took my very first "windows and doors" photos. This trip was another solo success.

My solo travels did not stop there either. The next biggest solo travels, by far longer, and further away, was my five-month 17-country Europe backpacking travels. I did some preliminary planning for that one, like researching the countries I wanted to visit, and perhaps the order of the countries and the towns and cities and activities, but I only booked my first two or three nights' accommodations, and basically spontaneously planned the rest. Here I stayed in hostels, ate by myself all the time, and did just about everything else solo. The countries included England (my first country!), Greece, Turkey, Italy, Slovenia, Croatia, Ireland, France, Austria, Slovakia,

Hungary, Germany, Switzerland, Belgium, Netherlands, Poland, and the Czech Republic. A few times I had a friend join me who lived there, and even stayed with her for a while, but by and large, this was my first epic solo successful travel adventure.

And my solo travels did not stop there…Most of Bhutan was solo, Vietnam, Cambodia, the Baltic Sea travels, the Île d'Orléans walking, Quito and the Galapagos Islands, and walking the Camino de Santiago, were all solo travels. On some of these travels like Bhutan, Vietnam, Cambodia, and the Galapagos Islands, I did either have a tour guide at times or joined a group of others, but I still went initially by myself successfully.

So why on this solo travels, here on the SWCP, am I having some challenges, I don't know. I suppose I had challenges on all these travels as well, and well in general, life has its challenges too. I suppose it is how one faces the challenges that count - with acceptance, bravery, and courage!

Because of my taxi ride, I also missed the section not only from Downderry to Portwrinkle, but also the three and a half miles from Portwrinkle to Freathy, which was where I was really supposed to end my walk today. This section would have started out walking across a golf course, and those haven't brought me luck lately anyway, and then there would have been a military range to either walk through or walk around on a road, depending if they were using the firing range today or not, which today they were not using. The bit after the military range into Freathy I also missed, which was about a mile of the three and a half miles. Someday I shall need to make up this entire seven-mile section. For now, I shall accept my missed miles with bravery and courage. (Note that I will make up the Downderry to Portwrinkle section in a few days.)

Back at the B&B, I gave the nice woman some of my laundry to wash after I asked her if she would, and then since of course it now wasn't raining, I wandered around the Cawsand/Kingsand area for a while. I went to a church in Cawsand, St. Andrew's Church, dating from around 1900 (a relatively young church), which was closed so I could not go inside to do my usual prayers. I said them outside instead. I went to see the harbour area. There were some boats floating in the waters in the harbour.

I also had a very nice solo dinner of a warmed kale and quinoa dish at a restaurant in Kingsand. My B&B was a half mile from all this, so I do need to add an extra mile round trip to today's stats that were not part of the SWCP. Tonight, I would sleep in a very large room in my B&B. I would say that today was a bit of an emotional-rollercoaster-type-of-day, but I need to just remember acceptance, and my bravery and courage.

DAY 53 STATS: 8 MILES OF WHICH ONE MILE I WALKED, THE OTHER 7 TAXI. 20 MINUTES OF WALKING. ONE EXTRA MILE. FLIP FLOPS. PUB IN DOWNDERRY IS "THE INN ON THE SHORE."

RAME HEAD TO CAWSAND/KINGSAND TO CREMYLL, MISSING FREATHY TO RAME HEAD – Thursday, 27 July 2017

"World's Best Cakes. How Baking Works. Bread Baking. Perfect Pies. Tartine Bread. Baking Artisan Bread. The Fabulous Baker Brothers. How to Make Bread. Baking by Hand. The New Artisan Bread in Five Minutes a Day. Artisan Pizza to Make Perfectly at Home. Dough-Simple Contemporary Bread." – Titles of a row of cookbooks on display at The Old Bakery Café in Cawsand.

Today's walk combined some of what I was planning on doing today, and some of what I was planning on doing tomorrow. Basically though to start, I missed about another three and a half miles from Freathy to Rame Head. I did this because from the description, it looked like there was a good share of road walking, and it just seemed easier to get a taxi to Rame Head instead. Also, tomorrow's forecast looks quite rainy, so this way I shortened tomorrow's walk. Once again, some disappointment on missing miles, but I need to accept this now, with not only bravery and courage, but also with gratefulness and with grace, as I remind myself of the quote from 20 July, "Wherever life plants you, bloom with grace."

Someday, I can return to the SWCP and make up all the miles I have missed! Which compared to the miles that I have walked, between last year with Scott and this year mostly by myself, actually isn't that much comparatively. In the approximate 407 miles since Minehead, I have missed just under 40 miles total, between both years that I have not walked at all. That's 10% missed, 90% walked. And even with missing these miles, I am definitely having amazing experiences on the SWCP that I have walked thus far!

I took a taxi at 8:30 and had him drop me off at the St. Germanus Church in Rame. It was closed. It seems like I have been coming across a lot of closed churches lately. I took a couple pictures of its exterior. Later I read that this "church has no modern utilities such as electricity, gas or water, and is still lit by candles during services." The other church that I have been to that is also powered by candles was St. Anthony across Gillan Creek. I still said my usual prayers outside of St. Germanus Church before I left. My usual prayers still consist of asking for my safety during my walk please, to be healthy, injury free, and blister free (so far so good, gratefully). To have good weather (well, I guess that does happen most of the time, gratefully). And for all things to happen positively during my walk (which they really do, gratefully). I still continue my prayers for the safety and health of family and friends. And I still pray for the world, for peace, love, compassion, and understanding.

I had a short walk on the road that led to the car park at Rame Head. It took me about ten minutes, so I counted that as an extra half mile. I stopped in the NCI Coastwatch Station there, as I wanted to ask exactly where the SWCP was since I came from the road. The man working there kindly pointed it out to me, just taking a short grassy path towards Rame Head, and I would see the marker pointing me in the right direction. I bought a cute little picture of a lighthouse and beach scene and some crayons for my niece to color. Ok, well for me to color. And it supports the NCI. There was an optional to walk out onto Rame Head itself with a chapel there, the chapel of St. Michael the Archangel which is about 600 years old, but I did not do that. I started on the SWCP towards Penlee Point at 9:00. The path was completely flat next to grass and some wildflowers. There were some sounds of waves coming from out on the water and staying on the water, rather than crashing on the rocks. Nice!

I passed by three horses, thought of Scott, and then heard the crashing waves on the rocky shoreline below. Looking back at Rame Head and its chapel, there was a really beautiful strip of rolling rocky brown coastline with the white capped waves crashing. A couple of joggers crossed paths with me going in the opposite direction. At one point, there was also an inland footpath to the Rame Church. I reached Penlee Point almost 45 minutes after I started walking. There was a bit of road walking, then a path through a forest of trees, then a bit more road walking and back to a path, all still in the trees. It was like this for about twenty minutes, and then I walked onto a paved narrow road lined with homes. I arrived next to the church in Cawsand that was closed yesterday, and the "Square" of Cawsand. I had walked two and three-quarters miles in just over an hour since Rame Head. It was all flat.

As I walked along the narrow street in Cawsand towards Kingsand, those two joggers who crossed my path earlier, passed by me again, looking like they had finished their morning exercise. I went into The Old Bakery Café in Cawsand for a snack of banana bread, Greek yogurt, and honey. I had left over yogurt and honey so after spreading that on the banana bread, I spread it on a piece of sourdough bread. I am pretty sure that it was all baked here based on all the cookbooks, and I rather enjoyed sitting in this quiet little café.

I started walking again at 11:05. I took a picture of the border of the two counties, Devon and Cornwall, a black symbol of some sort with the word "Corn" on the right, and "Devon" on the left. I think however, that this is no longer the official border, as it was changed in 1844 to the River Tamar running between Cawsand-Kingsand-Cremyll and Plymouth. So prior to 1844, Cawsand was in Cornwall and Kingsand was in Devon, and the actual border "was a small stream which runs 'underground' as you walk between Cawsand and Kingsand," per the booklet. Today I am still in Cornwall though in either village. But tomorrow I shall be in Devon once again, as I walked in north Devon weeks and weeks and weeks ago, and now will be in South Devon tomorrow once I get to Plymouth. This also means that I have gone through the entire county of Cornwall!

I wound my way through and up the narrow streets of Kingsand a quarter of a mile. I entered the edge of Mount Edgcumbe House and Country Park as three young ladies were riding some nice larger horses. I followed them for a short while on the very flat path, but soon they were faster than me. Scott would have liked this, and the horses earlier today. He would have stopped to pet them all. By the way, today's weather was warm, dry, and partly sunny all day! So refreshing after yesterday's weather. I wonder if there is a pattern to the weather I have been having. Like for every several days of good weather, I have a not-so-good day weather-wise.

The path was all flat for quite a while. I had views of the Breakwater Lighthouse in the Plymouth Sound, and eventually a navigation beacon in a camping park. At this point, the path climbed slightly through some trees. When there was this covered sitting area, Picklecombe Seat, which also looked like it had a little prayer spot of some sort, I took the opportunity to sit for a bit. The path continued through the trees, with a slight ascent and descent to avoid a previous landslip. Continuing through the trees, the path flattened out again, and eventually turned into a concrete walkway, but still in the trees. A lot of trees today.

I walked through the "garden" area of Mount Edgcumbe, and arrived surprisingly at the Cremyll Ferry and the pub there, three and a quarter miles after Kingsand, and one and three-quarters hours later. I wasn't expecting to arrive there that fast. I was not taking the ferry today however across to Plymouth as my B&B was still in Cawsand. I knew that my options for getting back to my B&B in Cawsand this morning were: 1. to walk back via inland paths through the park; 2. taxi, or 3. a bus that the B&B lady told me about this morning. Within five minutes of me arriving in Cremyll, after I carefully studied the information on the ferry for tomorrow, a bus just happened to pull up. Before I even had a chance to think about the options in depth, I therefore chose option three.

The bus dropped me off near the "Square" in Cawsand, which was literally a square paved area with a statue, and buildings surrounding the square. Since I enjoyed The Old Bakery Café this morning, I went back there for lunch, and had a good goat's cheese, rocket (arugula), and quince jelly sandwich. Quince is a fruit similar to pears. Both Cawsand and Kingsand villages "have pilchard fishing and smuggling in their history."

On my way walking back to my B&B, I stopped to look into one cute little gift shop. Back at my B&B, I peeked out the window not too longer later, and a passing rain shower would certainly have gotten me wet. Good timing. I ended up taking a short nap, and then went out to dinner, so I need to count walking back and forth to dinner as extra miles, as well as walking back from lunch.

Acceptance with gratefulness and grace.

DAY 54 STATS: MISSED 3.5 MILES FREATHY TO RAME HEAD. WALKED 2.75 MILES RAME HEAD TO CAWSAND, JUST OVER AN HOUR. WALKED 3.5 MILES CAWSAND TO KINGSAND TO CREMYLL, 1.75 HOURS. 2.0 EXTRA MILES FOR RAME CHURCH TO RAME HEAD AND LUNCH AND DINNER. PURPLE

SHOES. PUB IN CAWSAND IS "THE CROSS KEYS INN." PUBS IN KINGSAND ARE "THE HALFWAY HOUSE INN," "THE DEVONPORT INN," AND "THE RISING SUN." PUB IN CREMYLL IS "EDGCUMBE ARMS." Information on St. Germanus Church from chct.info/histories/rame-st-germanus.

DOWNDERRY TO PORTWRINKLE…PLYMOUTH – Friday, 28 July 2017

"It's not just about the walking – It's the vision you have and your sense of adventure and your joy in meeting new people and seeing new places." – A Friend on Facebook.

I woke up this morning and checked the weather forecast. It was supposed to just be cloudy with no rain till 4pm, a bit of a change from yesterday's forecast for today, so I thought I would take advantage of that and do a small part of what I missed a couple days ago, Downderry to Portwrinkle, two and a half miles. At breakfast the kind B&B woman called a taxi to take me to the SWCP sign at Downderry Lodge, about three-quarters of a mile from the Blue Plate Café where I ended the other day. I started the gentle zigzag uphill, which actually lasted fifteen minutes, till I felt like I reached the top, but it was still gentle feeling. Apparently, I had reached Battern Cliff, the highest point on the South Cornwall Coast Path at 462 feet. The climb itself was mostly in the shrubbery and thus blocked my views. I was then out in the open with views of the seas and headlands, but it was a cloudy murky morning, so the views were not as bright as they could have been.

The terrain was flat for a while, and then some gentle rolling ups and downs with flat in between the rest of the way until one lightly larger descent into Portwrinkle. Along the two and a half miles, I passed by a couple of sheep fields along the way. There were a few overgrown bushy spots here and there which were a bit wet as well, so once again, the long pants came in handy. Occasionally there were some views of Portwrinkle ahead, Rame Head and other headlands off in the distance behind. Below were a few rocky bits with some small crashing waves, and one small sandy beach. At one point there was a black and white triangular nautical marker, which I think I read that from that marker if you look straight out in the water fourteen miles offshore, you can see Eddystone Lighthouse. But I couldn't see it today with the cloudy conditions.

I entered the edge of Portwrinkle, a town where back "in the 17th and 18th centuries, almost everyone in Portwrinkle was involved in smuggling. Pilchard fishing was the other 'industry,' but smuggling was far more profitable," per today's booklet. One of the taxi drivers told me that apparently the harbour at Portwrinkle is the smallest harbor, so I took photos, of course. From a distance away as I approached Portwrinkle, it looked like there were only about four small boats in the harbour, and when I went to the harbour itself, only one white row boat was visible in my photos. Some white waves were crashing over the small short breakwall.

I was curious as to what was being smuggled in Portwrinkle that made it far more profitable than pilchard fishing. During an online search, I could not come with a specific sentence like, "People smuggled such-and-such in Portwrinkle." But I did find an article about "Smugglers in Cornwall," and found perhaps the answer to my question, plus a bit more information about smuggling: "Cornwall was suitable for smuggling in that it had a long expanse of rocky, virtually uninhabited coast, with few Revenue men to patrol it. The goods smuggled included tea, brandy, gin, rum and tobacco. Following numerous increases in tea tax, tea could be bought in Europe for one-sixth of the price in Britain, while French brandy was only one-fifth of the price. Around 1800 the Revenue men became more organized and proactive. Smuggled goods had to be dropped off in remote coves, and picked up again when the coast was clear [not sure if a pun was intended in that]. Tunnels and passages were dug out of the rocks to expedite movement. Once landed, much of the contraband made its way up country." Quite interesting!

I was also curious about pilchard fishing, as this was also quite common, so an online search I did found an article called, "Cornwall Good Seafood Guide," and I learned this about pilchard fishing: "Fishing has always been vital to the survival of the Cornish. The oldest, large scale, well documented fishery in Cornwall is the Pilchard fishery. Pilchards have been renamed as Cornish sardines in recent years, but they are the same fish; small, tasty, and high in omega 3 oils." One of the two original methods of Pilchard fishing was "using seine nets [which] was carried out all around the coastline of Cornwall. The seine nets used were large and very expensive. The fishery relied on late summer and autumn shoals [large numbers of fish swimming together] of pilchard that move north into Cornish waters following warm currents and planktonic food. The shoals were so large that they could be seen from the clifftops. Watchers called 'huers' were employed to keep a lookout for the return of the shoals. When the huers spotted pilchards coming into the bays they would call 'Hevva!' and wave white spheres called bushes (originally gorse bushes were used) to signal to the teams of men and women in the villages to jump into action." The men and women would use the seine nets, which were huge cotton nets, which by quite a labor-intensive process, were used to trap the shoal, and eventually scoop the pilchards out of the waters using baskets.

Wow. Quite interesting! Well now I have more insight about the SWCP itself! Remember in my introduction, the SWCP Association website told me that, "The South West Coast Path was originally created by coastguards, patrolling the south west peninsula looking out for smugglers. They literally had to check in every inlet so their cliff top walk was well used and gives us the amazing Path we use today. The Path has also been used by fishermen looking for shoals of fish and checking sea conditions."

Now all that makes more sense to me - smuggling, fishing, and the South West Coast Path - and I have more of an understanding and appreciation for the South West Coast Path. Glad I did the research. I would bet the "checking sea conditions" had to do with safety at sea, and perhaps even on land, perhaps even checking the weather conditions, or as people being used as "lighthouses."

Anyway, after my last bit of walking in Portwrinkle, I arrived at Whitsand Bay Hotel, my destination for this part of my day. I felt a bit underdressed in there as it was a fancy hotel, but sometimes I like to throw people off. They stopped serving food, so I called the same taxi as this morning, and I needed to wait about forty-five minutes. I completed two and a half miles in one and a quarter hours. Interestingly, I did not find the terrain "strenuous" as the booklet said that I read a couple of days ago, and I wondered why the booklet described it that way. Gratefully the weather remained dry, even with the clouds. My taxi arrived, with the same nice lady as this morning. She drove me to the Cremyll Ferry just in time to take the 11:30 passenger ferry boat, the Edgcumbe Belle, to Plymouth. Before I left, I noticed a sign that said, "Welcome to Cornwall," although in my case, I need to recognize that I have now gone through the entire county in England along the SWCP!

I took a few photos at Admiral's Hard where the ferry dropped me off in Plymouth across the water, and so now I was officially out of the county of Cornwall and in the county of Devon once again, this time South Devon. Wow, I have been in Cornwall since just before the village of Morwenstow back on June 20th! I have been in Cornwall for over a month, for about 296 miles! So cool! There was a blue marker at Admiral's Hard indicating that it was 352 miles to Minehead, but I read somewhere that that was not accurate. The booklet says that I have mostly walked (and biked and rode) about 411 miles since Minehead!

The next eight and a half miles through Plymouth, the largest city I have been in in nearly two months, was apparently mostly on concrete, sidewalks, streets, pavement, and tarmac, and whatever else you would like to call that. A few people have told me that parts of this stretch there really was not much to see or do that was that interesting, just city-type walking along busy roads and industrial areas. Except for me, of course, Smeaton's Tower, a former lighthouse from Eddystone, I was interested in that. I decided long ago that I would skip walking all but one of the miles, because one mile will be from my B&B to the Barbican/Mount Batten ferry that I will walk in a couple days, which is part of the SWCP, which includes Smeaton's Tower. Long ago when I decided this, I did not know that I would be missing other miles, so now I need to add these seven and a half miles to my missed-miles-to-do-at-some-time-in-the-future walk list. With that said, I took a taxi from the ferry to my B&B in Plymouth. Besides, it started to rain as I was waiting for the taxi. I waited for the taxi next to "The Vine," which on one side of the door said, "First Pub in Devon," and on the other side of the door said, "Last Pub in Devon."

Anne was a very nice lady at the Guest House. I had some tea, freshened up, and in the early afternoon, I ventured out into Plymouth to do some errands. The rest of today and tomorrow were planned "rest days." My first errand was to get some lunch, then to get cash out of a bank. Wow oh wow. I had to walk down to the very busy part of Plymouth from my B&B, where there were so many people around and so much concrete and so many buildings and so many cars and traffic lights and so much movement and busy, busy, busy. What a shock to the system, with the crowds, the concrete, the modern buildings, the cars, the traffic lights, the noise. More than the shock of the buildings I had back in Newquay. Just way too much going on. I guess I am really used to the quiet and calm and peace of walking along the coast with small villages in between all the beautiful nature!

I also needed a few things at a "bits and bobs" store, like some more soap and deodorant and such, and there a woman kindly told me of a vegan and organic store, called "Ethica," where I could get some more protein bars for snacks. That was a nice shop! I also stopped at the Minster Church of St. Andrew, which is in between the Barbican and Royal Parade areas of Plymouth, which had some nice stained-glass windows and large organ pipes.

On my way to and from the errands area mostly in the Royal Parade area, as it was only a few minutes from my B&B and on the way, I actually did walk over to the 72-foot Smeaton's Tower, a red and white striped lighthouse, the third lighthouse built on Eddystone Rocks, hoping that I could go inside and climb to the top. The small, but dangerous, Eddystone Rocks are about thirteen miles south west of Plymouth on an extensive reef in the Plymouth Sound, the cause of many shipwrecks. The first attempt at building a lighthouse on these rocks was around 1698 by Henry Winstanley but was destroyed by the Great Storm of 1703. The second attempt at building a lighthouse on the Eddystone Rocks was by Captain John Lovett and John Rudyerd in 1709 and stood for 47 years till 1755 when it was destroyed by a fire.

The third lighthouse on Eddystone Rocks was Smeaton's Tower, the one I was looking at. Built in 1759 by John Smeaton, who also designed the pier in St. Ives that I walked on back on July 6, and the harbour in Charlestown that I walked on back on July 22, also built this lighthouse. "He had decided to construct a tower based on the shape of an English Oak tree for strength but made of stone rather than wood. Local granite was used for the foundations and facing, and Smeaton invented a quick drying cement, essential in the wet conditions on the rock, the formula for which is still used today." About 120 years later, in the 1870s, cracks began to appear on the rock the lighthouse was standing on, making it necessary to build a fourth lighthouse. The stump of Smeaton's Tower still stands on its original rock, and the rest is here in the Hoe area of Plymouth.

The fourth lighthouse was built in 1882 by James Douglass and designed by Robert Stevenson, and was automated in 1982, 100 years to the day of its original opening. It has a helipad on top of this 161-foot tall lighthouse, which I have not been able to see from any distance. Today however, an outdoor concert of some sort, "MTV Crashes Plymouth," was going on and they had the Hoe area that surrounded Smeaton's Tower blocked off so

I could not really get too close unfortunately. Let alone go inside the lighthouse and climb to the top. I wasn't sure if the concert would continue over the next day or two, but I would keep an eye on it, as I would like to go up Smeaton's Tower if at all possible. As I did my errands and walked back, I got showered on with some rain.

After errands and before dinner, I finished reading the great little book, "Love on the Beach," by Sue Bunney that I bought in Gorran Haven just over a week ago. I really enjoyed reading about what it is like to live a quiet country life, a life that "consisted of the local cricket club, snooker, fishing and work, in that order." The two quotes that stood out for me most from this book of 77 pages, both of which I have mentioned before are, "The real things in life, such as mining, farming and fishing," and "Such is the force of the sea, unrelenting and unpredictable, you have to respect its power."

However, there was more to the book that also stood out for me. Sue Bunney talks about "the slower pace of life and the different priorities, plus the stunning scenery" of Cornwall. She mentions, "A Cornish childhood is unique, the beach playing a major role in the lives of Gorran children." Furthermore, "Because Cornwall has the sea on every side, except the bit which joins us to the rest of England, we all seem to form a close bond with the water." She mentioned places I have been, including Portmellon, Chapel Point, Mevagissey, and Gorran Haven. Sue Bunney has another book out, "My Cornish Life," which I might want to read. The book I read, and this walk I am on along the SWCP, even with the weather, makes me want to live a quieter, simpler, slower, calmer life in a smaller village by the seas. I am appreciating learning about mining, farming, fishing, and respecting the power of the seas. And yes, the scenery is stunning, and I can appreciate that bond with the water!

Speaking of farming, today was a day of research. (Note that I did not actually do all this research exactly on 28 July, but instead as I edited my book months later, as with much of the online research throughout this book, incorporating it all in.) I next wanted to research farming along the SWCP, and the best article I could find was about farming in Cornwall, but I would think that the rest of the SWCP has some similarities. A website called "Cornwall Food and Farming" is "an informative and fun way for primary and junior school aged children to get a better understanding of agriculture, Cornwall's main crops and food production," but I figured at 50, I can learn, too!

Farm animals include sheep, cattle, pigs, goats, and chickens. And even some llamas and alpacas. "Cornwall's mild climate means that Cornish vegetable farmers enjoy a longer growing season than the rest of the country. Cauliflower, potatoes and cabbage are grown all year. During the summer months we can look forward to other locally grown vegetables such as asparagus, new potatoes, courgettes [zucchini], lettuce, runner beans, broccoli and tomatoes. Wheat and barley are the most commonly grown cereal crops in Cornwall, [and also oats]. In early spring seeds are planted for arable crops like wheat, from which we get flour to make bread, barley, which is used to brew beer, and oats, with which we make porridge."

"Mild winters mean that grass can grow for most of the year in Cornwall. Grass is very important to Cornish farmers as most of them keep livestock, like cattle and sheep, which are grazing animals. In other words, these animals eat grass to produce milk and meat. A cow can eat 80 kilograms of grass a day. In October the maize crop is ready to harvest. Maize is grown in Cornwall to make maize silage, a valuable winter feed for dairy cows. The type grown for cattle feed is just one of many different varieties of maize that also gives us corn on the cob or sweetcorn, cornflakes, corn oil, popcorn and maize flour. Dairy farming is the most important sector of agriculture in Cornwall and the county is famous for the clotted cream, cheese and ice cream it produces." Clotted cream! See, I did learn something!

Anyway, the room of my B&B for the next couple of nights here in Plymouth was quite luxurious, with views from the window of the Plymouth Sound, a bay of the English Channel, and off in the distance the green hillside of Mount Batten across the water, where I will be walking in a few days. Scott should have been here with me to share this luxurious room with me. I also realized that it was appropriate that I finished Sue Bunney's book today, as I just left Cornwall this morning, and I am now in Devon.

Some stats: Up to today give or take, I have completed about 411 miles! Yes, not all of them have been by walking, and not all by my solo self, but as one of my friends just said to me on Facebook, "It's not just about the walking – It's the vision you have and your sense of adventure and your joy in meeting new people and seeing new places." Someone else said, "You rock – and it all counts." That means that if I add eight and a half miles to 411, then the next time I walk, I will be about two-thirds of the way to Poole!

DAY 55 STATS: 2.5 MILES AND 1.25 HOURS DOWNDERRY TO PORTWRINKLE. 7.5 PLYMOUTH NOT WALKING, AND ONE MILE THAT I WILL WALK IN A FEW DAYS. NO EXTRA MILES THAT I WILL COUNT. HIKING BOOTS FOR 2.5 MILES. PUB IN CRAFTHOLE, WHICH IS HALF MILE INLAND FROM PORTWRINKLE, IS "FINNYGOOK INN." PUB IN PLYMOUTH AT THE DEVON BORDER IS "THE VINE."
Information on the four Eddystone Rock Lighthouses from
trinityhouse.co.uk/lighthouses-and-lightvessels/eddystone-lighthouse; and
wikipedia.org/wiki/Eddystone_Lighthouse.
Information about Smugglers in Cornwall from
cornwall-calling.co.uk/smugglers.htm.
Information on pilchard fishing from
cornwallgoodseafoodguide.org.uk/cornish-fishing/history-of-the-cornish-fishing-industry.
Farming in Cornwall information from cornwallfoodandfarming.net/index.htm.

REST DAY IN PLYMOUTH – Saturday, 29 July 2017

"All I really need is love, but a little chocolate every now and then doesn't hurt." – Charles M. Schulz

The kind woman at my B&B in Plymouth washed in a proper washing machine my other half of laundry today. Now just about all my clothes are clean, since the nice lady at the previous B&B washed the first half in a proper washing machine in Cawsand a few days ago. After breakfast today, I stayed in my luxurious room till about 1:00pm doing miscellaneous things, including emailing a few B&Bs in case Scott comes over here, especially the ones that I had booked a single room, to see what the status would be of adding a second person. What?? Did you just type "in case Scott comes over here?" Yes, I did! We are thinking about it more seriously at this point after some discussion over video calling, given my emotional roller coaster day a few days ago.

I went out to lunch and since it was "only" lightly raining, I ended up slowly walking to the Barbican and harbour area of Plymouth, with shops and such. This was the mile walk that I would be doing tomorrow to get to the ferry to Mount Batten, but today I would just walk it today leisurely. I walked passed Smeaton's Tower again, but it was still blocked off from the concert, so I was still not able to climb up the tower. I did take a few more photos as I found a way to get closer to it though than yesterday. I saw the year of "1759" painted on the tower.

When I arrived at the Barbican area, I went into a few art galleries and antique shops. It was a busy section with many people, and the street I walked on, Southside Street, was actually quite nice. Besides, then I found an artisan chocolate café and shop, Chocaccino, so I had to go in! Everything looked sooooo good. I could have gotten a huge piece of Chocolate Hazelnut Heaven Cake, or the Chocolate Brownie, or the Chocolate Dulce de Leche Brownie Layer Cake, or the Chocoholics Dream Cream Tea (which I really should have gotten), or the Chocolate Truffle Cake, but I opted to go a bit smaller and get eight bite-size small pieces of chocolate, mostly of my favorite combination of chocolate and peanut butter. I sat in the shop and enjoyed, because after all, "a little chocolate every now and then doesn't hurt."

I went back to the very, very busy section of Plymouth that I went to yesterday, Royal Parade, to get some more cash while I was in this big city with banks. While I did not mind the busy area of the streets of Barbican, probably because it was more touristy, I certainly did not like this busy area where the bank was located. Just too much busyness for me after all my quiet and calm and peaceful days along the coast, getting my positive supply of negative ions, with small villages and so much nature and beauty. I was looking forward to getting back to all that tomorrow. It was still lightly raining as I walked back to my B&B in the mid-afternoon.

I received responses from five of the six B&Bs I contacted earlier today about adding Scott. One would not be able to add nor do they have another room, so I researched some other options in that town, Torquay. I may have found a couple possibilities. The others said it would be no problem to add him as I already had a double bed, some may just charge extra, which I expected and was fine with. I had the TV on in the background the rest of the evening, again no Doc Martin though, nor Poldark, went out to dinner at some point, and somehow the time passed on my planned rest day in Plymouth.

DAY 56 STATS: ONE MILE TO BARBICON/FERRY AREA. I DID NOT TIME MYSELF WALKING THERE SINCE I TOOK IT LEISURELY. NOT COUNTING THE EXTRA MILES WANDERING AROUND, GETTING CASH, AND WALKING BACK TO B&B. PURPLE SHOES. PUBS IN THE BARBICAN AREA OF PLYMOUTH ARE "CROWN AND ANCHOR," "THE NAVY INN," "THE FISHERMAN'S ARMS," "THE DOLPHIN," AND "THE THREE CROWNS."

PLYMOUTH MOUNT BATTEN TO WEMBURY – Sunday, 30 July 2017

"Life isn't about waiting for the storm to pass, it's about learning to dance in the rain." – Hanging on the wall in the Cliffedge Café in Bovisand.

I took the 9:00 Mount Batten Ferry, a small motorboat, from Plymouth to Mount Batten. Well when I got there at 8:50, the ferry driver was not there yet, and one other person was waiting. After the ferry driver arrived, he told us both that the first ferry doesn't leave till 9:15. Ok, I'll wait I thought, no worries. Next thing I knew he started the boat and we were on our way at 9:02. It was odd he said it wasn't leaving till 9:15, and then he left early. Oh, and I took a taxi from my B&B this morning to the ferry, since I did this walking yesterday, even checking out where the ferry was located near the Barbican area.

Anyway, once I arrived across the River Plym, there was a tiny bit of pavement walking, followed by some pavement steps up, a few steps down, and a path to a grassy area overlooking Plymouth. I could see the Breakwater and its Lighthouse, and Cawsand and Kingsand in the distance. That was days ago being at those tiny fishing and smuggling villages which are so different than the big city of Plymouth. It almost seems surreal to think that not only was I there a few days ago, but also thinking about the different lifestyles in just a matter of miles away from each other is quite impressive. Comparatively, it is like stepping back in time hundreds of years at those small villages, and then leaping into the modern world of Plymouth. And they are only miles apart.

I read about the impressive Plymouth Breakwater and its lighthouse as well. Because of the need of a breakwater due to the volume of shipwrecks in the Plymouth Sound, the Plymouth Breakwater "has the distinction of being one of the very first free standing breakwaters ever built." A major engineering project, the work started in 1811, taking thirty years to build, called The Great Undertaking, the breakwater is a mile long, 45 feet wide, and took three and a half million tons of rock to build. Soon a lighthouse was built on the western end of the breakwater and a beacon at the other end. Even with all this, shipwrecks continued to occur until the last one in 1913.

There were a lot of people out walking their dogs in the next section of grassy area as I continued to walk along the Jennycliff area. There was a big stone block of some sort marking the SWCP. I've never seen a large stone block like that before that was a marker. It was several feet tall and wide, and had the acorn symbol etched on it as well. Another large blue marker, similar to the one I saw when I arrived in Plymouth, told me that I had 175.5 miles till Poole. Alas this blue marker is not accurate just like the one when I arrived in Plymouth. Really, it is 212 miles to Poole at this point. In fact, if you add up the 352 miles from Minehead the other blue marker said, plus this blue marker, it would only be 527.5 miles along the SWCP, missing over 100 miles. (Hmmm I wonder if these markers were placed here back in the days when Mark Wallington was walking in his "500 Mile Walkies" book.)

I knew there was only one climb for today, and it was up via many steps which led into a tree lined section. After the climb, it was flat walking through the trees, till I was finally out in the open, then still flat walking as the path was lined with shrubbery. Continuous views of the Breakwater and lighthouse and Cawsand/Kingsand for a few miles behind me, along with some amazingly deep blue water and light blue sky, with a few fluffy white clouds.

For some reason, I had an unsettling feeling inside me through the enclosed trees, with the views of the busy, big city of Plymouth behind me throwing me off. But then I turned a corner literally, and figuratively I suppose, and views of green rolling hillsides just beyond with farmland and one shade of light green grass, trimmed with another shade of darker green trees. This was the refreshing SWCP scene that I have become accustomed to seeing and feeling more at home with! Back to those positive negative ions. Back to the calm and peace and quiet. Back to nature. It is so interesting how my life for nearly two months now, with the quietness, openness, slowness, constant seas and crashing waves, low population of people, nature, small villages, even with the not-so-good weather, and even with the close encounters with cows and golf courses, I have come to grow and love and get used to all this. Being in a big city was just unsettling. I definitely prefer the quieter, simpler, slower, peaceful, and calmer walking pace of life of the vast majority of the countryside and farmland and fishing villages and seas and waters of the SWCP!

I reached the Cliffedge Café in the area of Bovisand. I stopped in the café to get sandwich to take away and eat later, as I was not quite hungry then, but if I got hungry soon, then I would have it with me. I passed by the small Bovisand Beach, and did some road walking passing by a lot of chalet-type homes. The path remained quite flat until I arrived in Wembury a couple hours later, my destination for the day. There were a few very minor ascents and descents, and really this seems to have been one of the flattest stretches I have done. I also now realized that the views beyond behind me also included Rame Head. That was days ago! I contemplated the above quote I saw in the café. If I took it literally, I would have been dancing a lot the past several months, and perhaps the quote was telling me that maybe I should have walked/danced in the rain, because life includes challenges. If I take the quote figuratively, then perhaps it is about accepting the challenges as they are.

Then the views very close to my right got absolutely beautiful. Lots of brown rocky edges to the shoreline against the water, small white waves crashing, a great rocky cove and small beach, some brown rocks out in the short distance from the shore, with a few white waves crashing, and one small rock with what looked like a very tiny lighthouse on it. The booklet mentions a "white navigation beacon island," but I didn't know if this was what I was looking at, as the tiny lighthouse looked red and white to me.

More great brown rocks with white waves crashing as I continued walking. One man was fishing, standing on these brown rocks. In the distance were various sailboats, the kind with two triangular sails, and another one with a row of four large sails, much like a schooner. Blue waters and blue skies. I reached the homes at Heybrook Bay, passed by a tennis court, and a sign told me that I had one and a half miles to Wembury. I started to see a rock island in the waters, called the Great Mew Stone, a protected wildlife sanctuary. Note that today, as many, many days of my walk, I have been continuing to take lots of photos with benches in the foreground of the beautiful scenery. Still, I am thinking of a "Benches of the South West Coast Path" photography book.

There have been a lot of joggers out today, over the last several miles. That still always makes me feel overdressed. This time there were so many, I wondered if some running event was going on. I ended up asking someone who told me they were doing a "time trial," of the ten miles between Jennycliff and Wembury and back. He says it was a "social thing." What a scenic place to run! If I was a runner, I wouldn't mind running here for ten miles.

My first glimpse of Wembury Church up on a hillside appeared. I passed a small rocky beach with a few dog walkers and beach goers as the waves crashed again on the rocks. I got closer views of Wembury Church and Wembury Beach as I continued walking. Around noon, I was a few minutes away, and I could hear the church bells ring. Ahhh, one of my favorites sounds! Church bells near the crashing waves! A few minutes after noon, I arrived at Wembury Beach. A sign told me that I have completed 424 miles from Minehead, and I have 206 miles to Poole! I guess this is the "official" two-thirds of the way for me! (Or one-third for people going in the other direction.) Wow, amazing, simply amazing. (See the back cover of this book for a color photo of this sign along with kayaks and blue skies.)

I ate the sandwich I bought a couple hours ago as I sat at the upper edge of the beach. Yes, it was still good. There were people enjoying the beach because thankfully there was great weather today...sunny with some clouds, dry, and sometimes a breeze that made it cooler, but it was still warm. Perfect! Summer again.

I walked up to the church on the hill, and visited the inside and outside. Inside were some nice stained-glass windows from various centuries, the Werburgh Window dating from 1886, the Altar Window dating from 1902, and the Millennium Window dating from 2004. I bought a 29-page booklet that told "The Romantic Story of Wembury Church," of which I have yet to read. It starts off with a foreword written in 2009 by Michael Harman, Priest-in-Charge, who said, "This church dedicated to St. Werburgh, has stood for centuries, as solid as the granite on which it is built, weathering the channel storms, bathed in glorious summer sunsets, or just simply Here. It has been a constant beacon – not just to seafarers entering the [River] Yealm for whom it is the principal leading mark, or for ramblers on the Coastal Path, but especially for those who over the centuries have lived in this village, and for whom it has marked significant points in their lives."

Another "lighthouse-church tower," as even the booklet for today says that "the tower, with its commanding position on the coast, was (and still is) used as a navigation marker. It is said that a beacon was lit on the tower as a guiding light." I went inside, and realized finally an open church, as many have been closed the last few weeks. The views from above the church outside with the blue waters, the busy little beach, Great Mew Stone rock island beyond, the green hillsides and the blue skies with white clouds were just beautiful! Photos included the graveyard, the church, and this amazing scenery. Perfect! These views reminded me of the views from the Talland Church I saw a few days ago, both being up on top of a hill overlooking the scenery. (The Wembury Church view is one of the color photographs on the back cover of this book.)

I walked to my B&B on the road for about a half mile using my handwritten map that I drew long ago. At the moment it seemed like I could not get reception on my mobile in order to use GPS, so fortunately my handwritten map this time was sufficient. When I arrived, I was greeted by Phil, the very nice B&B owner. I remembered emailing him long ago asking him questions, and he even called another B&B for me. I figured I could sit down with him now and plan out my next couple of days because really, with several river crossings coming up, and perhaps a long-distance section where there wouldn't be any facilities or food in between, I was really confused when I planned B&Bs in this area long ago, and was not really sure how to take on the next couple of days.

Phil kindly helped me figure it all out. With the wrong timings of river crossings for ferries and/or wading, and the long distance I had originally planned, I had to change some of my original plans so that now I will need to do a circular-type walk tomorrow, then the next day skip a section and take a taxi, and shorten the day after, or something like that. Thanks, Phil, for the help! I sat in my room for a couple of hours double checking my plan for the next few days against the elevation, food opportunities, etc. I called Mom too, as usual.

Side note: Something might be wrong with my right knee. It felt a bit swollen and was aching today a bit. It actually started aching a bit a few days ago, but I didn't think much of it. I will need to be very careful from now on and keep an eye on it. I took some anti-inflammatories, and will use my hiking poles a lot to help support my knee, even if the ascents and descents are small, and I even happened to have brought a neoprene-type sleeve knee wrap with me, which I will start wearing tomorrow. I hope it doesn't get worse, and only gets better. When I got hungry for dinner, I needed to walk three-quarters of a mile to The Odd Wheel pub in Wembury and back.

So here is some good news...Scott seems to be on the plan for coming out here! He has talked to a few people about kitty and house care, and even started putting a few things into a packing pile. That, along with his inquiring about flights. I will continue to take care of B&Bs, travel insurance, luggage transfers, and trains. It is still not definite, but seems to be most likely. So excited! It would be great to have his company for the last few weeks of my walk, and share some of my amazing experiences and the beautiful scenery with him. I obviously have not walked all the miles by myself now anyway, between walking with Sasha, Lucy, Linda, Gordon, Jim and Henry, and the family of four, so why not walk with my husband. I am still having an epic walking adventure on England's 630-mile South West Coast Path, just now with a love story…

DAY 57 STATS: 6 MILES. 3 HOURS. TWO EXTRA MILES FOR WALKING TO B&B AND BACK AND FORTH TO DINNER. PURPLE SHOES. PUB IN WEMBURY IS "THE ODD WHEEL." Information about the Plymouth Breakwater and its Lighthouse from submerged.co.uk/plymouthbreakwater-building.php.

WEMBURY TO WARREN POINT, FERRY, AND NOSS MAYO TO STOKE BEACH CIRCULAR WALK TO NOSS MAYO – Monday, 31 July 2017

"Local produce for local people." – **On a fruit and veggie stand in Noss Mayo.**

After breakfast the B&B gentleman, Phil, drove me so that I could walk a half mile shortcut towards the Warren Point ferry. It was all inland and all flat on a gravel track road, and met up with the SWCP, but then I regretted that because it looked like the path would have been very nice to walk on for a mile and half. Well, the last quarter mile was the same anyway, so I backtracked about a quarter mile at least to see what I missed, then came back. Therefore, I missed a mile.

What I did see was the entry way into the River Yealm between the two grassy hilltops, then a lot of nice looking boats floating in the water in between, with a boat or two leaving or coming back on the river. There were also views of The Great Mew Stone I saw yesterday. I walked down to the ferry and it had one of those circular boards, where I opened the black board saying, "Drop the board for ferry," to reveal the white side saying, "Please close after use," which signals the ferryman that someone needs a ride. No batman symbol on this one. I called for the ferry, a very small motorboat, just after 10:00, and by 10:15 I was across the river, and started walking.

The walking started out on a road, and then turned into a path under some trees. Through the trees I caught glimpses of the river and the boats. Next was some gravel road walking near some homes. So far the terrain was all flat. In fact it remained very flat my entire walk today. More gravel road walking through some trees, with some views of the surrounding farmland and the tower of Wembury Church beyond.

Soon I was out of the trees and in the glorious sunshine and blue skies. More views of Wembury Church, The Great Mew Stone, and even Rame Head and Cawsand and Kingsand beyond and behind. The blue seas were dotted with white sailboats. The path today was now all a very wide track, the widest I have walked on the entire SWCP. I believe it was all called Revelstoke Drive because the person that owned this land long ago wanted to be able to ride his horse and buggy around all his land.

I turned the corner at Gara Point, and the views of Rame Head and that area disappeared, and views of the next small headlands ahead appeared, lined with a jagged rocky shoreline below. Beautiful. Small white waves crashed, the sounds and sights so refreshing. I passed the parking area for The Warren, and soon the flat wide gravel track became a wide grassy track, still wide enough for a horse and buggy. Small white waves continued to crash on the brown rocks below against the deep blue water and the light blue sky. Still dotted with sailboats. It was warm and sunny out, and a nice breeze. Lovely!

Earlier I passed by some fields inland with cows. Although three of the cows seemed to somehow got out of the field and onto the SWCP. They looked like they wanted to get inland. Then I passed by fields of sheep, some of which were also on the SWCP. The hillsides were those various shades of green with the grass, shrubs, and trees. A few leftover wildflowers added a bit of color. Just after noon, I took a break from walking and sat on a bench. To enjoy the views, and to have a snack. It was calm here at this spot, overlooking the scenery and enjoying the warmth. The view was of the small point, Stoke Down, and beyond was a long headland that in some days' time, I am sure I will be walking there.

After turning the corner at Stoke Down, the SWCP led inland through some trees. I ended up at a caravan park near Stoke Beach. This was my SWCP destination for the day, but before I headed inland back to Noss Mayo, due to my B&B being there, I walked down a short road to St. Peter the Poor Fisherman's Church, Revelstoke. In this one, I actually wrote my name in the little guest book. According to some information inside the remains of this church I read that this church is "an early 14th century church with south aisle and porch added in the 15th century. In 1840 the church was badly damaged in a storm, but occasional services were still held there until 1869 when the building was deemed to be unsafe for use. A new Parish Church, also to be called St. Peter's, Revelstoke, [was built] on a site facing across the river towards Holy Cross Church, Newton Ferrers. This was built in 1882. It is not known when the chapel at Stoke became known as St. Peter 'the Poor Fisherman' rather than just St. Peter's but perhaps it is reasonable to assume that it was so named at the time of the building of the new church so as to distinguish between the two."

This church was some very old remains with no roof, but you could go inside, so it was kind of like an open courtyard. Only it is still a church, and now I think it was still in use for occasional services and events "since a group of local people joined together to save the remains of the church, [with] repairs undertaken during 1971." It was kind of a strange feeling in there with its being open with no roof, as if you could feel the history.

There was also an old iconic Red Telephone Box converted into a miniature library and book exchange near the church, called "The Book Booth." I remember seeing this in England before, particularly in the Cotswolds, where one of these outdated Red Telephone Boxes, due to the mobile phone, was converted into one of the village's Visitor Information Center, complete with the village's history and old photos. Some other ways the iconic outdated Red Telephone Box has been converted into something useful include ATMs, art galleries, notice boards, school projects, couches, and locations for defibrillators.

I was doing a circular walk today for two reasons. One, my B&B was actually in this area and not further on. It was hard to find accommodations along this stretch when I did my planning months ago. Two, I was originally going to walk to Mothecombe, but was afraid of not getting mobile reception there to call a taxi back, and there seemed to be a lack of anything there, such as a pub or café that I could call from. I just did not want to get stuck in the middle of "nowhere." (Turns out there is a restaurant-B&B-beach house place in Mothecombe that I found out a few days later than today, and it puzzled me why I couldn't figure that out before, and why Phil did not seem to know about it.)

Anyway, for my circular walk I wanted to take the shortest route back to The Ship Inn in Noss Mayo for lunch. I asked someone at the caravan park to confirm my road walking and map reading skills, and they told me at one point there would be a footpath which would be shorter than road walking. However, I didn't quite understand where it was, but I knew the roads could take me there, so I started walking. I passed one footpath but it didn't seem right, so I kept going on the road. After a bit there was another footpath and just then my guardian angels of the day appeared, a family of three. They confirmed that this was the correct footpath to Noss Mayo. It was through some trees which led to a muddy gravel road for just a bit, and then out onto a road. I confirmed once again that I was going in the right direction towards The Ship Inn with another guardian angel, a teenage girl. I was only a moment away. I arrived, and I would say that shortest route back was about a mile and a half total.

I ordered some food at The Ship Inn, and then called my B&B to ask if they could come pick me up. I was not sure exactly how to find this B&B from here, and would rather not get lost, as it was on a farm somewhere not that close by. They would pick me up at 3:00, and I ate my lunch. The husband, Phil, picked me up, not in a car, but in a green golf-cart-type-farm-vehicle. I chuckled and thought to myself, ahhh my limo has arrived. At least there was no golf course around.

I was picked up this way because I was staying at the Worswell Farmhouse B&B, a working National Trust Farm. Phil told me that the cows and sheep that I walked near today were his. In fact, apparently all the land I walked on today was his, as this farm has been in the family for more than 65 years. In fact, the three cows that were not fenced in today, he put out there on purpose. I think he was saying they are females and needed to be kept away from the males until they gave birth. It was a bumpy ride on a rocky gravel track to the farm in the green golf-cart-type-farm-vehicle. I was glad for the ride, as trying to find this B&B would not have been easy.

Back in my room, I emailed a few more B&Bs in the increasing chance that Scott comes out here. I made a taxi reservation for the morning to take me to the other side of the next river after Mothecombe, River Erme, at Wonwell Beach. I wouldn't make low tide as it was very early in the morning and you can only get across at low tide by wading. (But don't quote me on this, and please do your own research on getting across River Erme.) This means that I will miss a few more miles, combined with missing the walk to Mothecombe, perhaps five miles total, but that is ok at this point. What is another few miles after all? I am still walking the majority of the SWCP. Acceptance with gratefulness and grace. I also contacted my next B&B to see if they could pick me up at the end of my walk tomorrow in Bigbury on Sea. He could. It would be a short walk tomorrow.

My "farm limo" brought me back down to the village for dinner. He had to be here anyway because of the 5K run going on. His "farm limo" was the sweep for the run, in case if injury. I heard the beginning speech and saw the runners start. I seem to be running into (pun intended) a lot of running events during my walk. Before I ate, I walked up to the church of Noss Mayo, St. Peter's Church, which must have been the one built after St. Peter the Poor Fisherman's Church became unsafe for use.

As I waited for my food at The Ship Inn again, the runners were coming back. Phil said the winners don't get anything. It is a community event, and soon there would be more Regatta events bringing the people of the villages of Noss Mayo and Newton Ferrers, both in this area across Newton Creek from each other, together. Another Regatta event that I have witnessed as part of my SWCP walk, being a witness to local village life!

During my "farm limo" ride back to the B&B, I was getting a Farming 101 lesson from Phil. They have wheat and linseed crops, plus cows, sheep, chickens, and pigs. The yearly cycle of crops and animals rotates throughout the year, so there is always something going on. They also sell fruit and veg (short for vegetable) at two honor stands in both towns. I saw the stand when I arrived in Noss Mayo, which said, "Local produce for local people." Phil also told me about the gestation cycles of the animals, some of which was just too much information for me. I had a very, very nice B&B room in this farmhouse, with views of the farm land out my window that once again, I would have liked to share with Scott. But maybe soon I will get to share my B&Bs with him.

DAY 58 STATS: BEFORE FERRY: EXTRA HALF MILE, THEN HALF MILE OF SWCP. MISSED A MILE. ABOUT A HALF HOUR…AFTER FERRY: FIVE MILES OF SWCP NOSS MAYO TO STOKE BEACH. EXTRA MILE AND A HALF BACK TO NOSS MAYO. THREE AND A HALF HOURS ROUND TRIP. PUPRLE SHOES…WILL MISS: ABOUT FIVE MILES FROM STOKE BEACH TO MOTHECOMBE AND ACROSS RIVER ERME. PUBS IN NOSS MAYO ARE "THE SHIP INN" AND "THE SWAN INN."
Information on the Red Telephone Box from ones I have seen in person and from npr.org/sections/parallels/2014/01/14/261397881/some-brits-not-ready-to-say-ta-ra-to-iconic-telephone-box.

WONWELL BEACH TO BIGBURY ON SEA, AND THURLSTONE TO HOPE COVE – Tuesday, 1 August 2017

"Hope is in the heart. Hope is everywhere." – My seven year old niece.

The taxi I arranged yesterday picked me up as planned, and as I left, Jackie of the Farmhouse B&B gave me a hug. We had some good conversations, and it was very nice to connect with her and Phil. It took a half hour to drive to the Wonwell "slipway" near Wonwell Beach, where I would start my walk. I needed to miss the five miles I mentioned from Stoke Beach to Mothecombe across River Erme to Wonwell, due to the longer walk that I had originally planned, and that I would not be able to make the low tide to walk across the river. Acceptance with grace.

After a quick look down at the upper part of the sandy beach, I started walking through some trees on flat terrain, which offered views of River Erme. A man with his dog was on the beach, and a flock of birds was sitting on a sandy spot in between the waters of the river. I heard the rush of the higher tides coming in, and within fifteen minutes I was out of the trees. I had a very short walk on the other end of Wonwell Beach and with a turn of the corner, I was out of the river area and back looking at the seas. A wheat field was on my left, and the sound of the waves was on my right. A good start to the day.

I had a view of a nice secluded rocky sandy beach cove, probably called Gutterslide Beach. Another one of those beaches that looks like you can only get to it by boat or kayak, but I wouldn't even know if that is possible. Today was a day of some ascents and descents, most gentle, but some steeper. The first uphill climb was gentle on a grassy slope, with a flock of sheep inland. At the top I got views of Bigbury on Sea, my first destination for the day. I passed by a herd of cows inland. I had a gentle downhill, and then a gentle uphill, and then I was on some flat paths, all through the grassy hillsides. I really liked the contrast of the light green and dark green grass and trees of the hillsides against the light blue and dark blue skies and water. I'm sure I have mentioned that my favorite colors are green and blue, and all their various shades. Looking in one direction ahead of me, because of the position of the sun, the view was of the dark brown rocks against the shimmering waters and small white waves. In the other direction behind me, the rocks looked lighter brown and the water a very deep blue. Beautiful!

I had another gentle downhill on the slope of a grassy hill, which headed a bit inland so that I got a view of one cluster of dark green trees against the light green grass. I could clearly see the SWCP cutting through the grass, and the blue skies above with white clouds making for a very picturesque scene. I took a panorama photo starting with the cluster of trees, the green hillside, the cliffs, rocks, water, and around to the other side of the hill. Then a gentle uphill climb again. More great views of coves with brown rocks, small white waves, the hillsides and cliffs of green grass, the turquoise to blue waters. This was just one small section, but when I looked at it, I heard myself say "Wow!" out loud. I was loving walking on these open green rolling hillsides and seeing these beautiful views.

I took a very steep zigzag descent down to a sandy beach very slowly. This had been the steepest section it seemed like in days, perhaps weeks. It had that small sandy gravel too, which can make it slippery. I was wearing my hiking boots this morning, as I knew of all the ascents and descents, and for this particular descent, I was very glad for my boots. As I descended, I had more views of the dark looking rocks and the shimmering waters. I reached the beach, Westcombe Beach, and took a little break at the beach. I needed to make sure my right knee was doing alright. It still seemed a bit swollen from a few days ago, but not as bad.

There was another steep but short ascent as I got closer to Bigbury on Sea. Followed by a short descent to Ayrmer Cove and a sandy beach. There were a few people on this beach. I was quite grateful for this warm-breezy-dry-mostly-sunny day! Looking back, I noticed that the color of some of the rocks of the cliffs were actually a light beige color, rather than a darker brown color. More benches were the foreground subject of some of my photos for today, and today's scenery had just been spectacular so far!

I arrived at the busy Challborough Beach with lots of people. With a half mile left in the first part of my day's five-mile walk, I arrived at Bigbury on Sea. A very busy beach, with a very busy parking lot and café, and a view of Burgh Island. Many people walk across the sand to get to the island when the tide is low. Or if the tide is high there is a "sea tractor" or "beach tractor," an elevated platform above wheels on a tractor-like chassis that is tall enough for high tide.

I was to be picked up by my B&B gentleman, as prearranged yesterday by email. I had an hour to wait, so I put on my flip flops and had some lunch in and amongst the beach-goers. Ken picked me up, and after some discussion, we decided to drop me off for my second walk of the day at the church in Thurlestone. I thought earlier today that I should do part of tomorrow's walk today because tomorrow's forecast looks quite wet and windy. Again, so disappointing. I have some really great days, but then the weather turns not-so-great again. Hopefully only though for one day. Because of this situation, I needed to miss some more miles, first from Bigbury on Sea to Bantham, which would have been one and a half miles, but that was around another river, River Avon, which had limited ferry service, only from 10:00 to 11:00, and then from 3:00 to 4:00, neither of which worked into my schedule today. I also missed Bantham to Thurlestone, probably another two miles because of the discussions I had with Ken. He dropped me off at the Thurlestone church, which was unfortunately closed. I put my purple shoes on for the rest of today's flat three mile walk.

The church was a bit inland actually, and after a quick visit to this 13th century All Saints Church as it was closed, I needed to walk a half mile from the church on a road and on a footpath towards the SWCP. I also needed to cross the footpath through a golf course. Uh oh. I kept my fingers crossed, and since the weather did not call for a downpour, I figured I was alright. I looked up at the skies including out to the water in the distance just to be sure. Still keeping an eye out for flying golf balls, I safely arrived on the SWCP. Whew. I now had about two and a half miles to Hope Cove, my second destination for the day. I started near Broad Sand, a small sandy beach. For a while, I needed to walk between the Thurlestone Golf Course on my left and another longer sandy beach, Yarmouth Sand, to my right with the sound of soft crashing waves to my right and the clunks of golf balls being hit to my left. A few small rocky coves with small crashing waves were on my right, and the golf course on my left, as I continued to walk. I could see Hope Cove beyond.

As I walked I noticed a quintessential directional post with acorns and arrows. One side had an acorn with an arrow pointing straight ahead, then a line, and then two arrows, one pointing to the left, the other pointing to the right, all as you were facing the post. In this case, you follow the arrow closest to the acorn above the line, pointing straight ahead, for the SWCP. On the other side of the post was an acorn with two arrows, one pointing to the left and one pointing to the right, then there was a line, and then a third arrow pointing straight ahead, as you were facing the post from this perspective. In this case, you follow the two arrows closest to the acorn for the SWCP, depending which direction of the SWCP you wanted to go, to the right or left, towards Minehead or Poole.

As the golf course ended, I noticed a sign, "Beware flying golf balls. Please keep to the Coastal Path and be aware of golfers." Then one more sandy beach with waves was on my right, Leas Foot Sand, shortly followed by another sandy popular beach, Thurlestone Sand. I also walked a short distance through the South Milton Ley Nature Reserve on a bridge over a stream of water, with "one of the largest reed beds in Devon."

I continued walking next to the popular sandy beach of South Milton Sand. To my left, safely behind a fence was a herd of cows, and these had horns! Most cows I have seen have not had horns. Also were a few horses that of course Scott would have loved to see. Then I passed by a sign that said I had one mile to Hope Cove. There was a big rock in the water off the beach that looked like the shape of a rock formation at Arches National Park in Utah, called Thurlestone Rock. According to today's booklet, this rock is "one of the most impressive natural arches along the coast." I then did a short bit of road walking, and then another sign ten minutes later that said I had one mile to Hope Cove. Then only a moment later I had three-quarters of a mile to Hope Cove according to another sign. Hmmm, the mileage on the signs seemed to be a bit off.

I walked on a popular wider stony track and reached the Hope Cove Viewpoint. From here you apparently can see Eddystone Lighthouse, but even though it has been a dry day, off in the distance the clouds obscured my view. According to the viewpoint sign and map, I could however see all the way to Dodman Point, some thirty-five miles away by sea, where even though I skipped the Dodman Point section itself, it was so interesting to think that about twelve days ago I was walking in that area!

I arrived at the main area of the village of "Outer Hope." Just beyond was the village of "Inner Hope." I love these names…Hope Cove, Outer Hope, Inner Hope. Gives me lots of hope, all around! I thought of two reminders my intuitive seven year old niece once said, "Hope is in the heart," and "Hope is everywhere." Indeed!

There was a beach, pubs, and a harbour with boats. The first harbour it seemed like that I have seen in a few days. I decided to come back later when I went out to dinner to take photos, as I would guess there would be less people around. I headed to my B&B. Carol offered me some tea and homemade cake and a homemade chocolate chip cookie. She was baking for an "Afternoon Tea" fundraising event for tomorrow, which perhaps on my rainy day, I will go to. It reminded me of the Cream Tea fundraiser at the St. Anta Church Hall in Carbis Bay. I spent a few moments making a different accommodation reservation in Torquay for a double room in hopes that Scott comes out. I cancelled my original reservation. If for some reason he doesn't come out, at least this small hotel is closer to harbour anyway than my previous lodging in Torquay.

A bit later, I walked down to the harbour of Hope Cove for photos. Sure enough, less people were out. Hope Cove "was originally a 13th century fishing village with the locals' income augmented by smuggling." I walked along the breakwater, which seemed to be a romantic thing to do, as I saw several couples also walking. I waited for one couple because the breakwater was not that wide. I took photos of the boats which were mostly sitting on the sand in rows, some kayaks, the breakwater, the rocks, the small headland beyond, and the setting sun. Ah, romantic. I then went out to dinner. A romantic dinner by myself.

There have been a few days when I have felt lonely walking by myself, but many other days when I don't. Today was one of those days where I did not feel lonely. Perhaps it really is the great weather that helps. In fact, I wonder if I had great weather days every single day from the beginning of my walk, if I would not really feel like I wanted Scott to join me. But his company would be good in either case now anyway. I also bet that if I had great weather days every single day, I wouldn't have missed any miles. Just not sure what happened to summer completely, but when it makes its appearance, it certainly is brilliant!

I started to think of all the people who have helped me and supported me thus far on my walk, whether on a daily basis, or only for a brief moment in time, in some capacity or another, for some reason or another. They are, in no particular order, and I appreciate them all:

Scott. My Mom. Sasha. The B&B people, whether just for the room and food, or also for rides, or also for conversations and company. Taxi drivers. The random people who walked with me on the spot for a few miles here and there, including Gordon. Lucy and other SWCP walkers that I have met up with from the Facebook Group page. A long, long list of various other "guardian angels."

DAY 59 STATS: WONWELL BEACH TO BIGBURY ON SEA: 5 MILES. 2.5 HOURS. NO EXTRA MILES. HIKING BOOTS. MISSED MILES: BIGBURY ON SEA TO BANTAM TO THURESTONE 3.5 MILES. THURLESTONE CHURCH TO COAST PATH: EXTRA .5 MILES. COAST PATH NEAR THURLESTONE TO HOPE COVE: 2.5 MILES. 1.25 HOURS. PURPLE SHOES. PUB IN BIGBURY ON SEA IS "PILCHARD INN." PUB IN THURLESTONE INLAND IS "THE VILLAGE INN."

Harbours, Boats, Villages, and Fishing on the South West Coast Path
Mullion Cove Breakwaters July 13
Gorran Haven Breakwater July 20
Clovelly Breakwater June 18

Harbours, Boats, Villages, and Fishing on the South West Coast Path
Boscastle (looking out to the seas) June 23
Boscastle (looking in towards the boats and village) June 23
Portwrinkle (smallest harbour) July 28

Harbours, Boats, Villages, and Fishing on the South West Coast Path
Church Cove (one of my possible book cover photos) July 13
Brixham Harbour Beautiful Dramatic Scene August 8
Branscombe Mouth Lone Orange Fishing Boat August 16

REST DAY DUE TO WEATHER IN "THE HOPES" – Wednesday, 2 August 2017

"Afternoon Tea. Scones and Home Made Cakes. Wednesday, 2nd August. 1 – 4pm. Fisherman's Reading Room. Inner Hope. Do come along and support the Reading Room." – Flyer for the Afternoon Tea today.

The forecast for today was…wind and rain. All day. Again. That's why I did some of today's walk yesterday. I spent the morning having breakfast, having a long video call with Scott, and typing my notes from yesterday's walks, as I did not do that last night. I peeked out the window at 10:30am to confirm the rainy and windy weather. Yup, it was confirmed, so I continued to type about yesterday. As I continued to type at 11:00, warm and dry inside, a heavy rain was happening outside. I was once again disappointed with all the bad weather I have been having, and I really don't want to walk in the rain all day, but I must accept it as it is since I have no control over it, and I must just hope for better weather from now on. I mean after all, I am in Hope Cove, Outer Hope and near Inner Hope, and I have hope in my heart. By noon, I was done typing and updating my recording of my daily statistics.

I contacted another B&B in Abbotsbury to see if they had a double room because the place I had there currently only had the single room. The new place had a twin room, but that was ok. It was a room for two, in hopes that Scott will still join me. Continuing concerns with a few things at home, but he also keeps making other small steps as if he is coming. He just hasn't booked the airfare yet. Anyway, one of the days in Abbotsbury happens to be our wedding anniversary if he joins me on the rest of my walk! If he doesn't join me, we had already known that I would be here on our anniversary and we would celebrate together when I return home from my walking adventure.

I ventured out to lunch in the rain. After eating, I went into the one art gallery that I saw in the village. My next adventure was to go to the local Afternoon Tea fundraising event that my B&B lady host was putting on to raise money for the local Fisherman's Reading Room to repair its roof. I walked a windy and wet short walk to the Reading Room, from Outer Hope to Inner Hope. Carol greeted me kindly at the door, I got some tea, and she pointed out the table full of goodies that people have baked. It was on a donation basis, so I made a donation and enjoyed tasting several homemade scones, cakes, and other locally made goodies while talking with the locals who live here in The Hopes.

The Reading Room was small, but dates back to 1908, over 100 years ago! Reading Rooms were a place for fisherman to relax after being out at sea. Reading Rooms provided newspapers, books, and snooker. I just looked up what snooker is because I am not familiar with that, and it looks like billiards. There are only a small handful of Reading Rooms left. I read information on the Reading Room, including that it was opened in May of 1908 as a memorial to the husband of a Mrs. Appleton, Mr. William Appleton, a lawyer and advocate, "a fine pattern of an English gentleman in its highest sense," who also enjoyed cricket, fishing, and "was a master at the beautiful game of billiards." "He loved the sea, rowing and sailing and sea fishing, and also all the sea-faring men and mariners. And there was good reason for his sympathy for them for he had much in common with them. They have to face danger, difficulty, unforeseen perils, death itself, in the pursuit of their ordinary avocations, and this gives them a true sense of the value of pluck, self-reliance and a dogged determination not to give in." (Quotes are from an article framed on the wall of the Reading Room, "Opening of Hope Cove Reading Room, May 18, 1908," and are from two people, Major Miles Halton Tristram and Mr. J.C. Carter, who spoke at the opening about Mr. William Appleton.)

I also read the Appleton Reading Room Standing Rules, also framed on the wall of the Reading Room. "Members shall be Fishermen, Coastguardsmen, Lifeboatmen, and Men of Hope, resident within one mile of the Room, and not under 16 years of age." "Smoking shall be permitted. All betting, gambling, or playing for money, or money's worth, are prohibited." "No noisy or boisterous games shall be allowed." "No oaths, or bad language, no quarrelling, no noisy talking, and no offensive conduct of any kind." I was told that they were perhaps quite religious. What another great experience learning about the importance of fishing and community!

I suppose if the weather was good today, and I was walking, then I would have not learned about Fisherman's Reading Rooms and Mr. Appleton, I would not have sat in one that is over 100 years old, and I would not have spent some time eating and talking with the locals of The Hopes, and experienced a bit more about fishing and community. Therefore, I guess it all turned out good for today even though I didn't walk.

After filling up on the goodies, I walked slowly back to my B&B. The rain for the moment had turned to a mist. On my way back, I visited a very small church, Saint Clements Church. I cannot find any information on this church, but it is quite small, and it therefore reminded me of the church with seating for only 33 people, St. Bueno's Church in Culbone that I saw nearly two months ago.

As I continued my way back to my B&B, I watched some big waves jumping next to the rocks of the cliffs and at the end of the breakwater, and some smaller waves going over the harbour wall that I walked on yesterday, all from the wind. I watched some kids standing at the edge of the breakwater jumping in the water, and perhaps testing the waves as they came over the wall. I was back in my room, and the weather forecast continued to call for rain for the rest of the afternoon. I would have tried to walk a couple miles perhaps if the weather had improved, but no such luck. I was once again reminded of the power of the weather and the seas.

I watched some TV, (again no Doc Martin or Poldark on), somehow found small things to do to keep me occupied, and a few hours later went out to dinner. I sure hope the weather is better tomorrow, but I don't know. No rain is forecasted, but it just might be quite windy…

DAY 60 STATS: REST DAY SO NO MILEAGE, NO HOURS. I WON'T COUNT THE BIT OF WALKING I DID IN THE TOWNS, AND THAT WAS IN FLIP FLOPS, EVEN IN THE RAIN. PUB IN HOPE COVE IS "THE HOPE AND ANCHOR INN."

HOPE COVE TO SOAR MILL COVE, AND SOUTH SANDS TO SALCOMBE – Thursday, 3 August 2017

"Of all the paths you take in life, make sure a few of them are dirt." – John Muir

I asked Ken and Carol if I could pay a bit extra for some extra bread and peanut butter to make a sandwich to take with me on today's walk. I was not sure about food along the way of my eight-mile walk, so I wanted to take something with me just in case. Sometimes it is a bit unclear to me if something will be open for food or not, as much as I do my research. I put some fresh fruit in my sandwiches as that was part of my breakfast, blueberries, strawberries, grapes, raspberries, all which jelly is made from anyway. Therefore, my sandwich will be like a PB&J sandwich, but with fruit instead of with J.

The forecast for today called for dry conditions, which was great, but quite windy. Not gale force, but not a gentle breeze either. I was a bit nervous about this actually, but I decided to give it a try, and if I didn't like it, there would be a hotel after about three and a half miles, Soar Mill Cove Hotel, and I could stop my walk there and get a taxi if I decided that option. They probably have food, too, but I still took my delicious sandwich. After breakfast, I said my thank yous to Carol and Ken, and started walking out their door, already feeling the wind. As I walked through the Hope villages, I went back and took a few quick photos of the outside of the Fisherman's Reading Room that I was inside yesterday, since I only took pictures inside yesterday.

The path started going gently uphill, and the path was quite wide and not close to the cliff ledge, so that put my mind at ease about not being blown over the cliff, even though pretty much right away I felt the wind pushing my body. Using my hiking poles to help stabilize myself, at least the wind was going in an inland direction, away from the coast and cliff ledges, so if anything, I would be blown inland. The path continued to be wide as I went up, alternating from grass to dirt. Note that I should mention here that most of the paths along the SWCP have been "dirt," also known as "soil, the ground, the natural terrain, the Earth."

The path flattened out, and as I looked back, I had views of Hope Cove, the beach, the rocks of the cliff below the villages, and the buildings of the villages going up the hillsides. There were some sheep quite close to the path where I was walking. Occasionally, I actually walked even more inland from the SWCP, paralleling the SWCP, right on the grass that the majority of the sheep were on so that I could be even more inland due to the wind. The views were still nice today, even with the layer of clouds. The green hillsides were covered in various types of grasses, and looking back at my photos, I could see the taller grasses leaning inwards from the wind. Views of The Hopes continued behind me as I walked.

Soon I arrived at an area where the path was so flat and wide, it was designated as wheelchair accessible. Some was gravel, and eventually pavement, as I got closer to the car park near Bolberrry Down. I had walked two and a half miles at this point, just over an hour. For the next mile, that path remained mostly wide and flat, but I really began to really feel uncomfortable with how windy it was. There had been only two other people out, a couple of joggers, but still my comfort level was being pushed. Well, I guess you could really say that my comfort level was being blown in the wind.

I still took in the views. To my right was the water below, but it was hazy off in the distance and with the cloud cover in the distance, the seas were not as blue looking as in the sun, and I couldn't see much beyond in the distance to my right. There were no sounds of crashing waves. It was pretty quiet out actually, except for the sound of the wind in the grasses, shrubbery, and in the air. To my left the views were of the green rolling hills inland, speckled with the whitish-grey color of the sheep. In front of me were the rolling green hills and headlands beyond.

A bit more flat trail, and then a small decent brought me to my first and only cove of the day, Soar Mill Cove. I took a few pictures of the cove with its small sandy and rocky beach. I knew that this was my potential stopping point, as I was quite near the Soar Mill Cove Hotel. I took a few deep breaths to figure out what to do. I was not comfortable with the wind, but it would mean missing more miles. But I have already missed plenty of miles, and my comfort level was more important. Courage. So, I decided to stop walking.

I did walk up another couple minutes to see if I could see what the terrain ahead of me was like, but it was around a corner, which seemed to get closer to a cliff ledge, and I definitely decided that no, this was not what I wanted to do. Besides, I didn't know what the terrain was like ahead – it could be closer to cliff ledges with several ascents and descents. I was completely convinced that the wind was too much for me, so I went back to take the inland half-mile path to the hotel.

Inside the hotel, I realized that the wind had made me a bit cold too, so it was nice to be in the comfort of the warmth inside of the hotel. I wondered if the winds today might have been classified as a "fresh breeze" or even a "strong breeze" today according to the Beaufort Wind Scale. I was also trying to recall if I had any other windy days where I actually ended my walk because of the wind. I know I didn't even attempt to walk some days at all when the forecast called for gale winds. And I think I've walked in some wind, but I don't recall if any other windy days made me end my walk early.

Anyway, the nice lady at the reception easily called a taxi for me. I had a rest in their lobby and ate part of my delicious PB&F (fruit) sandwich as I waited. I had the taxi take me to South Sands, a beach that was about a mile and a half from the "town center" of Salcombe, which was my destination for the day, whether I walked the entire way there or not. I missed three miles due to the wind, but such is my life on the SWCP. At least it stayed dry!

I sat on a park bench above the beach and ate the rest of my PB&F sandwich at South Sands. There were a few people on the beach. Back at the Soar Mill Cove Hotel I had switched from my hiking boots to my purple shoes, knowing that the rest of my walk would be on a road with pavement. The wind was much calmer here, actually non-existent. I wondered why it was so windy three miles from here, but not here.

I started walking the road, called Cliff Road, although it did not feel like I was on a cliff. I walked the few minutes to North Sands, another beach. I continued walking along Cliff Road towards the "town center" of Salcombe. I had views of the estuary that flows in from the sea. Or maybe it is really the estuary that flows out to the sea. In either case, it would be the Kingsbridge Estuary that flows into or out of the Salcombe Harbour that flows into or out of the English Channel.

I took a slight detour into a garden area, and then as I got closer to the town center, the street became busier and busier with lots of people. There had already been quite a lot of people since I was at South Sands, walking along the same road as I was, and it was even busier in the town center. I looked in a few shops but did not go inside any just yet. I made my way to what seemed like the main part of the town center next to the busy and large harbour. I took a few photos of the busy and large harbour with many types of boats, and then I turned around and realized that my accommodation for the next two nights was right there, The Victoria Inn.

I checked in a few minutes later. My room was in the back of the restaurant outside next to their outdoor seating area. It looked like it was in a small old stone building of some sort, perhaps it used to be the stables of a farm, I don't know. Obviously the inside had been remodeled. I realized that this is the only place I booked that did not include breakfast. I researched my day for tomorrow, including making taxi arrangements to pick me up at the car park of the Start Point Lighthouse, my destination for tomorrow. I went back outside and looked for a place for breakfast for tomorrow which starts at 7:00, and looked at where the ferry was located and its start time, 8:00, which I will need to take across the water to start my walk in the morning.

I was hungry again, so I got a good brie, arugula, and fig jam sandwich at a little café to take away. I took some time to go into a few shops, and then walked around the harbour area. There were kids enjoying jumping in the water and fishing for crabs. I walked along until I found a nice quiet bench to sit on overlooking the boats and the large harbour area to eat half my sandwich. There were nice green hillsides beyond the harbour with trees and homes. The weather was still dry, and not windy now, and the sun through the clouds felt nice and on the warm side. Ahhhh. Where were this sun and warmth and non-existent wind earlier today?

I was then in search of a church which I could see the tower of from a distance, but was not sure exactly where it was located, so I started walking in the general direction along another small street with a few more shops. My curiosity grabbed me first though, and I went into a little art place where kids of all ages can paint, not ceramics, but cardboard figures. It was cute in there. While in there, my eye caught a few "raw" and other protein bars, so I bought a few. I found it odd to find protein bars in a kid's painting place.

I continued my search for the church, when I happened upon of all streets, Church Street. I figured I must be in the right location, and sure enough just up the road was the church. The year carved on the outside of this church was 1843 of the Holy Trinity Church. I called Mom from outside the church as it was nearing 5:00, the time I usually call her. As I was standing there I noticed that I could see some boats in the distance through a hole in the trees. It made for a scenic spot, with the church, the graveyard, the trees, and boats beyond.

After my call with Mom, I took pictures of this scene when a man who just arrived on a motorcycle noticed me taking photos and asked me what had caught my eye for photographing, and I told him. He was very nice. What I didn't realize was that he was there to lock up the church. I just wandered inside, and sat down for a few minutes to do my usual prayers. There were some organ pipes, and a reflection of the large stained-glass window on the floor in my photos. I was done sitting and got up to leave when I realized the man on the motorcycle wanted to lock up. He was super nice about me being there though, telling me to take my time, and then wishing me a good rest of my holidays. Obviously, my camera and my accent gave away that I was not from around here.

I walked around Salcombe just a bit more, going down a small alley way, and then got some cash out of a bank machine. I always figure it is good to get cash when in a larger town that has a bank machine that will work for me, even if I still had some left from the last time I got cash. Many small villages do not have bank machines, and I never know exactly how much cash I will need till the next larger town. I went back into my room, with the intent of eating the other half of my brie sandwich and one of the protein bars I bought for dinner.

I video called with Scott for a while about his coming here. About an idea of perhaps him booking flights for Monday, but seeing what the consequences would be if he then switched it to Friday, and what would happen if he cancelled altogether. Yes, that was only a few days away and he had not yet booked his flights, even though he had done other things in preparation for joining me. In the meantime, I also made sure that another B&B would be alright if two people were in the twin or double room I had already booked, and they were fine with that, with no extra charge.

DAY 61 STATS: 3.5 MILES IN 1.5 HOURS WITH HIKING BOOTS. HALF MILE EXTRA. THEN ANOTHER 1.5 MILES IN 1.0 HOUR IN PURPLE SHOES. I MISSED THREE MILES. PUBS IN SALCOMBE ARE "THE FERRY INN," "THE VICTORIA INN," AND "THE KINGS ARMS."

SALCOMBE/EAST PORTLEMOUTH TO NEAR PRAWLE POINT, AND LANNACOMBE BEACH TO START POINT LIGHTHOUSE – Friday, 4 August 2017

"Warning. Fog signal may sound without warning. Please keep away from the revolving lens. Please do not touch the lens. Warning-do not look directly at the light source, which may dazzle." – Signs at the Start Point Lighthouse.

I woke up this morning to see an email that Scott booked his flights for Monday with a Tuesday arrival! That is only four days away. Yeah! I bought him travel insurance.

Since there was no breakfast at the Victoria Inn, I woke up early to get some egg sandwiches for take away at a small café by the harbour. I had to wait a bit for them because they were busy. Seemed like a popular place possibly for all the fisherman going out to the seas today. I walked a few minutes up the street to get the 8:30 ferry from Salcombe across the Kingsbridge Estuary to East Portlemouth to start my walk. It only took a minute or two to get across the water. I started walking along a road. I walked by a small beach and entered an area of trees. Through the trees, I had glimpses of the estuary and passed by a second small beach which had the sound of crashing waves, and the buildings of Salcombe built on the hillside in the background. So far, it was all flat terrain. I had a quick view of North Sands and South Sands across the water from yesterday. I was back in the trees momentarily, and then I was at the place where the estuary meets the seas. Back out in the open near the seas!

It was still flat walking through a hillside covered with ferns and other shrubbery. Below was the rocky coastline with small crashing waves. There were a couple of boats in the water in the distance. It was cloudy but I could see the sun. It felt warm, and it was dry, and no wind, and I was grateful. I reached the area of Gara Rock, about two and a half miles later, having only seen one jogger out this morning. Views ahead were of the rolling green hillside, as usual, but always different. I reached Seacombe about ten minutes after Gara Rock. It had still been all flat walking, with hillsides covered with fern, and also covered with grass. I walked near sheep that were all over - above, below, and even right on the path.

I passed by one man walking his dog. The terrain remained flat. I passed by a small sandy beach, Moor Sand. No one was on this beach. The coastline was still rocky. Views behind me were of the headlands of days passed by. A few sailboats were out on the seas today. I took a break at Gammon Head which was covered with colorful purple and yellow wildflowers. I passed by two sandy coves with waves, Maceley Cove and Elender Cove, just before Prawle Point, the most southerly point in Devon.

Unfortunately, today my knee decided to bother me a bit as I walked. I wanted to keep walking, but with a nine-and-a-half-mile day planned, I wasn't sure that was such a good idea to do the entire nine and a half miles with the way my knee was feeling. I looked at my map and noticed that there were some inland options I could try to cut some of the mileage down. I started on one of the inland paths which led to a road. It took me only a few moments to reach the road, and then I stopped and stood there to pull out my map again to see where my next step would be on the road. Literally. I was heading for the village of East Prawle, and needed to make sure I could find my way.

Just then a car started to come up the road towards me. Great! I thought. I will ask this person for something, for directions, or for a ride, I didn't know quite yet. I was not quite sure how I started the conversation, but a nice older, but not old, man who says he could take me to the pub in town so I could call a taxi that could take me a few miles ahead. Great, I thought. I got in the car. Now in the US, I would never do this. Here though, in small-town England, I felt safe. He had his dog in the car, too.

We ended up chatting and within the first few minutes I learned that he was an author and an artist. "Are you famous," I asked? Well, he did have one book that pretty much did very well compared to all his other books combined, he told me. A children's book, called "The Very Bloody History of Britain, Without all the Boring Bits." He was famous! I guess. Even though like the actors of Doc Martin, I did not know him. His name was John Farman. I asked if he had a copy of his book that he could autograph for me. He didn't, but one is available online.

As we kept talking he suggested that he could offer me a cup of coffee at his house in East Prawle, and then he could drive me a bit down the road to a place where I could restart my walk, instead of the need to call for a taxi. Now definitely in the US, I would not do this! Here though, in small-town England, I felt safe. I got the opportunity to go into a home in England that bits of it were quite old. We sat in his living room and talked for a few minutes. His dog, Roy, was recovering from surgery on one of his paws. He showed me some of his art, and gave me a postcard size image of one of his drawings of Ash Park in East Prawle, which I looked up online later and happens to be a holiday cottage in the area. The drawing is of the cottage surrounded by lots of trees, plants, and colorful flowers, with some steps that lead up from the garden to the cottage.

Then he kindly drove me to a nice beach, Lannacombe Beach, for me to start the rest of my walk. It was all so surreal actually. The whole story I am writing now - Just when I got to the road earlier as I was about to look at a map, here was a nice man who didn't know me either but helped me out. I saw his home, I got a couple rides from him (I offered to pay for the rides, but he refused), and he was a published author and an artist. Like I said what a surreal story. Just as surreal as my golf course-dumping-rain-brolly story. I asked John to please autograph the postcard he gave me. He signed his name, and wrote, "Best Wishes."

He wished me well for the rest of my walk, and I thanked him for his kindness. And that is the story of John and his dog Roy, and there were no boring bits. And wow, I just looked him up online, and he has about thirty other books out there. He went to Harrow Art School, the Royal College of Art, he is an illustrator and writer. His writing genre is "children's books, history, humor." He is famous! And he was one of my guardian angels. And a story that if I had continued walking around Prawle Point earlier today, I would not have met this nice man.

John dropped me off at the sandy Lannacombe Beach, about two miles from my destination for the day. Just a few people were out on this sandy beach covered by a lot of seaweed. By now the sun was completely out, blue skies, and it was warm, but with a gentle breeze. I sat and ate one of my egg sandwiches, made sure my knee was alright for the rest of the walk, and started walking again. I looked back at the beach, with white waves rolling onto the beach from the turquoise-to-blue waters. Above the beach were beautiful dark and light green covered hillsides, brown rocks against the shoreline, and a large lone cottage just beyond the beach.

This stretch had some continuing beautiful rocky coastline after the beach, with all the similar beautiful colors. The terrain was all flat, and the sun was brilliantly out. At noon, I passed by a picturesque sandy and rocky beach, Great Mattiscombe Sand, and my knee seemed to be doing just fine. A single family was enjoying this beach. Looking back the rock formations from the coastline were just amazing today. Like many large boulders. The waters were so brilliant today as well. Even though some say that some of the best lighting for photos is early in the morning and late in the afternoon, I think the midday sun offers great lighting as well, enhancing all the colors of nature.

As I turned a small headland, I started to see my destination for the day – the Start Point Lighthouse. I had my first view of it and started taking picture after picture after picture of it for the next almost-mile, as I got closer and closer. The lighthouse was sitting out near the tip end of a headland, and with the brilliantly turquoise and blue seas surrounding it, the greenery of the headland, a few lone large rocks just beyond it in the distance in the seas, it was glorious to be walking towards the lighthouse. This small section did a bit of gentle climbing and had some rocks to walk over as I had these constant views of the lighthouse. The sun continued to make it warm. I arrived at the paved road that leads to the lighthouse in one direction, and to the car park and the continuation of the SWCP in the other direction. There was a mileage sign:

Public Footpath to Start Point 1/4 m
Coast Path Poole 168 m
Coast Path Minehead 462 m

I have walked the majority of 462 miles to be here at this moment, to see this lighthouse! In fact, I have walked 372 of those miles, well biked some of those, and the rest needed to be by car and taxi. Wow, 462 miles. Now that is surreal!

Since this was my destination for the day, I walked down to the lighthouse so that I could take the tour of it, which I had wanted to do and planned to do, which lasted nearly an hour. I had looked up the information last night to make sure of the tours, and they were to be given on the hour from 11am to 4pm. The lighthouse was a white tower, with a few white buildings around it, and some of that signatory greenish-turquoise trim under some windows. I was given lots of information during the tour. We started outside, and then climbed up each flight of the spiral staircase of the 92-foot tower, to eventually reach the top where the Fresnel lens was rotating around.

I guess that it was Henry VIII who started "Trinity House," the organization that oversees the lighthouses today, to keep his navy safe. It took forty men two years to build the Start Point Lighthouse, because with no access to the point at that time by land, as there was no road, they had to bring in all the supplies from the sea. The lighthouse was built in 1836. The completion of its automation was in 1993.

The most interesting fact for me that I learned: The children of the lighthouse keepers had to walk on the SWCP itself four and a half miles a day each way to get to school! That's nine miles of walking a day for the children! Amazing! The SWCP! The one I am walking. The one I have come 462 miles thus far on. Now that's brave and courageous. Tomorrow, I will walk the four and a half miles that the children did nearly 180 years ago. Now that is also surreal!

The lighthouse is still in use today. Two refurbished former Lighthouse Keeper cottages are available year-round as holiday cottages, another one to add to my list of "expensive-places-to-stay-someday-along-the-SWCP."

The area of Start Point is "one of the southernmost points on mainland Britain, sticking out more than a mile into the English Channel." "James Walker, Chief Engineer to Trinity House designed the tower in the castle-like style he built some of his other lights, topped by a glazed lantern containing a large Fresnel lens." Unfortunately, as with many places along the SWCP, several shipwrecks have happened here at Start Point. For example, in "the great blizzard of March 1891 claimed two ships within a very short time," all per today's booklet.

It is time for me to talk about the important organization of "The Corporation of Trinity House," the organization that maintains over 60 lighthouses around England, Wales, the Channel Islands and Gibraltar, including all the main lighthouses I have seen (or will still be seeing) along the SWCP! I picked up some information about

Trinity House in the Start Point Lighthouse including that, "Trinity House is a charity dedicated to safeguarding shipping and seafarers, providing education, support and welfare to the seafaring community with a statutory duty as a General Lighthouse Authority to deliver a reliable, efficient and cost-effective aids to navigation service for the benefit and safety of all mariners in all weathers." Furthermore, according to the Trinity House website, "The safety of shipping and the well-being of seafarers have been the prime concerns of Trinity House since being incorporated by Royal Charter in 1514." That's over 500 years ago! In addition, their "long-standing familiarity with the channels, hazards, currents and markings of our coastline also qualify us to inspect and audit almost 11,000 local aids to navigation." Wow!

I should also like to briefly mention the Fresnel lens, and lighthouses in general, things I have learned about over my years as a "pharologist." My knowledge of physics is limited, so here is a brief explanation that my Dad helped me with for the Fresnel lens: A lighthouse must be visible on the horizon at great distances, even many miles. For this purpose a typical lighthouse had two main components: A lamp that was a source of very bright light, and some kind of lens to aim the light along the surface of a body of water where ships go by. Around 1800, a French physicist, Augustin-Jean Fresnel, developed the Fresnel lens, which greatly improved what lighthouses previously were using for the purpose of safety at sea. Fresnel made his lens shaped like large barrel made of glass, with the lamp inside. The glass was made out of a series of glass rings, of various thicknesses and angles, each acting like a separate lens, and each aiming the light all around along the surface of the water that surrounded a lighthouse so the passing ships could see the light at great distances. Ingenious! Fresnel lenses for lighthouses came in various sizes, called "orders," to suit the needs of the area depending on the distance needed for the light to reach.

Back in the day of lighthouse keepers, the lamps were wicks fueled with oil or kerosene, much like a candle, which a lighthouse keeper was responsible for keeping burning at all hours of the night, in any kind of weather. Quite an important and responsible job back in the day, sometimes a dangerous career to have, but one that definitely intrigues me. However now-a-days the lamps are all automated using electricity and are taken care of by Trinity House in England and Wales, or the Coast Guard in the US, and the need for the lighthouse keeper of yesteryear is sadly no longer needed. The lights of lighthouses also have unique flashing patterns, known as a "light characteristic" or "character," which is a series of light flashes and patterns and colors, unique to a lighthouse in a particular area. This flashing pattern is a way for ships to identify their location. For example, "flashing white every ten seconds," or "alternating red and white flashes every fifteen seconds." GPS also helps to aid navigation these days as well. So there you have it, "Fresnel Lenses and Lighthouses 101."

Also note that when I describe the lighthouses maintained by Trinity House as having "greenish-turquoise trim," as most seem to have this color against the white buildings, I made up that color scheme as that is what it looks like to me. I tried to find out if they have a name for this particular color but could not find one.

I had originally arranged for a taxi to pick me up at 3:00 at the car park of the Start Point Lighthouse, but since I was earlier than I thought, I texted him to see if he could pick me up at 2:30, and when I was done with the tour, I walked up the road to the car park. The views from this road were amazing of a very curved long headland ahead covered with checkered green and brown farmland and several small villages along the way. Places I will be walking…

My taxi was at the car park when I arrived as it was about a half mile walk on the road and I took my time. As we chatted on our way back to Salcombe, it turned out that this taxi driver lives in the same town as Mr. Farman and knows him and his dog Roy. Apparently Roy likes to sit on the bar stools in the pub, and may even have a few sips of beer. Remember, dogs are allowed in pubs and restaurants in England. But I wondered what the drinking age is for dogs.

I was hungry when I got back so I had a late lunch. I made a "to do and to pack" list for Scott to email to him for his coming over here. I eventually had dinner.

DAY 62 STATS: 4 MILES AND 2 HOURS FOR FIRST PART OF MY DAY. MISSED 3.5 MILES WHICH WILL BE ADDED TO MY FUTURE WALK LIST. THEN 2 MILES AND AN HOUR FOR THE SECOND PART OF MY DAY. NO SIGNIFICANT EXTRA MILES. PURPLE SHOES. PUB IN EAST PRAWLE IS THE "PIG'S NOSE INN." I GUESS THERE IS A LOCAL SHOP THERE CALLED "PIGLET STORES."
Some information and quotes on the Start Point Lighthouse from worldwidelighthouses.com/Lighthouses/English-Lighthouses/Trinity-House-Owned/Start-Point.
Information on the important organization of The Corporation of Trinity House from trinityhouse.co.uk/about-us.

START POINT LIGHTHOUSE TO STOKE FLEMING – Saturday, 5 August 2017

"This is the end of our village. We shall have to go elsewhere." Hallsands villager, 27th January 1917, from a long plaque telling the story of the "ruined village" of Hallsands.

"I have all my memories here, but it's no good sitting down moping. It was the dockyard that took all our beach. It blew for four days and four nights. The sea was like the mountains. I prayed God that the wind would stop…Once I thought of moving to Dartmouth, but this is where I belong with my memories." Elizabeth Prettejohn, last resident of Hallsands village, also from the plaque.

    I ate a quick first breakfast at the café across from my "B" (not B&B) at 7:00 again. My prearranged taxi, the same man as yesterday, picked me up at 8:00 and drove me back to the car park of the Start Point Lighthouse. This nice man wished me sincere well wishes for the rest of my walk onto Poole. This lighthouse sitting at the end of a green shrubbery-filled headland remained in my back-looking view just about my entire day! And what a great day it was! Great weather! Great scenery! Lots of nice places to stop! I did nine miles! And my knee was good!

    I started walking and immediately began appreciating this beautiful sunny-blue-sky-warm-slight-breeze summer kind of day! The first view was like the one from the road down from the lighthouse yesterday - the curved long headland ahead covered with checkered green and brown farmland and several small villages along the way, some of which I was about to walk to. The path started out on a gentle fern-covered hillside overlooking the sun shimmering brightly on the blue seas with the lighthouse standing tall and proud just beyond. It was quiet out – just the sounds of the breeze ruffling the plants, a few lapping waves, and a mixture of chirping birds, cooing birds, and the cawing of seagulls. One sailboat on the water added a splash of white to the blue, and as I walked the sailboat became illuminated by the shimmering sun. It was all so calm and peaceful. I remembered that I was now walking on the path that the children of lighthouse keepers walked on to get to and from school.

    I had a gentle decent to into the "ruined village" of Hallsands, which was "Lost to the Sea 26th January 1917" in a storm, with a previous storm also causing damage in 1903, both because of "the removal of 650,000 tonnes of shingle from [the area]. This took away the natural sea defenses and the village of Hallsands was severely damaged by storms in 1903 and 1917," per the booklet. "At the turn of the 20th century there were about thirty houses, a shop, post office, the London Inn and over 160 people living in Hallsands. The village was almost abandoned after the storm of 1917. However, a lifelong resident of Hallsands, Elizabeth Prettejohn, remained in her home until she died in 1964." The story of Hallsands, and other interesting information, is carefully told on some plaques displayed in the area. Hallsands "grew as a fishing village during the 18th and 19th centuries, [however] it was a very hard life for the small community, which could not be sustained by fishing alone. Some fisherman farmed the plots on the steep slopes at the top of the cliff. Most village men had other trades – tailor, carpenter and blacksmith – to bring extra in income. In many ways the village was self sufficient."

    The white building in this town was apparently used by the lighthouse keepers. If they could not see the white house, it was too foggy, and therefore they needed to sound the fog horn back in the day. I learned that tidbit yesterday on the lighthouse tour. From this vantage point, I saw a house below, something to do with the Hallsands story, the single sailboat floating on the deep blue seas, and the green hillside with the lighthouse beyond.

    I found out this about smuggling from the plaques: "The contorted remote coast of South Devon made it a perfect location for smuggling, which goes back to when King Edward I put taxes on the export of wool in 1275, to fund his wars. As a result merchants or 'free traders' looked for beaches and ports where 'Collectors' or tax men were not in attendance. When standards of living were low, luxury items such as tobacco, tea, and spirits if bought legally, were out of people's reach. Smugglers preyed on this and provided the luxuries of life at a price that ordinary folk could afford, and made a hefty profit in the bargain. It was estimated that towards the end of the 18th century, about two thirds of the brandy drunk in this country had been smuggled in." Enter the Coast Guard. "The Coast Guard has its origins in the efforts made to combat smuggling throughout the 17th and 18th centuries." And I believe it is because of all this that the SWCP itself became a reality as I wrote in the introduction to this book, according to the SWCP Association website that I utilized in my planning, "The South West Coast was originally created by coastguards, patrolling the south west peninsula looking out for smugglers. They literally had to check in every inlet so their cliff top walk was well used and gives us the amazing Path we use today. The Path has also been used by fishermen looking for shoals of fish and checking sea conditions." I loved learning more about fishing, farming, smuggling, and even other trades. And the connections with the SWCP. And the storms of 1903 and 1917 reminded me once again of the power of the weather and the seas.

    I zigzagged through some homes and walked down a concrete staircase leading to the quiet Hallsands Beach with its small lapping waves. It was peaceful. I walked on the quite pebbly sandy beach for a few moments, taking photos of its few small rowboats and motorboats resting on the sand. Then I found a spot where no one would see me, and I changed into a short sleeve t-shirt, the first time in a quite a while that I have been able to wear short sleeves. Summer! I walked on a mostly flat grassy hillside. It continued to be quiet except for some gentle lapping waves, a few chirping birds, the crunch of my feet on the gravel, and the squeak of opening and closing a gate as I went through.

And then I ran into the first person from the SWCP Facebook Group who identified me by the lanyard! What fun! I had it hanging from the back of my rucksack in kind of a ball shape. As we were passing each other at first, we just said hello to each other. Next thing I knew, I heard a voice that said, "I recognize your lanyard." I turned around not expecting to hear that, and at first I thought of the little "lead" I had on my mobile phone in my pocket attached to my wrist as a lanyard, but then I quickly realized that he meant the SWCP lanyard! "Oh, yes," I exclaimed, and asked, "Who are you?" "Greg," he said. I shook his hand saying that he was the first person to identify me by the lanyard. I now actually recognized the face and name, and said, "Are you Greg Power?" (Last name has been changed). Yes, he is, and I for some reason shook his hand again. To me, it was like meeting an old friend. At least someone I had a common bond with…walking and a love for the SWCP!

We chatted for a few moments about his walk yesterday, and where he was going today. I don't think he was doing the whole path in one go, but I just asked anyway. He introduced me to his dog Scruffy who just had fun at a beach and would like to go back to the beach. I told Greg there was a very nice beach just ahead for him in about a mile. It was fun to have someone actually see my lanyard. Too bad we were going in opposite directions, otherwise I would have asked if we could walk together for a while.

I entered the next small village of Beesands, and walked between a row of homes and the beach. I took photos of boats and an old rusty anchor and the shimmering seas and the lighthouse beyond. The anchor picture was a hit on Facebook. I got a bit confused making my way out of Beesands. The path led inland, which didn't seem right, even though I found out soon that it was correct in order to avoid the beach section at high tide. Instead, I ended up making up my own route which worked anyway. I first walked on a flat gravel path that several people were on that led to the far end of the beach which connected Beesands to Torcross. When I arrived there I asked a woman, my guardian angel of the day who was walking four dogs, if I would be able to get to Torcross this way since I seemed to be off the SWCP. She explained to me that the inland path was correct because of the tides, but since I was at low tide now I could walk the pebble beach around the rocks jutting out in the water, and I would be alright, as the beach would be continuous around the rocks. I would see some steps going up on the other side that would lead back to the SWCP. I thanked her and continued walking on this beautiful sunny-blue-sky-warm-slight-breeze summer kind of day!

The pebbles of this beach were actually quite difficult to walk on, as they were not like hard sand. Occasionally I walked on some interesting flat rocks to help with the footing, some of which were almost black in color with white stripes of some other type of rock. I took a photo of my purple shoes against the black of the rocks and the tan of the pebbles and sand. Soon there was a concrete walkway, and then I spotted the steps. It was a steep climb up the steps, but voila, when I got to the top, there was a SWCP sign and a moment later I was in Torcross. From above I had a view of the very, very long stretch of beach, Slapton Sands, leading out to more farmland-covered hills in the distance. Closer in were a short row of various boats and kayaks, and a row of the buildings along the paved sidewalk of Torcross.

I stopped for a second breakfast at a little popular café, as the breakfast I ate earlier was smaller and I was hungry. I actually ordered "English-style" bacon and "American-style" pancakes, which along with some sweet maple syrup was quite tasty. Maybe I needed the meat-based protein, as my meals the past several months have been quite vegetarian. I sat for a short while enjoying my breakfast and the weather.

I started walking again through the paved sidewalk of Torcross that was paralleling the beach. I took a great photo of two boats on the sand, with some blue barrels of some sort which looked like they were holding fishing ropes and twine, a few round buoy balls, all sitting as the foreground to the deep blue waters, and the light blue sky with its white fluffy clouds. Beautiful.

The SWCP then cut over to other side of a long road, as I needed to walk about two miles along Slapton Sands. Slapton Sands seemed to be a strip of land that had the seas on one side, and Slapton Ley, a freshwater lake, on the other side. There was also a road paralleling along Slapton Sands. To get the big picture of where I was walking, the most inland section would be the lake, then some land next to the lake which was the SWCP, then the busy road (the A379), then the beach of Slapton Sands, then the seas, all paralleling each other. I started walking the land between the lake and the road for a bit, but this actual SWCP part was a bit below the level of the road and so I was not able to see the seas, nor be near them, and I did not feel like I wanted to be there. I thought it was interesting that I really wanted to be nearer to the comforting seas, with the waves and their good for me positive supply of negative ions!

I wondered if there was a place to walk on the other side of the road, but not exactly on the beach itself because that would be hard walking on the pebbles and sand for two miles. I decided to go across the road to check it out. I carefully crossed the road, looking every which way more than once, as I still needed to get used to the traffic patterns in this country, and sure enough there was a very wide, mostly grass-covered track in between the road and the beach. I walked on that instead, and I was closer to the seas, could see and hear the waves, with their good for me positive supply of negative ions, and I more thoroughly enjoyed all that. I figured I was just paralleling the SWCP at this point, and I much preferred the sea and sand side of the road.

I passed by a monument that stated, "This memorial was presented by the United States Army Authorities to the people of the South Hams who generously left their homes and their lands to provide a battle practice area for the successful assault in Normandy in June 1944. Their action resulted in the saving of many hundreds of lives and contributed no small measure to the success of the operation. The area included the villages of Blackawton,

Chllington, East Allington, Sherford, Slapton, Stokenham, Strete, and Torcross, together with many outlying farms and houses." The booklet for today also told me that inland from Torcross is "Widdicombe House which was once owned by Captain Cook. During WW2 it was the headquarters of General Eisenhower while the US servicemen were training for the D-Day landings in the area." This is because "Slapton Sands was chosen as it is similar to Utah Beach in Normandy. Notice was given to 3,000 local residents to leave within six weeks and take all their possessions with them. The Americans arrived in December 1943 with 30,000 troops and 16,000,000 tons of equipment and full scale rehearsals for D-Day got underway early in 1944. After the D-Day landings of June 1944, people were slowly allowed to return to their homes from October of that year." Historic and thought-provoking.

I arrived at Strete Gate, where I met up with a SWCP sign once again. It took almost an hour to walk the two miles of Slapton Sands. I stopped for a rest at a picnic bench to enjoy the beach and the seas a little while longer. I contemplated getting a cookie at the café stand there, but did not partake. The SWCP continued through some shrubbery with views of a beach below, probably Landcombe Sands, and views behind all the way back to the lighthouse. Then the SWCP went through some trees, with a zigzaggy good uphill climb and out onto the streets of Strete. I stopped once again for a brief respite to enjoy the view now overlooking the blue seas beyond.

The SWCP wound its way to a grassy hilltop. There were a few cows, but not close for concern. Seemed like I had not seen cows in a while. There was still a view of Start Point Lighthouse and the rolling hills behind, and the large beach at Blackpool Sands and the town of Stoke Fleming ahead. I walked down a somewhat steep grassy slope with a foot print path, meaning that instead of steps per se, these steps were in the shape of footprints. Then I had a climb up the opposite side of a steep grassy slope going up. This section created a valley, Landcombe Valley, and it looked like you could get down to the beach from the bottom of either grassy slope. There were even some beach tents on a little grassy spot just above the beach. There were a couple of random trees on these grassy slopes, and the whole small green-shaded section made for some scenic photos.

I crossed the street, and walked through one field, then up and over another field. I overlooked Blackpool Sands beach. I walked down another grassy slope, through some trees, and arrived at Blackpool Sands, where I stopped for some lunch. The beach was busy with many people enjoying this beautiful sunny-blue-sky-warm-slight-breeze summer kind of day.

I left the beach to walk the last half mile or so into Stoke Fleming, my destination for the day. It started off in a tree-lined trail paralleling a road, then a short sidewalk, then I had to cross the street, and walk on a country road that was all slightly uphill. I arrived at St. Peters Church and stayed for a little while. I took some photos of a few kneeling pillows which had embroidery of various farmhouses, houses, cottages, and homes that I am guessing were all located in the Stoke Fleming area. This church was about 700 years old, and "like other churches on the coast it was used as a navigation aid," per the booklet. In fact, the tower is about 82 feet tall and stands about 400 feet above sea level. The next day I could see why – the tower was very tall and could be seen above everything else, much like a lighthouse. This is similar to the Wembury Church, amongst others, and is included in my "lighthouse list."

I wound my way through the paved paths and roads of Stoke Fleming, following the SWCP most of the way, and arrived at my B&B just a short distance off the SWCP using the GPS on my mobile phone. No one was home, but they had given me instructions on letting myself in. I spent some time changing seats on our return flight at the end of August, so Scott and I could sit together, since he booked the same flight. I updated his information on the airline website. I researched his trains after landing in London in a few days, even though I did not book anything yet. Yesterday I think I also switched another B&B to a double room. Scott will be walking with me soon based on all these plans!

I went out to dinner at a fancy restaurant where the portion size was a bit small, but it was still good. And well, I just had to get dessert - "dark chocolate and peanut butter cheesecake with salted caramel." I had rarely, if ever, come across a dessert with my favorite combo - peanut butter and chocolate. Other than those small ones in Plymouth. It was actually more like a chocolate peanut butter mousse in a glass, topped with strawberries and raspberries. It was delicious. Great way to end my beautiful sunny-blue-sky-warm-slight-breeze summer kind of day.

DAY 63 STATS: 9 MILES. 6.25 HOURS WITH SEVERAL STOPS. NO EXTRA MILES. PURPLE SHOES. PUB IN TORCROSS IS "THE START BAY INN." PUB IN STOKE FLEMING IS THE "GREEN DRAGON."

STOKE FLEMING TO DARTMOUTH – Sunday, 6 August 2017

"Happy birthday to you, happy birthday to you, happy birthday, dear coooows, happy birthday to you." – Me singing to a herd of cows.

During a video call, Scott told me he did house prep, and booked a shuttle to the airport, amongst other things to get ready to come over here! After breakfast, I walked out the door and the day began on a quiet country paved road. I'm not sure exactly why the SWCP in this section was inland, but it was, and I would guess due to some previous landslip, or no good route closer to the seas. Although, I could see the seas from where I was up above. After about twenty minutes on the road, I turned right to head down towards the seas once again. A sign told me I had two and a half miles to the Dartmouth Castle from here.

It was flat walking along the edge of a tan colored wheat field heading towards the sea. When I got as close as the SWCP took me to the seas, I turned left along a wide grassy flat hilltop. There was a slight downhill, and I looked behind me. The views went all the way back to Start Point Lighthouse, Hallsands, Beesands, Torcross, Slapton Sands, Blackpool Sands, to the tall church in Stoke Fleming used as an aid to navigation. Basically, I saw the entire section I walked yesterday! As I headed towards Dartmouth and the River Dart, there were several sailboats in the water as I continued to walk on the wide grassy flat hilltop. A cloud moved away to reveal the warm sun. In fact, the day remained dry, mostly sunny, and warm again and I was grateful. Maybe for the rest of August it will be summer!

I turned left to continue on some flat grass, but headed straight for herd of cows right on the SWCP. It had been a while since I have had a close encounter with a herd of cows. "I'm an expert at this by now," I said to myself chuckling. "I know all the tricks," yet I still remained humble. I watched as three other people ahead of me got through them. When I got there, I still felt somewhat nervous as they really needed to move out of the way as they were standing right on the path and there wasn't much wiggle room. For some reason, I started singing the "Happy Birthday" song out loud to them, and clapping my hands for them to move aside. That worked! I was proud of myself! That was brave!

Then there was another right turn. More flat and quiet walking, with views of the shimmering water under the sun. The path wound its way around and slightly down a hillside. There was another herd of cows, but those were sitting nice and still and were a little ways off the path. A sign told me I had two miles to Dartmouth. I walked through a bit of shrubbery as I turned left inland away from the seas and started walking along the River Dart. A flat area through forest of trees made for some shade for a while, and I eventually zigzagged down to a quiet tiny cove with quiet tiny waves. The views were basically now at the mouth of the River Dart. The cove was called Sugary Cove, and just beyond it was a quaint little park called Sugary Green. A sign explained that it was a place "designated for quiet recreation, so please enjoy the wonderful views and make use of the picnic tables provided, exercise your dog responsibly, and take your litter home and respect the natural and peaceful surroundings."

While I appreciated the peaceful surroundings, I did not make use of the picnic tables, and I arrived at the Dartmouth Castle and St. Petrox Church with one mile left to the large town of Dartmouth, my destination for today. I stopped for a cheese scone with butter at the little café overlooking the castle and the river and seas beyond. I visited the church that dates from 1647, which was located right above the river, and I enjoyed taking photos of the church and the tombstones with various boats that were sailing or motoring by. Also right next to the church was the castle that dates from 1481, which I did not visit. Per the booklet, "The Castle Tea Room (I did not see this) was built in 1856 originally as a 'light' to act as a guide to shipping entering the harbour." Another type of lighthouse!

It was a paved sidewalk walking into Dartmouth. As I slowly made my way into the busy town, a woman selling baked goods out of her little home through her window caught my eye. Instead of something sweet to eat, and even though I just ate a scone, I bought a freshly made slice of flaky crust topped with fresh beetroot, a bit of goats cheese, pine nuts, onion, and arugula. The woman recognized that I didn't have a British accent, and I recognized she did not either. She was from Estonia but has lived in England for twenty years. She bakes and sells her food right from her home. A nice touch as I walked into Dartmouth enjoying my snack. Meeting this woman reminded me of the Baltic Sea circumnavigation travels I did that I mentioned back on the 12th of June, since one of the seven capital cities I visited during that trip, Tallinn, is in Estonia.

As I walked on, looking back I had views of the river as it entered from the seas (or does it empty into the seas). Lots of boats, many of them sailboats, floated in the river. On either side of the river were the two towns of Dartmouth and Kingswear with green covered hillsides spotted with homes and buildings. I slowly meandered around and looked into shops, one of which was an antique store. I wandered down to the harbour to make sure I knew where the ferry to Kingswear was that I would need to take tomorrow.

I visited St. Savior's Church, consecrated in 1372, and built near the river because "parishioners no longer wished to struggle up the hill to reach the parish church of St. Clement," about three-quarters of a mile away. Then I made my way to my B&B, stopping a few times along the river to take photos of the many, many various boats, and the colorful homes going up the hillside across the river. I didn't quite remember booking this B&B, but it was definitely a half mile or more from the harbour up a road, and it definitely counts as extra walking mileage. I should have booked a closer B&B. I am not sure why I booked one further away. Now I understood why St. Savior's Church was built.

I spent some time figuring out next few days of walking and/or not walking, and/or waiting for Scott to walk with, including arranging a taxi for my walk tomorrow. I also spent some time finishing yesterday's writing because I didn't finish that yesterday. I also emailed Luggage Transfers, LTD about two B&B changes, and adding a bag for Scott. At the same time, back home, Scott was packing and was texting me and asking lots of questions about what to bring!

DAY 64 STATS: 5 MILES. 2.75 HOURS. EXTRA MILE AND A HALF FOR WALKING TO B&B ORIGINALLY, THEN WALKING BACK AND FORTH TO B&B AGAIN FOR DINNER. PURPLE SHOES. PUBS IN DARTMOUTH ARE "DARTMOUTH ARMS," AND "THE CHERUB INN." Information St. Savior's Church from parishofdartmouth.co.uk/StSaviours.

REST DAY IN DARTMOUTH – Monday, 7 August 2017

"Nothing soothes the soul like a walk on the beach." - Unknown

Today was a regularly scheduled rest day in my preplanned itinerary. Originally I was thinking though that I could walk some of tomorrow's walk, but with the possibility of rain (which it never did), and with Scott arriving tomorrow (!), I chose not to walk today. Scott and I can do some of tomorrow's walk later in the day after he arrives, and most of the rest of it the day after, as that was a regularly scheduled rest day as well. Why two regularly scheduled rest days so close? Because someone told me that the eleven mile walk from Dartmouth/Kingswear to Brixham, you have to do it all in one go, as there are no places in between convenient to stop for much. Well, the "expert" that I am now knows that a taxi can take you just about anywhere there is a road or a car park. I have figured it out, but more on that when it happens. Back to today.

I also chose not to walk today so that I can stay in mobile reception range as much as possible all day to help Scott get ready, especially packing, to fly here! First though, he wanted me to create a moment-by-moment "To Do" list for him from leaving the house to arriving at the B&B in Brixham, where I will be meeting him. So I did that this morning and emailed it to him. I also helped check him in for his flight online, answered many questions, in and amongst figuring out the next couple day's walking schedule and having some "brecko." I really enjoy planning travels, so I was glad to take care of all this.

By mid-morning I wanted to venture out a bit so I was not in my room all day, and to well, walk around a bit. The only plan I could think of for the moment in order to find something to do was to take the ferry from Dartmouth across the River Dart to Kingswear and go visit the Kingswear Parish Church there. I walked the half mile down to the harbour, and took the couple minute ferry ride across River Dart. A lot of people got off the ferry with me and walked in the direction to something I couldn't figure out, a line for something, but I walked out onto the street. Somehow I figured out later that they were going on a steam train ride. Across the street from this train/boat station was a cute looking teddy bear shop, so I went in and looked. I asked the woman there how to get to the Kingswear Parish Church, and she told me to just walk up the little street. According to a brochure I picked up in this church, "There has been a church building on this site since around 1170. However, only the tower of the present church is of great age, the rest having been re-built in 1847."

I realized that with my not walking today, that yesterday then would have been my last day walking solo along the beaches and seas and hillsides and villages of the South West Coast Path. (Well, mostly solo.) Now I can share my experiences with Scott. I have had mostly amazing, and some challenging, experiences on my own, and have really accomplished quite a lot. To date, I have covered 477 miles of the SWCP! Of those I have missed 90 miles, although 27 of those miles I did the first year I walked the 100 miles with Scott, so I really only missed 63 miles. Of the net miles then, (477 less 90), I have walked/biked 387 miles! Of those miles 387 miles, I have walked 38.5 with other people, so that is a net of 348.5 miles I have walked/biked solo, alone, by myself, on my own in 66 days! Amazing! Brilliant! Now that's courageous and brave! Not to mention the approximate 50 extra miles I have also walked.

After my church visit in Kingswear, I then took a few moments to figure out what to do next. I investigated what this steam train ride was all about. There was a brochure in the train/boat station that explained all the "Steam Trains & Boat Trips," and all the possible combinations. I went back and forth between deciding to take a cruise up the River Dart or the Steam Train from Kingswear to Paignton and back to Kingswear. Finally, I decided on the train. A half hour up, a half hour back. I could sit and watch the scenery.

In the meantime, Scott and I were texting about what shoes he should bring. The train ride started at 12:10pm. Outside at first were views inland, but eventually the train went near the coast. I was even seeing some of what was to come walking in the next few days for both Scott and me. Some nice-looking beaches with rows of those beach huts, and of course the hillsides and the seas. Scott and I still were texting as he asked me more questions about packing as I rode the train.

In between the ride up and the ride back, I checked Facebook and noticed a post about promoting the "England Coast Path," and a Facebook group to join. Most of it still being created, and the whole route, a new National Trail around all of England's coast, is expected to be completed in 2020 by Natural England, and will be 2,795 miles! It includes the 630-mile SWCP. A couple other ladies that I know from the SWCP Facebook Group are already in the England Coast Path Group. I joined the group for fun! According to the National Trails website, when completed, the England Coast Path "will be the longest managed and waymarked coastal path in the world." Wow, now that would be something!

Doing that steam train ride was a bit relaxing actually. I kind of liked just sitting and looking out the window for over an hour (there was a few minutes in between going and coming back). Scott and I texted a lot, and I just sat. Instead of walking. I also visited the little railroad train museum located at the train/boat station in Kingswear when I got back from my steam train ride. I took the ferry back to Dartmouth, with a view across the River Dart of the very colorful homes and buildings across the water with the green hillside above. I had a light lunch, walked around for a few minutes, and figured out where I would eat dinner later.

I went back to my room to video call Scott and help him finish packing. He had most things prepared and laid out, but I helped him by going through the packing list, told him which bag to put it in, check-in or carry-on, and made sure he had all his "bits and bobs" and everything necessary. It took an hour, but we got it done. Thanks to video calling, I could see his clothes and everything else. He had about a half hour left to shower and do one last chore. Then at 9:10am his time, 5:10pm my time here in England the same day, he got on the shuttle to the airport!

I eventually ventured back down the half mile again to eat a very delicious dinner. While I was eating, Scott checked in at the airport, checked his luggage, went through security, and went to the gate. And as I was typing this day up after dinner, Scott waited at the gate, tried to not fall asleep...and boarded the plane. I got teary eyed.

DAY 65 STATS: NO MILES. NO HOURS. TWO EXTRA MILES FOR WALKING BACK AND FORTH TWICE DOWN TO HARBOUR. PURPLE SHOES, BUT I SHOULD HAVE WORN FLIP FLOPS. PUBS IN KINGSWEAR ARE "THE SHIP INN" AND "THE STEAM PACKET INN."
Information on England Coast Path from nationaltrail.co.uk/england-coast-path.

SCOTT ARRIVES, AND SHARKHAM POINT TO BRIXHAM – Tuesday, 8 August 2017

"Love is walking in the rain together." – Unknown

This was the post on the Facebook Group page from Greg Power about his walk the other day when we met in person because he recognized my lanyard: "Beesands to East Portlemouth my favorite bit of path so far made better by meeting Debby Jagerman Dungan." I responded, "Awww. Thank you! Too bad we weren't walking in the same direction as we could have walked together." He responded, "Shame. Nice to have met you nonetheless. Scruffy said woof." Nice to have made a connection through Facebook with someone that has a common love of walking the SWCP. Yes, even with all the challenges, I think I have fallen in love with the SWCP!

As I woke up this morning, Scott landed in London! He got through Passport Control, picked up his checked bag, and took a connector train to Paddington train station. He did all this while I got ready and had breakfast. Yeah! He is in England! As I walked to get the ferry again to Kingswear, Scott changed his train ticket and got an earlier and faster train to Paignton, even though he will need to change trains there. It has been fun writing what he is doing in parallel time with what I have been doing, even though we were in different time zones and thousands of miles away. Now we are in the same time zone and at the moment only a couple hundred miles away.

As I took the ferry to Kingswear (again), Scott was on the train. He texted me a photo of himself on the train. I walked to the bus station, just up the street from the ferry/train station in Kingswear and took the 9:33am bus to Brixham while Scott was riding on the train. I texted Scott a photo of the bus. I got to Brixham just after 10:00, where we were to meet and see each other after over two months. I meandered around the harbour while I waited. I went into a shop or two, got some food, and went into a few more shops to pass the time till Scott would arrive. I took photos of several lighthouse miniature statues and other artwork in some of the shops. There was some famous boat in the harbour, "A replica of Sir Francis Drake's ship the Golden Hind which was built for a television series in 1963. Sir Francis Drake was the first person to circumnavigate the globe in the Golden Hind from 1577 to 1580." In addition, "Brixham was once the home of one of the largest fishing fleets in England and it still retains a large fishing fleet today," per today's booklet. Then I went to the B&B, as we pre-arranged that I would be able to check in at 11:30. We had a very nice room with very nice view overlooking the harbour and the colorful town of Brixham. I was so glad I could finally share a nice room with Scott.

Today, I kept seeing advertising indicating that this area is the "English Riviera," from Brixham to Babbacombe, including the towns of Torquay and Paignton, where we will be walking in a few days along the SWCP. Sounds romantic, fancy, and glamorous. "First referred to as the 'English Riviera" in Victorian times, thanks to visitors comparing it favourably to the French Riviera [with] a 22 mile stretch of outstanding South Devon coastline consisting of seaside resorts, rocky coves, picturesque villages and warm weather." Well, I might need to talk to them about those last words…

As I checked into the B&B, Scott changed trains, then took a taxi and arrived at the B&B at 1:55! It felt like yesterday that I saw him, even though it had been over two months. It was great to see each other, and I showed him our very nice room. I wanted us to do a three and a half mile walk today, so first after saying, "Hello, it's nice to be together," and all that lovey-dovey stuff to each other, we got some lunch. I wanted Scott to also stay awake to adjust to this time zone and fend off jet lag, just as I did back in Minehead by walking to Bossington. We went back to the B&B to get ready for our walk, as Scott needed to get his rucksack together, and I called a taxi.

The taxi took us to the car park at Sharkham Point. We started walking at 3:15pm. "We" is the operative word. Quite a late start in the afternoon for me. We didn't quite know where the SWCP was, as the car park was a bit inland, but one sign pointed us in the right direction, and after a bit of walking towards the water, and even going on a little side path, Scott found the correct path. Ironically, a light rain shower passed by as well, so we put on the rain gear, but it did not bother me because I was with my husband! After all, "Love is walking in the rain together."

The terrain was all flat, with ferns and other shrubbery on the hillside. We had views behind of the rolling green hills and headlands I have not yet been to, as for now there were still eight miles of coast between Kingswear and Sharkham Point that we will cover some or all of tomorrow. I took a photo of a bench in the foreground of this scene, one without Scott, and one with Scott sitting on the bench, as well as on a few other benches as our walk progressed. Ahead of us was a view of St. Mary's Bay, a beach below with a few people on the beach, and the headland of Berry Head beyond, one of our destinations for the day. The waters were a muted shade of turquoise and blue due to the cloud coverage above. I wanted to keep taking notes on my dictation app of my walk and keep taking photos as usual even with Scott there.

There was a slight climb uphill as we were in some trees, and other than some very small ups and downs, today was all flat. There was the sound of small waves lapping below, the sight of one huge freighter ship in the distance, and a few large rocks in the seas. Occasionally we walked in some "dark tunnels of trees," with peeking views until we were out in the open. As we went through at least three kissing gates, Scott and I followed our tradition from the other two times we were in England together (the Cotswolds and our 100-mile SWCP walk last year) of kissing when going through a kissing gate. It was very nice to have his company, to have him to talk to, to walk with him, and to share with him all the beautiful scenery!

We reached the Berry Head National Nature Reserve, and once we reached the car park, the path was wide and paved towards the café and the Berry Head Lighthouse. A lighthouse together! We stopped in the café, and I introduced Scott to the snack of cheese scones and butter. He enjoyed the snack. (Not quite cream tea yet.) We walked the short distance to see the Berry Head Lighthouse. At only sixteen feet tall, the shortest lighthouse in Great Britain, it was very cute in my opinion! Built in 1906, with a light range of about nineteen miles, it stands on Berry Head, from which "about 800 square miles of sea are visible," as told to us by a circular directional plaque. It was also one of the highest lighthouses in Great Britain, 190 feet above sea level, and also painted that same white with the same greenish-turquoise color trim of Trinity House lighthouses. I took photos of Scott standing in front of the fence surrounding the lighthouse.

Then we started walking towards Brixham. We entered some trees and it started to rain. At first the trees sheltered us, but as we went on, we needed to put the rain gear back on, as we had taken the rain gear off when we stopped for our cheese scone. Five minutes after we put on the gear, the rain began to lighten up, and soon it was non-existent. It was a passing shower. We were walking on a paved road, and then a sidewalk next to the street and the outskirts of Brixham. With my husband there, I didn't mind the passing rain shower because "Love is walking in the rain together."

We took a staircase down to walk on a small rocky beach, Breakwater Beach. At first we didn't think it was part of the SWCP, as we must have missed seeing a sign pointing us down the steps, but it turned out to be the SWCP. In fact, there was a little circular gold marker etched in the ground on one of the steps with an image of the acorn and the words "South West Coast Path." First time I had ever seen a marker like this. It reminded me of the many, many scallop shells etched in the ground along the Camino de Santiago. Then we took a detour off the SWCP. We walked on the breakwater near the harbour of Brixham, the long concrete pier was just over a half mile each way. Therefore, I counted this as one mile extra round trip. It offered great views of the large harbour of Brixham with its many, many sailboats and fishing boats and other sea-worthy vessels. The pastel colored buildings of Brixham painted a backdrop for the boats. Looking ahead, was English Riviera headland beyond.

At the end of the breakwater was the Breakwater Lighthouse. The second lighthouse of the day. It made the for the subject of some nice photos with the headland beyond, a few boats as they were coming in for the evening from being out on the seas, the sky above showing clouds, with a shape of blue sky peeking through the clouds that really looked like the shape of a heart. Romantic. The short lighthouse was painted white, and with either age or the sea water, several areas, such as its door, were rusted. There were several people fishing off the edge of the breakwater. The walk up and down the breakwater took over a half hour, and it was 6:40pm when we started to walk the last half mile back to the main harbour of Brixham. Of course, photos of Scott were taken with the lighthouse.

The walk back to the harbour took another fifteen minutes. As we were deciding about where to eat dinner, we had a view of the boats, some rowboats, and mostly sailboats, in the harbour. There were some darker clouds in the background behind a long row of the white masts of the sailboats, when some sun peeked out from behind where I was standing, and lit up the boats in the foreground and highlighted their reflections in the water. It was a very beautiful dramatic scene for several photos.

Today I had a walk, and then dinner with my husband! I've rarely started and ended a walk so late in the day, other than my own first day from Minehead to Bossington, and the day I walked with Linda from Gorran Haven to Pentewan. I didn't mind in the least. The point was that today I still walked the SWCP, and that my husband and I walked it together. Even with a bit of rain.

My kind, thoughtful, caring husband also brought me vitamins to take, and some peanut butter and chocolate flavored protein powder to mix with water (I had two glasses full). He also brought back to me my electric toothbrush and a base that worked that we could share, so I threw away the regular toothbrush I was using. And he massaged my feet! First foot massage in 480.5 miles.

DAY 66 STATS: HUSBAND ARRIVES. 3.5 MILES. 3.25 HOURS, NOT INCLUDING THE BREAKWATER WALK, WHICH ADDS A HALF HOUR. EXTRA MILE AND A HALF – HALF MILE THIS MORNING FROM B&B IN DARTMOUTH TO HARBOUR, AND MILE FOR BREAKWATER WALK. PURPLE SHOES. PUBS IN BRIXHAM ARE "THE MARITIME INN," "THE BLUE ANCHOR," "THE RISING SUN," AND "THE CROWN AND ANCHOR." Information on the English Riviera from visitsouthdevon.co.uk/explore-south-devon/english-riviera.

Harbours, Boats, Villages, and Fishing on the South West Coast Path
Penberth Cove (from above) July 9
Penberth Cove (close up) July 9
Porthgwarra Cove July 9

Harbours, Boats, Villages, and Fishing on the South West Coast Path
Portloe Harbour July 18
Coverack Harbour July 14
Cadgwith Harbour July 13

Harbours, Boats, Villages, and Fishing on the South West Coast Path
Ilfracombe Harbour area June 10
Cawsand/Kingsand (view from B&B window) April 17
Mousehole Harbour July 10

SCABBACOMBE SANDS TO KINGSWEAR (A "BACKWARDS" WALK) – Wednesday, 9 August 2017

"Welcome. Come on in and see what we do. This NCI Lookout is manned entirely by volunteers – looking out for those at sea and walkers (like you) who are enjoying the coastal path. Most of the time we just watch, log and make sure everything is okay. But in the unlikely event that something goes wrong and somebody needs help – we're here." – Welcome sign for the National Coastwatch Institution of Froward Point.

Scott and I really enjoyed an excellent breakfast at this B&B in Brixham. Amanda cooked very well, and she and Nigel were very hospitable as well. I had an avocado, tomato, feta, poached egg on toast with some great sauce on top. Scott had the "Full English," with a slight variation of extra sausage, as he is not a vegetarian. We will have more of the same tomorrow as we are staying here two nights.

Our pre-arranged taxi picked us up to take us to our five mile "backwards" walk today, meaning that the seas would be on our left-hand side, rather than the "normal" right-hand side. I did this due to the lack of facilities along the way, such as places to eat or to make a phone call to arrange a pickup taxi. With my help looking at a map in the little booklet, we found the car park that would lead us to a Public Footpath we needed to walk to get to Scabbacombe Sands, the start of our walk on the SWCP for today. Our end would be Kingswear. From the car park, there was a sign pointing us down the footpath that said "Link to Coast Path." We first walked on a gravel track road, then down and across a grassy slope. It took about fifteen minutes to connect to the SWCP, so at least a half mile extra of walking today. When we arrived at the beach at Scabbacombe Sands, we spent a little time being there on the rocky beach together, and taking pictures and spending a little time. No one else was on this beach.

To connect the dots of where we are walking today, when I ended a couple days ago in Dartmouth, Kingswear was across the River Dart, to which I had already taken the ferry. Then technically it is an eleven mile walk between Kingswear and Brixham, where I met Scott. I had skipped these eleven miles originally to meet Scott. Then when Scott and I walked yesterday the three and a half miles, from Sharkham Point to Brixham, that really was the last three and a half miles of the eleven. Then the five-mile part today, if we did it in the "forwards" direction from Kingswear to Scabbacombe Sands, is the first five miles of the eleven-mile walk. That leaves two and a half miles in between from Scabbacombe Sands to Sharkham Point. We will not be walking that at all, and I will add that to my future walking list.

The first of many short steep uphill climbs today was out of the beach on a green grassy and tree-covered hillside. As we walked up this first steep hillside, there were cows fenced in on the inland side, and six horses right on the SWCP. As I have mentioned before Scott loves horses. This time instead of me taking pictures to show him, we stopped and spent a few moments here so he could enjoy the horses. The views from the top of this climb were of the beach below that we were just on, the green rolling hills that we would not be walking on, with muted turquoise waters due to the cloud cover. I took pictures of Scott sitting on a log on the beach earlier, with the horses and cows just then, and again sitting on various benches throughout today.

The path flattened out for a bit, and there were those quiet lapping waves below. A zigzag uphill, and it didn't feel like we have come that far in our first hour of walking, and that is typical of the pace Scott and I have together. I was averaging a mile each half hour when I was by myself. Based on our past walks together, Cotswolds and our previous 100-miles of the SWCP, together we average one mile per hour!

At one point, Scott asked me something about which direction we are headed. "Towards Minepoole?" he asked. I laughed! Now that I think about it, though, that is brilliant – combining Minehead and Poole!

More flat walking then another uphill, then flat walking to Pudcombe Cove. We stopped at the overlook down to the quaint cove for our first snack stop. I noticed an apple tree, and Scott noticed blackberry bushes. I wondered if these were planted by the D'Oyly Carte Family who built the Coleton Fishacre art deco house that was inland from here. It appeared that the house was built between 1922 and 1926, and possibly has gardens, and is a popular spot to visit. In fact, you can do circular walks from the inland area around using the SWCP, and so this area was busier with people than a few miles back. Sure enough when we started walking again, there were even more people, and one of the many inland footpaths leading to Coleton Fishacre. There were even hydrangea trees right on the SWCP as we started another uphill climb through a forest of trees.

As we walked on a flat section lined by ferns, we watched someone with a large mowing machine mowing the ferns, to which Scott and I were completely puzzled by seeing this, wondering why he was mowing the hillside of ferns. Could it be trail grooming for the SWCP, or could it be for cows or sheep or horses to be able to graze here? We just didn't know. It started to rain so we put on our rain gear. It was a light rain, almost at this point just a drizzle, but looking out at the skies ahead of us, it seemed like the rain would not be ending soon. Interestingly, I got a bit disappointed again with all the rain I keep having on my long walk, apparently in summer, but with Scott with me now, it made me feel better about walking in it. Out on the seas, some quite large rock islands, the Mew Stone Shooter Rock and Shag Stone, which are nesting sites for birds, were in our view for quite a while, with several boats sailing by or motoring by, and one fishing boat sitting there fishing.

Another small uphill, more flat walking, and we reached the beginning of Froward Point. Soon we turned a corner to the right and saw the Dart River meeting the seas. We saw the Dartmouth Castle and St. Petrox Church from across the river that I was at a couple days ago. It was still lightly raining. We reached an area that Scott liked, the WW2 Brownstone Battery "built in 1942 as part of Britain's coastal defense," with a miniature railway and other remnants from the war. And the National Coastwatch Institution Station of Froward Point was there as well. There were a lot of uphill concrete stairs to climb within this section. At this point we had two miles to Kingswear. The above quoted sign at the NCI Station of Froward Point continued, "We're proud of our lookout and the equipment we have to help us do our job. We enjoy showing it off and pointing out interesting marine or bird life to passing visitors. So if you're interested, feel free to come inside."

We started yet another uphill climb through a forest, and when we reached a bench, we stopped for another snack for the day. The rain had stopped. Then we had a steep downhill continuing in the forest. We reached Kingswear Castle, which you are not allowed to climb on for it is unstable, and a small beach below. And yet another uphill climb with lots of steps. By now our legs were really feeling the workout. It reminded me in some ways of a few other days with many ascents and descents, including the day long, long ago that I had seven, or what actually turned out to be eight, ascents and descents. Although that day, back in late June between Trebarwith Strand to Port Isaac, was steeper than today.

With three-quarters of a mile left to go, it was flat road walking the rest of the way to Kingswear. We reached the train/ferry area at 3:00pm. Since I knew exactly where the bus stop was since I was there yesterday taking a similar bus, we took a 3:33 bus back to Brixham, and a half hour later, we were quite hungry and found a good little sandwich café to eat in. One final stop for the day was the All Saints' Church because Scott likes to visit churches too, but it was closed, just as the skies turned blue with white fluffy clouds. Apparently "All Saints in Brixham is the seamen's church. Every year they hold a Festival of the Sea in which thanks are given for the sea's harvest and the safe return of all trawler men." That seems like it would be a nice festival to attend.

Back at the B&B, I tried to contact another B&B about changing to a double room. I have emailed them twice, with no response, and so I called this time and left a voice message. I researched other options in that area in case they don't have a double room.

With the sandwich at the café I felt that I had eaten enough for today, except for some peanut butter that I had bought back in Plymouth, and another few cups of the great protein powder that Scott brought me, so I stayed in the room to type, as I wanted to keep my writing going, while Scott went out and got himself some dinner. He said that there was a group of people singing by the harbour near the Golden Hind replica.

DAY 67 STATS: 5 MILES. 5 HOURS. .75 EXTRA MILES. PURPLE SHOES, EVEN IN THE LIGHT RAIN. MISSED 2.5 MILES. A FEW OTHER PUBS IN BRIXHAM ARE "QUEENS ARMS," "THE BELL INN," "BULLERS ARMS," AND "THE NEW QUAY INN." Information about All Saints' Church from britholidaytips.com/torquay-sightseeing/torquay-churches-chapels/brixham-all-saints-church.

BRIXHAM TO TORQUAY – Thursday, 10 August 2017

"Donuts. Ice Cream. Tea & Coffee. Fish & Chips. Free Admission. Games of skill. Giant prizes. Fun for all." – Signs on the Paignton Pier.

"Life is good at the beach." " Sandy toes and salty kisses, sun-kissed noses and sweet reminisces." "Our beach hut." - Signs on a few beach huts.

"Oh I do like to be…collecting shells, licking ice cream, brushing sand from my toes, reading a novel, slurping coffee from a flask, paddling at dusk, fishing for the bbq, relaxing…beside the seaside." – Another sign on a beach hut.

We woke up to blue skies, sunshine, and warmth! And another excellent breakfast from Amanda and Nigel. Scott again had the Full English, and I had the "Amanda's Light," of fresh baby leaf spinach and watercress egg flan topped with feta cheese and sun dried tomatoes. Both mornings they also had granolas and mueslis, fresh fruit of oranges, grapefruit, strawberries, peaches, various berries, bananas, and figs. Yogurt and other toppings were used to make bowls with all this.

Today I went super light in what I was carrying in my rucksack. In fact, I didn't use my rucksack at all. I used a much smaller bag that I had that was still similar to a rucksack, but was not really a rucksack, but still held a few items. Combined with the forecast of absolutely no rain, that there were food stops roughly every mile and a half or two today, and that Scott would kindly carry a full water bladder of three liters, I chose not to carry much. (I should have had Scott with me all along just to carry my items, wink wink.)

What I did carry was extra socks, a thin long sleeve shirt in case I wanted to cover my arms since I wore a short sleeve shirt, small tubes of sunscreen and lip salve, extra mobile phone battery charger, our passports, wallet, mobile phone, camera, flip flops, a small water bottle anyway, booklets, sunglasses, sunhat, and that's about it. I loved going that light, but I know I can't do that often. Rain gear, lots of water, extra food, and first aid kit should really be carried. Scott had the first aid kit, and the water.

Scott unfortunately seemed to have lost his baseball hat the first day of walking, possibly it falling when we stopped to put on rain gear on one of the two places that we stopped, so we went into a store in Brixham on our way to start today's walk, and he bought a "proper" British sun hat. Similar to the one I bought in St. Ives.

We walked along the harbour as it curved out of Brixham, with views of the Breakwater Lighthouse and the English Riviera beyond that we will be walking around. In the water were fishing boats, motorboats, sailboats, tour boats, rowboats, ferries, yachts, and kayaks. We reached the little beach of Fishcombe Cove to which the pavement we had been walking on ended. (Pavement will be a large part of today's walk.) Views of the blue waters and a few boats and the lighthouse and the English Riviera continued. Soon after this first cove, was another small Churston Cove with another small rocky beach.

We climbed out of this cove uphill, one of the very few uphills today, as today was mostly flat, into some trees. In fact, we were in this flat path through the trees for quite some time, about a half hour. There were no views except for the trees, but we did hear that steam train that I took the other day out of Kingswear. When we were out of the trees, we entered out onto Elberry Cove, another rocky beach which we walked on for a short distance. All three of these beaches/coves had people enjoying the warm day. We had continuing views of the English Riviera ahead.

We entered onto a wide grassy flat area out in the open fresh air. There were people playing with their dogs on the grass, there were kayakers in the water, and the air was warm. At the moment, it felt just perfect. Summer! Then we reached the first busy beach, Broadsands. There were rows of colorful beach huts that it seemed I have not seen in quite a while. I still love them, and will continue to consider which beach would be my ultimate location to have a beach hut. Perhaps somewhere along the English Riviera?

The first row of beach huts we walked by were painted light pastel colors of pink, tan, green, yellow, and blue, repeating. The next several rows of beach huts were white, with doors and trim painted in various solid colors of white, blue, turquoise, yellow, red, pink, orange, purple, or green, or various striped colors of blue and white, white and purple, blue and purple, green and white, or red and white. Most beach huts were numbered, and people also put little, mostly nautical, decorations above or on the doors such as art work of ducks, sailboats, lighthouses, beach huts, surf boards, seagulls, fish, starfish, flowers, and the sun. I took a photo of Scott in front of a white beach hut with a blue door and a yellow painted sun decoration, amongst several photos of the beach huts themselves. I thought the beach huts were cute, and as I got to peek inside a few as we walked by, I saw that people were storing food, their chairs, and other beach supplies. Kids and adults alike of all ages were enjoying beach activities on this perfect weather day on the sand and in the water. Scott and I got something to eat as I listened to the sounds of the beach waves and children playing. Yup, it seemed like summer!

As we walked by more beach huts on our way out of Broadsands, we started walking on some more pavement that went under the bridge of the steam train, and then turned right to a path that paralleled the train tracks. The mostly flat path was just inland from the tracks, and we could see the tracks as we looked towards the water. The other day when I was on the steam train, I actually wondered where the SWCP was since the train seemed to be so close to the coast and I could not see a path. Now I know.

Once again, the path turned to pavement as we approached the very, very, very busy beach of Goodrington Sands. A sea of colorful umbrellas, tents, and other types of shelter covered the sandy beach, with loads of people enjoying summer on the English Riviera. More colorful beach huts outlined one end of the beach, and the blue water and beach waves outlined the other end. The kids were playing with pails and shovels, circular inner tubes, balls, boogie boards, and people were eating. There were waterslides and amusement rides and arcades all for the kids to have fun. I think this has been the busiest beach I have seen my entire walk along the SWCP thus far.

We walked up an incline through some garden section to a bike trail and some grassy patches. The SWCP markers around this area had been on the ground, small round metallic engravings of the acorn and the words "South West Coast Path," similar to the one a couple days ago. I took photos of one of the engravings with my purple shoes, and with my purple shoes and Scott's boots. We walked on the grassy patches to avoid the pavement of the bike trail, and then needed to walk on a sidewalk through a neighborhood as we reached the small harbour of Paignton where the tide had completely gone out, and many boats were resting on the seaweed-covered sand, surrounded by the protective seawalls.

We took time for another food stop at a little house garden café. After our small tasty meals, I introduced something to Scott that he has never had before – the infamous cream tea! Although we skipped the tea part, I explained to him the difference. We are in Devon now, so cream on first, then jam to top. But we tried it the Cornish way too, so he could taste them both. He loved it either way! While he wanted another scone, we didn't and continued walking. Since we could, we had a nice romantic walk along the red sandy beach of Paignton Sands. Red sand! First time I have ever seen red sand! Well, as romantic as it could be with all the crowds of people. The Paignton Pier extended out in the middle of the long beach into the water and was filled with amusement rides and games for the kids, and I suppose for adults, too. Scott remarked that it felt like we were in a scene out of the 1950's. I agreed. Actually, the "traditional Victorian pier [was] built in the late 1870s!"

The red sand beach of Paignton transitioned to the red sand beach of Preston Sands and continuing beach huts. At the end of the beaches, we left the soft sand, and once again were on a paved bike trail, but we walked on the grass next to it to another garden area with patches of grass. The last mile and a half or so of our eight mile day was paralleling a very busy noisy road, and once again we walked on the pavement of a sidewalk. Although, when we could, we walked on a small rocky beach and another red sandy beach, as we approached Torquay. There was more pavement and it was busy with people as we walked along the harbour of Torquay where we arrived at the end of our scheduled walk. It was from Torquay's harbour that "from here over 23,000 American troops left for Utah Beach in Normandy in 1944."

Scott wanted to go into a "Mountain Warehouse" store in this town, a store for outdoor clothes, shoes, and supplies, as he was curious about their shoe selection. We needed to walk an extra half mile round trip to the store and back, to which within moments when we got there, Scott did not see any shoes he wanted to try on. We made our way up another road a short distance to our hotel-type B&B. I had to rebook this one as the original B&B I had for Torquay was only a single, and we needed the double. I chose one online that was somewhat close to the harbour.

We went out to a nice Indian dinner later on. Other than lots of pavement, and even with the crowds of people, the day was fantastic with the warm weather, and the company of my husband, sharing with him all the sights and sounds of the SWCP! And yes, more than one quote for the day above!

DAY 68 STATS: 8 MILES. 6 HOURS. EXTRA HALF MILE FOR STORE. PURPLE SHOES. PUBS IN PAIGNTON ARE "THE SPINNING WHEEL INN" AND "THE SHIP." PUBS IN TORQUAY ARE "THE DEVON ARMS" AND "THE HOLE IN THE WALL."

TORQUAY TO MAIDENCOMBE – Friday, 11 August 2017

"Life is short. Eat dessert first." – Jacques Torres (Or in our case, eat dessert twice...)

My husband Scott is my biggest guardian angel. I mentioned this one other time when he happened to text me just at the right moment near Crackington Haven back on 22 June, when I needed him most. I don't know how he knew I needed him at that moment, but somehow he knew. But he is more that. Now he has appeared in England on the SWCP with me at the perfect time. Being with him for the past few days has made me realize just how much I missed him and how I am enjoying his company of someone to walk with. He has also been so supportive of me over the years of our various stages of our relationship and in my travels, but also in this walk of mine on the SWCP. He supported me from my first mention that I wanted to walk the entire 630 miles, through all the planning I did, to my potentially being gone for nearly three months where he could have been home alone without me. I really appreciate his support and company. Thank you, Scott.

This morning, we were unfortunately awakened at 5:30am to the sounds of cackling seagulls. I have heard this several times before, and have managed to sleep through it and not been bothered by the sounds. But not today. Fortunately I did not do yesterday's writing, so I utilized my time early in the morning to do the writing while Scott fell back to sleep. I also got two more B&Bs confirmed that it would be alright to add a second person to the double room I had already booked. After breakfast, on our way to start today's walk, I bought a better knee brace. Ever since my knee started bothering me, and seeming swollen actually, a couple weeks ago, I have been wearing the neoprene-type sleeve knee wrap that I bought before I left for England, but it was a size large, and was sliding down my leg. I bought a similar one today in a small size, which worked much better. I just want to keep my knee from getting more swollen at this point so that I can complete the SWCP.

Scott and I started walking by finishing walking around the harbour of Torquay, up a road, next to a hotel, on a path, up some steps, on another path, near some homes, up some more steps, on a flat path, next to a wall, and next to more homes, or something like that. We reached a NCI Station at a grassy area, and Scott went in for a few moments. There were views of Berry Head from a few days ago behind us. Amazing how far we have come in only a few days. We wound our way down to Meadfoot Beach, and then there was some road walking. We walked down a large grassy area and more of a trail overlooking Thatcher Rock, a large rock-island just off shore in the seas, which for a few moments felt more like the SWCP as we were more in nature than on roads, but that ended soon, and we were back onto a road. After crossing the road and starting on a trail that paralleled the road, it started to rain. It was a light rain, but once again, even with Scott here I questioned out loud, why do I keep experiencing rain? It is August after all. Shouldn't it really be summer? I've had rain in all three of the months that I have been here. I originally picked the summer months on purpose guessing that I would have three months of good weather, but no. Ok, enough of saying that. It is England, after all, and the coast.

The flat path led through some trees, crossed a road to more flat path through some trees, which actually helped block the rain as we walked through this section. We were on what was called Bishop's Walk, to which there were no coastal views. We reached Anstey's Cove and continued through some more trees, out onto a grassy area with some muddled views in the light rain. We went on one more path through some more trees, and reached the restaurant at Cary Arms in Babbacombe. Even with the light rain, all the trees provided their own peacefulness and a different feel than being right near the seas or seeing the seas, as well as providing shelter from the rain.

We had lunch in Cary Arms. And dessert, for me a warm chocolate brownie topped with raspberry ice cream, and Scott had some chocolate ice cream. As we were eating, the light rain fortunately stopped for the rest of the day, although it remained cloudy. It was on the warm side today, so that was good. There was a flat walk near the harbour of Babbacombe, which had a short breakwater, lots of rocks on a beach, and no boats. We started heading towards some red colored cliffs, like the red we saw yesterday of the sand, and cliffs as well, and towards a beach, but not quite to the beach. We could see a large previous rock fall/landslip of the red rocks, which seemed quite close to an area with some beach huts and buildings. There was a Cliff Railway in Babbacombe, similar to the one I saw in Lynmouth/Lynton back on 8 June, about 478 miles ago. The SWCP led uphill about half way next to the railway, under the railway, and back down next to the railway on the other side. We had a glance back at Babbacombe, a few headlands back, and Thatcher Rock. There was more walking in trees, then some walking near some shrubbery offering no views till we got to Petitor Road. We had a few moments of sidewalk walking.

We were stopped by two people, possibly a mother and daughter, who told us of missing boxer dog who had been recently reported missing, but was seen in this area, and if we could please keep an eye out for the dog. Of course, Scott, the animal lover, who has helped catch lost dogs before, would definitely keep an eye out for the lost dog. I figured our chances of seeing this dog was quite low.

We walked on a red colored path since we were probably on that red colored cliff, through even more trees for today. The terrain was flat then a slight decent, then flat again. I think today has had the most forests of trees to walk through than any other day on the entire SWCP. We barely got any views of the water just beyond and below, but I knew the water was there, even though there were no sounds today at all of waves crashing. It has been a couple of very different days than the rest of the SWCP in my opinion, with the many beaches, the red colors, more people, the English Riviera, and the trees. I wonder if we were in the trees so much in this section because it may have been an inland route due to the previous rock fall/landslip we saw earlier.

In the mid-afternoon we reached a road leading down to Watcombe Beach. And guess what we see? The boxer dog! No kidding. Of all places, and of all people to see the dog, we do. Scott, the animal lover he is, just takes charge and does his very best to help rescue this dog. I gave Scott my SWCP lanyard because I had the idea that if Scott could get hold of the dog and it had a loop on its collar, the clasp of the lanyard could go through the loop, and the lanyard itself could act like a short lead/leash. Scott tried and tried his best to get the dog. He even tried to entice it with some beef jerky he carried as snacks in his rucksack. With some patience, unfortunately there was no luck.

I managed to take one photo of the dog, and Scott even got on the phone and tried to make several phone calls to tell them where we spotted the dog to see if someone could come get the dog. The two people before that stopped us earlier mentioned a certain organization that could possibly help. Scott got a hold of them on the phone, but then was told to call some kennel, who told him to call the county, who told him to call someone else…After nearly an hour and a quarter of doing his very best, Scott could not catch the dog, nor contact anyone that seemed to want to come out to get the dog. I will say that this situation is amongst the list of my "most surreal" experiences I have had on the SWCP. Including the fact that Scott happened to be with me during this encounter, and of course wanted to help out, as that is the kind of person he is. (We never did find out later if the dog was rescued or otherwise found his way home.)

We continued the last mile of our walk on more red colored trail up and down and flat and up and down and flat, or something like that, through some more trees and woods. Somewhere along this mile I experienced the second time of the entire walk that I slipped and fell. I think I stepped on a wet tree root on the ground, which as I know, can be slippery when wet, so I am not sure why I stepped on the root in the first place. Fortunately, I did not get hurt. I did not even hurt my right thigh like I did when I slipped that first day leaving the B&B in Minehead before I even set foot on the SWCP. I guess I realized that fortunately, my right thigh had no long-lasting repercussions.

We reached Maidencombe and The Thatched Tavern at 5:00. A very nice classy pub, which also had a B&B. If I had known that this pub had a B&B, I would have had us stay here tonight, but as it was, we would need to get a taxi back to Torquay.

We ate a nice dinner at The Thatched Tavern. And dessert. What, another dessert? Yes, my husband's fault this time. A warm caramel chocolate brownie topped with chocolate ice cream for me, and Scott had some chocolate ice cream. Sound familiar? We called for a taxi to take us back to Torquay and arrived back about 7:15. I barely took any pictures today. There was not much scenery in the trees, and not many views of the seas and the coast. Today was probably the least scenic day of the entire SWCP in my opinion, but then again, the trees did have their own peacefulness about them, and the possibility of rescuing a dog added to the day. And of course, walking and sharing the day with my biggest guardian angel, my husband Scott.

DAY 69 STATS: 8 MILES. 6 HOURS (NOT INCLUDING DOG TIME). NO EXTRA MILES. PURPLE SHOES. PUB IN BABBACOMBE IS "CARY ARMS." PUB IN MAIDENCOMBE IS "THE THATCHED TAVERN."

MAIDENCOMBE TO DAWLISH – Saturday, 12 August 2017

"Protect wildlife, plants and trees. Take your litter home. Respect other recreational users. Consider your personal safety. Consider the local community." – Part of The Countryside Code.

After breakfast, Scott and I took a taxi back to The Thatched Tavern in Maidencombe to start walking. The walk started on a gravel road, then on a flat path through some shrubbery. A small climb allowed us to see some views of the water. With the cloud coverage, the water looked gray today, and there was not much to see out there other than a couple of large boats, including one freighter with four orange balls of some sort way in the distance that we have been seeing ever since Brixham. To our left were some small green rolling hills, and the weather was warm and dry, even with the clouds.

We came across a sign telling us of "The Countryside Code," an important code that "aims to help everyone respect other people, protect the natural environment, and enjoy the outdoors" as defined by Natural England. The sign stated, "Welcome to Maidencombe. However you choose to spend your visit, follow these simple steps from the Countryside Code and you will help wildlife and farmers, as well as having a great day out." The codes from the sign were:

> Know where you are allowed to go.
> Keep to paths across farmland.
> Use gates and stiles to cross fences, hedges and walls.
> Leave gates as you find them.
> Do not interfere with livestock, machinery and crops.
> Keep dogs under control.
> Protect wildlife, plants and trees.
> Take your litter home.
> Respect other recreational users.
> Consider your personal safety.
> Consider the local community.

There were some small rolling ascents and descents in between the flat paths, and we reached the Labrador Bay RSPB Nature Reserve. We climbed a short, but steep, uphill. Looking back we could see the checkered farmland of the hillsides with various shades of light green and tan, outlined by rows of dark green trees. A sign told us of the possibility of seeing Dartmoor ponies and "Please do not approach or feed the Dartmoor ponies as they are naturally curious and may bite or hurt you. These ponies will be returned to Dartmoor and must remain wild. If the ponies approach you, please clap your hands and shoo them away." We didn't see any today, which Scott would have liked to see of course. I was thinking that I had seen Dartmoor ponies before, but those were Exmoor ponies. We were now near Dartmoor National Park a bit inland from the coast, instead of Exmoor National Park where I was back on my first days of the SWCP.

We had a gentle downhill followed by another short but steep uphill. The path was of that red rock color, with grasses, shrubs, and trees on either side. Occasionally we had views of the gray water through the shrubs. Another small downhill led us into some pretty woods covered with ivy, ferns, shrubs, and trees. We ate a snack in the woods. Then we climbed the biggest uphill for today on a wide grassy path up the slope of a rolling hillside, which was not that big of a climb compared to many others on the SWCP. There was a herd of cows at the top, but they were too busy eating or sitting there to be of any concern. Otherwise I might have needed to explain everything I learned about cows, including the rules about cows, to Scott.

There was one more downhill, a short but steep uphill and we emerged out onto a road. A sign told us we had one mile to go till Shaldon, where we were to get a ferry across to Teignmouth. From this area we had a view of the large town of Teignmouth, and a red sandy beach bordered by a great red colored cliff. A few people were on the beach. Also in our view was, uh oh, a golf course. We descended a long wide grassy slope. We crossed a small portion of the golf course at hole number 17 without incident. The last bit of walking before reaching Shaldon was somewhat flat and a slight incline down through some trees. We reached Shaldon, but before taking the ferry, we walked down the one small street, taking photos of some rowboats and sailboats lying on a beach, to see what shops and cafés were there. We walked about two and a quarter hours to this point of our first four and a half miles.

There weren't really any shops, but the one thing that caught our attention was a local "garage and bric-a-brac sale" in someone's yard. Out of curiosity, we went to take a look. We looked around for a bit, and then one painting caught my eye – it had a small lighthouse on top of a breakwater wall, with fishing boats and rowboats in the foreground, some water, and a green hillside on the other side. Two people were standing on the wall. First, I love lighthouses. Second, it looked like a scene out of this very South West Coast Path walk itself that I have been doing. Perhaps even someplace like St. Ives, on a much smaller scale. Or Mousehole. Or a combination of any of the little fishing villages and breakwater lights I have walked by in these past 500 or so miles. This painting was paired with a second painting of a scene of some sailboats and other boats entering the mouth of a river, flanked by green rolling hills on either side, also much like the entrances to Dartmouth or any of the other entrances to rivers that I have walked by in these past 500 or so miles on the SWCP. Or perhaps it was even the entrance to where we were, the Teign Estuary into the River Teign.

I was so enthralled with both paintings because of their similarity to the SWCP that I felt like I really wanted to purchase them. But how would we get these paintings home? They were in frames and had glass over them. I asked the man how much they were anyway, and he described that they were a birthday gift some years ago, probably costing £45 ($60) each, and he would sell the pair for £30/$40. He believed the watercolors were painted in the 1930's. I contemplated purchasing them again, but we left the bric-a-brac sale to go get something to eat instead.

We went to lunch in a nice little café in Shaldon. We both ordered a very nice fig, goat's cheese, and prosciutto salad. We topped that off with getting variations on the cream tea. Scott got a fruit scone with the jam and clotted cream toppings, and I got a tasty apple cinnamon cheese scone with butter. As we were eating, we contemplated how to take those paintings back. We also looked up on the internet to see if we could find any information on the artist, but could not find anything.

As we sat there, I realized that I really wanted those paintings as a nice symbolic memory of the SWCP since they reminded me so much of the places I have been, so we went back to see if we could figure it all out. First, we negotiated a bit and settled on a price of £25/$34 for both paintings. Then the five of us worked together to figure out how to take them home safely. There were three people there, Martin and Des, the two who were selling the paintings, a friend of theirs, and us. First, we removed the frames and the glass. Those items were too heavy and breakable. Then we sandwiched the two paintings together between the hard backings of them, and then all of that was wrapped in thick paper and then bubble wrap. Finally, we placed the paintings in a bag with handles. And voila, I had my memories! And we still had two and a half miles left to walk today.

At first I carried the bag hanging in my hand, but after we took the ferry across the River Teign from Shaldon to Teignmouth, I quickly realized that the paintings would fit in my rucksack, and would still hold a few of my items already in there. Scott took my rain gear to carry. And even the SWCP Facebook Group lanyard came in handy, since the rucksack wouldn't zip shut, the lanyard helped keep the paintings strapped on to my rucksack. So not only had the lanyard been recognized by one SWCP Facebook Group member, it also may have acted as a lead/leash if Scott caught that boxer dog, and now it was a strap to hold my paintings in my rucksack!

The short ferry across the River Teign was packed with people, a few of whom had just been drinking we are guessing were a bachelor party, but we made it across safely in only a few minutes, as I crossed my fingers said a prayer and looked for the life vests just in case. This ferry runs all year, with restricted service in the winter, all day, and even some evenings in the summer. I read somewhere, but not sure where now, that apparently this ferry has been operating here since the 13th century (well hopefully not that exact ferry as that would be quite old), and it has had a black and white pattern on it for the past 300 years (well hopefully it has been repainted).

From the walk earlier as we were approaching Shaldon, I saw from across the water some beach huts on a strip of sand in Teignmouth that looked really colorful, as well as the harbour and town of Teignmouth in the background. The beach huts were not the bright or pastel colors of what I have seen along some beaches, but these were all earth-tone colors of greens, reds, grays, blues, browns, even blacks. Some had yellow and white trim, or red and white trim. They had looked more "rustic" as far as beach huts go, than the holiday-looking ones. I really liked the looks of these. When we got to the other side of the River Teign, we walked around the beach huts on the strip of sand to photograph them, both by themselves and also with the many rowboats in front of them resting on the sandy beach. What I wondered was if these beach huts were used for fishing equipment storage as "many beach huts were former fisherman's huts," that I researched and wrote about back on 13 June. In any case, I really enjoyed this series of beach huts, and wondered if this would be my ultimate location to have a beach hut.

As we started walking a few feet, there was an RNLI Lifeboat Station for Scott to look up close at a lifeboat. He learned that some lifeboats are open and others have closed cockpits. As we walked just a few more feet there was a lighthouse! Built in 1845, it is a "grey limestone circular tower lighthouse with a traditional light currently operated by the local Port Authority, [and] is 37 feet high and the light is visible for six miles." There is a blueish-colored top to the lighthouse, with a weathervane on the top as well. "The entrance to Teignmouth Harbour has always been treacherous and ships experience difficulty in avoiding the Ness Rocks." "Because of its [small] size, [this lighthouse] has mistakenly been referred to in guides as a toy lighthouse. However it is not; it is a real navigation aid." Wow, it did certainly look like it was for display-purposes only, and I am glad I found out the lighthouse in Teignmouth is a true lighthouse.

Basically, it took us an hour from the time we boarded the ferry, figured out that the paintings would fit in my rucksack, to the walk and photograph the "rustic" beach huts, to the RNLI Lifeboat, to photograph this lighthouse, and we had only walked less than a quarter mile, maybe even just an eighth of a mile! Then we really started walking again. By now the sky was blue with white fluffy clouds.

We walked along the Promenade of Teignmouth, then along a seawall heading towards another one of those great red cliffs, till we reached a set of stairs that led down and under some railroad tracks that we had been paralleling. A few trains even passed by us real close on our left side as we walked. A red sandy beach was on our right side below the wall. I was a bit nervous about walking on this seawall because the set of stairs that would go under the railroad tracks at the end of the wall the booklet said they would only be passable at low tide, and I had not looked up the tide tables. I kept looking at the shoreline, and it did seem like low tide, but I really didn't know the situation ahead. We got there and it was definitely not high tide, so we were good. Otherwise it would have been at least a half mile walk back or more to take an alternate route.

I tried to do some research on the geology of the red cliffs in this area, and what I gather is they could be made from New Red Sandstone from the Permian Period of about 280 million years ago, give or take a few million years, but don't quote me on that. But if that is correct, then those red cliffs are old!

A short walk on one road and a right to a busy road and another right to another short road led to a path between some shrubbery. There was a small descent and a small ascent, and we were out onto another road, took another right, and then within a few minutes Scott said out loud, "Here is a B&B if you want to stay here," jokingly.

I said, "No, we have another mile to walk to our B&B." He then told me the name of this B&B anyway as I was not looking at the sign and getting ready to walk another mile, when it turned out that was our B&B. Well what do you know? I pondered why I picked this B&B due to its location, as while it is exactly on the SWCP, it was still a mile to the main part of Dawlish. But well, we were here, so we checked in.

After a little while, we ventured out a mile to dinner via the SWCP into Dawlish town center. The path went along a small road, then a short walk on a busy road, through a small grassy park, and out onto a zigzag path down to the harbour, with a few row boats lying on the sand and concrete by the small harbour wall. There were views of Dawlish and the red cliffs of the hillsides beyond. We got as far as the railroad station "along the sea front being one of the most noticeable features" of Dawlish.

We were quite hungry by now, and needed to use the internet on our phones to find someplace to eat. I recalled seeing a Nepalese and Indian restaurant in the information book at the B&B so we figured out where that was and ate a great meal there. The other nights in Torquay, we ate a great meal at an Indian and Bengali restaurant. While I don't mind eating alone as I mentioned, it was great to eat meals with Scott.

(By the way, fast forward…the two paintings I happily bought in Shaldon have been reframed with new glass and are hanging on our living room wall, along with several other paintings purchased on the SWCP, including the very tiny two inch by three inch little artistic print of St. Brannock's Church that I bought way back in Braunton on my tenth day on 13 June, nearly two months ago. The other two paintings on our wall I have not yet purchased on my walk...)

DAY 70 STATS: 8 MILES. 4 HOURS, NOT INCLUDING THE BIG LONG BREAK BETWEEN 12:30 AND 3:30 IN SHALDON FOR FOOD AND PURCHASING MY PAINTINGS. AN EXTRA MILE GETTING BACK TO B&B AFTER DINNER. PURPLE SHOES. PUB IN SHALDON IS "THE FERRY BOAT INN." PUBS IN DAWLISH ARE "THE SMUGGLERS INN," "THE TEIGNMOUTH INN," AND "THE RAILWAY INN." Information on lighthouse in Teignmouth from simplonpc.co.uk/LH_SW.

DAWLISH TO STARCROSS VIA TRAIN, STARCROSS/EXMOUTH TO BUDLEIGH SALTERTON – Sunday, 13 August 2017

"Do one thing every day that makes you happy." – Sign on a Beach Hut in Dawlish by the Harbour.

After breakfast, Scott and I walked to Dawlish, again, so that counts as an extra mile, to the train station. After doing some reading, it seemed that from Dawlish to Dawlish Warren, two miles, we would be walking on a concrete seawall. Then from Dawlish Warren to Starcross, another two miles, we would be walking near a busy road, sometimes once again on concrete. We decided to skip these sections entirely. The gentleman at the B&B told us the best way to get to Starcross then was by train. A short little commuter type train, so we did.

This time as we walked to Dawlish, we took a slightly different route descending to the tiny harbour of Dawlish and walking on a path that took us next to some beach huts and through the tiny harbour itself. In the blue skies and sunshine, the solid colors of green, orange, blue, yellow, green, orange, blue, yellow of the beach huts were quite pronounced, as well as the red of the sandstone cliffs. I guess there was no red sandstone in all of Cornwall, but it is here in South Devon. We walked along a short seawall, and as yesterday, we walked on a sidewalk near a short road. The harbour had a few rowboats up on the shore next to its short seawall, and a couple of old rusty winches with rope and cable that I am guessing were (or are) used to pull boats out of the water, but don't quote me on that.

The train left Dawlish at 10:19am and arrived nine minutes later at 10:28 in Starcross. We saw out the window what we missed, including some red sandstone cliffs, walking near the water of the Exe Estuary, as well as the towns of Dawlish Warren and Cockwood, with its harbour and many boats. Next step for today was to take a ferry across the Exe Estuary to Exmouth. Whether we walked or took the train, this would have been necessary either way. We had over a half hour to wait for the ferry, as the next one was scheduled to leave at 11:10. It actually left a few minutes later, with a bit of a longer ferry ride than all the others I have taken, arriving in Exmouth at 11:32. We talked to a nice couple on the ferry who live in Teignmouth and were just out for the day to take a little walk together. They can hop on a train at any time to do a little day outing. What a great place to live – anywhere along the SWCP – just take a short train or drive someplace, and have a walk near the coast any day of the year. Weather permitting.

Scott and I began to walk along the busy Esplanade of Exmouth, passing above a busy beach, seeing lots of activities for families with kids. Soon we realized that we could take our shoes and socks off and walk on the sandy beach, with our feet getting wet and cooling down in the water, aka paddling. It was a perfect warm sunny day, with the sounds of beach waves, and us getting our fill of our good-for-us-positive-negative-ions. Before I go on with our walking day, let me say that I just finished the third National Trail book, "Falmouth to Exmouth, 172 Miles of Dramatic Coves, Cliffs and Beaches from Cornwall to Devon." Wow! 515 miles done, and one more book to go!

Towards the end of walking and paddling on this long beach, we stopped for a snack of what we had in our rucksacks, including some leftover food from last night's dinner, having walked about a mile and a half or two miles since the ferry. We just sat in the sand, enjoying the beach and the seas and the warm day. Unfortunately, the noise of some jet skis in the water was in the background of our picnic on the beach.

After our picnic on the beach, we walked the short distance of the rest of the Esplanade to the end, zigzagged up a concrete path to the top of Orcombe Point. We were now officially "at the beginning of an incredible journey through time." We were welcomed by an informational sign to the "oldest part of The Jurassic Coast World Heritage Site." This place is a "geological walk through time, which spans the Triassic, Jurassic and Cretaceous periods...older than dinosaurs." "Look at the red cliffs and be transported back 250 million years to a windswept desert that is even older than the dinosaurs." How cool is that?! (Due to my lack of geology knowledge, I now don't know if my comment yesterday about the New Red Sandstone and the Permian Period is accurate or not. However, the booklet does tell me that, "The red cliffs are of mudstone and sandstone. The colour in the rocks is caused by iron deposits as lots of iron compounds are red/orange in colour.")

I picked up a brochure at some point about the Jurassic Coast, spanning 95 miles of the coast in the counties of East Devon and Dorset, from Exmouth, where we are now, to Studland Bay, basically near the end of the entire SWCP walk. In other words, we will be walking the Jurassic Coast for the duration of my SWCP walk! We will be seeing really, really old things like the red rocks and sea stacks of Ladram Bay, formed in the Triassic period between 250 and 230 million years ago. We could look for fossils on the beaches in Charmouth and Lyme Regis. The golden sandstone cliffs of West Bay were from 180 million years ago, part of the Jurassic Period. The white chalk sea stacks of Old Harry Rocks near Swanage, an 80 million year old area, part of the Cretaceous Period. And other areas in between. How cool is that?! I am looking forward to this ever-changing colorful old, very, very old, landscape.

On top of the very, very old red cliff of Orcombe Point was a "Geoneedle," a tall thin pyramidal structure, further explaining the history of this area, and a compass on the ground with a circle in the center and four arrows pointing north, south, east, and west. Written on a plaque explaining the Geoneedle I read, "The different rocks exposed in the cliffs between Exmouth in Devon and Studland in Dorset show us how the world changed between 250 and 65 million years ago. Desert and seas, evolution and extinction, were all recorded in layers of sandstone, clay and limestone. Today this is a World Heritage Site and it is known as the Jurassic Coast. The Geoneedle marks the western end of the Jurassic Coast and its design symbolizes how the Earth's history is revealed in the cliffs." Then it explains three important eras of time:

"Cretaceous 145 – 65 million years ago (Purbeck)...Crocodiles and turtles, dragonflies and dinosaurs lurk in lagoons and tramp across mudflats. Millions of years later the tiny skeletons of plankton gently drift to the seabed through crystal clear waters of a vast shallow sea."

"Jurassic 200 - 145 million years ago (West Dorset and Portland)...Giant marine reptiles hunt in tropical seas. Ammonites drift in the currents and pterosaurs soar overhead. On the seabed bones and shells, plants and insects are shrouded in clay, sandstone and limestone. The remains of living things are transformed into stone creating world famous fossils."

"Triassic 250 - 200 million years ago (East Devon)...Wind blows sand and dust across vast deserts, whilst shifting rivers carve channels through the dunes. After sea levels rise the desert becomes a sea."

How cool is that?! That length of time is just so mind-boggling to me. There you have it, "Geology 101."

Well, not quite. Here is more "Geology 101" from today's booklet: "Inset into one side of the "Geoneedle" are pieces of the different building stone found along the Jurassic Coast...Sandstone, White Lias, Blue Lias, Hamstone, Forest Marble, Portland Stone, Purbeck Marble, and Beer Stone." I believe this is going in order from Exmouth to Studland. And I kid you not when the booklet says, "Beer Stone."

From atop Orcombe Point, we had views of the red sandstone cliffs beyond. It was flat walking for the next mile to Sandy Bay. We arrived here ready for lunch at a café overlooking the busy beach below, and had some food. We started walking again about 45 minutes later. It was a very scenic walk going in between a caravan park filled with little mobile-type home after home after rows and rows of homes on our left, and a military firing range, which I found odd that it was right above a beach, on our right. Ok, not so scenic actually. However after that, we did get a view of the quite scenic red sandstone cliffs just beyond, with a red sandy beach below, where the sand of the beach gave a very cool looking red tint to the water. There were several large rocks on this beach from rocks that had fallen from the cliffs. One lone motorboat was in the water here.

As we were walking through the caravan park, two walkers were walking in the opposite direction. They were walking pretty fast, perhaps to catch a ferry or something, but I noticed something ironic - they looked like me and Scott. She was wearing long pants and a t-shirt, like me. He was wearing shorts and t-shirt, like Scott. They both had sun hats on, like us. I should have taken a picture of at least them, or all of us together, but they hurried by too fast. They must be our long-lost twins.

We also saw Budleigh Salterton in the near distance, our destination for the day. We walked up a very wide grassy slope, next to more rows and rows of caravan homes. That transitioned to walking on a flat path next to a brown wheat field. There was also a row of thistles on either side of the path, which when in bloom of purple must have been a colorful row of purple. Next was a gentle uphill slope through the wheat fields. It was quiet here. Then we walked through a kissing gate (and kissed), and just like that, the terrain changed. It was now a pebbly path lined with shrubbery. It was as if we transitioned from farmland to an area that felt more like a "hike" in just a few feet.

We walked next to a golf course, but not for long, and then continued quite some ways through some shrubbery and some trees. There was a very, very gentle down slope feeling, but it was so flat we almost could not tell. There were no views at this time. At least out to the seas. Above, we saw an ultralight single person motorized plane flying overhead. I wondered out loud to Scott, how long would it take someone to fly above the south west coast of England, following the same SWCP I am walking? I suppose it is just a math problem. I just need to know how fast, how many miles per hour those planes can fly. So I tried to do some quick research. I don't know if this is accurate, but let's say they fly at 40 miles per hour. Since the SWCP is 630 miles, then that would take nearly 16 hours! So a couple of days at the least, but depending on fuel and food stops, let's say someone could see the entire SWCP from above in four days. Hmmm....perhaps something to do at sometime way in the future.

Another flat wide grassy path, a short concrete path, and we arrived in Budleigh Salterton. The first thing I needed to do when we arrived at the very rocky beach here, with rocks the size of one's fist, was go look at the beach huts. Solid blues, browns, grays, peaches, pinks, rusts, all quite those earthy colors again. Also on this a very rocky beach were various rowboats, fishing supplies, and a couple of men selling their freshly caught fish. Their sign said, "Just out of the net! Fresh fish for sale on Budleigh Beach. Mackerel (proper ones), Plaice (med-small) bootifull, dover sole (only small left), pan fry plaice, skate wings (cut to order)." Made for some fun photos, and I just loved seeing local fishing life in action. I realized again that it had been a beautifully sunny warm day all day today.

We walked more of the rocky beach, seeing more rowboats, some flipped upside down, resting on the rocks. We started walking on the sidewalk above the beach since walking on the large rocks for a period of time was tough, and came across even more beach huts. I took photos of these from behind as we were walking on the sidewalk, with the rocky beach and the seas peeking through in between the huts. These were also solid in colors of blues, green, browns, reds, and yellows. About half way down the beach, we turned around and walked back towards a main street in town with shops and places to eat.

We wanted a snack, considering though that our B&B for tonight was not in Budleigh Salterton. I booked one in Sidmouth, seven miles ahead. I was originally thinking of us getting a taxi to take us to Sidmouth, but when we stopped in a tea shop to get a snack of scones and asked to use their phone, since we could not get mobile reception, and asked for a taxi recommendation, they told us it would be much, much cheaper to take the bus, to which the last one for the day would be leaving quite soon. We needed to skip the scones unfortunately in order to make the bus, and took the 45-minute bus ride at 4:45, which arrived in Sidmouth at 5:30pm.

When we were waiting at the bus stop, there was a woman there who goes back and forth to work between Sidmouth and Budleigh Salterton on this bus. She was a nurse in a home for people with Alzheimer's and Dementia. As she shared some of her work and other stories, and we shared about my/our walk, it felt like a scene out of Forest Gump. Where he tells his story to those waiting for the bus on a bench. Obviously, our stories are not quite at all like Forest Gump's. Nonetheless, at one point I thought to myself, "Life is Like a Box of Chocolates," but I did not say it out loud.

Once we got back to Sidmouth, since we were hungry, we found a place for dinner near the sea front. After dinner we took a look at the sea, since we will be walking from there tomorrow, and then walked a half mile inland to our B&B, which counts as extra mileage. Walking more than six miles today with my husband was the one thing I did today that made me happy.

DAY 71 STATS: 6 MILES WALKED. 4 HOURS 15 MINUTES, INCLUDING LONG LUNCH BREAK. EXTRA MILES: ONE MILE TO TRAIN STATION IN DAWLISH, AND HALF MILE TO B&B IN SIDMOUTH. MISSED MILES: 4 MILES BETWEEN DAWLISH TRAIN STATION AND STARCROSS TO BE ADDED TO THE FUTURE WALK LIST. PURPLE SHOES. PUBS IN EXMOUTH ARE "THE BEACH," "GROVE," AND "THE BATH HOUSE."

SIDMOUTH TO BUDLEIGH SALTERTON (A "BACKWARDS" WALK) – Monday, 14 August 2017

"Foxes, moles, rabbits, weasels, dormice, badgers, fallow deer, hares." From an informational sign in Ladram Bay entitled, "Some of our other residents!"

After today, I will have completed 5/6 of the SWCP, or 525 miles, with less than 105 miles and 1/6 to go! Time is going by so fast actually. As much as I had some challenges, I am really, really going to miss this when it is over and be sad. I have fallen in love with the SWCP and all the beauty around me. But I can plan other trips, perhaps even coming back to walk any miles I have missed. In addition, with over 7,500 photos, so far, all my book notes and a book to write, a couple of photography books to do, scrapbooks to put together, talking to people about my walk, etc., all that will keep this trip going inside of me for quite some time!

Today Scott and I had the option of taking the bus in the morning back to Budleigh Salterton and walk forwards to Sidmouth, or walk backwards from Sidmouth to Budleigh Salterton and take a similar bus as yesterday back to Sidmouth in the afternoon. Last night I could not decide which option would be best. There were some climbs on the Sidmouth side, whereas on the Budleigh Salterton side, it was to be flat. Do we want to climb earlier in the day or later in the day? Also the weather forecast, depending on which weather source I used, either called for a bit of rain early in the day and a bit later in the day with dry in between, or rain on and off all day.

Since I could not decide last night, I figured that I would sleep on it, and wake up in the morning knowing the answer. Yup, I did. We would walk "backwards," do the climbs first, and have a leisurely rest of the walk into Budleigh Salterton, no matter which forecast would be correct. We started walking after breakfast, needing to walk the extra half mile from the B&B to the seas. We stopped and looked briefly in a couple of shops on the way.

We reached the sea front in about twenty minute's time, and it had been lightly, very lightly, raining. It was so light it didn't bother me in the least, and I was really hoping that the first forecast would be correct. We started on the path called the Millennium Walk next to a rocky beach, then the Clifton Walkway under a wall of a red sandstone cliff. Apparently, there was a ladder called Jacobs Ladder to walk up, but we walked on a more level paved pathway that went gently up towards a grassy area which was above more red cliffs. Both options would lead to the same place.

The uphill on the grassy area was a gentle slope, looking back on Sidmouth and more red cliffs covered with greenery, followed by a bit of pavement, a short time on a road, then onto a trail under some trees. Here the climb was a bit steeper until we reached Peak Hill. Then, guess what, it stopped raining! In fact, a bit of sun peeked out from behind the clouds. It felt muggy and warm, and it was dry. Perhaps the first forecast was correct after all! Which would mean it would remain dry till about 3:00pm. Would we make it to Budleigh Salterton by then?

The path then flattened out to a wide grassy path overlooking fields of cows and sheep. We could hear the sheep's "baaaaaas." The fields were rolling green and brown hills of that checkered squared off farmland. Scott commented that it reminded him of the Cotswolds. I've never thought of that, but indeed it did. There was a gentle downhill, then the path flattened out. Behind us we saw a view of Sidmouth, but if we were walking forwards then this would be the view ahead. There were several kissing gates today, and that meant that Scott and I exchanged a kiss each time. At one point, we took a short break at a scenic bench overlooking Sidmouth and a long row of red cliffs covered with greenery. I took photos with Scott sitting on the bench.

There was a descent through some trees, and then it opened up again, and we were walking next to a corn field. I think that was the first corn field I had walked by the entire time on the SWCP. We had views of some caravan homes again, but more beautiful were the views of the green rolling hills, the blue water, the red of the cliffs, and a few large red rocks, somewhat covered with green plants, sticking up out of the water. These were the red sea stacks at Ladram Bay. According to the booklet, they are "Otter Sandstone formed in the Triassic Period about 230 million years ago. This kind of sandstone is one of the most important sources of rare Triassic fossils in the world. The rhyncosaurus was an early mammal like reptile about one to two meters long walking on four legs, and fossils have been found here. The stacks were formed by the erosion of sea caves which eventually became arches. When the arches collapsed the stacks were formed." No wonder my first impression of all this red, and the shapes and formations, was that this reminded me of the state of Utah, especially Arches National Park. If Utah met the seas, this is what it would look like, I thought. It was stunningly beautiful.

As we approached Ladram Bay we were greeted with the sounds of a symphony of seagulls, and by the warm sun. The path flattened out with another view of "Utah meets the seas." We entered Ladram Bay, and slowly walked around to take photos of the great views of the red sea stacks with Sidmouth in the background, and another area of the red sea stacks near a beach. There was a kid's playground, miniature golf (fortunately there was no heavy downpour at the moment) with dinosaur statues, and arcade games. We stopped for lunch but we needed to wait about 40 minutes to order, as we were a bit early for their lunch menu. We started walking again after we ate, and went down to the beach to get a closer look at one of the red sea stacks. The sea stack had birds on it, and small green plants growing from them. Kayakers were paddling around them.

The path continued on some grass in front of some more caravans. Continuing views back behind us were of the red sea stacks in the water and Sidmouth which were stunning. At the top of the grassy area we looked back once again for those views with a herd of cows directly below us, with Sidmouth and the red sea stacks and cliffs in the background. I think this area of all this red is one of the most beautiful scenes along the SWCP for me. The area after the Gribbin Daymark walking towards Fowey was another. But there are so many more beautiful scenes, I would need to list practically the entire SWCP!

The path was flat and was next to alternating crops. First the light brown of wheat, then some short green unknown plant, more light brown wheat, and more unknown green short plant. I took a close-up photo of this green plant to see if I could identify it somehow, but never did figure it out. It was very, very quiet, except for a few lightly lapping ripples below. I looked directly straight out to the horizon and all I saw was the seas, the English Channel, so France was out there somewhere. We then walked through some shrubbery which blocked our views. I had noticed in the last few days that some of the shrubbery was blackberry bushes, and I have even seen Scott eating a few.

We paused at an area called Brandy Head. An information board at the area told me "Brandy Head derives its name from the smuggling activities which were once rife all along the coast. Amongst the shipments of contraband were often kegs of brandy. The safest time to land the booty was at night, out of sight of the customs men. More recently however, the Brandy Head Observation Hut was used in World War 2 to test new aircraft-mounted cannon and gun sights. This unobtrusive and small building holds a fascinating history that helped shape the Royal Air Force's role in the Second World War."

We continued to walk on flat with more wheat on our right, and then had some views of Budleigh Salterton, our destination for the day, for the second time. There was now a slight breeze and a light cloud cover. I looked around for signs of rain clouds. Not yet, but it was only about 2:15, a bit early for the predicted 3:00 rain. More fields of corn were now on our right, and a row of trees ahead of us separated where we were from and Budleigh Salterton. For a few moments, I actually felt like listening to some music, so I asked Scott if he wanted to listen also, so we listened to about three or four songs together on my mobile since I had reception.

Turned out the row of trees ahead of us was on the Otter River Nature Reserve, and there was no short way across the deep river, so the SWCP led us inland about a half mile between the corn fields and the trees, then across the river, and back down the river about a half mile towards the seas and Budleigh Salterton. The side going back was a gravel path, with many people enjoying the wildlife and birds of the Nature Reserve. "The Otter Estuary is a saltmarsh estuary that meets a freshwater river and is the home for many varieties of plants and birds."

Just as we were done with walking through the Nature Reserve, at 2:45, fifteen minutes before the predicted time, it started to lightly rain. We put on just our rain jackets and rucksack covers, and I say that the BBC Weather forecast, the first one, was correct. The other one, which shall remain nameless, was not correct. It was dry in the middle of our walk, which was my preferred forecast anyway. We had about a third of a mile left till the place in Budleigh Salterton where we ended yesterday.

We walked the Marine Parade of Budleigh Salterton, including seeing more beach huts, still trying to figure out which beach would be my ultimate location to have a beach hut on. These were the earthy tone colors of browns, grays, blues, yellows, greens, peaches. As I took photos of the front of them standing on the rocky beach, some of the beach huts, like I also noticed yesterday, were boarded up where the doors would be, I suppose protecting the contents inside from the elements outside, but that is a guess on my part.

There was one person sitting on the rocky beach in a lounge chair, reading. The person had a very colorful brolly (umbrella) over them to protect them from the rain, in a rainbow of yellow, light green, medium green, dark green, light blue, and dark blue from my vantage point. I thought this was not only a serene and peaceful place for this single person to sit and read, but along with the blue color of one beach hut, some green grass, the beige of the rocks on the beach, the muddled blue of the water, and the cloudy sky, made for some picturesque photos, some of my favorite.

We continued walking down Marine Parade and behind the beach huts, some of which had paintings on them like a palm tree, and three sailboats sitting on a patch of sand surrounded by water. Nice art work. A bit further down Marine Parade were some light yellow painted beach huts which had in front of them an old red quintessential British telephone box. I took a photo of this as well, the red box, the yellow beach huts, green grass, rocks of the beach and similar water and skies of my umbrella photos. I liked the juxtaposition of this old red telephone box at the beach with the beach huts.

Historically, "Salterton was the home of fisherman and salters who panned salt in the large tidal estuary. As well as salt, there were three lime kilns…producing lime for farming and building…[And] 'Budleigh Babberton' in JK Rowling's 'Harry Potter' is named after Budleigh Salterton," all according to today's booklet.

Finally, some more rowboats resting on the rocky beach made for some final photos for today, and we arrived back to where we ended yesterday, and then decided to go to the scone place, The Cozy Teapot, where we couldn't get scones yesterday due to the timing of the bus. Today we had about an hour to wait till the bus. We each had a date and banana scone, Scott had a cheddar and tomato scone, and I had a cheddar cheese and olive scone. I decided that eating scones is one of my favorite things on this walk, especially when I can try different flavors. Of course, the classic cream tea scones with jam and clotted cream, or clotted cream and jam, is also a favorite!

We took the bus back to Sidmouth at 4:15. By now we knew this routine, and arrived at 4:50. We visited the St. Giles & St. Nicholas Parish Church briefly, originally dating to the Middle Ages and was reconstructed around 1860. I still say my usual prayers, even when Scott is with me in a church. We went back to the B&B after the church, which I need to count that extra half mile back to the B&B again. I was so full from scones and whatever else I ate today that for dinner I just ate a banana, and a few protein powder drinks, while Scott went out and got some Indian food for himself and for our lunch for tomorrow.

DAY 72 STATS: 7 MILES. 4 HOURS, NOT INCLUDING LUNCH BREAK. EXTRA MILE FOR BACK AND FORTH TO B&B. PURPLE SHOES. PUB IN SIDMOUTH IS "THE MARINE."

Beach Huts of the South West Coast Path
Saunton Sands June 13
Dawlish August 13
Three from between Brixham and Torquay August 10

Beach Huts of the South West Coast Path
Westward Ho! June 17
Beer August 16
Budleigh Salterton with Red Telephone Box August 14
Budleigh Salterton August 13

Beach Huts of the South West Coast Path
Teignmouth August 12
Three from Swanage August 28 and 29

SIDMOUTH TO BRANSCOMBE MOUTH – Tuesday, 15 August 2017

"South West Coast Path. The longest National Trail in the UK. 630 miles continuous coast path from Minehead (Somerset) to Poole (Dorset) via Lands End. 70% of the path is within Designated Heritage Coasts, areas of Outstanding Natural Beauty, or National Parks. 95 miles of World Heritage Site." An informational sign about the SWCP and local walks in the area leaving Sidmouth.

Today was a day of at least 900 steps and three climbs! Scott and I left the B&B in Sidmouth, and this time we did the extra half mile in ten minutes time. It was already a warm, blue sky, sunny, dry day! Leaving Sidmouth, after being near some red sandstone cliffs and a few rowboats, the start of today's walk included some road walking through a neighborhood to go around due to the original SWCP having fallen away some time ago. The sign leading us on this route said, "Coast Path Route. Follow Cliff Road for 200m. Turn left for 100m. Straight on for 130m. Turn right to return to cliff edge." We got back to the original path in fifteen minutes time, and saw views behind us of Sidmouth and beyond. Today we would walk in the "forwards" direction.

The first climb started out on long grassy slope, and looking back we could see Sidmouth, the green grassy and tree-covered hillsides, and the red sandstone cliffs and the red sea stacks in the water. Then we were on a trail in some trees with the first 95 steps of the day. However, on these uphill steps there was a slight path to the side of them at times, which I found easier to climb, rather than climbing the steps themselves. So even though today is a day of 900 steps, I did not technically step on them all. As we reached the top of Salcombe Hill, there was a small group of National Trust people doing some trail maintenance on some of the steps. I thanked them for their work!

There was a viewpoint labeling where we were looking at in just about all 360 degrees of views. We could see all the way back to where Scott and I started walking together the day after he arrived, Scabbacombe Head. The sign said that was 26.5 miles away, and Berry Head was 22 miles away. Straight out ahead in the seas 130 miles away is Brittany in Northern France, and 90 miles away both are Guernsey and Normandy in France. Looking ahead is Portland Bill which is 34 miles away, where we will be in several days' time. Great perspectives of where we have been, where we will be going, and France.

The terrain was now flat, and we had some beautiful views just ahead of the long thin Salcombe Mouth beach below with some rock fall at one end of the beach, green fields speckled with brown cows, and the red sandstone cliffs. Then there was a long descent down with 200 steps, to which about two-thirds of the way down, I again took the gentler grassy slope down the rest of the way. Easier on the knees, especially my right one. There were two large mushrooms on the grass, which reminded me of some discussion on the SWCP Facebook Group page a few days ago. There was a continuing gentle downhill on some more grass, and then there was some walking inland a bit to avoid some unstable cliffs. It was very quiet around today. There were no waves crashing. Just the sounds of some birds cooing.

It was time for the second climb, which started on a long grassy slope next to some cows. There was a zigzag uphill alternating between steps and trail, with a total of 148 steps, to the top of Higher Dunscombe Cliff. There were some great views behind us of the red sandstone cliffs, Sidmouth, and the green grassy hillside we recently climbed down. The lighter green grass was checkered and squared off by rows of darker green trees, and we could see the paths themselves of the SWCP cutting through the scenery. We had just walked by the cows we saw earlier without incident. The skies were a great deep blue with white fluffy clouds.

The terrain flattened out and we walked between shrubbery on our right and corn fields on our left. More corn fields! We needed to walk around a small field with three horses on it, to which Scott did his best to interact with them from a safe distance, and from above we could see the next beach below, Weston Mouth, which had a few people on it, which was even longer and thinner than Salcombe Mouth beach. Green covered cliffs were above this beach leading down to the beach, and from where we were standing, this vertical view of the beach, the green cliffs, and a few small headlands beyond was breathtaking. We then walked on a really great stretch of path, a flat wide grassy path sprinkled with yellow and other colorful small wildflowers. The views out towards France of the blue shimmering water were just stunning! The sun was out and it was warm and all was good with the world!

The second descent for today was through some trees then on a grassy slope, and about 150 steps down to Weston Mouth beach. It was noon when we arrived at this rocky beach. These rocks were this size of fists, golf balls, and smaller. My purple shoes posed for a photo with the rocky beach, the blue seas, and the blue and white sky. On this beach is "The Watch House, a former Coastguard lookout for 18th and 19th century smugglers." Scott and I sat for an hour on this beach, to eat the Indian food lunch that Scott bought last night, to just sit, and to enjoy the warm sun and the beauty around us!

Our third and final climb for the day started with 130 steps, then a grassy slope, and then alternated between steps and a side path, and an uphill path in some shrubbery of another 100 steps. We reached the top about twenty minutes after leaving the beach. Again, the views looking back were green and red and blue. The views to our right side were blue and blue and white – blue skies and blue waters and white clouds. I have decided that for today, blue is my favorite color! Especially on a day like today. I also realized that it seems like the waters these days have been more bluish in color than turquoise.

Then this thought popped into my head…time is going by fast on this trip. Over two and a half months already. Wow! Even though I've had some challenges, I have never wanted the time to pass by as quickly as it has.

Me and Scott and Benches and Scenery on the South West Coast Path
Scott arrives and sits on a bench between Sharkham Point and Brixham August 8
Me taking a photo with a bench between Sidmouth and Branscombe Mouth August 15 (photo credit: Scott Dungan)
Scott sitting on a bench between Sidmouth and Branscombe Mouth August 15

The path flattened out with fields on the left, and the continuing blue, blue, blue on the right. More views all the way back to Scabbacombe and Berry Head. Scott pointed out that there was a family of pigs in the brown dirt as we walked diagonal on grassy field to our left. It looked like a family with mama pig and several little piglets. We couldn't get very close to them, but could see them all running around, and could definitely tell the difference in size between mama and the piglets. Cute! A row of trees on the horizon inland next to a grassy area was where we walked next. We then arrived at another big wide flat grassy area where there were actually a couple of cars parked. We figured the people may have gone down to some beach below, or were out for a walk in the great weather. The views out on the horizon from here were amazingly blue, blue, blue, white, and with the sun shimmering on the blue. Cows and a bench for Scott to pose on for photos were in this area as well.

There was a bit more flat walking, and then with one mile left in our walking day, we walked on a dirt road in the shade of some trees. There was a side trail down to the church in Branscombe, but we decided to skip it for today because we were being picked up in Branscombe Mouth by our B&B gentleman, and I did not know how far it was exactly to the church. Inland we saw a view of the village of Branscombe, and then we emerged out in the open with a view from above of the thin long sandy Branscombe Mouth beach and some "white-colored" cliffs beyond, not red! In fact, "around here you will notice the colour of the cliffs changing from the red Triassic sandstone to yellow/white. The cliffs are of Upper Greensand and what we see is more yellow/brown than green, [a] result of chemical reaction between the oxygen in the air and the iron minerals (called glauconite) in the rocks themselves. This Greensand is about 100 million years old and is of the Cretaceous period of geological time," per today's booklet. Today's beaches seem to have been thin and long. Another bench from this view was a place for Scott to sit and smile for photos.

We had one final descent on some grass, then the last steps, the number of which is unknown, and finally a short steep grassy slope. We reached the café at Branscombe Mouth, and had a small snack. The B&B gentleman picked us up just before 4:00, close to our pre-arranged time of 4:00, and took us to Seaton where I booked the B&B for tonight. We had cream tea at the B&B, offered by the woman there. It had been great weather all day sunny blue warm!

We went out to dinner in Seaton at a burger place called Flipside. We needed to walk about a half mile down a street that paralleled the Esplanade of Seaton. They had meat for Scott and veggie for me. They also had an extensive beer list, and while we don't drink beer, it was entertaining to read about all the flavors of beer and the countries they came from practically worldwide.

Note that there are two "Seaton's" along the SWCP. One was in Cornwall near Downderry, and this one in Devon, about 143 miles apart from one another. In fact, when I was originally booking B&Bs, I had confused these two locations, and one of the B&B owners needed to explain to me that his B&B was nowhere near where I had told him I was walking from that day.

As we walked back to the B&B, we first strolled a half mile to the end of the Esplanade of Seaton before turning around to walk back to the B&B. It was getting darker out now as we did this, but there were still people out enjoying the evening, even a few kayakers still on the water.

By the way, I double checked the stats in the booklet for today's steps, and it seems to be 90, 200, 148, 150, 130, and 100, which is actually 818, but there were some steps that the booklet did not have a count for, and since I did not count the steps today, then 900 it is, according to the booklet.

DAY 73 STATS: 7 MILES. 5.5 HOURS. EXTRA HALF MILE FROM B&B TO START WALK. AND EXTRA HALF MILE TO DINNER, BUT HALF MILE FROM DINNER IS PART OF SWCP, SO REALLY TODAY IS 7.5 MILES. PURPLE SHOES. PUB IN SEATON (DEVON) IS "HOOK & PARROT."

BRANSCOMBE TO BEER TO SEATON (TO LYME REGIS) – Wednesday, 16 August 2017

"Every part, because the scenery changes with every mile, and each mile has something unique to offer!" – What I say to people when they ask me my favorite part of the SWCP.

"Blue skies and happy days." – A sign on a beach hut in Seaton.

I ate a breakfast with some good homemade granola and some porridge. Scott had the Full English. At 10:00 we got a ride back to Branscombe from the B&B gentleman, but instead of dropping us off at Branscombe Mouth beach where he picked us up yesterday, we asked if he could please drop us off at the church in Branscombe village itself, about a mile inland. Other than this "extra" mile from Branscombe village to the beach, we would only have four miles to walk today, and we would like to visit the church, the one we did not get to visit yesterday, as well as the village, as I researched it last night and it looked like there were quite a few things to see there.

Scott and I were dropped off at The Church of Saint Winifred, and we were glad we got dropped off at this church. In fact, we spent forty minutes at this very old church. I usually don't read tombstones, but right away I read one that happened to date back to 1667. That is 300 years exactly before I was born. Wow! Time is such a mind-boggling concept. There were even older tombstones at this church – 1606, 1585, and 1583. The church itself "is one of the oldest in Devon. It may be a thousand years old."

The next stop in this quaint little village of Branscombe was a house near the church that I saw in the little booklet called Combe Cottage, and described as "a delightful chocolate box picture and featured in puzzles." It was filled and decorated with colorful flowers. The front wall of the cottage, with its windows and doors, was surrounded by colorful flowers. Reds, oranges, yellows, pinks. One of the doors was marked "Longview Cottage," which in its doorway had many types of gardening tools and supplies leaning against the walls. Across the road was filled with colorful flowers, and there was even a garden filled with colorful flowers. We saw a sign that said, "Doreen's Garden. Welcome all friends!" Another sign told us that it was free of charge to visit the gardens, but a donation to the "Devon Air Ambulance, who have airlifted many residents and visitors, would be gratefully appreciated."

As we were just about to enter the garden, after making our donation, we met Doreen! A very nice elderly lady. We chatted for a few minutes with Doreen. One comment she made was that she likes all the colors of her flowers even if it is "out of fashion." I didn't think it was out of fashion at all, and commented how lovely it all was. Most flowers were Dahlias, although there were many other varieties of flowers as well. I should have asked her if she maintained this large garden and all its colorful flowers by herself. We wandered the garden which not only had flowers, but trees, shrubs, grass, small statues, a small stream at the bottom, benches, all nicely groomed and well taken care of. It was a peaceful little place situated just below the green grass and tree covered hillsides.

You could even see the church tower from her garden, and I took some great photos of the church tower in the background with the green hillsides surrounding, and all the colorful flowers in the foreground. Reds, oranges, yellows, pinks, purples, and the green leaves of the flowers. We spent twenty-five minutes in all at this puzzle-perfect place. I think I shall need to find the actual puzzle someday to complete and frame.

Our next stop in Branscombe village was The Forge, a blacksmith shop, "built around 1580 and believed to be the only working thatched forge left in the country, from more than 200 years of blacksmiths." Some pieces on display made of wrought iron were flowers, candlesticks, sculptures, fireplace accessories, door accessories, wine racks, and furniture. I asked the man there if he was "Andrew," the name on the business card. Andrew was the 83 year old father, a Master Blacksmith, who has pieces for sale in the shop. So does this man who was one of the sons, and also the brother, and a grandson of Andrew all have pieces for sale.

Our final stop in Branscombe village was at The Old Bakery, now a tea room and café, for some lunch, as we had spent quite a bit of time in this village. This place "dates back to the late 18th century. It is believed to have been the last working bakery to use traditional ovens fueled by wood." Scott ordered the Ploughman's Lunch, a British plate that I have seen many, many times, but never have ordered. It had salad, cucumber, tomato, pickled onion, chutney, apple, bread, butter, cheese, ham, and chicken. Quite the variety.

We chatted with the woman who worked there and told her of my walk along the SWCP. She commented, out of the blue, that I am "a brave lady," and that I must be "super fit." That word, brave, again! And yes, I suppose by now, I am quite fit, especially with all the ascents and descents I have done! I also remarked to her, as I do to anyone one when we talk about my walking the SWCP, that first I have not quite walked every mile, mostly due to weather, or sometimes out of choice. Second, if asked about the scenery and what my favorite part has been, I say, "Every part, because the scenery changes with every mile, and each mile has something unique to offer!"

Finally at about 12:30pm we started walking on the flat Public Footpath for the extra mile for today that led back to the beach where we would start back on the SWCP. This Public Footpath was in a scenic valley with some cows, and with views of the green hills surrounding us. We did a quick stop at the rocky beach at Branscombe Mouth for a few photos, including of a lone orange fishing boat, some rowboats, and several people enjoying the beach, including some people flying kites. From an information board from The National Trust at the beach, I read about lots of information: "Since the 17th century fishermen have found the sea at Branscombe to be very fruitful. Crabs, lobsters, and fish are in plentiful supply here. For centuries Branscombe villagers have been farming the clifftop fields and many are still used for livestock today. In recent years farmers have diversified, and now produce a range of goods from beer to cheese! Walking east from Branscombe is like walking through time as geology changes from Triassic red mudstone to Greensand and finally the distinctive Cretaceous white chalk cliffs." Information on fishing, farming, and geology!

We "officially" started walking the SWCP at 12:45pm. There was a very short grassy uphill climb, and then we could hear the crashing waves as we walked through a small caravan park. There was a choice of routes now, on top of East Cliff, or the Hooken Undercliff. Since the "official" SWCP goes on the Undercliff, we went that way. It was mostly a flat path which paralleled between the high cliffs above to our left, and a long beach with constant crashing waves below to our right. There were lots of shrubs and trees, but we did get views of both the cliffs and beach. I would alternate between taking photos of the cliffs on our left, and the long beach on our right with the seas beyond. It took almost an hour to walk the Hooken Undercliff section which was one mile of the two miles we had till we would get to the town of Beer. Yes, a town named Beer. The very last part of this Undercliff area was a steep climb up that actually scared me a bit because it was very close to the edge, one of the very, very few times I have felt this way on the entire SWCP about being so close to an edge. I needed to walk fast to get out of this small section as quickly as possible to make myself more comfortable. Note that the Hooken Undercliff is an "area of land that collapsed in March 1790." That is not a typo of 1970, the booklet said 1790.

Random Scenic Photos
Combe Cottage Colorful Flowers with The Church of Saint Winifred August 16
The Little Chapel on the Hill Ilfracombe June 10
Porthcurno area near Minack Theater July 9

Scott was taking his time on this steep climb, so I waited for him in an area I felt comfortable, and then together we reached a grassy area on top of the cliff with one mile to Beer. It was quite windy on top, and I wondered if we had done the East Cliff walk instead if that would have been windy as well. I would like to say that I am going to have a beer in Beer, but since I don't drink beer, I am not going to have a beer in Beer. Although, "Apart from quarrying, farming, fishing and smuggling, lace making was very important in Beer's history."

As we turned a corner at Beer Head, we were out of the wind already and on a flat grassy area. At first there was a view of Seaton and beyond, and then a view of both Beer and Seaton, with their beach huts visible. The cliffs near Beer were more of the white color, and then closer to Seaton, they were back to the red color. There was a little road, called Little Lane, and then Common Lane, leading into Beer.

We spent over an hour in Beer going up and down the main street, looking at a few shops, going into St. Michael's Church, which had an anchor decorated with pink and white flowers in front of it, and going down to the rocky beach. It was Regatta Week here in Beer, but this time I did not get to see any events going on like I did back in Charlestown, but there were a lot of people around, and many various types of flags decorated the main street. A banner told us "Regatta Day is always the 2nd Thursday after the 1st Monday in August." The first Monday in August was August 7, so the second Thursday after that would be August 17 tomorrow, so we were actually one day early for Regatta Day itself. I saw other signs that the actual Regatta Week started August 12, and the week would include, but not limited to, a rowing championship, kayak and canoe fun, lugger racing, sausage sizzle, regatta talk, junior fun disco, children's arts and crafts, circus skills workshop and demonstration, small boat angling competition, barrel rolling in the street, a coastguard display, bingo, and of course Afternoon Cream Tea. And on Regatta Day itself there would be the sailing races, children's fossil fun, the best decorated raft, the best decorated beach hut (I would have liked to have seen that), and finally a fireworks display.

We finally went down onto the rocky beach with its boats and beach huts and lounge chairs, for many photos. Mostly brown shades of beach huts, but some of other colors of blues and pinks and greens, where the beach huts were sitting underneath the white cliffs. The lounge chairs on the rocky beach were mostly red and white striped, with one blue and white striped one mixed in for color, and a few people were relaxing on them. I think they were for rent. Lots of fishing boats were on the beach as well, along with fishing supplies of buoys and ropes and nets and crab and lobster pots. Signs were around informing you of the several places to eat in Beer, serving anything from all day breakfasts to local crab sandwiches to fish and chips to cream teas. Fishing trips were available, including mackerel fishing, deep sea fishing, and pleasure trips. Self drive motorboats were for hire.

A "Wet Fish Shop" was selling all kinds of fish, subject to availability – plaice, lemon sole, dabs, brill, turbot, Dover sole, John dory, skate wings, cod, haddock, Pollock, whiting, hake, megrim, huss/rock, mussels, mackerel, sea bass, and scallops. Some fish were smoked – haddock and mackerel. Some fish were cooked – crabs, lobsters, prawns, cockles, whelks, shell on prawns, and crab meat. Fish cakes were made of smoked haddock with spring onion, or cod with pancetta. I wish I had noticed the fish cakes, as those sounded good. Once again, I just love experiencing and seeing all this local fishing life so important to the SWCP. Even though I have never heard of many of these types of fish.

We did a short climb out of the town to start the SWCP again, sat on a bench to enjoy the sunny warm day and look down upon the beach of Beer with all the boats and beach huts and lounge chairs and people, and the white cliffs covered with green grass and trees beyond before we walked on. The seas were blue and a bit turquoise, and the skies were blue with white fluffy clouds. We started walking again on a busy paved path to Seaton Hole. We needed to take the inland route through some busy roads in Seaton due to a previous landslip years ago, since the low tide route across a pebbly beach was not passable at this time. In fact, a sign told us, "Coast Path to Seaton. Please note the route to Seaton via the beach is not accessible at high tides. The road through to Seaton is permanently closed 200m ahead due to major cliff falls. To follow the inland alternative route turn left onto Old Beer Road."

The inland route went through a bit of trees on a path, and the rest was mostly sidewalk until we reached the paved path along the Esplanade of Seaton. After taking photos of a long row of beach huts, we were back in the spot in Seaton where we were yesterday having already done the last half mile continuing down the Esplanade to its end last night. This row of white beach huts with grey roofs, and solid front colors of various shades of yellow, turquoise, pink, red, blue, green, etc., some also having some alternating colors in stripes, was sitting under the red colored cliffs.

We took a double-decker touristy bus to Lyme Regis at 5:00 because that was where our B&B was for the night. The bus ironically went back to Beer first, so we got to see the town once again from the bus. We arrived in Lyme Regis at 5:30 and walked a few minutes to our B&B. We were greeted by a very nice woman and her seven year old daughter. As we asked where the places to eat dinner were, the seven year old kindly ran to get us a map, "The Lyme Regis Guide," and explained to us how to get from their home to a few restaurants. She really wanted to make sure we knew where we were going. I told her that I have a seven year old niece and showed her a picture. I asked her what grade she will be going into after their summer holiday, and she told me "level three." I guess that is the equivalent of second grade that my niece will be going into. The little girl was quite cute, friendly, and helpful.

Originally I had planned to walk all the way to Lyme Regis for today, but from Branscombe Mouth that would have been eleven miles. The last seven miles between Seaton and Lyme Regis were mostly through what is called The Undercliffs (different from the Hooken Undercliff we just did). The Undercliffs between Seaton and Lyme Regis is a National Nature Reserve, a Site of Special Scientific Interest, and is "probably the wildest and most unspoilt area of the entire Coast Path." There was only one way in, and one way out. It would take about three hours to go through, and I just did not feel like us doing this section today. Especially that it was nearly 4:30 when we arrived in Seaton. It would have been a very long day. Skipping this section also allowed us to take our time this morning exploring Branscombe, and this afternoon exploring Beer. I will add The Undercliffs between Seaton and Lyme Regis to my future-to-walk list.

The one thing we missed "walking" through by not walking The Undercliffs from Seaton to Lyme Regis, although we drove through it on the bus, was going from my third county of Devon into my fourth county of Dorset! Therefore, that is a total of four counties I have been in along the SWCP (Somerset, Devon, Cornwall, and Dorset), one county twice in the north and south (Devon), and one county in its entirety (Cornwall)! I will be in Dorset from now to the final day of walking.

Scott and I went out to dinner and had burgers again at a place in Lyme Regis. Meat for Scott, veggie for me. We briefly looked at the sea front of Lyme Regis, but it was windy and getting late, so we went back to the B&B. Our B&B was a half mile from the sea front, so that would be an extra mile for that today round trip. Of course, Scott posed for many photos throughout the day in all of the places we visited and walked, on this "blue skies and happy day."

DAY 74 STATS: 4 MILES. ABOUT 2.5 HOURS, NOT INCLUDING ALL THE TIME IN BRANSCOMBE OR BEER. EXTRA MILE FOR BRANSCOMBE TO BRANSCOMBE MOUTH. EXTRA MILE FOR DINNER TO/FROM B&B. PURPLE SHOES. MISSED SEVEN MILES SEATON TO LYME REGIS. PUB IN BRANSCOMBE IS "MASON ARMS." PUB IN BEER IS "BARREL O'BEER." Quotes about the Church of Saint Winifred, The Forge, and The Old Bakery are from a brochure I picked up in Branscombe called "Discover Branscombe Trail" written by The National Trust.

"REST DAY" IN LYME REGIS: LYME REGIS TO CHARMOUTH VIA A BEACH WALK, WALK LYME REGIS, AND SCOTT DOES LYME REGIS TO SEATON UNDERCLIFFS – Thursday, 17 August 2017

"Life's Just Better In Flip Flops." – On a beach hut in Lyme Regis.

The couple of the B&B in Lyme Regis, Ruth and Phil, along with their seven year old daughter, were very nice, and we chatted for a bit this morning at breakfast. Scott and I were trying to figure out how to manage the next nineteen miles of walking that I had scheduled for the 18th and 19th, and with a little advise from them, we figured it out. Therefore, a slight change of plans for our scheduled "rest day." Instead, we will walk on a beach from Lyme Regis to Charmouth. This will allow us to skip the three-mile "official inland" SWCP for this section tomorrow and replace it with this beach walk. As long as the tides are low, walking this stretch of beach is possible. Phil checked the tide tables for us, and it was low enough for us to complete the walk today safely. Otherwise, we would not do this. Phil said he has done this beach walk, which is Charmouth Beach, in forty minutes.

To start, Scott and I first needed to walk down to the sea from the B&B, an extra half mile. We started out walking on the seawall in Lyme Regis towards Charmouth. We went down some steps to get to the Lyme Regis end of the beach. I carefully assessed the tide situation again just to make sure. At this point, just to the other side of the seawall from where we descended it was already impossible if you wanted to keep going towards Lyme Regis, but it was free and clear to Charmouth for us. I also looked at how many other people were on the entire stretch of the beach, and there were lots of people all along the entire stretch. As we started out walking the first part, I continued to watch and monitor, but realized that we would be alright the entire walk.

This beach is known for their fossils…ammonites to be specific…from the Jurassic Period of 200 to 145 million years ago! Therefore, the "lots of people" I noticed on the beach a few moments ago were out on the beach looking intently for these fossils, some with chisels in hand. Ammonites are an extinct group of squid-like creatures shaped like a spiral. Without quite knowing what to look for exactly, we did see several of these spiral-shaped ammonite images just on some large boulders. Scott started to collect a few interesting looking rocks. Me, I started to collect small pieces of sea glass that I did not expect to find here…whites, browns, greens, blues! I found that looking for sea glass was quite peaceful, centering, and meditative for me.

The terrain on this beach walk varied, from little rocks and pebbles, to soft sand, to large boulders, to some strange mushy black stuff. I could not figure out what this mushy black stuff was, and I just wondered if it was tar. There were small cliffs to our left, and the beautiful seas shimmering in the sunlight to our right. We had the sound of the waves crashing on the beach the entire time. Towards the Charmouth side, the waves as they went back to the seas took rocks with them and created a great tumbling sound, the sound of rolling rocks. The skies were blue with white clouds, and it was relatively warm out. As we walked we had views of green rolling hills and headlands beyond, including Golden Cap, a hill we will be climbing tomorrow, the highest point on the south coast of England at 619 feet. Behind us was Lyme Regis.

We arrived at Charmouth a leisurely hour and a half later after we started walking. More than twice the time it took Phil. That just meant that Scott and I took our time and enjoyed the walk and the looking and collecting at a leisurely pace. It was a very nice beach walk, peaceful, centering, and meditative, including taking photos of the beach, the seas, and the fossils.

The Charmouth end of the beach was quite busy with people, including many more who were hammering away looking for the ammonite fossils. In fact, there was a fossil shop down near the beach, and I bet that was where one could get lots of information about the fossils, perhaps even being able to rent the chisels from the shop. I don't know for sure though, that is a guess. There were also some beach huts here in Charmouth. There was a row of all gray beach huts, another row of alternating all blue and all green beach huts, and a row of all light peach beach huts.

It was time for lunch so we walked a half mile inland to Charmouth and found a little café. After eating, we took a bus back to Lyme Regis and got back in the mid-afternoon. I wanted to walk part of the SWCP from where we started this morning backwards to where the long Undercliffs section would end in Lyme Regis. So we did this by walking down the Marine Parade walk towards the harbour of Lyme Regis and a bit beyond. It was super busy with people along the Marine Parade. There were some beach huts along the beach, these were white with alternating colors on the doors. There was a rocky beach with some people, and then an even more busy sandy section of beach with colorful brollys, sun shade tents, lounge chairs, and kids galore. There were some games and activities going on for the kids to enjoy. We found a shop selling gelato. Double chocolate and salted crunchy caramel. We sat by the harbour with its many sailboats to eat the gelato.

We walked to some beach huts along another stretch of beach, these were mostly white, with earth-tone colors for the doors. We finally walked to where the Lyme Regis Lawn Bowling Club was playing, the place where the SWCP emerges from the shrubbery, and where I wanted to get to today, about a half mile total of walking, at a leisurely pace again. I wore my purple shoes for this, but I easily could have worn my flip flops. I mean after all, life is just better in flip flops.

And then Scott made a last-minute decision to walk the Undercliffs section! Just like that. At the spur of the moment. That's my husband, for sure. Or at least walk part of it, turning around at some point, but which to make a long story short, turned out to be all of it! At this late in the afternoon, I did not have the desire to walk the section today, and I wanted the rest of the day as a "rest day." I will save this Undercliffs section for a future walk. The Undercliffs "covers an area of about 800 acres and is probably the wildest and most unspoilt area of the entire Coast Path. Some say it is the nearest thing you will find to a rain forest in Britain." The Undercliffs is now a National Nature Reserve and was caused by landslips starting back to 1765, and also 1823, 1839 (the Great Slip), and 1840. A sign tells you as you enter, "Please note that it takes approximately three-and-a-half to four hours to walk. The terrain can be difficult and walking arduous. There is no permitted access to the sea or inland along this stretch of the path." I remember though that Sasha said in her book that it took her two hours and ten minutes to walk this section, or at least the main part of it. Anyway, Scott grabbed a fish fillet meal to nourish himself for the walk, we kissed, and off I went to leisurely walk around Lyme Regis, while Scott went on a "leisurely" seven mile walk!

I walked in a park up a slight hillside where I had views above down to the busy beaches and harbour of Lyme Regis below. I heard a little live music of blues rock on the Marine Parade. I went into a few shops. I bought Scott an old little horse book as an anniversary present, as our fourth wedding anniversary is tomorrow! I went back to the B&B, caught up on writing, and did a few other miscellaneous things.

In the meantime, Scott texted me when he could, depending on any mobile reception that he could, or mostly could not, get. After about an hour and a half since I hadn't heard from him, I figured that he was going all the way to Seaton. I did eventually hear from him and sure enough he walked all the way to the burger place we ate at the other day! It took him three hours and twenty minutes to do the seven miles including breaks, side trails (which he shouldn't have done), and the seven miles included a bit before and after the official Undercliffs section. He showed me his pictures. His mobile phone battery was down to a mere 5% when he got back via taxi after eating a meat burger. I should have given him my extra mobile phone battery to take.

I decided to have Scott write a bit about his Undercliffs experience. Here is most of what he wrote: "It was covered like a canopy. Like a jungle with birds up high in the dense trees, and their unfamiliar calls. At one point I heard noises and crackling and rustling sounds in the surrounding dense fauna. Three deer! Mud. Mud. And watery trail from recent rains. Steps leading up and down with washed out sections. It was easier to step on the rungs so as to not get my feet into the wet muddy gaps. I felt anxious at times at how long it would take given my late start and my not being familiar with the trail and some confusion between the park boundary and Seaton towards the end. A couple times I decided to explore some small side trails. Not the wisest of choices, overgrown and very brushy, and quickly went back to the main trail, although I took videos.

The terrain generally descended, although there were other ups and downs occasionally. Soon I passed a second sign that gave me a description about the Undercliffs. I stopped off at what was an Undercliffs version of a viewpoint, which was a view of a patch of water, but mostly sky because of the dense foliage. The leaves of the trees above created a canopy. One other person walked up behind me, and we chatted briefly, and she went off in the opposite direction.

As I continued on, at times when the path opened up, it was beautiful. It would open up to views of the coast. Soon I came to the halfway point of the Undercliffs identified by a large sign at a bridge. After I short break, I continued on.

I was running out of cell phone battery to call a taxi when I arrived in Seaton. And to text my wife. When I arrived at the same burger place we ate at the other day, after eating, the burger place helped me call a taxi to take me back to the B&B where my wife was waiting with cash to pay the taxi driver. I had missed the last bus." That was Scott's Undercliffs experience!

At some point, I went out myself to get some dinner, a veggie burger, and then later met Scott outside the B&B as he arrived by taxi so I could pay the taxi driver, as he was too late to catch any buses, and I had the cash. I felt like I did a lot on my "rest day." And Scott did, too! I'd like to add to my future-walk list not only the Undercliffs, but also to do some ammonite fossil hunting!

DAY 75 STATS: BEACH WALK: 3 MILES. 1.5 HOURS. ANOTHER HALF MILE ON MARINE PARADE, CASUAL SLOW WALKING. EXTRA TWO AND A HALF MILES: BACK AND FORTH FROM B&B TWICE, AND EXTRA HALF MILE INTO CHARMOUTH TOWN. PURPLE SHOES. PUBS IN LYME REGIS ARE "COBB ARMS," "THE ROYAL STANDARD," "SHIP INN," AND "THE PILOT BOAT INN." PUBS IN CHARMOUTH ARE "THE GEORGE" AND "THE ROYAL OAK."

LYME REGIS TO STONEBARROW VIA TAXI, THEN WALK STONEBARROW TO WEST BAY (OUR FOUR YEAR ANNIVERSARY) – Friday, 18 August 2017

"The best things in life are the places we've been, the people we love, and the memories we make along the way." - Unknown

I gave Scott the old horse book as my anniversary gift I bought yesterday to him this morning. He was appreciative. We said our thank yous and goodbyes to the nice couple, Ruth and Phil, but their daughter was not available unfortunately. She was reading. Ruth says she enjoys reading more than television. Good for her! This was the Charnwood Guest House, and I mention it for the great hospitality by the family. Since we did the beach walk yesterday from Lyme Regis to Charmouth, we took a taxi to Stonebarrow, which was actually an extra mile and a half beyond Charmouth. We skipped this portion because it was inland walking, all on a road. Instead, we saw the road from the windows of the taxi.

We walked out to the top of Stonebarrow from the car park where the taxi dropped us off and wandered around the top for about ten minutes looking at the views of where we have come from, and views ahead of where we are going, the next hill called Golden Cap, and beyond. We started walking the SWCP, for our official four year wedding anniversary walk, which started down some steps and down a gentle grassy slope before it flattened out on a wide grassy path. If I had still been walking the SWCP on my own, we would have celebrated our anniversary together when I returned home later this month. This way, we could celebrate together today. The skies were blue (for now), and the blue water shimmered in the sun. There were sounds of small waves crashing below. Lots of purple heather or some plant colored the greenery we were walking through.

There were a few small rolling ups and downs in between the flat through several grassy fields. The views ahead were of that checkered farmland, one old lone building, and Golden Cap. Soon we had one mile to go of the two miles to Golden Cap from Stonebarrow. We needed to walk across a field with some cows, including mamas and babies, but they were fortunately easy to walk around. I remembered all the rules I learned just in case.

But then…another herd of cows, right on the SWCP, right in our way, right on our four year wedding anniversary walk, as we started to climb Golden Cap. There was no great easy way around them, especially not on the uphill side as that was way too close to the edge of a cliff. Downhill would have been in the wrong direction and through lots of shrubbery and trees. There were a lot of cows. I repeat, a lot of cows. Mamas and babies, too. I quickly told Scott all the rules I could recall at the moment as my heart was pounding. Do not walk between a mama and her babies. Do not look at them in the eyes. Do not run. Stay calm. Do not walk straight towards them. Do not walk in such a way that will separate one cow from the rest of the herd. Talk to them by saying Mooooooooove or sing Happy Birthday and clap your hands.

I got really nervous with this herd. The most nervous around cows in all my experiences because some of those rules we were going to have to break. There were too many to not separate the herd. I was having trouble staying calm. We may have had to separate a mama and baby if absolutely necessary as there were too many to get around otherwise. Breathe. Anyway, to start we saw a small walking path in the grass below the hill they were on and slowly started to walk that way, but we still needed to get back up to the SWCP otherwise we would be bushwhacking through the shrubbery and trees. Scott suggested that we stop for a few moments and see what they were going to do. He was so calm in this situation. His first experience with cows. Me, even with all my previous experiences, I was not calm. As we stood there, some of the cows started to mooooove on. It was hard for me to wait though as Scott still wanted to see what they would do.

I decided to start talking out loud to them which had worked for me in the past, and also the talking helped me calm down. As we finally started slowly walking, some cows continued to move away, while others did not, but we kept walking as calmly as we could, quite close to some, slowly, until finally we were past them. Whew! I did not like that one bit. What was only a couple of moments seemed like an eternity. I wondered why they don't fence the cows in when they are that close to the SWCP. On the other hand, England is full of Public Rights of way. I was grateful that Scott was with me during this cow experience today, probably the worst one of all. I don't know what I would have done if I was by myself.

After that I had to keep moving to shake off the nerves, so I started up a grassy slope getting closer to the top of Golden Cap. At the top of the grassy slope were two National Trust people doing some trail maintenance on the SWCP. I should have asked them about why those cows were not fenced in, but I thanked them for their work. I looked back at the cows now a good safe distance from me. There was a zigzag path up the rest of Golden Cap, the highest point on the south coast of England at 619 feet. All in all, other than the cows, the climb itself was not that difficult, as we did it in stages, and of course the cows slowed us down.

At the top of Golden Cap waiting for us was Kaz, a woman from the SWCP Facebook Group, who was originally going to walk with me one of these days when I put my request out there about a month ago for walking partners. Today she had time for a short walk with both of us, mostly to meet me, as she has been following my walk on the Group page. I looked back at the views of the checkered green farmland, with a few scattered buildings, a few herds of sheep (and cows), a long sandy beach, the towns of Charmouth and Lyme Regis beyond. The seas were a muddled blue color now under the cloud coverage in the sky. Scott took a couple photos of Kaz and me at the top of Golden Cap for me to post on the SWCP Facebook Group page. She walked up from the other side from Seatown. "Golden Cap gets its name because just under the surface is golden Upper Greensand rock. The Upper Greensand is a Cretaceous rock formed about 100 million years ago. When the rock is 'fresh' it is a greenish colour but becomes the golden colour you see when it reacts with the oxygen in the air," per the booklet.

We chatted with Kaz for the next little-over-a-mile into Seatown, so I didn't pay a lot of attention to the terrain as I usually do, but I believe there was a gentle descent down from Golden Cap, first on some steps, then on a grassy slope. There were views of Seatown and its beach below ahead of us, and some more checkered farmland beyond, and looking back behind us up at Golden Cap. A bench at one point offered us a place to sit, and I took photos of Scott and Kaz sitting together. The terrain flattened out through a wheat field which had the wheat in shapes looking like triangular piles. We walked onto a short road to a pub in Seatown. The three of us chatted the entire time about walking, jobs, what made me decide to walk the entire SWCP, etc.

We all sat for a bit at the pub in Seatown and talked a bit more. Scott and I wanted to eat, but we needed to wait till they served food at noon, about a half hour away, so soon we said goodbye and thanks for meeting us to Kaz, as she took off to wander around the area some more on her own as she likes to do. It was very nice to meet another person from the SWCP Facebook Group. The Group has become a great source for me of connecting with those people in England who love and appreciate the SWCP!

Scott and I sat and ate in the pub. I had a thought as we were eating. I know how people in Cornwall eat their scones when having a cream tea, and I know how people in Devon eat their scones when having a cream tea, but I wondered how people in Dorset eat their scones when having a cream tea. I couldn't find anything online, so I guess I will have to ask someone, or better yet, we will need to have at least one cream tea before Poole and find out!

As we were getting ready to walk the last just-over-three miles to West Bay, we walked down to the beach of Seatown for a few photos. It was a good thing we did this, as I looked behind us and saw a very ominous dark cloud carrying a big rain squall headed our way. I felt a few rain drops and said to Scott, "Ummm…We are not walking yet! Let's go back inside the pub and wait." I figured it was a passing rain squall, as that was what the forecast said, although it seemed to have arrived earlier than forecasted. As we sat inside the pub for a half hour, I peeked outside several times, and sure enough it was raining. A lot. And we even heard thunder. I was so glad we did not get caught in that as we were walking! I thought of Kaz out there, and found out later that she needed to run back to her car from her walk, got rained on a bit, but made it back alright.

Finally, I looked outside again and saw perfect blue skies and white clouds now behind us (for now), which was the direction of the weather pattern today, so I figured it was now alright to walk. As we left the pub and walked across the pebbly beach, which seemed to have an orange tint to it, I could see the ominous dark rain cloud moving ahead. A lone white upside down rowboat sat on the upper end of the beach along with a red Coastguard box that contained a life raft. With the white rowboat, the red box, the orange tint of the pebbly beach, the green hillside, and the ominous dark blue sky in the distance, I took a few quite dramatic looking rain squall pictures. I could even see the rain streaks coming down in the sky in the distance in these photos.

Scott and I then started up a short grassy uphill climb which actually felt steeper than Golden Cap. After the climb, the terrain flattened out, had a slight downhill, and another short but quite steep uphill climb again on a grassy slope. I felt the warmth of the sun and started singing, "Out came the sun and dried out all the rain." Sometimes I walk faster than Scott, so I looked behind from this vantage point and took a photo of him climbing the grassy slope with the town of Seatown a bit in the distance.

At the top of that climb the sign said we now had two miles to West Bay, our destination for today. We had views of a long sandy beach ahead of us, which would be the very, very, very long Chesil Beach, lots of green farmland on the hilltops, and the Isle of Portland beyond. There was a steep but short downhill, and the terrain flattened out again. Then I looked behind us again. Oh, no! Another ominous dark rain cloud. It was still off in the distance, but approaching. I really wanted to try to make it to West Bay without getting wet! We picked up the pace a bit, and with one mile left we were at the beach at Eype Mouth. I looked again, and the ominous dark rain cloud seemed to be moving inland rather than toward us.

Storms, Skies, and Sun
Seatown after the Passing Storm with Rowboat August 18
Seatown after the Passing Storm with Dramatic Skies August 18
Large Yellow Sun Rising in Early Morning walking to Scabbacombe Sands April 25

It was flat the rest of the way into West Bay, and still walking a bit faster, we arrived, dry! It actually never did rain during the time we spent in West Bay. Looking out at the seas, there were still some clouds, but not rain clouds, and even a break in the clouds allowed the sun to light up the water.

We wandered around West Bay a bit looking for someplace to eat, but we seemed to have arrived in that window of in between lunch and dinner times. We finally found something for a quick snack. West Bay was in the shape of the letter "U," with the harbour in the middle of the three sides. I took photos of the various boats in the harbour, and we also stopped in St. John's Church. We knew the name of this church, since in big letters on the white building it said, "St. John's Church." There was also an old looking Methodist Church, but we could not go inside that one.

I called the gentleman from our next B&B who I had pre-arranged that he would kindly pick us up in West Bay. We were staying in Abbotsbury, further on for two nights. He arrived within twenty minutes, and we checked into our B&B. Abbotsbury is a town where you step back in time a few hundred years. Brown stone buildings with thatched roofs. There was a chapel on a hill that we could see from the window of our room. And a Swannery (more on all that tomorrow and the next day).

We freshened up, and went out to a four year wedding anniversary dinner. Unfortunately of the two restaurants in town, the one we chose was noisy and my food was not that great.

What an adventurous day! On our anniversary! I am glad I was with my husband through it all. It was nice to walk through some places, create memories…and adventures… with someone I love along the SWCP.

DAY 76 STATS: 6.5 MILES. ABOUT 3.5 HOURS, NOT INCLUDING LONG LUNCH/RAIN BREAK. EXTRA MILE FOR WALKING BACK AND FORTH TO DINNER IN ABBOTSBURY. MISSED ONE AND A HALF MILES CHARMOUTH TO STONEBARROW. PURPLE SHOES. PUB IN SEATOWN IS "THE ANCHOR INN." PUBS IN WEST BAY ARE "THE GEORGE" AND "THE WEST BAY."

WEST BAY TO WEST BEXINGTON TO ABBOTSBURY (SOME WALK, SOME TAXI) – Saturday, 19 August 2017

"Oh! I do like to be beside the seaside! I do like to be beside the sea! I do like to stroll along the Prom, Prom, Prom! Where the brass bands play, "Tiddely-om-pom-pom!"" – From the song, "I Do Like to Be Beside the Seaside" by John A. Glover-Kind.

Scott and I got a ride from the B&B gentleman in Abbotsbury back to West Bay, and soon we started walking. There was a short but steep uphill climb to the top of the cliffs which I did in about five minutes. We had views of West Bay behind us and beyond. The path turned flat next to a golf course, and there was a view of a long sandy beach below us with the sounds of crashing waves. Somewhere around here was the cliff fall that I read about on 29 June: "Broadchurch Beach: West Bay cliff fall blocks coast path" which forced the closure of the cliff-top path along East Cliff between West Bay and Freshwater. There should be a diversion in place to keep us walking in a safe area, and I was looking out for it, but at the moment, I could not really tell where the diversion was exactly.

We had a short decent, followed by a short ascent of about 62 steps, as I counted them. We had more views back behind us of the beach at West Bay and the other hills and flat area we just were. Looking back, I could see evidence of some cliff fall as there was a pile of lots of rocks on the sandy beach below, but I was not quite sure if that was the cliff fall from around 29 June since there seemed to be no diversion around the area we had just walked. Turns out what I did see was indeed the cliff fall, and the diversion was only a quarter mile inland running along the golf course, not completely inland as some other diversions I have taken, so that it seemed to me like there was no diversion in place, when in fact there was.

We walked a short distance on a small pebble beach and then the path went in front of some caravan homes. Here there was an inland section through a camping area, which was to get around a river, not any cliff falls, followed by one more very short uphill. Looking back again at the sandy beach below with a few people strolling the beach, the seas today were turquoise and blue, and we could see headlands way in the distance, of where we had walked days ago.

It was back to flat walking on top of the cliffs, and then another bit that went inland on some grassy fields and back to the Hive Beach Café at Burton Hive Beach. This inland bit was a diversion put in place some years ago. We arrived at the café hungry in the late morning, so we had a second breakfast of waffles, bacon, and maple syrup. I had that in Torcross a few weeks back too, although that was with pancakes instead of waffles. It was tasty both times. We started walking again after a quick visit to this beach which had people on it and a few rowboats, one filled with crab and lobster pots. The path continued to be flat in front of another row of caravan homes, where we were paralleling a long beach.

Some suggest that this area is the start of the long pebble Chesil Beach, an 18 mile beach from perhaps even West Bay to the Isle of Portland. They say it has 180 billion pebbles! They say walking on it is not the easiest to do as the pebbles roll a lot beneath the feet, and I don't think that there is any hard sandy area to walk on. Scott and I walked just above the beach on a more solid path following the SWCP. There were small white and yellow daisies, and other short vegetation in the pebbles here in an area that paralleled the beach. It looked like a scene from a desert, and we heard the waves crash on the pebbles. In the distance I could see the Isle of Portland. The SWCP took us inland a bit on a very flat area in order to go around a marshy lake, the Burton Mere. There were meadows to our left filled with wildflowers, and now instead of the sound of crashing waves, we heard the sound of the breeze in the tall grasses and marsh reeds.

    I also noticed that some of the markers now for the SWCP were short limestone waymarkers, like a block of stone, about a couple feet tall. They have actually been like this on and off for a few days now. They reminded me of similar stone markers on the Camino de Santiago in Spain. It was a sunny warm dry day with blue skies, white clouds, and occasional breezes. We continued on the flat next to the marshes for quite some time, and eventually saw West Bexington ahead. We also saw a way out of the marshes to the pebbly Chesil beach, so we decided to venture out to take a look at the billions of pebbles and to hear the crashing waves.

    Since it only seemed like a half mile to West Bexington, we decided to walk on the pebbly beach the rest of the way, even though we knew it wouldn't be the easiest. I now understood why the SWCP took us a bit inland behind the marshes. It was a good workout on the ankles and calf muscles to walk on the pebbles, and it was definitely slower going than a harder surface. But I wanted to walk on the pebbly beach anyway. Scott posed for some pictures on this beach with its billions of pebbles, turquoise waters, and a sky so big and blue with white fluffy clouds. A couple people were fishing from this beach. The pebbles were marble-sized on average in the colors of white, tan, light brown, reddish, and black. Although, the pebbles on Chesil Beach can vary from "pea size" near West Bay to "the size of your hand" at Portland, per the booklet. It took us twenty minutes to go the half mile. It was a good half mile, being right next to the crashing beach waves, with a slight breeze, and all those good-for-me-positive negative ions. It was actually meditating to walk on the pebbles for this short bit. But that half mile was enough, and we arrived at West Bexington in the early afternoon.

    As I walked towards a restaurant to get something to eat, I walked past a very nicely dressed grandfatherly-aged gentleman, strutting along, almost dancing, I heard him happily singing out loud, sharing his joy with anyone who was listening on this sunny warm glorious day. Something like, "Oh, I do like to be beside the seaside…"

    I really don't think he was actually singing to anyone in particular, other than to himself, and probably didn't care if anyone was listening or not, but I was listening, and I began to form a smile across my face. I was passing by him just coming off walking that half-mile meditative stretch on a pebbly beach, in my hiking clothes, carrying my rucksack, and just removing my proper British sun hat. He continued, "I do like to be beside the sea…"

    Those were the only words I heard, but it was enough to make my smile widen. I smiled not only because here was this happy gentleman just enjoying his day so much that he felt compelled to sing out loud, but also because the words for some reason immediately grabbed my attention. I had never heard these lyrics before. The grandfatherly gentleman noticed my smile and commented, "Glad I could make you smile." I didn't say anything in response other than make eye contact and keep smiling, as I wanted to keep hearing what he was singing. Since we were walking in opposite directions, alas I did not hear any more. I didn't want it to seem like I was eavesdropping so I didn't stop, and I kept walking. Fortunately, I had heard enough though. Enough to know that even in these few words I heard, in these two little sentences, what he sang spoke to me, and rang true to my heart. I knew that the seaside is definitely where I like to be beside.

    I felt immediately that these lyrics represented my walk on the South West Coast Path in many ways, after 77 days thus far of walking beside extensions of the Atlantic Ocean in the forms of channels and seas. The words made me realize my love for my being beside the seaside, and how I fell in love with the South West Coast Path. The lyrics represented my love for hearing the ocean waves crash on the beaches. For seeing the rocky coastlines and the beaches and the coves and the bays that the waves touch. For seeing the greens of the hillsides and valleys and headlands, and the blues and turquoises of the waters. For being with nature, the various plants and grasses and shrubbery and trees and wildflowers. For the birds and sea life and animals. For smelling the salty and fishy sea air. For feeling the sea breezes and winds. For walking near mountain goats and sheep and horses. For getting my beneficial and positive supply of negative ions. For appreciating the timeless fishing villages, and the people who fish on the seas. For walking in my bare feet on the sand and in the waters. For all the harbours and the many types of boats floating or resting in them. For appreciating the mining and farming industries, and learning about smuggling of the past. For all the people I had met along the way, and the friends I have made, whether for a brief moment in time, or for a few hours, or for a lifetime. For the Trinity House and the HM Coastguard and the National Coastwatch Institution and the Royal National Lifeboat Institution. For all the churches and chapels and lighthouses. For still deciding which beach would be my ultimate location for a beach hut. For celebrating my 50th birthday in an epic way. For meeting local people and delving into local culture and local ways of life. For the food and the desserts and the cream teas. For following the arrows closest to the acorns. For walking and walking and walking. For filling my heart and soul and spirit with everything that I have experienced along my nearly three months on the South West Coast Path. Even on my days off, even with the uncooperative weather and missing miles, and even the cows and the golf courses. I had fallen in love with being beside the seaside on the South West Coast Path!

    Here are most of the lyrics to the song "I Do Like to Be Beside the Seaside" that I was fortunately able to find later by searching on the internet with just the few words I heard the happy gentleman sing. They were written by John A. Glover-Kind, copyright unknown.

Now everybody likes to spend their summer holiday
down beside the side of the silvery sea.
I'm no exception to the rule, in fact, if I'd me way,
I'd reside by the side of the silvery sea.

But when you're just the common or garden Smith or Jones or Brown
at business up in town, you're got to settle down.
You save your money all the year 'til summer comes around.
Then away you go to a place you know, where the cockle shells are found.

Oh! I do like to be beside the seaside!
I do like to be beside the sea!
I do like to stroll along the Prom, Prom, Prom!
Where the brass bands play, "Tiddely-om-pom-pom!"

So just let me be beside the seaside!
I'll be beside myself with glee
and there's lots of girls beside,
I should like to be beside, beside the seaside, beside the sea!

Oh! I do like to be beside the seaside!
I do like to be beside the sea!
I do like to stroll along the Prom, Prom, Prom!
Where the brass bands play, "Tiddely-om-pom-pom!"

So just let me be beside the seaside!
I'll be beside myself with glee
and there's lots of girls beside,
I should like to be beside, beside the seaside, beside the sea!

  Now while not all words are entirely appropriate for me (I would change the word "girls" to "boys"), I decided that day that the wisdom that came from a joyful happy nicely-dressed grandfatherly-aged gentleman singing would become my theme song for my nearly three-month, mostly solo, mostly walking adventure on England's 630-mile South West Coast Path!

  Scott and I stopped for some side salads at an expensive restaurant in West Bexington. As time passed, we decided to take a taxi and skip the last three and a half miles of the four left to Abbotsbury. For no real good reason other than we felt like we wanted a shorter walking day, and we were curious about visiting The Abbotsbury Swannery.

  We asked the taxi driver to take us directly to the Abbotsbury Swannery which is "the only place in the world where we can walk through the heart of colony of nesting Mute Swans," over 600 of them! When we got there we were told that their feeding time would be in about twenty minutes at 4:00, their "Tea" time. Where else in the world would we ever get to see this? There was a sea of white feathered birds at the edge of a lagoon, being fed by children of all ages, including us! The average wingspan of a Mute Swan is seven to eight feet.

  According to the Abbotsbury Swannery booklet that I bought, the "Abbotsbury Swannery conserves the only managed colony of nesting mute swans in the world. Swannery records date back more than 600 years. Today, there are often more than 600 free-flying swans on site at any time and up to 150 pairs may nest on a clearing of only two acres. The Swannery is an integral part of a nature reserve recognized as a wetland of international importance. It supports a superb variety of wildlife." A sign informed us that they also get fed at noon, their "Lunch" time. The sign continued, "Children may be asked to feed the birds, but due to the sensitive nature of the nest-site, entry is by invitation only. We ask helpers to refrain from picking up feathers on the actual nest-site. Thank you."

  I took a lot of pictures of the white swans with their black and orange-reddish beaks. I was lucky to catch some photos where the curve of their necks when two were standing next to each other would make the shape of a heart. Romantic looking. The white of the swans was a great contrast to the blue of the waters they were floating in, the green rolling farmland hillside behind them, and the blue skies with white clouds above.

  As we walked out of the Swannery, I found a small actual acorn on the ground. The SWCP symbol! The National Trails symbol! I had never really thought about what an acorn was until this moment, so I looked it up online later…The acorn is the nut of an oak tree. I wondered how many oak trees I had seen along the SWCP and not realized it. I wondered why National Trails chose the acorn as its symbol. I recalled the information I read about the third lighthouse built on Eddystone Rocks, Smeaton's Tower, which I wrote back on the 28th of July which said, "He had decided to construct a tower based on the shape of an English Oak tree for strength…"

Just before we walked the half mile back to the Abbotsbury village, I called Mom as it was close to 5:00. As we continued walking, we stopped to see the Tithe Barn which we could not go inside, however it "was built around 1400 and was one of the largest in Europe, being 275 feet long and 31 feet wide," and the St. Nicholas Church, which we were able to go inside. The Church bells rang 5:30 as we were inside, and per the brochure I got inside the church, "The Tower contains six bells, dating from 1636 to 1776; the bells were rehung in 1897." The church itself dates from the late 14th or early 15th century. I said my usual prayers.

Scott and I went out to dinner to the other option in town. I found that my food tasted better than yesterday's so we made this our anniversary dinner instead. And it was a quieter atmosphere. More romantic. We walked back to our B&B after dinner, walking next to all the brown stone buildings with thatched roofs of Abbotsbury. I took a few "windows and doors" photos of this history.

Hearing the song lyrics earlier by the joyful happy nicely-dressed grandfatherly-aged gentleman made me want to look up the song lyrics in more depth this evening, and I even read some more information about the song "I Do Like to Be Beside the Seaside" on the internet. "It was a popular British "music hall" (theatrical entertainment) song, written in 1907 by John A. Glover-Kind, and was made famous by a music hall comedian and singer, Mark Sheridan, who first recorded it in 1909. It speaks of the singer's love for the seaside, and his wish to return there for his summer holidays each year. It was composed at a time when the yearly visits of the British working-class to the seaside were booming." Furthermore, the song "captures the spirit of the times when ordinary working people in Britain flocked to the coast in their thousands by train to resorts...for daytrips and their first proper holidays. [John A. Glover-Kind] encapsulated the sense of fun that many must have felt."

I also remembered a quote that I saw on the 10th of August on a beach hut: "Oh I do like to be...collecting shells, licking ice cream, brushing sand from my toes, reading a novel, slurping coffee from a flask, paddling at dusk, fishing for the bbq, relaxing...beside the seaside." Now I understand that quote even more!

I can also confirm that the seaside and the coast and the beaches are still booming over 100 years later. And I can totally understand why. I decided that this gentleman who was singing this song earlier today was another guardian angel of mine, and that over the last few months I definitely have this love for being beside the seaside that Mr. Glover-Kind and Mr. Sheridan expressed in the song. Perhaps I need to return each year to the South West Coast Path for my summer holidays as well. After all, I do have that future-to-walk list...

Oh! I do like to be beside the seaside!
I do like to be beside the sea!
So just let me be beside the seaside!
I'll be beside myself with glee
and there's lots of [boys] beside,
I should like to be beside, beside the seaside, beside the sea!

DAY 77 STATS: 5.5 MILES WALKING. 4 HOURS, PLUS A BIT IN ABBOTSBURY. MISSED 3.5 MILES WEST BEXINGTON TO SWANNERY IN ABBOTSBURY. NO EXTRA MILES. PUPRLE SHOES. PUBS ABBOTSBURY ARE "ILCHESTER ARMS" AND "SWAN INN." Information on the Seaside song from wikipedia.org/wiki/I_Do_Like_To_be_Beside_the_Seaside and songfacts.com.

ABBOTSBURY TO EAST FLEET TO NEAR FERRYBRIDGE (SOME CAR, SOME WALK) – Sunday, 20 August 2017

"I am a little church (no great cathedral); far from the splendour and squalor of hurrying cities; I do not worry if briefer days grow briefest; I am not sorry when sun and rain make April." Excerpt from a poem by E.E. Cummings called "I am a Little Church," written in 1958, displayed in The East Fleet Old Parish Church in East Fleet.

Before we started our short walking day, we took a side trip walk up to the St. Catherine's Chapel, an old limestone constructed chapel, perched up on a hill above Abbotsbury, the one we saw from our window of our B&B. From the sign outside the chapel, "This chapel was built in the late fourteenth century by Abbotsbury Abbey and was dedicated to St. Catherine of Alexandria, one of the most popular saints in late medieval England. The hilltop location recalls the monastery of St. Catherine on Mount Sinai and suggests that the chapel was a place of pilgrimage. Overlooking the sea, the chapel was used as a beacon, thereby ensuring its survival after Abbotsbury Abbey was dissolved in 1539." Furthermore, from some information displayed at the local pub in Abbotsbury, "It is thought that the chapel survived the 16 century Dissolution due to its usefulness as a coastal beacon and sea mark. In later times a navigation light was kept burning at the top of its stair turret." Wow, another form of a lighthouse! We spent about ten minutes inside and outside. It was empty inside, with good acoustics. It is so interesting to be inside structures that are hundreds and hundreds of years old. You can almost feel the spirits. I need to count this as an extra mile and a half of walking today, round trip.

On our way back to the B&B, we had views of some of the town of Abbotsbury nestled in the green hills, with the church tower rising above. We picked up a couple of sandwiches for today's short walk, as there would be no food stops during the walk. We said our thank yous to Irene, and then Kevin dropped us off at East Fleet, six miles ahead on the SWCP from Abbotsbury. No good reason for missing another six miles other than we just wanted a short day today, and it was forecasted to rain today, even though not till about 4:00. I believe we missed some green rolling hills from Abbotsbury down to the area where the SWCP starts along The Fleet Lagoon, "England's largest lagoon and the richest in wildlife in the United Kingdom." Hopefully those will be the last missed miles that I will want to walk sometime in the future, and add to that list.

Before I go on with our day, more about The Fleet Lagoon. Parallel to each other, first and outermost there are the seas, then there is the 180 billion pebble Chesil Beach, and then innermost is the Fleet Lagoon. Therefore, many of those pebbles of Chesil Beach form a barrier between the seas and Fleet Lagoon. "The Fleet's only connection with the sea is at its extreme eastern end, and consequently the influences of tidal currents and saltwater weaken along its length. In these changing conditions a number of different habitats have developed, and together these support the greatest variety of wildlife of any lagoon in the UK." The Fleet Lagoon runs from near Abbotsbury to near Ferrybridge and the Isle of Portland and is eight miles long. The definition of a lagoon is, "an area of shallow coastal water that is wholly or partially cut off from the sea." There is an abundance of bird and animal life, plant life, 150 species of seaweed, 25 species of fish, and more along The Fleet Lagoon. (All this information was obtained from a brochure entitled, "The Fleet Lagoon," from the Dorset County Council.)

Kevin dropped us off in East Fleet, but not quite at The East Fleet Old Parish Church, another small old church, where I wanted to start today's walk, because he was not allowed to drive the rest of the roads. Therefore, we walked on the roads about a half mile to visit this tiny church. It seemed as small as St. Bueno's Church in Culbone and Saint Clements Church in Hope Cove. In fact, the measurements might only be 17.25 feet by 13.25 feet.

The "Old Parish Church, now a mortuary chapel, stands at East Fleet. The walls are of local rubble with freestone dressings and the roofs are covered with stone slates. The Chancel is uncertain but mediaeval date. The church was damaged and partly destroyed by a gale in 1824," according to today's booklet. In fact, from some information hanging on a wall in the small church, "This Chancel is all that remains of the old Church which was inundated in the great storm of 1824, when the Nave was wrecked…In 1824 a great tidal wave washed over the ridge of Chesil Beach and over the Fleet Water and passed onwards, the water reaching a depth of about thirty five feet at this point." In addition about this small church, "During the old smuggling days this vault is said to have been used by smugglers for the storage of wines, spirits and other contraband. A secret underground passage runs from this vault…" The quote from above is about this church.

After the small church, Scott and I walked a short footpath to the SWCP and started officially walking at nearly noon. We walked the four miles from East Fleet to our B&B, which was about a mile before Ferrybridge near the Isle of Portland. The terrain was all flat the entire way. It was quiet, too. No sound of crashing waves as Fleet Lagoon and Chesil Beach separated us from the seas. The only sounds were occasional birds chirping. We saw signs that part or all of this area was a Nature Reserve. Occasionally our views were blocked by some high shrubs. We mostly had views of the reeds right in front of us, a sandy shoreline close to us, the lagoon itself, and Chesil Beach just beyond. At times there were small rowboats on the shore, some of which looked quite old and no longer usable. Across the lagoon, on the beach, there were a few small buildings, perhaps fishing huts. Every once in a while an old pier that led out to the lagoon rested on the shore with many of its wooden boards crumbled or entirely missing.

We also walked around a military firing range, the Tidmoor Firing Range, closer to the Fleet Lagoon because it was open. If it was closed, the red flags would have been flying, and we would have had to take an inland diversion route, but we didn't need to do that. Even with the military firing range, this part of the walk was still close to the lagoon. However, a bit later we needed to walk around a second military area, the Wyke Regis Training Area Bridging Camp, where we mostly only had views of the not-so-scenic buildings and a very serious-looking barbed wire fence. There was also a camping/caravan area we walked through at one point.

To find our B&B, we needed to look for a green sign that said "Farmhouse B&B" somewhere along the SWCP. I wanted to make sure it would be easy to spot, so I called the woman of the B&B to make sure we would see it clearly. She said yes. We kept walking and walking. We were getting closer to Ferrybridge and I started to question if we had walked passed it and missed it somehow. I called again. No answer. Five minutes later, we saw the sign. She called back just as we started down the short footpath to the B&B and farm, located at the edge of the town of Wyke Regis.

Not before we stopped to take photos of their three alpacas. They also have horses, sheep, ducks, chickens, pheasants, pigs, dogs, and other animals on this farm. I chose this B&B for two reasons. One was the animals, because when I looked at their website months and months ago, I thought it would be fun to stay on a farm. The second reason I chose this B&B was its close proximity to the Isle of Portland. I originally, and now we, would be here for three nights as a home base for walking around the Isle of Portland over the next couple of days. This was one of the B&Bs that I already had booked a double room so only needed to let them know I added a second person.

Most of our walk today was cloudy and it seemed a bit chilly out, and we actually did have a little rain drizzle about twenty minutes before we got to the B&B sign, and as we walked up the short footpath. We were in the B&B by mid-afternoon, I think the earliest arrival time since Scott has been here, similar to when I used to arrive at

B&Bs when I was walking on my own. We had a classy room with a view of the garden with some of their animals. Scott was thrilled with all the animals, especially the horses. I was glad I could share this particular B&B with him.

For some reason, I wanted to take a nap, and I thought it was nice to be in our room this early. It also gave me time to catch up on writing and research our plans for the next two days around the Isle of Portland. We got Indian food delivered to the B&B so we wouldn't have to go out later for dinner. As predicted it was raining and kind of felt a bit stormy outside from about 4:00 onwards. I even think I heard the fog horn of one of the three lighthouses we will see tomorrow on the Isle of Portland.

DAY 78 STATS: 4 MILES. 2.25 HOURS. EXTRA MILE AND A HALF FOR CHAPEL. EXTRA HALF MILE FOR OLD CHURCH. MISSED SIX MILES ABBOTSBURY TO EAST FLEET. PURPLE SHOES. PUB IN WYKE REGIS IS "WYKE SMUGGLERS." Information about the Old Parish Church in East Fleet from british-history.ac.uk/rchme/dorset/vol1/pp109-110.

FIRST HALF OF ISLE OF PORTLAND – B&B IN WYKE REGIS TO FERRY BRIDGE TO CHISWELL TO PORTLAND BILL LIGHTHOUSE – Monday, 21 August 2017

"The flashing pattern of a lighthouse light is called its Character…Lizard flashes every three seconds…Eddystone flashes every ten seconds…Bull Point flashes every ten seconds…Hartland Point flashes every fifteen seconds." - Information at the Portland Bill Lighthouse.

During breakfast at this farm this morning, the chickens and ducks and geese were watching us eat. They were out on the patio just outside of the dining room table. Then Scott and I got to go outside and see the two big pigs, George the long haired black and white furry pig, and Mildred the short haired gray pig! We even got to pet them. So cute! We wandered around their large yard for a moment to look more at their animals, plants, and ponds.

Today I went quite light with the contents in my rucksack. In fact, almost every day for the last week or so, I have been going quite light. I have not even been using my standard rucksack. Just a small cloth bag that kind of looks like a rucksack, but is much lighter, that I mentioned back on 10 August, when we walked from Brixham to Torquay. I didn't put much in it today, and would only do this only when there was no rain forecasted, even though I still took a rain jacket, and when I know there are food and water stops along the way, even though I still take a bottle of water. I also take extra socks, a long sleeve shirt if I am wearing short sleeves, the battery backup for the mobile phone, sunscreen and lip salve, and other similar items I had back on 10 August. Scott still carries his regular rucksack and carries a bit more than me so that we are covered in any situation. One thing I also finally realized, well Scott suggested it, is while I still take the small booklets needed for each day, I have been taking photographs of the pages out of the heavier guidebook (the last of the four guidebooks in use) on my mobile phone. We are finding that the SWCP has been well marked enough that we don't really need to refer to the topo maps and information in the guidebook, but just in case, I can look them up on my mobile. I would not do all this if I was walking by myself.

We started walking on the SWCP again after the short walk from the Farmhouse B&B, taking a few more photos of their alpacas, which I found out their names are Kim, Barney, and Angus. The walk was flat, still near The Fleet Lagoon, and just over a half mile of about fifteen minutes to get to the beginning of Ferry Bridge. We had similar views as yesterday with the lagoon and Chesil Beach just beyond and a few boats and buildings on the water and on the beach.

It took us a half hour to walk across the Ferry Bridge itself, about a mile and a half long, as we walked on a side trail on the left side of the bridge. While the bridge was busy with cars, we seemed to be just that far enough away that it wasn't too bothersome or noisy. We were not walking on pavement either, and it was all flat. We arrived on the other side of the bridge and onto the Isle of Portland, followed the SWCP signs around a marina, and then made our way to Victoria Square in the town of Chiswell so that we could walk half way around the Isle of Portland counter-clockwise to the Portland Bill Lighthouse, our destination for today, so that the seas would still be on our right. While I don't think the Isle of Portland is technically an island, because it is connected to the mainland by Chesil Beach and Ferry Bridge, it is "about five miles long and two miles across at its widest point," per the booklet, and the path around it is an official part of the entire SWCP.

A short walk on an Esplanade near this end of Chesil Beach brought us back to the sounds of the seas, as the waves took the small pebbles back and we could hear the rolling and tumbling of the pebbles. We looked back on the long pebbly 18-mile Chesil Beach and the very blue seas. There were a few rowboats sitting on the beach, and I singled one of them out, an orange rowboat surrounded by a few crab and lobster pots and rope, taking its photo sitting on the pebbles, with the deep blue seas, the deep blue skies and white clouds, and part of the Isle of Portland in the distance.

There was a short but steep climb up a hill, when a sign told us we had three and a quarter miles to the Portland Bill Lighthouse. We had already walked three and a quarter miles, mostly across the bridge, and we took a snack break. From the top of the hill, we had views of the buildings of the town below, and Chesil Beach and the Fleet Lagoon as they curved their way back into the distance.

The path was pretty much all flat all the way to the lighthouse. At first it felt like we were hiking in the mountains as there were a lot of rocks around us that reminded us of rocks we see when hiking back home. There were two slight inland diversions due to previous rock falls, one of which took us to some large rocks that were carved into animal shapes. Turns out many of the rocks around are limestone, from quarrying, which has been "going on for centuries and there are still some quarries in operation today," per the booklet.

The path turned to flat wide grass. It was a beautiful sunny warm day! Out to our right were views of nothing but blue! I start singing out loud, "Oh, I do like to be beside the seaside, the seaside is where I like to be…" which were not quite yet the correct lyrics to my theme song, but it was fun to sing the song anyway in my own way.

We had views, and then approached the first of three lighthouses that we would be seeing, although the third one will be more on tomorrow's walk. For today, the first lighthouse was a short one in height, which was the first true lighthouse built on the Isle of Portland, built at the beginning of the 18th century but rebuilt in the 1860's. It is now a private house and holiday cottage, all white in color. We should have rented that, and I can add that to my "expensive-places-to-stay-someday" list! I cannot find any other name for this lighthouse except "The First Lighthouse," thus appropriately named. Although it may also be called the "Old Higher Lighthouse."

A few minutes later of walking we reached our second lighthouse, the Portland Bill Lighthouse, established in 1906, which is technically the third lighthouse built historically over time. A tall red and white stripped lighthouse, with a bit of that "Trinity House greenish-turquoise" color trim, this is the lighthouse that is currently in use, and is 135 feet tall with 153 steps to the top. We walked around the outside to photograph the lighthouse, and then enquired inside about bus times back to Wyke Regis and tour times for the lighthouse, including climbing those steps. We had forty minutes to wait for the tour, so we ate a quick lunch at the café by the lighthouse.

The half hour tour was filled with information which unfortunately when I am given that much information all at once, I don't remember much of anything. Needless to say, the views from the top of the Fresnel lens of the lighthouse on the inside, to the views of only blue, blue, blue (seas and skies) beyond, with the sun shining brightly and shimmering on the seas, were spectacular. It was like we could see out to the edge of the world.

From the top of the lighthouse in the other direction, we had a sneak peak at the other half of the Isle of Portland, including what looked like a whole small village of beach huts, and the third lighthouse, which is actually "The Second Lighthouse," or "the "Old Lower Lighthouse." Beyond that, the cliffs of the hillsides way in the distance, even past the Isle of Portland, looked like they were snow-covered, as the rocks were white in color. I was definitely looking forward to seeing the village of beach huts up close tomorrow, the next lighthouse, and the white cliffs along the SWCP in the days ahead of us. Geologically, we will be getting to the Cretaceous 145–65 million year old white chalk cliffs and sea stacks. For now, we are in "almost all limestone–Portland Stone–about 130 million years old." "Buckingham Palace and St. Paul's Cathedral are made from Portland Stone."

We had a bit of time before our bus, so we wandered around, and took more photos of the lighthouse from various angles, including photos of Scott standing in front of the lighthouse. This gave us a perspective of how tall the lighthouse really is, a lot taller than Scott. There was also an obelisk in this area, the Trinity House Obelisk, which is actually a form of a lighthouse as well, as it was "built as a daymark at the very tip of Bill Point. Although a pair of lighthouses had operated at Portland Bill from 1716, Trinity House also decided to place a 23 foot tall obelisk at Bill Point in 1844. It acted as a warning to ships of a low shelf rock at Bill Point, which extends 100 feet out into the sea. At the time, the present 1905 lighthouse did not exist, making the obelisk an important daymark at the very southern tip of Portland." Therefore, we really saw four lighthouses around the Isle of Portland.

We took the 4:10 bus back to near our B&B, and walked about five minutes to our B&B. Later we went to the local pub for dinner. Today was first half of the "Portland Circuit," tomorrow will be second half.

I heard from my friend and inspiration, Gordon, today. He sent me an email asking where I was, how many days I had left till Poole, and if I was still enjoying my walk. I appreciated hearing from him and responded, "Thank you for contacting me. I am well! The weather lately has been beautiful (mostly) and my husband had joined me for the last three weeks. We are doing the other half of the Isle of Portland Circuit tomorrow, and should be in Poole (Swanage) the 28th or 29th. I am still enjoying the extended walk, and am getting sad that it will be over soon, but enjoying each day. How is life-after-the-Coast-Path for you?"

Gordon responded back, "You still have a week to enjoy the remaining Jurassic coast. It is fascinating how it changes over such a short stretch ending in Swanage. There are no more pebbles as in Chesil Beach! Your husband has joined you for three weeks! I have some wonderful memories and meeting strangers, friends and family. Doing the SWCP in one hit has its own kudos (especially carrying the tent!), you know who the genuine walkers are...they are fit. Today I have been picking stones with the grandchildren aged six and two-and-a-half before we sow grass and clover seeds. An organic farmer thing. Almost as enjoyable as the SWCP. Next month my wife and I plan to explore Crete, which will include some mountain walking, culture and history as well as the beach. October I am going on a trekking trip to Nepal with some friends. The things you have to do to wind down after the SWCP. Retirement whilst you are fit is great. Keep active when you get back to Seattle. Let me know when you wash the feet on Studland beach."

I responded that he had some nice travels planned, is having a good time with his grandchildren, the best joys in life, and that I would keep in touch after I finish. What a brave and courageous man. He is still my inspiration.

DAY 79 STATS: 6.5 MILES. 3.5 HOURS. NO EXTRA MILES (TOO SHORT TO B&B FROM BUS STATION TO COUNT, OR TO PUB). PURPLE SHOES. PUBS ON ISLE OF PORTLAND ARE "THE LITTLE SHIP," "ROYAL PORTLAND ARMS," "THE BRITANNIA INN," "THE ROYAL EXCHANGE," AND "THE PULPIT INN." Info on the Trinity House Obelisk from portlandhistory.co.uk/trinity-house-obelisk.

SECOND HALF OF ISLE OF PORTLAND – PORTLAND BILL LIGHTHOUSE TO CASTLETOWN – Tuesday, 22 August 2017

"At certain times of the year our ducks quack during the night!" – A "warning" sign in our room at our "Farmhouse B&B."

Before I get started about the walk for today a few random thoughts:

Things that I am still not used to even after over two and a half months of being in England: Dogs in pubs and restaurants; driving on the opposite side of a road and being a front seat passenger on the opposite side of a car.

Things that I am quite used to after two and a half months of being on the SWCP: Walking for hours and hours; climbing hills; carrying only a little on my back and not having many belongings in general; not driving, not doing dishes; walking (just about) everywhere.

Things that I am still not used to after two and a half months of being on the SWCP: Walking near busy roads with lots of cars, near crowds of people, or walking inland.

Things that I am definitely used to after two and a half months of being on the SWCP: Being by the seas!

Blister update: The blister on the outside of my big right toe came back again a few weeks ago, but it was not bothersome, so I left it alone, and once again it broke itself and formed a callous. However, now a blister in the same spot has formed on the outside of my big left toe, but it is also not bothersome so I am essentially leaving it alone, except for wrapping it in some of that sheep's wool I bought. I still believe that all my blister theories are working as I have had no major blisters, especially none that have gotten really bad or have prevented me from walking like during my Camino walk in Spain. And to recap all my blister theories (again though my disclaimer is that these have worked for me) are showers in the evenings, keeping the feet dry as possible over night, flip flops as soon as I can after walking each day and in the evenings, letting the feet air out, sleeping with bare feet, changing socks often, double layer socks. And really also comfortable and well-fitting hiking boots and shoes, especially my purple trainers!

Furthermore, other than my longest walking day of walking fifteen miles back on July 1st, and for a few days thereafter, my feet have not really ached too much at all. Comfortable boots and shoes, and also I bet that is because I have been taking care of my feet in general and not walking long mileage per day. However, I do still have a bit of a swollen knee, but fortunately that has not prevented me from walking.

Back to today…The earliest bus back to the Portland Bill Lighthouse was at 10:30 with an 11:00 drop off, so we took that one. While at the lighthouse before walking, I took some pictures of Punxsutawney Phil with the lighthouse in the background. There was even a red telephone box in these fun photos as well. I haven't taken any photos with Phil since the Half Way Marker. Although at the moment, it was actually lightly raining and cloudy. We went to the café to get some sandwiches for take away, and by the time that was ready, the rain stopped, and the sky turned to blue and white clouds, so we went back to take more pictures of Phil in the sun instead of the clouds. The fog horn of the lighthouse was also going off. That was fun to hear working. It wasn't loud for us. Fortunately, it remained dry and warm, even though somewhat cloudy, the rest of the day.

We finally started walking but it took a long time to not get very far due to taking lots and lots photos. First were more photos of the Portland Bill Lighthouse, as we walked away from it. Benches offered a place for Scott to sit and pose. Then we were by that "village of beach huts" I saw yesterday from the top of the lighthouse, so of course I had to take lots of pictures. Some of these beach huts started out in the foreground of pictures, along with a rowboat sitting on the land, and in the background, a few sailboats on the seas, along with the lighthouse. These beach huts were mostly solids in colors, earthy tones of browns, reds, blues, greens, mauves, oranges. At the same time, the third lighthouse of the Isle of Portland that we saw, which was really the "The Second Lighthouse" was visible, and became a backdrop subject for some of my beach hut photos.

These beach huts actually felt like they were more like homes, because they were bigger than others I have seen, most had a window and a door, perhaps they even had small rooms inside them, and looked more like a miniature home rather than a storage hut. In fact, according to the booklet, "There are over 300 beach huts in Portland. Many of them are around Portland Bill, but there are some at Church Ope Cove. Originally they were fisherman's huts, but more recently they have been converted into leisure use. They often change hands for many thousands of pounds." I think I have decided that if I was to ever have a beach hut this would be the place. This would be the ultimate location to have my own beach hut! In fact, since these here seemed like miniature homes, I wouldn't mind living here and having my beach hut be a mini-home, too. I would also be in close proximity to not one, not two, not three, but four lighthouses. I could walk to Chesil Beach or the other small beach and cove on the Isle of Portland. And from the Isle of Portland I would be no more than a four hour drive from anywhere along the SWCP. Now I know there still some possibilities I have not walked to yet, and I know that there are many, many,

many great sandy and/or rocky beaches I have walked by or on that are all in second place behind this for my ultimate location for my beach hut, some of these beaches miles and miles long, some smaller and shorter, all of them scenic, not to mention secluded and isolated coves, and so many others, but I really do like the idea of a mini-home-beach-hut!

As we continued our leisurely stroll around the mini-home-beach-huts, the Portland Bill Lighthouse was visible for the background of some more photos. Then Scott and I walked up a short footpath, as we got closer to The Second Lighthouse to see if we could go inside. This Second Lighthouse "was built at the same time as the First Lighthouse and is often referred to as 'the low light' being lower down the hill," or "Old Lower Lighthouse." Both the First and Second Lighthouses were replaced in 1906 by the Portland Bill Lighthouse.

This Second Lighthouse is now used a bird observatory and a field studies center, as well as accommodations, so unfortunately we could not go inside as it was not exactly open to the public. We were told that there were a few displays inside, I'm guessing bird-related. I did take photos however of the lighthouse up close, with it being all white. I might be able to add this to my "expensive-places-to-stay-someday" list, along with yesterday's lighthouse. Two expensive places to stay on the Isle of Portland. As we walked back on the road to get back to the footpath, The First Lighthouse was visible up the small hill, so I took photos of it along with some wheat fields and some sunflowers in the foreground. There were a few horses as well on the footpath for Scott to enjoy.

Finally, we went back to the SWCP to continue walking. I would say that we covered an entire half mile in 45 minutes, between taking photos of Phil at the lighthouse, all three lighthouses, the beach huts, and trying to visit The Second Lighthouse. The path had been flat grass, easy walking, and then at this point as we turned around and looked back, we could actually see all three lighthouses in a row, and could even get all three lighthouses in a photo together, along with some mini-home-beach-huts.

After this scenic area, the rest of most of the walk today was not that scenic in my opinion by comparison. First, we walked through a rocky section of an old quarry. Then we walked on some grass next to a road, where we took a short lunch break with the sandwiches we bought earlier, at the Cheyne Weare viewpoint for about twenty minutes. After a short stretch that the booklet described as "the route is steep in places and you need to be careful to follow the faded arrows on boulders," we only saw one faded painted arrow, the rest was easy to follow, and we didn't seem to run into any steep sections probably because we followed the arrow, we reached Church Ope Cove, with its interesting beach huts all huddled here together on this small cove. This little cove was interesting to look at, with more earthy toned colors of the beach huts, a rocky beach, and the turquoise and blue seas.

We ascended a bunch of steep steps up, in chunks of five steps at a time, and it seemed like there was around ten of these chunks. Maybe that was the steep section the booklet was referring to. A mile of flat gravel walking on the track of an old railway was next. There were a few people doing some rock climbing with ropes on the cliff edge next to the SWCP. We could hear the sounds of waves crashing amongst themselves in the water and along a small rocky coastline below. Views beyond were of the turquoise and blue waters, and those white cliffs of the hillsides I saw yesterday that looked like snow.

In the mid-afternoon we had about one and three-quarters miles to go back to Chiswell and Castletown, the end of our Portland Circuit walk. We had a short uphill zigzag climb, and then the very not-scenic-at-all area of a flat area on a road next to some walls and barbed wire of some buildings used for the Young Offenders Institution, used for some other purpose now, and then next to the Verne Prison after some flat in between.

We then had a good view of the harbour of the Isle of Portland that we were near yesterday with the town of Weymouth and Chesil Beach beyond once again as we started a descent into Castletown. The descent started out gradual, then was flat, and then there was a quite long but gentle descent, known as the Castletown Incline, and finally out onto a road. Around the corner was the bus stop at the Portland Castle where we took a right turn yesterday, but today came from the left hand side. We completed the Isle of Portland, also known as the Portland Circuit, at 4:00pm.

We took a 4:30 bus back to near our B&B again. A bit later on I picked up some Indian take away for dinner, as today they would not deliver for some reason like they did the other day. Scott went out and explored the farm since this was our last night staying here, and spent some time with his favorite animals, the horses, one named Radar. From the previous two nights, although it was not too bothersome, we can confirm that at least during this time in August, their ducks do quack during the night.

DAY 80 STATS: 6 MILES. 4.5 HOURS, INCLUDING LOTS OF TIME AT THE BEGINNING FOR PHOTOS. I NEED TO COUNT AN EXTRA HALF MILE FOR PICKING UP DINNER. PUPRLE SHOES. MORE PUBS ON ISLE OF PORTLAND ARE "EIGHT KINGS" AND "CORNER HOUSE INN."

An Ultimate Beach Hut Location – Isle of Portland – August 21 and 22
Including The Second Lighthouse/Old Lower Lighthouse and "snow-covered-looking" cliffs in distance

NEAR FERRY BRIDGE TO WEYMOUTH TO OSMINGTON MILLS – Wednesday, 23 August 2017

"Courage! What makes a King out of a slave? Courage! What makes the flag on the mast to wave? Courage! What makes the elephant charge his tusk, in the misty mist or the dusky dusk? What makes the muskrat guard his musk? Courage! What makes the sphinx the Seventh Wonder? Courage! What makes the dawn come up like thunder? Courage! What makes the Hottentot so hot? What puts the "ape" in apricot? What have they got that I ain't got? Courage!" – The Cowardly Lion from the Wizard of Oz, who realizes that he has had his courage all along!

Hmmm...I realized that lately I haven't had, or needed, many guardian angels that help out in times of necessity. Except I still have Scott...And you know, all along I have had Myself! Yes, I have been my own guardian angel all along! Protecting myself, helping myself, taking care of myself, encouraging myself. Not once, even with all the fluctuating weather, even with my feelings at times of loneliness, even with all the cows and golf courses, and even with missing miles, did I never ever ever want to give up entirely on my SWCP walk. Perhaps maybe I am a little bit like the Lion in the Wizard of Oz, who always had his bravery and courage all along.

The last three mornings at this Farmhouse B&B, the woman has made some really good homemade granola, and she served not the little button mushrooms one usually gets with the Full or Half English, but small Portobello mushrooms instead, topped with some small skinny green, crisp and salty tasting herb, that tastes like the sea. I asked her what it was, because I had never seen it nor tasted it before, and I thought it was quite delicious. It is called Samphire, also known as sea asparagus. It is a sea vegetable that grows along the shorelines in marshy shallows or on salty mudflats, and it might even be considered a vegetable. It can be eaten raw, boiled, or steamed. I wondered if they got it somewhere along the Fleet Lagoon, and I also wondered if I could get any in the US. The woman of this B&B also had some fresh honey right on a honeycomb that we scraped right off and that I put on some toast. I must say that this place has had some of the better breakfasts I've had.

This B&B also had a book entitled "The Dorset Tea Trail, A Guide to the Tea Shops of Dorset," by Jean Bellamy. I read some more history on tea. "Tea was discovered accidently five thousand years ago, legend says. Apparently the Chinese Emperor Chen Nong was sitting in his garden sipping a bowl of hot water when the breeze blew some aromatic leaves into the vessel. He so enjoyed the flavour that thereafter he ordered his hot water already infused with the leaves." The book also mentioned Anna, Duchess of Bedford, who started the tradition of afternoon tea in 1840, as another book I read mentioned back when I was in Port Isaac. This book was a list of "tea rooms" and "tea gardens" that came about "towards the end of the 19th century when cycling in the countryside became popular, and when the first cars were seen on the roads. Country people opened their doors to travelers cycling or motoring out from the towns, offering them a pot of tea or homemade lemonade, scones, and a slice of cake. From this humble start the tea rooms we know today began." I still need to find out if Dorset has their cream tea like Cornwall or Devon.

Scott and I pet the pigs once more, and said our goodbyes to the horses, the alpacas, the chickens and ducks and geese. We had a view of the entire Isle of Portland that we walked around the last two days as we were leaving the farmhouse on its short footpath back to the SWCP. We needed to repeat a half mile walk back to Ferry Bridge, so I shall count that as extra mileage. We crossed the street of the bridge and instead of going right towards the Isle of Portland we went straight towards Weymouth and started new mileage on the SWCP. It followed a paved bike trail for about a mile. We did a quick stop at the ruins of Sandsfoot Castle, apparently built between 1539 and 1541, in a garden/park, where we could "still see some evidence of the original castle walls."

The next bit of walking was through some neighborhoods on sidewalk and grass which led to another park, a walk on a short seawall, near the Nothe Fort, which was "built between 1860 and 1872, [and] was manned during WW1 and it saw action in WW2," and then down to the harbour of Weymouth, with its many boats in the water between the two sides of the town on either side of the River Wey. We took a little "rowboat ferry" across the harbour into Weymouth, powered by an older man. The couple minute row somehow reminded me of a rowboat ride I took in Vietnam years and years ago around a floating fishing village there. It was very early in the morning one day back in 2007 near Cat Ba Island in Halong Bay. I wanted to see what local life was like in a village where people not only fish for a living, but their homes were built on small floating wooden planks. It was a meditative morning as I was rowed around this floating fishing village in Vietnam, seeing local life in action. What intrigued and inspired me most though about the experience was that the rowboat was powered by a woman. She rowed me around the floating fishing village, using the strength of her body. She did not speak much English, and I did not speak Vietnamese, but I could still sense not only the strength of her body, but also the strength of her spirit.

Today, as Scott and I were rowed across the river, we noticed and liked the meditative sound of the dripping water off the oars into the water as the older man rowed. We arrived on the other side of Weymouth, and stopped at a café for a small snack.

The next part of the walking was along the long Esplanade of Weymouth. We started on pavement, but soon realized that the long busy beach next to the Esplanade was sandy and walkable, so we took our shoes and socks off and walked barefoot on the sand and in the edge of the water, aka paddling. It was a nice feeling, and it seemed like we have not had the opportunity to do that in a while. As we walked, we noticed that the beach got less and less populated. We realized that it was because the sandy beach turned into a rocky beach, and with the difficultly of walking on the rocks, we returned to the pavement of the Esplanade. I walked though with my flip flops on now for a little while. There were some beach huts, but not individual ones like we have seen, but one building with a row of them all together. For some reason this building looked like it was built in the 1920s to me. It was painted white with blue doors and trim on some columns that had that old look to it, some even a bit rusty.

After a bit, we went back down to the beach again as it became mostly sandy, but still with some small rocks, and the tide was low enough. I continued to wear my flip flops as the rocks hurt my bare feet. Looking back, we could see the entire Isle of Portland. The small white waves were crashing on the beach as we walked. We arrived at the crowded Bowleaze Cove and passed the art-deco Riviera Hotel built in 1937 "and was used by the American forces as a hospital in WW2," and got back to what felt more like the SWCP, as we were now on a grassy path up on a hillside. We looked back on the curve of the beaches we just walked, to the town of Weymouth, and back to the Isle of Portland.

I put my purple shoes back on. The SWCP was quite flat and next to us spread out for a long time, the inland green rolling hillsides were covered with tent campers. Lots and lots of them. No caravan homes, just tents. We enjoyed that so many families were out enjoying their holidays. Some of the tents were quite large, accommodating whole families and all their camping belongings. Barbeques, towels and toys for going to the beaches, games to play. Nearby was an Outdoor Education Center, and we wondered if the kids could enjoy that as well. With so many colorful tents, the green hillsides look like a colorful sea of shells or pebbles on a beach. (Yes, I have been beside the seaside for 82 days now.)

I decided I needed a photo of Punxsutawney Phil with one of the quintessential SWCP wooden markers with its yellow arrow close to the acorn. So I pinned Phil to my rucksack as I have been doing for his photos with safety pins, propped my rucksack against a wooden marker that said "Coast Path," and took his photo with the seas in the background. Silly, but oh so fun.

With the SWCP being very flat since we left our B&B, we finally had one very small uphill. At the top of the hill we had a great view of a small beach below and the green rolling hills and the light tan rocks on the cliffs beyond. I wondered how far down it was to Swanage and Poole, the last days of the entire SWCP. We sat on the grass for a small snack. There were still many camping tents around on the green rolling hills, but I don't think we were yet at the white cliffs area that looked like snow to me that I saw from the Portland Bill Lighthouse.

At this spot where we stopped for a small snack, I also decided I needed another photo of Punxsutawney Phil in front of a SWCP stone marker, also with a yellow arrow close to the acorn, this one telling us that Osmington Mills was in one mile.

We had a slight descent into Osmington Mills, which just about consisted of our B&B, The Smugglers Inn, and a small combo café/thrift/bric-a-brac store. We checked into The Inn, and then went to the café/thrift/bric-a-brac store to get a snack of cream tea since we didn't make a dinner reservation till 7:00 and had several hours. We drank a lemongrass ginger tea with our scones, clotted cream, and jam. Still not knowing if Dorset is like Devon or Cornwall, I had each half of my scone one like Devon, and the other like Cornwall. Still delicious either way!

We also looked through the thrift/bric-a-brac store stuff, and Scott found two great small paintings of a lighthouse and a church scene, that I really liked. They reminded me of the two larger paintings we bought back in Shaldon, and I just had to buy them to go along with those other two, and my little church painting of St. Brannock's Church. These two paintings were only £4/$5.50 for the set, with the tag that showed the price describing them as "sea scapes." They actually look like they were painted with something fuzzy. The lighthouse is sitting on a little hilltop, with its beam of light casting out over the seas, and its reflection in the water of an area that could become a harbour as you can tell the seas were flowing into the area. A couple houses are next to the lighthouse, and a sailboat is out on the seas. The painting is quite dark actually with the background mostly gray, and so what I first thought was a yellow ball of sun, but I then wondered if it was really a night scene with a full moon.

The fuzzy paining of the church also has a house next to it, a fence in front of it, what looks like a sandy beach and the blue seas. Here the skies are painted more of a white and light blue with brown streaks, and again that yellow ball, perhaps of the sun. Or the moon. I just don't know. Both scenes once again reminded me of the SWCP! Back in our room at The Smugglers Inn, I removed the frames and glass the paintings were in so as to not break that the rest of my walk. By now I was an expert at this. It was fun that I now have two sets of unique paintings as memories from the SWCP. I reframed them, and now both sets, plus the little church painting, so five great paintings are now hanging on our living room wall, all great memories of my SWCP walk!

Later Scott and I had dinner at The Smugglers Inn, parts of which date back to the 13th century. According to "A Brief History of Smugglers Inn" that was in our information book in our room, Smugglers Inn "was once the home of the leader of the most notorious gang of smugglers in the area during the 18th and 19th centuries, Emmanuel Charles. He imported brandy that was so disgusting that none of the locals would drink it." The very detailed information continued later on: "Legends of the smuggling days of old have often held a romantic flavor, yet there is nothing vaguely romantic about the savagery and violence that often accompanied it."

The information said this about female smugglers: "Not only were women useful to the smugglers as signalers and carriers of messages from members of the gang to each other, but they actually brought goods in from the shore for them. The voluminous skirt was a particularly useful fashion, for the women wound yards of silk and lace round their bodies and reached home as a rule quite peacefully with their contraband."

In the early 1800s efforts were made to stop smuggling including the Preventative Waterguard with "a large number of cruisers and boats under the command of naval officers, whose duty it was to patrol the coastal areas while revenue cruisers sailed further out to sea and riding officers [on horseback] guarded the land. Over the next few years [after 1815], a whole series of measures were taken to increase the numbers of those employed in the prevention of smuggling and to improve cooperation between them. In 1822 the Preventative Services were given a further overhaul. The Waterguard, Revenue Cruisers and Riding Officers were amalgamated under the control of the Board of Customs and given a new collective name, The Coastguard. Terraces of cottages to house the Coastguard officers were built at strategic spots all along the coast."

"The Coastguard Service came into operation on 15th January 1822. Coastguards served on ships and on shore. By 1839 there were over 4,553 Coastguards." Painted on the outside wall of The Smugglers Inn is a verse from "A Smuggler's Song," written by Rudyard Kipling, but here are a few verses:

If you wake at midnight, and hear a horse's feet,
Don't go drawing back the blind, or looking in the street
Them that ask no questions isn't told a lie.
Watch the wall my darling while the Gentlemen go by.

Running round the woodlump if you chance to find
Little barrels, roped and tarred, all full of brandy-wine.
If your mother mends a coat cut about and tore;
If the lining's wet and warm – don't you ask no more!

Five and twenty ponies
Trotting through the dark-
Brandy for the Parson, 'Baccy for the Clerk.
Them that ask no questions isn't told a lie.
Watch the wall my darling while the Gentlemen go by!

Wow…more on smuggling…with its connection to the Coastguard…and thus the connection to the SWCP!

DAY 81 STATS: 8 MILES. 5 HOURS. EXTRA HALF MILE FROM B&B TO FERRY BRIDGE REPEAT. PURPLE SHOES AND BARE FEET AND FLIP FLOPS. PUBS IN WEYMOUTH ARE "THE RED LION," "THE SHIP INN," AND "THE BLACK DOG." PUB IN OSMINGTON MILLS IS "THE SMUGGLERS INN." Information on Samphire from bbc.co.uk/food/samphire and bbcgoodfood.com/glossary/samphire.

OSMINGTON MILLS TO LULWORTH COVE – Thursday, 24 August 2017

"There is an uphill for every downhill, and a downhill for every uphill." - Turkish Proverb

It was a warm quiet morning already at 10:00. The sun was out through a thin layer of clouds. The joggers and dog walkers were out as well. I realized that some of my favorite walks, aside from those walking along the beaches and the coastline, are those when I am on top of the cliffs, out in the open, and I can see for miles and miles in all directions, and that's what it was like as we started our walk leaving Osmington Mills. I was able to get mobile reception on my phone so I brought up the "I Do Like to be Beside the Seaside" song and started to dance around just because it felt like that kind of morning.

The path was pretty much flat for the half hour and first mile to Ringstead Bay. There was a bit of path through some trees, but otherwise the path was out in the open next to some grassy fields. We went down to rocky beach for a look at some rowboats sitting on the rocky beach, and some sailboats and rowboats floating in the water. Someone was bringing up their crab and lobster pot, others were bringing up the sails, and two little kids in wet suits were playing in the water. It was good to see this local morning activity.

We stopped at a café to get a couple of sandwiches because for the next five miles, there would be no food stops. The next half mile, or even longer, after we got our sandwiches was all inland on a dirt track road. It started out flat and then changed to a slight incline up on the track road which turned into a paved road. We stopped at a little wooden chapel, St. Catherine's by the Sea, originally built in 1926, but rebuilt in 2010. There were several benches in the small graveyard behind the church which offered great views of the seas and Isle of Portland still in view beyond. It was a peaceful tranquil spot. Especially in the warmth of the sun. Scott posed for some photos sitting on a bench with the views in the background.

There was a bit more slight incline up on a grassy slope, then Scott and I were on top of a cliff looking down at a green cliff edge below, the beaches, and the places we just passed – Osmington Mills, the colorful-sea-of-shells-or-pebbles tent camping area, the long beach all the way into Weymouth, and all the way around to the Isle of Portland. And the blue waters in between this circular bowl. The path was flat on top of this grassy cliff we were on.

There was a hang glider, and I wondered if anyone has ever done hang gliding along the entire edge of the SWCP, much like I wondered about that ultralight motorized plane a while back. Another math situation I could figure out, depending on how fast hang gliders go. How long would it take someone to continually hang glide the edge of the SWCP, hoping that the winds would cooperate for them? Let's say a hang glider travels at about 20 miles per hour, then it would take about 31.5 hours to hang glide the entire SWCP!

A few hours after we started our walk, we stopped to eat our sandwiches near the White Nothe Former Coastguard Cottages and a WW2 lookout at White Nothe, and after walked out a short ways to a spectacular viewpoint overlooking all the green-topped rolling hills of the white-tan colored cliffs we will be climbing up and down soon, and the beaches below. These are the white cliffs that I saw from the top of Portland Bill Lighthouse that looked like snow. We had arrived! Definitely not snow though, but absolutely beautiful. Both Scott and Punxsutawney Phil posed for photos on a bench at this beautiful spot. Soon we started walking again, with three and a half miles left to Lulworth Cove, our destination for the day. At a half-hour per mile pace, I figured we should be in Lulworth Cove around 2:35. Boy was I wrong…

The path started out quite flat next to some wheat fields. I took a couple of photos facing inland of only just the light brown of the wheat fields and the blue and white-cloud sky. We continued to have views of the green rolling hills and white-tan color cliffs. I could see the several of the four hills we would soon be ascending and descending, not realizing that a couple of these descents would be among the toughest I have done the entire SWCP. The first descent was gentle, but the loose rocks, pebbles, and gravel made me walk quite slow so as to not slip and slide. We had the sound of the crashing waves on a small beach below which was soothing as I walked this section. We got closer to the beach, which was called Middle Bottom, although I think that it should be called First Bottom. The first ascent felt like we were climbing out of a bowl because the shape of the grass-covered hills inland, called The Warren, and the grass cliffs blocking our views on the right, created this bowl-shaped effect. With descent and ascent number one done, the view ahead included the amazing white-tan cliffs, the arching rocks of Durdle Door with its long sandy beach, and lots of people.

The second descent was one of the steepest and slowest and toughest for me of the entire SWCP! It was not very long, but its steepness made me a bit nervous. With loose gravel that could be slippery, I utilized the grass to walk on instead, which could have also been slippery, but for me was a better surface. I was really glad I had my hiking poles with me today as planned, as these helped me brace myself descending into Bat's Head. The second ascent to Swyre Head was long and semi-steep. There were several well-worn paths, of which I chose the inner-most path closest to the fence line.

The views from up here included the hills we were recently on behind us, a sandy beach, the white-tan edge of the cliffs, and all the way out to the Isle of Portland. The views ahead were of getting closer to the beach and the arch rocks of Durdle Door, and now we could see a steady stream of people going up and down a path leading to the view point of Durdle Door. It amazed me how many people were on this path. We could see a bunch of them stopping at the view point for a look, and then we could see some of them continuing on down the steep-looking set of steps to the beach below. "This has got to be one of the most populated areas I have seen on the SWCP," I declared out loud to Scott. Seems like even more so than Lizard Point, which takes second place. A herd of cows added a speckle of black and white to the green covered hilltops a bit inland.

The third descent was another steep, slow descent, relying on my poles. Another one of the steepest and slowest and toughest descents for me of the entire SWCP! The bottom of this descent was called Scratchy Bottom, I'm not sure why, perhaps it should be called Third Bottom. From here, there was a view of the sandy beach below which was a continuation of the beach starting at Durdle Door. We had closer views of Durdle Door itself from here as well as a few other rock formations in the water, and another arch in the cliff we had just come down from.

The ascent from this spot, ascent number three, was quite short and gentle and it was the place where the steady stream of people had collected to view the arch in the rocks. Durdle Door was formed about 140 million years ago in the Jurassic Period, and is "one of the Coast Path's most iconic landmarks." With camping nearby, as well as several car parks, I also wondered if tour busses drop of people as well to take a look with these crowds. We stopped ourselves and had a snack, and mixed in with the crowds. We noticed that we could just make out the Portland Bill Lighthouse structure at the tip of the Isle of Portland out in the distance.

We then walked on the busiest mile of the entire SWCP I have been on, our fourth ascent. It was the path I saw earlier when I noticed the steady stream of people. The stream was still steady with lots and lots people, as well as a steady slight uphill incline. Weaving in and out of the people, seeing the busy car park and camping area, we then took a right turn down, the fourth descent, along with yet more people going both up and down, into the town of Lulworth Cove, our destination for the day that soon we saw just ahead. A large grassy area filled with rows and rows of cars was also below near Lulworth Cove. This fourth descent was gradual, on some rows of concrete bricks, but the hiking poles still came in handy. Fortunately, my right knee survived all these ups and downs.

We arrived at the Lulworth Cove Inn, about 45 minutes after my predicted arrival time (I thought I would play that game just once more), just on the other side of the car park and checked in. This day of ascents and descents compares to some of those other days where I have had several ascents and descents in one day. But I think that some of today's were tougher. I was grateful that at times there was a breeze today that made it sometimes feel cooler, even though it was generally a warm day, and definitely a dry day.

Soon after checking in, Scott and I went out and walked down to the very round cove of Lulworth Cove. Still busy with people, we viewed the boats floating in the water and the cliff tops surrounding the water. A few rowboats were resting on or near its pebbly rocky beach. Lulworth Cove was the probably the most circular in shape cove I have seen. We were hungry so we got a small snack, then went back to the room so that I could research tomorrow's walk. We needed to make sure the military firing range would be open, and we saw that we have possibly another four ascents and descents to look forward to! Hiking poles are ready! Scott suggested that I should wear my hiking boots tomorrow. I should have worn them today as well, but I had my purple shoes on.

We had a view from our room of a part of Lulworth Cove in the distance after the short road leading down to it. A few hours later we went back out for dinner. I ordered a "Super Food Salad" with various greens like kale and spinach, quinoa, pumpkin seeds, blueberries, avocado, and a pomegranate dressing, one of the best salads that I have had on the entire SWCP. A good healthy meal to end a good, yet tough, day.

DAY 82 STATS: 6 MILES. 5.25 HOURS. NO EXTRA MILES AS BOTH B&BS WERE RIGHT ON THE COAST PATH. PURPLE SHOES, BUT SHOULD HAVE WORN HIKING BOOTS. PUB IN LULWORTH COVE IS "LULWORTH COVE INN," AND A BIT INLAND IN WEST LULWORTH IS "THE CASTLE INN."

LULWORTH COVE TO KIMMERAGE BAY – Friday, 25 August 2017

"Military Firing Range. Keep Out. Unstable cliff ledges. Beware of falling rock. Danger. Unexploded shells. Do not touch any military debris. Keep to the Range Walks. Follow the Yellow Markers." – Some of the many signs in The Lulworth Military Firing Range.

There are two routes out of Lulworth Cove. One is to walk around the cove itself on the rocky beach and climb out slightly around the other end. "This route is OK at most states of the tide," per the booklet. With our 10:00 start, and with the high tide for the day being at 10:30, Scott and I just did not know if this option would work for us. Therefore, we went for option two, a bit longer in length, but no questions of tides.

It was the inland route which started off on a sidewalk leading out of town, curved around to a slight uphill climb of Bindon Hill, flattened out, and then descended 333 steps, "the longest continuous flight of steps on the SW Coast Path." While I avoided most of the actual steps themselves by going on the little side trail next to the steps, as it was easier on my knees, this descent made some of the others I have done seem a lot easier. Well except for a few of those from yesterday. Before the descent down, we had a good view of the round Lulworth Cove with its sailboats and buoys floating in the turquoise and blue waters, surrounded by the small hills on either side of the entrance. Beyond that the seas were a great blue today, with the blue of the skies and white fluffy clouds. We could even still see the Isle of Portland in the distance.

When we arrived at the junction at the bottom of the steps to where the short climb was that came out of the cove, the first route I mentioned, we realized that perhaps we could have done the cove walk as I saw one other person on that path. Perhaps, though. Better safe than sorry. From here, we could see the circular shape again of the cove with its beach underneath the short hillsides, and a few people on the beach.

Today's walk was largely through The Lulworth Military Firing Ranges, a 7,000 acre area that includes seven miles of the SWCP. One needs to make sure it is open, and therefore no firing is going on, to be able to walk through. Last night I checked several websites which said it would be open. If it were closed, it would be a long way around, or some other plans would need to occur to walk today. One of the signals for the ranges being closed is the flying of a red flag.

As we were descending the 333 steps section, a red flag was flying. What?? I checked the websites last night and they said it was open. I was a bit upset needless to say, but we decided that we should still walk to the actual entrance where there was a gate to see for sure what the status would be. They were open! I'm not sure why the red flag was flying up above. There was no red flag flying at the actual entrance gate, the gate was unlocked, and a sign said, "Lulworth Range Walks. Open. Enjoy The Walks." At 10:50 we entered the ranges, and even saw a few people walking inside the gate. "There have been firing ranges in this part of Dorset since WWI but during 1943 the range was extended and has been in use ever since," per today's booklet.

The range walk on the SWCP started out on flat wide grass leading to the picturesque Mupe Bay. On the way there there was a herd of cows, and goats, inside a fenced area. I think the only other time I saw goats on the SWCP was a few on a hillside long, long ago, the mountain goats back on 8 June in the area called "Valley of Rocks" near Lynmouth and Lynton. The time where there were a couple of goats, and me, on a narrow ledge. Anyway, today as Scott and I walked along the grassy path, these goats were of no concern, the blue water was to our right, and to our left was a constant barbed wire fence with signs every once in a while saying, "Military Firing Range. Keep Out."

Above Mupe Bay we stopped at the benches which offered us a snack stop and some great views - the grassy hill with the steep trail we were about to climb, the white-tan cliffs with a rockfall that went right down to the edge of the turquoise and blue water, two yachts in the waters of the bay, and more hills and cliffs beyond. The scene to me looked like a lake in the mountains. Of course this really isn't a lake, but the edge of the water with the rockfall and cliffs looked like a lake scene in the mountains to me nonetheless. The sound of small crashing waves serenaded our short break.

Then we began a steep ascent up a hillside. Well, the "mountainside," as this climb felt like that to me because even though there were steps, they were covered with loose rocks. I took it slow, stopped carefully for photos, and arrived at the top in fourteen minutes time. I wondered if this was the longest time it had taken me to go up any ascent on the SWCP. There were great views at the top of what we just saw of Mupe Bay below, but from a higher perspective, and the great blue waters and blue skies beyond. The two yachts below became three as another one motored in.

The path then flattened out for a bit. There were a lot of warning-caution-danger signs on today's walk..."Keep out"..."Unstable cliff ledges"..."Do not go near the cliff edge"..."Beware of falling rock"..."Danger. Unexploded shells. Keep out"..."Do not touch, objects may explode"..."Danger. Do not touch any military debris. It may explode and kill you." OK, no worries, I got the messages, the warnings-cautions-dangers - I will definitely stay on the trail and not touch anything!

Before the next climb down, the views from here looking to where we would be walking were brilliant. Of a beach below, white-tan cliff edges covered with green grass on top of the rolling hills, the etch of the SWCP we would soon be walking on, and all the blues and turquoises. Just lovely! A photo of this scene is on the back cover!

The next climb down was a steep one, with both steps and side trails that I took slowly. There was a military beach at the bottom with no public access. Next was a small uphill and a flat section that prepared us for the next climb. We saw in the distance some tanks, which are used for target practice. For ten minutes this time, there was another steep uphill, and while I went slowly, it was easier than a lot of other climbs have been lately because it was on a wide grassy path. There were no steps and no rocks or pebbles. From the top were amazing views looking back on the amazing landscape we have come from – glimpses of the white-tan cliffs, the green hillside we had just come down, with the etch of the path we walked, and inland were green grass covered hillsides sprinkled with checkered farmland. We could see herds of cows, and farm houses inland, and with the bright, warm, sunny day, this was a great spot for a food break.

Next was a steep descent, even though it was also mostly grassy. We arrived at Worbarrow Bay, a large round bay with a thin line of a beach, which gave us more amazing views of where we just walked - the green on top of the hills, and the white-tan cliffs that lead down to the turquoise and blue waters. We stopped at a bench briefly for some photos. I found it interesting that this military range offered such amazing landscape.

Then it was time for an inland detour to see a village, Tyneham, which was taken over by the military in World War 2 for D-Day preparations. "The villagers were given 28 days' notice to move all their possessions by 17th December 1943." More specifically, per a display in the village, "Winston Churchill's War Cabinet issues clearance notices to all 106 properties in an area of approximately twelve square miles, including Tyneham Village. They have one month to leave. As properties belong to the Squire, who will receive compensation, most inhabitants were given only the value of the produce in their gardens."

The area near Torcross and Slapton Sands were other such villages, although the difference is that the Torcross and Slapton Sands villagers were allowed to return to their homes months after D-Day. Because it is inside the Lulworth firing ranges, the village of Tyneham remains abandoned. Scott and I started on an inland flat track to Tyneham, where I first took off the hiking boots that I had been wearing and put on my flip flops for the short walk.

Most of the buildings of Tyneham are crumbled with no roofs, and plants are growing out of the fireplaces. Plaques describe what each building used to be – a shepherds cottage, a post office, a labourers cottage, and others. The old telephone poll still stands and an old telephone is still in an old Red Telephone Box, although it is a rebuilt display made to look like the one from 1929. The schoolhouse and the Tyneham Church of St. Mary the Virgin are the most intact buildings because they have been restored, and inside the school and church are displays, old books, children's nature study lesson and books, learning about habitats and wildflowers and plants and trees and birds and butterflies and animals, and an old piano. It was like stepping back in time over 70 years. From some information on display, "Before the Second World War, Tyneham was just one of many small, isolated Dorset villages, relying largely on farming and fishing for its livelihood." When the inhabitants left the church, "they pinned a note to the church door. It read:"

"Please treat the church and houses with care. We have given up our homes, where many of us have lived for generations, to help win the war to keep men free. We will return one day and thank you for treating the village kindly." "In 1945, with the Cold War looming, the newly elected government decided to retain the valley and the villagers could not return."

Scott and I spent forty minutes in the historic village. I put my purple shoes on for the remainder of today's walk, as there would be no more steep or rocky ascents or descents. We took a different connecting path to the SWCP which had a slight incline uphill. Technically we missed a small section of the actual SWCP, but I am saying that we made up for it by walking the two inland paths and seeing the great historic village. It would be similar mileage. I do think though that we may have missed one more steep ascent. Well, really I guess I shall add that bit of the actual SWCP that we missed to my future-to-walk list.

We connected back up with SWCP and the path was flat behind some shrubbery then opened up to views of lots and lots of flat checkered green fields, a couple of them with sheep way in the distance, the deep blue Kimmerage Bay, the Clavell Tower, and the headlands beyond. I wondered if any of what we were seeing beyond was Swanage or even Poole. With only days left of my walk, I actually started to feel a bit sad that soon this scenery, and my walk, all I have had experienced, and all that I have fallen in love with, would be soon over. A sign told me I had eleven miles to Swanage, then Poole would be about seven miles beyond that.

But for now, I did not dwell on that too much. The path went around a green hill that we didn't need to climb, and then descended slightly. It flattened out, went around some green fields, one of which was one with sheep in it that we saw from above. We walked near the cute little sheep that appeared to have been recently sheared. At 4:05pm we left the Lulworth Military Firing Range, seven miles and five and a quarter hours later. A sign on this side of the gate we walked through confirmed once again that, "Lulworth Range Walks. Open. Enjoy the walks." I was glad it was open today, as even with a few climbs, it was some amazingly beautiful lovely brilliant scenery. We arrived at Kimmerage Bay, our destination for today.

We had to walk a mile inland to Kimmerage itself, to the restaurant there where our prearranged pick up from our next B&B gentleman would be. Scott spotted a footpath that we took leading to a road leading to another footpath, and when we arrived at the restaurant, we were hungry, so we ate there, sharing a very good baked butternut squash and oven roasted vegetables with sweet potato and couscous. We also finished a sandwich we got from our B&B this morning in Lulworth Cove. Yes, it was still good.

David picked us up at our prearranged time, and drove us the twenty minutes to our B&B in Worth Matravers. We drove through the narrow country lanes that I have been driving around now for nearly three months. The ones where if a car is coming from the other direction, someone needs to kindly pull over and let the other pass by where there is room for two cars, since really they are like single-lane roads. I have never been nervous when in a car, as people here are used to doing this, while it is something different than what I am used to back home. The tall shrubbery that lines the narrow roads make it hard to know where you are really going since you cannot see, but those that drive here are used to that. Still, when I think of going back to roads with at least two lanes, and freeways with four lanes, or more, and going that fast, I don't really know how I am going to handle the busyness of all that back home after being on these quiet country roads with no traffic whatsoever for the last nearly three months. I wonder if I am going to want Scott and I to move to a smaller quieter town. Near the beaches. Beside the seaside.

Back at the B&B Ann made us dinner. I had forgotten that I preordered this extra feature of this B&B long ago. Ann will also make us a packed lunch for tomorrow, in addition to breakfast and dinner tomorrow morning and night as well. It was all part of the cost of the room. The rides would be an extra cost. We did however, need to share a bathroom at this B&B with the other guests.

I found out that the area we are in now, from Wareham to Swanage, is called the Isle of Purbeck, as the land sticks out like an island into the sea. It is an Area of Outstanding Natural Beauty. Yes, indeed!

I have actually walked through many "Areas of Outstanding Natural Beauty" along the SWCP which are "exactly what it says it is: outstanding landscape whose distinctive character and natural beauty are so precious that it is safeguarded in the national interest." There are AONB landscapes for nature, people, business, and culture throughout the UK. Basically, AONBs are protected lands for conservation and enhancement of natural beauty of the landscape, "protecting some of UK's most important and sensitive habitats." There are 46 AONBs in the UK, 34 in England, "just over one-fifth of the English Coast is AONB, and over 19,000 km of footpaths and bridleways pass through AONBs including ten National Trails." Including parts of the SWCP. Including areas in Cornwall, Devon, and Dorset, that I have (or will) walk through, in no particular order, such as exactly or near, and not necessarily limited to: Land's End; the Lizard Peninsula; the cliffs north of Boscastle; estuaries of the Fowey, Fal, and Helford Rivers; villages and small towns such as Tintagel, Mevagissey, Polperro, and Fowey; Lulworth Cove; Chesil Beach; the Jurassic Coast; "from Coombe Martin to the Cornish border;" "from Torbay to the outskirts of Plymouth;" the Isle of Purbeck; and more. In fact the "South West Coast Path plays an important role in the popularity of the AONB."

There is one more organization to talk about which plays a role in managing AONBs, "Natural England." Natural England is "the government's advisor for the natural environment in England, helping to protect England's nature and landscapes for people to enjoy and for the services they provide." They are responsible for "promoting nature conservation and protecting biodiversity; conserving and enhancing the landscape; securing the provision and improvement of facilities for the study, understanding and enjoyment of the natural environment; promoting access to the countryside and open spaces and encouraging open-air recreation; and contributing in other ways to social and economic well-being through management of the natural environment." What beautiful concepts in action AONB and Natural England are!

I also found out that this particular weekend is a "Bank Holiday," which "is a colloquial term for a public holiday in the United Kingdom. There is no automatic right to time off on these days, although banks close and the majority of the working population is granted time off work or extra pay for working these days, depending on their contract." I think that public transportation runs on a more limited schedule during these holidays as well. That might explain the lots of people at Durdle Door yesterday as well.

DAY 83 STATS: 8 MILES, INCLUDING THE 7 MILES THROUGH THE RANGE, AND THE TYNEHAM DETOUR AS SIMILAR MILEAGE TO COAST PATH. 6.25 HOURS. EXTRA MILE TO KIMMERAGE VILLAGE. HIKING BOOTS, FLIP FLOPS, AND PURPLE SHOES. "PUB" IN KIMMERAGE VILLAGE IS "CLAVELL'S VILLAGE CAFÉ AND FARM SHOP."

Information on AONBs from gov.uk/guidance/areas-of-outstanding-natural-beauty-aonbs-designation-and-management; and from landscapesforlife.org.uk.
Information about Natural England from gov.uk/government/organisations/natural-england/about.
Information about Bank Holidays from wikipedia.org/wiki/Bank_holiday.

KIMMERAGE BAY TO WORTH MATRAVERS – Saturday, 26 August 2017

"Hand built strata; Held by gravity; Between turf and sky; Dark brought to light; Exposed to weather." – From a row of Poetry Stones along the South West Coast Path.

After breakfast, Scott and I got a ride back to the restaurant in Kimmerage by David of the B&B. We went to go visit the church just across the road, St. Nicholas, another church which like many churches I have seen along the SWCP have parts dating back to the 12th and 13th centuries, but then was extensively rebuilt in 1872, while we waited for Jill and Brian. Today we would walk part of our day with a woman and her husband from the SWCP Facebook Group, a couple who responded to my walk request quite a while ago. They parked their car a bit up the road from the church and restaurant at a car park and will do a circular walk. We waited nearby and soon saw them as they came out of a footpath. We met each other and hugged. Jill has been following my progress through the pictures I post on the Facebook page. I appreciated the nice hug from her.

We all needed to walk the extra mile back to Kimmerage Bay, and Jill knew of a nicer footpath than the one Scott and I took yesterday. This one was more shaded and next to corn fields. It took us twenty minutes to walk the extra mile. At the edge of Kimmerage Bay with the Clavell Tower in the background, we did a quick photo session. Scott took pictures of me, Jill, and Brian proudly showing off our SWCP Facebook Group lanyards so that I could post the pictures on the Facebook Group page; they took pictures of me and Scott, which were actually the first "together" pictures we have of us on our shared walk since Scott arrived; and we took pictures of the two of them.

We started with a slight climb to Clavell Tower, built in 1830 by "Reverend John Richards Clavell as an observatory and folly." In 1833 "after Clavell died and passed the estate to his niece the tower became a destination for picnics and family expeditions. From the 1880s until 1914 it served as a lookout post for the coastguards but it was then left empty and became increasingly derelict." "In the early 21st century the tower was in danger of falling into the sea and so from 2005-8 it was dismantled and moved further inland. Now it can be rented as a holiday home," per today's booklet, and as we walked by some current renters were sitting outside this 40-foot round structure on its porches. I recently looked up more information online, and while it has not been a lighthouse, its interior looks quite lavish, and I think I should add it to the list of "expensive-places-to-stay-someday" list for that time in my life when I have a lot of extra money, such as when this book becomes a best seller, which at this point with the growing list I have been keeping would be quite a very expensive trip. In the meantime, the Clavell Tower is fully reserved until July 2019.

The path was relatively flat after the tower. It was quiet as there were no waves crashing. We started walking about 10:30 really, but it took us quite a while to just get through this first bit, between chatting and taking photos that I made the official start time for the day be 11:00. I asked Jill about cream tea in Dorset, since she lives here I figured she would know, and because I still did not know if it is the same as Cornwall or as Devon. Jill said it is the same as in Cornwall, with jam first, cream on top. So there was my answer. Jill also suggested however that we try the "Dorset Apple Cake" sometime soon before my walk ends, a local specialty. I decided I was now on a quest to find and try this new cake.

The inland scenery on today's walk was quite beautiful, filled with farmland, including barrel rolls of hay, and great shades of green color. To our right were the blue waters and somewhat blue sky. Behind us were the white-tan cliffs and green hills we walked yesterday in the military firing range area of Lulworth. While it was a beautifully warm and dry day, it was a bit hazy out. I also realized that it seemed like we were no longer walking above the white-tan cliffs and were back to brownish-colored cliffs. There were splashes of yellow and white wildflowers as we walked. I mostly chatted with Jill as we walked the mostly flat path, while Scott and Brian chatted together.

About an hour after we began "officially" walking, we started one of the two biggest uphill climbs of the day. The climb started out gentle and zigzagged its way up, and then the steep part began which took me about nine minutes to get to the top, including a few photo stops. At one point I stopped and looked back to see a brown patch of farmland with more barrel rolls of hay and a large tractor. On either side of this were green grasses, and inland more varied greenery, and on the other side the blue seas. Just beautiful. Green and blue still my favorite colors.

It was steep to the top, but no steps, only "footprint" type steps and a grassy slope to the top of Houns-tout Cliff. The views of the farmland I just saw and the white-tan cliffs of yesterday, and even the Isle of Portland from days ago all behind continued to be beautiful as the four of us stopped and sat on a bench and ate. Scott and I got some sandwiches from our B&B this morning, and Jill made us some as well. That was very sweet of her. We all sat there and ate and chatted for about 45 minutes. We had another walker take a photo of all four of us sitting there, and we had Jill take a few more pictures of me and Scott together. Since Jill and Brian were doing a circular walk today

Some of the only photos of Scott and me together on the South West Coast Path (And Fog)
At Kimmerage Bay with Clavell Tower in the background August 26 (photo credit: Jill and Brian)
Near some beach huts in Lyme Regis April 30 (photo credit: a kind woman who offered to take our photo)
Scott pointing to "What you can see from Land's End" – Fog – From our 2016 100-mile walk mentioned July 8

back to their car, it was from here that they would walk back following a path along the ridge top. We said our goodbyes, nice to have met and walked with you, and hugged again. It was nice to walk with yet more members of the SWCP Facebook Group and meet new people, and make new connections.

My purple shoes were the subject of a photo I took from sitting on this bench looking at the great views. I also took a few quick photos of Punxsutawney Phil at the bench with the great views behind as I thought this would be a great scenic spot for him to pose as well. At 1:15 Scott and I started walking again. We soon had a short but steep descent, all with steps, and no side path option, but I don't know how many steps as I didn't count, and the booklet didn't say. We had a view of a bay below called Chapman's Pool, filled with about a dozen expensive-looking boats and yachts, and I could hear people down there enjoying the beach. There were a lot of people out walking today on this part of the SWCP. I guess this is a popular section to do, and/or the good weather had brought people out to enjoy walking.

There was a nice inland diversion through a grassy field to a road and next to some sheep. We were in a beautiful valley. One of the more scenic inland diversions of the SWCP. It was all flat and ended up at a few quaint houses in an area called Hill Bottom before heading back out. We needed to stop for a few minutes to tend to a blister that Scott had developed on the back of his heel. We put on a piece of sheep's wool and used a few plasters (band aids) to keep it secure.

The path back out began with a slight incline uphill, and then the path flattened out for quite a while. It was on grass then a trail next to a stone wall. There were words on the wall written in five stone plaques, known as Poetry Stones, which read:

Hand built strata
Held by gravity
Between turf and sky
Dark brought to light
Exposed to weather

They were created around 2012 using "dry stone walling [which] is an ancient building method where structures are made from stones without any mortar to bind them together."

As we walked along the long flat stretch, we had views of the green covered hill we just came down just before inland diversion, the bay with boats below, and the miles we had recently done, and walked over the last few days, again including the white-tan cliffs and the Isle of Portland, over thirty-five miles away.

We had a steep descent and ascent with 185 steps down and 218 steps up! I used the poles a lot, and while on the way down I did every step, on the way up, I used side paths a bit. We reached the top at St. Aldhelm's Head and another bench with another beautiful view was waiting for us. Scott and I sat on this bench and enjoyed the views while eating once again. I guess we were burning a lot of calories during our walk today. A half hour later, after Scott posed for photos on this bench, and note that I have also been taking many bench-only photos for my "Benches of the SWCP" photography book someday. We started walking again, visiting a National Coastwatch Institute Station where they were serving refreshments, so we nibbled again, and made a donation.

We visited the quaint St. Aldhelm's Chapel which dates from the 12th century and was square in shape. A plaque inside the chapel told us that that Parish Church in Worth Matravers and this Chapel are 800 years old. A booklet about this unique chapel told me that "Two points immediately strike the visitor as being most unusual. First, the angles of the building are pointing approximately to the cardinal points of the compass, not the walls as is customary. Secondly, the 7.77meter [25 feet square] square shape is most unusual for an ecclesiastical building. These two features – the square shape and the orientation – have caused people to speculate that the chapel did not, in the first instance, have a religious origin. However, the beautiful vaulting of the 12th Century roof and the existence of the medieval graves outside near the walls, together with its position within a circular earthwork, suggest that it was a religious building from the beginning."

St. Aldhelm's Chapel was indeed small, much like The East Fleet Old Parish Church, Saint Clements Church in Hope Cove, and St. Bueno's Church in Culbone. It was cool in temperature inside, with its stone walls and interior arches. There was no electricity, just the lighting from candles, such as was the case in St. Germanus Church in Rame, and St. Anthony Church across Gillan Creek. As we walked out of the Chapel, a woman was there with her young child and with her own father. Scott seemed to recall that she told Scott they were visiting the Chapel because her parents were married there years ago and she was taking her father to visit there today many years later.

As we continued walking, I could hear waves in the water, but as I looked out, it seemed more like perhaps it was the coming together of a few different patterns of currents in the water. We had a distant view of Anvil Point Lighthouse which we will be walking next to tomorrow. The path continued to be all flat, next to grassy ledges and blackberry bushes on our right. A few more wildflowers were around.

At 4:30 we reached Winspit Quarry. There was a footpath here inland to Worth Matravers for our B&B, but we decided to walk to the next quarry, Seacombe Quarry, and take the inland footpath from there. That inland footpath would be a bit shorter than the one at Winspit, and it would also cut out about a mile of walking between the two quarries tomorrow, which we would be doing now instead. The path between the two quarries was all flat on a grassy path. A half hour later, we headed inland for the one mile of extra walking to "Worth." The footpath started out flat, then had a bit of incline, and 73 additional steps for the day. We took a flat path after going over a wall-type style out to the road that was very close to our B&B and to the Square and Compass Pub.

I wanted to go inside and look in the pub because of its uniqueness, something that had to do with either its low ceilings, or its small door, or that there is a narrow passage from the front door to the bar, or its original interior, or its small size, or that drinks are still served through two hatches as they were served long ago, or something like that that our B&B gentleman told us about, but it was very crowded, and there was a long line to get in. Instead Scott and I went into the Fossil Museum at the pub filled with fossils and other archaeological finds primarily from the local area, collected by one of the owners of the pub and his father through 60 years of collecting. The interesting display included fossils, flint tools, coins, brooches, buckles, shipwreck bits, and "miscellany of farming bygones." Scott and I went back to the B&B, and Ann made us a very good dinner again, for me a vegetarian bean burger, and a meat dish for Scott.

DAY 84 STATS: 8 MILES. 6 HOURS. TWO EXTRA MILES. PURPLE SHOES. PUB IN WORTH MATRAVERS IS THE "SQUARE AND COMPASS."
Information on St. Nicholas Church in Kimmerage from
dorset-churches.org.uk/kimmeridge.
Information on Clavell Tower from
dailymail.co.uk/travel/travel_news/article-5228329/Is-Britains-booked-hotel-room.
Information on Poetry Stones from
southwestcoastpath.org.uk/newsapp/article/49.
Information on Fossil Museum from
squareandcompasspub.co.uk/mindswep/squareandcompasspub.co.uk/fossil-museum.

WORTH MATRAVERS TO SWANAGE – Sunday, 27 August 2017

"What will you do now with the gift of your left life?" – Carol Ann Duffy, as seen in a plaque along the South West Coast Path.

After breakfast, Scott and I left the B&B in Worth Matravers after thanking David and Ann for their great food and hospitality. We walked a few moments to the infamous duck pond of Worth Matravers, filled with the three resident ducks, but please do not feed them. I don't really know if this duck pond is infamous, but I do believe it is the center of the village. "Of course quarrying has been going on in Worth Matravers since medieval times and smuggling was a thriving business in the 19th century. Lots of the houses are made with local quarried stone," per today's booklet, including from Winspit Quarry, which "produced Purbeck Stone up to WW2," and from Seacombe Quarry, both of which we walked by yesterday.

On our way out of "Worth," as the village is known as locally, Scott and I went to visit the St. Nicholas of Myra Church. "The church is one of the oldest in Dorset: much of the structure is Saxon, with 12th century Norman re-fitting inside and doors and buttresses. It was restored in 1869 after a period of decay." As I was walking around the church outside and inside, and saying my usual prayers, I wondered if this would be the last, or one of the last churches I will visit on my SWCP walk. I wonder exactly how many churches I have visited these last almost-three months. I did not keep a list, and probably will not go back through my book and count them, but I would imagine that since this is my 86th day, I have maybe seen an average of one church every four or so days, so maybe twenty churches and chapels, give or take, might be a good guess! That is a lot of my "usual prayers," and I am grateful that my prayers have been heard and that I have had safety during my walk, I have been healthy, injury free (my knee has not prevented me from walking), blister free (other than small ones that have not prevented me from walking), had good weather (well, not all the time, but most of the time), and all things have happened positively for myself during my 630-mile adventure. My family and friends are safe and healthy. And I will continue to pray for the world, for peace, love, compassion, and understanding.

Scott and I needed to walk the extra mile back out to the SWCP on the footpath we took yesterday. However, on the field we walked on yesterday, right in the path that led to the footpath were some cows. And some bulls. Yikes! I saw them as we walked to the church, and I was already worried when we were at the church. I thought I was done walking through herds of cows, with only a few days left in my entire walk. Fortunately, when we were near the duck pond I noticed a different way to get back to the footpath, thus bypassing most of the cows. There were a few, but not close enough to make me worry. I wondered if that would be the last herd of cows I would need to walk near on my SWCP walk. I remembered back to the two cows on the SWCP that someone else talked to, where I learned to talk to them. I remembered the time a herd of cows blocked a stile right in my path that I needed to climb, so I requested if they could please "moooooooove," which worked, along with my record-breaking climb up and over that stile. I thought about the time I sang "Happy Birthday" and clapped my hands to some cows. And the day I carefully walked by five cows, only to be told by someone there would be a whole other herd ahead. And the herd that scared me the most with Scott that we walked slowly through towards Golden Cap. I thought of all the cow rules I had learned. And of all the many, many cows that were all either a safe distance away or behind fences.

And you know, as much as I would say that getting through herds of cows was amongst the toughest experiences for me during my entire walk, I will no doubt still miss the cows of the SWCP.

We were officially back on the SWCP and it was already a sunny warm perfect day! I wondered briefly if I had this kind of weather all along if would have been able to walk every mile, and walk more often by myself. Thinking back, it had been disappointing of how some of the weather had been – rainy, windy, thunder, gale winds, extreme heat, fog, downpours - even in June, July, and August. But, I guess this is England and its coast, and perhaps I should have expected this, and I must accept and respect the power of nature, the weather, and the power of the seas. For the most part, actually, I have had many, many, many spectacular weather days, with great warmth, brilliant sun, and lovely blue skies! Even some of the cloudy and rainy days had been warm. I never had any snow, so that is good.

Anyway, today the sun was gloriously shimmering on the water. After a couple of noisy motorboats went speeding by in the seas, it was quiet and peaceful. After about a half hour of walking mostly along grassy fields, we stopped at a grassy area of these rolling hills for a snack, and to savor the moment of the beauty of nature, water, warm weather, and the SWCP. The waters were a brilliant deep blue with a few various boats in them, the small cliff ledges of the small rolling green hills were tan in color, and the skies were a beautiful light blue with very few white clouds around. Out on the horizon I could see nothing else.

Then I had an idea! A brilliant idea! I, or we, could stay in south west England for another couple of weeks and walk the miles I missed! I wouldn't have to do the miles I missed this year that Scott and I already did our first year in 2016, since I have technically already walked them. Just the new-approximate-90 miles that I missed. Then I could complete every foot of the SWCP! Perhaps the weather will be perfect, or more perfect now, later in August and into September. I wondered if I could use Sasha's home as a base and get transportation. I would need create a map to map out the areas to see where I missed and see what other places might make a good base. My mind raced with the planning as we were sitting there. How much more would it cost? Who cares, I said, I've already spent quite a lot. What about my job? My boss may not like it, but the woman that was covering for me would then get some more time working there. How long is my Visa in England good for? I thought it would be good only for 90 days, but I looked on a UK website later and it might be good for six months total. I was excited with my thoughts, and kept day dreaming as we continued walking.

The green grassy hillsides were covered with meadows of small wildflowers as we continued walking. It felt like a meadow hike in the mountains back home. There were purples, pinks, yellows, and whites. Not large wildflowers, just small ones, but noticeable for a few miles of walking. I still do not know the names of my wildflowers along the SWCP, but perhaps it doesn't matter, as long as I was recognizing and appreciating their colors and their beauty.

We walked by one area called Dancing Ledge. I read a sign that said, "Climbing and Coasteering at Dancing Ledge. Organized groups must have a National Trust license for climbing or coasteering at Dancing Ledge, Hedbury or East Man." Yesterday David told us about Coasteering, the first time I have ever heard of it. I guess people climb along the rocks just at the edge of where the cliffs meet the waters, and perhaps you go horizontally climbing rather than vertically. After doing some more research, apparently you can "swim, climb, scramble and jump your way along the stunning Jurassic coastline." You can "explore caves, ride the swell, and leap off cliffs." Looks like you wear a wet suit, a helmet, and a life jacket. I would think it could be dangerous with the possibility of incoming high tides, waves, and rocks, but I am sure that Coasteering is done with the utmost safety, in good weather, and with the right conditions. Hmmm, perhaps something to try at some point, like when I come back to the south west coast to stay at all my "expensive-places-to-stay-someday." Dancing Ledge was actually originally a quarry, and the name comes from "the waves break or 'dance' over the ledge."

As we walked on, a sailboat with an orange sail caught my eye in the water. About an hour later, we had our first sighting of the Anvil Point Lighthouse. We arrived at the lighthouse around noon. It was not open to the public, unless you rent out the lighthouse keepers' cottages, adding yet another one to that "expensive-places-to-stay-someday" list. These cottages have retained the "original black chimneys, which have been lost from many other lighthouse keepers' cottages around the country." The Anvil Point Lighthouse opened in 1881, and together along with the Portland Bill Lighthouse, they "guide ships along this part of the English Channel. It is now fully automated and has a range of about nine nautical miles," per today's booklet. This lighthouse is white in color with that "Trinity House greenish-turquoise trim," and is a shorter lighthouse, only about 39 feet tall. I thought about the shortest lighthouse in Britain that I saw of only 16 feet tall, Berry Head Lighthouse, and one of the tallest lighthouses I saw, the 135 foot Portland Bill Lighthouse. The path to the Anvil Point Lighthouse for the last few miles had been relatively flat the whole way, with some very minor ups and downs.

I believe that Anvil Point Lighthouse is the last lighthouse that I will be seeing along the SWCP. I did keep a running list of not only the "traditional lighthouses" that I have seen, but also of other structures used as lighthouses or aids to navigation. I have seen approximately 35 traditional lighthouses, harbour lights, daymarks, beacons, obelisks, castles, ruins, church towers, and chapels, whether currently in use or not, all of which had or continue to serve the extremely important purpose of guiding ships, and the people on those ships, along the seas and oceans and waters in safety. This "List of Lighthouses/Aids to Navigation along the SWCP" is included at the end of this book.

Scott and I took photos at the lighthouse, with each of us posing (yes, Scott has been taking pictures of me all along since he arrived, too), and then we continued on to the Durlston Castle where we stopped for some lunch. The path here was gravelly and wide and filled with lots of people. When we continued walking, we stopped at The Great Globe, a big sculpture of Planet Earth, with many information boards around it about the sun, the moon, the stars, the planet Earth, quotes about nature and the world. The path continued on "Isle of Wight Road" which was a tree covered forest-type road. A sign here stopped me in my path and made me contemplate life for a while. It said, "What will you do now with the gift of your left life?" – Carol Ann Duffy.

I had never heard this quote before, and I did not know where it came from, perhaps a poem or a book, and I did not know who Carol Ann Duffy was, so at the moment I just took this quote for what it was with those twelve words only, with its literal instinct to mean to me that from this exact moment, going forward, of what will I do with the rest of my life, with the gift that I have of the rest of my life, that life is a gift, and how will I live the best possible life that I can from this moment on…

At one point we were out of the trees for a moment, but then went back in the trees momentarily, before emerging on a road, and then out to a grassy area of Swanage called Prince Albert Gardens. It was warm and sunny and beautiful. There were many views of many boats floating and moving in the water, the busy beach of Swanage off to the left beyond, and the last few hilltops and white headlands I will be walking on and near my last day, including Old Harry Rocks. I could see more white headlands way in the distance and I wondered if one can continue walking along those headlands.

We walked to the National Coastwatch Institution Station at Peveril Point, and they were serving refreshments like the one was serving yesterday. It seemed like they were both open with snacks for the Bank Holiday weekend. We only had a half mile left to walk to our B&B at this point, but as I shall tell, it took us quite a while to get there. So I shall add fifteen arbitrary minutes to our arrival time to this point and call that the ending of walking time for today in the stats.

I read a sign at the NCI Station reminding me once again of the importance of the NCI and its people. "This station is operated by the National Coastwatch Institution, a national voluntary body which maintains a visual and radio distress watch around the U.K. and acts as a support to H.M. Coastguard. All NCI stations are manned by unpaid trained volunteers. As a registered charity we depend on public help for our running costs. All donations help save lives. Thank you."

We first spent some time at the NCI Station having a snack, and of course making a donation, and then somehow Scott noticed an older man sitting on a park bench seeming to simply be sitting, being, and enjoying the warm sun of the day. Scott went over to him and chatted with him for a while, while I took photos of the area after our snacks. I eventually joined them, and soon another noisy motorboat boat went speeding by, making a lot of noise. The older man said, "You don't see much going at that speed." I have always listened for words of wisdom from older people, and I thought to myself, yes that is true, and that is why I have been walking for nearly three months. To slow down. To see things at a walking pace. Not at a fast speedy pace. Life should be like that all the time. To experience life at a walking pace.

Scott told me that he and the older man chatted about all kinds of things, from boats and butterflies and birds to fossils and geology and marine life. A while later as Scott and I were about to leave Peveril Point, Scott ended up talking to the older man once again wanting to ask him if I could mention him in my book. He said, "Oh she is writing a book, then she needs to include a poem written by a local woman who grew up in the Swanage area." The poem was located near her home someplace quite near Peveril Point where we were.

In the meantime, while this conversation was going on, which I did not know about, I had started walking down the Foreshore, a concrete walkway area on the way to Swanage. I looked into the waters to see rowboats, motorboats, fishing boats, and sailboats, some with large sails, and many boats with colorful reds and yellows and blues and whites. Perhaps there could have been yachts or schooners or ferries or tour boats or kayaks as well, some of the many, many types of boats that I have seen along my SWCP walk. Perhaps this is the last harbour full of boats along the SWCP that I will be seeing. And appreciating, especially the livelihood of fishing.

I ended up at a Lifeboat Station and watched as an RNLI crew launched one of their orange Lifeboats into the waters by people wearing black and yellow clothing, red life vests, and white helmets. I remembered seeing action like this long, long ago, on the 2nd of July at the beach at Trevaunance Cove. Once again I am reminded of the importance of the RNLI and its people, who save lives at sea with their lifeboats and stations, and with their lifeguards on the beaches.

Then Scott decided to seek out exactly where that poem was that the older man told him about, and in searching and asking a few other people living around there, we ended up at her home, in her back yard, sitting at an old white iron table and chair set, surrounded by sculptures and art created by her and her husband, and meeting the woman who is an artist and a poet! I could not believe that Scott persisted in trying to not only find this woman's poem, but also found the local woman herself, Carlotta Barrow.

Here is the poem, "Growing Up on Peveril Point":

Arriving by night, when only three,
Down slippery steps to the sparkling sea.
Morning sun across the bay
Lights fishing boats on their way
Past glimmering cliffs, first catch of the day!

Winter, trudge the beach at school,
Chapped knees and chilblains as a rule!
Summer light and what delight
To swim and row and fish the ledges,
Climb the cliffs to the very edges.

Autumn and a golden glow
From leaves and trees and russet hedges
Sloes and berries, apples, too
Mushrooms for our winter stew.

Gales bring driftwood to the beaches,
Where we collect from far out-reaches.
Friends and neighbors gather round.
The blazing fire with its crackling sound,
In the place I love the most
The house on the point at the end of the coast!

  We talked to Carlotta Barrow for at least twenty minutes. I believe that the place we were sitting is actually her and her husband's "Waterside Artists Studio and Sculpture Garden." Carlotta told us of how her family came to this area when she was three years old, arriving by night, and she waking up in the morning to see its beauty, and has never left. She gave us brochures of art and sculpture in the area, one of them being, "The Swanage Seen Art Trail," including some of her art and sculptures. She showed us her two poetry books. I bought one of them, "Durlston Bay And Other Poems from the Jurassic Coast." The other book was, "Poems Inspired by the Purbeck Coast and Beyond." She told us that the above poem, as well as other stories about "Living Here," was on display at the bunker just next to the NCI Station, including information about her mother, an author, Dim Pares. Carlotta was sweet and kind. I asked her if she could please autograph the book I bought from her. She wrote, "To Debby, Congratulations on the Coastal Path Walk, Carlotta Barrow." I thought what a great connection to have made on my nearly-last day on the SWCP. Thanks to Scott.

  We went to the bunker to look for her poem and stories, and other information displayed at the bunker included a description of The Beaufort Scale, the one telling me about calm air, breezes, wind, and gales, and storms. The scale that I have become quite familiar with. Another information board told me a bit about local fishing: "Fishing has been carried out in local waters for thousands of years. Evidence of this can be found in some local gardens where the shells of Limpet, Winkle, Whelk and even Oyster, turn up regularly. At the Iron Age excavation in Portland the Winkle shells which have been exposed are about a metre thick and 3500 years old. Today the main catch is Brown Crab and Lobster with Spider and Velvet Crab and Whelks being more seasonal. There is also a fin fishery of, seasonally, Plaice, Dover Sole and Flounder Flatfish and Grey Mullet, Bass, Pollock, Black Bream Wrasse and occasionally Red Mullet and Cod. Any Salmon or Sea Trough caught accidently have to be returned to the sea as do any of the quota species above when the relevant quota is reached." There was also information on various shipwrecks, waves, tides, and climate change.

  By now it was late afternoon, and Scott and I finally started walking down the Foreshore together, the half mile section towards our B&B. Views of the boats in the water continued, and then a busy beach with people swimming and enjoying the sun. We arrived at our B&B which was near a busy area with lots of shops and restaurants and pubs. It was definitely a Bank Holiday weekend, and a glorious summer day.

  Back at the B&B I became more obsessed about the idea of staying in England and doing the 90 miles that I missed, and was curious as to where along the entire SWCP the small sections of anywhere from one to seven miles each were located. Since I had no full map of the SWCP with me, and no way to print a map, I hand-drew my own map of the SWCP on a piece of paper, and wrote down some of the larger towns as reference. Then I went through the list of missed miles here and there and colored in dots on the paper of them all. They were scattered all along just about the entire path. It was actually a cool fun little map that I drew, and it looked like I could use a few general areas as bases to stay in and branch out from there. I thought maybe to shorten the 90, maybe I could skip any pavement walking and/or skip anything small under two miles, but ultimately I thought no, I want to be able to walk all 630 miles completely, so I shall not miss the pavement nor the small sections.

  But then I decided that now would not really be the right time in my left life for me to stay longer in England, so I sadly dropped my brilliant idea of doing the rest of my missed miles now, and staying beyond what I had already planned for this summer.

Instead, I did my "every-two-or-three days" Facebook posts on my personal page, and on two SWCP Facebook Group pages. On the original SWCP Facebook Group page, with a modified version on the second SWCP Facebook Group page, I wrote: "Kimmerage Bay to Swanage the past couple of days. Including walking with Jill and Brian of this Group for several miles! It's been so great to have had the chance to walk with a few of you from this Group over the last few months, and to just be able to connect with you all through my photos. This Group has really enhanced my walk along the Coast Path. While I still have a few more days here, including the last miles of walking, I will miss this part of England when I get back home. Those of you who live close by are extremely blessed to have this glorious path in your backyard. Honestly, I've had to miss about 110 miles over the last three months mostly due to weather, (a few miles here and there missed can add up), but the 520 miles of the SWCP that I did do, plus about 73 other extra miles, will always be in my heart! Stay tuned for at least one more post when I get to South Haven Point."

Note that above I mentioned that I posted on two SWCP Facebook Group pages. Yes, two! That is because at some point along my walk, I somehow discovered a second SWCP Facebook Group, so I joined that one as well, and therefore have been posting photos since my discovery on both pages.

Yes, I really do appreciate both SWCP Facebook Group pages. They both have been invaluable to me. From seeing other people posting their photos and sharing their walking experiences to asking for advice or assistance when needed and getting good responses. From finding people to walk with to hearing words of encouragement and support when needed. From making new friends to being able to share my walk with everyone through my own photos and posts. Lucy, the admin of one of the groups, has been extremely helpful and supportive to me, so a special appreciation goes out to her.

I thought further about my walk, and more accurately reflected on the mileage than in my posts: Three months. Actually 513 SWCP miles walked (or biked) this year! I missed 117 total this year, with 27 of them had been done last year, so a net of 90 missed miles. And of those miles I did walk this year, nearly 350 of them have been alone, solo, by myself, on my own! Plus about 73 extra miles, with most of those miles also solo. I should be proud of all this. I should consider myself brave and courageous. While I did not, or could not, walk every single mile, I still tried, and I feel like I have succeeded. Weather was something I could not control. I am safe and healthy. I am 50 and in great shape. I walked. And walked. And walked. My epic adventure.

630 miles is the equivalent of walking from Portland to San Francisco, the two cities my sisters live in. 630 miles is the equivalent of 24 marathons. My 513 miles walked is the equivalent of walking of the entire coastlines of the states of Washington and Oregon, plus a bit into California. My 513 miles is the equivalent of almost 20 marathons. I walked over 80% of the entire SWCP. I walked the equivalent elevation gain and loss as climbing Mount Everest three times.

I may not have walked every mile, nor walked it all by myself, but I can power up a hill, and I have conquered countless ascents and descents. I have been by the calming, yet powerful, seas and waters day after day. I have heard my favorite sounds of the waves of the waters, whether a quiet meditative wave on a sandy beach, or the tumbling of pebbles and rocks being taken back to the seas, or the crashing of larger waves against the rocks and coastlines. I have smelled the sea and salty and fishy air. I have been taken back in time by visiting fishing villages and learning about smuggling. I have met and connected with great and interesting people, including authors/writers, artists and poets. People have called me brave and courageous. I have put my feet in the water, paddled, and felt the sand between my toes. I have taken over 10,000 photos between my camera and my mobile phone! I have seen, and prayed in, countless historic churches and chapels. I've had my first, and several delicious, cream teas, loving them both with jam on top and cream on top, and even experienced Cream Tea and Afternoon Tea events with the locals.

I have come to love all the various colors and shades of blues and turquoises and blue-greens and green-blues and azures and cobalts and sapphires and indigos, and all the various colors and shades of green (light green, dark green, emerald green, mint green, lime green, sea foam green, verdant, viridescent, forest green, moss green, olive green, cyan, grass green, and seaweed green), all now my favorite colors. And purple, my purple shoes.

I have made friends and connections in this country, and have walked with some of them. I have walked and stayed with a great friend of mine. I have watched my first few episodes of Doc Martin, seen some of the TV actors that I did not know. I have read books by local authors about local life. I have met local people and delved into local culture and local ways of life. I have walked through four counties, in five parts, and one county it its entirety.

I have fallen in love with the SWCP and everything about it. I will miss the SWCP. I will long to be back. I feel like I want to live by the ocean. With a steady supply of those positive-good-for-me negative ions.

I have had so many guardian angels, including and especially my husband. The biggest guardian angel that I have had though has actually been myself! And I need to recognize this. For I had planned this entire epic adventure, and the planning, especially the B&Bs have all worked out. For I have found my way when lost, and I have walked at times in the rain. For I have gotten myself past several herds of cows, some near a stile that I needed to climb. For I have walked the majority of the SWCP solo. For I have been my own companion the entire time. I have written. I have walked. And I have realized that I do like to be beside the seaside.

I have followed the arrow closest to the acorn around the most breathtaking beautiful stunning amazing brilliant and lovely coastlines. This walk will be in my heart and soul and spirit, and will be a part of me for the rest of my life.

What will I do now with the gift of my left life? Or maybe it should be my "right life" as I have had the seas and oceans and waters and beaches on my right side just about the entire time?

In either case, even though I don't have a clear plan for the next 50 years, I know I can dream something, try something, do something, whatever I want that to be. 513 miles is an amazing accomplishment!

I do know that in my left life, I will walk as much as possible. If I don't get the opportunity to live near the ocean and beaches, I will visit as often as possible. There are plenty of lakes and bays near where I live, and the Pacific Ocean itself is just a three hour drive.

In fact, I really could come back to the SWCP and fill in the gaps, fill in the blanks, complete the pieces of the puzzle, connect the dots, and walk the 90 miles which I have now mapped out. Maybe not right now. But some day. Hopefully someday soon. I could even add another 2,165 miles to that as soon the England Coast Path opens up…

But I still have a few more days here for now…

DAY 85 STATS: 6 MILES. 4.5 HOURS. ONE EXTRA MILE. PURPLE SHOES. PUBS IN SWANAGE ARE "THE ANCHOR INN," "THE SHIP INN," AND "THE RED LION."
Information on St. Nicholas of Myra Church from stnicholascenter.org/galleries/gazetteer.
Coasteering information from dorsetcoasteering.co.uk; and landandwave.co.uk/coasteering-dorset.
Anvil Point Lighthouse info from
worldwidelighthouses.com/Lighthouses/English-Lighthouses/Trinity-House-Owned/AnvilPoint.

REST DAY IN SWANAGE – Monday, 28 August 2017

"Oh I do like to be beside the seaside
The seaside is where I like to be
I like it the most
When I walk along the South West Coast
The seaside…my purple shoes…and me."

What have I learned on this 630-mile adventure?...I can't control the weather...Guardian angels show up just at the right time...I am brave...I am not fond of walking near cows...I am in good shape for 50...I love the ocean and seas and water...I do like to be beside the seaside...In fact, I made up the lyrics above.

I also learned that while I can think of a plan for "tomorrow," I need to live for today, because what happens tomorrow may depend on what happens today. Now this can be a philosophical lesson, in addition to a lesson about the weather. For example, if I could not walk "today" due to the weather, then my plan for tomorrow would need to be modified. And even visa versa. If I knew that I would have not-so-good weather "tomorrow," I would need to modify today. Life in general is like that, too. Tomorrow might depend on today, and today might depend on tomorrow.

I learned to really appreciate the extensive fishing and farming livelihoods along the SWCP. I learned a lot about interesting smuggling that occurred along the SWCP of yesteryear. I learned about the tragic shipwrecks and the much needed lighthouses. I learned about the World War 2 historical aspect along the SWCP. And the historical mining and quarrying industries. I learned about the history of tea and Afternoon Tea. I learned about some geology, especially the last few weeks along the Jurassic Coast. I never did learn to identify birds and wildflowers, but concluded that it didn't matter as long as I appreciated them. I learned to appreciate the importance of many organizations along the SWCP, including but not necessarily limited to the South West Coast Path Association, National Trails UK, National Trust, Natural England, Luggage Transfers LTD, Trinity House, Royal National Lifeboat Institution, National Coastwatch Institution, HM Coastguard, the Maritime and Coastguard Agency, Areas of Outstanding Natural Beauty, and even the SWCP Facebook Group pages. I learned more in depth about the reasons why the SWCP was originally created – "By coastguards, patrolling the south west peninsula looking out for smugglers. And by fishermen looking for shoals of fish and checking sea conditions."

There were all the inspiring books I read about walking the SWCP book in one go from my great friend Sasha Harding's book to Mark Wallington and "his" dog, to the late Overend Watts, and most recently John Haughton's limerick walk. Those other inspiring books I read about walking around the British coast from Ruth Livingstone to Helen Krasner. And the book I read while walking about life in Cornwall by Sue Bunney. Not to mention the four guidebooks from National Trails, and the invaluable booklets written by Dave Westcott from the SWCP Association.

Well what is a rest day for other than…to walk? After writing some this morning after breakfast, Scott and I finally got out of the B&B at 10:45 and walked along the promenade above the beach in Swanage. While tomorrow will be my official last day of walking, I wanted to do a mile of tomorrow's walk today. Just because. We walked along the promenade and beach all the way to some steps that led up to the Pines Hotel.

There were a lot of various rows of beach huts along the way, some of the last ones I will see, and I still love seeing them. At first these beach huts were white in color with doors of sharp blue, red, or yellow. Another row of beach huts looked older and made out of wood and were solid brown or red, and had flat roofs. Yet another row of beach huts, with pointed roofs, were either solid brown, solid red, solid blue, or white and blue. One of these had a pot of yellow flowers painted on its blue wall. Another beach hut had other painted flowers and a sign that said, "Welcome to the beach." Another row of beach huts, also with pointed roofs, were white with various shades of blues and greens. (Sounds like I am describing the SWCP scenery.) Another row of beach huts were made out of red bricks, with red, green, yellow, or blue doors and trim. Another row of beach huts looked quite old, also made out of red bricks with blue doors and rusty locks on the doors. And a final row of beach huts were painted dark blue and light blue, just like the seas and skies, with names such as, "seagull, sailing, sunray, puffin, and pelican." Swanage sure has a lot of various beach huts. I wondered how many beach huts I have actually seen all along my SWCP walk.

A lot of people were out enjoying the beach, the warmth, and their beach huts. Today was Monday of the Bank Holiday weekend, the reason for the beach being busy. As Scott and I walked near the sand, and on the sand, I saw one last headland I would be walking on tomorrow. When we arrived at the steps of the Pines Hotel, I was not sure if these steps were the exact ones that were for the SWCP for tomorrow, but it was close enough for today, and therefore we could start walking at the hotel tomorrow for my last day of walking and my last six and a half miles.

Scott and I walked back to the other end of Swanage where we started. To walk "backwards" we walked on the side roads and streets and sidewalks instead of by the beach, and this will count as an extra mile. On one of the side roads was yet another row of beach huts. These were painted blue and white, each one with a different painting pattern than the others. We stopped by one of the hotels along the way because Scott had looked in one of the art and sculpture brochures Carlotta Barrow gave us yesterday, "The Swanage and Purbeck Sculpture Trail," and Scott wanted to find one of her sculptures that was mentioned called "Suzannah." He found it in the garden of the hotel, and it is made of "Portland Stone," and costs £500 ($700) to purchase, a sculpture of the upper half of a girl.

A month ago, my great friend Sasha said she would come out to Swanage, the place she grew up, and meet me here to walk with me on my last day, whether I happened to be here by myself or with Scott. She told me a few days ago that she will be here today around lunch time, and she called at noon as we were walking back. She was here along with her husband and her two dogs. For now, they will take their dogs for a walk after being in the car from their long ride from Falmouth, and will call again in about an hour and a half. It was nice to hear her voice. In the meantime, Scott and I were hungry, even though we will go out to lunch with Sasha and her husband in a while, so we went to a café in Swanage for a snack.

After our snack, Scott and I had some time before Sasha would call, so we wandered around and ended up finding a gallery that carried of all things, Sasha's art and her sister's art. That was a fun coincidence. I bought a few greeting cards, three with Sasha's fun images, and one of her sister's.

Sasha called and we met Sasha, Jack, Jess, and Mouse, and had lunch with them. Scott and I thus ate again. We spent time talking about lots of bits and bobs, especially about walking the SWCP. I told her how I missed 90 miles and she agreed that yes, I did not have good luck with the weather, and that I would just need to come back! When I mentioned my brilliant idea from yesterday of staying here now a few more weeks, it actually felt alright to me that I did not stay now at this point in time, and therefore would have something to look forward to in the future, maybe even possibly next year.

We decided what time tomorrow we would all start walking together on my last day, and what arrangements would be made. We talked about how Sasha grew up here in Swanage, and that it was strange for her to see me in her home town. I asked if the house she grew up in was still in her family, and it was not. I mentioned my quest from several days ago to try to find some Dorset Apple Cake. She told us of a second thing to try as well - Dorset Knobs. Dorset Apple Cake is a cake made with flour, cinnamon, butter, brown sugar, egg, milk, sultanas (a dried white grape, similar to raisins), and apples. There are variations on this recipe, but I think the main ingredients are that it has brown sugar, cinnamon (or allspice), and apples. One recipe recommends using the traditional English Bramley apple or some tart tasting apple. The cake can be made as a loaf cake, or in a round tin. A topping might include demerara sugar (a type of sugar with a molasses type flavor), or flaked almonds.

Dorset Knobs are a "unique savoury biscuit made by the Moores family since 1880. Once created each biscuit has three separate bakings lasting a total of four hours. The whole process taking eight to ten hours!" "Dorset Knobs are made from wheat flour, white sugar, water, oil and yeast (originally the recipe used butter instead of oil). They are baked, then left in the oven till dried out. Dorset Knobs are light, crisp, dry biscuits about the size and shape of a golf ball, and a shelf life just about as long."

Golf balls! Speaking of golf courses, I can't believe that one of my most surreal, and quite challenging experiences, had been on a golf course, taking cover under a brolly during a downpour of rain. From my first walk near a golf course between Appledore and Westward Ho! back on the 16th of June to visiting the St. Enodoc Church located in the middle of a golf course. From being driven to a farm in a little golf-cart-type-farm-vehicle to finding a golf ball on the grounds of St. Uny Church near Carbis Bay. From being near a miniature golf course with dinosaurs statues on it to walking near, or through a few other golf courses, some for longer distances, without incident. I was never one to like to play golf, and still I don't think I shall be taking up golf any time soon.

After a while of sitting and eating and talking with Sasha and Jack, they had some bits and bobs to go do, so Scott and I went back to the B&B to rest, since it was after all a scheduled rest day, and for me to catch up on more writing. We tried to find some Dorset Apple Cake and Dorset Knobs on our way to the B&B, but could not. It was 3:30 and it has been another great sunny warm day today!

Now an update on blisters and my right knee and such. First, one of my toe nails is actually falling off! I noticed it a few weeks ago. I actually thought there was a new blister on a new toe at first, but then I realized that the toe nail was loose and it made me squirm if I tried to touch it even though it didn't hurt. Just the thought of it made me squirm. After I saw the movie "Wild" I had commented how I hoped all my toe nails would stay intact, and well, what do you know, one of them actually was not intact!

The minor blisters on the big toes of both feet, the only blisters I fortunately ever had, are calluses now. And unfortunately, my right knee is still a bit swollen from over 100 miles ago. Perhaps this is a good reason not to walk anymore for now other than tomorrow. Physical therapy and some rest are in order. I also realized that for the entire three months, I have managed to put on enough sunscreen so as to never get sun burnt. And other than my longest day of walking, and a bit here and there, in general my feet after all these miles do not hurt! My purple shoes, hiking boots, and flip flops worked well!

Back in the B&B room I realized that I felt tired. It was strange to realize that I feel more tired on a rest day of not walking and not doing much, compared to a day of walking for miles and miles and miles. Perhaps the walking just is a natural part of me now, a normal part of my everyday life. Perhaps it is part of who I am now and who I have become. Perhaps walking energizes me.

Tonight I cried to Scott. Not over missing the 90 miles, but because tomorrow it will be all over. My walk. It went by so fast. I really have fallen in love with the SWCP, with all its beauty, and calmness. I have fallen in love with walking as well. I will truly miss all this!

Hours later, Scott and I went out to dinner at the same place we went to lunch, and then strolled around for a few minutes in the comfortable evening air beside the seaside.

DAY 86 STATS: 1 MILE. HALF HOUR. ONE EXTRA MILE. FLIP FLOPS. OTHER PUBS IN SWANAGE ARE "THE BLACK SWAN INN" AND "THE CROWS NEST INN." Information on Dorset Apple Cake from bbcgoodfood.com/recipes/dorset-apple-cake and fussfreeflavours.com/dorset-apple-cake. Information on Dorset Knobs from moores-biscuits.co.uk/dorset-knobs.html and cooksinfo.com/dorset-knobs.

LAST DAY. SWANAGE TO SOUTH HAVEN POINT (POOLE) – Tuesday, 29 August 2017

"Walk and be Happy. Walk and be Healthy." – Charles Dickens

Last night I looked at my daily "to do" list one last time. I checked the final elevation on the SWCP Association's website, and I checked the last day's weather on BBC Weather. I prepared my clothes and my socks, and got my rucksack ready. I took the appropriate final SWCP Association booklet by Dave Westcott, "Walk 70 Swanage to South Haven Point," and I took photos of the appropriate pages of the fourth and final National Trails guidebook that would be finished today, "Exmouth to Poole, From Jane Austen's Cobb to Lulworth Cove – Over 100 Miles of Historic Coastline." I read in the booklet about Swanage that "Apart from the traditional fishing and smuggling, Swanage was largely an industrial port exporting the local Purbeck stone."

I woke up this morning feeling a mix of sadness, nervousness, excitement, and feelings of a great sense of accomplishment. Strange that I felt nervous today. I think the only other times I felt nervous the entire time was as I was waiting at the airport to board my flight to England nearly three months ago, my first few steps on my very first day of walking, and when encountering cows. I felt sad today that after today my long walk would be over. I also felt sad that I missed the net of 90 miles. But more importantly, I was excited and accomplished that I came all the way over here from 4,700 miles away from home and did this. I planned this all using the internet and email, and booked 50 accommodations to which I kept on schedule to keep all my reservations, and to which all of them were great places to sleep and eat breakfast. I figured out transportation when other than my feet were needed. I walked nearly 350 of the 513 miles I walked solo! I never once felt like giving up completely. I have seen or met famous people including actors, authors/writers, artists, and poets. I have walked near mountain goats, horses, and the cutest sheep. I fortunately did not see any adders nor have any ticks. I looked at many headlands behind me that I had walked, and saw many headlands ahead of me that I was about to walk. I walked on top of hillsides and down into valleys and bays, beaches, and coves. I have described how "the scenery changes with every mile, and each mile has something unique to offer," and really the scenery changes with every stride. I made some friends, ate some great food, and consumed way too many delicious chocolate, desserts, and cream teas. I figured out my ultimate location for a beach hut. I listened to some live music at a restaurant, a pub, and a music festival. I would like to think I lost weight from all the walking, but with all the food, desserts, and cream teas, I am not sure if I did. I certainly built up some muscles in my legs though, and I feel healthy. I fell completely in love with the seas, waters, oceans, beaches, boats, harbours, villages, and the entire SWCP. I followed all the arrows closest to the acorns. I truly celebrated my 50th birthday in epic and monumental style during my walking adventure on England's 630 mile South West Coast Path!

I tied up the laces of my purple shoes one last time, and at 9:00, Scott and I were picked up by a friend of Sasha's, along with Sasha, Jack, Jess, and Mouse. Other than her friend, the six of us (four people and two dogs) would walk my last six and a half miles of the SWCP together. To South Haven Point. All along I have been referring to this place mostly as Poole. Technically, I will be ending at South Haven Point, which is "the entrance to the Poole Harbour," with Sandbanks and the town of Poole on the other side of the harbour entrance, but is the official end of the entire walk. Or the official beginning if you were walking towards Minehead.

We were driven to near the hotel that Scott and I walked to yesterday, and at 9:10 we walked down to the beach to start walking. The beach was just about completely empty and so quiet this morning compared to the crowds of people yesterday. I guess the Bank Holiday was over. The sun was peeking through a light cloud layer, tempting us with a warm day. The rays of the sun shone down through the clouds on the waters and shimmered as if they were congratulating me. The sound of light beach waves hit the sand that I would be listening to almost for the last time. The dogs were happy to run around. It was a nice peaceful way to start my last walk. I could see one more headland that I would soon be walking on.

We all walked on the sandy beach beyond where Scott and I stopped yesterday. We crossed over a few "groynes" (low timber barriers on a beach used to help prevent erosion), and found the set of steps that would take us off the beach and onto the last headland that I would walk on. The path turned flat for a while, and seemed to be lined with shrubbery, including blackberry bushes. We eventually had the last climb of my walk, a gentle short uphill with some steps. I took out my hiking poles one last time because for some reason I was under the impression that it would be a longer steeper climb than it was, but I could have done this climb without the poles.

Looking back were views of the last inland checkered farmland, the last rolling hills, the homes and buildings of Swanage, and the empty beach below. Not the last beach though. A herd of cows was safely at the top of an inland hill, the last herd that I shall see. Sasha and I walked together mostly, while Scott and Jack walked together. As I took photos of the scenery, some with her dogs in the pictures, Sasha and I compared notes on the SWCP, and talked about how this walk was not only a physical roller coaster, but an emotional roller coaster as well at times, as we had also talked about one of the other days that we had walked together. She had experienced a mix of emotions just as I did during her walk. We agreed though that the walk is definitely nourishing for the soul!

"You are brave coming over from America all by yourself to do this," she said to me. Yes, the word "brave" mentioned to me once more, out of the blue! Sasha has been a huge source of support, friendship, and inspiration for me in several ways over the last year, including for my SWCP walk. I appreciate all of what she has done for me, and what she has said to me, and her book for inspiring me, and that she has walked with me a few times this summer. She is truly a great friend, and I was saddened that we live so far away.

The path turned towards Old Harry Rocks, some large white sea stacks seeming as if they were floating in the seas, next to the white chalk cliffs, and was flat walking all the way there. These were those white chalk rocks at the end of the Jurassic Coast from the Cretaceous period of about 65 million years ago. I had walked through time the last few weeks from 250 million years ago to 65 million years ago. Still boggles my mind when I think about the concept of "time."

We all arrived at Old Harry Rocks about an hour after we started walking from Swanage. We all sat on the grass above the white cliffs and white rocks and took photos, slowly walked out of the Old Harry Rocks area, and continued to walk and chat. A few sailboats sailed by, and a motorboat or two motored by as well. About a half hour later we continued on, walking on a very wide grassy area, with views of upcoming beaches and the tip of the beaches very near the ending point. The path turned into a very wide flat gravel track that the six of us, four people and the two dogs, could walk side by side.

An hour later we stopped at the Middle Beach Café. I did an internet search last night for Dorset Apple Cake and this café came up with having some. So we stopped and three of us, me, Sasha, and Scott, had Dorset Apple Cake. My quest was a success. It was a moist cake with bits of apples and sultanas, topped with that demerara sugar. It was good! Although, I never did get a chance to try any of the Dorset Knobs. I had two and a half miles left of the entire 630 miles as I enjoyed the cake.

About a half hour later we started walking near long rows of beach huts along Middle Beach. Yes, these would be the last beach huts I would walk by. I think Sasha said her family had one here long ago. These beach huts were mostly solid shades of brown, some boarded up with wood in shades of blues and whites. One beach hut was yellow. I thought of the Isle of Portland as my ultimate location for a beach hut. I thought about all the photography books I could create from my walk - "The Beach Huts of the South West Coast Path," "The Benches of the South West Coast Path," and "The Windows and Doors of Appledore, Clovelly and other places along the South West Coast Path." Or perhaps books with photos of all the harbours and boats, or of all the lighthouses, or even all the photos of my purple shoes with the scenery.

Speaking of my purple shoes, Sasha, Jack, Scott and I all took off our shoes or trainers or sandals, in my case, my purple shoes, and walked about a mile and a half along the beach at the edge of the sand in bare feet, where the sand meets the water. My last beach walk, my last paddling. At first the beach was crowded with people. We had to dodge the kids and the swimmers and the kayaks and the pails and shovels and the sand castles. As we walked on, the crowds thinned out, to just a few people. I took photos looking back at the headland with Old Harry Rocks at the tip, and looking back at Scott and Jack walking with Mouse behind us. Sasha and I were walking with Jess.

And then we walked through the…naturist beach section near the Studland Nature Reserve. Yes, people without any clothes on. Or according to Sasha, they all had their "bits and bobs" hanging out all over the place. It was odd to walk through this section completely dressed, with rucksacks on, and I wondered why the SWCP practically ends here (or starts here if you are walking in the opposite direction), but I bet the naturists are used to it as after all, it is part of the SWCP. I was not sure though that we were at all used to it, as Sasha and I kept joking and giggling about it as we walked through, trying not to look. I had my sunglasses on so no one knew where my eyes were looking anyway, and really I did not want to look. We joked and giggled though how people were still wearing hats. We guessed they just didn't want to burn their heads. Note that I did not take any photos in this area.

Eventually people were dressed again, although there weren't very many people at all in general any longer, as it was a quieter part of the beach. The sound of small crashing waves continued the entire beach walk, with a few seaweed-covered rocks at the edge of the waters. I tried to savor the last time I would hear my favorite sound. I collected a few sea shells as a souvenir of my last day of walking, although I probably technically wasn't supposed to. In the distance I saw the first headland that I would not be walking on. It was another sunny warm dry day today, almost hot out, which I appreciated for my last day. Summer on my last day! Not a drop of rain, no extreme heat, no relentless winds, no gale force winds, no fog, no downpours, no thunder. In fact, according to the Beaufort Wind Scale, I would say that today was "calm."

Sasha kept asking me all day how I was feeling. I am sure she just wanted to make sure that I was alright. I remarked mostly that I didn't know each time she asked. I realized that my nervousness this morning was actually not knowing what exact emotion I would be feeling as I was walking, and especially when I would arrive at the final South West Coast Path Marker. We all walked off the beach and the sand as we were getting very close to the marker now. We all put our shoes or sandals or trainers or purple shoes back on. It was 1:43pm.

A quintessential British Red Telephone Box was the first sight. The second sight was the cars lined up for the vehicle ferry across Poole Harbour, "one of the largest natural harbours in the world," to Sandbanks and Poole. And as we turned a slight corner to the road, I could see the blue of the marker. 50 more feet to walk. On a sand covered sidewalk. Sasha and Jack and the dogs stayed back to give me some private space. Scott walked behind me as I walked. What would I feel? What would I think? What would I do now with the gift of my left life?

At 1:48pm on the 29th of August 2017, I touched the blue South West Coast Path Marker! Wow! I did it! I made it! 630 miles! I had only seen pictures of this blue marker, and now here I was standing there with it. I almost hugged it!

Before I could really asses my feelings and thoughts, Scott took pictures of me with my first touch of the marker, and then I posed for several more, on both sides of the blue marker. I took photos of my purple shoes with the blue marker, and with the engravings on the ground. The marker I believe is in the shape of a sail of a boat, but in some ways to me it looks like the shape of a heart. I wondered if its color of blue is meant to represent the seas and the skies. Carved on the marker are images of a couple of lighthouses, a fishing boat, seagulls, the Clavell Tower, St. Michael's Mount, dolphins, deer, and egret, a shore bird, a tin mine, and people walking with rucksacks on. I thought back to the monument in Minehead and my first days on the SWCP.

The engravings on the ground at this blue marker were of ammonites and lighthouses and St Aldhelm's Chapel and fish and crabs and starfish and sailboats and birds, and even the monument in Minehead. The letters NSEW told me the directions. And the engravings said, "South West Coast Path – National Trail – The Ever-Present Sense of the Sea." Yes, I do like to be beside the ever-present sense of the seaside. "To Minehead. Start/Finish. 630 Miles. Each One Different." Yes, that is what I said when people asked me - that the amazing SWCP scenery was different and changed with every mile.

I took photos of the marker itself, and of course, as I would not forget, I took photos of Punxsutawney Phil attached to my rucksack with the marker, as he has walked along with me in my rucksack the entire time. Sasha rejoined us at this point, as I motioned her over to please be here with me. She took pictures of me and Scott. Scott took pictures of me and Sasha. I was extremely glad to be there at the SWCP Marker with these two people, my husband and my great friend, at this moment.

I was very glad that I could share some of my last few week's experiences with Scott, including but not necessarily limited to walking on beaches together, introducing him to cream tea, sharing nice B&Bs together, seeing his joy when we came across horses and in trying to rescue a dog. We can both look at the living room wall with the five painting memories I collected along my walk, four of which he was with me when they were purchased.

I took photos of the last signpost, or first signpost if you just started walking in the other direction, which read, "South West Coast Path. South Haven Point. Old Harry 4. Minehead 630." Complete with the acorn symbol, the sign itself being the arrow. The arrow closest to the acorn.

I, and we, spent twelve minutes taking all these pictures. Then I walked off into the sunset, just me and my purple shoes…

Actually, at 2:00pm on the 29th of August 2017, I walked away from the marker and the South West Coast Path. I glanced back quickly, to once more make sure I left nothing behind as I always have done, and to look back in a quick reflection of feelings and thoughts. Then I turned around, and as I walked forward into the gift of my left, and right, life, I felt…like I had an epic 50th birthday celebration walking adventure. I felt like I fell in love with the South West Coast Path. I felt like the beauty of the scenery and the headlands and the beaches and the harbours and the seas and everything else in between will forever be in my heart and soul. I felt calm and relaxed. I felt like I was ready to see what would happen with the gift of my life at a walking pace. I felt accomplished, brave, courageous, proud, healthy, and happy!

DAY 87 STATS: 6.5 MILES. ALMOST 5 HOURS. NO EXTRA MILES. PURPLE SHOES AND BARE FEET. PUBS IN STUDLAND ARE "BANKES ARMS," AND LASTLY, "THE PIG ON THE BEACH."

Last Day. Swanage to South Haven Point (Poole). August 29
"The rays of the sun shown down through the clouds on the waters and shimmered as if they were congratulating me."
Jess, Scott, Jack, Mouse, and Sasha.
Sasha, Me, Jack, Jess, and Mouse. (photo credit: Scott Dungan)

Last Day. Swanage to South Haven Point (Poole). August 29
The Dogs, Sasha, and Me at Old Harry Rocks
Jess, Sasha, and Me with trainers off walking the last mile and a half
Me at the "last" signpost (or the "first" signpost) – 630 miles to Minehead
(All photos credit: Scott Dungan)

Last Day. Swanage to South Haven Point (Poole). August 29
"I did it! I felt accomplished, brave, courageous, proud, healthy, and happy!"
Me and Sasha at the blue South West Coast Path Marker. (photo credit: Scott Dungan)
Me and Scott at the blue South West Coast Path Marker. (photo credit: Sasha Harding)

IN THE MEANTIME (29 AUGUST 2017 TO 26 MARCH 2018)

AKA Postscript, After Thoughts, Afterword, Follow Up, Miscellaneous Notes, In Between, and What's Next

"Close your eyes and tap your heels three times and think to yourself, 'there's no place like home.'" – Glinda, the Good Witch, from The Wizard of Oz.

The Rest of Tuesday, 29 August 2017 and a Bit of Wednesday, 30 August 2017

Scott, Sasha, Jack, the dogs and I were all driven back to Swanage by Sasha's friend. For the moment, we said goodbye to Sasha, Jack, and the dogs, but would see them once more later in the evening. I was not quite sure what to do now actually. I didn't have to do any more walking, and there was still plenty of the day left. Therefore, Scott and I treated ourselves to a few pieces of chocolate from Chococo, "The place to eat, drink, and delight in fine chocolate." Well, ten small pieces of chocolate total. A celebration dessert.

We went back to our B&B to rest, and so that I could just "be" for a while. Contemplative. Meditative. Reflective. Sasha and Jack and the dogs were going down to a beach in Swanage a little while later, so after a while, we met up with them once again for a short bit. We sat on a small rocky beach in Swanage, feeling for the last time those positive-good-for-me negative ions.

Finally, Scott and I went out to dinner, and had another final celebration dessert, some amazing chocolate cake of some sort. I mean after all I just walked the majority of the SWCP.

The next morning for our last "brecko," Scott had his last Full English, I had a "Greek-style" breakfast of hard boiled eggs, feta cheese, tomatoes, pita bread, cucumbers, and olives. Sasha then kindly drove us to the train station as we headed back on our way to the airport to fly home. Although there is part of me that feels that the South West Coast Path is like home.

Back Home – Reliving the SWCP with Fish and Chips, Cream Tea, and a Friend

I missed the SWCP so much that a few days after we arrived home that in order to relive my SWCP walk, Scott and I went to one of our local fish and chips restaurants and indulged, bringing back memories of my walk and our walk. I also knew there was a British shop and restaurant in a town near our house, so one day I drove there specifically to see if they had the ingredients to make our own cream tea. They did! I bought some of their homemade scones, and some clotted cream that they actually imported directly from England. At my favorite local grocery store I bought some strawberry jam, and along with some tea Scott and I already had at home, we had cream tea! Now that is really reliving the SWCP. Of course, we ate the scones both the delicious Cornwall and Devon ways!

I also emailed my friend and inspiration Gordon to let him know I had finished my walk a few days ago. He was happy for me, and also invited us that if we ever are able to visit his area of England, we could stay with him and his family on his farm for a few days, and do some "local walking (great scenery) and see the sights." I appreciated the invitation, hospitality, and his friendship.

The Punxsutawney Phil Photography Contest

Now for something totally fun. Remember all those pictures of Punxsutawney Phil I took along the way, and remember that I was taking them for a photography contest? Well, I took fourteen of my photos of him in the various locations along the SWCP that I mentioned in the book. With them, I created a large collage. This is the list:

Minehead Monument – First Day
Godrevy Lighthouse near Gwithian
First and Last Gift and Refreshment House in England at Land's End
Land's End sign pointing to New York and John O'Groats
The Most Southerly Gift Shop at Lizard Point
Lizard Point with Lizard Lighthouse in the background
Lizard Lighthouse
Half Way Marker in Porthallow
Portland Bill Lighthouse
A SWCP wooden marker with an arrow and acorn
Osmington Mills one mile stone marker
Sitting on a bench at White Nothe overlooking white cliffs on way to Lulworth Cove
Sitting near a bench at Houns-tout Cliff between Kimmerage and Worth Matravers overlooking farmland and seas and cliffs
South Haven Point Marker – Last Day

I sent this collage to the "Worldwide Adventures of Phil" photography contest and entered it in the International category, describing the collage as, "Phil walked and hiked with me in my backpack for three months,

Punxsutawney Phil on the South West Coast Path
First Place International Category
Worldwide Adventures of Phil Photo Contest 2017

from beginning to end, on the beautiful 630-mile South West Coast Path trail in England. Together we were by the ocean and beaches and hills and fishing villages daily, and visited lighthouses and other landmarks."

And guess what!? I WON! First Place! Yes, I did!

I received a certificate commemorating this event, framed the collage and the certificate, and added this to a wall in my living room along with the other time I won First Place of Phil in the Cotswolds, and my Honorable Mention along the Camino de Santiago in Spain. Now how fun is that to have won first place for a second time, both being in England, this time with Phil on the SWCP!

And speaking of Phil and Groundhog's Day, since my walk last summer, I have now turned 51. On Groundhog's Day. Again.

The Toe Nail and The Knee

Two days after my walk, with the nail that remained loose on one of my toes, but still somewhat attached at the cuticle, I decided to be brave, and take some small scissors and trim the hanging toe nail off back to the cuticle so that it would not snag and rip off if I put on any socks. Since it made me squirm, it took some real courage to do this, but I was successful, and just like cutting toe nails, it did not hurt to do that. I could not believe that I actually lost a toe nail. For a while when I still wore flip flops and painted my toe nails, I only had nine toe nails to paint. I used a light color nail polish so it wouldn't be that noticeable. You know, I never painted my toe nails while walking the SWCP. I researched that it takes three to six months to grow back a new toe nail, and I would say that about three months later, indeed a new toe nail had grown back.

Then it was time to take care of that knee that was still on the swollen side. I went to an orthopedic, got an easy diagnosis where he gave me a treatment protocol of physical therapy, along with stretches, strengthening exercises, rest, and massage. After the treatment, the knee has thankfully returned back to normal. Which is good, because...I decided to go back and walk the 90 miles I missed! But more on that a bit later...

A Sixth Painting

For the past several years, my step-mom has been taking painting classes. For her recent class, she asked me if she could paint one of the scenes from my SWCP walk from one of my photos. I thought that would be great, and she chose a photo I took on the 24th of August at the beach of Ringstead Bay near Osmington Mills. I described the beach as, "We went down to rocky beach for a look at some rowboats sitting on the rocky beach, and some sailboats and rowboats floating in the water. Someone was bringing up their crab and lobster pot, others were bringing up the sails, and two little kids in wet suits were playing in the water. Good to see this local morning activity." In the background was a headland. After she completed the painting, she kindly gave it to me, which I very much appreciated. I bought a frame for it and added it to the living room wall along with the five other paintings I had, now all my memories from my SWCP walk.

Reading Another Book

Another way I relived my SWCP walk in the meantime was I read a second book by Sue Bunney called "My Cornish Life." Another book of some of her own personal life, family, history, and her stories, along with more of living life in Cornwall. The book includes more insight into fishing, farming, shipwrecks, mining, smuggling, cricket, the fishing villages of Gorran Haven and Mevagissey, and of course the beaches and the seas. I read this book in an eBook version on my mobile phone, and read a few pages a night until I completed the book, and learned quite a few things.

I learned that smugglers were sometimes called "free traders," and salt was another item smuggled. "The salt tax doubled the price of salt and had a huge impact on the pilchard trade in Mevagissey. Salt was the preservative which kept the fish cured and so vital for the industry. When the new tax was introduced, the Mevagissey men invented some ingenious ways of getting around the problem. They knew they had to have salt to survive. One Mevagissey man...stated to an enquiry, 'we used to tie the salt bags round the women's legs, under their long skirts, and smuggle it in.' Salt became as precious as brandy and silk."

I had described most of my colors of the seas as blue or turquoise, and at one point Sue describes the seas like this: "People really appreciate good weather in Cornwall and when the sun shines Cornwall is at her very best. The light which so many artists rave about, dances on the sea picking out the different shades of sparkling azure blue and illuminating the craggy rocks and headlands." Sun shines. Sparkling azure blue.

Sue describes this about Gorran Haven when she and her husband Rob would go out fishing in the morning from the perspective of the seas: "I always enjoy looking back at the village as it begins to wake up. The early morning sun beginning to light up the old cottages which are clustered around the harbour, and the tiny church of St Just, watching, as it has done for centuries, those who go down to the sea in boats. The eager dog walker throwing sticks into the sea and enjoying the luxury of an empty beach, the odd visitor who has woken early and is walking along the old quay enjoying the peaceful scene, and the child on their first holiday morning, busily digging in the sand." Ahhh, the SWCP!

Sue Bunney describes Cornwall in her book: "Cornwall has something for everyone, from the sweeping beaches of the wild north coast to the more gentle, hidden coves of the south." I have walked along both. She continues, "With its rivers and moors and history of smugglers and miners, farmers and fishermen,... [yes, indeed as

I have learned]…it also holds another attraction, it is a land of secrets." Please read her book to find out her secrets about Cornwall.

Sue Bunney also confirms for me one of my mysteries – about beaches that seem so secluded that the only way to access them is from the sea. For example, she says, "One of our favourite beaches is Great Perhaver, just a stone's throw by sea from Gorran Haven, but that short distance hides a variety of challenges. The only access is by boat, and landing on the beach when the sea is calm can be perfect, trying to land when the wind is southerly can be more tricky…In spite of this, the isolation of the place still beckons."

Some of my favorite quotes from Sue Bunney's book about the power of the seas and the weather include: "Equally beautiful but dangerous, the power of the sea is forever awe inspiring." "Living in Cornwall all the year round you soon become acquainted with the state of the tide and the seasons, and very quickly learn to appreciate the power and majesty of the storms, and the fickle moods of the sea."

I have learned a lot about life in Cornwall from both of Sue Bunney's books, "Love on the Beach" and "My Cornish Life," and since I have not told everything in both books, they are great reads to get insight into a life beside the seaside that I can only imagine.

The "Ultimate Location for my Beach Hut" Additional Thoughts and Locations

Now I know I mentioned that the area in the Isle of Portland near The Second Lighthouse with the beach huts that looked like they were miniature homes in close proximity to four lighthouses, walking distance to Chesil Beach, and no more than a four hour drive from anywhere along the SWCP, would be my ultimate location for a beach hut, but in reviewing my entire walk along the SWCP, I decided that there are so many other beaches that could be my ultimate location to have a beach hut as well, some of which already have beach huts located on them, and others which do not. Some of which were accessible by land, others of which might only be accessible by sea.

Some of my favorite beaches that could also be my ultimate location for my beach hut were the long sandy ones that I walked their entire length. There was the long three-and-a-half mile sandy beach of Saunton Sands that I walked its entire length on the sand itself, where I saw my very first beach huts. Nearby was the three mile long sandy Woolacombe Beach where I walked along its sand dunes, voted the best beach around, which when I walked it was mostly empty. There was also the long sandy two-and-a-half mile Perran Beach that I also walked the length of on its sand mostly in bare feet, where I ended at a music festival in Perranporth. And the Gwithian Towans Beach, another three-mile sandy beach where I stared out walking above in the sand dunes, but then found my way down to walk on its sand, with a view of the Godrevy Lighthouse in constant view behind me. With hearing constant crashing waves on the sand, these long beaches were among some of my favorites, and thus yes, one of my ultimate locations for a beach hut, even if I would have to build one.

Then there were some of the shorter and smaller beaches, but for their amazing scenery (well every beach had amazing scenery in its own way), and relaxing feelings, some of these are also my ultimate locations for a beach hut. For example, among Sasha's favorites were the beaches at Crantock and Holywell. And I really enjoyed the quieter beaches of Hallsands, Beesands, and Torcross. Even the rockier beaches of Budleigh Salterton, and the rocky and sandy beach of Trevaunance Cove near St. Agnes, where I sat for a long time, are great locations for a beach hut.

Even the busy beaches along the English Riviera like Broadsands and Goodrington Sands had their own charm. And Paignton Sands with the old traditional pier and its red colored sand could be an ultimate location as well. All the beaches near small fishing villages and other quaint villages also would make great ultimate locations for a beach hut, which would also take me back in time. Places where I could easily get something to eat, such as Clovelly and Appledore/Instow, Boscastle and Port Isaac, Cadgwith and Coverack, all great places for a beach hut.

I also appreciated the beach of Gunwalloe Church Cove Beach with its historic Church of St. Winwaloe right next to it. And the very scenic beach at Kynance Cove with the large rocks of Asparagus Island to look at and enjoy. The rustic beach huts of Teignmouth made me like that beach as well. And the collecting and looking at old fossils and sea glass along the beach between Lyme Regis and Charmouth also make this beach one of my ultimate beach hut locations.

The 18-mile, 180 billion pebble Chesil Beach, while I did not walk on much of it itself, but did near West Bexington, is another ultimate location. The beaches in Swanage which had so many different beach huts at the end of my walk, except for the naturist beaches, would be other ultimate locations.

Although, there were a lot of great small rocky and sandy coves, both named and unnamed, all along the SWCP, secluded and isolated, that I rather liked that seemed like the only way to get to them was by boat or kayak. Such as the small narrow cove just past the Lizard Lighthouse; or the picturesque Mupe Bay near Lulworth that with the rockfalls and cliffs at the edge of the water looked like a lake scene in the mountains; or the cove on the way to Porthpean Beach, where I described it as "spectacular of this little deserted beach and cove area just beyond with various shades of brown of the rocks, various shades of green of the hillsides, various shades of the blue skies, and one motorboat speeding by leaving a white line in the various shades of blue waters."

And all the beaches and coves in between these all along 630 miles, which just because I didn't mention them doesn't mean they couldn't be included in this list of my ultimate locations for a beach hut. Oh my, so many to choose from.

But really, if I needed to chose my ultimate location to have a beach hut, say aside from on the Isle of Portland, and whether my choice currently has a beach hut or not, I would say…the spectacular deserted beach and cove area on the way to Porthpean Beach! And maybe I could even build my very own mini-home-beach-hut there!

The Book Writing and Editing

I started delving into the editing and writing of this book quite soon after I returned from my walk. I never realized how much time it would take to write a book. But also how much I enjoyed it because as I did my process, I was able to relive my walk in many different ways. I started by going through each day that I had written in my B&Bs each night, day by day by day, and reading each of those days twice. In the "first round" of reading, editing, and writing, I did several things. I read each day and completed the sentences to my notes, and embellished on those sentences and paragraphs with the thoughts and experiences I remembered. Basically, general editing and writing. I looked through each and every single one of my photos, over 10,000 of them, to remember more moments and be able to describe the scenery in more detail. Some photos also helped me add quotes and information. Reading and looking at my photos really allowed me to relive my walk! In this first round of reading, editing, and writing, I also read each day out loud to my Mom over the phone for several reasons. One, it helped me to do some further editing, and two, so that she could hear each and every day of my walk in detail. Now she will still be the first person to buy my book, but this way she had a sneak-peak. Thanks for your support, Mom, and for listening to my book every day! This first round of editing took about three months to do, as I basically tried to stay on a schedule of editing one SWCP day per day.

The "second round" of editing went a bit faster, taking about a month and a half, so an average of editing two SWCP days per day. This round was researching information and facts, both by going through the SWCP Association booklets and researching online. I really actually learned a lot from this round, that really enhanced the information included in this book and my reliving my walk on the SWCP. It made me appreciate the walk and the location and the people and the history even more. In some ways, this research part took me back to my school days of long ago, doing book reports and research projects. I realized that all my schooling had led me up to this moment of doing what I am calling my "ultimate research project."

Next I had a list of miscellaneous and random notes to fill in some blanks, make a few changes, write this "In The Meantime" section, etc. Once this is complete, well then, as I already mentioned, since I decided to go back and walk the 90 miles that I missed (more on that soon), I will have more to write, and most likely do similar rounds of writing, editing, reading out loud, researching, and photo-looking to the days of my 90-mile walk. Then I will read the entire book all once again, every single day, to see if I have any other modifications and to be sure it all flows and creates a book, which will be "round three."

I will also need to decide on photos to include in this book, which I started as I looked through the 10,000 photos mentioned above to narrow them down. At that time, I chose about 200 photos as possibilities, but may need to narrow those down further, plus include some from the 90-mile walk. I did decide though that if I really do include photos in this book, then they will need to be black and white versions because color versions would increase the printing and selling price of this book substantially.

I started some formatting of the book properly for printing, such as choosing a font type and size, page size, and margins, but may need to redo all that again once the entire book is complete.

I will also need to write my epilogue/random after thoughts/reflections, go through some more miscellaneous random notes for the book, design the front cover, include maps and a bibliography, and a list of organizations, and the list of lighthouses, and a list of "expensive-places-to-stay-someday," and perhaps other lists. I will also need to do title, dedication, and acknowledgment pages, design the back cover, do a copyright page and a table of contents, and whatever else is required for writing a book!

As I did the second round of editing, I also kept track of how many pages each day was, and added them up. At that time I was around 315 pages, depending on the font I will choose. Wow, I actually stunned myself that I was actually writing a book! I say that is brave!

Thank You, Once Again

I would also like to thank, once again, the SWCP Association and Dave Westcott, for their permission to quote from their booklets. Since the SWCP Association is a Charitable Incorporated Organization, they highly accept people becoming members. From their website and brochure, "It costs roughly £1,000 each year for every mile of this glorious Path to be kept open, safe and clearly signed, so we're asking for your support to help us look after and love the Path. Whether you use it to walk the dog, have family picnics, to escape on holiday for some fresh sea air or enjoy it as a serious walker, if you love it, please help us protect it for future generations to enjoy. If you love walking the Path, please think about supporting us to improve and promote it. By becoming a member, you are helping us conserve every mile you experienced. Full details are online at www.southwestcoastpath.org.uk or by telephoning us on 01752 896237." Since I do love the SWCP, I am a member, have been for several years, and actually renewed my membership in the meantime. The SWCP Association did not ask me to promote them in this book. I just appreciate them very much.

One Final Disclaimer

I would like to add one final disclaimer at this point in addition to the others I mentioned scattered throughout the book. This book is not a guidebook or booklet, not a suggested itinerary, and not anything official when it comes to things like cows, adders, ticks, blisters, emergency numbers, directions, tides, and information, and all other things I mentioned. I am not responsible for anything, including but not limited to, your safety, getting lost, weather, etc. Nor is this a history book, and I hope all the information from other websites and books is correct. I am also not liable for any personal injury or loss of any kind suffered as a result of reading this book.

And now for the best part!...

Returning to the South West Coast Path

And finally...As I was writing and editing this book over four and a half months, my ending kept changing. Would I end the book with the 513 miles I did in 2017, plus the 27 from the original 100 miles in 2016, and say that someday I would go back to complete the other 90? Would I think about walking my miscellaneous "future-to-walk" list – St. Michael's Way (either all 13.5 miles of it, or the nine miles I had not done), The Saints Way (all 28 miles of it), Lundy Island, and the Isles of Scilly? Would I end with thinking about walking the England Coast Path? What would be my conclusion?

Well at the moment, the book is not ending yet. As I was editing and writing each day, reliving my walk though my words and looking at my photos, even writing about the disappointments with the weather and feelings of loneliness and occasionally getting lost, I just had the desire to go back and walk the 90 miles I missed and be beside the seaside once again! I had the excitement I felt when I had this brilliant idea a few days before my walk ended. I consulted with my loving and supportive husband about my desire and excitement, and he was agreeable to my going back and walking. Thank you, Scott! I am going back to fill in the gaps, fill in the blanks, complete the pieces of the puzzle, and connect the dots, and walk the 90 missed miles!

I took out that little map I hand-drew the few days before the end of my walk on a piece of paper with the dots of all the missed spots. But it was too small to work with. Instead, I made a photocopy of a larger map I had that had been hanging on my refrigerator for over a year now. It is a map of the SWCP that I had bought a while ago from the SWCP Association. It is green in color for the land, and blue in color for the waters, still my favorite colors, and has the words of many towns and villages along the way showing how many miles each town and village is from both Minehead and South Haven Point. It actually took three pieces of paper to make the photo copy of this map so that I could color in dots on a larger map in the color red of all the places I missed.

Then the planning began. I will say in brief that planning these 90 miles was in some ways more complicated and tougher than planning all 630 miles in a row because the 90 miles were scattered throughout the SWCP in random locations and longer distances between each red-colored dot. To simplify the planning, I decided that I wanted to see if I could stay in one location as a base for several walks. Using the red dot map as a guide, I was able to figure out that yes, I could do this. For example, I could use Bude as a base to walk the Morwenstow to Duckpool section I missed, and the Millook Haven to Crackington Haven section I missed. I could use Mawgan Porth as a base for the Porthcothan to Mawgan Porth, and the Porth Beach to Fern Pit Café in Newquay sections. My friend Sasha is kindly letting me stay with her for a few sections missed near Falmouth. And so on.

The transportation however, to get from one base to another, proved to be a difficult task for me as I am not very familiar with buses and trains and locations in England. I did my best to come up with an itinerary based on my bases and a bit of research on the internet, but then I had the generous help of Lucy from the SWCP Facebook Group page to refine some of my transportation options and get some other help and advice for how to plan this 90 miles. I emailed her a preliminary spreadsheet I had created for my walk, and she provided me with lots of helpful information, websites, feedback, and especially help with public transportation options, including even specific bus or train numbers and routes. And within a matter of about a week, I had my 90-missed-mile itinerary planned!

I picked some dates along with this planning, Monday, 26 March 2018 through Monday, 7 May 2018, to be exact. Six weeks. 90 miles. I had also done research on the towns used as bases for accommodations, and picked a few B&Bs I had stayed in previously, and different ones for some other bases. I got on the internet and either booked them online or via email, as I had done before. Within a matter of about another week or two, seventeen B&Bs and other accommodations were booked and arranged. And I booked my flights!

I also incorporated that Scott could join me the last ten days of this new walk, purposely reserving double rooms rather than single rooms. Again, it might be a near-last minute decision for him to join me based on some circumstances back at home. I figured that with six weeks that the loneliness I experienced before would not happen to me at all this time around. I would be walking most of my 90 miles once again by myself!

I also hoped that the weather would cooperate, but picking spring over summer, we shall see. What I do know is that only one of the missed sections is the longest at seven miles, the Undercliffs between Seaton and Lyme Regis, which has to be done all at once. All other sections are anywhere from a half mile to seven-and-a-half miles, but even the longer sections I can break down into shorter sections, so most are an average of four miles, and I gave myself plenty of days in each section. I am hoping that with the shorter sections, even if I have a few rain drops, I can manage to complete the 90 miles, and thus complete every mile of the SWCP! I have also built in extra "rest/alternate" days to walk in most locations so I have a choice of days to walk depending on the weather. There are also some days specifically for transportation, as getting from one red dot to another red done sometimes might take several hours by bus or train. I really hope the weather will be more cooperative this time. Please no strong rains or relentless winds, no gale winds, no excessive heat, no thunder, no fog, and no downpours.

And now no hurricanes or blizzards or snowstorms or bitter cold please either because as I have been editing this book and planning my new walk during the winter months of late 2017 and early 2018, I have read that the south west part of England, as well as England, the United Kingdom, and Ireland have experienced these very strong weather patterns. In fact Hurricane Ophelia passed through Ireland and the United Kingdom during October 2017, and Storm Emma brought snowstorms and snowfall to even the south west coast of England in early March of 2018, a rare occurrence for that area! This was all even followed by a second snowfall about ten days before my departure which included more ice and snow. In fact Storm Emma washed away part of the A379 coast road in Slapton where I walked back on the 5th of August 2017, and also damaged a few other areas along the SWCP. I send to the people living in all the areas affected by these storms my well wishes and hope everyone and everything returns to as normal as it can as soon as it possibly can.

For my new walk, I decided to save the "future-to-walk" list for another adventure. I also decided to save my "expensive-places-to-stay-someday" list for another adventure as well. Although, maybe I will find some more ultimate locations for a beach hut.

And you know, I never really completely unpacked from last summer. I kept a pile of clothes, my hiking boots, my purple shoes, and other items to take in a corner of our house. Including my SWCP Facebook Group lanyard. I even bought a new base for my electric toothbrush. I hope I have learned enough about cows, and there might be one golf course that I need to walk hear, but I am sure I can handle all that. Me and my two pairs of purple shoes that are still in good shape are looking forward to once again following the arrow closest to the acorn and being beside the seaside…

And I am looking forward to having some more delicious cream tea…

SPRING 2018 (27 MARCH TO 6 MAY)

TRAVELING BACK TO THE SOUTH WEST COAST PATH - Tuesday, 27 March 2018

"Filling in the gaps!" – Woman at the B&B in Braunton.

Ok now that I think about it, maybe I am having a slight mid-life crisis. You see the ironic truth as to why I was able to go back to England so soon after last summer, and for so long again of six weeks, is that when I got back home from the SWCP towards the end of last summer, I found myself without a job and collecting unemployment. It was some "unforeseen circumstance" that happened at my job that ironically was written about in the letter that I had my boss sign before I left for England last summer that I showed to the Border Agent at Heathrow Passport Control. I did not in the least anticipate that this would happen. It was a stressful time all of a sudden not having a job, and all of a sudden needing to take classes on learning how to write a resumé, cover letters, and interviewing techniques, which I haven't had to do for over twenty years. I did not like it one bit. I desperately tried to apply for jobs, even had a few interviews, but alas no job offers came through. Long story short, I took the time to regroup my left, and right, life. Instead of desperately looking for a job for a while, I had the opportunity to take an online class to further my education to add to my resumé. I worked out a lot. And to look at the whole situation on the bright side, being unemployed and taking an online class gave me the flexibility and the time to start to read, edit, and write this book! In and amongst all this, I also decided to go back to England to walk the 90 miles I missed last summer in order to complete the entire SWCP! Therefore, with my time and flexibility, I also planned the new walking adventure on England's 630 mile South West Coast Path to begin right after my unemployment benefits ran out. Maybe this was not a wise choice financially and I should have hopped on the job-searching once again, but I felt like I wanted to do this now because once I find employment again, it might be a while before I could take much time off. Let alone the six weeks that I am about to do. Perhaps all this is a slight mid-life crisis that I did not expect to have. On the other hand, the job loss just happened to me, and I look at it all as more of an opportunity. And what a great opportunity to be back on the SWCP!

So here I was, about fifteen minutes from landing in London again, making my way to Braunton to walk the first two miles I missed because of the day I did not see the obvious big red sign with white letters leading me to a closure, where I had to walk back to the big red and white sign, only then being offered a ride a few minutes later by some guardian angels and a guardian dog, which I gratefully accepted.

This time as I went through Passport Control at the Heathrow airport, there was no long set of questioning me like last summer. I guess six weeks was a lot less time than 89 days. This man at Passport Control was very nice, actually having a conversation with me about my walk after he asked me what I would be doing in England. He kindly suggested making sure that I go from the Jurassic Coast area westward where it is all beautiful. I said that that is exactly where I am going!

Soon I boarded a train from Paddington to Barnstaple after taking the Heathrow Express train from Heathrow to Paddington. I boarded the Paddington to Barnstaple train an hour and a half earlier than the one I originally booked. After flying from Seattle to London on the same overnight flight I took last summer, and after watching two movies and taking a couple-hour naps laying down on three seats since miraculously no one was sitting next to me, I paid a small price to take an earlier train since I booked the later one just in case my flight was delayed or it took longer to get through Passport Control. Therefore, I arrived in Barnstaple a couple hours earlier than planned rather than wait in the Paddington train station.

Out of the window of the train, I saw fields of sheep with tiny baby lambs. So cute. Maybe I will see sheep like I did before on the SWCP, this time with baby lambs. I arrived in Barnstaple welcomed with dry skies with patches of blue, and a bit of a light breeze. I appreciated the dry weather already. Before I caught the bus to Braunton, along with my new wheeled suitcase (more on that later) and one of my two rucksacks that I brought (more on that later), I decided to walk about a half mile to the Pannier Market to see if they still had that beautiful china dish set of white with red, pink, and peach delicate flowers that one vendor was selling individual pieces of so that I could possibly try to buy some small piece that would most likely not break. Unfortunately no such luck with that today. They did not have that china for sale. Perhaps I will get a chance somehow during this next six weeks to buy some china somewhere else.

Back outside I heard the familiar and common cooing sound of the common wood pigeon, and made my way to the bus station to take the bus to Braunton. I also asked a helpful person working on the bus about my planning for a few days ahead about which buses I should take to get from Braunton to Bude. By 2:30 in the afternoon, I was in my first bed-and-breakfast, doing my best to not fall asleep, as I was still not over jet lag.

The nice woman of the B&B asked me what I was doing in England and after I explained my story, she said, "Oh, you are filling in the gaps!" "Yes, exactly!" I replied. Yes, I am filling in the gaps, filling in the blanks, completing the pieces of the puzzle, connecting the dots, and walking the 90 miles that I missed last summer!

Trying to keep myself awake till at least 9:00pm, I went out for a snack, and then walked to the St. Brannock's Church in Braunton, the same church where last year I purchased the little two-inch by three-inch artistic print, which had since been framed and hung on our living room wall along with the four other paintings of my memories of the SWCP. Some of these same little prints were still for sale today. It was really good to know that I was familiar with the town of Braunton, and remembered the directions of how to walk to the church. Inside the church, I said my usual prayers just as I did last summer, with being grateful that I arrived back in England and on the SWCP safely. As I crossed the street back and forth to and from the church, I remembered that I need to be aware that the traffic moves in the opposite direction than what I am used to, so once again I looked both ways about ten times, waited till there were absolutely no cars coming whatsoever, and ran as fast as I could across the street. Ok once again, I am exaggerating, but the point is that I still need to be very careful about crossing the street for the next six weeks.

I walked back to the B&B to call Mom at my usual 5:00pm my time, 9:00am her time. Some things just don't change. When a restaurant around the corner from my B&B opened at 6:00pm for dinner, I ordered a nice healthy salad. I skipped dessert. As much as I tried to stay away for a few more hours, I fell asleep around 7:00 or 7:30pm, sleeping till 7:00am the next morning, with the exception of being awake in the middle of the night for two hours. That should cure the jet lag.

DAY ONE (OR DAY 88) STATS: NO OFFICAL SWCP MILES OR HOURS. PERHAPS 1.5 MILES OF EXTRA WALKING IN BARNSTAPLE AND BRAUNTON. PURPLE SHOES. (NOTE THAT FOR THIS 90 MILES, IF I ALREADY LISTED PUBS IN THE TOWNS PREVIOULY, I WON'T LIST THEM AGAIN.)

BROADSANDS TO BRAUNTON, CROW POINT LIGHTHOUSE, AND CROYDE BAY TO BAGGY POINT - Wednesday, 28 March 2018

"My mind and heart and soul were still here the entire time. Like being back home." – Me.

For old-time's sake, I had the "Half English" for breakfast today with scrambled eggs, warmed tomato, warmed mushrooms, and toast. Excited to be walking on the SWCP again, although it did feel a bit surreal that I was actually here again so soon after last summer, I was kindly given a ride to my starting point for my first day's walk to make up the two missed miles in this area. With a 9:05 drop-off, I needed to put the waterproofs on (the rain gear) due to a light drizzle, which stopped not much more than five minutes later. I was dropped off at the white house where that obvious big red sign with white letters was telling me of the path closure and diversion route that somehow I missed reading last year. However before I started the walk from there today, I decided to backtrack a bit.

I walked on a non-SWCP beach, Broadsands, to walk to the lighthouse at Crow Point. I remembered reading about this in my booklet that this replaced the ruins of the Braunton Lighthouse I saw last year, and since I like lighthouses, I took the walk that seemed like a two-mile round-trip walk all along the beach. The lighthouse was a short white stilt tower with the light on top, and from here I had views across the River Taw to Instow and Appledore. A light rain started again but stopped not much more than five minutes later once again. The sun was trying to break through the clouds.

I wore my purple shoes today, knowing how well they worked for me last year, even with a forecast of light rain since the terrain today would be all flat, and the original two miles that I needed to walk was not that long. For these six weeks, I actually packed my two pairs of purple shoes again, so in case one pair got a bit wet, I still had my second dry pair. I of course also packed my one pair of good hiking boots, as well as my two pairs of flip flops. Even though there were these few passing rain showers, the air felt like a mix of warm and cool. I walked back on the sandy beach to the white house. The third and final rain shower of the day passed by briefly.

About an hour later, it was now time to walk my first official walk on the SWCP to make up the 90 missed miles. Since the big red and white sign was still there, I started out walking on the road of the "Diversion South West Coast Path Temporary Alternative Route." I walked by the approximate spot where I got the ride from last year. Soon I decided to walk up on a raised grassy path about ten feet higher than the road but paralleling the road. It seemed like the place to walk, even though the grass was a bit wet. I managed to keep my purple shoes dry however.

Less than a half hour later I arrived at the other side of the diversion area. A jogger passed me by on the road below, and still wearing my rain gear, I once again felt over-dressed. It was dry out now, although there was now a cool breeze, so it wasn't as warm out as it was a bit ago, so the rain gear kept me warm. I was walking parallel to an estuary of the River Taw and there were several boats scattered and laying around. Some of these boats definitely looked broken and abandoned. I think there was a flood in this area at one time, thus the broken boats and the need for the diversion route perhaps. Other boats in the area looked like maybe they could still be in use, but I didn't know for sure.

There were yellow daffodils in bloom as I walked. Signs of spring. I saw some yesterday at the church too. I crossed over a stone wall near a toll place, the "Mid Toll Road Car Park" that I actually paid the toll on this road when I was driven in earlier of £2/$2.80 as the road into the area I walked is a private toll road, about a half hour after I started since the white house. "All tolls go to the maintenance of the road and marshes." It had been completely flat walking and I could see the marshes across the road. I stopped at a bench to remove the rain pants I was wearing but kept the rain jacket on for extra warmth even though I was also wearing two shirts and a warm jacket. Under my hiking pants I had on a new pair of fleece-lined jogging pants that kept me nice and warm too. I purposely bought these new fleece pants because I knew that I would be walking the SWCP this time in the "spring" rather than the "summer."

I passed by a sign that said I had a half mile to Braunton. Here some of the boats lying around actually looked like they could be miniature homes. About an hour after I started the official walking, I reached the traffic circle at Velator, the place where I was dropped off last year by car, the place where I started bike riding on the Tarka Trail the next day last year. I now had walked the two miles I missed last year and thus completed my first official SWCP missed-miles! Two miles completed, about 88 more to go!

I took off my rain jacket as it was warming up a bit now and walked to Braunton town on the Tarka Trail, the road that passed by the bicycle shop where I rented the bike from last year, and I stopped in the information center and museum in town for a look around. Since I still had all day today to walk the two miles, which along with the extra two miles to the lighthouse, all of which did not take that long, I had previously planned that I wanted to go to Croyde Bay for the rest of the day today to have lunch, to get a cream tea (!), and after being reminded of the walk by the woman at the B&B, to walk to Baggy Point. The people at the information center helped me confirm bus times to Croyde, and soon I was on the bus, being dropped off near The Thatch pub. This time I was not picked up by a delivery guy in a small white van.

I had looked up tea rooms in Croyde, and with the GPS on my mobile, I tried to find the first one, but alas it was closed today. So I walked to the second one, about a mile on the other side of Croyde and closer to Baggy Point. I walked on the road through town, then connected up with a short part of the SWCP to the tea room. I had a soup for lunch and ordered my cream tea. Since I was in Devon, I ate my scones with clotted cream first then jam on top. They also gave me strawberries to put on top of the cream and jam. I figured that soon I will be in Cornwall, so I will have another cream tea someplace with jam first then clotted cream. Both ways are still delicious.

After my food, I walked the mile walk out to Baggy Point on the SWCP close to seas. I was back to my favorite sound of the crashing waves, and back to those good-for-me-positive negative ions! Yellow daffodils were in bloom, as well as gorse in bloom somewhat with their yellow flowers. Yes, spring! It was dry but quite cool with the breeze, but my clothes keep me warm. I had on a warm hat and gloves as well. The skies were blue and the sun was shining. I was happy! I sat for a few minutes to really appreciate that I was back on the SWCP. It still felt surreal, but it felt amazing. I took a photo of my purple shoes at Baggy Point.

I walked back on another path that was a bit higher up for variety. When I arrived back in Croyde about an hour and fifteen minutes later, I asked someone at the National Trust car park if there was a bus stop on other side of Croyde Beach that I could catch a bus back to Braunton. She said there was, so I walked across the entire beach on the sand, taking my socks and purple shoes off to paddle across the small stream about half way down, even with the cool air and cool water. It was a short walk across the stream and I kept my shoes off for a few minutes to allow my feet to dry before I put my shoes and socks back on. I sat on the same rock I sat on last year and watched the waves and the few people enjoying the beach today. I took a photo of my purple shoes on the beach with the sand and the blue seas and the blue sky with white fluffy clouds. It really did feel really good to be back along the SWCP!

I double checked with someone on the other side of the beach once I got to the road where bus stop was. I walked up the road towards Croyde town about five minutes. I had 25 minutes to wait for the bus. Back in Braunton I picked up some food at a grocery store to eat in my room later for dinner, called Mom, video called with Scott, and I was back to some of my other evening to-dos just like last summer. Such as writing up the notes I took from my day as the first draft of this book, setting my alarm on my mobile for the next morning, backing up photos on my laptop and a couple flash drives, washing my socks in the sink (this one had one faucet), checking the news, checking the weather for the next few days, getting my rucksack ready for the next day's walking (or get my luggage together if the next day was a transportation day), etc.

Like I mentioned, it felt surreal that I was back so soon already in England and on the SWCP. It had been only about seven months, and I was recalling how when I left the SWCP last year, I felt sad and wondered when I would return. I did not really think it would be this soon. I figured more likely in the summer of this year, or depending on the job I had that I ended up not having, perhaps this would have had to wait till 2019. But I was here now, due to all those turn of events in my life that I had not planned with my job loss, and so in many ways that loss was all for the best. It made me think that sometimes things in life happen for a reason, even if the reason is not evident right away. The job loss was so that I can walk these 90 miles now, look for a new job after, and complete this book. It really feels like yesterday that I was here. That I never really left. I suppose physically I left, but my mind and heart and soul were still here the entire time. So now I was physically here as well. Like being back home.

DAY TWO (OR DAY 89) STATS: FIRST TWO MILES ON THE SWCP COMPLETED! ONE HOUR FOR THAT. PERHAPS ANOTHER FIVE OR SIX MILES EXTRA: TWO FOR CROW POINT LIGHTHOUSE, TWO FROM THE THATCH TO THE TEA ROOM TO BAGGY POINT, AND ONE AND A HALF OR TWO BACK ON THE BEACH TO THE BUS STOP. SIX ADDITIONAL HOURS FOR EVERYTHING ELSE. PURPLE SHOES.

TRANSPORTATION FROM BRAUNTON TO BUDE – Thursday, 29 March 2018

"A Walk on the Beach is Good for the Soul." – A painting on the wall in my room of the B&B in Bude.

Last night Kara from the B&B I would be staying at in Bude helped me with figuring out buses to get me there from Braunton, a bit better plan than from the helpful person on the bus a few days ago. Even with the helpful person from a few days ago, in my own research I kept coming up with different variations of times and bus changes. Kara looked it up for me and gave me the simplest and easiest answer. First I took Bus #21 back to Barnstaple from Braunton, taking twenty minutes leaving about 7:50am. Next it was Bus #85 leaving ten minutes later, taking about an hour to get to Holsworthy. Doing all this, I was able to take my luggage with me and thus did not need to use Luggage Transfers.

I did a quick visit to the church in Holsworthy, which was right across the street from the bus stop, St. Peter's and St. Paul's Church, with its 86 foot tall tower. Holsworthy is inland and not on the SWCP, so this was a "bonus" church that I otherwise would not have seen. I had about an hour to wait for the last bus, #6 to Bude, which took about twenty minutes. It was raining while I was waiting for the bus in Holsworthy, but I was alright with that since I wasn't walking today. I sat under the shelter of the bus stop, and kept myself warm and dry. I saw the border sign as I crossed into Cornwall (Kernow) from Devon while on the bus.

Once I arrived in Bude, I tried to remember on my own how to walk from the bus stop at The Strand in Bude to the B&B and remembered most of it, but had to use the GPS on my mobile for the last little bit, arriving about three hours after I left Braunton. I was staying at the same B&B I stayed in last year, which I did not mention the name of before, but I will know as Kara has been quite helpful both years, Sunrise Guest House. Kara and I talked about driving and walking options for the next two days, and we got it all sorted out, as I would be using this B&B to do two missed walks. I had a cute small room again, but this time with a shower, not the sitting shower/bath tub I had last year. Since I wasn't doing any official SWCP walking today, having just scheduled today as a "transportation" day in my itinerary, I went for a walk to go out to get some lunch first. I did think of packing a bathing suit with me to swim in the Bude Sea Pool, but at the last minute I realized that it would just probably be too cold to go swimming this time of year, in March, so I ended up not packing my bathing suit.

After lunch, I strolled down to Summerleaze Beach, taking the advice from the painting on the wall of room of my B&B, and knowing quite well that "a walk on the beach is good for the soul." Although I was going to go to the beach anyway even without this advice. I saw some familiar sites as I walked towards the beach – an RNLI Lifeboat Station, and some beach huts! I walked on the sand of the beach towards the water's edge, but a rain cloud in the distance told me not to go down to the crashing waves just yet. Instead I walked on the pathway above to Crooklets Beach about a half mile where I ducked under the shelter of a café just in time. Not only was that a cloud of rain, but a bit of hail as well! What?!? Hail!?! Well that's new weather for me to experience on the SWCP, one that I had not even thought of. May this be the only time that I experience hail on the SWCP. It didn't feel that cold, but I guess the cloud above was that cold. Fortunately, there wasn't much hail, and it didn't last for very long, stopping in under ten minutes. With no other clouds looking like that in the sky, I walked back from Crooklets Beach to Summerleaze Beach first on the sand, then on the wall around the sea pool because the tides were coming in. The sea pool sign said it was open year-round, but no one was swimming today. That would have been something to experience to have been swimming as it was hailing. I walked back into town, picked up some dinner for later, and went back to my B&B in the mid-afternoon.

I stayed in my B&B the rest of day and evening and night, organizing my belongings, since I had not done that yet since I arrived back on the SWCP. Therefore today was a "rest" day in addition to a transportation day. I did my first Facebook posts to my personal page and to the two SWCP Facebook Group pages. I told everyone that it was great to be back!

Another painting on the wall in my room told me that "Life is Better at the Beach." I know that, too!

DAY THREE (DAY 90) STATS: NO SWCP MISSED MILES. NO HOURS. ABOUT A MILE WALKING ON THE BEACHES, AND SOME WALKING TO AND FROM THE B&B. PURPLE SHOES.

MILLOOK HAVEN TO CRACKINGTON HAVEN – Friday, 30 March 2018

"TAKE CARE – this is one of the steepest and deepest valleys on the Cornish coastpath!" – Cornwall in Focus.

I was slightly nervous for today's walk, which was unusual. This was the place where last year I lost the path somehow and ended up at a road getting a ride into Crackington Haven, and I hoped I would not lose the path again today. I also was wondering if the path would be quite muddy today due to the weather they have had in England the past several months, including the two snowfalls that occurred earlier this month. What also made me nervous was the booklet telling me that near Dizzard Point, "The path down is very steep and rough with about 180 steep steps." I researched this walk online and an article also told me in bold letters, "TAKE CARE – this is one of the steepest and deepest valleys on the Cornish coastpath!" Then my mind wandered...What if this very steep and rough descent into one of the steepest and deepest valleys was quite muddy!? On the other hand, I did plenty of other climbs similar or with even more steps last year, and I would wear my hiking boots today, so why was I nervous?

I even texted Scott last night about my nervousness, to which he supportively also reminded me how many other steep and rough descents I had done last year. Some of which he and I did together which I thought were the toughest. Could this one be any worse? I doubt it. With that gentle reminder, I texted back, "I got this!"

I woke up to a mostly sunny, and hopefully dry, weather forecast for the next four or five hours, enough time to do the walk before any rain could start. After breakfast, Kara kindly dropped me off in Millook Haven. She knew exactly where the sign was from the road leading into the SWCP at the four and a half mile marker leading to Crackington Haven, a bit before the place a lost the path last year. At the moment, the sky was blue, and the sun was out. The path did indeed start out muddy as I wondered, but it was negotiable mud where I didn't necessarily need to step right into any of the deeper parts, which were not that deep to begin with. Just slippery. I wore my hiking boots today, as my purple shoes would have turned brown, and I also smartly brought my hiking poles. The poles definitely helped me with balancing and negotiating through the mud.

After the first half mile, I sat down at a bench to type notes on the dictation app I still was using, drink some water, and listen to birds chirp and waves crash. It was a peaceful morning. I was again in a surreal moment that I was here again on the SWCP! However, as soon as I continued walking I got a bit nervous as this seemed to be the place where I may have lost the path last year. I was walking on the edge of a grassy field which headed inland for a bit, when I saw the sign pointing me to make a right turn into some woods. Yes, this must have been the place. I wondered what I was doing or thinking last year to not see this obvious sign. I did not recognize being in the woods at all. Perhaps I was typing on my mobile some notes on the dictation app, staring at my phone while walking on the grassy field, not looking around to see the sign. Then I would have walked past the sign, and continued inland until I emerged on the road. Note to self: Do not type on your dictation app while walking the SWCP.

Heading now into the woods I felt the nervousness disappear. I had to leap over a small stream while walking in amongst the trees. The path to this point had been mostly flat, and once I was out of the woods, a sign told me I had three a half miles till Crackington Haven, so I had walked a mile already in about 35 minutes time. I walked along the edge of another grassy field which had a slight uphill slope. I had beautiful views of farmland inland behind me as I looked back around, as well as views back to Widemouth Bay. The sounds of constant crashing waves filled the crispness of the morning air. It felt a bit warm with the sun, and cool from the morning crispness, at the same time. It felt good.

I walked along the edge of more grassy fields, all of which had many areas that were wet and soggy, leftover from the weather of the past few months. My hiking poles were useful here, as well as my waterproof boots, and when I could I would take a look around to find the least wet and soggy area to walk through. I kept walking through gates, kissing gates, and going up and over stiles. There were more soggy grassy fields when I reached the sign that told me I now had two and a half miles to Crackington Haven about a half hour later. Back to my average walking pace of about a mile per half hour.

There was another patch of trees to walk through on a muddy path and another soggy grassy field. I stopped to take my warm jacket off actually, as the weather was great. Dry and sunny and getting a bit warmer. I stopped at a bench to take photos of it with its signs: Poole 500 miles in one direction, and Minehead 132 miles in the other direction. Hmmm. 632 miles?!? I thought the SWCP was 630 miles. Another sign on the bench said I had two and a half miles to Crackington Haven. Hmmm. Didn't I already pass a sign with this mileage on it? Millook Haven was two and a quarter miles back from this bench.

And then it was time for that steep and rough descent into the one of the steepest and deepest valleys. I was down in about twelve minutes, taking it slow. And you know what? It was not muddy like I was nervous about. And it was not any tougher than any of the descents I did last year. In fact, some descents from last year were much tougher. Still, I was grateful that it wasn't muddy or tougher. I counted as I descended confirming the 180 steps. It took me ten minutes to ascend out of the steep and deep valley up the other side, which was also not muddy.

Walking on another grassy field, I passed by the first two people I had seen all morning. They were walking in the opposite direction with larger rucksacks on. Saying just hello, they seemed to be determined to keep walking on, although I did check to see if they wore a lanyard from the SWCP Facebook Group but I did not see one.

I had a small descent along with a short, but muddy, ascent. The hiking poles have been brilliantly helping me on all the descents and ascents, and with the mud. Onto yet another grassy soggy field, I continued to hear the sound of crashing waves below me. I had been on top of cliff tops all morning with views below of the rocky coastline, the blue waters, the headlands behind me, and the green covered hillsides ahead of me. Still my favorite colors of blue and green. There were some rocky and sandy beaches below, but I saw no way down to them, and the waters seemed too rough for someone to even get there by boat or kayak. But I don't know for sure if there is no access to these beaches. Most of the beaches though were quite rocky. It was still dry out and continued to border on the warm side. There were some clouds and some blue skies. Yellow gorse was also starting to bloom on the path today. Soon I had a view of a church inland, St. Gennys Church, and passed by four people with two dogs on a flat section along a ridge.

Green Rucksack, Lanyard, Muddy Boots, and Fun Signs
My Small Green Rucksack with SWCP Facebook Group Lanyard above Crackington Haven March 30
My Muddy Boots above Crackington Haven March 30
Batman on Yellow Circle for Helford River Ferry July 16; "Welcome" sign outside Cadgwith Cove Inn July 13

I had another gentle descent into another valley, and while the ascent out of the valley was also on the gentle side, it was somewhat long in length and thus made it seem harder than the ascent out of the steepest and deepest valley. And this ascent was muddy in lots of places. I reached the half mile sign to Crackington Haven a few minutes before noon. I went out to sit on a bench on a side path on a ridge with several people around to celebrate my accomplishment of not losing the path, navigating the mud, conquering one of the steepest and deepest valleys on the Cornish coastpath, and completing another section of the missed SWCP 90 miles!

I ate a cheese and chutney sandwich that Kara had made me this morning on her homemade bread. It was tasty after walking for nearly three hours. I took photos of my muddy boots in the foreground, and with great views of Crackington Haven, with its buildings and its beach below. My muddy boots were also in the foreground of photos with the other half of the beach below, the green rolling hills, the next headland called Cambeak, the blue waters, and the blue sky with its white clouds. I also posed my green smaller rucksack (more on that below) in the scenery. The rucksack was sitting on the bench with my hiking poles, and the SWCP Facebook Group lanyard attached to it.

Let me talk about my new wheeled suitcase and my two rucksacks for a moment here. First of all, the wheeled luggage that my husband so kindly bought for me at the last minute for my walk last summer was just too large in size for six weeks for this trip, as much as I appreciated the purchase for last year. Knowing that some of time during this trip I would not be using Luggage Transfers the entire time, and wanting to pack less stuff too than I did last year, I still wanted a wheeled suitcase, but a smaller one. With no job at the moment, I also did not want to spend a lot of money on new luggage. Therefore, I took a chance and went to a thrift store about two months before I left for these six weeks. I found a smaller wheeled suitcase, the carryon size, but when it came time to pack my stuff, it was actually too small, especially since I wanted to pack my hiking poles and hiking boots in it. This practice-packing happened a couple weeks before I left, and I actually started to panic. How would I ever find some wheeled luggage bigger than the carryon size, but smaller than the large size, and not pay a lot for it? I looked online, and to buy something cost quite a lot.

Therefore, I took another chance and went back to the thrift store about a week before I left. And guess what?! I found one, the perfect size. It wasn't too big; it wasn't too small; it was just right. With tax it was only about $15/£11. Later I researched the actual brand and model online as it looked like a top-of-the-line brand, and it was worth at least $300/£220. Wow! And that is the story of my new wheeled suitcase.

As far as my rucksacks go, I brought two with me this time. I brought the one I had last year, which I don't think I mentioned the brand and size last year, but is the Osprey Talon 22 Liter, but at times it felt a bit too large last year, and for this year since most of my walks would be a lot shorter in length than last year, I wanted something smaller to use for the walks. I still took the Osprey because it acted as my carryon for the flights to carry my laptop, camera, and other items that I did not want to check in, and I also used this one when I would take public transportation along with the wheeled luggage. For walking however, I brought a smaller rucksack, a green one that I bought in Spain on my Camino de Santiago walk several years ago. It is some Spanish brand and I don't know the liters it holds, but less than 22, and it was perfect for these six weeks. Interesting how not only did I buy my original pair of purple shoes on my Camino walk, but I also bought this small green rucksack. In addition, instead of a water bladder this year, what I did this time was I bought two plastic water bottles with pop-up type lids at the Paddington train station and used them the entire six weeks, fitting them in the outside pockets of my small green rucksack. It was just right.

Green rucksack. Purple shoes. I was colorful. Perfect...

Anyway, I sat for 25 minutes on this bench above Crackington Haven, and when the air started to turn cooler and I had to put my warm jacket back on, I walked the last half mile gentle descent into the small village of Crackington Haven, which I recognized from last year. I walked on the beach for a bit to try to clean some of the mud off my boots in a puddle, but they were still quite muddy. I had about 45 minutes to wait for the bus back to Bude, so I ate a rich vegan chocolate brownie at a café while I waited. Yes, chocolate. Some things don't change. It was a celebration, after all. While the bus was about ten minutes later than the schedule said, I was back in my B&B in the mid-afternoon. I got this! Well, I did this!

Later on, I went out again to get some dinner for take away from a vegetarian food cart. I took my mushroom wrap to Summerleaze Beach once again to get some more negative ions and hear more crashing waves. The tide was in further this time and there was no way to walk down to the sea pool or all the way to Crooklets Beach like yesterday. I paused once again and reflected on the surreal, but amazingly great, feelings of being back on the SWCP.

DAY FOUR (DAY 91) STATS: 4.5 MILES. 3 HOURS. ONE EXTRA MILE IN BUDE TO AND FROM B&B FOR FOOD AND BEACH. HIKING BOOTS AND POLES. Quote about the walk, "Walking Crackington Haven to Millook Haven," from cornwallinfocus.co.uk/walking/cancleav.

Arrows and Acorns with Scenery
Looking back after Soar Mill Cove April 22
Between Wembury and Warren Point July 31
Between East Portlemouth and Prawle Point August 4

Arrows and Acorns with Scenery
Looking back sometime after Prawle Point April 23
Gurnard's Head from 2016 100-mile walk with Scott
Between Portscatho and Portloe July 19

Arrows, Acorns, and Wooden Sign Posts with Scenery
Pointing towards Golden Cap August 18
Pointing towards Combe Martin and Hunters Inn June 9
Getting close to Start Point Lighthouse April 23

BUDE TO DUCKPOOL TO MORWENSTOW - Saturday, 31 March 2018

"Rare breed sheep on these cliffs." – Sign along the SWCP today.

Today I decided to repeat about four miles in order to walk the just over three missed-miles from last year, for a total of about seven miles walking. I was originally going to only walk the three "required" miles (which I originally thought was four miles), between Duckpool and Morwenstow, but after no luck finding a taxi or a ride to Duckpool, I started walking from Bude to Duckpool and onto Morwenstow, which was just fine with me anyway. It meant more time on the SWCP. I wanted to end in Morwenstow either way in order to eat lunch at the Rectory Farm Tea Rooms there when I was done with my walk. The forecast for today was dry, with perhaps a few sun breaks, so that was great, too.

I won't describe too much of the repeat walk miles since I described this section in more detail last year, but the first mile or so out of Bude was mostly flat as last year, but on wet soggy grass this year. Hiking boots were once again quite useful. I sat on a beach for a moment after that first mile to get out my hiking poles for the 100-step climb I needed to ascend, which I descended last year. The walking continued on flat wet soggy grass, as I had views behind me of Bude, and recognized certain places of walking from last year. About an hour and a quarter after I started walking I only had one more mile left to go till I reached Duckpool. On the way, I saw the cutest sheep and their cutest little baby lambs. I remembered seeing this a few days ago from the window of the train where I wondered if I would see baby lambs on my walks, and sure enough, I was happy to see them.

I wasn't so happy to see a herd of cows however. Fortunately, they were just off to the left side of the path, just enough out of my way that I passed by them easily, although I kept peeking from the corner of my eye at them just to make sure they were staying still, which they were. The sun was doing its best to peek out behind the clouds, and while it remained dry, it was actually on the windy side this morning, and remained that way most of the day. Not just a gentle breeze either. But also not as windy as that day I had last summer walking from Hope Cove to Soar Mill Cove back on the 3rd of August, and definitely not gale winds.

I walked a few more ups and downs, saw a few more sheep and baby lambs, heard the crashing waves, negotiated around and through some muddy places, looked at the rocks on the coastline pointing out into the water, and arrived at Duckpool two hours after I started walking from Bude. I recognized the car park there and sat down to have a snack of leftover breakfast.

As I was ready to start my new miles, the sign pointing towards Morwenstow said I had two and three-quarters miles. Originally I thought I missed four miles, then I thought it would be just over three miles because the booklet adds up to about three and a quarter miles, but this sign said less than three miles. In either case, it didn't matter. I was walking the missed miles of the SWCP! I walked up the first zigzag climb, taking about seven minutes for the ascent. The sun was peeking through the clouds. By the way, today's walk was a "backwards" walk because I was walking in the direction of Poole to Minehead, with the seas on my left. Now again, this could be the forwards direction if you were walking from Poole to Minehead, but since I did the majority of my walk from Minehead to Poole, for me this was "backwards." I missed this section last year due to the excessive heat I experienced, where after walking several long days in a row in the heat, I decided to make one of my hot walking days shorter, and especially because the day I was going to walk this section it was not only the longest day of the year, but it was the hottest June day in 41 years, the 21st of June 2017.

Looking behind me, I had views back to Bude and the sandy and rocky beaches in between with their white waves, as well views of the green-covered hillsides and the paths that I had been walking on. The view ahead of me was of a large cliff leading down to rocky coastline that I would soon be walking on top of, and big white satellite dishes. The path was flat and lined with the yellow flowers of gorse starting to bloom. A couple walking passed by me ahead of me. And a great flock of sheep, with several baby lambs, passed by me as well, and I was able to get some great close-up photos of them! Cute!

Now remember that gorse is a prickly plant. And also on this path was a lot of mud. Repeat, a lot of mud. I had to make a choice…Walk in the middle of the path where there was the most mud, or walk on the edge of the path with less mud but closer to the prickly gorse. Hmmm. I decided that since I had protective clothing on with my warm jacket and I could use my hiking poles to brush away some of the gorse, and since the gorse was not that grown over, I chose the less muddy option closer to the gorse on the edge of the path.

The next part of the path was a very soggy grassy flat area next to the big white satellite dishes, the GCHQ Listening Station, "the government's eavesdropping station," followed by lots more mud. But with my hiking poles, searching around for the least wet and muddy parts, I made my way through just fine. I recalled that a few days ago I was nervous about walking with the potential of a lot of mud, but I have since become accustomed to this situation, and my hiking boots have worked very well even though by the end of the muddy days they were covered in mud. I just cleaned them off as best as I could later on.

I had a descent, passing by a couple going in the direction toward Bude. On this descent, I needed to find some grass to walk on with more traction than the slippery mud on this part of the path. I arrived near a sandy and boulder-filled beach at the bottom of this valley, after one short final muddy section which I took very slow descending. Hiking poles helped me get through all this.

I stopped at the bottom of the valley to look and listen. To the waves crashing, and to a few birds chirping. A sandy and rocky beach. The turquoise waters of the seas. Ahhh the SWCP! Here I was sheltered a bit from the wind that was still blowing above, as I stood on a bridge with a nice sounding stream at the bottom of this picturesque valley.

I had a slow ascent up out of the valley due to some more mud. A few people were descending across the valley from me where I had just descended, and a person with two dogs was on the beach below. There was lots of yellow gorse around. I came across a "warning" sign telling me that there was some "Rare breed sheep on these cliffs," and if I had a dog with me to "Please ensure your dog is under control, preferably on a lead and does not stray from the path." I did see a flock of sheep in the far distance inland and wondered if this was the rare breed.

I continued walking on another very muddy but flat section, using my poles for balance here and the edges to walk on because sometimes there were larger puddles of mud to negotiate around. I arrived at a "Disused Lookout" and used this shelter for a moment to get out of the wind, fix my wind-blown hair, and look out to the seas. This was followed by one more descent and a real good ascent that I took slow. I was getting hungry and looking forward to having some food at the tea room in Morwenstow.

One more flat soggy grassy area, and a short side visit to Hawker's Hut that I missed walking by and going in to last year. Recall that Rev. Robert Stephen Hawker was a 19th century cleric, poet, and eccentric who wrote sermons and poetry and contemplated the sea in this hut. I went inside the tiny hut, noticing a book to write in. I wrote, "31/3/2018 Debby Dungan USA Completing the 90 miles I missed last summer when I walked from Minehead to Poole. Love the Coast Path." I also drew the shape of a heart. I took photos while sitting in the hut looking out through the door to the seas and contemplated for a moment.

I continued walking just a short distance more on that flat soggy grassy area, and then I saw the church tower in Morwenstow that I recognized. I walked inland on the same grassy footpath that I did last year, although it was soggy and muddy today. Although this year, I did not walk with that nice older gentleman from Yorkshire that I walked with last year. Fortunately, there were no cows this year as there were last year. Four and a half hours after starting from Bude, and two and a quarter hours after starting from Duckpool, I arrived at the church in Morwenstow, completing another section of the SWCP!

I visited the Parish Church of St. Morwenna and St. John the Baptist inside to say my usual prayers and enjoy the peacefulness of the church. I noticed that some of the bench ends in the church dated from 1575! It still boggles my mind, the concept of time, and that these churches have been around for centuries.

I went to the Rectory Farm Tea Rooms and had a warm bowl of soup, which was nice because it had been cooler out today with the wind most of the day. I was grateful that the day remained dry however. I recalled that I had a bowl of soup there last year too, even though it was hot out, and that the man working there told me that I was "knackered" last year after walking in the heat. This year, I did not feel that way.

And of course, I had to have a cream tea! This time I ate it the Cornish way, jam first then clotted cream, since a few days ago I ate my cream tea the Devon way, clotted cream first then jam. I called Kara to kindly pick me up as we had pre-arranged. I had a half hour to wait, so I waited in the peaceful church.

DAY FIVE (DAY 92) STATS: 7 MILES, ABOUT 4 REPEAT AND ABOUT 3 NEW FROM THE MISSED-MILES. 4.5 HOURS. HIKING BOOTS AND POLES.

SCHEDULED "ALTERNATE" DAY, SO A REST DAY IN BUDE – Sunday, 1 April 2018

"The mud will wash off, but the memories will last a lifetime." – Unknown

After breakfast, it was time for some boot maintenance and cleaning and washing off from the last few days of the mud, mud, and more mud off my boots. I cleaned my muddy boots by using a spoon that was in my B&B room to scrape the chucks of mud off into a paper bag that I had from some take away food. I then placed the boots near a heater to dry. Last night I also took out the inserts to let them dry separately.

I had scheduled today in my itinerary as an extra "alternate" day in Bude in case I could not get either of the two walks done that I did the past two days due to potential uncooperative weather. I chose Bude as a base for the two walks (Millook Haven to Crackington Haven and Duckpool to Morwentsow) because Bude was about half way between the two walks and was a larger town to stay in, and I already knew the B&B that I booked. Since I had dry weather the last two days and did my walks, today thus became a "rest" day. I spent a few hours typing up the notes from my first two days into draft one for this book, including looking through the photos I took and looking through the booklets for any additional information. I figured if I can catch up today and keep caught up, then the book could be completed faster.

After a few hours of writing I was hungry for lunch, so I went to the same vegetarian food cart that I ate at a few days ago. It was near a paved trail by a canal so after I ate I walked up and back on the non-SWCP paved trail slowly for about thirty minutes. Then I made my way back into town just as it started to lightly rain, picked up some more food for take away for dinner later, and went back to my B&B just in time for it to rain harder most of the rest of the day and night. Good thing I had cooperative weather the last two days for my official walks.

I did some more book writing and basically caught up on writing four of the last five days since arriving in England. I had also scheduled tomorrow as a second alternate day in Bude in case I needed it for the two walks I did, so instead of having a second rest day in Bude, I made arrangements to travel to my next B&B in Mawgan Porth a day early, including figuring out transportation to get from Bude to Mawgan Porth, my next central location for three walks.

My Mom asked me, well she really told me, that I should not feel lonely during this trip like I did a bit last year. I agreed with her because first of all, I am here for a shorter amount of time, six weeks, rather than three months. Second, I will soon be staying with my great friend Sasha. A few weeks after that, I will be staying with Lucy from the SWCP Facebook Group as well. Finally, Scott will be joining me the last ten days of these six weeks, which we actually did decide and plan this time well ahead of time. We had even booked his flights and did other arrangements before I left for the SWCP. Really, I just do not think that any lonely feelings should appear again since after all, I am back on the SWCP to appreciate once again all that it has to offer along this place that I fell in love with last year, beside the seaside!

DAY SIX (DAY 93) STATS: NO SWCP MILES. ABOUT TWO MILES EXTRA FOR WALK ALONG CANAL AND BACK AND FORTH TO THE B&B. PURPLE SHOES.

TRAVEL DAY FROM BUDE TO MAWGAN PORTH AND ANOTHER REST DAY – Monday, 2 April 2018

"Dear Debby. Welcome back to Seavista! We are delighted you are staying with us again! Please let us know if there is anything we can help you with, whether it be restaurant recommendations, suggestions for things to do and see in the area or anything to improve the comfort of your stay with us. We remain at your complete disposal and hope that you will enjoy your visit here in Mawgan Porth. Kindest regards, Kate and Oz." – Loving welcome note in my room from Kate.

I actually originally scheduled two alternate days in my itinerary in Bude to do my two walks in the area to accommodate for the weather, the location, the distances, and the number of my walks in this area. As mentioned, in most areas I have scheduled "alternate days" in my itinerary, but I shall explain again in further detail. These are days so that in each section I can choose the best days possible to walk based on the weather forecast. A few places have no alternate days, so I have to hope for the best possible weather. Other places I have one or two alternate days in my itinerary, so I have choices. On the alternate days I can do whatever I want - write, walk around whatever town I am at, sit and walk on a beach, do a repeat walk, do some other non-SWCP walk, or whatever.

Since I had already completed the two walks near Bude, and since I used yesterday as a writing and short walk day, I decided to get to my next B&B a day early in order to have an extra alternate day in my next area, Mawgan Porth. Thus, a couple days ago I emailed loving Kate of the great Seavista Guest House, where I stayed last year and had some great Super Food Porridge breakfasts, to see if she had my room available for an extra night. She had a different room available, which was just fine. I researched bus schedules from Bude to Mawgan Porth, and I kindly asked Kara at the B&B in Bude if I could leave a day early. Kara was alright with that, to which she still charged me half a night's rate, which I was happy to pay, as it was not that much.

I would have had to take three buses today, but I asked Kate if after my first bus to Wadebridge, a two and a half hour ride, if taking a taxi at that point would be a reasonable price. Kate lovingly said that her Dad could pick me up at the bus station in Wadebridge, for a small price. Less than the price of a taxi, maybe a bit more than buses, but I was happy with that so I didn't have to take two more buses, which would have taken a longer time. And honestly, even with my wheeled suitcase and using the Osprey rucksack on buses, putting both of them in the boot (trunk) of a car was easier.

On Bus #96, the long ride was nice because I actually passed through places I have been both this year and mostly last year, and I could see them out of the bus window. Crackington Haven, Boscastle, Tintagel, Port Isaac, signs pointing to Trebarwith, and Polzeath. The bus wound its way through those narrow country roads that when two cars (or buses) are heading towards each other, one has to kindly move over as much as possible to let the other pass. I arrived at Wadebridge on schedule, and Kate's Dad was waiting for me. He drove me to the B&B where Kate welcomed me with a hug. I guess yesterday when I mentioned Sasha, Lucy, and Scott as people I will be with this spring, I should have mentioned Kate as well. I consider her a friend, too! I was also greeted with the loving welcome note above in my room on their stationery.

I went to a small café to get some lunch, then spent at least an hour walking down the long sandy beach in Mawgan Porth from the road to as close to the water's edge as I could get without getting my purple shoes wet. I walked to one end of the beach as far as I could, and back to the other end as far as I could, both times being stopped by a stream but close to the hillsides on either side of the beach. I also sat on a large rock for a bit filling up with, you know, those good-for-me-positive negative ions, and listening to, you know, my favorite sounds of the crashing waves. And the sounds of the trickle of a stream. Spending time at the beach was a great way to spend a rest day here in Mawgan Porth.

I went back to the B&B to continue to catch up on writing. Usually for my scheduled "longer" travel days, such as today, I did not also schedule a required walk, so I can do whatever I want on these days as well, just like on the "alternate" days. Therefore, I have scheduled quite a few rest days on my 90-mile six-week walk along the SWCP. I feel like this will actually be a great mix for me of having many days of walking, and also many days of doing whatever I want, especially spending time at a beach!

DAY SEVEN (DAY 94) STATS: NO SWCP MILES. ABOUT A MILE OR A BIT MORE WALKING TO AND FROM B&B AND ON BEACH. PURPLE SHOES. PUB IN MAWGAN PORTH IS "THE MERRYMOOR INN."

HARLYN BAY TO TREVOSE HEAD LIGHTHOUSE TO HARLYN BAY – Tuesday, 3 April 2018

"Please follow the short diversion through the gaps in the stone hedge. Once work is completed this will be the permanent route for the coastal footpath." – A National Trust sign along the SWCP.

I woke up to sun and blue skies with some white clouds this morning, and to the sound of sheep, and probably baby lambs, baaaaaaing. Although I couldn't see it, but there must have been a farm across the street from this B&B.

Aside from seeing Kate again, the breakfast I ate this morning was why chose to stay at this B&B again on this trip, and was glad I even now had an extra night here than originally planned, thus an extra breakfast. Today's breakfast started with a delicious homemade pear, apple, lime, and cucumber juice. I helped myself to a small bowl of delicious homemade muesli topped with various seeds, yogurt, and fresh fruit. This was followed by the delicious "avocado, poached egg and potato hash served on lightly toasted English muffin with lime and chili flakes." This B&B was the place last year that even with all the great breakfast choices I only ate the delicious Super Food Porridge, so this time I thought I would eat different things each morning.

After my delicious breakfast, I walked down to the bus stop near the Mawgan Porth beach that I walked on yesterday. The tide was in, quite close to the upper end of the beach, with no way to walk out as far as I did yesterday. It is just amazing to me about nature and tides and how they remind me of the power of the seas that I must respect. I took the half hour bus ride on Bus #A5 to Harlyn Bay and the beach there. Today's missed walk was actually only the mile around Trevose Head near the lighthouse. Last year I had missed just this small bit because of the weather, wind and rain, where I decided to walk inland on roads instead of the SWCP to get to the lighthouse. This year, instead of just walking the one mile only, and since I had an extra day in this area now as today was really supposed to be the day I would have travelled from Bude to Mawgan Porth, I figured I would make it a longer walk of five miles and walk round trip from Harlyn Bay to the lighthouse and back to Harlyn Bay. Thus I am repeating about a mile and a half from Harlyn Bay to the place where I turned inland in the "forwards" direction, walk the new mile in the forwards direction, then walk the two and a half miles "backwards," repeating it all again as I walk backwards.

The bus dropped me off at the beach and I started to walk on the sand. There was a stream in the middle of the beach that unless I took my shoes off would have probably gotten my hiking boots too wet for my walk today. I did not quite remember how to get around the stream, and even though I consulted my booklet, I asked someone at the lifeguard hut. He instructed me to walk off the beach just ahead, cross over a bridge, and then down the other side back onto the beach. Then about half way down the beach there would be some stairs to climb up to get back on the SWCP. Ah, yes, then I remembered.

I did remember this part of the path being mostly flat, with some very minor ups and downs. This year of course it also had some muddy spots as I walked above the beach, and predicting the mud is why I wore my boots today. There were a few people on this path as I walked. In fact, the entire time I was on this path today, there was quite a good amount of people walking today, just enjoying this stretch of the SWCP. I started having views of the Padstow Lifeboat Station and some large rocks jutting out into the waters called Merope Rocks. The path continued to be flat and was not as muddy as I predicted as I continued walking.

About 45 minutes after I started walking, I recognized the path that was next to a field where I turned inland last year. This year, it was quite muddy and had some puddles, so I walked along some narrow edges to avoid getting my boots too wet. Then I started on new path, the last mile out to the Trevose Head Lighthouse. There was actually a short diversion to walk on. A National Trust sign told me, "Due to cliff failure and rock fall here, works have begun to change the route of the coast path at this point. Please follow the short diversion through the gaps in the stone hedge. Once work is completed this will be the permanent route for the coastal footpath." There were new signs and gates as I walked, and I could even smell the new wood used for the gates. I appreciated the work that goes into keeping the SWCP safe and useable.

I passed by a sandy cove below the short cliffs with holes or a cave or something in the rocks. It was a great little sandy cove, and it looked like a great little secluded spot, although I could not figure out a way to get down there. There was another sandy beach I walked above as well.

The SWCP then went on the inner side of a small ridge, but I first went out to the tip of the ridge above the Lifeboat Station to a bench to take a few photos of the tip of the ridge, the waters beyond, a few large rocks in the waters, and the headlands in the distance. Knowing that I would be walking backwards on the SWCP soon, I took a short alternate route back to another part of the SWCP to continue walking.

By the way, note that this time I did not take Punxsutawney Phil with me to photograph him. Since I won first place last year (!), I was quite happy with that, and did not need to enter the contest again this year. Although, I am continuing to take photos of benches, and if I see any windows and doors, and of course beach huts and harbours, I will take those photos as well.

A few moments later I saw the top of the Trevose Head Lighthouse come into view. And within another few minutes after walking near some grass and negotiating some more mud, I arrived at the lighthouse, taking pictures of it from various angles as I got closer and made my way to the place by the road where I was last year. It took an hour and a half to get here. I took a few more photos and celebrated that I completed another missed-mile on the SWCP by starting to walk back to Harlyn Bay! The booklet reminded me that "Trevose Head projects further than most of the Cornish north coast, so the positioning of the lighthouse in 1847 was crucial for shipping," although that is some repeat information from last year.

In walking back, this time I took the inner path along the small ridge which was the actual SWCP, and at one point I realized that there were areas along the SWCP today that I did not hear the waves crash. Parts were just quiet. The weather remained dry my entire walk, with a breeze which made it feel a bit cool. The sun gave way to a mostly cloudy sky as I walked back. I ate lunch at a food cart by the beach at Harlyn Bay while I waited for the #A5 Bus back to Mawgan Porth. This morning I bought a "return" bus ticket, meaning a two-way ticket, as it was cheaper to buy this rather than two "single" tickets, one for each way. I did this since I knew I would be taking the bus both to and from Harlyn Bay. If I would only have been taking the bus one-way, then I would have bought a "single."

I was grateful for a beautiful day weather-wise with dry mostly blue skies, being by the blue and turquoise seas, near and on beaches, seeing rocks and small hillsides on the water's edge, and seeing people enjoying the day with their kids and dogs. I am definitely in love with the SWCP.

DAY EIGHT (DAY 95) STATS: 5 MILES, OF WHICH ONE MILE WAS NEW, WITH 4 REPEAT MILES. 3 HOURS. HIKING BOOTS, BUT POLES NOT NEEDED. PUB IN HARLYN BAY IS "THE HARLYN INN."

WATERGATE BAY TO PORTH BEACH TO FERN PIT CAFÉ, NEWQUAY – Wednesday, 4 April 2018

"Chia Pudding - Chia, nuts, and seeds soaked in blended banana and coconut milk with maple syrup served with a sprinkle of granola, fresh berries, and bee pollen." – This morning's breakfast.

Today's delicious breakfast at the Seavista in Mawgan Porth started with a small bowl of the muesli with seeds, fresh fruit, and yogurt again. The smoothie of the morning was with banana and berries. Finally, I had a delicious chia pudding, which I had to order yesterday since the chia needed to soak overnight. The description was "chia, nuts, and seeds soaked in blended banana and coconut milk with maple syrup served with a sprinkle of granola, fresh berries, and bee pollen." I found a surprise of a bit of peanut butter in there as well. A great breakfast to start my six-and-a-half-mile walk.

Last year I had missed from just past Porth Beach to the Fern Pit Café because I needed to meet my great friend Sasha, and at the time I was already running late, so I had taken a taxi. It was mostly city walking anyway, but in order to complete all 630 miles of the SWCP, today it was time for this walk. I figured I would get some nature-time in before getting to the shock of a big city however, so I took Bus #A5 to Watergate Bay to start my walk, as I remembered that this walk was on the clifftops above beaches and the seas. Sure enough, from the first moments of walking, I could see and hear the crashing waves, the beaches, the coastline, and the seas, and hear birds chirp and seagulls caw. Ahhh, the SWCP!

I passed by some fields on my left with a couple of signs along a fence informing me, "Please keep out – Corn Bunting habitat," and "Do not enter – Corn Bunting nesting." Later I looked up something about these birds and a website called RSPB, The Royal Society for the Protection of Birds, which told me about the corn bunting that "This nondescript lowland farmland bird is the largest of the buntings and is most usually seen perched on a wire or post. It is a stout dumpy bird brown which flies off with a fluttering flight and with its legs characteristically 'dangling'. Its dramatic population decline in the UK makes it a Red List species." Similar birds are the reed bunting, the skylark, and the yellowhammer.

I was curious about this new organization I just discovered, RSPB, and found out that they are "passionate about nature, dedicated to saving it" since 1889 and are now "the largest nature conservation charity in the country." Then I was curious about what Red List meant and found out that there are three categories of conservation importance. Red being the highest on the list with the "highest conservation priority, with species needing urgent action," because of their historical population decline. The next highest category is amber, and the lowest is green. I found it interesting that I walked by a red listed habitat area. Later I also listened to a recording of a corn bunting song and wondered if I had heard any at all as I walked by the fields.

I wore my purple shoes today because I figured most of today's walk would be city walking. I did my best to keep them purple, as I had to navigate several muddy spots along the path above the crashing waves. Following the same path as last year, I walked across the sand of Porth Beach about an hour after I started walking just as the sun peeked out of the clouds. It had been overcast with a light wind till this point. Just beyond Porth Beach a woman had stopped to watch a bird and to listen to its song. I stood with her for a few moments to not disturb her peace with the bird so that it wouldn't fly away, and to listen to the bird's song with her. I wondered if it was a corn bunting.

About fifteen minutes later I arrived at the restaurant that I called the taxi from last year that drove me to the Fern Pit Café. The light wind and cloud cover continued. I would say that yesterday and today the temperature was probably about 50F/10C, but with the light wind, it did seem a bit cooler and a warm jacket and warm hat kept me feeling warm. I was now starting my missed miles for today.

The SWCP started along the edge of some grassy fields lined with benches. Of course, a few photos were taken with the benches. I was still hearing the waves crash on the beaches below, which was nice to hear especially with the city buildings on my left. But then I hit the pavement and a busy noisy road with lots of businesses. I only needed to follow that for a few minutes though and then walked on a smaller side road following the SWCP sticker signs on poles. And following the directions in today's booklet. I reached above Towan Beach with its rolling small white waves and a few people down below. There was a house with a red roof on top of a rock island that was sitting on the beach. Per the booklet, "The House on The Island (Towan Island) is known locally as 'The House in the Sea' and is joined to the mainland by a suspension bridge 90 feet above the sea. Before the house was built in the 1900s the island was used as a vegetable garden. The house has been owned by various people...and is now available as a holiday home or a boutique retreat!" Hmmm. Perhaps yet another place to add to my "expensive-places-to-stay-someday-along-the-SWCP" list.

I wound my way through some more streets and above the Newquay Harbour. Many fishing boats, sailboats, and rowboats were in the harbour, some floating on the water, others resting on the sand, surrounded by a few breakwalls. "From the 18th century the harbour became important in the export of mined tin and copper and later china clay," according to today's booklet.

Shortly after the harbour I arrived at a white oddly-shaped building, Huer's Hut. According to the booklet, "During the time when pilchard fishing was the main industry a 'huer' would watch for shoals of pilchards from this building. When a shoal was sighted the hue and cry went out and all the fishermen would make for their boats, being directed to the shoal by sand signals from the huer. There is even a story that a funeral was abandoned when the hue and cry went out so the pilchard catch was not missed. This building probably dates from the 14th century and was thought to have been a hermitage originally." From the website "Visit Newquay" I read further that in addition to being a possible hermitage, Huer's Hut may have also been a "religious retreat for contemplation or an early shipping beacon akin to a lighthouse or maybe a combination of all three." Reading about this was so interesting, and I remembered reading more about pilchard fishing and huers doing some online research I talked about on 28 July 2017, and now I was at an actual place representing the important fishing industry. And adding yet another type of lighthouse to my list as well.

Since that was all pavement walking, I was now back to walking on a path and arrived at an Old Lifeboat House, a large white building, which was built in 1899. I did not walk on an optional path on Towan Head to an Old Coastguard Lookout, where once "the activities of smugglers could be seen." I appreciated that I was still learning about the fishing and mining industries and smuggling as I walked my missed miles on the SWCP. The path then followed above some rocks on the sand at the beginning of Fistral Beach, then above Fistral Breach. By now I was quite hungry, so I stopped to eat lunch above Fistral Beach about two and three quarters hours after I started walking.

The walking continued along a sandy path above the beach next to a...golf course. My first golf course of these six weeks. No incidents occurred as there was a tall fence protecting me from any flying golf balls, and the weather continued to stay dry and light winds with cloud coverage. A walk on a road was next where I had views all the way across Fistral Beach, as I was perpendicular to the long white waves. I wondered if I could have walked along the length of the beach itself today. The road turned into a stony track, curved around and led right to the Fern Pit Café. I will admit though that a few times today not only did I follow SWCP signs and the booklet, I also used the GPS on my mobile just to make sure where I was going through this city, including getting to the café.

I was planning on eating at the café today all along, but now I was glad that I stopped earlier and ate because the Fern Pit Café was actually closed. A sign also said that access to the ferry crossing was closed too, so for those who wanted to cross the River Gannel today I don't know if there was an alternate way down to the ferry, or even if the ferry itself was even running. For me however that didn't matter, as I had now completed another missed section of the SWCP! I arrived three and a half hours after I started walking, including the lunch stop. I walked up and around the road a few more minutes to a bus stop in front of a hotel. I had to ask someone along the way where the bus stop was. I had about a half hour to wait for the bus back to Mawgan Porth.

DAY NINE (DAY 96) STATS: 6.5 MILES OF WHICH ABOUT 2.0 WERE REPEAT AND ABOUT 4.5 WERE NEW MILES. 3.5 HOURS. PURPLE SHOES THAT STAYED MOSTLY PURPLE. SEVERAL PUBS IN NEWQUAY, BUT SOME CLOSEST TO THE SWCP ARE "WALKABOUT," "THE FORT INN," AND "THE RED LION." Information on RSPB from rspb.org.uk/about-the-rspb. Information on conservation list from rspb.org.uk/birds-and-wildlife/wildlife-guides/uk-conservation-status-explained. Information on corn buntings from rspb.org.uk/birds-and-wildlife/wildlife-guides/bird-a-z/corn-bunting.
Some information on Huer's Hut from visitnewquay.org/explore/huers-hut.

PORTHCOTHAN TO MAWGAN PORTH – Thursday, 5 April 2018

"Happiness This Way." – With an arrow pointing to Porthcothan Beach on a sign for the Porthcothan Bay Store.

"This is my Happy Place." – Business Card for Porthcothan Bay Store.

I missed today's four-and-a-half mile section between Porthcothan and Mawgan Porth last year due to wind, rain, and a long-mileage planned day. But before I began my walk today to walk those miles, I first needed to move to a different room in the B&B, to the same room as I had last year, because of the non-availability of the room I was in when I added a fourth night to stay here a few days ago. Also before I began my walk today, I had another delicious breakfast, the Super Food Porridge, the one I had every morning when I stayed here last year, made with "coconut milk, coconut oil, nuts, chia seeds and a drizzle of honey and seasonal compote," and also some fresh fruit and some edible flowers.

After breakfast, I took Bus #A5 to Porthcothan, the same bus I took the other day to Harlyn Bay but alighted (got off) the bus sooner, this time buying a single ticket. I immediately noticed a welcome sign that said, "Happiness this way," when I got off the bus at the Porthcothan Bay Store pointing towards Porthcothan Beach, and knew I was in the right place! That, along with the mostly sunny and completely dry forecast today, I knew it would be a happy day! I walked into the Porthcothan Bay Store to pick up a sandwich as I figured I might take my time today walking and would get hungry before arriving back in Mawgan Porth, perhaps eating the sandwich at the infamous Bedruthan Steps along the way. As I purchased my sandwich, I noticed their business card with the saying, "This is my happy place," with an arrow pointing to a photo of the beach at Porthcothan. Definitely going to be a happy day!

I started my walk by just going down to the sand of the beach for a look and listen. Yup, a happy place! The waves were so soothing to listen to as they rolled down the stretch from the seas down to the beach, hearing the rolling crashes. The beach was not that wide and it was surrounded by short hillsides on either side with the constant rolling waves coming in between the two hillsides. I stood for a bit. I even took some videos which I don't take very often at all. As I took some deep meditative breaths and left the beach, I noticed some daffodils in bloom as I started my walk. I heard the birds chirp in the fresh crisp morning air. Perhaps corn buntings? I recalled that last year I did see some more corn bunting signs the day I walked towards Porthcothan. Seemed like it was a great spring weather day today.

It took me an entire ten minutes just to walk the short length next to the beach on the SWCP, which may really only take a minute or two. Listening. Looking. The continuous rolling crashing waves, the edges of which would hit the rocks of the short cliffs causing white spray to splash up. I took more pictures and more videos. I decided right then and there that this was my new ultimate location for a beach hut! This was my happy place. Or owning a home overlooking this long beach would be wonderful, too.

Walking only a minute or two later was my second ultimate location for a beach hut, another sandy beach with more rolling waves. A moment or two after that I was walking with looking back at views to Trevose Head Lighthouse, along with looking at the turquoise and blue waters. A few minutes later there was a secluded cove. Then large rocks appeared in the water with birds sitting on them. A mere fifteen or twenty minutes, and I was just completely in awe by the beauty in this section!

This all of a sudden made me realize that I was now very glad that I actually missed 90 miles last year. And that I was glad at the moment that I was unemployed. The combination of all this has given me this amazing opportunity to come back to the SWCP and see and hear and feel all this beauty again so soon! I even wondered if I should ever like to repeat some of the walks I did last year in the rain, including the one leading to Porthcothan, so that I can enjoy them even more. Yes, I had fallen in love with the SWCP and all that it has to offer.

As I continued to walk there were people fishing, people jogging, and people walking. There were benches for people to sit and look and listen. There was a very short descent to a small rocky beach with a few people on the beach. I stopped for a few minutes to look and listen. The waters were so blue and turquoise in color as the waves on this beach also came rolling in between two short hillsides. I passed by a sign that said I had three and a quarter miles to go to Mawgan Porth, meaning that at this point I had taken 45 minutes to walk a mile and a quarter.

There was a short ascent up out of the beach where I had views back of where I had just walked and all the way back to the lighthouse. I walked on a grassy field. So far there have been a few muddy spots and only a bit of soggy grass. I didn't know how muddy it would be today, so I wore my hiking boots. I could have worn purple shoes to this point, since I have been able to negotiate around a few muddy spots. I sat on a bench to look and listen.

After my sit, there was a long stretch of flat grass. I thought about the lawn mowing conversation I had with Gordon last year where he told me that the National Trust does bring a "weed eater" machine to areas to create the mowed look, and then sheep help keep it groomed. There was some yellow gorse in bloom today. The signs along this stretch of the SWCP had been the acorn symbol on granite slabs of rock. I passed another sign telling me I had two and a quarter miles till Mawgan Porth, an hour and a half after I started walking today. I turned a slight corner and saw a secluded sandy beach cove below the cliffs, and views of the grass covered hills leading down to the waters I had been walking on. There were many people out in this area today enjoying the great spring weather.

I noticed that it was quieter now with smaller waves crashing below me. I passed another secluded sandy cove. After that long flat stretch, I arrived at the infamous, and popular, Bedruthan Steps after two hours of walking, seeing the few large rock islands in a row as I approached. There was a big red safety warning sign about going down to the beaches below with the tides, saying "Beware of being cut off by in-coming tides. Note the beach is covered up to two hours before high tide." I looked down below and there were some people down there though dodging waves and scrambling on rocks, and I wondered why they were down there now since the low tide would be in three and a half hours. I stopped to sit and eat my sandwich.

As I ate, I watched a lot of people go down to the Bedruthan Steps, including families with children, so I decided to venture down myself, since I figured that parents would not allow their children down there if it wasn't safe with the tides. In fact, I did notice that in the twenty minutes time I was eating, the tides and waves were already receding. Bedruthan Steps are a group of large rock island stack formations just offshore, although "It is likely that the name refers to the set of steps (staircase) down to the beach rather than the legend of the giant Bedruthan who used the rock stacks as stepping stones," according to today's booklet. The formations of these rock stacks actually reminded me of The Twelve Apostles rock stacks I once saw in Australia.

I climbed down the very steep zigzag staircase of 120 steps, holding onto the handrails quite tightly as it was quite steep going down, definitely the toughest descent of the day, and even the toughest descent of my last week. Even tougher than the descent into the steepest and deepest valley on the Cornish coastpath near Crackington Haven! And this staircase was not even part of the official SWCP. I noticed other warning signs along the steps as I descended. "Do not enter water at any time, dangerous currents," and "Danger of rock falls. Do not sit below or attempt to climb the cliffs."

Once I was down to the sand and rocks, I walked a bit on the first part of the beach. Continuing on there was one spot I just had to wait a moment for water to recede in order to get across just like other people were doing. I noticed that the children were loving it down here, so happy to be there. This must be their happy place!

I walked around a bit on the sand looking and listening. I was below the cliffs looking up at the rocks and seeing people walking up above on the SWCP. I was near large boulders sitting on the sand in the water. I was close to the crashing waves. There were waterfalls and caves. Lots more people showed up. It was a happy spring day.

After a half hour down there I climbed the 120 steps back up with many more people coming down, which was followed by some much easier steps as I continued on the SWCP. Looking back, I had views of rocks and hillsides and headlands and the lighthouse. There was some more flat walking first on grass then on a path. It was quiet. No sound of crashing waves. Just birds chirping. And the sound of the wind. And voices of people passing by. I had views out in the distance on the horizon of just the turquoise and blue seas, with nothing beyond. I had been walking very slowly all day. I was just feeling quite happy.

I had a slight descent onto another path, around a corner, and then views of the beach at Mawgan Porth appeared. It was a long but gentle descent above the beach down to the beach and the few buildings below of shops and restaurants. I thought that the path would continue all the way to start of beach, but due to a cliff rock fall there was a diversion in place through some streets and homes which I started walking on. Then instead I decided I would rather walk on the beach, so I back-tracked a bit to a place I saw access to the beach and thus completed another missed-mile section walking on the beach into Mawgan Porth four hours after I started today! It was a slow-paced, spring, and happy day!

DAY10 (DAY 97) STATS: 4.5 MILES ALL NEW. 4 SLOW AND HAPPY HOURS. HIKING BOOTS, NO POLES, BUT COULD HAVE BEEN PURPLE SHOES.

TRANSPORTATION DAY TO SASHA'S – Friday, 6 April 2018

"Though miles may lie between us, we are never far apart, for friendship doesn't count miles, it's measured by the heart." – Unknown

This morning's final delicious breakfast started off with a tasty lime, kiwi, apple, cucumber, and kale smoothie juice. I also helped myself to a small bowl of muesli with seeds, fresh fruit, and yogurt once again. I decided to try something different today once again, and while it was delicious, I wished I had gotten the Super Food Porridge again instead. I had waffles with bacon and maple syrup. It reminded me of the couple of times I ate something similar last year. I definitely am going to miss these breakfasts here at this B&B.

I waited a few hours in my room before I needed to begin my transportation day to get to Sasha's. I said my thank yous and good-byes to Kate. I will miss her and her B&B. I feel at home here. It was great to have some time to talk with her about life and things over the past several days, and I appreciate that we have become friends. We gave each other a hug.

Her Dad kindly drove me to the Newquay bus station where Sasha was to pick me up in the late morning to bring me back to her home. Somehow though there was a mix-up between Sasha and me, and we unfortunately could not find each other after waiting over a half hour, so I ended up taking two buses to get to Falmouth via Truro, and finally a taxi to get to her house. I was alright with that though, as that was my original plan anyway so she wouldn't have to drive to get me in Newquay. I felt bad that we could not find each other though because she did drive from Falmouth to Newquay to pick me up. I tried to call her at one point but I apparently called her home landline number, not her mobile, so she never got my voice message. And she emailed me, but I did not even think to check email while waiting until it was too late and she had turned around to drive back home. I felt bad for the mix-up, but it all turned out just fine.

When she answered her door after I knocked, all was good and we hugged, and it seemed like yesterday that I was just here. A surreal feeling once again. It was great to see her, and I was also greeted happily by her three dogs, as she had gotten one more dog since last year. After settling in and chatting a bit, we took a drive with her three dogs and went on a flat walk in a National Trust area to walk the dogs, a non-SWCP area near her home. We chatted the whole time about life and about the SWCP. It was really great to have someone to talk with about all sorts of bits and bobs, especially talking about the SWCP knowing exact locations of where we were reminiscing about. We also sorted out details of my walks for the next three days. She will kindly help me out with several rides which I really appreciated.

Sasha had also created two more books that over the course of the last several months that I had also purchased and read. One book was about another long walk that Sasha did, the 140-mile walk around the island of Anglesey off the northwest coast of Wales. Taking eleven days to complete the walk, "A Brush with Anglesey – An Artist's Continued Search for Inspiration along Britain's Coastline," is similar to her book "A Brush with the Coast – An Artist's Search for Inspiration along the South West Coast Path" in that it is filled with her adorable paintings and her inspirational story of walking around this island. She had two dogs with her for this walk, and her husband even drove their newly purchased old camper van from campsite to campsite around the island as she walked. What fun!

Sasha's other new book was a children's book which I bought a copy for my niece, but Sasha also kindly gave me a copy of my very own. Entitled, "Plop!" it is based on her love and knowledge of the coast as well. The back cover describes the book as, "While playing on his favourite beach, a scruffy, brown dog finds a curious trinket in the sand and nuzzles it over his head for safekeeping. But what happens when it slips from his neck and lands – PLOP! – in a rock pool?" My niece loves the book, and so do I!

Sasha cooked dinner for me, herself, and her husband Jack, and we all enjoyed a nice dinner together. I watched some TV with them, and feeling tired, I went to bed early. It was so great to be with a great friend again!

DAY 11 (DAY 98) STATS: NO SWCP MILES. ABOUT TWO MILES WALK WITH THE DOGS. PURPLE SHOES. MANY PUBS IN FALMOUTH.

PORTREATH TO PORTHTOWAN – Saturday, 7 April 2018

"Happy. Smile. Love." – Painted on a painted rock that Sasha and I found above the Porthtowan Beach under a bench.

After brecko of a bowl of cereal at Sasha's house, I decided to wait a few hours to start today's four mile walk from Portreath to Porthtowan. It was lightly raining out, but the forecast said it would stop raining around 11am or noon, and the sun might even appear. Last year I missed this section, from Porthtowan to Portreath, because of the forecast of thick cloud and fog the day I was supposed to walk it. This year I decided to walk it "backwards" so that I could end in Porthtowan where there would be a couple of cafés to get some good food after my walk as I waited for Sasha to pick me up. Sasha kindly both dropped me off and picked me up today, which I really appreciated, so that I could complete another missed section of the SWCP.

Sasha drove me a half hour as we chatted and I ate a peanut butter sandwich in the car. I had her drop me off at the Portreath Arms just before 11am, the place where I met a family that I walked with last year towards Gwithian. Before starting on the SWCP today, I took a short side walk to the harbour at Portreath to see the waves hitting against a breakwater and small white building on its far end which "was used as an observation post for the harbour master to guide ships into the harbour in stormy weather." I walked up the paved Lighthouse Hill, but did not see any lighthouses so I'm not sure why it was called that. A sign at this point said I had two and three-quarters miles to Porthtowan, however I was sure I had four miles according to today's booklet. Well three and three-quarters miles actually to be a bit more exact. I needed to continue walking on a paved road for a few moments longer to a car park due to a diversion due to a landslip. Here a sign now said two and a half miles to Porthtowan, but I still think it is just under four miles.

As I started walking on a muddy and wet trail, I overlooked a three-quarter circular cove with small sandy secluded beaches below that no one probably goes to. I had views of headlands beyond that I walked on last year, and views even out to the Godrevy Island Lighthouse on the way to Gwithian, Hayle, and St. Ives. I wore my hiking boots today because of the rain this morning, which had stopped, and because of the muddy days I have already had. I turned right around a corner and all the views behind me disappeared until I was a bit further on and looked back again to see all the way to Godrevy Lighthouse against some blue skies.

Today was a day of walking near a military area, and soon I saw a MOD Property (Ministry of Defence) sign warning me, "Dangerous cliffs and old mine workings. Keep to the footpath." I followed this advice the entire way into Porthtowan. The path had been flat and continued to be flat for a bit. It actually became warm out and there was no wind, so I stopped to take my hat and jacket off, and to get out hiking poles for a decent of about 70 steps down a valley, and an ascent of about 70 steps up out of the valley. More views behind me appeared out to Godrevy as I looked back after the climb. A family of four passed me by in the opposite direction, and I also saw one person heading in my direction. The path continued to be flat for quite a while with on and off muddy and puddle spots. I could see the view ahead of me of a mining chimney and headlands beyond that I walked on last year. It was relatively quiet of the sound of waves, but birds were chirping and seagulls were cawing. Straight out to my left were views of nothing but water and sky, and out to my right was the fence of the MOD Property.

I heard the sound of waves once again as I walked above a deep cove. A few trail runners passed me by as the sun started to peek out of the clouds. Then lots of waves crashed at another cove as I descended a few steps, which I did not count, but the booklet said 65 steps. I looked up at the big ascent I was about to climb. A large rock stood in the water with lots of birds sitting all around it, called Gullyn Rock, so I wonder if the birds sitting on it were gulls. This was down into a valley called Sally's Bottom.

I climbed a steep 117-step climb up, which I counted, although the booklet said 110 steps, still with the MOD Property fence on my right. The views from the top down to the cove below and beyond to the hilltop I just walked were beautiful, especially with the warm sun out and the blue skies with white clouds. Spring!

Another trail runner passed me by. I passed by some brick structures which were "shelters for the military personnel that operated gun emplacements during WW2," with one last look at Godrevy Island Lighthouse behind me in the distance. I walked on flat path until I arrived at the mining chimney which "was part of a steam pumping engine which serviced a local mine that closed in 1927," and other industrial mining ruins, which had lots of mud and puddles in places and the hiking poles helped me to navigate and balance around them. The views ahead of me were now of Porthtowan on the hillsides, beaches below, and rolling white waves heading towards the long coastline, with the Wheal Coates mining ruins above that I had walked by last year.

As I walked on a long wide flat stony road, I saw long white rolling waves below. Soon I had one more view back to Godrevy with the coastline below the green and brown hillsides I had just walked on being touched by the waves below. I turned a corner to overlook the beach at Porthtowan with its rolling white waves crashing on the sandy beach coming from the turquoise and blue waters. I walked a short distance down a paved road into the town and walked out onto its beach two and a quarter hours after I started walking. The sign here confirmed three and three-quarters miles, and with my average of about a mile every half hour, that seemed correct. I had now completed another missed-mile section of the SWCP!

For some reason I could not remember either of these two towns that I just walked from and to in my mind yesterday when I was planning this walk. Then last night I remembered Portreath when I recalled the Portreath Arms was where I met that family to walk with. I still could not recall Porthtowan however until I was descending the road into town and recognized the buildings, especially the Zennor ice cream shop where I had an ice cream last year, a Belgian chocolate flavor. This year I did not have ice cream. Instead I had a healthy lunch at one of the cafés. After eating, I called Sasha as we prearranged I would do, using the café's landline phone as I did not have mobile reception, and sat on the beach for about a half an hour while I waited for her listening to the crashing waves and watching kids playing. It was peaceful to just sit on this beach for a while.

When Sasha picked me up she brought her three dogs with her and we went on another walk. Up and out of Porthtowan on the SWCP in the direction of Chapel Porth. We probably walked at least a slow mile out and a slow mile back, not quite will the way to Chapel Porth, so this was repeat walking for me. The sun came out even more and it felt like a warm spring day, even bordering on summer actually. We discussed birds and she told me that perhaps the chirping birds I have heard are more likely meadow pipits, so maybe not corn buntings, and the cooing birds are wood pigeons.

At one point Sasha and I briefly sat on a bench to enjoy the warmth and the views of the beach below and the hillsides where I had walked earlier today. As I stood up I noticed a painted rock under the bench with the words "Happy. Smile. Love," and a few hearts all in black on a pink background. I guess I found one of those treasure-hunt rocks that seem to be a popular thing to do. I wanted to keep it, but I left it under the bench for the next person, taking only its photo. A few days later I found out that there is actually a Facebook Group page called "Kernow Rocks" where the instructions are if you find one of these painted rocks you take a photo of the rock, post on the Facebook page where you found the rock, then hide it somewhere else for someone else to find. Since I did not re-hide this rock, I did not post my photo however. Sasha did decide to paint a rock herself, since she is an artist after all, and we happened to find a rock in the shape of a triangle which she thought she could paint a sailboat on.

I thanked Sasha for a great day, including the rides, and especially the walk together, and she felt the same - that it was a great day together!

DAY 12 (DAY 99) STATS: 5.75 MILES, 3.75 NEW AND 2 EXTRA WITH SASHA. 2.25 HOURS FOR THE NEW WALK. HIKING BOOTS AND A BIT OF HIKING POLES.

ST ANTHONY IN MENEAGE TO HELFORD – Sunday, 8 April 2018

"The walk along the Helford River is very uneven in places and largely through trees with occasional glimpses of the river and opposite shore. It is best done in the spring before the trees are in full leaf and the bluebells are in flower." – Today's Booklet.

Without Sasha's kind driving today, I don't think I could have done today's walk. There were no buses, or at least no convenient buses, especially on a Sunday, to and from where I walked today. Taxis would have been quite expensive. So thank you, Sasha, for making today possible so that I could walk the three miles that I missed two years in a row! Not just last year, but this was the only section Scott and I missed during our 100-mile walk two years ago.

After winding our way through the very narrow back roads, Sasha dropped me off at the church in St. Anthony in Meneage. The one powered only by candles that I did get to see two years ago with Scott because of a ride we got to there from our B&B. Today I went inside the church once again to look around, and to say my usual prayers. I also actually wrote in the guest book of this church, which I rarely do. For the comments I said, "Peaceful." I walked around the outside of this church as well and took a great photo of the church with its tower and a "car park" of boats right next to the church. I thought about the juxtaposition of this, the very old church next to the modern boats, but it really showed the significance and importance of both – the history and religion coupled with the fishing industry.

I did buy a small booklet about this church called "St. Anthony in Meneage, The Story of the Parish Church, By The Revd H. H. Dixon." I found the last paragraph to be a nicely written summary which said, "St. Anthony in Meneage has had a long and varied history. Beginning, no doubt, as the little wattle and mud church of some long-forgotten hermit, it grew first into a small Norman church of nave and chancel, and later into an enlarged Early English church in its present form…To all our visitors we offer a welcome, and we hope that they will carry away with them happy memories of the Meneage – the monks' land – and of the little Church of St. Anthony in its happy setting of wooded hills and water."

I started walking about 9:30 up the road a tiny bit from the church away from its happy setting, and made a right turn onto a grassy field where my hiking boots got a bit wet from the morning dew on the grass. Looking back I could see Gillan Creek and a few homes on the green hillsides. Not too much further, I took a left turn at a sign that said two and a half miles to Helford. The flat, sometimes muddy, path started out with grassy fields on my left and shrubbery and the Helford River on my right.

Soon I was in a more wooded area with shrubbery on both sides and small trees. Since I was walking in spring, the trees were not in full leaf and nothing was overgrown, and most importantly, the sun was shining warmly through the trees. I had occasional views of the river, including that of a view of a small cove. Sailboats were going by. The ground was uneven with lots of rocks and pebbles and tree roots and small twigs, but nothing that couldn't be walked on. Although, it was very muddy in many places, so at times even with trying to avoid the mud and walk on the edges or elsewhere, my hiking boots got muddy nonetheless as I wiggled my way through the leafless trees. Without the leaves I continued to have plenty of views of the river and the sun continued to shine through.

At a small beach cove I had views across to green grassy fields on other side of the river, most likely where I walked last year after the ferry crossing into Helford Passage. I noticed a large freighter ship in the distance in the waters, and motorboats and canoes were coming down the river. As the mud continued, I was glad that I wore hiking boots with all the muddy spots. I did not see any bluebells in flower, but there were some white and some pink primroses in bloom. I continued walking through some trees that offered shade, and then I had a view to out across the river to Helford Passage. The sounds for today were of the motorboats, the voices of people in the motorboats, and my boots sloshing around in the mud.

About an hour after I started walking, I emerged out of the trees and was near some homes. There was a small display of old bottles for sale, but I did not buy any. Although looking at the photos I took of them later I wished I did buy some, but I think I was afraid they would break, just as if I were to buy some china. They were colorful, as some were clear, but others were blue, red, yellow, green, or purple in color.

I walked a short distance on a gravel track and then down a paved road with sign telling me I had a half mile to Helford. I took a left up a couple of steps to another muddy path in some trees and next to some homes. I emerged at the car park and café that looked familiar because this was where Scott and I were dropped off two years ago, and I was dropped off last year when I didn't do this missed section I had now just completed.

I walked through the village of Helford which "was once a thriving haven with trading ships bringing rum and tobacco from the continent," some smuggling information, and onto a paved path leading to the ferry to cross the Helford River. I called Sasha as we had arranged that I would call her just before boarding the ferry. Here I had mobile reception. I opened up the sign to summon the ferry, but no Batman symbol like last year, just the plain yellow circle this time. About an hour and a half after I started walking today, I took the ferry across the river for my third time, but this time I finally completed the three-mile section I missed two years in a row! Thanks to Sasha!

While I waited for Sasha as we agreed to do a dog walk after my walk, I had a healthy lunch at The Ferry Boat Inn. Sasha dropped her car a bit away from Helford Passage so she walked with the dogs to meet me, then we walked back together on the SWCP to Durgan and a bit beyond that small village going inland from there. Therefore,

I did a bit more walking of repeating about three-quarters of a mile of the SWCP. It was a great day weather-wise! Sunny and warm, probably at least 60F/15.5C. Spring! Back at Sasha's, I was thankfully able to also do some proper laundry today.

DAY 13 (DAY 100) STATS: 3 MILES. 1.5 HOURS. PLUS AN EXTRA MILE MOST OF WHICH WAS REPEAT. HIKING BOOTS BUT NO POLES.

FERRIES FALMOUTH-ST MAWES-PLACE & A NON-SWCP WALK ATTEMPT ST MAWES TO ST JUST – Monday, 9 April 2018

"The Scallop Shell is the ancient symbol of pilgrimage. It marks the many routes of the 'Camino' pilgrimages across Europe, often found on gateposts, walls and lampposts. Traditionally a pilgrim places their hand on the shell, joining hands with centuries of Christians who have passed this way before." – Explaining a basket full of scallop shells in the St. Just in Roseland Church.

Today my main goal was to take the ferries connecting Falmouth and Place, via St. Mawes. Two years ago, at the Prince William Pier in Falmouth was where Scott and I ended our 100-mile SWCP walk, and last year, while I did the walk starting in Place with Sasha, I missed the ferry experience since Sasha drove us. So this year, for fun, I wanted the ferry experience. Even if that meant I just take the ferries only today. But on recommendation from both Sasha and Lucy because of the walk's and the church's beauty, I also decided to do a non-SWCP walk in St. Mawes to the church in St. Just in Roseland. Or at least attempt to do the walk…

Sasha kindly dropped me off at the pier to catch the 9:15 ferry to St. Mawes. It was a twenty minute ride across the River Fal. Before taking my walk, I took the ferry to that place called Place, just to see if from this perspective, then stayed on the ferry back to St. Mawes, all just to say that I did these two ferries. I had to explain to the Place ferryman why I did not get off the ferry. On my way over, I was tempted to get off and repeat some of the SWCP in that area, but I already had my other plan of the non-SWCP walk. I was back to St. Mawes with all that by 10:30, and I guess I completed another piece of the SWCP, one without any walks! Note that I bought a combination ferry ticket called the "Roseland Ramble" that paid for back and forth on the two ferries today.

After finding a quick bite to eat, I started walking on the road leading to the St. Mawes Castle, confirming with someone on the way that I was headed in the right direction for my walk to the Parish Church in St. Just in Roseland. At some point I noticed a tile in a wall of the very familiar scallop shell symbol of the Camino de Santiago, painted yellow with a blue background. I wondered what that was doing there, and thought perhaps someone had maybe done a Camino walk in Spain and placed that there from that for their own memories. I did not think too much about it after that.

After walking past the castle, I walked on a smaller road that curved around and down, which soon led to a path. I asked one other couple once again just to make sure I was going in the right direction, and I was. The river should remain on my left throughout this walk until I arrived closer to the church.

The path was flat and easy going through a few grassy fields. There were a few muddy spots, but they were easy to navigate around in my purple shoes. Purple shoes were not the shoes to do this walk today in however. After about a half hour of walking I got stopped by a huge muddy soggy wet boggy puddle area. Bigger than any muddy soggy wet boggy puddle area that I have experienced the past two weeks on the SWCP. I tried to walk around it, through it, over it, but it was so wet, I unfortunately got my purple shoes a bit brown and even my socks wet in my attempts. I even wondered if I had hiking boots if I would have even been able to get through this muddy, soggy, wet, and boggy puddle area. I have not experienced this much mud and wet area on the SWCP, so I was at least "glad" that this happened on a non-SWCP walk, and not on a SWCP walk where I would have had to stop my walk. Today, I had no choice but to stop my walk at this point and go back towards St. Mawes. I did think of even taking my shoes and socks off and walking the area barefoot but opted not to take that option. Needless to say, I was disappointed with this whole situation, especially with the quite warm sunny summer-like day I had.

I turned around and made my way back to St. Mawes, but wanted to still somehow make the best of my day and make it to the church in St. Just in Roseland. I asked yet another couple if they knew if there was a bus to the church instead. They told me yes, and if I to go to the visitor information office, they can help with bus times and the bus stop was right there. Once I got the visitor information office, alas I was about ten minutes too late for the bus to St Just in Roseland and the next one wouldn't be for a few hours. However, the kind lady there said she was getting off work in a half hour and would drive me the few miles. A guardian angel. I was grateful. In fact, all of the people I asked questions to today have been guardian angels. While I waited the half hour, I got some lunch. It was so sweet of her to drive me, which was on her way home anyway.

She also helped me with bus times back from St. Just in Roseland to St. Mawes, and with that timing, I had about 45 minutes to wander around the quaint turn-of-the-13th-century church in its beautiful location by the St. Just Pool, a tidal creek. The tombstones were scattered around in several areas on patches of grass on the hillsides and in the general surrounding subtropical gardens area. The setting for the church had flowering trees, plants, and even what were most likely palm trees. Inside the church there were a few things that caught my attention. A place for

Prayer Pebbles, where you "select a pebble to represent you or the person you wish to pray for," and place it in a bowl of water. There were also colorful Prayer Crosses that were made by members of the church.

Finally, there was a basket full of scallop shells along with a photo of the yellow scallop shell symbol on the blue background that I saw earlier today. Indeed it was from the Camino de Santiago. A flyer explained, "The Scallop Shell is the ancient symbol of pilgrimage. It marks the many routes of the 'Camino' pilgrimages across Europe, often found on gateposts, walls and lampposts. Traditionally a pilgrim places their hand on the shell, joining hands with centuries of Christians who have passed this way before. We hope your visit to St. Just Church today will inspire you, as you continue on your own pilgrimage, following in the Way…" In addition, the brochure for this church said, "For centuries St. Just in Roseland has been an inspiring place of pilgrimage for so many people." Wow! I am just amazed at how I have come across a few scattered reminders here and there along the SWCP, and now this non-SWCP walk, that remind me and connect me to my walk along the Camino Francés/Camino de Santiago in Spain.

Whether I walked to this church or got the ride from the kind lady at the visitor information office, it was worth coming to this church either way, as it made me stop to think for a while about my walk along the SWCP, that perhaps this is more than just walking for the adventure of walking 630 miles. Perhaps I am on some sort of pilgrimage, some sort of spiritual journey. I wondered if all the guardian angels I have had have been part of this journey, and being taken care of by them, and the possibility of also being taken care of by the "universe" and by a guardian angel above all guardian angels who oversees my guardian angels that I only briefly thought about last year on the 3rd of July. I wondered if my loss of a job has all been a part of this journey. I wondered if sometimes walking by myself, sometimes feeling lonely, sometimes walking with others, have all had some spiritual significance. I wondered if the weather, from rain to wind to hail to thunder to heat to fog, has all been part of this journey for me. And getting lost and missing miles are all part of this as well. Do I feel any different? Am I experiencing any transformations? I remember that last year early on in my walking adventure, I did not feel that I was on some spiritual journey at all. Perhaps I am realizing now though that there is something bigger out there. Not in a religious sense for me, but in some other spiritual or greater sense that is hard to explain. Maybe there just is something greater than me out there that is watching over me.

Perhaps I am also experiencing a greater connection with nature. A greater connection with the negative ions of the seas. A greater connection to the beaches, the sand, the views of what's around me, including looking behind me to see where I have been, looking ahead of me to see where I shall be going, and looking out into nothing but seas and skies. A sense of living life more than just going to work every day and traffic. A deeper appreciation and thankfulness and gratitude for everything in my life and all the experiences along all my SWCP walks. A desire to experience life at a walking pace.

I do remember that they say that walking the Camino de Santiago, a pilgrimage, is like a reflection of life - the ups and downs. Not just physically of the ascents and descents (although I felt physically fit with the ascents and descents), but with the elations and happiness and good times, along with the challenges and struggles and difficult times. Both in the experiences, like with the weather, and in the emotional rollercoaster, if you will. It happened to me on the Camino in Spain. It happens to me in life. And it certainly has happened for me on the SWCP.

I took the bus back to St. Mawes, the twenty minute ferry ride back to Falmouth, and a bit after I arrived, Sasha kindly picked me up to take me back to her home. Sasha has been a great guardian angel these past several days. I shall miss my time with her, her husband, and their three dogs. She truly is a great friend!

DAY 14 (DAY 101) STATS: NO SWCP MILES. ABOUT TWO TO THREE NON-SWCP MILES. OVER AN HOUR OF WALKING. PURPLE SHOES THAT UNFORTUNATELY GOT A BIT BROWN AND WET, BUT LATER DRIED OUT. PUBS IN ST. MAWES ARE "VICTORY INN" AND "ST. MAWES HOTEL."

TRANSPORTATION FROM FALMOUTH TO GORRAN HAVEN – Tuesday, 10 April 2018

"The tiny church of St Just is nestled into the side of the cliff and stands sentinel above the waves guarding the village. Where there is a service at St Just, its one bell echoes across the little harbour and beach calling the people to prayer, as it has done for centuries." – From Sue Bunney's book, "My Cornish Life."

Sasha kindly dropped me off once again at the bus stop in Falmouth. After thanking her very much for everything, and hugging, she said to keep in touch so that I can let her know how I am doing on completing all the bits and bobs of my SWCP walk. I laughed again. Every time she uses that term, I find it great and funny. I felt sad leaving her, and I shall miss her.

Today my goal was to get to Gorran Haven for my next missed-miles walk for tomorrow. Optional for today could be to do a repeat walk to Portmellon or Mevagissey. First, I took a bus to Truro. Then I was supposed to take another bus to Gorran Haven, but since the bus station in Truro was closed, and the buses picked up at various locations in Truro, and even with me asking several people who work for the buses, no one seemed to know where I would go to get the bus to Gorran Haven. Besides, I would have had to wait an hour and a half anyway according to the schedule that I looked up online. Instead of a bus, I decided to just take a taxi, albeit on the pricey side, to Gorran

Haven, but was worth it, for the shorter amount of time, ease, and comfort, along with my luggage that I was carrying.

After arriving at my B&B I was hungry for some lunch so I went down to the area near the beach of Gorran Haven that I remembered so that I could go the Coast Path Café that was good from last year to eat. Alas, they were closed on Tuesdays, and will unfortunately also be closed tomorrow. Instead I went to a place called Cakebreads that I read about in one of Sue Bunney's books. I was after all back at the place where I originally bought one of her books, and where she writes about in her books.

After eating, I walked to the St. Just Church to first find a bench at the end of a short path with a view that was also mentioned in one of Sue Bunney's books, which I found and took a few photos of the bench with views of the beach below, with its harbour and breakwater, and with the hillside above. I went into the church for some peaceful reflection and gratitude time. Through the quietness of the church, I was able to hear seagulls cawing outside as well as the small waves hitting the beach. After that nice time, I took a walk on the small beach and along the breakwater itself, still in peaceful reflection and gratitude. As mentioned, I was considering doing a repeat walk today, but decided against it when looking up at the hillsides surrounding Gorran Haven I saw they were blanketed with fog. Reflection and gratitude for my friendship with Sasha, and for my being once again on the SWCP.

I picked up a few items for dinner from Cakebreads, which aside from baked goods, which I did not get, is also a small café and a small store. I took the few items back to my B&B room for later. I sat listening to birds chirping, seagulls cawing, and chickens clucking, as I took the time today to catch up on writing and a few other things on my to-do list, thereby making today a "rest day."

DAY 15 (DAY 102) STATS: NO SWCP MILES AND NOT MUCH EXTRA WALKING. FLIP FLOPS WALKING AROUND GORRAN HAVEN.

HEMMICK BEACH TO DODMAN POINT TO GORRAN HAVEN TO MEVAGISSEY – Wednesday, 11 April 2018

"It has been used as a navigation aid for centuries but it is also a perfect spot for a picnic." – Sue Bunney in her book "My Cornish Life" about Dodman Cross.

Tony of the B&B in Gorran Haven kindly gave me a ride down to Hemmick Beach this morning, the place that last year that I decided to take the inland paths through Dodman Point and into Gorran Haven, instead of going around Dodman Point itself on the SWCP. This year, I wanted to complete the part around Dodman Point, and continue on to Gorran Haven repeating some of the SWCP. Since the weather was a summer-like day today, I also decided to continue walking after a break in Gorran Haven onto Mevagissey.

Starting out from Hemmick Beach, with one mile to go to Dodman Point, there was a slight uphill on a grassy path then onto a path with great views of the beach below, a large lone house next to the beach, the headlands I walked on from last year, green checkered farmland inland, and the path to Dodman Point ahead. After the slight uphill, the path flattened out. There were a few muddy spots, blooming yellow gorse, and some white flowering bush as well that I am not sure the name of. There was one muddy spot that I had to walk through that I could not negotiate around and thus got the tips of my boots muddy.

The large lone house next to Hemmick Beach "holds a special place in [the] hearts" of Sue Bunney and her family. In her book that I read in the meantime between my SWCP walk last summer and this spring, "My Cornish Life," Sue Bunney tells of how her husband Rob's father "was born in the small cottage which stands near the entrance to the beach. The family had lived there for over a hundred years, with no mains water or electricity…Walking along the path from the Dodman, and looking down at the first sight of Hemmick always lifts the heart. This is a real Cornish cove, with a stretch of golden sand divided by the rock formation into different areas, thus providing the illusion of owning your own patch of the beach for a day." Here I was looking down on that very special place.

I passed by a National Trust sign welcoming me to the Dodman and telling me of Dartmoor ponies that were grazing in this area. The sign said, "Welcome to the Dodman. Dartmoor ponies are grazing in this area. Whilst passing through, please observe the following points for safety and welfare of both you and the ponies. Close all gates. Do not feed the ponies as this may encourage them to bite. Keep dogs under close control. Take care when passing close by them. Be aware that these are wild ponies." The sign continued, "They are a rare, native breed originating from the wet and windswept moors and mires of Dartmoor. Dartmoor ponies are extremely hardy, thriving on rough grazing they cope well on exposed cliffs and are very capable of withstanding inclement weather. It is these characteristics, coupled with their genuinely docile nature, that make them ideal in helping us to improve and diversify wildlife on this coastal slope grassland."

I had another slight uphill, as Dodman Point is "the highest point on the south coast of Cornwall," according to the booklet, at 374 feet above sea level. There was a bit more uphill on a grassy slope. There was another National Trust sign welcoming me once again to the Dodman and this time telling me of Dexter cattle that are grazing in the area. The sign started out similar to the Dartmoor ponies sign, but explained that, "Dexters are an old breed of small cattle originally from the mountainous west coast of Ireland. They are believed to be similar to domestic cattle of Iron Age Britain, linking them historically with the archeology of the Dodman." This sign also repeats that these cattle are extremely hardy like the ponies, coping well on exposed cliffs and with inclement weather, and help improve and diversify wildlife, as well as apparently being docile. I did not see any cattle today, but it was good to know that the cattle are docile.

After I reached the sign that said a quarter mile to Dodman Point, the path flattened out again. I passed by one man walking his dog. I arrived at the large 20-foot tall granite cross about forty minutes after starting my walk this morning. That was a slow mile probably because I took a lot of photos and looked at the scenery. An engraving on the cross told me, "In the firm hope of the second coming of our Lord Jesus Christ, and for the encouragement of those who strive to serve Him, this cross is erected, A.D. 1896." The booklet, and on the SWCP Association website, also told me that this cross built by Rev. George Martin was built "as a navigation aid for shipping, after two naval destroyers had collided near the point earlier the same year." Wow, another type of lighthouse, per se, added to my list of lighthouses that I stared last year. And not a daymark or a church tower, or even a Huer's Hut, but a cross! In addition to Sue Bunney's quote above about the Dodman Cross, she continues, "The cross stands as a beacon, sending a message of peace. Sitting on the steps below the cross…while gazing out into the bay towards Falmouth, or up along the coast to Fowey and Plymouth, is one of life's great pleasures."

I remembered that I skipped this section around Dodman Point last year where the booklet said that the path to Dodman was "steep and strenuous in places." I thought that this climb was quite gentle actually. I was not sure why the booklet described it that way. For today's weather, there was a very slight breeze out, but almost non-existent. There was some cloud coverage but the sun was just behind the clouds this morning, and it would be a dry day, as I took a photo of my boots at Dodman Point. Out in the distance there was a view of nothing but blue waters and blue skies. Except for one fishing boat and one sailboat. I took a deep breath and all was good with the world.

I took a short side trip to visit an 18th century Watch House. "The Admiralty set up a chain of watchhouses along the coast, so that the Navy at Plymouth could keep an eye on shipping in the English Channel," according to today's booklet. A sign inside the Watch House told me, "This hut was originally established as a signal station in 1795, as part of Admiralty defences in the Napoleonic Wars. The lookout was also used to aid the revenue vessels to identify 'free traders.' If the revenue men caught smugglers as a result of signals from the watch house the signalers would have been entitled to a portion of the prize money." Sue Bunney describes this as, "The men manning the little house had been watching for free traders sailing quietly along the coast hoping to land their illegal cargoes of silk and brandy without being caught. Later the watchers would have been scanning the sea for the shoals of pilchards coming into the bay." Ahhh yes, the reasons that the SWCP was originally created – the coastguard looking for smugglers and shoals of fish, and checking conditions of the sea.

I saw a few of those Dartmoor ponies a bit beyond the Watch House grazing near some trees. The path continued to be flat, then on some grass, and then back to a dirt path until I arrived at the one and three-quarter mile sign to Gorran Haven where I had started last year from the inland path. This was about an hour after I started walking this morning. Another section of missed miles had been completed! From here, I had a view of the somewhat long Vault Beach below and the grassy hillside above it.

I was startled several times this morning with loud booms coming from what sounded like way out in the water. At first I thought it was an earthquake, but I don't know if they get those in England, and I didn't feel the ground shake. Perhaps it was an explosion of something that was so loud it echoed out into the water, and that thought made me a bit nervous. Then the loud booms happened a few more times, and I got worried not knowing what it was. Fortunately, after negotiating around and through a very muddy area, two people were coming in my direction so I asked them what the booms were that kept continuing. He said it was a Navy vessel that he pointed out to in the water doing some firing drills. Mystery solved and the worry went away. The booms happened for a little while longer, and then stopped for the rest of the day.

Walking back to Gorran Haven, I will make this description shorter since I walked this last year, but it was flat, with lots of yellow gorse in bloom. There were lots of sheep and baby lambs below near Vault Beach as I walked parallel above the beach. I could hear small crashing waves and had views back to Dodman. Soon I turned a corner to the left with minor ups and downs and views of Gorran Haven. I arrived back in the small town about two hours after I started walking this morning. I went back to my B&B for a short break of changing into fresh socks, putting on more sunscreen as now the sun was out and it was warm, and thus also getting my proper British sunhat out, the one I bought in St. Ives last year. I couldn't believe I was actually getting a chance to wear this hat again!

I had a quick lunch of haddock fish and chips, and then it was time to walk the three and a half miles to Mevagissey, repeating part of the walk that I did last year in light on and off rain with Linda. This year it would be in the warm sun on a summer-like day! I really enjoyed this walk last year, so wanted to do this section again.

Winding my way through the streets and neighborhoods of Gorran Haven, near the B&B I stayed at last year, soon the pavement ended and the path began. Walking on a grassy field, I was glad I saw one gate that I had to walk through that was not marked as the SWCP but was correct anyway. I didn't remember this gate from last year but must have walked through it. I walked through more grassy fields with lots of sheep and the cutest baby lambs. There were a few muddy places and a few people out today enjoying the weather.

Looking out I had views of headlands beyond, including a view of the Gribbin Daymark which is between Par and Fowey. I passed by an area I remembered from last year of small waves gently crashing on the rocks below.

I passed by Chapel Point with its white buildings, walked on a flat grassy area that looked like a big lawn mower went through, and soon had views of Mevagissey with its harbour lighthouse. A sign told me I had one mile to Mevagissey as I walked the roads through Portmellon Cove, past the Rising Sun pub. The rest of the walk was road walking to the place above the harbour where I would be zigzagging down to the harbour.

Just then however an elderly man with his dog met up with me so we started talking as we both sat on a bench overlooking the harbour. I wanted to change into flip flops, and he was sitting there while throwing a ball for his dog to run after. This kind elderly man told me that he has lived here all his life, here in Mevagissey. Whereas one of his brothers now lives in Portloe and the other in Australia, but he stayed here. He was a lobster fisherman. I pointed out to the waters saying that the waters were his "office," and he agreed. He still has a small fishing boat below in the harbour. Currently, he has a problem with one of his shoulders and one of his hips that he hopes to get fixed soon.

The best part of his story, after I shared my story of why I am here in England on the SWCP, is that he said that he has had a good life! He said that not many people can say that they have had a good life, but he can. I told him I was happy to hear that he had a good life.

What a great short conversation on a little bench overlooking the harbour of Mevagissey. I love stories of meeting people like this. Like talking to the elderly man I chatted with leaving Woolacombe last year who was in the Merchant Navy during his life. I guess the words of wisdom from both these elderly men could be that last year we decided that, "Perhaps the walking will help extend our lives," and this year the words of wisdom would be to just be reflective and appreciate having a good life.

I recalled more words of wisdom I have taken to heart along my walk. There was that older man in Swanage last year sitting on a park bench near the NCI Station at Peveril Point as we watched a noisy motorboat speeding by: "You don't see much going at that speed." Yes I agree, as I have really come to love experiencing life at a walking pace.

Of course my friend and inspiration Gordon's perfect words of wisdom for me also came to mind: "It takes courage to walk this path alone. It also takes courage to make a decision to not walk from time to time." And of course the words of wisdom from the nicely-dressed grandfatherly-aged gentleman in West Bexington: "Oh, I do like to be beside the seaside. I do like to be beside the sea…"

As I got up to leave the little bench overlooking the harbour of Mevagissey, I shook this elderly man's hand and wished him well. As mentioned, he had been throwing a ball for his dog to catch but at that moment the dog could not find the ball. The man pointed out to me where it was down the hillside and I saw it. Since his hip would not allow him to go down the hillside to get the ball, as I walked towards the harbour I got the ball, and while it took me two throws to get the ball back to his dog, the dog was able to find the ball. The man waved to me thanking me for that. I waved back.

I still wondered though what the words of wisdom were from that elderly man dressed in all red with a bright green rucksack cover that I crossed paths with back on the 27th of June as I walked from Port Issac to Polzeath last year who was moving right along.

I walked along the harbour of Mevagissey taking photos of the various colorful fishing boats floating in the water and the harbour lighthouse about an hour and a half after I started walking from Gorran Haven this afternoon and stopped to get a second small lunch at the same café Linda and I had a cheese scone in last year. I walked in and out of a few shops around the harbour. I called Elaine of the B&B in Gorran Haven so that she could kindly pick me up as we had prearranged. What a great summer-like day!

I wanted to see how many times I had seen Dartmoor ponies along the SWCP last summer since I had seen some today. So later on I took some time to go through my book and make a list of all the times I not only saw (or could have seen because a sign told me they may be in the area) Dartmoor ponies, but also Exmoor ponies, and other horses that I am not sure of the breed. For example, while I did not see them, I could have seen Dartmoor ponies back on the 9th of July last year between Porthgwarra and Lamorna Cove. I also could have seen Dartmoor ponies on the 12th of August just past Maidencombe on my way to Dawlish. I did see Exmoor Ponies on my first day last year, the 4th of June, between Minehead and Bossington. I did see Shetland ponies with Scott our first year someplace, and I could have potentially seen Shetland ponies near Godrevy Lighthouse last year but did not.

There is also a long list of places either I, or both Scott and I, saw horses, not knowing their breed. In no particular order, seeing both wild horses and people riding horses, there were some horses between Crackington Haven and Boscastle who were quite close to a cliff ledge. I saw a few horses between Widemouth Bay and Crackington Haven, and between Clovelly and Hartland Quay I saw two beautiful brown colored horses. Rame Head had a few horses in the area, as well as people riding some at Mount Edgcumbe Park. There were some horses inland near Lansallos near Fowey/Polruan, and people were riding some on a beach near Marazion. With Scott our first year together, we saw a few horses near some mining ruins between Zennor and Pendeen. There were about six great horses right on the SWCP near Scabbacombe Sands that I saw with Scott, and I saw some near Thurlestone Rock last year as well. There were also horses in a few other scattered areas like the Isle of Portland and Branscombe Mouth, and even while staying at a Farmhouse B&B in Wyke Regis, which Scott really enjoyed. Of course I bought several books about horses for Scott, and there is a pub called "Coach and Horses" in Horns Cross near Bucks Mills.

Coastline, Hillsides, Headlands, Farmland, and the Path
Great view towards Fowey and Polruan July 23 and April 12
View of coastline and the Start Point Lighthouse August 4 and April 23
Descent towards Man Sands April 25

Coastline, Hillsides, Headlands, Farmland, and the Path

Looking back at Watermouth Harbour and headlands between Combe Martin and Ilfracombe June 10
185 steps down and 218 steps up between Kimmerage Bay and Worth Matravers August 26
Car Park with my shade from a car on hot day at Welcombe Mouth,
with the Path and hillsides and headlands, between Hartland Quay and Morwenstow June 2

Coastline, Hillsides, Headlands, Farmland, and the Path
Open green rolling hillsides between Wonwell Beach and Bigbury on Sea August 1
Mupe Bay August 25 and May 6
View looking back to farmland from Houns-tout Cliff August 26

Coastline, Hillsides, Headlands, Farmland, and the Path
Hemmick Beach and farmland near Dodman Point April 11
Wheal Coates Mine and Towanroath Engine House and the Path in one direction July 2
Wheal Coates Mine and Towanroath Engine House and the Path in the other direction July 2

DAY 16 (DAY 103) STATS: 7.5 TOTAL, WITH ABOUT 2.0 MILES NEW TO A BIT BEYOND DODMAN POINT, AND ABOUT 5.5 REPEAT CONTINUING TO GORRAN HAVEN TO MEVAGISSEY. ABOUT 3.5 HOURS, NOT INCLUDING THE BREAK IN GORRAN HAVEN. HIKING BOOTS.

MEETING SUE BUNNEY, THEN MILE IN PAR AND WALK TO FOWEY – Thursday, 12 April 2018

"All you need is Love and the Beach." – Etched on a glass jar in a shop in Polkerris.

This morning at breakfast Elaine of the B&B in Gorran Haven asked me if I would like to meet Sue Bunney, the author of the two books that I read, where I learned a lot about local Cornish life, and have quoted many times in my own book! After all, Gorran Haven is the area she writes about in her books. You see, yesterday I asked Elaine if she happens to know Sue Bunney, and I explained the story to Elaine of how I bought Sue Bunney's first book last year when I walked through Gorran Haven, and that I have read her second book since then as well. I said to Elaine, "Of course I would like to meet Sue Bunney!" It turns out Elaine knows Sue and her husband Rob and their son. So Elaine made a couple phone calls and made arrangements to visit with Sue and Rob on our way to Par this morning. And just like that, I met Sue Bunney!

Sue, Rob, Elaine, and I sat in Sue's living room drinking tea and talking for 45 minutes. I told Sue of how I bought "Love on the Beach" when I was in Gorran Haven last year, and that I read "My Cornish Life" on eBook. I told Sue that I have been mentioning and quoting her from both her books in this book, and I asked if that would be alright with her. She said that would be great, and asked what I wanted to quote. I could not think of all the many times I quoted her at that moment, only the parts about the 'power of the seas.' She chuckled saying that that is what other people also pick up from her book.

Sue told me a brief story, to which I hope I got all the information correct, but something about how her grandfather was a 'real' fisherman because back in those days the fishing boats were not built with motors and modern equipment, so fishermen had to do many things by hand including raising the sails, along with maneuvering fishing nets by hand as well.

We all chatted about other things such as how Sue is reading books ironically about the area near where I live, while I was reading her books about where she lives, and a few other topics of conversation like the weather. Then Sue very kindly gave me a printed copy of her "My Cornish Life" book, complete with photos that she kindly autographed for me as well! Wow, what a great gift! She wrote, "To Debby, Enjoy your walking and Cornwall. Best wishes, Sue." That was so sweet and kind of her. I really appreciated that, and shall treasure the book as well as meeting her in person. We also took a photo together with me, Sue, and Elaine taken by Rob. Wow, what a great honor to meet Sue Bunney, and to come full circle that I came back to the place where I originally bought her book and now I have met her.

After the visit, Elaine kindly drove me the 30-minute ride into Par. During the ride, Elaine told me about how important the mining and fishing industries are in this area, and that she considers both of them to be "high risk" industries. But because of the close-knit communities, if an unfortunate disaster happens, everyone comes together to support each other and to help out.

Elaine dropped me off at Richard's Fruit, Veg and Fish Shop across the street from the Par Inn, where a board outside advertised, "Richard's Catch of the Day from our Bay – local fish, flowers for all occasions, fruit 'n' veg, local meat, dairy and other local produce." After safely putting my autographed book into my rucksack for the day, I took a right turn on the road just after the shop to walk the mile or so that I missed last year because Matt kindly drove us to the other end of Par. I figured that since the weather would be great again today, I might as well also walk all the way to Fowey, which is where I would be staying anyway tonight with Lucy from the SWCP Facebook Group page at her B&B.

The road was next to homes and past a post office and a few more homes. I took another right turn with a sign telling me I had a half mile to Par Beach. This path was next to a stream, and I crossed a road and walked through a path with some trees. I took a few turns, ending on another road leading to a car park next to the beach. I had a couple of options to walk on at this point and chose the option of walking the length of the beach on its sand! It was a quiet beach with only very small waves. There were people walking their dogs, and a few families with children already playing in the late morning. Near the end of the beach, I turned left out to another car park, took a right across a bridge over a stream, climbed up eighteen steps, and emerged on the SWCP that I walked last year with Matt on to Polkerris. From the time I was dropped off at the shop by Elaine, it took me forty minutes to walk all that. At first I thought that maybe it was little over a mile, but I did stop a few times, so let's call that a mile total, and another section of my missed-miles from last year was complete!

I was walking on a flat path along grassy fields above the beach. And well, I had some great views out to my favorite golf course! I wondered if my friends from last year that I hid under their brolly during the downpour were playing golf today on this gratefully warm day. Not a rain cloud in sight today! I passed by a few horses (more horses!) and took photos for Scott, followed by a slight uphill and more flat walking. So far I have been able to walk on edges of any mud with my purple shoes which I decided to wear today, but I did bring my boots with me just in case in my rucksack.

I had a view down into Polkerris, with its breakwater, and then a descent into Polkerris. There were a couple groups of people taking either a surfing or a paddle boarding lesson. It had now been just over an hour since I started walking. I stopped here for a few minutes and went into the little shop down by the beach, and what do I see etched on a large glass jar, but the words, "Oh I do like to be beside the seaside. I do like to be beside the sea." Well, what do you know – my theme song! Too bad the jar was too large and breakable otherwise I would have bought it. Another jar read the quote above, "All you need is Love and the Beach." Indeed.

I walked zigzag uphill through some trees to a grassy area covered with yellow dandelions. I did not take many notes from this point on since this was a repeat walk from last year, however as I walked I heard my favorite sound of a few small lapping waves hitting rocks on a small beach. Then there was this herd of cows...safely behind a fence. It took me about forty-five minutes after the zigzag uphill to reach the Gribbin Daymark. I was hoping that it would be open to climb today since I missed climbing it last year, but alas it was not open today either. There were however several people having picnics with several kids running around.

One of my favorite views and places was next, which was why I wanted to repeat this walk. I walked down a big wide grassy path with amazing views of more green grass and some cows and a cove and a beach and some trees and the white and tan colored small cliffs and the grassy and brown checkered hillsides of farmland and yellow gorse in bloom and the turquoise and blue waters and the towns of Fowey and Polruan beyond. I took my time walking this short section because this is just one great view!

I walked to Polridmouth Cove with its lake to have something to eat and I sat on the same logs that I sat on last year with a view of the Gribbin Daymark. I spent about fifteen minutes here. It had been quite warm walking today and dry, with the sun sometimes out but some cloud coverage as well. However at this spot that I was sitting at there was a slight breeze that made it seem cooler.

After this spot, I needed to be on the lookout for something I missed seeing last year – the twenty-foot red round navigational aid on red poles with a red ladder, a lighthouse per se. It took a bit of walking, but I finally spotted it on a hillside near the river leading in between Fowey and Polruan. I took a few photos as I saw it for a bit, and then it disappeared. I had a slight uphill climb, and walked past St. Catherine's Castle.

It turns out I was able to wear my purple shoes all day today keeping them mud-free and dry as there were places to navigate around any muddy spots. I stopped at the same Readymoney Beach that I stopped at last year to change into my cushy flip flops. Yes, I had three pairs of various shoes with me today! I have to keep the feet happy. Finally, I walked on the road into Fowey to the same bagel place from last year to have a sandwich and of course, their "Ultimate Chocolate Cream Tea" – "Two scrumptious chocolate chip and orange scones, served warm with chocolate hazelnut spread, and clotted cream, and served with a pot of tea for one." Delicious.

I sent a message to Lucy telling her that I had arrived in Fowey, and she met me at the bagel place, and we walked together to her B&B and talked for quite a while. It was good to stay with another friend that I know. After talking, I went to my room to write. What a great day – a beautiful walk, great weather, another friend, and meeting Sue Bunney!

DAY 17 (DAY 104) STATS: 7 MILES TOTAL, ONE NEW MISSED-MILE, AND SIX REPEAT MILES. 4 HOURS. PURPLE SHOES.

PENCARROW HEAD TO POLRUAN AND FOWEY – Friday, 13 April 2018

"At Pencarrow Head there is a path that cuts across the headland itself, but the true Coast Path takes you around the headland." – Today's Booklet.

After breakfast, I walked from Lucy's to the main part of Fowey to take ferry to Polruan. Today I only really needed to walk the approximate half mile or so around Pencarrow Head that I missed last year because when I walked with Lucy to Polperro, we took a side path cutting through the headland, rather than around the headland. However, only walking that short distance today was not enough, so I made it about a three-mile day walking back from Pencarrow Head to Polruan and the ferry back to Fowey.

I took the ferry from Fowey to Polruan at 9:10 and within two minutes I was across the River Fowey. I picked up a sandwich at a café before my planned walk on the road to get to the car park for Pencarrow Head and Lantic Bay. I started walking on the road, but really was not too happy with the idea of doing this actually. Yes, I could have walked the SWCP from Polruan to Pencarrow Head and back again round trip, but I thought walking on the road and doing a "circular-type" walk might be a better option. Which after I started walking on the road, I realized that I did not particularly like that option.

But just then a miracle happened. Really. It must have been. I saw a woman just getting into her car with her teenage daughter, and I kindly explained to them that I was not from around here, that I wanted to walk from Pencarrow Head and Lantic Bay, and if they were going in that direction, would they please be able to give me a ride to the car park there? Well what do you know, they said it would be no problem at all. Really? Really! I must say that they have been the biggest guardian angels thus far on my 90 missed-miles walk, and probably one of the biggest ones of my entire SWCP walk. Because after being driven on the long road, I really think that if I ended up walking on the long road I would not have enjoyed it. Or at least I would have turned around and walked the SWCP instead round trip, which perhaps is what I should have done all along.

Anyway, the mother and daughter kindly drove me the couple of miles and dropped me off at the entrance to the footpath for Lantic Bay. I was so grateful. I thanked them so very much. They did not want to take any money. I really hope something good happens to them. I started walking on a small path then on some grassy path, and five minutes later I was at a SWCP sign above the Lantic Bay Beach with a view down to the beach, and the hillsides surrounding the bay that I recognized. I started walking in the direction towards Polperro since that was the direction to walk around Pencarrow Head.

The path started out flat with good views of Lantic Bay Beach below and the surrounding hillsides as I walked. Yellow gorse and creamy-yellowish colored primroses were in bloom and the birds were chirping in the mid-morning. Soon I turned left around the headland and had views of the headlands beyond that I had walked last year. As I continued walking I had views of some rocks below where last year Lucy and I saw a seal. Well, Lucy saw it and I think I saw it. I walked on a bit further until I saw the side path down the hillside from last year that Lucy and I walked down, but just to make sure that was the correct path, I walked a bit beyond that and through a gate, to which I saw another side path, so perhaps that was the correct one. I walked on just a bit further just to make sure, and then I decided to stop at a spot overlooking a small field of creamy-yellowish colored primrose wildflowers which overlooked the rocks below, the seas, the headlands, and the quiet scenery of the morning. I listened to some small lapping waves. There, I had done it. I completed the approximate half mile around Pencarrow Head that I had missed last year. It took about twenty minutes to do that, so perhaps it was a bit further than a half mile, but in any case, another missed section of the SWCP completed, on the true SWCP! Then it was time to walk back towards Polruan.

I turned around to now walk "backwards" from this point back to Polruan on the SWCP. Although on the way back, I realized that I had just taken another accidental short cut, so instead I took the actual SWCP back following the arrows up a short hill to a sign telling me that I now had two and a quarter miles to Polruan. I listened to the waves crashing on the sand of the beach at Lantic Bay. Ok, so now I had really completed the missed section on the true SWCP!

I walked back to the SWCP sign above the beach that I had recognized a bit ago, which told me I had one and three-quarters miles to go to Polruan. It had now been about forty minutes from this sign, around the headland, and back to this sign.

I had a descent at this point that I remember doing the ascent of last year with Lucy. It was near here that Lucy and I had our conversation last year about the arrow closest to the acorn!

There had been no one out this morning thus far that I had seen either walking the SWCP or down on the beach. I did hear a motor of a fishing boat and saw the boat as it chugged by in the waters. I heard small waves crashing and birds chirping. The path flattened out, and I passed by some small purple wildflowers around in the grass, which I later found out from Lucy that they were violets. There were a few short, but somewhat steep, uphill climbs giving me a good morning workout. Looking behind me were views back to Lantic Bay Beach that soon disappeared as I went up and over the tall part of the hillside I was walking on. Now the views in front of me were all the way out to Gribbin Tower. Four people walking to Polperro passed me by as we talked for a moment of where we were walking to and from on this cloudy, but dry, and mostly warm morning.

The path remained flat on the way back passing through some pretty areas with grass and purple and yellow and white wildflowers, and of course the yellow gorse, and the white flowering bush too that I also saw a few days ago on the way to Dodman Point. Spring flowers! Later I found out from Lucy that the white flowering bush is called blackthorn.

Then I didn't expect it, but I had a view of the red lighthouse of Fowey that I saw yesterday from this perspective. I walked through a grassy field then into a neighborhood in Polruan, passed by a school and a sign saying I now had a quarter mile to the harbour and the ferry back to Fowey. I was hungry now, so I stopped on a bench to eat by a National Coastwatch Institution and St. Savior's Chapel ruins. From this bench, I had views of St. Catherine's Castle, the red lighthouse, and Gribbin Tower as I ate my sandwich. It took me one and three-quarters hours to do the entire walk today to this point, including the missed part around Pencarrow Head and the repeat walk back to Polruan. I was still so grateful to the woman and her teenage daughter, my guardian angels, who drove me to the Lantic Bay car park. I might have still been walking to there now, or just starting around Pencarrow Head now, if it was not for them.

St. Savior's Chapel "was built in the 8th or 9th century [and] was well visited, being at one end of The Saint's Way and along another pilgrim route from Plymouth to St. Michael's Mount." In fact, "because of its location, it was used as an early kind of daymark, to help ships navigate into the River Fowey." What I was looking at today looked like just the ruins of a corner of two walls that was still standing. Thus I not only saw another kind of lighthouse, but I also had reminders of the Camino de Santiago pilgrimage routes once again that I have come across during my SWCP walk!

I walked around St. Saviour's Point, which actually did not look familiar to me from last year. I passed by a sign saying that I now had 500 yards to the harbour in Polruan and the ferry back to Fowey and I walked on roads next to some homes of Polruan. I saw some local morning activity as I walked where a man in a pickup truck, loaded in the back with fruit and vegetables and baked goods, stopped by someone's house. A couple of women were out to meet the man as he was delivering the fresh food to them, and they bought exactly what they wanted right out from the back of the truck!

As I arrived at the ferry, I realized that last year when I was following Lucy in this area on our walk, we must have walked a different way to get to the area of the National Coastwatch Institution and the chapel ruins because I did not recall walking around St. Saviour's Point or on the roads. So it is a good thing that I walked this way now, because now I have completed another less-than-quarter-mile missed section that I didn't even know I had missed!

I took the 12:10 ferry back to Fowey, although this time it took a few extra minutes as the driver stopped in the middle of the river for a few minutes to take a phone call. While I was sitting eating my sandwich earlier, I had looked up "things to do in Fowey" since I had the rest of the day left, and I discovered a "second-hand and antiquarian books" bookshop in Fowey that looked interesting to go into. And I was so glad I did!

I was looking at a section in the bookshop on "coastal walking" and I found two treasures, two booklets from several decades ago! One is called "Cornwall's Coastal Footpath," by W.V. Hunter and Tor Mark Guides, possibly dating from 1969, 1970, or 1980, according to some research I did looking for the book online! The second booklet is called "The South West Way: A Complete Guide to the Coastal Path: 1982," from the South West Way Association! Now how amazing is that?! The South West Way. That was what the SWCP used to be called. These were guidebooks for the SWCP from decades ago. What treasures! How fun! I was so excited about these finds that I want to describe them in my own book in more detail. I could really describe so much of them as they are so interesting to look at and read, but I will try to keep it as brief as possible.

Cornwall's Coastal Footpath

The introduction of "Cornwall's Coastal Footpath" booklet says, "The aim of this booklet is to introduce holidaymakers and others to the pleasures of exploring the Cornish coast on foot along the old coastguard footpath. It is intended to be a series of short rambles rather than long hikes, being for the casual walker and not the inveterate hiker with his ruck-sac and boots." (So am I an inveterate hiker?) That introduction paragraph continues about how back decades ago, "certain stretches of the coast are better suited to pleasant walking than others...by contrast, there are other stretches of the coast where the path is difficult to find or follow, beset by gorse and with the occasional ploughed field intervening."

This booklet continues with some history. "The origins of Cornwall's coastal footpath are interesting and by no means common knowledge. It came into being in the eighteenth century at a time when the prevention of smuggling first began on a nation-wide scale. Other short sections came into use as short cuts from one cove to another, used by fishermen and farmworkers just as was the case inland, but the full extent of the path which at one time extended round every yard of the seaboard of Cornwall had its origins in the preventive service [of smuggling]." The paragraph continues about the smuggling of "Brandy, silk, tea and a host of other highly dutiable goods [which] were brought over clandestinely from France, notably from Brittany, to the quiet and deserted coves and harbours of Cornwall." The history continues, "After about 1850, as a result of this surveillance...smuggling died away. The paths were thereafter used by the men of the coastguard service on bad weather watch," namely to prevent shipwrecks.

The history continues, "When the number of coastguardsmen dwindled, hand in hand with the decline of coastwise shipping as well as of inshore fishing and of wrecks, the paths were much less used and became overgrown. gorse, bracken and brambles grew over them in the sheltered valleys and farmers ploughed across them here and there." Continuing, "The balance is now being re-dressed somewhat...the gradual clearing of badly overgrown sections of path, the provision of signposts to show the way, and the acquisition of land made available to the public by the National Trust, have given us back some of what had been lost of the magnificent walk there is around this part of England's shores." This is all so interesting to read about!

Specifically at the time this "Cornwall's Coastal Footpath" booklet was written, "This Cornish coastal footpath is part – some will say the best part – of the South-West Peninsula Coast Path, which is officially promoted and safeguarded by the Countryside Commission as one of Britain's long-distance footpaths. With a length of 515 miles in all, running from Minehead in Somerset round to Poole harbour in Dorset, the South-West Peninsula Coast Path is far and away the longest of its kind in England." Ahhhh, so the SWCP used to apparently also be called the "South-West Peninsula Coast Path," and by the measurements of that time, it was calculated as 515 miles! Thus perhaps why Mark Wallington entitled his book "500 Mile Walkies." I wonder if he used either of these booklets as his guidebooks since his book was first published in 1986.

"Cornwall's Coastal Footpath" booklet then includes a few paragraphs about advice, such as the use of Ordnance Survey maps since there are no maps in this booklet; how the "cliff tops...are exposed and open to every wind that blows," (and I can attest to that); that "shoes should be stout enough to cope with rough ground;" and most interestingly that "bare ankles for lady walkers are inadvisable on rougher sections where dwarf Cornish gorse and the occasional bramble line the path." All good, and interesting, advice. I guess that is why I have been wearing long pants. But I do wonder what the men of the time were advised to wear?

Finally, the rest of this booklet specifically talks about the sections of walking spanning from "The long and very overgrown coombe which runs to the sea at Marsland Mouth [which] is the border between Cornwall and Devon," to the Dodman, the "373 feet high and the boldest headland of Cornwall's channel shore," and all sections in between, not necessarily in order, and some sections described in the direction of walking from Minehead to Poole, with other sections described in the direction of walking from Poole to Minehead.

While I could write a lot of specific descriptions about the walks in this booklet, here are a couple of random sentences from the section of about the Trevose to Treyarnon to Porthcothan to Bedruthan Steps to Mawgan Porth that I walked last year and about a week ago. "From Trevose, going southwards, there starts what must be one of the finest uninterrupted stretches of all of Cornwall's coast path. For something like eight miles there is no intermission in a fairly well defined, easily trod path with incomparable, rapidly changing views…The coast path south from Trevose runs on the seaward edge of the golf links past sandy Constantine Bay and round an area of shallow turf-covered cliffs to the beautiful little inlet of Treyarnon. One passes the Youth Hostel and struggles across the broad but shallow Treyarnon stream as best one can on improvised stepping stones. The rocks here are flatter than hitherto with angular islets and rock stacks offshore on the next stage of about two miles to Porthcothan beach. The cliff line is deeply indented but the way easy and not difficult to follow. At the beach a sandy track leads us up to the coast road to cross the sizeable stream here via a bridge before one turns seaward again and leaves the few houses behind. Porth Mear, about a mile further on is a completely deserted cove where a small stream comes down to the sea…As we round [Park Head] a fine vista opens up of Bedruthan Steps and the high coastline towards Newquay. Curiously enough, along the cliffs by the usual viewpoint over the Steps, iron was once mined, although there are now no surface traces of this former working. A fine walk takes up past Trenance Point round and down into Mawgan Porth, a popular beach in the summer season." That is just about all the description there is for those approximate eight or nine miles.

The last sentence of this "Cornwall's Coastal Footpath" booklet describes Land's End as, "This final most westerly headland of Britain, world famous as the Land's End, was known as Pedn-an-Laaz – the End of the Earth in the old Cornish language – though this is a name few visitors have ever heard." Interesting!

I really love the language and the descriptions in this little booklet. I could include so much more from the "Cornwall's Coastal Footpath" booklet in my book, but let me just move along to the second booklet. Although I will also say that there are also a lot of great black and white photos in the 48-page "Cornwall's Coastal Footpath" booklet of the scenery taken decades ago of places that I have walked the last few years!

The South West Way

The second booklet from 1982, "The South West Way," in its introduction says, "The South West Way is by far the longest of the Official Long Distance Footpaths; it runs from Minehead in Somerset right round the South-Western peninsular to South Haven Point on the south side of Poole Harbour in Dorset. We ourselves reckon this is some 550 miles, others differ but all agree it is a fair step!" The introduction continues, "This Footpath Guide attempts to provide in one single unit all you need to know to do a reasonable day's walking without let or hindrance. The information is updated annually and members (see Invitation to Membership page 65) are advised by News Letters of important changes during the year. The path was enacted in the National Parks and Access to the Countryside Act of 1949. It must seem amazing therefore, to those who do not know the fact, that it is still unfinished after three decades!" The introduction to this 68-page booklet about the entire SWCP continues, "It is sometimes called the South-West Peninsula Coastal Path, which is more of a mouthful." This all was really interesting to read!

The introduction also states, "The path does undoubtedly pass through some of the finest coastal scenery in Europe and, with its enormous variety and contrast between bustling resort and quiet cove, is a never ceasing source of delight. Its other feature is the tremendous amount of interests of all kinds along its way." (Indeed! Not just in England, but in Europe, too!) "This path is the longest Long Distance Footpath – we think it is the finest – we hope you will too! We certainly know of no other Long Distance Path that has as much contrast and variety as ours. Try it!" (Ok!)

This booklet describes the path in an "anti-clockwise" direction from Minehead to Poole, and includes a list of accommodations of about ten pages, including beds and breakfasts, hostels, and guest houses, and a few pages for camping. The prices for the non-camping accommodations ranged from about £3.00 for a hostel to £19.90 for B&Bs and guest houses, with an average range of about £6.00 to £9.00, according to my quick glance at the ten pages. That ranges from about $4.00 to $26.00! Of course, that is back in the early 1980s. I wanted to see if any of the accommodations I have stayed in the last few years were around decades ago, but it was too time-consuming for me to try to figure this out.

Anyway, this great booklet continues with general information such as about the weather. "No, we ourselves offer no advice or predictions on this subject, to do so would only include us in the ranks of those who are wrong! However, there is a local weather forecast service available, three times a day for Devon and Cornwall, which covers by far the greater part of the path. This can be obtained by telephoning either Exeter (0392), Plymouth (0752) or Torquay (0803). Then in each case, 8091." Clearly before the internet and mobile phones.

There is a section called "A Word for Beginners," which has two subsections called "For those who have never been walking," and for those who have "walked but not on long distance path." Both sections have paragraphs of advice, the last couple sentences being, "The usual remarks about carrying stand-by supplies, therefore, certainly apply, better to carry an extra couple of bars of chocolate than to go hungry. [And] Last, but not least, before you start, cut your toenails!" See, I guess eating all my desserts was approved by the South West Way Association back then. And even though I did cut my toenails many times last summer, I somehow still managed to lose one.

There is also a section listing other books and guidebooks available, including "Cornwall's Coastal Footpath." The next sections of "The South West Way" booklet talk about train and bus services, ferries and tide tables (which the list of ferries appears to be quite similar to what I have experienced), and maps that can be used. There is also a section where, "Our Path, we reckon, needs about six weeks to accomplish. That being so we have tried to divide it up sensibly into six roughly equal sections." However, at that time, it appears that not many people have walked the entire path in one go, so they write about a lot of cautions about walking their suggested itinerary.

Finally, starting on page 41 of the booklet, they describe small sections of The South West Way path, with various distances of each section, some sections being described in only one paragraph, and others taking a few paragraphs to describe. Again, I would love to include a lot more in my book, but here are a few random examples.

Minehead to Porlock Weir – "The official path does not start where you would expect it to at the western end of the sea front road. Look for an inconspicuous opening between two cottages on the sea front a little to the east of the harbour. The Official route, although a good moorland walk, does not follow the traditional coastal route."

Combe Martin to Ilfracombe, Harbour – "This stretch has been a disgrace for a very long time and our serious suggestion was that a bus should be taken for most of it. However, a great deal of work has been done in recent years and with the results of an Enquiry pending at Widmouth, there may well be further improvements during 1982. The path currently leaves Combe Martin Sea Front by a lane but unfortunately, soon comes up the main road which has to be followed for some way."

Westward Ho! to Clovelly – "This section is now greatly improved, our sincere thanks to all those concerned. The path begins a series of ups and downs which will escalate to become much more common and much steeper in the sections ahead; you have been warned!...Once you are on the Hobby Drive, it is a pleasant easy stroll along and down to Clovelly."

Bude to Crackington Haven – "This section can surprise the unwary. It starts easily enough but before you have finished it, you will know in no uncertain fashion you have really had a walk!"

Trevone to Porthcothan (since I included this from the other booklet) – "There have unfortunately, been recent cliff falls just beyond Trevone. Diversions have been made but they are not currently properly waymarked. At Harlyn Bay despite a definitive right of way being shown on the map, it is not possible to make progress to the west of the stream mouth except by making use of the beach for the first few hundred yards."

Porthcothan to Newquay, Harbour – "Good easy walking nearly all the way. There is a little problem sometimes behind the beach at Mawgan Porth and the best route is probably over the sands when possible." (No mention of Bedruthan Steps.)

Mullion Cove to Lizard – "Very spectacular. A wonderful section this, it can be accomplished, too, without great effort! Unless the weather is beastly, you will certainly enjoy this stretch."

Fowey to Polperro – "A regular ferry crosses to Polruan. This section is one of tremendous contrasts; parts of the path in National Trust ownership are exceedingly well maintained – the remainder is at present badly neglected by Cornwall County Council. The section most difficult to follow is just beyond Colors Cove."

Hope Cove, Inner Hope to Salcombe, Ferry – "Excellent coast walking, some of the finest in South Devon. This section also makes an easily accomplished day walk from Kingsbridge using Hope and Salcombe buses."

Seaton to Lyme Regis (where I will be walking in a few weeks, now called the Undercliffs) – "Be careful to come inland to the road up to the golf course to get back on to the coastal path. The section through the Landslip is in a National Nature Reserve and can be very rewarding to some but extremely frustrating to others. Views are extremely limited and the path in places puts on a fair imitation of a corkscrew or helter-skelter; you are unlikely to get lost but most unlikely to know where you are. Suggested times to walk the Landslip range from one and a half hours to four hours."

Charmouth to West Bay – "Interesting walking with spectacular views from Golden Cap, the highest mainland point on the south coast of England."

Lulworth Cove to Kimmeridge, Gaulter Gap (Severe) – "The coastal path through the Army Ranges is now open again at certain times, see below. It is a very fine walk indeed but a tough one."

Swanage to Sandbanks (South Haven Point) – "At Ocean Bay Stores at the north end of Swanage sea front it is usually better to keep along the pedestrian promenade and then walk two hundred yards along the beach turning up some steps rather than take the poor Official route along the main road and then through a housing estate. There is a last good stretch around Ballard Point and the Foreland. The final lap from Studland to Shell Bay is along the coast – watch for sand-storms if it is windy!"

So there you have it, the SWCP aka The South West Way aka the South-West Peninsula Coastal Path, as it was back in 1982! There is also a page on an "Invitation to Membership," showing that the dues were £4.00 ($5.25) for individuals and £5.00 ($6.50) for a joint subscription for married couples." Today they currently are £22.00 ($29.00) for single membership, and £29.00 ($38.00) for a joint membership or an "overseas member," which is my membership.

Finally, the booklet ends with a history of the South West Way Association starting with its Official Formation in May 1973. It was "formed to promote the interests of users of the South-West Peninsula Coast Path." In 1976 the first Footpath Guide was issued, and in 1978 the first Printed Footpath Guide was done, which I tried to find online, but the earliest one I could find was from 1980, so two years before the one I bought in Fowey. Finally, in 1982 for the Future, "We feel there are considerable grounds for optimism in 1982. Maintenance should be better than it has been for a long time. Work is proceeding on further improvements on several stretches of the path; we hope, therefore, we may have more good news shortly."

I really loved reading the varying wording and descriptions in this booklet! And I certainly appreciate ALL the improvements that have been made on the SWCP the past several decades to make the entire SWCP walkable! It would be fun to compare these 1982 descriptions to the descriptions in the most recent SWCP Association guidebook, but that would take too long for this book. I suppose if you do own the current guidebook, you can compare the descriptions above. If not, at least you can compare them to my descriptions throughout this book.

One final note, I discovered one more thing on the back cover of "The South West Way" booklet, the important "Country Code," an earlier version of "The Countryside Code" that I mentioned on the 12th of August. This one you can look on that date in my book and compare the two. In 1982 The Country Code was, "Guard against all risk of fire. Fasten all gates. Keep dogs under proper control. Keep to the paths across farm land. Avoid damaging fences, hedges and walls. Leave no litter. Safeguard water supplies. Protect wild life, wild plants and trees. Go carefully on country roads. Respect the life of the countryside."

For my purchases today of these two booklets, they were both only £3/$4.25 each. Although "The South West Way" booklet was priced at 90p back in 1982, which is about $1.25 now. I need to say that these two booklets are my most treasured purchases along my SWCP walk, along with my five paintings hanging on my wall, and some old postcards that I found in Weymouth, which you will be reading about in a few weeks! And I still really appreciate my guardian angels from this morning.

DAY18 (DAY 105) STATS: ABOUT 3 MILES TOTAL. ABOUT A QUARTER MILE TO GET TO MISSED SECTION, THEN ABOUT A HALF MILE NEW AROUND PENCARROW, THEN REPEAT A HALF MILE BACK AROUND PENCARROW AND ANOTHER 1.75 TO POLRUAN/FOWEY. ABOUT THREE HOURS. PURPLE SHOES.

SEATON TO DOWNDERRY – Saturday, 14 April 2018

This church is a "stone building, just a stone's throw from the beach." – Information on the Church of St. Nicolas in Downderry.

After the original bus I was going to take to today was cancelled, I said my good-byes and thank yous to Lucy, and instead I took the next bus from Fowey to the train station back in Par, then a train to Liskeard, then just missing my bus to Seaton by about two or three minutes, I took taxi to Seaton for today's easy and short walk. When I was explaining my SWCP plans to the taxi driver, he did the wave of the hand and arm waving out the window of a car moving up and down in the wind like a roller coaster that made me chuckle because of the many times I got symbol that last year. Now that I think about it, that roller coaster wave is kind of not only about the ups and downs, the ascents and descents, of the SWCP physically, but also like the emotional roller coaster that Sasha and I have talked about.

From where the taxi dropped me off in Seaton, I needed to walk "backwards" along and up a road to the SWCP sign where I was dropped of last year to walk backwards towards Millendreath and East Looe. It took me about ten minutes to walk there, to the sign that said a half mile to Seaton Bridge and one and a half miles to Downderry in one direction, and in the other direction it pointed to Millendreath. Then it was time to walk forward and walk the same road in the "forwards" direction on this road that I missed last year, just this short half mile, that now I technically walked twice. So I walked down the hill on the road, one of those narrow country roads, passing by homes on my left and views of the waters through some trees on my right. Soon I had a view of the beach that connects Seaton and Downderry. I walked on a bridge over a stream, next to the beach to Waves Bar, where last year I sat waiting for the rain to stop. So now I completed one more missing section of my walk – that short half mile on the road from the sign in Seaton to Waves Bar (twice)!

It was then time to repeat some beach walking before I needed to complete one more missing section. The repeat part was walking on the beach between Seaton and Downderry. Because this morning Lucy reminded me about checking about tides when walking on a beach, I randomly asked someone walking their dog on the beach before I set off just to make sure I would be alright. He said the tide was going out now so I would be fine for several hours. As I walked, I listened to the small waves crashing on the beach. There was lots of smelly seaweed to navigate around. There were actually many people walking dogs on this beach. I noticed lots of various sizes and shapes of pebbles, rocks, boulders, and red and green smoother flat rocks leading out to the seas.

I walked past where I went inland last year to a café in Downderry, having now completed the repeat walk, but continued walking on the beach for a short while longer, across a stream, up some steps, next to school, taking a right on the road for a bit, and carefully walking around a sharp left turn on the road until I arrived at the sign that said two and a half miles to Portwrinkle, the place where I was dropped off last year to do that walk. Therefore, now I had completed another three-quarters of a mile that I missed from the other end of Downderry to that sign!

Therefore, within an hour and fifteen minutes, I completed the two small missed sections on either side of the repeated beach walk today!

I was technically done for the day with my required walking. It seemed silly that I was done by 11:30 in the morning with such an easy and short walk, but since I did not know what the weather would be like when I planned my trip months ago, I gave myself plenty of time to do this walk today just so I could guarantee that I completed it. I was done with yesterday's walk early as well, and made the best of the rest of yesterday finding those two booklets. Today's weather was once again fortunately dry, although there was some cloud cover and a slight breeze that made it cooler, but that was just fine. I would make the best of the rest of this day as well.

I was hungry so I headed back from the Portwrinkle sign, carefully walking on the road around the sharp turn till I reached some sidewalk, to the same café I stopped at last year. On my way back into Downderry to the café, I stopped inside the small Church of St. Nicolas. This church is a "stone building, just a stone's throw from the beach, [and] dates from 1905." A relatively young church then compared to some that are several hundred centuries older. I liked the play on the word "stone" in this bit of information I found about this church.

I went to the Blue Plate Café for some lunch. Since I had nothing else to do today and wanted to make the best of my day, I went to my accommodations, the Inn on the Shore, changed from my purple shoes of the day to my flip flops and walked slowly on the beach once again from Downderry to Seaton filling up with some of those good for me positive negative ions. I walked the road back to Downderry instead of the beach, since that is another SWCP option, just to experience that. My room at this Inn was right above the beach and had a view of the seas from the side window, and I could hear the waves crash on the beach through the window. I was even able to see this Inn from the beach below as I walked, as it was located on top of the short hillside above.

Speaking of the emotional roller coaster, this had been the first day this trip so far that I have felt some lonely feelings. Well except for the day after I left Sasha a few days ago. I'm not sure why. Maybe because now that I have finished staying with three friends, Kate, Sasha and Lucy, I miss them, even though it won't be too long till Scott gets here, and even though I really have not minded at all walking by myself so far this entire trip. Maybe because I have a beach and a room with a view and the wave sound that I can't yet share with Scott. Or some combination of the above. But I know that the feelings shall pass and I will be just fine.

DAY 19 (DAY 106) STATS: 5.5 TOTAL INCLUDING .5 NEW ON THE SEATON END, .75 NEW ON THE DOWNDERRY END, AND 4.25 REPEAT OF BOTH THOSE SECTIONS PLUS BEACH WALKING A COUPLE OF TIMES AND EXTRA ROAD WALKING. 1.25 HOURS BEFORE LUNCH. SLOW WALKING WHICH I DID NOT CLOCK FOR AFTER LUNCH. PURPLE SHOES THEN FLIP FLOPS. Information on Church of St. Nicolas from stnicholascenter.org/galleries/gazetteer.

CLIFF TOP CAFÉ/WHITSAND BAY TO RAME HEAD AND CAWSAND – Sunday, 15 April 2018

"Oh, I do Love to be Beside the Seaside!" – As printed on a mug and a wall hanging that I bought.

Well with the weather forecast for today constantly changing, it was a whirlwind day deciding what to do. I guess it was bound to happen that I would encounter some rain during these six weeks. I mean, after all, I have been fortunate that the only rain I have had in nearly three weeks so far either happened when I was on a travel or a rest day, or just the few passing showers on my first day in Braunton. But no worries, today I only got caught in the rain for a mere two or three minutes.

Because the forecast originally called for rain all day, I was actually not going to walk at all and have an unplanned rest day and so I called a taxi last night to take me directly from my Inn in Downderry to my B&B in Cawsand. Not the same B&B I stayed in the Cawsand/Kingsand area last year, but a different one, one that was much more centrally located. Located basically right across the road from The Old Bakery Café actually where I ate last year and will eat again this year. This B&B had a great view from my room window – of the buildings of Cawsand and Kingsand, the building with the clock tower, the small beach below, and on down to Mount Edgcumbe Park, into Plymouth, the Plymouth Breakwater Lighthouse, the headlands beyond, and the waters in between. And I can hear the waves crashing on the beach and crashing on the breakwalls protecting all the buildings. What a great B&B room that I will be enjoying for two nights. With yesterday's room too, that will be three nights in a row that I heard my favorite sound of the crashing waves at night.

After the taxi dropped me off at my B&B, since it actually had not been raining this morning as originally predicted, I checked the forecast again. It now called for no rain till about 12:45, so that would give me almost a few hours window time to do some of my walk today, and the rest tomorrow. Basically, between the two days, I need to walk from Portwrinkle to Rame Head, about a six-mile section that I missed last year because of a combination of some road walking and the weather. I gave myself two days to do this walk this year in case of rainy weather, so I could either do the entire walk in one day or split it up into two days. Since the forecast called for some rain in the early afternoon, I decided to do some of the walk today, and the rest tomorrow.

John from the B&B in Cawsand was kind enough to drive me to the Cliff Top Café above Whitsand Bay. It would be a two mile walk to Rame Head and then two options of walking back to Cawsand after that. I went to the café to get a snack before starting my walk, which started on a road for a few minutes until I reached a sign that said four and a half miles to Cawsand in the direction I was going, and back to Portwrinkle in the opposite direction four and a quarter miles. I already started to have views of Rame Head. A "Welcome to Whitsand Bay" sign greeted me. On it I read that Rame Head and Whitsand Bay are Sites of Special Scientific Interest where "The SSSI protects some very rare plants, such as shore dock, slender bird's foot trefoil and early meadowgrass." However, I had no idea what these rare plants looked like to see if I could find them. The sign continued, "The Dartmouth grit and slate cliffs, dating back 400 million years, have also yielded important marine fossils." That's old. And that this area is "A diver's delight [because] Royal Navy frigate HMS Scylla was sunk by controlled explosion in 2004 to create an artificial reef. It has since been colonized by over 270 marine species." I am not a diver. A few yellow and white daffodils were in bloom however, and I did recognize those.

The path began to wind its way, with minor ups and downs, through a few homes and chalets, overlooking Whitsand Beach with its very long coastline of white rolling crashing waves. At first I was walking on a path, then on a road and then back onto path, with a slight descent allowing me to get closer to the beach below the hillsides, although the path never went down to the beach itself. Views to Rame Head continued ahead of me, and views behind me continued of the long beach surrounded by the hillsides, and further back headlands of where I once walked. I wondered if at the right tide times, if one could walk the entire several-mile long beach of Whitsand Bay.

The path flattened out to a grassy path as I was getting closer to being at the end of the long Whitsand Beach. I was able to listen to the waves crash that entire time. I passed by a few more homes, crossed a small road and climbed up a few steps. The path slightly ascended uphill overlooking the long coastline of white waves out to the headlands beyond. The view was quite amazing, although it was a bit cloudy out, so I bet in the sun the view would have been even more amazing.

It was only about noon by this time and I felt a few drops of rain. I already had my rain jacket on for warmth as it was a bit cool and breezy out, so I stopped to put the rain cover on my rucksack. The drops of rain were early according to the forecast, but they stopped once the rain cover on my rucksack was on, so the rain cover worked! Speaking of rucksacks, I already mentioned that for these six I brought with me two rucksacks. The black one I used last year and the smaller green one that I originally bought in Spain on my Camino walk. So far I have only used the black one once, on the day I walked from Par to Fowey where I brought my hiking boots with me in case I needed them. All other days, I have been using the smaller green rucksack.

As I ascended slightly I had another closer view of Rame Head. Before I knew it, I was on the grassy area near the NCI Coastwatch Station that I started from last year on my way to Cawsand and Kingsand. Three horses were on the grassy area eating so I took their photo with Rame Head in the background. I wondered if these were the same three horses that I saw last year just past Rame Head. Just as I ascended the grassy area, about an hour after I started walking, and a half hour before the predicted rain time, a bit more rain started. For about two or three minutes as I headed towards shelter in the NCI Coastwatch Station, I walked in some rain. Arriving at the station, I thus completed part of another missed section from last year! Then it stopped raining.

I wanted to go see if the St. Germanus Church in Rame was open because last year when I was dropped off there it was closed. I walked the road the half mile to the church, and it was open. From a brochure of this and another church that I bought it tells me that "the first stone building was consecrated in 1259, the slender unbuttressed tower with its broached spire (an unusual feature in a Cornish church), the north wall, north aisle and the chancel are all probably of this date," with restorations in 1848 and 1886. In addition, "The church still has no electricity and is lit by candles, the organ is hand pumped." I recalled that the only other two churches I have visited that have no electricity and are lit by candles are the St. Anthony Church near Gillan Creek and St. Aldhelm's Chapel near Worth Matravers.

Since I had already started walking back toward Cawsand and Kingsand on the road as I went to the church in Rame, I just walked the one mile back to the two towns on the road and went right to The Old Bakery Café for a great healthy lunch of a "goat's cheese, rocket and pomegranate jelly" sandwich, which I also had a similar sandwich last year, and a nice "fig, Stilton cheese, and walnut salad," which included mixed leaves, mint couscous, lentils, tomatoes, and olives. I was hungry. After eating, since I had already changed into my flip flops after wearing my hiking books for the walk, I took a leisurely walk through the narrow roads of Cawsand and Kingsand, and I even walked on the correct SWCP road by The Rising Sun Pub which I just discovered because apparently last year I took the other parallel road, which I think both are official ways to walk towards Mount Edgcumbe Park. I walked out to the beginning of Mount Edgcumbe Park and walked in the park a leisurely short distance on a wide path lined with wildflowers and eight benches with views of the Plymouth Breakwater Lighthouse. (I counted the benches as I walked back.) As I wandered back in through the narrow roads of Cawsand and Kingsand, I took a few window and doors photos to perhaps add to my photography book someday.

I remembered a little gift shop up one road, so I went in and I was actually glad I did. I bought two items, a mug and a small wall hanging with a wooden seagull, which say...

"Oh, I do love to be beside the seaside."…..Perfect!

DAY 20 (DAY 107) STATS: 3.5 MILES TOTAL INCLUDING 2.0 MILES ON SWCP, 1.5 ON ROAD. ONE HOUR OFFICIAL WALKING. HIKING BOOTS.

PORTWRINKLE TO CLIFF TOP CAFÉ TO RAME HEAD TO CAWSAND – Monday, 16 April 2018

"By the Sea All Worries Wash Away" – Displayed in dining area of B&B in Cawsand.

Last night I watched a couple of TV shows as I sat in my room writing. They were documentary-type shows about the lives of Prince Harry, His Royal Highness The Duke of Sussex, and the future Meghan Markle, Her Royal Highness The Duchess of Sussex. A British Royal marrying an American actress. A love story. Since the wedding date is not until the 19th of May, I unfortunately will no longer be in England myself like I was in Bhutan for that royal wedding so I will therefore not get a chance to meet any of the British royalty. However, I will watch the wedding on TV back home. Although with the time difference, I will need to decide if I shall get up during the middle of the night to watch the wedding live.

After breakfast, John of the B&B in Cawsand kindly drove me to Portwrinkle today so that I could start today's walk to the Cliff Top Café to complete the other approximate four miles of the six-mile missed section to Rame Head, but it ended up being a walk all the way to Cawsand instead, doing a total of nine miles and repeating several of those miles. I was dropped off at the smallest harbour of Portwrinkle. The tide was out compared to last year when I was here, so I saw more of its small breakwaters, but there were no boats in the harbour today except for a few lining the beach and path above. I still took some photos. There were already views all the way out to Rame Head, and behind to headlands and villages and towns that I have already walked. The blue and turquoise waters were shining under the blue skies with a few white clouds.

As I walked out of Portwrinkle, I walked on the grass and pavement areas lined with benches to sit on for the views. I walked past the large Whitsand Bay Hotel and passed a sign saying two miles to Tregantle. I took a short detour down to get closer to Finnygook Beach for a few photos. The path down to the small sandy beach was lined with those white flower bushes called blackthorn, and the seas were blue and turquoise. A sign said two and a quarter miles to Tregantle, but I don't think I walked backwards a quarter of a mile since I was walking forwards.

A slight uphill then took me to a...golf course. But with the weather today of partly sunny, partly cloudy, some wind, but dry with no rain forecasted, I was not worried. A sign did warn me however, "Beware! Falling golf balls. Keep to public footpath," but with the wind today, I did not see anyone playing golf. I walked past hole 5 with par 4, and then past hole 6 with par 3, all on flat grass. There were a few benches here offering views all around. The views out to Rame Head continued, as did the views behind, and below was a long coastline with waves and beach.

Once out of the golf course the walking continued to be mostly flat on grass to the Tregantle Firing Range. There were two options for this – if the range was open I could walk through, if not I would need to walk around the range which does not add that much extra mileage. Today the firing range was open because I checked a website last night and because when I arrived no red flags were flying. However, just as I was about to enter, I noticed a herd of cows...right on the path. And I know the rule is to walk around them, not through them, but walking around them in a firing range where there might be something explosive lying around, I just did not want to do. Nor did I want to walk through the herd of cows. Therefore, I decided to walk the alternate way around the range.

I started walking on the edge of a grassy field, followed by a path for a while that paralleled a road on one side, and on the other side was a fence, and beyond the fence was the firing range and well, more cows. A bit over an hour after I started walking this morning I passed by a sign that said two and three-quarters miles back to Portwrinkle and two miles to Whitsand Bay, which was about where I started yesterday at the Cliff Top Café. Soon the path walking turned into some road walking on a major road, until I was able to turn right on a smaller road until I was finally around the firing range and back on a path. I passed a sign that said four miles to Rame Head. The path was all flat paralleling a road and paralleling the long beach with its constant rolling waves.

I passed through the small village of Freathy, walking on the road, and then arrived at Whitsand and the Cliff Top Café, although I did walk a short distance on some grass next to homes and chalets in this section, but mostly on the road. It was just after noon, about two hours after I started walking, and I had now completed yet another missed-mile section of four and a half miles! I stopped in the café for some lunch.

I tried to call Penny and John of my B&B to see if they would come pick me up since I had completed this section, but they were not available, so with the good weather today, I walked all the way back to Cawsand via Rame Head, repeating the two mile section I did yesterday, and two and a half additional miles from Rame Head into Cawsand on the SWCP that I did last year. I did not take many notes since this was all repeat walking.

As I walked above Whitsand Beach this time, the tide was further out than yesterday. I passed by two horses that were right on the path when I got to the far end of the beach. During this section today not only did I listen to the waves, but I also listened to some music since I was able to get reception on my mobile and I was walking a repeat section. I haven't listened to music these past several weeks. And yes, just as I thought yesterday, the views out from here overlooking the long coastline of white waves out to the headlands beyond in this blue-sky-and-some-white-cloud weather were even more amazing than the cloudiness from yesterday.

Passing by some yellow gorse, I soon arrived at Rame Head, turned a corner to the left, and the views behind me disappeared with new views appearing of small white waves hitting the rocky coastline below the green hillside. I passed by five more horses, one of which was also right on the path, so in both cases when I came across these horses, I walked a distance away from them off the path on some grass to give them their space. Horses don't make me nervous like cows do, but it was still a good idea to not walk right next to them.

The walk was flat all the way to Penlee Point with views looking back to Rame Head. I turned another corner to the left and had a view of the Plymouth Breakwater Lighthouse. I shivered at the idea that soon I would be back in a big city for a few days, but I missed walking some miles in Plymouth so I needed to return. Continuing on flat roads and tracks and narrow concrete paths in some trees, I emerged at The Square in Cawsand, just over two hours after I started walking from the Cliff Top Café.

I went to The Old Bakery Café once again for a healthy snack of the same fig, Stilton cheese, and walnut salad I had yesterday, and their banana bread toasted and topped with Greek yogurt and honey, which I also ate last year. I also got one of the same sandwiches I had yesterday to take away for dinner for later. I wore purple shoes today because of the dry forecast and because when I walked yesterday there was little mud, and the couple small spots of mud I did come across were easy to walk around. I liked the quote displayed in the dining area of my B&B at this morning's breakfast…"By the Sea All Worries Wash Away."

DAY 21 (DAY 108) STATS: NINE MILES TOTAL. FOUR AND A HALF NEW. FOUR AND A HALF REPEAT. FIVE HOURS TOTAL INCLUDING A BIT OVER A HALF HOUR LUNCH. PURPLE SHOES.
I confirmed the Titles for Harry and Meghan from royal.uk/prince-harry-and-ms-meghan-markle-announcement-titles.

REST DAY IN PLYMOUTH – Tuesday, 17 April 2018

"Beach House Rules: Wake up smiling. Flip flops are mandatory. Hang up your towel. Hard work not allowed. Keep the sand outside. Relax, swim, play. Eat plenty. Nap often. Soak up the sun. Be grateful for this day." – On a sign in a shop in the Barbican area of Plymouth.

Today was a rest day in Plymouth for a few reasons. One was that I gave myself three days to do the seven-and-a-half mile walk around the streets of Plymouth in case of uncooperative weather when I planned my itinerary, or to split it up over a few days if I wanted to. Two was that the forecast for today turned out to be rainy and even possibly gale force winds. Three was tomorrow and the next day should be nice and sunny and warm. Four was to just do a few necessary errands and have leisurely day in the shock of a big city. I used Luggage Transfers today so that I could just concentrate on doing my errands and have my leisurely day.

I took a few pictures out the window of my B&B in Cawsand of the waves crashing against the seawall just below the buildings and clock tower right at the edge of the water. It felt quite dramatic that all these buildings were that close to the water, but I figured that they were safe enough from any large storms. After breakfast and saying my good-byes and thank yous to Penny and John, John kindly dropped me off at the Cremyll ferry that I had already taken last year, and about ten minutes later I went from the county of Cornwall to the county of Devon once again. I was in north Devon weeks ago when I was in Braunton, then Cornwall, now south Devon. At first it was not raining when I got off the ferry so I decided to walk from Admiral's Hard where the ferry dropped me off to the Royal Parade area of Plymouth to start some of my errands, but not walking via the SWCP, just using the shortest way the GPS on my mobile phone told me which was just over a mile of walking. Some drizzle began as I got closer to my first errand of a bank to get some cash so I was able to get some shelter in the bank. My next errand was to the vegan and organic store that I discovered last year, which also offered some shelter from the rain, so that I could get protein bars for snacks, toothpaste, lotion, and soap.

I walked another few minutes to the Barbican area of Plymouth that I rather liked last year and did bit of browsing in shops including a few charity shops also known as thrift stores. I had a fun conversation about the television shows I watched a few nights ago about the upcoming marriage of Prince Harry to Meghan Markle. One of the charity shops had many great sets of English Bone China sets of dishes and tea cups that I would have loved to bought, as they reminded me of the set in Barnstaple, but alas they would be just too breakable for me to pack in my wheeled luggage. They were so colorful from some with brownish-reddish flowers to grey flowers to pink flowers to a set with purple and yellow and orange flowers. Other sets were had blue flowers, or green and blue and brown leaves, or orange poppies with green leaves, or delicate pink flowers, or blue flowers, brown churches and farm buildings, green ivy leaves, and more. I would have loved to have them all.

Finally, it was on to my last "errand," the chocolate café, Chocaccino, for first a savory lunch, and then I indulged with sweet desserts to celebrate the completion of all the miles I have successfully done thus far the past three weeks, about 38 of my missed miles, plus about an additional 45 miles of either repeat walking or extra walking! I ordered the delicious "combination" lunch which included a choice of a savory dish and a choice of three desserts. My savory lunch was a chicken salad. I know, that is not vegan. My three desserts included a pecan chocolate cake, a brownie layer cake, and a chocolate brownie with cranberries. So delicious, and that should be enough chocolate to last me for quite a while!

As I was eating, I realized that I am a woman of opposites. I tend to be vegetarian, I would like to be vegan, but I eat chicken and bacon. I really want to stay away from sugar, but I eat chocolate. I find the shock of a big city too much for me, yet I have three days here in Plymouth. I love to walk on the SWCP, but I just prefer not to walk in the rain and wind and the fog.

After my delicious lunch, I walked to my Guest House near the Hoe area, walking about a mile through the Hoe area to get there that was closed last year for that music concert. I walked by Smeaton's Tower that I shall hopefully get to climb up the tower tomorrow or the next day. As I walked to the Guest House, it was not raining but it was quite windy. I don't think that it felt like gale winds though. Even with being in a bit city, I was grateful for this day.

DAY 22 (DAY 109) STATS: TWO NON-SWCP MILES. DID NOT COUNT THE HOURS FOR MY LEISURELY DAY. PURPLE SHOES.

PLYMOUTH – Wednesday, 18 April 2018

"Hundreds of thousands [of pilgrims] subsequently visited Santiago de Compostela. Many pilgrims sailed from England through Plymouth which was one of the only two ports licensed for this journey. The pilgrims often wore a sign indicating their destination. Those going to Santiago de Compostela wore a scallop shell. This eventually became a general symbol of pilgrimage." – A sign on a wall in Plymouth that I noticed which included an acorn and a large yellow scallop shell.

To start my long walking day all on pavement, I walked a mile back to the ferry at Admiral's Hard to officially start walking the Plymouth waterfront on a gratefully blue sky sunny day. I passed by Elvira's Café, the first and last pub in Devon called The Vine, a playground, walked around Royal William Yard, climbed up a few steps, strolled on paved path with benches and views of Plymouth Sound and Drake's Island, sauntered down Durnford Street, took a right turn on another street, noticed The Wall of Stars, made another right turn, curved around to the left, ambled by some local Industrial Heritage signs, then wandered onto Grand Parade all in about an hour's worth of walking since I officially started at Admiral's Hard. There were lots of various SWCP signs along the way so I mostly took photos of just the various signs today, some of which looked quite old, and others I had never seen before in all my miles on the SWCP. I included a list of the signs I saw today just before my stats below, along with some information and a discovery I made connecting Plymouth on the SWCP in England to the Camino de Santiago walk I did in Spain.

I stopped for a second breakfast at a restaurant before wandering on. I walked by the Hoe area and since I knew that this was where Smeaton's Tower Lighthouse was, I took a short break from my rambling to climb the 93 steps of the 72-foot red and white striped tower, with its spiral staircase and some quite steep and close together steps, for the experience, and for the views, on this blue sky sunny day. This was the third lighthouse built on the dangerous Eddystone Rocks in 1759. It was dismantled and moved to the Hoe in the 1880s. I read some information about the lighthouse on information boards as I climbed. "Its design and construction were considered great achievements of the age, and the Lighthouse stood marking these dangerous rocks for 123 years." The present Eddystone lighthouse was built in 1882 which replaced Smeaton's Tower and is thirteen miles out in the water south west of Plymouth. The views that I saw from the top of the tower were to the waters of Plymouth Sound straight out, to the right out towards Mount Edgcumbe and Penlee Point, and to the left out to Jennycliff and beyond. Various boats were moving about in the waters. From the top of the tower where the glass was to let the light shine through, I was fascinated with the replica of the candle holder with room for twenty-four candles which was the way this lighthouse used to be lit for the safety of passing ships. There was also an original small table on display that dated back to 1759. I was glad that I finally got a chance to climb this former lighthouse.

I continued my promenade around the Hoe area, arriving at the Sutton Harbour Bridge near the Barbican area. Technically the official SWCP allows you to walk across this bridge, but it was closed, so I had read on the SWCP Association website that you can take the short ferry ride instead across the harbour to avoid walking around the harbour, so I did. I marched past an aquarium, followed acorns either painted or on stickers on light poles of the streets, and red square signs, and a very large SWCP red and white marker with the words "South West Coast Path" in red and white, taller than me, which looked like a rocket. I wondered about the history of this interesting and unique SWCP sign. I walked on a paved path lined with garbage and through an industrial area on Cattedown Road.

I will say that the three and a half miles from Admiral's Hard to the Sutton Harbour Bridge were mostly fine scenery-wise, and worth walking even though it was all on pavement, and occasionally near a road. The path had been well marked. Since crossing Sutton Harbour, the signage continued, for example an acorn on every light pole and other markers, but this area that I walked through, an industrial area, including some large oil tanks, and then across a bridge and on a sidewalk near the busy A379 road had to be the worst section of the entire SWCP. Not scenic at all, and I really wondered why this was an official part of the SWCP. It made walking around the Hayle Estuary that I did last year seem so much nicer. But enough complaining, I was grateful to be walking this entire eight and a half miles in the warm sun and blue sky, even with a breeze every now and then.

After the busy road, I took a right turn on a paved path, past a statue of a rhinoceros, took another right turn down a smaller road and about five minutes later I passed a sign that said that I had two and three-quarters miles left to Mount Batten and that I had come two and a half miles from Barbican. I was still stomping through an industrial area. Not only have I been able to follow many SWCP signs and markers and arrows and acorns, I have also been reading the booklets for today very closely as I walked just to make sure I didn't get lost.

Another paved pathway took me around a boat yard with two and a half miles to Mount Batten, my destination for the day to catch the ferry back to Plymouth. When I was at Sutton Harbour earlier, Mount Batten looked so close, and in fact the Sutton ferryman told me it was a half mile way, but needing to walk there around all this was five miles. I stepped along a short quay onto some roads in a neighborhood, and a path between some homes. I roamed around the Hooe Lake at low tide with very old abandoned wooden hulls of boats lying on the sand.

A wooden sign there pointed in three directions – the direction I was headed with Wembury in seven miles, the direction I came from back to Barbican three miles and Tavistock seventeen miles, and in the third direction, pointing inland on the "Coast to Coast Path" four miles to Wembury, fifteen miles to Ivybridge, and 118 miles to Lynmouth. I wondered what this "Coast to Coast Path" was and later researched it. Basically it is an inland route linking Wembury in south Devon on the English Channel to Lynmouth and Lynton (where I walked through last year) in north Devon on the Bristol Channel. Looking at a map it goes through the length of the county of Devon, and I suppose if one wanted to skip walking the county of Cornwall entirely on the SWCP they could take this Coast to Coast Path. But who would want to miss that, I can't imagine? Or I suppose one could do a circular route with the Coast to Coast Path and the Cornwall part of the SWCP if one wanted to miss the rest of Devon and Dorset in the south and a bit of Somerset in the north. But who would want to miss that, I can't imagine either?

Anyway, I walked through an archway of the Radford Castle and then through a path, probably the only non-pavement path of the day, lined with small trees but next to a smelly water treatment plant. The "castle" was not actually a defensive castle, but a "mock castle lodge built in the early 19th century," but looked like a small castle. That path led into a nice neighborhood where I stopped for some water at the Royal Oak Pub, circa 1799, with its pub food, accommodation, homemade food, quiz nights, and real ales. There was a carving of an oak tree in the brick of its front wall. I sat for a few moments on their benches enjoying the warm sunny blue sky day drinking some water that the bar tender kindly gave me, noticing a large metallic carving of an acorn. Oh yes, acorns come from oak trees and the pub is called the Royal Oak. The pub also said "Walkers Welcome." Actually, if I had known about this place to stay, I might have considered it. It seemed quite historic and I was intrigued by this pub.

In fact, it reminded me that a few days ago, I had asked Lucy why National Trails chose to use the acorn as its symbol, that I wondered back on the 19th of August when I found a small acorn on the ground. I had learned at the time that the acorn is the nut of an oak tree, and I recalled a quote about Smeaton's Tower, "He had decided to construct a tower based on the shape of an English Oak tree for strength…" Lucy told me that oak trees are very British. She said that both National Trails and National Trust use some part of the oak tree as their symbol – National Trails uses the acorn, and National Trust uses oak leaves. Lucy thought that perhaps since National Trails manages fifteen other trails in addition to the SWCP, then it is not just about the coast. It also about all the other locations all over the countries of England and Wales, so perhaps the acorn is more appropriate to trails all over both countries. The oak is also the national tree of England. I also looked up the general symbolism of the acorn and the oak tree, and found out that they represent potential, honour, longevity, endurance, and…strength.

I continued on next to a grassy park, carried on around the lake, on a road next to more homes and businesses of some sort, and into the village of Turnchapel. I passed Clovelly Bay Inn, meandered up a narrow road, which was the most climbing I had done all day except for Smeaton's Tower, as the pavement had all been flat. I went next to a car park, down some steps which was now above a marina with a SWCP sign saying I now only had a half mile to the Mount Batten ferry.

I roved next to what looked like the top of a lighthouse of some sort with a light inside and an airplane-weather vane on top, and soon I had a quarter mile till the ferry. I arrived at the ferry five hours after I started walking, strolling, sauntering, ambling, meandering, marching, wandering, stepping, stomping, roaming, roving, rambling, and promenading this morning, which included the time I took to eat the second breakfast, climbing the lighthouse, and waiting a bit for the Sutton Harbour ferry. I had now completed the eight and a half mile section of the SWCP that I missed last year, which I originally thought was seven and a half miles, with a few miles of the most unnecessary walking of the entire coast path! Why they don't let you walk from Admiral's Hard to the Barbican and then let you take the ferry to Mount Batten officially, I don't know. But I need to look at all the small gems I saw today anyway such as all the various new signs, the Royal Oak Pub, learning about the "Coast to Coast Path," the connection I made mentioned below between the Camino de Santiago and the SWCP, Smeaton's Tower, the two ferries, the abandoned hulls of boats around a lake, and not to mention the amazing fact that I had perfect weather today for this walk! From across the Plymouth Sound I had a view back to the Hoe area with the tall red and white striped Smeaton's Tower.

I was hungry about a half hour before I arrived at the ferry but figured that since I was close to the ferry which would take me back to the Barbican area, I would eat when I got back. I had worn my purple shoes today, and once I arrived in the Barbican area, I switched to flip flops. When I was on the ferry, I sat next to an older couple, where the gentleman told me that in 1941 it cost 3p to take this ferry, perhaps the equivalent of a few cents or less! Today it cost me £1.50/$2.00.

After eating lunch, I walked around the Hoe area again and stopped on the grassy area next to Smeaton's Tower to sit down and enjoy the sun. Along with everyone else. It was a popular place today with the great weather for people to socialize. Oh, and I wore jeans today, the only time I have done that for a walk. Otherwise it has been hiking pants.

As I walked back to my guest house I noticed a small section of the SWCP that I actually missed this morning as I had accidently walked in front of some buildings instead of walking behind them, so with my flip flops and jeans on, I did the short bit next to some benches and a wall with tiny models of some of Navy ships and submarines, known as "The Millennium Wall."

I thought that as I walked through all those industrial areas and busy roads of a big city today, I now had views once again out to the green hillsides of the SWCP of Mount Edgcumbe, Penlee Point, Jennycliff, with small quaint places like Cawsand and Kingsand hidden away taking one back in time and to a quieter slower place which I so much prefer.

SOME SIGNS SEEN TODAY: Note that these are not listed in any particular order, and some that were on the ground I took photos of with my purple shoes!

Many signs on light poles: Black acorns with black arrows. Black acorns painted on a white background with black stripes on the top and bottom of the white paint on light poles. The SWCP sticker I have seen many other places which is black with white "South West Coast Path," white acorn, and white arrow pointing in one direction, the other direction, or both directions.

Red squares, but in the shape of a diamond configuration, with a white outline and white words of SWCP and a small white acorn, a gold star, and white arrows pointing in the direction of walking. Seen on walls and on the ground. Similar square/diamond on the ground but black background and brownish words.

Small gray acorn with black and gray circles around acorn, and small white acorn with black and gray circles around acorn. Seen on walls and on the ground.

Various black acorns spray painted on white poles. Various white acorns spray painted on black poles. White acorn and arrow spray painted on a green pole. White acorn spray painted on a blue pole.

New wooden pole with acorn, yellow arrow, "Coast Path," and "Gifted by SWCP Association" emblem.

Very old looking red metallic signs bolted around light poles with part of it having "SW Coast Path" and an arrow carved out of the red metal, and an acorn carved out of the red metal on another part of it. I liked these the best and wondered how old they were and what their history was.

Concrete looking poles with "South West Coast Path" in capital letters in white, and red metallic pointers at the very top with acorns carved out of a white circle. Again I wondered their age and history. I was also walking the Waterfront Walkway according to a similar pole.

One final acorn on a wall I noticed when walking back along the Hoe with a large yellow scallop shell. Engraved was the description of the "Way of Saint James." "Saint James, one of the Apostles, was martyred in AD44. Legend has it that he spent a number of years preaching in Spain and was subsequently buried there. His supposed burial site was discovered in the early 9th century and became a focus of pilgrimage. Hundreds of thousands subsequently visited Santiago de Compostela. Many pilgrims sailed from England through Plymouth which was one of the only two ports licensed for this journey. The pilgrims often wore a sign indicating their destination. Those going to Santiago de Compostela wore a scallop shell. This eventually became a general symbol of pilgrimage." That was the most fascinating plaque I had read, and yet one more great connection with England and Spain, and my own adventures and journeys along the SWCP and the Camino de Santiago! I did wear a scallop shell attached to my rucksack during my Camino walk. Scallop shells and arrows and acorns!

DAY 23 (DAY 110) STATS: 10.5 MILES TOTAL. 3.5 FROM ADMIRAL'S HARD TO THE SUTTON FERRY AND 5.0 FROM OTHER SIDE OF SUTTON HARBOUR TO MOUNT BATTEN FERRY ALL OF WHICH WERE NEW MILES. ONE MILE EXTRA WALKING TO ADMIRAL'S HARD IN THE MORNING TO START THE WALK, AND ONE MILE BACK TO GUEST HOUSE AT END OF THE DAY. PURPLE SHOES, A BIT OF FLIP FLOPS. PUBS I SAW ALONG THE WAY WERE "THE VINE," AND "ROYAL OAK PUB."

REST DAY #2 IN PLYMOUTH – Thursday, 19 April 2018

"UK temperatures top 29C [84F] in hottest April day since 1949. Temperatures have soared to over 29C in parts of London, making it the warmest April day for nearly 70 years. The average maximum temperature for the UK in April is 11.9C [53F]." – Headline and news article on BBC News for today.

Today was a beautiful warm sunny blue sky day again in Plymouth. I would guess that yesterday may have been at least 60F/15.5C, with an occasional breeze, and today was even warmer without a breeze. Today I had originally scheduled in my itinerary to be an alternate or extra day to do the walk that I did yesterday in case of uncooperative weather. With yesterday being a good weather day, and since I had completed the walk in this area, I took today as my second rest day in Plymouth, just like I took the other rest day two days ago. With the great weather today, I woke up really wanting to do a walk, but it was just more convenient and sensible to keep today as a rest day. So I just enjoyed the sun having a leisurely day in Plymouth. I was able to find the quieter spots of the big busy city.

I spent a bit of time in the morning typing up my day from yesterday first. Usually I do this each evening after my walk, but knowing I had today, I waited to do the writing. After I was hungry so I walked the mile around the Hoe area back to the Barbican area again (which I actually do like to be in this area) to eat a healthy lunch of a good roasted butternut squash, lentil, and feta salad with greens. After my healthy lunch I went into a few antique shops and looked around leisurely for a while. I walked through the Elizabethan Gardens, which were not blooming, and then it was just time for a cream tea! I had not had one in a while, so it was time. Since no one was watching me, I made sure I had some of my scones the Devon way, and the others the Cornwall way. Still both delicious!

As I sat there enjoying, I was not sure what to do next. Since I felt like walking though, I realized that I could walk around the Sutton Harbour which I did not do yesterday. Therefore, with my cushy flip flops on, I set off on a slow leisurely walk. This walk was not part of the SWCP, and I noticed signs that it was actually called the Harbour Trail going from the Mayflower Steps and Barbican area around to the National Marine Aquarium. I walked to the aquarium and back to the Barbican area. It was all on pavement, but I still enjoyed it going around all the boats in the harbour and passing by many various restaurants and pubs. I did not notice how long it took me to do the walk, but I believe it was a mile around, so I walked two miles back and forth.

Once I got back to the Barbican, I thought that since I have no idea if I will ever get to Plymouth again, I would enjoy five small chocolates at the same chocolate shop I had the three desserts at a few days ago. As I walked back to my B&B slowly and leisurely along the mile-long Hoe, I sat on a bench of the grass overlooking Smeaton's Tower and the water in the quite warm sun. I loved this weather. Like yesterday, lots of people were also on the grassy area enjoying the day.

Later on, I completed writing up my day from yesterday, reorganized my belongings, and slightly changed my walking plans for tomorrow.

I also read an interesting and fascinating small booklet that I bought yesterday at Smeaton's Tower called "The Lighthouse Keeper's Lot, An insight into the life of a lighthouse keeper, 1698-1982." Some highlights included, "The life of a lighthouse keeper was not for everyone. The weather had a major influence on the working day, which meant there were very busy times coupled with long periods of boredom. Shore based lighthouses would often provide a home for the keeper and their families, whereas an off shore 'rock' lighthouse, was staffed by single men…The principal duty of the keepers was to maintain the light. The light source was lit half an hour after sunset and kept burning until half an hour before sunrise. Regular checks were performed in order to ensure the light was on. In stormy weather the keepers had to remain in the lamp room and tend to the light all night."

Further information about the light itself said that, "The most important element of any lighthouse is the light. This is shone throughout the night for the benefit of passing ships. In medieval times this light was usually created by fire in an open brazier, burning wood, peat or coal. [However], many wooden lighthouses caught fire and burned down. The candle was a surprisingly effective alternative. Candle chandeliers were used when a stronger light source was required. It was claimed Winstanley's Eddystone Light (1698), the world's first rock lighthouse, used 60 candles with a hanging oil lamp. Rudyard's Eddystone Light (1708) was lit with 24 candles. So too, for many years, was its replacement, Smeaton's Tower (1795)." Ahhh, the replica of the candle holder I saw yesterday.

The booklet further described how glazed lanterns were tried to protect the light sources, then "oil lamps using rape seed, whale or fish oil were tried but remained largely inefficient until the introduction of Argand's lamp in 1784. This lamp had a hollow circular wick and a glass chimney, reducing oil consumption, delivering a good draught and giving a much brighter light. Curved metal reflectors were also being installed behind the new oil lamps to better direct the light. Twelve oil lamps, each backed with a reflector were fitted in Smeaton's Tower in 1810-11." Wow, I am fascinated with the lighthouses and the progression of how they were lit to protect those at sea.

Continuing on, "Lighthouse candles had to be tended, and the wicks trimmed, approximately every thirty minutes. Oil lamps needed tending every two hours…In 1822, Fresnel invented the annular lens; a central lens surrounded by concentric rings. The introduction of optics in the form of lenses and prisms better focused and intensified the light beam. The first optic was installed in Smeaton's Tower in the late 1840s, enclosing a central oil lamp. When the Douglass Light was completed in May 1882, the large new drum optics rotated around the light source, for the first time producing a distinctive flash or character."

Finally, "Electricity began to be used to power some coastal lighthouses during the 1870s…The Douglas Lighthouse was finally converted from oil burning lamps to electric power in 1956. On 18 May 1982, the last duty keepers left the Eddystone. The light became automatic and today's modern light source is solar powered." I really do find it fascinating to read about the progression of the technology of lighthouses, and am intrigued by the "romance" of being a lighthouse keeper. I am also saddened that the important profession of the lighthouse keeper of yesteryear is no longer needed.

As I checked BBC News I saw that today had been the hottest April day in the UK since 1949, especially in parts of London. While it was not as hot here in Plymouth as my very, very hot days when I walked from about Bucks Mills to Bude over the course of four days last summer in June, it might have been a lovely and comfortable 65F/18C today in Plymouth. Summer in spring!

DAY 24 (DAY 111) STATS: NO SWCP MILES, BUT A LEISURELY FOUR MILES TO AND FROM B&B AROUND THE HOE, AND BACK AND FORTH ON THE HARBOUR TRAIL. DID NOT KEEP TRACK OF TIME. FLIP FLOPS. "The Lighthouse Keeper's Lot" booklet was published by Plymouth City Council, supported by Arts Council England.

WEMBURY CHURCH TO YEALM FERRY AND NOSS MAYO TO MOTHECOMBE – Friday, 20 April 2018

"Baby Lambs! Please keep all dogs on a lead. Thank you." – Sign as I was walking closer to Mothecombe.

A general note by the way, last year I used Luggage Transfers for my entire walk. This year I started out by taking my own luggage with me as I traveled from location to location, but now I have been using Luggage Transfers the past week or so due to these locations and logistics of my walks. I was going to stop using them in a few days, but it is just so much easier to not travel with my own wheeled luggage that I just might arrange to have them transfer my luggage the rest of my walk. Sometimes you just have to pay to make life easier.

On to today's absolutely beautiful walk, both in scenery and in weather. I took a taxi from my Guest House in Plymouth to the church in Wembury as buses for transportation were too complicated or not at the right timing, so I chose to just take a taxi. Sometimes you just have to pay to make life easier.

I visited the Wembury Church that I also visited last year inside, and took a few scenic photos from above the church and graveyard outside which overlooked the seas, the Great Mew Stone large rock, the green hillsides and farmland, and just the beauty of this area. I already had photos of this from last year, but it was worth it to take some more photos, as with the tombstones and the church in the foreground and the coast and farmland scenery in the background, it is quite a beautiful location. (See photo on the back cover of this book once again of this scenery.) I walked down to the beach at Wembury briefly before I started my walk. Today I actually figured out a way to combine two walks that I originally had planned to walk over two days, but with one of the walks only being a mile and a half, and with the beautiful weather, and with the location of the walks, I combined them into one walk in one day. Therefore, that meant that I am a day ahead of schedule in my planned walks.

I started walking already with a blue-sky-sunny-warm day and I was grateful. Summer in April! The sign told me I had one and a half miles to go till the Yealm seasonal ferry, some of which I technically did last year, but I missed part of this walk because the B&B gentleman I stayed with last year in Wembury dropped me off at a place where I walked an inland path towards the ferry. Today the new path started out with a slight uphill then flattened out. I passed by a flyer sign telling me about the "River Yealm Ferry Service – The Yealm Ferry operates a seasonal service between Warren Point (Coast Path to Wembury), Noss Mayo (Wide Slip) and Newton Ferrers (Harbour Office Pontoon) April to September 2018, 10am to 4pm daily. (May be restricted to 10am to 12 noon and 3pm to 4pm in bad weather and quieter times.)"

The views of the water, the Great Mew Stone, and the green covered hillside on the other side of the Yealm River Estuary were already beautiful. The flat path turned into a flat grassy path, and soon I had views of the mouth of the river with hillsides of green grass and trees across where I walked last year. Looking back, I continued to see the Great Mew Stone, the green hillsides, the coastline, the blue waters, and the headlands beyond, which was actually back out to Rame Head, where I was days ago. I will say that I love this scenery a whole lot more than the Plymouth industrial areas. Especially on a warm day like today. Or on any day really.

I crossed a small bridge over a small stream and walked on more grassy path. There was farmland around me inland to my left, and perhaps across the river I saw the farm that I stayed in at last year, the one with my "farm limo," a green golf-cart-type-farm-vehicle. There were views of sailboats floating in River Yealm, and looking back out to the mouth of the river, the waters were so blue, with a few sailboats, and out to the Great Mew Stone. After the grassy path, I was back to a dirt path with no mud at all. In fact, I wore purple shoes today knowing that today would be dry, not too many ascents and descents, and I kind of figured out what the path would be like based on what the similar area was like last year.

There were butterflies and bees and flies flying and buzzing around. Sounds and sights of summer in April! I walked parallel to the river and arrived at the gate that I stopped at last year when I back-tracked a bit, and soon I was at the sign that said a quarter mile to the ferry. It was a track road that was quiet as I heard just a few birds chirping, some flies buzzing, and some quiet lapping ripples in the river. About 45 minutes after I started walking, a sign pointed to the "Ferry Slipway," and soon I opened the board to signal the ferry, as the half circle of a black sign told me to "Drop the board for ferry." Once open, the sign was a white circle, with instructions to "Please close after use," exactly like last year.

I waited a few minutes for the small motorboat and was across river within a few minutes. Therefore, I had completed the missed mile from last year from the Wembury Church to the gate, walked a half repeat mile, and repeated the ferry since I started walking this morning! My plan for today to connect the two missed sections was to walk the roads from the ferry to the place above Stoke Beach and Peter the Poor Fisherman's Church to start the next missed section. I passed by the Ship Inn in Noss Mayo, the church in Noss Mayo, and used my GPS to help find the shortest distance on the roads, recognizing some of them from last year. I originally thought I would be walking a mile and a half on the roads, but it was more like two miles.

The SWCP sign I started at in order to walk to Mothecombe said I had three and a half miles to go to the Erme Estuary, but the booklet said five miles, and after I completed the walk today, I bet the booklet was correct. The path began on a wide flat grassy area which was actually the continuation of Revelstoke Drive that I walked on last year to this point. I was back to seeing the blue waters with the rocky coastline below the caravan park that I walked near last year as I looked back. I passed by a herd of cows ahead safely behind a fence. It was nice and quiet on this wide flat grassy road with just the subtle sound of the waves on the rocks below the hillsides behind me. I bet this road would have been quite muddy and soggy weeks ago, but today it was completely dry. I chose to walk very slowly today in the warm weather because the sun felt good, as I heard more subtle waves on the rocks below me. I spotted a couple of kayakers below in the water.

Just over a couple hours after I started walking this morning, I stopped for a snack sitting by the Tea House ruins. Per today's booklet, "The Tea House (or Painting House) at the top of Beacon Hill has been there since the mid-18th century. According to a local taxi driver, the Tea House was used to entertain Queen Victoria when she visited the area. Although Victoria did visit South Devon in 1846, there is no evidence that she came here." I had stopped in the Ship Inn earlier hoping to get a sandwich to take with me on today's walk, but they were not serving food yet. Fortunately, I always carry snacks with me of nuts and protein bars, the ones I bought in Plymouth a few days ago, so I enjoyed those under the warmth of the sun. Who knows, maybe Queen Victoria did enjoy the beautiful views from here on a warm day as well.

After my nice break, I descended slowly on a short but steep grassy path covered with small yellow wildflowers, small purple wildflowers, and white and yellow daisies. I actually sat on the grass for a moment to take some photos to include these little wildflowers, and also to include my purple shoes in the foreground with the beautiful green rolling hills and headlands ahead of me with a bit of brown farmland, the deep blue waters, a few trees, and the blue sky. Today these colors seemed so vibrant. I saw and heard a small group of rocks in the water with waves crashing as I continued walking on some flat grass after the descent. It was so peaceful out today.

I had a slight ascent and realized that it was not just warm out today, it was hot. Not as hot as those really hot days I had last year, and I am definitely not complaining, but a comfortable heat of maybe 70F/21C. There were views of amazing green rolling hills ahead checkered with some brown farmland. There were dark rocks below leading to the waters of light blue in the distance. It actually looked like there was some white coloring on the rocks which I guess might be from seagull droppings. There was also lots of yellow gorse in bloom, and I walked on another flat green grassy path.

I turned right to a short descent that curved left to a flat path. I saw Burgh Island in the distance near Bigbury-on-Sea and the headlands beyond. Then I walked next to my "dream farmhouse" that would be a great location to live. Just inland was a large brown house and in front of it was a grassy field that edged up to the SWCP. I bet the views from that farmhouse were beautiful out to the seas, and within a few steps from my home I could be walking on the SWCP. Later tonight I read in the booklet that I was possibly at Carswell Cove, and the booklet describes, "As you look towards St. Anchorite's Rock from above Ryder's Hole (which I was at a bit earlier), you can see a boathouse/beach hut at Carswell Cove below. This is a private beach hut which belongs to Carswell Farm. It can sleep two and can be rented for a couple of nights. It even has its own outside hot tub!" So I think my "dream farmhouse" may have been Carswell Farm, and while I did not see the boathouse/beach hut, I looked it up online and it looks amazing. One website describes the Carswell Beach Hut as, "The beach hut is down a steep cliff path after a fifteen minute walk from the parking spot, but every step just puts the whole world further behind you. The hut sits in a tiny cut in the rocks perched above your personal strip of sand and private beach. The gentle wash of the surf fills the cove as you light the BBQ and laze in the wood fired hot tub, relaxing after a day of exploring rock pools and swimming in the sea." I think that not only have I found another place to add to the "expensive-places-to-stay-someday-along-the-SWCP" list, but I have found my true ultimate location for a beach hut!!

I had a small decent with some steps to a grassy area where there was a bit of bogginess to the grass so I had to walk downstream a short distance to find a section that I could leap across to keep my purple shoes dry. Then the grassy area ascended. I stopped for another snack break sitting on a smaller rock next to the large St. Anchorite's Rock overlooking the amazing vibrant scenery on this beautiful hot day. I had been out for four hours now with one and a half miles to go. There was another flat grassy path and then oddly, I had to cross a large patch of dirt of farmland. This is one of those brown patches that created that brown and green checkered look I saw earlier today.

The path took me closer to many of the rocks that I had seen earlier, walking just above them and around them, including the rocks with the white coloring. I was able to hear the waves more from here and it was calming and peaceful. This place was called Butcher's Cove. The path took me even closer to those rocks with the water splashing in between them and a small waterfall running down the small valley I was approaching. I crossed a small bridge over the stream that created the waterfall, and then I had a good short but steep ascent with a few steps.

I walked around the edge of a grassy field with sheep and baby lambs up above and started to have views of the River Erme. As I walked through a gate, I noticed a sign in the shape of a sheep, painted like a sheep, with the words "Baby Lambs! Please keep all dogs on a lead. Thank you." A flat path paralleled the river, and I walked into the shade of some trees for a few moments. I climbed down some concrete steps with an old-looking "Coastal Footpath" sign and arrived onto the sand of a beach. Several people were enjoying the hot day on the beach where I had to leap across a stream to keep my purple shoes dry. The path led into some more trees with an ascent of steps and more trees. I arrived at a sign that said I was at the Mothecombe Slipway with the Low Tide Crossing pointing to the Erme River, and two and a half miles back to St. Anchorite's Rock.

I checked the tide chart that was on display, with the low tide for 20 April at 15:54, which was about an hour from when I arrived, and while I did not need to walk across the Erme River Estuary today, I happened to arrive at low tide, where you have one hour on either side of low tide to walk across the river. Good timing. Otherwise, if someone arrives here at any other state of the tide and needs to get to the other side, they would need to call a taxi to get around to Wonwell. I walked down to the river, which was now like one long sandy beach, and with other people also walking around, I took off my shoes and socks and walked about half way across and back just for the fun of it and to say that I had walked across some of the Erme River Estuary. I figured that walking half way across was more than some people do when they arrive a higher tide. And with that, I had completed another missed-mile section from last year, from the place above Stoke Beach and Peter the Poor Fisherman's Church to Mothecombe and a bit on the Erme River Estuary! And what an absolutely beautiful section it was on a great weather day!

Therefore, I completed two sections today in a total of five and a half hours, including the road walking in between, walking slowly to enjoy the day, and taking breaks to enjoy the day. I would say that I walked a total of eight and a half miles today. One and a half from the church at Wembury to the Yealm River ferry, two miles on roads, and five miles from above Stoke Beach to River Erme.

I walked up a road to the Schoolhouse Café in Mothecombe for a late lunch. They kindly called a taxi for me that I took back to my B&B in Noss Mayo. I had a nice romantic dinner by myself on this warm evening as I sat outside on the upstairs patio of The Ship Inn seeing the tower of the church above the town of Noss Mayo as I ate. An absolutely beautiful day!

DAY 25 (DAY 112) STATS: 8.5 MILES TOTAL, ABOUT 6 NEW MILES, AND THE REST REPEAT OR ROAD WALKING. 5.5 HOURS. PURPLE SHOES. PUB IN NEWTON FERRERS, WHICH IS ACROSS NEWTON CREEK NEAR RIVER YEALM AND NOSS MAYO IS "THE DOLPHIN INN" AND CAN BE WALKED TO FROM NOSS MAYO. NOTE THAT WHEN I WAS IN NOSS MAYO THIS YEAR "THE SWAN INN" HAD BEEN CLOSED DOWN, SO THE OTHER OPTION IN NOSS MAYO IS "THE SHIP INN."
Information about the Carswell Beach Hut from canopyandstars.co.uk/britain/england/devon/carswell-farm/carswell-beach-hut, and from carswellcottages.com/holiday-cottages-south-devon-coast/the-beach-hut.

BIGBURY-ON-SEA ACROSS RIVER AVON TO BANTHAM TO THURLESTON–Saturday, 21 April 2018

"Please wave or shout to attract attention. For your own safety wait here to be directed to the pick-up point." – Instruction sign to cross River Avon via ferry.

I took a taxi this morning to get from Noss Mayo to Bigbury-on-Sea. Sometimes you just have to pay to make life easier. The woman driving asked me, "Are you traveling by yourself?" I answered that for over four weeks I am until my husband joins me. She replied, "You are a brave lady." Wow that word "brave" once again! It has been a while since I had heard or thought about that word. So when she said it, I was happy to hear the reminder again.

I was dropped off at a road above the car park in Bigbury-on-Sea, so I needed to walk down to the car park where I ended my walk and was picked up from last year. What a difference a season makes. Last year the car park was full of cars and people. Today, there was hardly anyone around. I had a view out to Burgh Island. I had one and a half miles to the ferry across River Avon, which only runs from 10:00am to 11:00am and then again from 3:00pm to 4:00pm, seasonally. I had conflicting information about today if it was running yet or not. One website said it doesn't start till the 25th of April, another website said not till May, and a third website said it had already started back on 2nd of April. My next B&B woman said the 2nd of April date was accurate for this year, so after I was dropped off at just before 10:00 I had a bit over an hour, but not more than that otherwise I would not make the ferry, to walk the one and a half miles, which usually averages me 45 minutes.

The weather forecast for today said there could be a passing shower or rain this morning with clearing and warmth for this afternoon. Just as I was at the car park and starting on my walk the only passing rain shower happened, enough to get my rain jacket on, and that was all the rain thankfully for the day. I considered going out to Burgh Island today actually, but preferred to make the ferry between 10 and 11, so I did not go to the island.

I started on a small path above beach which turned into a grassy path, then crossed a road to another long grassy path that had an uphill slope for a while as I walked next to cauliflower fields. Looking back behind me, I had views to Burgh Island. I arrived at Mount Folly Farm where a sign said a half mile back to Bigbury-on-Sea and a mile to the ferry. I crossed the road again and here the sign said a half mile to the ferry and a mile back to Bigbury-on-Sea. Hmmmm. There was a downhill slope on some grass with views of the mouth of the River Avon with Bantham Ham across the river. This grassy slope led to a path by small beach that lead to a flat grassy path. Before I knew it, there was a sign pointing to the Seasonal Ferry. I took a right turn and I was at the instruction sign for the ferry at a place called Cockleridge Ham. That only took me about 30 minutes, and I was surprised at my faster walking time this morning.

The sign said, "Cockleridge to Bantham Ferry. The ferry operates on demand between 10am and 11am and again between 3pm and 4pm. From Monday the 2nd of April until Saturday the 22nd of September. The ferry does not operate on Sunday. Please wave or shout to attract attention. For your own safety wait here to be directed to the pick-up point." Wow good thing I had been a day ahead of schedule on my walking, otherwise I would have arrived here on a Sunday and would not have been able to take the ferry, thus probably would have needed a taxi to take me around.

I held my arms up high in the air and waved them around as best as I could. I heard a shout back at me although I couldn't hear what he said, so for fun I shouted, "Ferry." I saw the small motorboat coming across the water and noticed that he pointed ahead to a different part of the beach that I was standing on indicating that I should walk down the rocky and sandy beach a short distance to the pick-up point just down the beach a very short distance. Within a few minutes I was motored across the river in the boat. Another missed section of the SWCP completed!

I walked up out of the ferry landing area after paying £3/$4 for the ferry ride. A sign told me I had one and a quarter miles to Thurlestone, my destination for the day, going through the car park of Bantham Beach, but according to the booklet, the official path goes around Bantham Ham and is two and a half miles to Thurlestone, so I started that on a paved path road that turned into some wide grassy paths around the small peninsula. I stayed well in the middle of all the paths because off in the brush were warning signs for Adders. Snakes. I really did not want to come across any of those, and fortunately I did not. It would probably be worse for me to see a single Adder than all the cows I have encountered combined. I had a view of part of the beach below with rocks and turquoise waters and soft sand and it was a pretty view. After going around the little peninsula, I went down to the beach on this blue sky warm day. I took off my purple shoes and socks and sat for a while on a rock. I ate a small snack. There were paddle boarders and surfers out in the turquoise waters. Small children in wet suits were playing in the sand. I listened to the rolling white waves coming in to hit the sand and rocks. I had views of the grassy hillside ahead, and out to Burgh Island and Bigbury-on-Sea as well. It was quite a quaint picturesque area.

I sat for a while since I had less than two miles to walk, and then walked through and in between some of the dark colored rocks, some of which were covered in green seaweed, and the water, paddling in my bare feet. I walked across the beach occasionally paddling in the cold water to the less popular end of the beach with small pebbles and seaweed. I sat again to let the feet dry off before I put my shoes and socks back on. I left the beach with a sign that said one mile to Thurlestone.

I walked around the edge of a grassy field that at first was flat then slightly uphill the grassy hillside with sheep inland. I had views back to another beach below the hillside and across to Burgh Island, Bigbury-on-Sea, and the headlands beyond. At the top of the hill I had views ahead to what I recall was Hope Cove and the headlands beyond as I started walking along the edge of Thurlestone Golf Course. A faded information board sign greeted me to the golf course. The sign had light colorful images of a few birds and wildflowers. The sign told me, "Ahead lies Thurlestone Golf Course, stretching for one and a quarter miles alongside the Coast Path. Founded in (unreadable), the golf club now has thirteen hundred members. Unfortunately the slates and gravels which make up the cliffs along this stretch of coastline are vulnerable to erosion from the sea and over the last hundred years several yards of the course have collapsed into the water, bringing golfers and walkers into even closer contact."

The board also talked about wildlife on the golf course including that it "provides a habitat for many birds including Rock Pipits, Pied Wagtails and Wheatears. In the scrub and hedgerows you may be lucky enough to see a Cirl Bunting one of Britain's rarest birds. Overhead Buzzards and (unreadable) can be seen." There was also a small paragraph about Coastal Plants, but unfortunately most of that to me was unreadable, perhaps something about a pink flowers, perhaps Sea Campion and Sea Beet.

About two and a half hours after I started walking this morning, including my time getting across River Avon and my time at the beach, I passed by the footpath that crossed the golf course where I had walked inland from the Thurlestone Church last year. Therefore, two missed sections of the SWCP completed, from Bigbury-on-Sea to the ferry this morning, and from Bantham to Thurlestone after that!

I then repeated some walking, continuing near the grassy hillside with a few sandy beaches below, some with rocks, and one longer sandy beach, around the golf course, with views out to the blue waters, Hope Cove and beyond on this warm day. Not hot like yesterday, but dry and warm. I arrived at the clubhouse of the golf course where I figured it was time to make peace with golf courses as I thought about the downpour on the golf course in Par last year, and had some lunch in the clubhouse.

I briefly sat on the Thurlestone Beach before walking the mile and a half on roads inland to my working-farm-bed-and-breakfast. I chose this place because it seemed centrally located for my walks in this area and I booked three nights here. The view from my room was of part of their garden, and part of a hillside with a few sheep.

DAY 26 (DAY 113) STATS: 4.0 SWCP MILES TOTAL INCLUDING 1.5 MILES BIGBURY-ON-SEA TO RIVER AVON FERRY PLUS 2.5 MILES BANTHAM TO THURLESTONE GOLF CLUBHOUSE. 3.5 HOURS INCLUDES WAITING FOR FERRY AND LOTS OF BEACH TIME. EXTRA MILE AND A HALF ON ROADS TO B&B. PURPLE SHOES.

SOAR MILL COVE TO SOUTH SANDS – Sunday, 22 April 2018

"When the fog clears, sunshine follows." - Bronnie Ware

Since I had been one day ahead of schedule the past few days, Marion of this working-farm B&B helped me organize my next few days. I made a few phone calls this morning to rearrange B&Bs, Luggage Transfers, and reserve taxis. More on all that later.

Marion also kindly dropped me off at the Soar Mill Cove Hotel this morning as we drove through some fog to get there. I was already starting to get nervous. After she drove away, it was completely foggy. I could not see that far in front of me and I said to myself, "No way am I walking in this." I hoped that it would burn off soon as the weather forecast did not call for fog, and I wondered if perhaps it was just localized, so I went inside the lounge area of the hotel, and I waited. And waited. And waited. I glanced through magazines. I talked with a large family. I took their family photo as they all gathered on the couch. I told them why I was waiting. I looked out the window. Still foggy. I looked through more magazines. I looked at the menu of the hotel restaurant. I waited. I recalled that last year I sat in this same lounge area because I did not want to walk in the strong winds.

Finally about an hour and a half later one of the family members said to me, "Look, the fog is lifting. You can see the sea!" I was delighted, but there was still some lingering fog, so I waited another half hour just to be sure. Then at noon, I walked outside to blue skies with white clouds and I was grateful. Yes, when the fog cleared, there was sunshine. During the two hours that I waited, I was actually afraid that I might not get the chance to do this walk at all today and thus not complete all the SWCP miles. But that was not the case, and I nearly skipped with joy down the grassy field from the hotel down to the beach at Sour Mill Cove.

Well, I didn't really skip, but at one point when there was a short boggy section, I did leap a bit to avoid getting my purples shoes wet. Once down at the beach, I walked onto the beach for a few photos, and then started the three miles to South Sands. The path started to slightly climb on some grass then turned into a dirt path as it continued to climb. There were amazing views of Sour Mill Cove and its small beach, the hill I had climbed down from last year to get into this valley and up to the hotel, and more views back to headlands beyond where I had walked last year. Sour Mill Cove had a few large rocks sitting in the middle of the turquoise water, the hillsides surrounding above were covered with green grass and the light brown color of the cliff edges, and with the blue sky, white clouds, and yellow gorse it was a beautiful early afternoon and I was glad the fog lifted. I took so many photos of this scene in just the first quarter of a mile.

The path flattened out after a long but gentle climb, and I realized that I was glad that I did not walk this section in the wind last year, as one short area was closer to a hillside where I might have felt uncomfortable with the thought of being blown over. I crossed over a few bridges over streams then a bit more climbing. Someone hand-drew arrows on white paper to mark the path as I went along and this continued all day. I wasn't sure if this was really for the SWCP as there were plenty of regular acorns and arrows, so I wondered if perhaps there was some event that these particular arrows were specifically for, such as an organized run. The climbing became gentler until it flattened out again, and remained flat for much of the rest of the walk.

There was a slight breeze on this warm day, and it was nice and quiet, except for a few chirping birds and an ever so light sound of lapping waves from way down below. The views out to the blue and turquoise seas and the lighter blue sky and nothing beyond were just so beautiful and peaceful and calming, especially after a bit of a stressful morning waiting for the fog to lift. A couple of white sailboats dotted the blue seas.

Several people were out walking today. There was lots of yellow gorse, and inland were large fields of yellow rapeseed. I remembered seeing these bright yellow fields in the Cotswolds years ago, and it was refreshing to see them here along the coast. With a farmhouse and some cows, along with the bright yellow rapeseed, and with green fields, it all made for some scenic inland photos on my left. The path remained flat as I passed over a beautiful cove below on my right. About an hour and fifteen minutes after I started walking a sign told me three miles to Salcombe, which meant I had about a mile to South Sands. All the other signs I had seen today pointed to Salcombe but did not give mileage.

When I passed the sign that said two and a half miles to Salcombe, there were about ten horses right near the path, so I slowly moved around them, giving them plenty of distance between us, and took some photos for Scott. There was a long but gentle descent with small loose rocks that I walked slowly on so as not to slip that led to Starehole Bay with some very blue waters. Walking around Starehole Bay and its corner called Bolt Head was on some stone path and a few stone steps up and around and a few steps down the corner of this rocky outcrop. It was then flat, with a view down the Kingsbridge Estuary into Salcombe, and I even walked through a few trees.

I realized that I was actually glad I did not do this entire stretch in the wind last year, even though most of it was flat on wide grassy paths and inland enough. I would just not have enjoyed and appreciated the scenery as much as I did today. Last year I felt sad for missing many sections of the SWCP. But looking back I am glad I followed my instincts, intuition, courage, and bravery to make the decisions I did. The end result was that I could once again enjoy the SWCP during this almost-summer-like spring this year!

About an hour and 45 minutes after I started walking I arrived at the South Sands Hotel, where I was dropped off last year to walk to Salcombe. I stopped in for some lunch and realized I had walked from one fancy hotel to another fancy hotel today. I was originally going to walk the repeat to Salcombe, but with my late start and bit of stress from the morning, I decided that since I completed the missed section of three miles, I would be happy with my day! After picking up a sandwich in the café next door which would be my dinner, I called Marion and she kindly picked me up.

Then I was in for an experience at this working-farm B&B that I have never done before in my life. Feeding time at the farm! First of all, this house and farm dates back to 16th century. That in and of itself is fascinating and historical. Beams in the ceilings, for example. I went with Marion for over a half hour as I watched her first feed some chickens and feed some baby lambs in a barn. After, we walked through the graveyard of a church, which had amazing views of the graveyard and church in the foreground and farmland in the background including yellow fields of rapeseed, to one of her fields. Here I watched Marion feed some sheep and baby lambs. She threw down some grain or something for them to eat, and also fed the baby lambs some milk from bottles. I was even allowed to pet the baby lambs. We walked to a second field to feed and put a blanket on her horse. Of course, though, there were her cows in this field, so I faced my fears, summoned up my bravery and courage, and made peace with cows, as I walked quite close to them in her field - but on the far side of Marion. And that was my half hour of farm life!

As we were in these fields feeding the animals, there were other fields all around us with green farmland, bright yellow rapeseed, and the tower of the church. It felt so peaceful to be out in the countryside. As we walked back to the house, I stopped by the church once again for a few more photos. The Church of All Saints in South Milton has origins dating back to the 12th century, and was rebuilt and enlarged in the 13th and 15th centuries. The church was not open to go inside, but the outside made for some very beautiful photos. A nice ending to a nice day. Once the fog lifted and the sunshine followed.

DAY 27 (DAY 114) STATS: 3.0 MILES. ONE HOUR AND 45 MINUTES. PURPLE SHOES. Information on The Church of All Saints from britishlistedbuildings.co.uk/church-of-all-saints-south-milton.

ELENDER COVE/PRAWLE POINT TO LANNACOMBE TO START POINT LIGHTHOUSE – Monday, 23 April 2018

"It's a Boy! Royal Baby: Duchess of Cambridge Gives Birth to Boy." – BBC Breaking News

After saying my goodbyes and thank yous to Marion, leaving a day earlier than originally planned, I took a taxi past the village of East Prawle towards the car park of Prawle Point to see if we could find the footpath that I took last year up from Elender Cove where I somehow met a famous author and artist who gave me a couple of rides and I visited him in his home. Today the taxi driver was able to find the public footpath, and I had a quarter of a mile to walk down to Elender Cove to officially start walking on the SWCP the three missed miles around Prawle Point to Lannacombe.

The path started out flat overlooking the beautiful cove with its deep blue and turquoise waters surrounded by small white crashing waves against brown rocks at the coastline under the green and rocky hillsides of Gammon Head above. I had a bit of scrambling on some rocks to do and a bit of an uphill climb out of the cove. A few purple wildflowers lined the path. The path remained flat to and around Prawle Point with its National Coastwatch Institution lookout and a visitor center. "Prawle Point is the most southerly point of Devon and there has been a lookout here since Anglo Saxon Times. 'Prawle' means lookout in old English," according to today's booklet.

I followed a gentle descent down to a large grassy area. At a sign that said two miles to Lannacombe two friendly cows came up to the gate that I needed to walk through, probably just asking me for food. Before I opened the gate, I talked to them calmly, as Marion taught me to do yesterday, and as I opened the gate, the cows kindly backed up to let me through. They really did seem friendly and just curious. For the first time, I did not feel nervous as I walked passed them this time. Please note though that I would never take cows for granted to be friendly and curious however.

I had very flat walking for quite a while, with rocky hillsides and grass to my left, which then turned into some crops to my left. I thought perhaps the crops looked like rutabaga or turnips or some other root vegetable. As I was taking photos of the crops, a woman passed by me and so I asked her if she knew what the crops were. She thought maybe they were sugar beets. It turned out that the crop was a "fodder beet" because I asked the woman at my B&B later this evening. She told me that fodder beets are not used for human consumption but are used for feeding cattle.

As I walked along there were small waves crashing on brown rocks quite close to me on my right, and a view back to Prawle Point behind me, including seeing the Prawle Arch rock formation at the tip of Prawle Point. The path continued to remain very flat with grassy fields and then turned into large dirt patches of crops that have not yet been planted or had just not yet begun to grow. I passed above a beach as well that was also quite close to me. I passed by a sign that told me I had one and a half miles to walk till Lannacombe. There were more dirt patches of crops as I continued walking as well as a herd of cows on the other side of an electric fence. At some point along the way a small sign reminded me that I was on a Public Right of Way, with the following requests: "Please keep to the path; keep dogs under close control (not applicable to me); leave gates as you find them; respect private property; and follow the Countryside Code."

Then the scenery changed from all those crops to a dirt and rocky path with shrubbery and plants all around, and rocky hillsides up to my left. It was like I went from some domesticated lands to some wild lands. I had to watch my footing carefully as I navigated through the rocks on the path. Soon I had a half mile to Lannacombe, and at the quarter mile sign, I had a slight uphill climb followed by walking back down very slightly, near a bit of tall shrubbery, and finally on a track road into the small beach at Lannacombe, where last year the author/artist dropped me off. About an hour and forty minutes after I started my walk on the SWCP at Elender Cove this morning, I had completed yet another missed-mile section! I stopped briefly for a snack.

After those three miles, I walked a repeat walk from Lannacombe to the Start Point Lighthouse of two miles because I had plenty of time today, because my B&B would be easier to walk to from there, because I remembered this walk being very beautiful, and because I like visiting lighthouses. The path started out flat in and out of land owned by Down Farm. As I entered the farm a sign explained, "The 350-acre traditional Down Farm produces cattle for beef and sheep. We grow grass for making hay and silage, along with cereals including Wheat, Barley and Oats. We also run bed and breakfast in our farmhouse and have a self-catering cottage available. Our family has been farming here on this coast for over 140 years. Our farm lies in the South Devon Area of Outstanding Natural Beauty and on the Heritage Coast. It is also a Site of Special Scientific Interest. Our Conservation Stewardship agreement means that we use careful grazing to keep the bracken and scrub in check: this helps rare wild flowers and insects along the coastal edge. – Richard and Judy." My B&B for tonight was at this Down Farm.

The path continued around a rocky beach from above with views back to Prawle Point. It was so great to see all the distance I had just walked from. I walked around a headland I had seen ahead of me all morning that I was walking towards. Just around that headland, I started to have a view of the lighthouse that would remain in my view the rest of the walk. This was the beautiful part of the walk, with this constant view of the lighthouse.

I climbed up and over a small hill, and on the other side was the sign that points to Poole of 168 miles and to Minehead of 462 miles and a quarter of a mile to Start Point. In the distance beyond the water, there were familiar views to Hallsands, Beesands, Torcross, Slapton Ley, Blackpool Sands, and the headland beyond. A great view!

I had not checked the schedule of Start Point Lighthouse to see if it was open today or not, so I walked down the road towards it, but alas it was not open today. That was alright though since I took the tour last year. I took a few photos of the lighthouse, and started to make my way to the Down Farm B&B. I stopped briefly for another snack before walking up the road from the lighthouse, through the car park, and down the road for what seemed like almost a mile. I took a left down another road to the B&B and was staying at another working farm, with this house dating back to the 1390s! That is so fascinating to me.

As I walked into the house, greeted by Judy, her husband Richard came rushing out saying, "It's a boy!" At first I thought that perhaps one of their children or some other relative of theirs had a baby. It turned out it was William, Duke of Cambridge, and Kate, Duchess of Cambridge, giving birth to their third child, who is the fifth in line to the throne. Wow, I was in England for this event, I thought to myself, here at this moment! With the baby unnamed for now, the headlines read, "Prince George and Princess Charlotte have arrived at hospital to meet their new baby brother." (Well, even though I won't be in England for Prince Harry and Meghan Markle's wedding, at least I was in England for this birth.)

Judy told me about the thick walls that were built in homes without all the modern equipment and machinery used today. The thick walls were made of stone on the bottom, and also made out of horse hair, earth, and reeds. I find it fascinating that places like homes and churches are still standing over 600 years later!

Today I went from point to point – Prawle Point to Start Point. The weather for today was definitely not as warm as it has been, with cloud coverage and some breeze. Even so, it remained gratefully dry.

DAY 28 (DAY 115) STATS: 3.0 MILES ON SWCP FOR MISSED-MILES. 2.0 REPEAT MILES. AT LEAST ONE MILE EXTRA TO B&B. 3.5 HOURS TOTAL. PURPLE SHOES.

REST DAY IN BRIXHAM – Tuesday, 24 April 2018

"A series which helps prospective buyers find their dream home in the country." – The premise for a TV show called "Escape to the Country."

Being one day ahead of schedule, I booked an extra night at my other favorite B&B in Brixham, Beacon House, because of the delicious breakfasts. Kate's in Mawgan Porth is my other favorite. I took a taxi a long distance to Brixham because one of the roads near Slapton Ley, where I walked last year, was damaged from the storms over the winter here and subsequently buses were not running as usual. In addition, taking a taxi, even if a bit expensive, gave me easy door to door service and I was also able to take my luggage with me and save on using the Luggage Transfers service. Finally it turned out the taxi driver I had this morning was the same one I had last year from and to the Start Point Lighthouse, so it was like seeing a friend.

This is the same B&B in Brixham as last year that Scott met me at, although a different room, but with the same great view of the harbour. Amanda and Nigel greeted me warmly. I was looking forward to her breakfasts, and I was back in the "English Riviera" area of the SWCP.

My original plan for today was to walk the two and a half miles that I missed from Scabbacombe Sands to Sharkham Point. Alas today turned out to be a rest day instead. When I arrived in Brixham it was only lightly raining with the sun trying to come out. Since I only had two and a half miles to walk, I figured that since I had pretty much not walked in rain gratefully this entire four weeks, I would give it a go. I picked up a sandwich to take with me and found a taxi.

We drove to the Scabbacombe Sands car park but on our way the rain was getting heavier, and it looked foggy. I told the taxi driver that if it looked like this when we arrived at the car park, I would have him take me back to Brixham. Well needless to say it was even foggier at the car park itself. My courage told me to not walk today. I wanted to enjoy my walk, and to be able to see the views. The taxi driver thus took me back to Brixham, and we hoped together that tomorrow's weather would be a vast improvement.

Back in Brixham, I ate my sandwich sitting at a café near the harbour where I ordered something to drink. I went back to my nice B&B to finish yesterday's writing. Then I took a nap. It seems that I nap on my rest days. I guess I needed to rest on my rest day. I watched some TV, eventually went out to eat again, and watched more TV. I didn't even take one photo today.

I have actually been watching a bit of TV in the evenings some of my days the past several weeks. I got addicted to watching four different shows, all with similar themes. The shows are "Location, Location, Location," "Love it or List it," "Escape to the Country," and "A Place in the Sun." The general theme for all four shows is basically the same where the hosts are real estate agents showing people who are looking to buy their dream homes three or four properties around the UK or other countries. The "Location, Location, Location" show helps people find a home in the perfect location. The "Love it or List it" show actually has one host showing new homes and the other host showing renovations on the people's current home, and the people decide whether they are going to sell their current property and buy a new one, or stay in their updated current property.

"Escape to the Country" is about people who want to leave living in the city and move to their dream home in the country. (Sounds like me!) "A Place in the Sun" shows properties overseas in other countries and people can decide if they want to stay in their current location or move abroad or buy a second property. What I really enjoy about all these shows, even though many of the episodes I have been watching are several years old, is that not only do I get to see the interior of some great international homes, but also some of the shows show some great properties in locations I am familiar with, such as the Cotswolds, and even several places along the SWCP in villages and towns that I have walked in, or nearby in the counties of Somerset, Devon, Dorset, and Cornwall. I get to see insides of homes that are centuries old, or modern, or a combination of both. I also get to see properties in other countries like Ireland, Spain, France, and Italy. It all just makes me dream about living here.

One TV show that I have not been watching, but really should be, is more episodes of Doc Martin. I ended up watching only the first four episodes of season one last year and really enjoyed them. Apparently I still have the rest of season one, and then seven or eight more seasons, and about 57 or more episodes, to watch.

DAY 29 (DAY 116) STATS: NO SWCP MILES. NO HOURS. NO EXTRA MILES. WAS WEARING HIKING BOOTS FOR THE TAXI DRIVE BUT CHANGED TO PURPLE SHOES WHEN OUT IN BRIXHAM.

SCABBACOMBE SANDS TO SHARKAM POINT (AND BRIXHAM TO BERRY HEAD AND BACK) – Wednesday, 25 April 2018

"Rise and Shine - It's Beach Walkin' Time!" – Hanging on the wall in dining room at breakfast of my B&B in Brixham.

Because of yesterday's disappointment of the fog and rain and not being able to walk, I wanted to ensure that I would be able to do the walk today. Therefore, last night I checked the weather forecast, from three different sources, and it looked like the best time to walk, with full sunshine, was early in the morning between the hours of 6:30am and 9:30am. How would I work that out though, as I usually eat breakfast at 8:00?

I thought about it and figured that walking two and a half miles would take be about an hour and a half to two hours, about my usual pace, plus there were two climbs today, as well as a footpath to get me to the SWCP. I thought for the first time, what if I was able to do the walk before breakfast? Let's calculate the timing…If I get up just before 6:00, get a taxi to take me to Scabbacombe Sands at 6:15, start walking at 6:30, walk till 8:30, then arrange for a taxi back from Sharkam Point, I would be back for a 9:00 breakfast.

I went downstairs last night to talk to Nigel about my plan and to see if I could have breakfast at that time. He said that time would be no problem, but I might want to book the taxi last night for this morning to ensure that I had a ride. I went back to make a few phone calls, but no taxi numbers that I called had a taxi available. I went back downstairs to ask Nigel if he had any other taxi numbers and he went to look. A few moments later he said that he did not, but then he kindly, miraculously, like a guardian angel, offered to take me to the car park for Scabbacombe Sands at 6:15 in the morning. He would coordinate with walking his dogs before he had to be back at the B&B to serve breakfast to his other guests.

As we looked at a map, I also realized that once I got to Sharkham Point I could walk back on the roads to Brixham, taking about a half hour instead of trying to arrange for a taxi to pick me up at a place I probably would not have mobile reception anyway. I would still be back by breakfast time, and I could even call Nigel once I was closer to town and had mobile reception if I was going to be later than 9:00. I thanked Nigel so much and really appreciated the ride. I even thought to myself if he had not offered this to me, I wondered how I would have been able to do today's walk in the bright sun. I may have had to gone later in the late morning or early afternoon when it was predicted that rain would occasionally fall, and I really just did not want to do that. Anyway Nigel offered, so I didn't have to wonder.

And you know also, if I wasn't one day ahead of my schedule from several days ago, and if I didn't arrive in Brixham a day early, I may have had to walk in the late morning or early afternoon today anyway with the possibility of rain, and not in the bright sun, since my original plans would have been to arrive in Brixham early this morning and do the walk in the afternoon. Life certainly does have an amazing way of working itself out at times. For this, I was grateful.

This morning Nigel dropped me off at the car park for Scabbacombe Sands at 6:35, and the sun was already rising as a full bright sun. I took a great photo of the rising sun over the seas as I started down a green grassy slope with a few green trees and a sign saying, "Scabbacombe Sands Link to Coast Path." I had a fifteen minute walk on this grassy slope heading downhill towards the SWCP. I was familiar with this walk because Scott and I did this last year on his second day here, but we headed towards Kingswear that day with the seas on our left, and this time I would be headed in the Brixham direction with the seas to my right. I started my early morning walk down the grassy slope to the sounds of birds chirping and cows mooing (on the other side of a fence), and to the sound of sheep baaing and the lapping waves on Scabbacombe Beach. The grass was wet with the morning dew, but my hiking boots kept my feet dry.

After I took a few early morning photos of the large yellow sun rising, and a few sheep on the path, and the beach down below of Scabbacombe Sands surrounded by green hillsides, I took off the jacket I had put on because I didn't know if it would be chilly this early in the morning and I had my first of two climbs for the day. This one was long and started out steep but became gentler towards the top. Good exercise first thing in the morning. As I climbed, I looked back and had views to Scabbacombe Sands, the hillside Scott and I climbed last year where last year there were some horses right on the path, and one boat motoring by in the early morning sun. The greens and blues had a different tint to them this early in the morning. Different shades of my favorite colors. When I got to the top of the climb I stopped for a snack of a protein bar as I had not eaten anything yet and it would be several hours before I would have a proper breakfast.

The path became flat on grass, and the glorious sun was shimmering on the seas. I already had views ahead of Sharkham Point and Berry Head as a rabbit hopped across the path. The flat path continued until I had a gentle descent down a grassy field with views of the next beach, Man Sands, a large white house ("former coastguard cottages - now holiday cottages" – to add to my "expensive-places-to-stay-someday" list), the green checkered farmland inland, Sharkham Point in the distance, and the next climb I would soon be doing. It was so quiet and peaceful out this morning. Perhaps I should do more walks this early in the morning.

Inland on the other side of Man Sands beach was what looked like a small lake, but I'm not sure what it was exactly, perhaps more like a pond, as I walked across some of the rocks on the beach, then over a bridge made out of larger rocks which was over the stream running off from the lake or pond, and then walked on some sand of Man Sands beach. A sign told me I had three miles to Brixham just under an hour after I started walking from the car park. The full bright sun was shining brightly and shimmering in the water.

The second climb of the morning was another long climb and moderately steep. I didn't think I would see anyone else walking this morning, but I did pass by a man and his dog. I wore my hiking boots today because I knew of the climbs, and also it turned out that there was a lot of wet grass from the morning dew to walk through even after the original grassy area earlier. At the top of this climb were views back to Man Sands, the large white house, the green hillsides, the deep blue waters, and back to the hillside on the other side of Scabbacombe Sands. One brown field of a crop inland completed this beautiful scene.

The path flattened out again with brush and shrubs on either side of me as I continued to face the sun as it continued to warm me up. I had a gentle zigzag decent, still in the brush and shrubs and some trees. A woman jogger was going up this zigzag, and after her when I passed another man with his three dogs, I figured I was getting closer to Sharkham Point and Brixham.

I walked above a small secluded and isolated-looking beach as the path continued to be flat with more shrubbery. The flat turned into a grassy field as I approached Sharkham Point, my destination for the early morning. From here I could look back at the views of where I had been walking this early morning, with so much green on the hillsides with deep blue waters and light blue skies. I read a sign that said, "Please help The National Trust to care for this property by not leaving litter, lighting fires or damaging trees or plants, and keep your dogs under close control." It was just so amazingly beautiful out this morning.

I had views ahead to Berry Head with its lighthouse as I walked around Sharkham Point before making my way inland just a bit to find the car park to start my walk on the roads back to Brixham. I also took photos of a bench where last year I took a photo of Scott sitting on the bench. The sun was still out but now a few white clouds were out as well with views all the way back to Man Sands and Scabbacombe Sands.

Just as I was trying to figure out where the car park was to start my walk back to Brixham on the roads, a guardian angel appeared out of the small paths in the area, the only other person around at this moment. A man carrying a fishing pole had just come back from doing some fishing. Ironically we were both going to ask each other where the car park was as there were lots of small paths in the area that weren't clear as to which ones would lead to the car park. Together we found it as we spotted his car. He seemed nice enough, and I would not do this back home, but I decided to ask him kindly for a ride as far as he was willing to drive back to Brixham so that I would not have to walk some of the roads. I shall forever be so grateful to this kind man because he actually drove me all the way back to the harbour area of Brixham. I could not believe that was happening to me. It would have been a long walk back on the roads I realized, and here I was meeting up at that exact right moment with the only other person this morning at Sharkham Point with a car. Life certainly does have an amazing way of working itself out at times. For this, I was grateful.

My walk today, in the bright shining sun, had been surrounded by two guardian angels, Nigel and this man carrying a fishing pole. Not to mention my timing of being a day ahead of schedule. You know, a few weeks ago at the St. Just in Roseland Church I really started to wonder more in the possibility of a guardian angel above all the guardian angels, and in the greater universe in general also taking care of me. But after my ride this morning, with the rain and fog yesterday, with no taxis available, and with avoiding a long walk on roads with only one other person at Sharkham Point, I think I need to believe that there is not only a greater universe in general, but also that there is a guardian angel above all guardian angels, and that there is someone or something out there that is greater than me that is watching over me and helping me out when I absolutely needed it. Not to mention that I have also walked in about 95% dry conditions the past just-over-four weeks, compared to some of the weather conditions I had last year. Life certainly does have an amazing way of working itself out at times. And for all this, I am truly grateful.

By 8:20 I was in the car park with the man carrying his fishing pole and with his ride, by 8:30 I was at the harbour in Brixham, and by 8:40 I was back at my B&B, twenty minutes early for breakfast. I had an excellent breakfast consisting of a large bowl of mixing granola and muesli together, topped with yogurt and lots of various fresh fruit, followed by "Amanda's Light" breakfast of "avocado and sweet cherry tomatoes topped with lemon basil dressing and feta cheese all on toast." It was a delicious breakfast after my early morning beautiful sunny walk.

During breakfast, I chatted with a couple also staying here, and when I mentioned that I had been walking the SWCP on my own thus far this spring, once again I heard the words, "You are a brave lady." Amazing how that word, brave, has come up for me so often last summer and now again this spring. Part of me doesn't consider myself brave per se actually, even with all the times that I have heard this. To me, walking the SWCP, along with all my other travels, including all my solo travels, is just me doing something that I love – walking and traveling! It doesn't feel that unusual or courageous to me. Perhaps to others however, I suppose it is brave and courageous, so I shall appreciate all the times when someone has called me brave, or has told me that it takes courage, and I shall take it all as a compliment and make those words ingrained more in me. And I have experienced some challenges during my walking, had to make some decisions about when to walk and when not to walk, and have walked many of the miles on my own, so yes, I should say that I am brave. Back on the 9th of June, as I was at the huge pile of rocks on the highest point in all of the SWCP, the Great Hangman, which reminded me of the Cruz de Ferro rock pile on my Camino de Santiago walk, I mentioned Native American "Pocket Spirits." Perhaps I should now get the one that stands for "courage," which is represented by a symbol of an "Eagle Circle."

After breakfast, I took a nap, and eventually made my way out again to get some lunch of a healthy smoothie bowl topped with seeds and fresh fruit and edible flowers. Then I decided to risk getting caught in the possibility of rain in the afternoon and walked the flat, mostly pavement, to the Berry Head Lighthouse of one and a half miles each way from Brixham starting at the harbour that Scott and I walked last year, just to visit the lighthouse. I took a couple photos of the lighthouse once I arrived there, and saw a rain cloud as I made my way back. I went super light walking, just wearing my rain jacket, and also wearing jeans and purple shoes. Somehow I managed to make it back to the harbour area of Brixham just in time. I got caught in some rain as I made my way to a café that I went to yesterday for dinner to get some food for take away for my dinner later today. The rain lightened up to a shower as I made my way back to my B&B for the rest of the evening.

Today was a day of guardian angels, the greater universe in general, a guardian angel above all guardian angels, someone or something out there that is greater than me, the amazing ways life works itself out, and gratitude. And a day of reflecting on the words brave and courageous. All of this, after I followed the quote above to "rise and shine" and wake up early in the morning to do a beautiful sun-filled walk.

Oh, and Scott will be here in two days! I am sure that I mentioned that at some point this past four weeks that this time Scott and I preplanned that he would join me in Lyme Regis for my last ten days of walking.

DAY 30 (DAY 117) STATS: 2.5 MILES NEW, 3 MILES REPEAT, SO A TOTAL OF 5.5 MILES. 1.5 HOURS NEW MILEAGE, PLUS SOME TIME GETTING TO THE SWCP DOWN THE GRASSY SLOPE. ABOUT AN HOUR FOR REPEAT WALK. HIKING BOOTS FOR EARLY MORNING WALK, PURPLE SHOES FOR LIGHTHOUSE WALK IN THE AFTERNOON.

DAWLISH TO STARCROSS – Thursday, 26 April 2018

"The Black Swan has been the town emblem for well over forty years…There are records of black swans being on the Brook in the early 1900s." – From information board about "The Waterfowl of Dawlish Water."

It was sad to say my goodbyes and thank yous to Amanda and Nigel. They had been very nice hosts, kindly offering me an early morning ride, and providing me with another excellent breakfast. Along with a big bowl of granola and muesli with yogurt, lots of fresh fruit (pears, peaches, figs, berries, and grapes), and even freshly made warmed pieces of rhubarb, today's "Amanda's Light" breakfast was a "fresh baby leaf spinach and watercress egg flan topped with feta cheese." I had another long taxi ride to get me to Dawlish for my next walk, but again it was worth it for easy door to door service. Since I woke up this morning Scott and I have been texting getting him prepared to fly here!

After my taxi ride, I dropped off my luggage at my next B&B and started my walk to Starcross. It would be all flat mostly on pavement. I started walking first on the seawall just above the reddish-brownish colored sandy and small rocky beach of Dawlish paralleling the railroad tracks. I did check tide tables this morning and since I was here at low tide after walking on the seawall for a few minutes, I decided to walk on the beach instead. I confirmed with a couple of people that I could indeed walk to Dawlish Warren on the beach at this time and that there would be an exit from the beach, and since these people just came from there they confirmed it all for me. Otherwise I would have needed to take the alternate routes of the seawall, or even if really necessary on the main road if the tide was higher. As I walked on the sand and small rocks in my purple shoes, to my right were the small waves rolling up onto the beach. Looking back behind me was back to the small hillside Scott and I walked down last year, and headlands beyond. To my left was the seawall with the railroad tracks above, and the red cliffs above that were covered with green shrubbery.

Yes, the red colored scenery of this area! In fact, "The striking red cliffs along here are of Permian sands and they have been eroded by wind and rain to produce remarkable shapes. Ancient winds piled up these sands on what was a gravelly desert floor. In effect, you are looking at fossilized sand dunes. These red cliffs beside the railway are evidence of the desert conditions when they were formed some 280 million years ago." (This was information from the booklet for today who referenced "Geology in Devon" by Devon County Council.)

About a half hour after I started walking with my nice gentle stroll on the beach, I exited the beach just before a large red cliff called Langstone Rock in front of me. I walked on a short red path then on top of the seawall for another short bit still paralleling the railroad tracks. I crossed over the tracks by a pedestrian bridge with steps up and down to a car park in Dawlish Warren. A sign told me I had two and a half miles till the ferry at Starcross, even though I won't be taking the ferry, but that was my destination since that was where Scott and I took the train to last year to get the ferry. The sign also pointed a mile and a half back to Dawlish on a Public Bridleway. Another sign cautioned, "Coastal walk to Dawlish along sea wall can be dangerous at high tide. Use Coast Path." As mentioned, I checked the tides before I walked from Dawlish to this point. Before I continued walking towards Starcross, I stopped for some lunch at a café.

Once I continued walking, I was on a sidewalk next to a road and to my surprise I got caught in a thirty-second passing rain shower. I was not prepared so I got a bit wet, and once I put my rain jacket on, the shower had passed. I looked up at the sky and I guess there could have been the possibility of another passing rain shower so for now I kept the rain jacket on. The forecast didn't call for this, but at least it wouldn't be constant rain. Next I walked on a paved bike and walking path, with the railroad tracks now on my right side, and a few sheep in between me and the railroad tracks. The paved path turned into a wide sidewalk but it was still a bike and walking path as I entered the village of Cockwood. There were a very light few drops of another passing rain shower. I walked next to The Anchor Inn Pub and around the harbour of Cockwood at low tide with some various boats sitting on the sand. Well according to the booklet, it is always low tide here. There was some construction going on, but the biking and walking path was still available to bike and walk on.

I crossed the road and walked more on a paved wide sidewalk which was still the bike and walking path. I was next to a busy road on my right side with the railroad tracks to the right of the road. Other than the beach walk earlier, there really have been no views of the seas or coast today. A sign told me I had three-quarters of a mile left to walk till Starcross. I passed by a sign saying that the ferry from Starcross to Exmouth does actually not start running till 28 April, so it is a good thing that I did not need it today.

As I entered Starcross, I went into a charity shop, which is what I would call a thrift store. I did that yesterday too in Brixham, and a in a few other places like Plymouth. I still have wanted to buy some china like a tea cup and saucer or something small that would not break, and I have seen some, like all those in Plymouth, but haven't bought any because I am afraid they would break trying to pack it in my luggage. However, today I found a small piece of china that was a little round dainty tray only about three inches in diameter and shallow, painted with a couple of gentle light pink flowers, that seemed like I could pack it easily enough so as to not break it. In fact, the lady at the charity shop packed it for me very nicely in some bubble wrap. The back of the little tray describes my little treasure as being made in Audley Staffordshire England. I was happy to have finally found a piece of china!

I asked someone in this shop about trains and buses back to Dawlish. The bus would leave sooner than the train, so I went to the steps of the train station first to walk to the place that Scott and I got off the train last year in order to complete another missed-mile section of the SWCP of four miles in about two and a half hours! The bus stop was right next to the train station so I walked back a few feet and as I waited under the covering of the bus shelter another passing rain shower went by. Good timing.

Well I have now completed all the missed SWCP miles I set out to walk thus far by myself! Now Scott was packing and getting ready to fly to England to meet me in Lyme Regis tomorrow and walk the rest of my missed SWCP miles with me!

I took the bus back to Dawlish, answered a few questions from Scott about packing, and soon he was on the shuttle from our house to the airport. On my way out to dinner, I walked by the river running through Dawlish, known as "Dawlish Water" or "The Brook," and saw a few different waterfowl including a few black swans, and their baby cygnets, in the water. According to an information board about "The Waterfowl of Dawlish Water," it told me that "The Black Swan has been the town emblem for well over forty years…There are records of black swans being on the Brook in the early 1900s. However some time between the two World Wars, the line was lost. In the late 1940's, Captain C.R.S. Pitman…presented a pair of Black Swans to Dawlish…[and] Black Swans have inhabited the Brook ever since."

As I was eating dinner Scott arrived at the airport, checked in, and went through security.

DAY 31 (DAY 118) STATS: 4.0 MILES. 2.5 HOURS. PURPLE SHOES. PUB IN COCKWOOD IS "THE ANCHOR INN." PUB IN STARCROSS BEFORE THE FERRY IS "THE GALLEON INN," AND PUB IN STARCROSS A BIT BEYOND THE FERRY IS "THE ATMOSPHERIC RAILWAY INN."

TRANSPORTATION DAY – SCOTT ARRIVES – REST DAY IN LYME REGIS – Friday, 27 April 2018

"I can see the sea!" – On a cup coaster in our B&B room in Lyme Regis.

Last night as I watched my favorite TV shows about properties, Scott boarded the airplane to fly to Heathrow. This morning as I woke up, Scott landed in England. As I got ready to start my day, he went through passport control and picked up his luggage. As I had breakfast, he took a bus from the airport to the Woking train station. As I was in a taxi from Dawlish to Lyme Regis, Scott was on a train to Axminster. As I waited in the sitting room of our B&B in Lyme Regis, I found out that the new Royal Baby's name was Louis Arthur Charles, and Scott was still on the train. I called Scott a few minutes before he needed to get off the train just to make sure he was awake. I was glad I was not walking today, as it had been quite rainy and windy this morning.

Scott got off the train, got in a taxi and arrived at the B&B in Lyme Regis at 12:15! After over four weeks it was great to see each other again! We had a view of the seas in the distance and a church nearby from the window of our very nice room in Lyme Regis of this B&B that we will be staying in for five nights together. In fact when I originally entered the room of our B&B, which the door was labeled "Debby and Scott," I thought to myself, "Wow! I can see the sea!" It wasn't until later on that I discovered the cup coaster in the room saying the exact same thing. I booked this room for five nights because of the Undercliffs walk I needed to do this year, along with another walk, and wanted to make sure I had plenty of options for the best weather to do these walks. And because of the fossils and sea glass.

Now I am in the county of Dorset. And the Jurassic Coast. After giving Scott some time to settle in, we wandered down the road from our B&B to find some lunch. On our way we stopped in the church we saw from our window, The Church of St. Michael and St. George, which was consecrated in 1837. It looked different from other churches as this one had five conical shaped spires, rather than the tall square-shaped church tower that most churches I had been seeing have. For now, the rain had stopped. We ate lunch at a vintage retro 1950s café with photos and books about Elvis Presley and Marilyn Monroe. After eating, this café was next to an antiques and fossil shop so we spent a lot of time casually looking around. I even saw some more great china sets, but once again did not buy any because I was afraid of breaking them. We looked at fossils and learned a bit about finding them on the beaches near here, which would prepare us for a few days ahead.

We strolled along the Marine Parade waterfront of Lyme Regis running parallel to the rocky then sandy beaches, and then ambled up into the seafront gardens where I walked through last year when Scott was walking the Undercliffs. Looking below at the beaches as we sauntered through the gardens, the rocky beach below was empty of people, and the sandy beach that last summer was packed with adults and kids was empty and quiet today except for one woman walking her two dogs. Beyond the beaches was a view of the harbour with its boats surrounded by the breakwater to the right. Beyond the water to the left were the hills of Stonebarrow, Golden Cap, and beyond. There was a very light rain falling as we meandered up some steps and through the garden, eventually making our way back to the B&B so that I could finish yesterday's writing that I actually started earlier today when I was waiting for Scott to arrive.

Eventually we went back out to dinner walking along the quiet waterfront once again listening to the small waves on the beach with the tumbling sound of rocks as the water took them back to the seas. We photographed my purple shoes and Scott's shoes on the sand and on the rocks. We also walked by some...beach huts!

And a side note that as I was editing this day nearly five months later, I was curious where Ruth Livingstone was in her walking around the entire British Coast. As of 20 September 2018, she has now walked an impressive 3,901 miles and is currently along the coast of Scotland!

DAY 32 (DAY 119) STATS: NO SWCP MILES. LEISURLEY EXTRA WALKING IN LYME REGIS PROBABLY ABOUT TWO MILES ROUND TRIP. PURPLE SHOES.

THE UNDERCLIFFS: LYME REGIS TO SEATON – Saturday, 28 April 2018

"Coast Path. Please note that it takes approximately three and a half to four hours to walk to Seaton. The terrain can be difficult and walking arduous. There is no permitted access to the sea or inland along this stretch of the path." – Sign for the Undercliffs.

I have now found my third favorite B&B breakfast at the Dorset House in Lyme Regis. In fact, that was why I picked this place to stay when I did my itinerary planning. This place is more expensive to stay than other B&Bs, but knowing that Scott would be sharing this place with me, I wanted something nice. Their website's menu, the other reason why I picked this place, which describes them believing that "Breakfast is the most important meal of the day," and that "Locally sourced, homemade food is our passion," had a variety to choose from, so I decided to try to eat something different each of the five mornings we would be eating breakfast here. Today and every day, I started off with a bowl of their homemade organic granola, topped with all the fresh fruit and compote they displayed, and organic yogurt. That was followed today by a bowl of their Superfood Porridge topped with cashew butter, cacao nibs, banana slices, coconut flakes, and a bit of maple syrup. Scott ordered the Full English with bacon, sausage, baked Portobello mushrooms, baked tomatoes, baked beans, bread, and poached eggs. That should start us off quite well for today's walk through the Undercliffs.

By the way, did I ever mention that the new electric toothbrush base charger that I brought with me for these six weeks stopped working several weeks ago? Similar kind of situation like last year. This year, I started using my electric toothbrush like a normal toothbrush. Well Scott came to my rescue again and brought me another brand new electric toothbrush base charger.

After a great breakfast and packing our rucksacks for the day, Scott and I stopped by a small café to get some take away sandwiches for our walk through the Undercliffs. Last year I did not walk them because it was a "rest day" for me when Scott walked it spontaneously. And honestly, the thought of walking through "forest" for hours last year made me feel a bit nervous, so last year I chose to not walk this seven and a quarter mile part of the SWCP. However now in order to say that I have completed all the 630 miles of the SWCP, it was time to walk through my nervousness.

I will admit that part of the reason I had Scott join me on the rest of my SWCP missed miles at this point, aside from spending time with him and sharing some of the SWCP with him again, was to walk with me through the Undercliffs so I would not be doing this section by myself. Even so, I woke up in the middle of the night last night worrying about it. Would it be muddy? Were there ticks? Were there adders? Would it be dark? Would it feel spooky? Were there really no views? Was there really no walking on a beach?

I was even nervous as we sat through breakfast wanting to leave already so that I could start walking sooner than later to just get there and hopefully put all my worries to rest. In some ways I wish that some people hadn't described this walk to me like they did, making it sound spooky, including the words "difficult and arduous" as described on the path itself, so that I wouldn't be nervous. I have done plenty of forest walks in my hiking days back home, and had no problems. The good news was that the weather would be great today, even waking up to looking outside at the sun trying to peek out from behind the white cloud layer.

Anyway, back at the café where we bought our sandwiches, Scott also spontaneously bought the ingredients for cream tea, without the tea – scones, clotted cream, and jam. I was deep into my nervousness at the time that it didn't even occur to me what he was buying. I was not even thinking that we would be eating cream tea at some point during our walk.

Before I go on about our walk, here is how today's booklet describes what the Undercliffs are. "The Undercliff is a National Nature Reserve and a Site of Special Scientific Interest and is managed by Natural England. It covers an area of about 800 acres and is probably the wildest and most unspoilt area of the entire Coast Path. Some say it is the nearest thing you will find to a rain forest in Britain." The booklet describes a place called Goat Island, which I will describe more of later. It also talks about that some of the Undercliffs was inhabited, which I will describe more of later at Rousdon Cliffs. Furthermore, "Due to the Undercliffs being almost inaccessible a wide variety of plant and animal life has developed along this stretch of the coast. Up to 100 species of birds have been recorded including nightingales, birds of prey, sea birds and migrants. Also roe deer have been spotted, badgers, rabbits, grey squirrels, lizards and a very large variety of plants." I'm really not sure why I was nervous. This all sounded quite interesting.

Historically, the Undercliffs, which were "formerly open rough pasture, grazed by sheep and rabbits," formed over the centuries due to a series of landslips. "Recorded slips took place in 1775, 1829, 1839 (the Great Landslip – more detail later), and 1840."

Scott and I walked along the Marine Parade waterfront of Lyme Regis next to the beaches, through a car park next to the Lyme Regis Bowling Club with its lawn bowling green, and passed the bench where we sat last year as Scott made his last-minute decision to walk the Undercliffs. It was 10:30 with a sign telling me it was seven and a quarter miles to Seaton as we walked up a few steps near caravan homes and then an uphill climb already into some trees. There was already some mud, but at this point it was negotiable to walk around. I was wearing my hiking boots and had my hiking poles with me for this walk, which were invaluable today. Not too long after we started we now had seven miles to go, then a few feet later, six and three-quarters miles. Hmmm. At this point we were out in the open, not in the "forest" just yet, as the technical part of the Undercliffs had not yet started. At this point, we had views down to the harbour of Lyme Regis below and out to the hills of Stonebarrow, Golden Cap, and others beyond. This was an area called Ware Cliffs, where according to their information board, "you can stroll through fields and woodland, and discover a lovely viewpoint over the Cobb (harbour)." Well there was a view from here at least before entering the Undercliffs. There was some grass in the foreground and a bench which I took photos of Scott sitting on with the view.

There was a flat grassy area with more negotiable mud on the path and we still had the views for a bit and then passed the six and a half miles to go sign. Finally after about twenty minutes of walking thus far since just passed the lawn bowling green area where we entered the trees, we saw our first information sign saying, "Welcome to Axmouth-Lyme Regis Undercliffs National Nature Reserve." Presented by Natural England, the sign told us this about the Reserve: "Past and present earth movements known as landslips have produced a spectacular wilderness that is now predominantly woodland." (I wonder why no one told me this would be spectacular so I wouldn't be nervous.) The sign continued, "Landslips can occur at any time on the reserve and this creates temporary open ground habitat which is colonized by grassland and scrub before finally becoming woodland over time." (That sounds nice.) "This cyclical and active process creates a diverse mix of habitats which are home to many different plants and animals." (That sounds nice, too.) My nervousness lessened quite a bit.

The sign continued, "The reserve is internationally important for its wildlife, geology, fossil and active geomorphology. It forms part of the Dorset and East Devon World Heritage Site and is also part of the Sidmouth to West Bay Special Area of Conservation. We hope you enjoy your visit." Well I think that I shall do my best to enjoy! There was also a map on this sign pointing to "You are here" at the Ware Cliffs area, the beginning of the Axmouth to Lyme Regis Undercliffs NNR.

This sign also supplied important safety and caution information, such as requesting to "please keep to the way-marked Coast Path at all times," that the path between Axmouth to Lyme Regis (or Lyme Regis to Axmouth in our case as we were walking "backwards") "runs for over five miles through the reserve and it takes most people at least three and a half hours to complete," as well as other information about the terrain. Surprisingly the path started out to be very wide, flat, and dry, surrounded on either side with various green foliage. There were already lots of the various species of birds chirping, but I wasn't sure which of the 100 species they were. There was a second similar sign posted to the first one, and then finally the third sign, a wooden one:

"Coast Path. Please note that it takes approximately three and a half to four hours to walk to Seaton. The terrain can be difficult and walking arduous. There is no permitted access to the sea or inland along this stretch of the path." In other words, there is only one way and one way out. (Note that Seaton is a bit beyond Axmouth.) This was the sign I had known about in the past. While it was a great warning and caution sign, I took a deep breath, and then the enjoyment began.

To start, below my hiking boots was mud…and tree roots…and rocks. It was all flat and negotiable to start, but it was muddy and I had to watch my footing very carefully so as to not slip and fall. Birds continued to chirp. There were a few steps with wooden slats and watery mud in between. And more mud. After about a half hour of walking there was a boardwalk to walk on for a short distance. All around us so far were trees, plants, foliage, brush, ivy, vines, ferns, green, green, green, and even a few wildflowers. And you know what, it was not dark and spooky like I imagined. So far no ticks or adders. Yes, there was mud. Lots of it, and yes, my boots were getting muddy, but not soggy wet. Yes, Scott was with me, and that helped, and yes it was quite different and, in some ways, I was glad I wasn't walking this section by myself for my first time walking through this. It did have its own charm however. So far no beaches to walk on that was for sure, but all the trees and plants and foliage was different from any other part of the SWCP that I had been on (other than that shorter Hooken Undercliff section Scott and I walked last year from Branscombe to Beer), and while the mud made the walking tough in some ways, there was still plenty of beauty all around. My nervousness had disappeared.

About an hour after we started walking, we arrived at a section called Pinhay Cliffs. A sign here told us that Pinhay Cliffs are "A stunning wealth of wildlife and natural habitats can be found within every ridge and crevasse of the reserve," including that the ground is home to plants and insects, to look out for various types of shrubs, grassland can be home to orchids, nesting birds may be in chalk cliffs, there are ponds, pools, wet flushes, springs, and reed-beds each with their own unique flora and fauna, and various types of trees. With all this various beauty, what was there to be nervous about? This sign also had a "You are here" section and showed us how far we had walked since Ware Cliffs, and how much further we had to go, about a quarter of the way done by this point.

And we had a view of the water from here, with one fishing boat in the water below! There was even a bench to sit on to enjoy the view. I thought they said there were no views.

After another bit of walking another "Welcome to Axmouth-Lyme Regis Undercliffs National Nature Reserve" sign showed us how far we had walked now beyond Pinhay Bay. The path was quite flat surprisingly again for a little while, and it felt like it was paved. At 11:50 we passed by a sign that said we had completed two and a half miles and had five miles to go. That adds up to seven and a half, even though the original signs said seven and quarter, so I shall now go with the larger of the two numbers. One-third done.

We were then back to a smaller path with mud, mud, mud, and more mud. Here and there were some steps going up and some steps going down. Lots of green foliage continued, including some spots of white wildflowers. At 12:20 we had some views of the tan colored cliffs above and "inland" to our right. The hiking poles were definitely helping me with stabilization through and around the mud. At one point, I could actually hear some crashing waves below, and continued to hear lots of the various birds chirp in this lush green forest.

We did occasionally see other people on the walk today. There were originally two people who were ahead of us, then they were behind us, and we think they turned around at some point to go back to Lyme Regis. We saw a man and his dog going in the opposite direction. We saw two women. We saw another man and his dog. We saw a solo man. Near the half way point, we saw a group of three people walking in the opposite direction. One of them jokingly said to us, "You have seven hours left to go." I replied, "You have eight hours."

At this point we were at Rousdon Cliffs, the half way point. Already. Three and three-quarters miles done, three and three-quarters miles to go. It was 12:35, about two hours after we started walking. A sign at Rousdon Cliffs with a subtitle of "Turning back time" told us of some history of the area, including signs of human habitation. "The ruined buildings near the footpath were once a freshwater pumping station and an engineer's house. Water was pumped up to the Peek Estate and used for drinking water. Other signs of human habitation within the Reserve include East and West Cliff Cottages, found at either end of the Pinhay Estate, and Landslip Cottage at Downlands Cliff. The owners of Landslip Cottage, the Gappers, sold afternoon teas to tourists visiting the landslip, then a major attraction." Another "Welcome to Axmouth-Lyme Regis Undercliffs National Nature Reserve" sign again pointed to "You are here."

Here we decided to stop and have a picnic. We found a spot to sit in a small cleared area, although I was a bit concerned about ticks, but fortunately we never came across any at all today. First we ate half of the sandwiches we bought this morning. And half of the cream tea. Seemed like an appropriate place for this since unbeknownst to us someone happened to have sold afternoon teas near here anyway years and years ago! And yes, now that I wasn't nervous, I remembered Scott had bought the ingredients this morning, and he handed me the scones, jam, and cream. I happily took them, cut one scone in half with the wooden knife given to us at the café, and on one half I put jam topped with cream, and the other half cream topped with jam. I took a few photos of our cream tea picnic half way along the Undercliffs. I randomly gave one of the halves to Scott and I ate the other one, although I can't remember which of us ate it the Cornish way and which of us ate it the Devon way. By the way, at some point along the Undercliffs in the direction we were walking, I believe we went from the county of Dorset into the county of Devon.

As we enjoyed our picnic, we listened to the sound of the tumbling waves below bringing rocks back to the seas. At 1:05 we started walking again, first taking a photo of our boots coated with mud, as well as the bottom of our hiking pants also quite muddy, and soon there was more mud to walk through and around and negotiate. Mucky, wet, squishy, slippery mud. Green foliage continued. Some wildflowers such as primrose were around.

At 1:20 we had a really good view back to a long secluded-looking beach below (hence the sound of the tumbling rocks in the waves earlier) and the headlands and hillsides beyond in the distance, including Golden Cap. Yes, another view! As we walked on, to our right we had more views of the tan colored cliffs "inland." The path in general so far had been relatively flat, but the roots and the rocks and the mud made the walking not as easy. Occasionally there had been some less muddy and non-muddy stretches as well making parts of it easier. I would bet in the summer after all this mud dried up, the walking would be easier overall.

We walked a few yards off of the SWCP at an area called the Sheepwash at 1:45. "This sheepwash was built in approximately 1800…The sheep, sometimes brought from miles around, were washed before being sheared…It is said that washing sheep prior to shearing increased the value of the fleece at market by up to one third…When the sheepwash was being worked the landscape would have been very different. The 1840 Tithe map shows much of the Undercliffs as pasture and there would have been open fields and hedgerows here. After the Great Landslip in 1839 much of the land was abandoned and the woodland has grown up since."

By now I was actually getting a bit tired of walking with, and negotiating around, all the mud, all the mucky-wet-squishy-slippery-sometimes-inch-or-more-deep mud, as it was a bit tiring doing this after a few hours rather than just being able to walk on dry land. However we were still in the beauty of all the green of the trees, plants, foliage, brush, ivy, vines, and fern, surrounded on all sides of us, including overhead, which was still quite unique. There had been more wildflowers along the path, some purple flowers, perhaps bluebells, and others white flowers, which were either wild garlic or wild onion. The sounds of birds chirping continued as we kept walking. (Later I asked Lucy what the wildflowers were and she told me that the purple ones were indeed bluebells, "our native wildflower Hyacinthoides non-scripta and not the invasive Spanish bluebell, which is threatening our own variety," and the white flowers were wild garlic, "known as Ramsons and Latin name allium ursinum.")

The path was still flat for a little while longer, then it started to climb mostly with steps. And climb and climb. It actually felt like we were coming out of Undercliffs as the trees were thinning. Then all of a sudden the path widened and the sky was visible without trees, and at 2:05 we were at an area called Goat Island. The sign here explained part of what happened, and when it happened, that created this different landscape than all of the rest of the SWCP. The sign entitled "Goat Island, Where the earth slipped away," a well-documented one of the series of landslips that formed the Undercliffs, another Natural England sign explained:

"On Christmas Eve 1839 an enormous section of cliff slid seaward in an event known as the Great Landslip. A deep Chasm formed behind the landslide block, which later became known as Goat Island. Rainwater had soaked into permeable cretaceous rocks increasing their weight and these slipped towards the sea on the impermeable slippery clays lower down in the geological strata. The landslip carried with it wheat and turnip fields, which were later ceremonially harvested on Goat Island during a festival to celebrate the event. The landslip became very famous and was visited by thousands of people including Queen Victoria." This sign also pointed to "You are here" and indicated that we had two miles still left to go till Seaton from here. (I recalled that Queen Victoria may have also visited The Tea House in the 1800s that I sat near on my way to Mothecombe about ten days ago.)

But now I had walked and completed the Undercliffs!

Well, thanks to my husband, my guardian angel of the day, for flying all the way out here just to walk this section with me! We stopped to sit on a bench to eat the rest of the sandwiches and the other half of the cream tea to celebrate, overlooking the seas beyond and below us. I saw one fishing boat out in the water and wondered if it was the same one I saw hours ago. We took a photo of the mud caked onto our boots and the bottom of our pants legs, then proceeded to clean the mud off the boots figuring we were done with the mud for the day. We started walking again at 2:45.

No sooner did we start walking again after a short section on some grass, the path had more mud! And more steps going down and up! So much for the clean boots. I even wondered if this bit was still considered part of the Undercliffs because of the terrain. Finally, the path flattened out and was next to some green fields and also a field of yellow rapeseed. Soon we had one mile left till Seaton, continuing around some more fields, and passed by the other wooden sign with three-quarters of a mile left, similar to the one we saw miles and hours ago:

"Coast Path. Please note that it takes approximately three and a half to four hours to walk to Lyme Regis. The terrain can be difficult and walking arduous. There is no permitted access to the sea or inland along this stretch of the path." So then I wondered if this was the official end/start of the Undercliffs. In any case, at some point since Goat Island, I had walked and completed the Undercliffs!

Scott and I walked on a track road, and through the Axe Cliff Golf Club without incident, onto a paved road with a slight descent, turned left onto the busy Axmouth Road, crossed over the Axmouth Bridge going over the River Axe, took another left, and walked to the far corner end of the Esplanade at Seaton, where I had Scott and I walked to last year. And officially at 3:45 I had completed another missed section of the SWCP, the one that made me the most nervous, which turned out to be quite unique and beautiful and interesting, and thanks to Scott, with seven and a half miles, five and a quarter total hours, of which about four hours were walking, and of those about two and three-quarters hours were in the Undercliffs, I had completed another missed section of the SWCP!!

About fifteen minutes later, we walked down the road parallel to the Esplanade to a bus stop and took Bus #9A back to Lyme Regis, crossing once again from Devon to Dorset. By the way, the weather for today was actually perfect for the Undercliffs being in the trees much of the walk. It was cloudy out and around 50F/10C or maybe even a bit warmer, and dry. Any warmer than what it was might have been too hot to be in there, and gratefully it was not raining, nor windy, nor foggy, nor hailing, nor thundering.

After resting up a bit we made our way out to a well-deserved dinner. And you know what, now that I know what the Undercliffs were like, I would walk them again. Even by myself. Even with no beaches to walk on, because the forest with all its foliage was actually quite beautiful, interesting, and unique. Although if I ever get to walk the Undercliffs again on my own, I would prefer to walk in similar or better weather, and hope that perhaps it would not be quite as muddy.

DAY 33 (DAY 120) STATS: 7.5 MILES INCLUDING THE UNDERCLIFFS. 5.25 HOURS. HIKING BOOTS, EVENTUALLY CAKED WITH MUD. PUB IN SEATON ALONG THE ESPLANADE IS THE "HOOK & PARROT." PUBS INLAND LESS THAN A MILE IN AXMOUTH ARE "THE SHIP INN" AND THE "HARBOUR INN." Some information on the formation of the Undercliffs from wikipedia.org/wiki/The_Undercliff.

The Undercliffs April 28
Me with sign (photo credit: Scott Dungan); Muddy Boots at Goat Island
Scott with sign; Me in the Foliage (photo credit: Scott Dungan)

STONEBARROW TO CHARMOUTH TO LYME REGIS – Sunday, 29 April 2018

"Notice. Any person willfully injuring any part of this county bridge will be guilty of felony and upon conviction liable to be transported for life by the court." – An old sign in the concrete of a bridge between walking from Stonebarrow to Charmouth.

Another great breakfast to start my day consisted of Lyn's spelt pancakes with berry compote, along with her "cake of the day" treat, her small sampling of ice cream, and another bowl of her great homemade granola with fresh fruit and other toppings. Every day Lyn and Jason also supply us with a small treat in our room of chocolate covered cacao nibs.

After breakfast, Scott and I took a taxi to the car park at Stonebarrow. Since we did that last year too, I technically missed the inland diversion route of a mile and a half of walking from the beach at Charmouth to the car park at Stonebarrow, so that mile and a half was my first of two missed sections for today. Before we started the mostly road walking "backwards" from the car park to Charmouth, we wandered briefly around the top of Stonebarrow, with views out to Golden Cap and beyond to the Isle of Portland in one direction, and views out to Charmouth and Lyme Regis in the other direction, taking a side path around to the corner from last year where the diversion started due to a landslip cliff fall at Cain's Folly, and where we started last year heading for Golden Cap. This time we walked a short distance on the wide grassy path of the SWCP which consisted of mud and ended up back out to the car park. The walk continued going down the long road of Stonebarrow Lane with a slight descent that the taxi had just driven us up. After that road, following Coast Path Diversion signs and the booklet, we took a left on Bridge Lane crossing over a bridge to which I noticed an old sign on the bridge declaring, "Notice. Any person willfully injuring any part of this county bridge will be guilty of felony and upon conviction liable to be transported for life by the court. T. Fooks." I wondered how old this sign was, and was very careful as we crossed the bridge.

The walking here was all on a flat sidewalk that led to a footpath with a sign at that point that said we had a quarter mile to the seafront of Charmouth and to the Coast Path. We walked on another road next to some homes and to the car park, the Charmouth Heritage Coast Centre, and the beaches of Charmouth. That all took an hour, and just like that I had completed yet another missed section of the SWCP!

I took a few photos of some alternating blue and turquoise-colored beach huts with Stonebarrow, Golden Gap, and the other hillsides beyond. We wandered into the Charmouth Heritage Coast Centre and watched a short film on interesting history of the Jurassic Coast and fossils. It reminded me of the changing colors of the rocks along the Jurassic Coast, from red to gray and golden color to white, from East Devon to West Dorset and Portland to the Purbeck area, from the Triassic to the Jurassic to the Cretaceous periods, from 250-200 to 200-145 to 145-65 million years ago. The film also mentioned a lot about fossil hunting and collecting and ammonites and a woman named Mary Anning, a female fossil collector back in the 1800s, who I had never heard of before and decided then and there that I must find out more about her as she sounded intriguing to learn about.

After the film, Scott and I had a really enjoyable time at this beach in Charmouth. Since it was low tide at 12:39, as shown on a flyer after a bridge going towards the beach, and there were lots of people on the beach, I basically walked on the beach from Charmouth in the direction of Golden Cap, and got almost to the valley before the climb up Golden Cap. At least a mile walk on the beach. It was so peaceful and calming to just slowly stroll along, getting a fill of those good for me positive negative ions, listening to the small waves, yet staying away from the gray and golden colored Jurassic 200-145 million year old cliffs themselves as I actually heard some small rockfalls. I also heard water trickling down from the cliffs onto the beach. The beach consisted of sand, pebbles, and rocks. I took photos of my purple shoes against the sand and rocks, and also took a photo of my footprints in the sand. While I did this Scott also strolled, but he stopped to look for rocks and fossils as I walked so didn't make it quite as far as I did.

After getting almost to the valley before Golden Cap, I turned back around, caught up with Scott, and after my calming long walk on the beach, since we were both quite hungry by this time, we walked back to the road by the Charmouth Heritage Coast Centre and headed into Charmouth to get some food at a café we ate at least year. Unfortunately for us they only took reservations for their Sunday brunch. So we turned back to eat at the café near the Charmouth Heritage Coast Centre where we originally were and ate there instead, thus walking an extra unnecessary mile round trip. But that was just fine because that was the start of my second missed section, walking the diversion route from Charmouth back to Lyme Regis.

Last year we had walked from Lyme Regis on the beach to Charmouth, taking a long time due to our looking at rocks and fossils and sea glass, but since I wasn't sure if walking that was considered an official route, I figured I should walk the three miles on the official diversion SWCP route, backwards from Charmouth to Lyme Regis, even though it would be inland and on some roads. I used the booklet very closely to follow these three miles as it seemed easier to do this with all the different turns and paths and roads winding our way through homes and fields and such. We started by ascending through a couple of grassy areas next to alternating green and blue, then a set of pink, beach huts, lined with a row of benches slightly climbing, arriving near some homes where we walked on roads taking several turns here and there and at some point arrived at a farm, a gravel track, a barn, and walked through a field and out onto the busy A3052 road, past a hotel, and through a path in a small forested area.

This emerged onto the 15th hole of the Lyme Regis Golf Club, and as we walked through this, I looked up at the sky to check the weather. It had been cloudy and on the cool side today with some breezes, but gratefully it remained dry. Scott wondered why we were walking through a golf course, and I explained to him that I had probably walked through, or around, or near, about a dozen golf courses on the entire SWCP. I reminded him of my downpour in Par, and while I will never take up the game of golf, I do have some fond memories about golf courses, and have made my peace with them.

Occasionally, such as on the A3052 road again and another road after the golf course and as we finally descended three fields, we had views of Lyme Regis with its homes all on hillsides and the harbour below with its breakwater. Before these three fields however, was another small forested area which the ground happened to be blanketed in beautiful meadows of wildflowers. We actually got a bit turned around in this area, as there were several paths to follow, but eventually found the first of three fields.

We reached another short road, a car park, and finally had 114 steps to descend to the foreshore and seawall and some other steps we took last year to get to the beach in Lyme Regis to walk to Charmouth. There was a sign saying, "Welcome to the Jurassic Coast World Heritage Site," with some reminder information. "The Jurassic Coast covers 95 miles of incredible coastline from East Devon to Dorset, with the rocks recording 185 million years of the Earth's history. This story is made visible by coastal erosion and landslides. Erosion exposes the ancient rocks and fossils which offer a unique insight into the Triassic, Jurassic and Cretaceous geological periods of Earth's history." The sign continued, "Erosion of the soft cliffs along this coast also creates ideal habitats for rare plants, insects and animals. Because of these rare plants and insects, the sea cliffs are of international importance for nature conservation. The cliffs are also home to a variety of reptiles, dormice and bats."

One and a half hours and three miles after leaving Charmouth I had completed my second missed section for today! Honestly, the beach walk from last year was much nicer, but it was still alright to complete this section today and the other one earlier today. Later on, Scott and I again went out together for a nice dinner.

In my itinerary for these six weeks, I purposely added two extra days in the Lyme Regis area for two reasons. One was to have the option of choosing the best weather days for the walks I had completed the last two days, especially for the Undercliffs walk. The other reason was because I remembered how meditative it was for me last year to look for sea glass, and I wanted to be able to do that again. Plus have a chance to really look for fossils that are in this area. I knew that there were "guided fossil walks," so after looking at a flyer sign and researching on the internet, I found out that there would be these guided walks tomorrow and the next day. We decided that tomorrow we would go on our own, and do the guided walk the day after in the Lyme Regis area. There were guided walks in the Charmouth area as well, but they were yesterday and today, so we missed those. It really didn't matter to me which location we fossil-and-sea-glass-hunted - I was just looking forward to lots of meditative beach time the next two days.

DAY 34 (DAY 121) STATS: 6.5 MILES TOTAL. 1.5 MILES IN ONE HOUR FOR FIRST MISSED MILE SECTION. 2.0 MILES ON BEACH EXTRA. 3.0 MILES AND 1.5 HOURS FOR SECOND MISSED MILE SECTION. PURPLE SHOES.

COLLECTING FOSSILS, SEA GLASS, POTTERY, AND OTHER OBJECTS ON THE BEACH AT LYME REGIS – DAY 1 – Monday, 30 April 2018

"Collecting from beach material IS acceptable practice." – Part of the Fossil Collectors' Code of Conduct. (Emphasis added.)

Another great breakfast where today's "on the side specials" included a rhubarb apple compote, which I put on top of my granola, and a seaweed biscuit. For my main course I had the "baked garlic and lemon mushrooms on sourdough," one of their homemade breads. Scott had his Full English again.

Today was the first of two great meditating relaxing days at the beach. I am usually not one to just sit on the beach for hours and hours and hours, but with the activity of fossil hunting, and collecting objects, I thoroughly enjoyed my time not walking much or sunbathing on the beach. After breakfast, Scott and I made our way down to the beach between Lyme Regis and Charmouth and ended up spending over four hours, to be exact, looking for fossils and ammonites, and collecting sea glass, pottery, metal, and other random objects. We really had no idea how to properly hunt for fossils or what to really look for, but we did follow some information and rules on a sign about Fossil Collecting that we saw yesterday at the beach in Charmouth:

"The best place to look for fossils is amongst the loose pebbles on the beach. Help us look after this World Heritage Site by not digging or hammering in the cliffs. Follow the fossil code: No digging in the cliffs or ledges without permission. Report any important fossils," such as a rare or special fossil. I don't think though that we found any real important fossils in order to become famous and expert paleontologists. Although I don't even know that we would know what a rare or special or important fossil was if we did find something that could be like that. We were just having a lot of fun. If we did find something, we should report it to the Charmouth Heritage Coast Centre or the Lyme Regis Museum so that they could take photographs and record information and the finder's details, but the finder would still be the keeper. In fact they say, "The fossil is still yours to take home and it helps us to record valuable information about the fossil finds from the coast." We were actually told that collecting on these beaches near Lyme Regis and Charmouth were the only places where you can actually really take things from the beach home with you.

The sign also advised us to stay away from the cliffs due to possible rock falls, and to check the tide times to avoid being trapped by incoming tides. We did both. I also read some information in a couple of the brochures I picked up yesterday at the Charmouth Heritage Coast Centre in their "Fossil Hunting Guide." More safety advice included to be suitably dressed, such as wearing footwear with a good tread due to pebbles, rocks, and boulders. I wore my purple shoes.

This brochure also mentioned the Fossil Collectors' Code of Conduct, which is "a voluntary code of conduct that is in place on the West Dorset Coast, in order to encourage safe and responsible fossil collecting." The Code of Conduct includes, "Collecting from beach material IS acceptable practice (emphasis added); Digging in the cliffs is NOT acceptable practice (emphasis already added); and Do not over collect – leave some for others to find." In other words, please share kindly and respectfully.

Basically Scott and I sat in one spot and searched that area finding and collecting, and then slowly moved to another area. Or we would very slowly walk and look down to find and collect. I found it all very meditating. We barely moved down the beach from the steps at Lyme Regis in the over four hours we had, as there was so much to look at and to find.

I did take a few photos today, mostly just of the seas, the rocks and sand and the beach, my purple shoes and Scott's shoes with this scenery, and the hills of Stonebarrow, Golden Cap, and beyond. It remained dry today, with even some blue skies, but it was cool out and we wore warm clothes.

I will describe more tomorrow about what we found today since after our guided fossil walk tomorrow, we understood more of what we did find today, but in brief I collected sea glass of various colors, broken pottery pieces, and one really good one ammonite that I was excited to have found on my own today without even knowing much about them. I also found a possible old coin worn out and covered in some sort of corrosion or something, which I actually should have taken to someone to look at and possibly record my finding, but later forgot about doing that.

I also found a complete unbroken bottle, because at one point as I was down on the ground and happened to look under a large boulder where the bottle must have been protected by the incoming waves of the seas, weather, and other elements, and thus had not been broken. I have no idea how old this bottle was, and could have been quite modern actually, being perhaps a leftover from someone's recent picnic. It has a screw top lid area so I don't know if that is an indication of how old it is or not. It is clear in color and about six and a half inches tall. Perhaps I should have taken that to someone to look at and possibly record my finding. Unfortunately, there was no message inside the bottle.

Scott found several interesting rocks, some with swirl shapes of ammonites, and one cool piece of pottery painted with a younger image of Queen Elizabeth II on it (more on the origin of the pottery pieces tomorrow). Some of the sea glass colors I found included various shapes and sizes of different colors including white, lots of shades of green, shades of brown, and even rarer shades of blue.

After all that beach time, which I was glad to share with Scott, we went back to town to eat a late lunch, went into a few shops, asked about some of the rocks and fossils we found at one of the numerous fossil shops in Lyme Regis, walked through the seafront gardens again, noticing that the lampposts in the town of Lyme Regis each have large images of ammonite sculptures (more on ammonites as well tomorrow), ate some dinner, and finally went back to our B&B.

With no required missed walks today, we probably walked about a mile total all day. Again the weather was dry all day, a bit breezy and cool the first part of the day but warmed up as the day progressed, but a jacket was still required. It was a great meditative day collecting on the beach of Lyme Regis. I felt like a paleontologist.

DAY 35 (DAY 122) STATS: PERHAPS A MILE OF WALKING ON THE BEACH OVER THE COURSE OF FOUR HOURS, PLUS WALKING AROUND LYME REGIS LATER IN THE DAY. PURPLE SHOES.

COLLECTING FOSSILS, SEA GLASS, POTTERY, AND OTHER OBJECTS ON THE BEACH AT LYME REGIS – DAY 2 – Tuesday, 1 May 2018

"She sells sea-shells on the sea-shore,
The shells she sells are sea-shells, I'm sure,
For if she sells sea-shells on the sea-shore,
Then I'm sure she sells sea-shore shells." – By Terry Sullivan about fossilist, geologist, and paleontologist Mary Anning.

My breakfast for today to get ready for a second day of meditative fossil, sea glass, and pottery hunting started with Lyn's "on the sides" of a "cinnamon and star anise spiced dried fruit compote," which I put on top of my granola along with yogurt, and a "chocolate and almond brownie square," to which Lyn had leftovers and allowed us to take a few for today's beach time, but were eaten long before we arrived at the beach. I also had the Vegetarian Breakfast which included a homemade sausage of squash, beets, and feta, along with some spinach, tomato, and mushrooms. Scott once again had his Full English.

Yesterday after our day on the beach, Scott and I had also gone into the Lyme Regis Museum to sign up for today's Guided Fossil Walk. The meeting time for this today was at 10:30am to coincide with the lowest tides possible. The meeting time for all the guided walks varies, depending on the tides. The meeting place for the guided walk was back at the Lyme Regis Museum. It would be about a two and a half hour time with our guides, Paddy Howe, Geologist and Fossil Hunter, and his son. As we waited a few minutes because we arrived a bit early, I noticed a connection between the Lyme Regis Museum and the woman I heard about a couple of days ago, Mary Anning. A plaque told me "Mary Anning 1799-1847. The famous fossilist was born here in a house on the site of Lyme Regis Museum. The house was her home and her fossil shop until 1826. More about Mary Anning inside the museum." There was also a small drawing of a building that said "Mary Anning's house and shop drawn in 1842. It was demolished in 1889 to make way for the museum." As part of our payment for the guided fossil walk today, we would get free entrance into the museum later, where I must find out more about Ms. Anning.

Yesterday I had also seen a very large ammonite fossil saved in a wall near the museum with its plaque saying, "This fossil is the shell of an ammonite Arietites cf. buckland and dates back approximately 200 million years to the early Jurassic period. It is amongst the largest of the ammonites found locally. The ammonite was discovered in 2013 by Paddy Howe, Lyme Regis Museum geologist, approximately ten metres from this location during the seawall construction works." We were about to meet Paddy Howe!

Paddy and his son arrived and immediately took us and a group of about a dozen or more other people down the seawall making our way to the staircase leading to the beach near Lyme Regis. Before we went down to the beach to start looking, Paddy first told us all about all the possible things that we could find on the beach. If I heard correctly, he told us that from the Cretaceous period of about 114 million years ago from the green layers of flint we might find fossils of sea urchins. He also said that from the 200-million-year-old Jurassic fossils we may find dinosaur vertebrae or other bones filled in Calcite crystals, and even fossilized dinosaur droppings called Coprolite. We might even find fossilized sea lilies, iron pyrite also known as Fool's Gold, and of course ammonites.

We were also told of some of the rules of fossil collecting even though Scott and I had read about it already, but Paddy needed to tell the entire group. Again, if you see anything in the cliffs, you have to get permission first to dig for it, unless of course if you don't dig for it right at that moment you will lose it, so dig for it then you can get permission later. You can keep your collection, but they want to be able to record it. Anything lying around on the ground is fair game to keep without permission. Don't go near the cliffs due to possible rock falls. I actually wondered a reasonable question, but didn't ask - if you were not allowed to go near the cliffs due to possible rock falls, and if you saw something important in the cliffs that you needed to dig and collect, how would that work?

Here are some of the rock and fossil findings that one can potentially find on the beaches here, as well as some of what we did find between yesterday and today. This information is from the Charmouth Heritage Coast Centre "Fossil Hunting Guide" that I got a couple days ago. The rocks one can find include flint (white in color), chert (orange in color), mudstone, limestone (light grey in color), and beef rock (a type of limestone that looks like a piece of steak). Of these, limestone may be the only type of rocks that might contain ammonites. Scott found many pieces of beef rock. One can also find a few minerals like Calcite crystals (white to orange in color), and iron pyrite or Fools' Gold, which I actually found a couple of small pieces of and kept a couple of them each measuring from a half an inch to an inch.

The main fossils one can find are the ammonites. They are "extinct sea creatures that had a chambered spiral shell. They are related to modern day nautilus. At Charmouth there are three main types of ammonites you can find." First are Beef Rock ammonites that have a faint outline of the ammonite on them, which Scott found a few. Fool's Gold ammonites come from "rusty brown pebbles on the beach…where you may find sections or even a whole Fool's Gold ammonite in just one patch." That was the really good one that I found yesterday, and today Scott found a couple more! They are really small all less than a half inch in size of the ones we found. The one I found was still attached to the pebble, and the others were just by themselves. Very cool! Calcite ammonites are "beautiful crystal ammonites found in some of the light grey pebbles on the beach and are often the hardest ones to find." We did not find any of these, but Paddy found one less than a half inch in size and gave it to us!

Belemnites are "the fossilized remains of ancient squid-like creatures and are the most common fossil found here at Charmouth. Sometimes tips of the fossils have been broken off and look like small tubes." We found several of these with the help of Paddy who pointed them out to us. Crinoids or Sea Lilies are related to starfish and sea urchins. I think Scott found a small piece of one of these. One can also find fossil seashells such as the "remains of fossilized sea snails, oysters and clams." I found a fossilized clam shell, although it looks like a scallop shell! Perhaps another connection to the Camino de Santiago…

Scott may have also found a rock with the fossils of tube worms in it, small marine worms that "would have been living in the Cretaceous seas at Charmouth" and these were "the remains of ancient worm homes." We could have also found fossil wood like driftwood, and perhaps even a fossilized bone from some ancient marine reptile, but did not find any of those.

While Scott was good at finding rocks and fossils, I enjoyed collected more sea glass with similar colors as yesterday. I found more pottery pieces as well, including one broken but mostly intact pottery piece in the shape of a fish in brown and blue coloring, to which I dropped a moment after I picked it up and broke it into a few pieces, which I saved all of them so I can somehow perhaps glue them back together. On the back of this piece it said, "Wade Porcelain Made in England," and I researched that and found the fish's image and that it is an angel fish and while I could not find an exact year, several places had them for sale labeling them as "Vintage item from the 1960s" and sold as a pair in a box called "Aqua-Dishes in Scintillite" which is porcelain achieved with "subtle effects of colour and glaze that beautify and enhance…the clay." That piece was fun to find!

Other pottery pieces I found included several in various shapes and sizes of solid colors of greens, blues, yellows, and reds. Some pieces I found you can see the remains of things painted on the pottery like decorative edges, flowers, patterns, and one piece had an image of a sailboat. Some pieces were of the blue and white patterned pottery, and I even found the underside of two pieces that I can put together that say "Indian Ornament T. B & S.," which upon researching that I found out that maybe that is from a company called Thomas Booths and Sons from 1872 to 1876! Wow!

Scott and I spent three hours with our guides and we found some great things! After our amazing fun meditative three hours with Paddy and his son after the guided fossil walk ended, Scott and I spent another hour on our own once again continuing to look for more things. Although, the word "walk" was not much today as after a total of another four hours like yesterday, we probably walked less than a mile round trip today. We had brought food with us today to eat throughout our several hours of sandwiches we picked up earlier this morning so we would not be hungry. The weather today actually did include one passing rain shower this morning just as we all started walking on the beach, but dried up and was on the cool side the rest of the day, but not cold, and we kept feeling warm enough. I only took about another half dozen photos of the same scenery as yesterday of the rocks and sand on the beach, the water, the hills and headlands beyond, and the blue sky with white clouds, which all still made for some scenic photos of our time at the beach. A crab and lobster pot, as well as other people looking for things on the beach, also made their way into the foreground of a couple of these photos.

After our time at the beach, Scott and I went to the Lyme Regis Museum to take advantage of the free entrance fee we got as part of paying for the guided fossil walk. One of the first things I noticed in the museum was a collection of round coins which looked like maybe the one I found yesterday called "farthings," a previous monetary currency of the UK, which might have been equal to a quarter of a penny, some made of bronze and earlier ones made of copper. The ones in the museum dated from the 1600s! The ones displayed had images of anchors and ships, hearts and flower pots, frying pans, and coats of arms on them. Also on display were French copper coins also from the 17th century from trading.

I looked at my coin again later on and with the corrosion I was not able to tell anything on it. I should have taken it to the museum today but left it in our B&B room from yesterday and with the museum closing soon, I did not have time to go back to get it. I hope I don't get in trouble for having someone not look at it to record, but I will do my best to find a coin shop back home to see if it is anything of importance, and if so, I will take a photo of it to email to the museum later on at some point. I really hope it is of something of importance!

Then I found out something really cool - that the sea glass and pottery pieces (also known as china pieces!), and metal objects, I had found on the beach were from an old town "tip," a rubbish/garbage dump that was unearthed when there was a landslip in the area in May 2008. A few BBC News articles I looked up online about this landslip entitled the "Worst landslip exposes landfill" and "Landslip is worst in 100 years" warned people to stay away from the area for a while. A few days later another article entitled "Landslip beach closed for years" because "washing machines, fridges, metal cylinders and bottles have blocked part of the World Heritage Jurassic Coastline beach path." This article further said, "Exposed items, which are not deemed hazardous, will have to be left to wash into the sea. The landfill site, which dates back to Victorian times, closed in the early 1970s." Wow, have I possibly been finding pieces of pottery or sea glass possibly dating back to the Victorian times! If so, that is better than buying full pieces of china in some ways. Hence the name of Thomas Booths and Sons, or the Wade Porcelain pieces. Or maybe even that possible coin.

In a bit more research, I found out that the name of the landfill was the Spittles Lane Landfill. It was strange to think that I was still finding things not only ten years after the landslide exposed the landfill, but possibly finding things 150 or so years old. This is yet another link I have come across to Queen Victoria, just as The Tea House near Mothecombe and the Great Landslip in the Undercliffs, and who knows, maybe I did find something that will eventually make me famous...

Some of the metal objects I found most likely from this "tip," which I did not keep, were some old nails and screws, wire, a drawer handle, lots of various electrical parts from household items and automobiles like spark plugs and other stuff. Some of this stuff I actually thought could have been from a shipwreck or something, but I am not quite sure about that, and was most likely from the "tip."

Anyway, back to the museum. There were so many other various objects displayed in the museum, along with a lot of history, that it would take me another several pages to write about, so I shall just focus on the information I found out about Mary Anning from some information displays in the museum. She was a geologist born and living in Lyme Regis all her life. Becoming a geologist, "her work played an important part in the birth of geology as a science. She not only found the first skeletons of ichthyosaurs and plesiosaurs to be scientifically described – she studied the fossils and anatomy, and worked with many of the early geologists." More information continued that Ms. Anning "was the right person, in the right place at exactly the right time. Lyme Regis was the right place for a pioneer fossilist. The fossils were there, and so were the well-off visitors to buy them. The town was in the middle of a long stretch of Jurassic lias rocks…rich in fossils…frequently exposed by landslides. Mary was born at just the right time. Scientific interest in geology was starting, and in her lifetime it was considered the most important science. Her finds include the first complete plesiosaur in 1823, many ichthyosaurs, new species of both plesiosaurs and fish, and the first British find of a flying reptile [pterosaur]. She also made collections of starfish, ammonites and belemnite ink sacs. She also studied the fossils, and dissected living sea creatures to work out anatomy." She sold many ammonites in her fossil shop, apparently the first fossil shop in Lyme Regis, which was now where this museum is located. Many of her findings are now on display at the Natural History Museum in London.

What a fascinating woman. I bought a small book about her called, "Mary Anning of Lyme Regis" by Crispin Tickell, to find out more. The book describes her as "probably the most important unsung (or inadequately sung) collecting force in the history of paleontology." The book also told me more about Ms. Anning as a woman. It describes her as "a woman in a man's world. Science was still largely the province of the leisured gentleman amateur." In fact, "until recently almost none of her discoveries displayed in museums or collections in different parts of the world carried her name. Instead they carried that of the donors…During her lifetime only two of the species she had identified were named after her…Some may have believed this unfair, even at the time. She obviously felt it strongly." Later the book says, "Whatever others may have found then and since, Mary Anning remains without peer as the prime collector of Lyme Regis."

The book continues, "What were her special strengths? First she had the sharpest eyes in the business. She saw what others failed to see…She had immense patience and persistence, and from experience knew when as well as where to look. She was out in all weathers, and physically courageous and tough…Once a fossil had been located, she took extraordinary pains in extracting or directing its extraction without damaging it. Yet perhaps her greatest skill was in putting the pieces of a fossil specimen together." Furthermore, "It is no wonder that even in her life time Mary Anning was the stuff of legend…She has inspired cartoons since 1830, poetry (or verse) since 1838, literature since 1951 and 1969, novels (particularly for children) since 1966, television since the 1970s, dance since 1987, and film since 1982…She has been enlisted in many causes, from science to feminism, and is now what she was in her lifetime, a boon to the tourist industry. A stained glass window in her honour was installed in Lyme Church within three years after her death. She even has a road named after her." Wow! And finally, "Of the verses which may be related to her, the most famous is the tongue twister song by Terry Sullivan in 1908:

"She sells sea-shells on the sea-shore,
The shells she sells are sea-shells, I'm sure,
For if she sells sea-shells on the sea-shore,
Then I'm sure she sells sea-shore shells."

(Say that ten times fast.)

I am glad I discovered learning who Mary Anning was, and I am glad she is recognized now by others about her important life. I say that she is courageous, and brave!

I noticed later on that the Lyme Regis Museum also offers guided "Mary Anning Walks," which if I had realized earlier, I would have liked to have gone on that walk as well. Also, note that aside from the beach between Lyme Regis and Charmouth, there is also another beach on the other side of Lyme Regis called Monmouth Beach that is also good for seeing some of the largest preserved ammonites. Scott and I did not go there, but would have needed to carefully watch out for going at low tides, plus would have had to walk on pebbles to the far west end of the beach, according to booklet for this area.

Since I met Paddy Howe today, Geologist and Fossil Hunter, perhaps even a famous one, I wanted to recall all the other "famous" people I have met, or saw, on my SWCP adventure between last summer and this spring. In fact, meeting these people randomly really added meaning to my walking adventure. In addition to Paddy Howe, I also met a couple of authors, poets, and artists. Of course, there was meeting author Sue Bunney this year after reading two of her books, and talking with her and her husband in their living room drinking tea, where she kindly gave me a copy of one of her books and autographed it saying, "To Debby, Enjoy your walking and Cornwall. Best wishes, Sue."

I also met John Farman, author of about thirty books and an illustrator who kindly gave me a couple rides last year in the Prawle Point and Lannacombe areas. I also sat in his living room and talked for a few minutes, and he autographed for me a postcard of one of his drawings saying, "Best Wishes. John Farman."

Thanks to Scott, I met a local poet in Swanage last year, Carlotta Barrow, where we ended up talking with her right at her home in her back yard and studio, sitting at an old white iron table and chair set. She kindly autographed for me one of her poetry books saying, "To Debby, Congratulations on the Coastal Path Walk, Carlotta Barrow."

What a great collection of autographs I can add to my other memories of my SWCP walk!

A few famous people that I saw last year were some actors from the TV show Doc Martin when I was in Port Isaac during their filming of new episodes for their next season. I at least saw Ian McNeice, who plays Bert

Large the father, and Joe Absolom, who plays Al Large the son, and while I did not get their autographs, I did get some photos. And I enjoyed watching a few episodes of the TV show as well.

Of course, I also was able to spend time with my great friend and inspiration, artist and author, Sasha Harding!

The last two and a half relaxing days on the beaches, including the two-mile walk round trip a few days ago towards Golden Cap, plus the last two days looking and collecting, had been wonderful, including spending this kind of time with Scott. I would normally never be able to sit on a beach that long, but having things to look for and collect really did feel quite calming and meditating. I really did feel like a paleontologist, geologist, and fossil hunter. And collector of other fun things!

DAY 36 (DAY 123) STATS: PERHAPS A MILE OF WALKING ON THE BEACH OVER THE COURSE OF FOUR HOURS, PLUS WALKING AROUND LYME REGIS LATER IN THE DAY, SIMILAR TO YESTERDAY. PURPLE SHOES.

WEST BEXINGTON TO ABBOTSBURY – Wednesday, 2 May 2018

"Oh! I do like to be beside the seaside!
I do like to be beside the sea!
I do like to stroll along the Prom, Prom, Prom!
Where the brass bands play, "Tiddely-om-pom-pom!"" – Once again, from the song, "I Do Like to Be Beside the Seaside" by John A. Glover-Kind.

Last night gale winds and rain were predicted overnight and into this morning, but it said that should stop by 11:00 in the morning for today. Sure enough, it was windy and rainy overnight, and actually sooner than predicted, that stormy weather stopped, the sun mostly came out all day, and it was dry. There was a breeze at times which made it cooler, but when there was no wind and no clouds covering the sun, it was warm. By later in the day the skies were quite blue with white clouds. My final breakfast consisted of the Superfood Porridge once again, and Scott had his Full English.

After saying our thank yous to Lyn and Jason, for door to door service and ease, Scott and I took a taxi from our wonderful five days in Lyme Regis to Abbotsbury. As prearranged, once we arrived at our B&B in Abbotsbury in a home that is 350 years old conveniently located in the main part of the village near restaurants and pubs and shops, the B&B gentleman kindly drove us to the car park near the restaurant in West Bexington from last year when I heard that joyful happy nicely-dressed grandfatherly-aged gentleman sing my theme song.

"Now everybody likes to spend their summer holiday
down beside the side of the silvery sea.
I'm no exception to the rule, in fact, if I'd me way,
I'd reside by the side of the silvery sea."

Needless to say, I had some of the lyrics in my head all day, and would occasionally sing the words I knew out loud, which my husband kindly tolerated.

We had a four mile almost all flat walk to Abbotsbury which started with a few minutes of walking on the pebbles of Chesil Beach. We had gone from the million-year-old fossils of Lyme Regis to the billions of pebbles of Chesil Beach.

For the next mile, sometimes we walked on a narrow path, and sometimes on a wide track, but it was all parallel to Chesil Beach and the crashing waves of the sea on the pebbles. Occasionally there were some large puddles of water on the wide track, but the parallel narrow path up a few feet allowed my purple shoes to stay dry. After about a half hour of walking, the path and track turned into a paved road, but still paralleled the beach and the waves. My favorite sound of the crashing waves, with the tumbling of the pebbles being taken back to the sea, was heard the entire time so far.

About forty minutes after we started walking, a sign told us we had two and a half miles to Abbotsbury. As we walked, hillsides were inland on our left covered with green, and speckled with farmland, cows, sheep, and farmhouses. I took several nice photos of this inland scenery today with the green of the farmland, the blue of the sky, the white of the clouds, and the brown or white specs of the farmhouses. We passed by several WW2 pillboxes on the beach and had a view of the Isle of Portland ahead. Soon we stopped for a snack and sat on a few of the pebbles of the beach to eat, and to enjoy the great weather with the big blue sky and the sound of the waves. The beach itself was too difficult to walk on because of all the pebbles, otherwise I am sure we would have walked on the sand if there was sand. Last year we walked about a half mile on the pebbles. I took a few photos of our shoes against the pebbles, a close up of the pebbles themselves, and the Sea Campion white and pink wildflowers that seemed to be growing right out of all the pebbles.

"But when you're just the common or garden Smith or Jones or Brown
at business up in town, you're got to settle down.
You save your money all the year 'til summer comes around.
Then away you go to a place you know, where the cockle shells are found."

After we kept walking, and about an hour and a half after we started walking earlier, a sign now told us we had a mile and a half till the Swannery in Abbotsbury. We were at a car park, and briefly walked up a short boardwalk to a ridge of the curved Chesil Beach. From this vantage point, you could see a very long distance up and down the beach with its billions of pebbles, to the Isle of Portland in one direction and even to Golden Cap and Lyme Regis in the other direction. A sign near this boardwalk told us, "The Fleet and Chesil Bank are internationally protected for geology and wildlife." The scenery from this vantage point was breathtaking.

We knew there were some Subtropical Gardens up the road from this car park, and with the shorter walk today we thought we might go wander around the gardens. As we were sitting in their restaurant having lunch, we decided not to see the gardens after all, since we had the beauty of nature already all around us as we were walking. We spent about an hour and a half though, between walking up and down the road and taking our time eating.

Back on the SWCP there was a bit of pebble walking to start, and then with a mile left to go to Abbotsbury, the path turned into a wide grassy path with dried up mud. The path curved inland with a flock of sheep with baby lambs on our right, and behind us was the curve of the ridge of Chesil Beach. Ahead we could see up on the hill where St. Catherine's Chapel was sitting. All the green grass speckled with the white sheep made for great photos with the blue and white sky.

Still my favorite colors, blue and green, along with their various shades of turquoise, blue-green, green-blue, azure, cobalt, sapphire, indigo, light green, dark green, emerald green, mint green, lime green, sea foam green, verdant, viridescent, forest green, moss green, olive green, cyan, grass green, and seaweed green. And purple, my purple shoes.

With three-quarters of a mile to go, the only slight uphill climb of the day was on a grassy field. We passed another WW2 pillbox and the grass flattened out. We had a view of the white of the swans in the Swannery in the distance, along with the beginning of The Fleet. We walked through a gate next to a long old dry-stone wall which started to take us back in time, as the grassy path curved around the hillside that the chapel stood on. Even the brown of the dry-stone walls along with the green grass and blue and white sky made for a scenic photo.

"Oh! I do like to be beside the seaside!
I do like to be beside the sea!
I do like to stroll along the Prom, Prom, Prom!
Where the brass bands play, "Tiddely-om-pom-pom!""

A sign then gave us a choice of walking to the chapel, to the Swannery, or into Abbotsbury. I chose Abbotsbury since we had visited the other two places last year. The official SWCP was the one to the Swannery, which we walked last year coming back from the Swannery into Abbotsbury after visiting the swans.

With a half mile left, we walked through a short bit of trees, more grassy path, and walked next to another old dry-stone wall with views out to St. Nicholas Church, the Tithe Barn, and some other large brown stone buildings. We walked onto a short track road where last year we walked up to the chapel. We were out onto the main road of Abbotsbury four hours after we started walking, and I completed another missed section of the SWCP! Of those four hours, about two and a half were spent walking the four miles from West Bexington to Abbotsbury.

As we were approaching Abbotsbury, a village that takes one back several centuries in time with its brown stone buildings and thatched roofs, I knew there were a couple of tea rooms so Scott and I went into one of the tea rooms, The Old Schoolhouse Tea Rooms and Tea Garden, for a cream tea! After our snack, we wandered around some of the smaller side roads of the old village, wandering back in time. We also visited St. Nicholas Church, and as we left, the bells rang 5:00pm. Inside I said my usual prayers.

Later in the B&B room I was glancing through a brochure about "The Making of Chesil Beach" by the Chesil Bank and the Fleet Nature Reserve. In it I recalled that along the 18-mile Chesil Beach, the size of the pebbles varied from pea size to the size of a hand, depending on what end of the beach you were on. The brochure further told me, "This grading has proved a blessing for fisherman and smugglers landing on the beach in fog or at night. Picking up a handful of shingle they could tell exactly where they were simply by the size of the pebbles." I was still learning about fishing and smuggling with this small pebble of interesting information!

"So just let me be beside the seaside!
I'll be beside myself with glee
and there's lots of girls [boys] beside,
I should like to be beside, beside the seaside, beside the sea!"

DAY 37 (DAY 124) STATS: 4.0 MILES. 2.5 HOURS OF WALKING WITH AN EXTRA HOUR AND A HALF FOR A LONG LUNCH. PURPLE SHOES. PUB ABOUT A MILE INLAND UP THE ROAD FROM WEST BEXINGTON IN THE VILLAGE OF SWYRE IS "THE BULL INN."

EAST FLEET TO ABBOTSUBRY – Thursday, 3 May 2018

"Just to let you know…there are some cows ahead." – My husband.

After breakfast in our 350-year-old B&B with Maria and Steve, Maria kindly dropped us off at a store just up the road from a long footpath that led down to the SWCP. We carefully crossed a busy road, holding hands, walked down a smaller road towards the East Fleet Farm, and walked down the long footpath lined with grass on either side heading straight towards the Fleet Lagoon, where we took a right-hand turn at the end of the footpath onto the SWCP. All that took about twenty minutes, so I will round that to an extra half mile. Today would be a "backwards" walk as we would walk from East Fleet towards Abbotsbury. Technically from where we started today, at a sign that said seven and a quarter miles to Abbotsbury, approximately the first mile was repeat walking after we made the right turn from the footpath. This first mile took us to The Old Church, where we started from last year, walking to our B&B near Wyke Regis in the direction of the Isle of Portland.

The first thing I noticed as Scott and I started walking was the blue water of the Fleet Lagoon and the light blue sky on this sunny day. There was a bit of crispness in the air this morning, and with a slight breeze most of the day, it felt cool, but the sun was out and the sky was blue and it was gratefully another dry day. For a little while the path alternated between a grassy path, a gravel track, another grassy path, and then a small path. I could hear the very faint small ripples of the water of the lagoon. Scott and I passed through several kissing gates, which meant that each time we well, kissed. After about forty-five minutes we reached The Old Church, with a sign saying six miles to Abbotsbury, so then we began the missed miles.

We walked by a large field inland of some green crop that might have been wheat or barley in its early stages, but I don't know for sure. As we went through one kissing gate, I remarked about the familiar and helpful acorn symbol, the one with the white acorn on a black background, that I have seen hundreds of times, the one that I have appreciated hundreds of times, knowing that I was walking in the right direction.

We listened to the sounds of a lot of the bird life of the Fleet Lagoon and saw several types of birds as we walked along. At one point we saw several of them sitting on one of the many abandoned row boats that line the shore of some places along the lagoon. On the other hand, perhaps some of the many row boats that line the shore are not abandoned and are still in use. Some of these row boats were sitting on the shore itself, and others were floating in the water.

Scott and I walked by the brown dirt of another field of a crop that either hasn't been planted yet or has not yet started to grow. We had a grassy area to walk through with continuing farmland inland on our right, and the lagoon with Chesil Beach just beyond to our left. With the sun behind us and the slight breeze it felt cool out. We passed a few more WW2 pillboxes. We passed more of the same green fields of a crop that I did not know what it was exactly.

We walked through the gate of a long old stone wall and along a long field of bright yellow rapeseed in bloom. That crop I can identify, as Scott and I saw a lot of that in the Cotswolds several years ago. I also saw some of these bright yellow fields a few weeks ago as I walked from Soar Mill Cove to South Sands, as well as in South Milton on that same day when I had my working-farm experience, seeing the bright yellow fields and farmland and church, all making for some very scenic photos. Scott and I also saw a rapeseed field towards the end of our Undercliffs walk a few days ago. Today I took a lot of photos of the great colors of the bright yellow flowers of rapeseed and the deep blue sky with a layer of white clouds in the middle. As a view of the Isle of Portland behind us disappeared, we passed by a sign saying five miles to Abbotsbury. Here a field with about a half dozen horses were standing and eating, and made for the foreground of a few photos with the bright yellow rapeseed in the background. Scott enjoyed seeing these horses.

Some large buildings appeared and we walked by the Moonfleet Manor, and another brown dirt field of a nonexistent crop. An old-looking wooden SWCP sign told us four and three-quarters miles to go, and then we walked by another green crop field with more yellow rapeseed fields in the distance, and still the blue waters of the lagoon on our left.

About two hours after we started walking, we stopped at Herbury "Island" to eat some sandwiches that we had picked up early this morning at a little café in Abbotsbury before eating breakfast. According to an information sign for Herbury "Island," it is actually "a headland which protrudes into the mid Fleet. It provides a superb buffer zone preventing disturbance to winter birds feeding in and flying along the Fleet and summer and migrant birds feeding on its shores." Although then the sign says, "The neck of Herbury floods in high water and is permanently wet. This attracts a range of wildlife and makes Herbury really an island…The Coast Path runs along the back of Herbury."

After our fifteen-minute break, we had four and a half miles go to Abbotsbury. We started heading inland as we had to walk around Herbury Island inland rather than on the edge of The Fleet. Here we had the same green field crop on our left that I had been seeing today as we were walking on a grassy path, next to an old stone wall, and another green field crop on our right, as we headed towards some more yellow rapeseed fields. Before we arrived at the rapeseed fields though, we turned left at a four and a quarter miles to Abbotsbury sign. We walked by more fields and more of the Fleet Lagoon lined with more of those row boats. At almost three hours after we started walking we had three and a half miles to go. I commented at how flat the SWCP has been all these miles.

Then something I had never experienced on the SWCP before in any place at all happened. As we walked around a very large dirt crop field there were lots of some kind of flies. And I mean lots and lots of these flies or some kind of flying bugs. Fortunately, they were not biting, and when we just started to notice them, two people walking in the opposite direction told us that there were lots more all through walking along the edge of this field for perhaps at least a quarter mile. I picked up my pace and actually jogged a bit to get through this very buggy section. Swatting them away did not help, as there were so many of them. I actually felt like this experience was worse than walking through a field of cows.

After gratefully getting through that as fast as I could, the sign on the other side of the field said we had three and a quarter miles to go, but the field definitely felt larger than it actually was with all the flies. For some reason, Scott walked his normal pace through this which was odd, so I waited for him safely out of the fly zone at the other end of the field and a bit beyond. We were at an area called Langdon Hive.

When Scott was safely out of the fly zone too, he handed me something though. Something I could not believe he found. One small piece of pottery! Like the pottery I had collected at Lyme Regis. Wow! Interesting that he found one small piece here, and how in the world did he find that one tiny piece in all of the brown dirt, especially with all the flies. I wondered how the piece of pottery got there, and I really wondered if there was a lot more in the area. Perhaps another landfill was buried underneath the dirt field. Who knows.

Anyway, we had to walk around a small boggy section so I wouldn't get my purple shoes wet, and soon we had finished walking near the Fleet Lagoon and were headed inland towards Abbotsbury, walking next to a few trees and then on, and next to, and through, large fields of grass. We passed by a three mile sign and walked through more large fields of grass. And then it happened...

COWS. A moment earlier my husband casually said to me, "Just to let you know...there are some cows ahead." I really didn't want to hear that, but at least he was with me this time. Although last year when he was with me near the top of Golden Cap in a herd of cows, it was not fun at all. This time at least the cows were busy eating, but somehow, and I don't know if it was because of us, or because they just happened to want to move to a different place, but as we were crossing the field, they began to follow us. Yes, follow us. Or it appeared that they were following us as they were going in our direction and we were in front of them. Maybe they were headed in our direction anyway even if we weren't there. I walked as calmly as I could but did not feel comfortable at all, and I did walk a bit faster pace to keep my distance from them. But Scott was behind me and was closer to them. I motioned for him to hurry up and began to panic slightly.

Fortunately, the cows veered towards some creek of water as we walked out of the field and turned right safely out of their way. May that please be my last encounter with cows on the SWCP. Note that later on this evening, Scott showed me a video he had taken of the cows walking towards him. I could not believe it and thought that was not the smartest thing to be doing, and was a bit upset that he did that, but the video was kind of interesting to watch now that the experience was over. I guess Scott has a different level of tolerance for flies and cows than me.

It was getting warmer being inland with no breeze, so I took off one of my two layers of shirts that I had on. I took a photo of Scott standing on this green hillside we were on with those cows in the background. Soon we had a view of St. Catherine's Chapel in the distance on top of its hillside as a yellow arrow close to an acorn was curved telling us to take a right turn. We were still next to large grassy fields. We had two and a quarter miles left to go and I thought that all of these grassy fields could have been very wet, soggy, boggy, and muddy, but fortunately they were not, except for a few spots that we managed to negotiate around.

As we had a slight descent down another grassy field, we had a great view of all the green fields and farmland and countryside with darker green hedges separating the fields and some patches of small trees in various areas of the landscape. All the green through the rolling hillsides was so beautiful. It got a bit breezy again so I put my second layer back on. With two miles left to go, we stopped for a snack just before crossing a road. I realized that today's mileage, actually around eight miles total, was similar mileage to the Undercliffs, as well as similar mileage to Plymouth, but all three definitely completely different scenery! These three sections are the longest missed sections I have had to walk this year in and of themselves. (Although I did walk some similar long days of around eight miles this year as well, but those included some repeat miles.)

The weather got warm once again so I took off the second layer once more as we ascended a grassy hillside. With one and three-quarters miles left, we went over an old stone wall by climbing up and over and down a stile, and then up and over and down another stile and through some trees. One more stile to climb up and over and down, and onto another field of...cows. But these were very busy eating, were a bit further away, and were not moving, yet with just having that other experience, it was still a bit nerve wracking as I looked behind me several times just to make sure they decided not to mooooooove, which they did not.

We climbed over another stile and walked by more fields with a view looking back on all the fields and green landscape we had just walked through. A view of the Isle of Portland was beyond. The green scenery once again was beautiful. The last bit of walking was on the ledge and ridge along the top of a hillside with just over a mile to go. Below and beyond were views of the Swannery below, St. Catherine's Chapel on the hill, the village of Abbotsbury, and a flock of sheep and baby lambs. We were quite near these sheep and I tell you that I much more prefer walking next to sheep than cows any day. And I much prefer sheep over a lot of flies, too.

It became breezy again, so I put the second layer back on. We descend the grassy hillside out onto a road that led to the Swannery car park. About five hours after we started walking this morning, I completed another missed section of the SWCP!

Then as we walked back towards Abbotsbury, just as we got closer to the church yard, I had a good cry. "I only have about three miles left to walk of the entire SWCP," I said out loud to Scott. Three more miles and my 630-mile walking adventure will be all over. On the one hand, that is amazing and I should be very happy and excited. But I cried because I will miss this. I will miss walking. I will miss so much of what I have experienced and seen and felt and heard over the last few years. Even with all the cows and weather and other challenges I had, I will really miss this. I had fallen in love with the SWCP, and I will really miss the SWCP!

So, we went and ate one more cream tea to cheer me up at the same tea room as yesterday. Both yesterday and today, we had half our scones the Cornwall way, and the other half the Devon way. This will end up being my last cream tea along the SWCP, and I will miss cream tea, too! I took photos of the collections of china on display in the tea room, including many colorful various patterns painted on tea cups, saucers, plates, and tea pots, because I still like seeing china, and would still like to get more someday.

In our B&B in Abbotsbury, they had an old-looking booklet published in 1984 entitled "Dry Stone Walls" by Lawrence Garner. I thought it was quite appropriate seeing this booklet here since the last couple of days we had seen several dry-stone walls taking us back in time. I had also seen them occasionally throughout my SWCP walks, and I remember them from walking in the Cotswolds as well. From this booklet I discovered some interesting facts about these timeless walls. "A dry stone wall is one built entirely or mainly without the use of mortar; it relies for its strength and durability on the skilful placing of stones so that each one is locked securely in place." So interesting! "Many of the walls that enclose some of Britain's highest terrain have stood for two hundred years."

The booklet continues describing the development of the dry stone walls in three distinct stages. The first stage dates from the fifteenth century, then the sixteenth century saw a boom in wool production with the need of these dry stone walls to enclose livestock, including sheep. Then the third stage where "The great period of wall building that started in the late eighteenth century and continued into the early nineteenth…was the golden age of the professional waller. For the first time walling became recognized as a specialist craft and sophisticated techniques were established to make it possible to build sound walls at considerable speed. The methods developed in the eighteenth century remain virtually unchanged today."

The booklet has detailed description of the construction process of various types of dry stone walls, as well as great black and white photos of the building process and types of walls. In fact, there are regional stones and styles of dry stone walls. "Although the basic principles of dry stone walling remain the same everywhere, regional variations arise for two reasons – the characteristics of the local stone and the prevailing agricultural conditions." The walls differ in Scotland, Wales, The Lake District, The Pennines, and even the Cotswolds and the South-West. "Cotswold wallers have many difficulties to contend with. The distinctive Jurassic limestone tends to be soft and vulnerable to frost and road salt." In addition, "A variety of stone enclosures is to be found in Devon and Cornwall. Free-standing dry stone walls of the conventional kind are to be seen on the moorlands such as Dartmoor, where granite provides substantial stone…The characteristic feature of the south-western peninsula is the stone hedge in its various forms, basically an earth bank faced with stone and topped with turf, brushwood, stone or a permutation of these…'Slab' material, such as quarry waste or slate, can only be used vertically with its length into the bank and there are two main ways of laying it – in straightforward courses of upright stones or in a herringbone pattern with stones leaning opposite ways in alternate courses." I do remember seeing the herringbone pattern at some point along the SWCP, and I am sure I have seen dry stone walls of various construction styles and stones along my walk.

The booklet continues, "Devon wallers using granite or limestone frequently favour a technique called 'chip and block,' where gaps caused by the irregularities of the rough stones are filled in by smaller chips." With so much more detail in this small 32-page booklet, I briefly considered wanting to learn the craft of creating dry stone walls someday.

I decided that since today became the last day I had a cream tea along the SWCP, I would reminisce about the approximate twenty cream teas (or variations thereof) I had both last summer and this spring. It all started in Ilfracombe on the 10th of June last year, when Jo introduced me to my first ever cream tea, where I learned about cream tea, and where I fell in love with eating the scones topped with both jam and clotted cream, and clotted cream and jam. My second cream tea was on the 26th of June in Port Isaac at my combination B&B and tea room, where I learned about the perfect cup of tea. My third cream tea was at a tea room in the village of St. Mawgan inland from Mawgan Porth, followed by my fourth cream tea at a fundraising event at the St. Anta Church Hall in Carbis Bay on the 6th of July where I enjoyed cream tea with the locals. Marazion was the place for my next cream tea after a bike ride, and then there was the delicious sweet variation of cream tea in Fowey, a warmed chocolate chip and orange scone topped with chocolate hazelnut spread.

When Scott joined me last year, together we had a snack of cheese scones topped with butter near the Berry Head Lighthouse, and two days after that, I introduced him to his first ever cream tea in Paignton, where he fell in love with eating scones both the Cornish and the Devon ways. We also enjoyed variations of the scone in

Delicious Cream Teas and Other Delicious Food

Left: My first cream tea in Ilfracombe with both Devon (cream first, jam on top) and Cornwall versions (jam first, cream on top) June 10. Right: Cornwall version with strawberries in Port Isaac June 26.

Devon version, Croyde Bay, March 28.   Cornwall version, Morwenstow, March 31.

Left: Cornwall version with black currant jam and strawberries, St Anta Church, Carbis Bay, July 6.
Right: Goat Island, Undercliffs completion (both versions), April 28.

Left: Favorite Superfood Porridge with edible flowers, Mawgan Porth, June 30.
Right: Three desserts, Plymouth, April 17.

Shaldon a couple days after that, where Scott ate a fruit scone with the jam and clotted cream toppings, and I ate an apple cinnamon cheese scone with butter. By now we were addicted, so we had some savory scones days later in Budleigh Salterton, where we each had a date and banana scone, Scott had a cheddar and tomato scone, and I had a cheddar cheese and olive scone. And only a day after that, which was the 15th of August, the woman at our B&B in Seaton greeted us with cream tea.

At a small combo café/thrift/bric-a-brac store in Osmington Mills, Scott and I ate a cream tea snack to hold us till our dinner reservations later on that day, still delicious either way, which would turn out to be my last cream tea of last summer. I had six on my own and six with Scott last year, not all necessarily the traditional cream tea, but all delicious regardless.

To hold me over till this spring, in the meantime back home, I purposely went to a British shop in a town near our house to buy homemade scones, clotted cream imported from England, and also bought some jam at our local grocery store, so that we could relive the SWCP at home enjoying a cream tea. Number thirteen. On the 28th of March on my first day of walking this spring, I had to have my first cream tea, which I ate at a tea room in Croyde Bay as I was feeling how surreal and amazing it was to be back on the SWCP. Here I ate my cream tea the Devon way, clotted cream first then jam on top, but only three days later, at a tea room in Morwenstow I ate my second cream tea of the spring the Cornish way, jam first then clotted cream on top. Both delicious. Since I was in Fowey again this year, I ate the delicious sweet variation of cream tea again, their "Ultimate Chocolate Cream Tea."

During a rest day in Plymouth I had my fourth cream tea of the spring, and then on the 28th of April Scott bought the ingredients of making a cream tea for our Undercliffs walk together, where we sat and enjoyed cream tea twice that day, once at the half way point, and the second time at Goat Island, to celebrate my completing the Undercliffs walk.

Yesterday was the sixth time having cream tea this spring here in Abbotsbury, with today being the last cream tea, the seventh of this spring, and the twentieth of both last summer and this spring. What fun to reminisce about cream tea, and still delicious both ways!

DAY 38 (DAY 125) STATS: ABOUT 8.25 MILES TOTAL. A HALF MILE EXTRA AT THE BEGINNING OF THE DAY. 7.25 FROM EAST FLEET TO ABBOTSBURY, WITH ABOUT 6.25 OF THOSE NEW MILES AND ONE MILE REPEAT. THEN ABOUT A HALF EXTRA MILE REPEAT BACK FROM SWANNERY TO B&B. FIVE HOURS. PURPLE SHOES.

REST DAY IN WEYMOUTH – Friday, 4 May 2018

"Minehead 11-8-55. Dear Auntie, we are having a very pleasant time here though the weather is now rather uncertain. We are most comfortable and the garden is delightful. We are keeping well and are taking it easy. Hope to see Paul and Jen on Saturday. Hope you are well. Love from all. Dorothy." – As written on the back of an old postcard that I bought of the quay and harbour in Minehead.

I had scheduled today as an alternate day in Abbotsbury to get the two walks done in order to choose the best weather, but since we completed them, I changed plans for today to get us closer to a beach instead for a "rest day." After breakfast and saying our goodbyes and thank yous to Maria and Steve of our B&B in Abbotsbury, Scott and I took a taxi to Weymouth where I found a hotel literally across the road from the Esplanade and the beach. Our room even had sea views! We dropped off our luggage in the lobby, as the room was not ready yet on this cloudy-turned-sunny dry day, and started our restful day.

We didn't do a lot today, but somehow the time passed by, and we had a few nice experiences. First, we went on a slow ramble around a place called Radipole Lake in the middle of the larger town of Weymouth, completely not on the SWCP, that Scott found in doing some research of something to do today in Weymouth. Although a sign there did link this lake to the SWCP by talking about a "Legacy Trail" where one can walk from an area of farmland landscape to this lake and onto Chesil and the Fleet and to the Isle of Portland. Radipole Lake itself was inland from the Esplanade of Weymouth by about a mile and is a place for bird watchers. We strolled around the lake slowly for at least an hour looking at some of the wildlife one can see such as swans, cormorants, grebes, ducks, mallards, kingfishers, butterflies, dragonflies, and water voles.

After our saunter we made our way back to the many shopping and food streets of Weymouth that we had discovered that had lots and lots of various shops and restaurants. We meandered into a few of the shops after eating some lunch.

We then strolled up and down some of the long beach of Weymouth, and even paddled in the water, for quite a while. The coolness of the sand and the water on my feet felt refreshing. The weather was nice, being on the warm side. There were views from the sandy and pebbly beach across the water to Osmington Mills, Lulworth Cove, and the large white cliffs of that area. The white cliffs of the 145-65 million-year-old Cretaceous period.

I really wanted to go back to one shop we had found earlier that had a lot of old, mostly black and white, photographed postcards of various villages and scenes of places all along the SWCP! I was amazed to have found this. They had boxes and boxes of these old postcards. We spent nearly an hour going through them all, hurrying towards the end as the store was closing, to choose some of my favorites that reminded me of places I had walked all along the SWCP. I could have purchased so many of them, but I "limited" myself to twenty-seven of them which made a good representation of my 630-mile walking adventure. Some postcards had writing on the back, such as the one from Minehead in my quote above (names changed), which seems to be dated from 1955, which would make this postcard 63 years old! The photo of this one is of the quay and harbour in Minehead with boats, buildings, and a hillside in the background. It even had a two pence stamp on it with an image of Queen Elizabeth II. Here is a sampling of some of these old postcards, in order from Minehead to Poole, with description of the photo and other interesting things such as stamps, dates, postmarks, what's written on the back, and/or publishing information:

High Street, Clovelly – Photo includes donkeys walking up the cobbled street with a sign for the New Inn. Stamp is a half pence, and the postmark date might be 8 September 06, so this postcard might be well over 100 years old from 1906! Did I really find postcards this old?!

Boscastle from the Harbour – Photo includes the breakwater, the harbour, and the buildings in the valley, probably taken from the hillside above at Penally Point. No writing, dates, stamps, or postmarks on the back, even though it says, "This is a real photograph." I would be certain that this image is from well before the flood of 2004.

Bedruthan Steps, Newquay – This photo looks a bit colorized showing the large rocks at low tide with the headlands beyond from the vantage point of above. Nothing written on back and no dates.

Porthtowan – Photo is black and white of the beach at Porthtowan with rolling waves and the hillsides beyond. On the back the date is written "17-4-19" so this one appears to be from 1919!

Early Morning St. Ives – Black and white photo of boats in the harbour of St. Ives looking out to the breakwater with one of the Harbour Lighthouses at the end of the pier. The sun is rising in the clouds. This one has a two pence stamp similar to the one in Minehead, and the postmark looks like 16 September 1957.

Porthcurnow Beach – (That's how it is spelled on the postcard.) Photo is of the rock formation from the vantage of the hillside above near the Minack Theater, and of the hillsides and beach below. No writing or dates on back. However, many of these postcards have the publisher on the back of them, so I researched this one, "Pictorial Stationery Co. Ltd. London. Peacock Series. Art Monotone." Per a website, this publisher was "Founded in 1897 [in] London. The company started publishing postcards in 1902." 1902!

Mousehole Village near Penzance – Photo is colorized of a view from a road above the harbour looking down on some roofs of buildings to the harbour with its breakwaters, more buildings, and green hillsides beyond. The back says, "We are spending the afternoon here, just having a rest on the rocks. We are having a glorious time and lovely weather." (Glad they had good weather.) Postmark date is 8 August 08, so probably 1908(!), with the stamp being a "Half Penny"!

Summer Evening, Mullion Cove, South Cornwall – Photo is from the path above Mullion Cove looking down on the grass, the breakwalls of the small harbour, and the hillsides and rock islands beyond. Written on the back is, "Dear All, had a showery journey down, but lovely since. Had a fine rough sea on Saturday night. Went to Coverack on Sunday and Traboe for a cream tea. Spent this morning in Helston (Market Day.) All good wishes, Edith and Don." Postmark is most likely 1952 with a two pence stamp. (Some rain, and a cream tea!)

Asparagus Island, Kynance Cove – Black and white photo of the rock formations at low tide. No writing on the back, but I did research the postcard manufacturer, "Judges LTD, Hastings." Still known as Judges Postcards, it was called Judges Limited between 1910 and 1984.

The Lizard – Photo is from beyond the Lizard Lighthouse looking back at the lighthouse with the coves and hillsides in front so the lighthouse is in the distance in the background. I have similar photos I took. Some writing on the back says, "Dear Mr. and Mrs. Potts, Having a lovely time, having showers, the little coves and bays are very low down and so beautiful. You can get among the rocks and it is lovely and warm. Hope you had a happy birthday. All the best." Postmark is from 27 June 1966, and the stamp is three pence. (Interesting to read about the weather in some of these photos, and to see the price of stamps going up. I wonder if the cove they are talking about is the same one I liked just past the lighthouse.)

Church Cove, The Lizard – Postcard photo is of a building on the right side of the cove, several rowboats, and the hillside on the left side of the cove. Comparing the postcard to photos I took, the building is still there, but the rowboats in the photos I took are more worn down as if they have not been used for a while since this postcard.

Fowey and Polruan – I bought a little envelope containing six small "real photo snapshots" of these two towns. They are described as "Fowey and Polruan, Fowey Harbour from Castle, Ready Money Cove, Fowey from Hall Walk, Fowey from Polruan, and Bodinnick." I decided to mail these postcards to Lucy several months after I arrived home as a thank you gift to her for all her helpfulness, so for myself I made copies of the small snapshots.

The Harbour, Polperro – Photo includes a few rowboats floating in the water, buildings, and the hillside above. One of the buildings is where the Polperro Heritage Museum of Smuggling and Fishing is now I believe. On the back of the postcard is written, "Thursday 23 June 1930. Still having delightful time and weather. Went to Lansallos yesterday afternoon. This is a very good view of this part of the harbour. Must point out interesting bits to you when we return. When the tide goes out, this part is quite dry. Hardly believe it, can you? Lots of love." Postage is one penny.

The Harbour and Quay, Brixham – Photo is of various boats in the harbour with the buildings above. This photo appears to be colorized. No writing or postmarks on back, but it says, "This is a genuine Photogravure

Memories of the South West Coast Path

Two old guidebooks, six paintings on living room wall, and sample of six old postcards.
(See specific list on page 380)

Production." I researched that photogravure is "an image produced from a photographic negative transferred to a metal plate and etched in." I wonder now if some of the other postcards that I have said "colorized" are actually this process as well.

The Ness and Lighthouse, Teignmouth – A view of a grassy area in front of the lighthouse looking out to the lighthouse and the hillside beyond. This photo is either colorized or a painting or the photogravure technique. The publisher of this postcard is "The Knight Collection of British View Cards." Upon research, it is possible that this company was only in business from 1904 to 1908!

Lyme Regis, Ware Cliff - View of two people sitting on an open area with trees and shrubs and the hillside above surrounding them. Photo seems colorized. The postmark on the back is mailed from Lyme Regis dated August 06, so 1906, with a half penny stamp! Writing says, "Dear Kelli, Very warm here today. Plenty of people about. I have enjoyed…" then unfortunately I cannot read the rest. I wonder if this person walked the Undercliffs.

Charmouth – Photo is taken from the beach at Charmouth with a few rowboats in the foreground, the hillside just beyond (probably before it was closed from a landslip), and Golden Cap in the distance. No writing on the back, but also by "Judges Ltd Hastings," similar to Asparagus Island, Kynance Cove.

The Esplanade, Swanage – The back of this postcard says it is "reproduced from water color drawing," and is a color view of the Esplanade from above, the beach, the waters of Swanage Bay, and the white cliffs beyond. There is a horse and buggy with a few people sitting in the buggy in the drawing.

What a fun and historical collection of the places I have been, reliving my memories of the SWCP through old photos and postcards dating back fifty to hundred years old, and even older! Most of these I paid today 50 pence/67 cents, or £1/$1.33 for, and a few were £2/$2.67.

These postcards, along with the two old guidebooks that I found in Fowey, "Cornwall's Coastal Footpath" and "The South West Way," and the five paintings I have on my living room wall, have all got to be the most amazing finds I just happened to have found all along the SWCP, and amazingly all related to the SWCP in one way or another! I will treasure these always as my most valued treasures, along with all my own memories documented in this book and all my own photos, from my walking adventure on England's 630-mile South West Coast Path!

After dinner and a short rest, Scott and I strolled on the beach once again around sunset time. It was a calming and peaceful day. Even though I cried again because I am going to miss all this!

DAY 39 (DAY 126) STATS: NO SWCP MILES. PROBABLY TWO OR THREE LEISURELY MILES ALL DAY. PURPLE SHOES AND FLIP FLOPS AND BARE FEET. Most publisher/postcard manufacturer information from sandgrownlass.co.uk/old-postcards/postcard-publishers.
Some information also from hertfordshire-genealogy.co.uk/data/postcards/publisher-knight-brothers.

TYNEHAM TO WORBARROW BAY – 630 MILES COMPLETED! – Saturday, 5 May 2018

"Walk and be Happy. Walk and be Healthy." – Charles Dickens

Part One:

In the middle of the night last night from our room right across the road from the beach in Weymouth, I could hear the small ripple sounds of the small waves rolling onto the beach. That was nice and soothing to hear my favorite sound during the night. Before Scott and I started my final mile and a half walk needed in order to complete the entire SWCP today, we picked up some sandwiches for the walk, and took a taxi first to drop off our bags in Lulworth (although the place we stayed at wouldn't let us drop them this early in the morning, so this taxi driver handed off our luggage to the taxi driver that would pick us up later on today), and then we were dropped off at the car park at the abandoned village of Tyneham for my last missed section. Last year when we took the inland detour to Tyneham from Worbarrow Bay, we took the other inland detour out to a different part of the SWCP, thereby missing the SWCP between Worbarrow Bay and where the other inland detour to Tyneham met each other. It was only about a mile and a half section, but in order to complete the actual entire SWCP, I wanted to walk this section.

To start the walk for today, we repeated the slight uphill of the other inland detour out of Tyneham, which took about ten minutes. This had views looking out to Worbarrow Bay with all the beautiful large white cliffs surrounding it, and the greenery of grass and shrubs and trees in the foreground. Even some yellow gorse was in bloom. We took a right turn towards the bay to walk the last mile and a half of the SWCP. I was feeling a mix of emotions – Anxiousness, which was odd, but I was wondering how I would really feel in about forty-five minutes; Happiness – that in about forty-five minutes I would have walked every mile of the SWCP; Sadness – that in about forty-five minutes I would have walked every mile of the SWCP that I fell in love with, and I would miss it. It was a brilliantly sunny day out and very warm, almost hot. A great day for my last walk, and I was grateful.

The path was a wide flat grassy and dry dirt path with amazing views out to Worbarrow Bay as we walked towards the bay and the large white cliffs. The water was such a deep blue out today, the grasses and trees and shrubs were so green, the cliffs were so white, and even on top of those cliffs I could see a couple of bright yellow fields of rapeseed in bloom. I was still seeing all kinds of shades of my favorite colors, blue and green, on my last SWCP walk. All those beautiful views continued for the mile and a half, even with the barbed wire fence and warning signs on my right about The Lulworth Military Firing Ranges area that we were walking through. They were open this weekend, and when I planned my itinerary, I actually had to adjust a few days in order to make sure that I would be in this area during a time when the range was open. The warning signs told us, "Danger unexploded shells. Keep out." And later, "Military firing range. Keep out."

On my left were the edges of some big cliffs that looked like they abruptly dropped, so I walked as far to the right side of the path as I could. Today was technically a "backwards" walk so that we could end the walk at Worbarrow Bay and have some beach time before going back inland to Tyneham to get our second taxi. At one point I stopped to take a photo of my purple shoes with the beautiful scenery of the bay and cliffs.

The water of the bay was so blue as we descended, my last descent of the SWCP. This descent started out gradual then got a bit steeper, but not too steep as I did not need to use the hiking poles that I brought with me today just in case I needed to use the poles since I was wearing my purple shoes for the last time. The views below also included a secluded cove to the left with an outcrop of land just before Worbarrow Bay.

As I walked down that last descent, I kept wondering what emotions I would feel at my final moment. Just like last year walking from Swanage to South Haven Point with Sasha asking me all day how I was feeling as we walked.

I passed through one last kissing gate (with Scott) and saw an information sign about Worbarrow.

I heard the waves crash on the beach.

I breathed in the sounds of the waves and the warmth of the day and the beauty of the scenery.

I walked down the last eleven steps onto the wide path of the SWCP that to the right goes to Tyneham in one mile, and to Kimmerage in two and a half miles, and to the left down to Worbarrow Bay beach. One final SWCP sign told me there was three quarters of a mile to Flower's Barrow and four miles to Lulworth Cove. That was it!

At exactly 11:34am on 5 May 2018, about an hour after we started walking with about two miles total including the inland detour, I had completed another missed section of the SWCP. Most importantly, I had now completed every single mile of the 630 miles of the South West Coast Path!!

I did it!! I stood there for a few moments on the wide path and breathed in once again the sounds of the waves and the warmth of the day and the beauty of the scenery…and the great sense of accomplishment…Scott congratulated me and hugged me, and I smiled with a couple of tears.

Part Two:

At that moment, what did I feel? I actually felt…hungry. Therefore, after a couple photos on the wide path of the SWCP at that spot, and after a little skip, hop, and jump in my purple shoes, Scott and I walked down to the beach to eat our sandwiches. I took off my socks and purple shoes as we sat by a babbling stream on the beach of Worbarrow Bay. I could hear both the stream and the waves on the beach. Several people were on the beach enjoying the warm day with no wind no rain no fog no excessive heat no thunder no hail. Just a perfect spring, actually a perfect summer-like, day.

I took a couple of photos of my purple shoes by themselves sitting on a rock with a view of the beach of Worbarrow Bay, the blue waters, and the white cliffs surrounding. All other photos I have taken of my purple shoes today were when I was wearing them. But these photos were the shoes by themselves. Perhaps a symbol that they, along with my hiking boots, had helped me accomplish my walk. That the purple shoes now needed to perhaps get repaired a bit actually before they would be able to walk again, but that I appreciated all my shoes and boots! (See back cover of this book for a photo of my purple shoes at Worbarrow Bay.)

After eating, we paddled in the cold water amongst a mix of sand and pebbles, and it felt like a good refreshing massage for my feet. I realized that fortunately I had no blisters these past six weeks, no toe nails that fell off, and no problems with my right knee. Scott took a few photos of me standing on the beach of Warbarrow Bay with those white cliffs in the background.

We went back to just sit for a while at this beach. I had the passing thought that I wondered when it was, two years ago, that Scott and I started walking my initial 100 miles of the SWCP. I knew it was in May sometime, but could it be exactly today, the 5th of May? Later I looked in my calendar and it was the 7th, but we had flown to England on the 5th, so just about exactly two years later, I had completed walking the entire SWCP.

Scott and I spent two calming and relaxing hours at the beach of the bay celebrating my accomplishment, mostly just sitting. I was just soaking in not only the sun and the warmth, but also the thoughts and feelings of what I had just accomplished. Reminiscing about the approximately 135 days of my life the past three years that I have spent in the South West corner of England, on the South West Coast Path.

As we had a prearranged taxi time however, we walked back to Tyneham and I wore my flip flops on the flat wide three-quarters of a mile gravel path, and also through a short Woodland Forest walk, back to the car park and the abandoned village of Tyneham. We spent a few minutes looking at a few more village remnants that we did not see last year including some buildings from a farm, including a horse stable and a farm barn that was also used as a theater. Displayed were an old horse-drawn wagon and some gardening tools.

As we were riding back to Lulworth in the taxi, I glanced that it was a beautiful 17C/63F, although it felt warmer. For our final nights along the SWCP I had booked a really nice room at The Castle Inn Pub.

Me on the South West Coast Path (all photos taken by Scott Dungan)
With a SWCP wooden signpost on Isle of Portland August 22
On a beach in Lyme Regis with Golden Cap in the background May 1
Worbarrow Bay, just before I completed 630 miles! May 5. I did it!

Part Three:

After checking into the pub, I wanted to extend my beach time and celebration time so we walked the half mile down to the beach at Lulworth Cove and sat on that beach for a half an hour, watching some people still enjoying the beach on this warm day, and watching a family of ducks with nine cute baby ducklings swimming in the water and waddling on the beach.

Then Scott and I had a good laugh because as we were walking back to the pub for dinner, I noticed a SWCP sign pointing to Stair Hole Cove, and I realized that I had actually not done that quarter of a mile last year. I did not even know until this moment that I missed this short bit. Last year we walked straight down the long hillside path from Durdle Door directly to the Lulworth Cove Inn, not even seeing the sign pointing to Stair Hole Cove.

So at 11:34 this morning, I had actually not completed the entire 630 miles of the SWCP. I still had a quarter mile to go! Before we went back to The Castle Inn Pub, I declared to Scott, "We have to do this now please!" So in my flip flops and jeans, we walked on a wide white paved path up to Stair Hole Cove, took a few photos of the holes and arches in the rocks by the water, and then photos of Lulworth Cove below from above. A sign from here said a quarter mile to Bindon Hill and one and a half miles to Mupe Bay, where Scott also took a few photos of me in my jeans and nice dinner shirt overlooking Lulworth Cove. There was also a final bench up here that became the subject of a few photos with the cove below that could possibly be in that "Benches of the South West Coast Path" photography book someday.

I walked down the wide white paved path and about forty steps down to the beach of Lulworth Cove. Therefore, at exactly 6:30pm on 5 May 2018 I had completed another (unknown) missed quarter-mile section of the SWCP. Most importantly, I had now completed every single mile of the 630 miles of the South West Coast Path!!

I did it!! I stood there for a moment and breathed in once again the sounds of the waves and the warmth of the day and the beauty of the scenery…and the great sense of accomplishment…

What was ironic about this was that after we got back to The Castle Inn Pub from Worbarrow Bay, I did all my Facebook posts telling everyone that at 11:34 this morning I had completed the SWCP. I really did not feel like doing another post about this quarter mile section, so I left the Facebook posts as is, and now anyone reading this book who read my Facebook posts will know that it was a quarter mile off, due to something I did not even realize till now.

This is what I wrote on Facebook before my realization:

"As of 11:34 this morning, I officially completed walking all 630 miles of the South West Coast Path!!! (With images of clapping smiles, thumbs ups, hearts, flowers, champagne bottles popping, and party poppers exploding.) Tyneham to Worbarrow Bay. I will write one more post tomorrow. Now it's time for a celebration walk down to Lulworth Cove and dinner and dessert."

Part Four:

So what were my emotions as I sat there earlier today at Worbarrow Bay when I thought I had completed the SWCP, and later in the day when I actually did complete the SWCP? I realized that over the last few years I had definitely fallen in love with the South West Coast Path! I felt a large sense of peacefulness and calmness that I had set out on an epic 50th birthday celebration walking adventure, and even though it took me into my 51st year, I had done it! I felt brave as I thought about the fact that a majority of the 630 miles I had done on my own, solo, alone, by myself. In fact, I had walked about an amazing 420 miles on my own, about two-thirds of the SWCP by myself! That does not include all the extra and repeat miles that I walked alone as well.

Just as I turned around to look back at the blue marker at South Haven Point on 29 August 2017, and as I walked forward into the gift of my left, and right, life, I felt…like the beauty of the scenery and the headlands and the beaches and the harbours and the seas and everything else in between on the South West Coast Path will forever be in my heart and soul. I felt like now I was really ready to see what would happen with the gift of my life at a walking pace. I felt accomplished, brave, courageous, proud, healthy, and happy!

DAY 40 (DAY 127) STATS: 4.0 MILES TOTAL. FINAL 1.5 MILES ON THE SWCP IN ONE HOUR! AND THEN LATER THE FINAL .25 MILES! EXTRA MILES INCLUDE A HALF MILE FOR BEFORE MISSED WALK, THREE QUARTERS OF A MILE FOR AFTER MISSED WALK, AND ONE MILE BACK AND FORTH FROM B&B. PURPLE SHOES.

EXTRA WALK – LULWORTH COVE TO MUPE BAY TO LULWORTH COVE – Sunday, 6 May 2018

"Over the last several years I have fallen in love with your lovely corner of the world all around the SWCP. **My adventure and journey has created so many memories for me, not to mention thousands of photos. When people ask me my favorite part, I cannot choose one. I tell them that each mile has its own special beauty."** – Me, as part of my final Facebook post.

Because I had scheduled an extra alternate day in the Lulworth area to do the Tyneham to Worbarrow Bay walk, and since I completed that yesterday, Scott and I had one more day today to do any walk in the area that I wanted to do. The first of two options were to Durdle Door. However, that would have been quite the crowded walk to do and place to go since this was a quite popular destination. With this being a Bank Holiday weekend, and a Sunday, and amazing summer-like weather, people were already on their way to Durdle Door as the large grassy car park at Lulworth Cove was already filling up in the morning, and the walking path going uphill from the car park already had a stream of people.

Therefore, for our final extra walk today I chose to at least go from Lulworth Cove to Mupe Bay and back, a four-mile walk round trip, and a walk we had done last year from Lulworth Cove to Mupe Bay and beyond. Last year to get around the possible high tides around Lulworth Cove itself, we took the alternate inland route complete with its 333-step descent, "the longest continuous flight of steps on the SW Coast Path." This year we thought we would go around the cove itself if possible. I checked the tide tables, and it did say that high tide would be at 11:16 in the morning, so I did not really know if walking the cove was even possible, but I thought we would walk down to the cove after breakfast anyway to look and evaluate the situation. If the tide was too high and we could not walk around the cove and would have had to walk the alternate way around, I would have to come up with something else to do today because I did not really want to descend the 333 steps today. I wanted a more leisurely day, since after all, I had completed the entire 630-mile SWCP.

After breakfast on our way down to Lulworth Cove from our B&B, we stopped at one café to get some sandwiches to take with us for lunch, and we stopped at a restaurant to make dinner reservations since we figured the few options in the village it might get crowded later with all the people already in the area.

We arrived at Lulworth Cove about a half hour before high tide and saw that it was perfectly fine to walk on the rocky beach around the curve of the cove. In fact, there were already many people on the rocky beach settling in for the day, not only on the area of the cove we were standing at, but all the way around as well. I would imagine that this many people would not be there if high tide meant getting stuck by the tides. I actually wondered if last year if we had walked down to the cove and looked to see then perhaps we would have been able to walk around the cove instead of taking the alternate route with the 333 steps. At least this way though I can say that I have walked both options now. (Disclaimer here, please check tide tables and make your own knowledgeable decision to walk around the cove. It is quite possible that since there is the alternate route, that at certain high tides it is not possible to walk around the cove.)

With my purple shoes on once more, it took us about twenty minutes to walk on the rocks to get around most of the cove. It was not easy going to walk on these rocks as there was no compact sand to walk on, but it wasn't difficult either. When we got to the other side, we decided to bypass the set of steps that lead out of the beach to the SWCP and instead walk to up a side path to the top of Pepler's Point that other people were taking. From here we were able to look down on Lulworth Cove with its several luxury yacht sailing boats and a few fishing boats floating in the blue water with the white cliffs covered in greenery surrounding the cove. We had views of the 333 steps on one side, and the path leading to Durdle Door on the other side.

We walked on a wide grassy path which led to the gate of the Lulworth Ranges, still open today. We walked the flat path overlooking the seas in the warm sun to the benches above Mupe Bay. On our way we had a view of the rocks and a small cove before Mupe Bay, along with the large white cliffs covered with greenery surrounding the bay and beyond out and across to Worbarrow Bay. This place was the scenery that last year reminded me of a lake in the mountains. I stopped and breathed in the amazing views and the beauty of it all. I would miss this for sure. I shed a tear.

I was originally thinking that we would eat our sandwiches at the benches above that look down on Mupe Bay. However, I noticed some steps leading down to the beach there and also saw a few people already on the beach below, so I said to Scott, "Let's eat down there." What a great bonus to go down and eat and sit on this beach for a while. There were a few luxury yachts floating in the bay, and a handful of people. Definitely not the crowds that were going to Durdle Door.

After we ate and sat on the sandy and pebbly beach for a while, with feeling the heat of the day increasing, I felt like taking a quick dip in the water. I did not pack my bathing suit with me however, since I did not even bring it at all with me for these past six weeks because I did not think that there would be any warm enough summer-like opportunities to swim in the spring, but with the heat of the sun today, and the blue of the sky with not a cloud in sight, I figured any clothes I got wet today would dry quickly. So spontaneously Scott and I dove into the cool turquoise and blue waters of Mupe Bay!

It was so refreshing! It was great. It was cleansing. It was freeing. It was like a polar bear plunge swim, which I have actually never done in my life, as the water was quite cool. It was summer in early May. I loved it. After diving in once and then standing up to experience this reaction, I dove in again. After getting out of the water completely and sitting back down, less than five minutes later, I dove in a third time. I definitely should have brought a bathing suit with me last summer in order to have done this last year as well when the weather cooperated.

I took a short nap in the warmth of the sun as my clothes began to dry. (Another nap on a "rest" day.) I actually brought my rain jacket with me today, as I always do no matter what the forecast because this is the coast after all, and I used the jacket to lie down on which worked well to catch the water dripping from my clothes. I was glad my rain jacket came in handy this past six weeks for something since I really only wore it a couple of times, probably amounting to no more than an hour's worth of rain (and hail) the entire six weeks!

I also sat and contemplated some about my 135 days over the last three years on the SWCP. I learned so much about the history of the SWCP. It all started with my reading on the SWCP Association's website, "The South West Coast Path was originally created by coastguards, patrolling the south west peninsula looking out for smugglers. They literally had to check in every inlet so their cliff top walk was well used and gives us the amazing Path we use today. The coastguard's children used these paths to go to school, while their wives used them to get from one fishing hamlet to the next. The Path has also been used by fishermen looking for shoals of fish and checking sea conditions." I indeed did learn a lot about smuggling, the coastguard, and fishing. I also learned a lot about farming, mining, shipwrecks, lighthouses, and World War 2. I appreciate all that I learned. I even learned about a lot of various organizations all connected to the SWCP in one way or another. There were all the books I read as well, from guidebooks, to personal experiences walking the SWCP or walking the coast of Britain or living here, from both men and women. I read books and booklets providing me with all kinds of information. I found treasures of paintings, old postcards, and old guidebooks.

While I did not pick up learning the British accent, I did learn some British words: car park, rucksack, waterproofs, trainers, brolly, take away, lovely, brilliant, and cheers! Some of my favorite words I learned are knackered, paddling, brecko, and bits and bobs. I enjoyed so much British food, even though I skipped the Full English. Cream tea, of course, was the winner, with the many desserts coming in second. I watched a few episodes of Doc Martin, and saw some actors. I became a paleontologist, geologist, and fossil hunter for a couple of days. I listened to some music on the speakers of my mobile, and listened to some live music as well. I walked through millions of years of time, from the Triassic to the Jurassic to the Cretaceous periods. I saw and/or visited about 40 various types of lighthouses/aids to navigation.

I started each day with a quote, wrote down my daily stats at the end of each day, and looked up pubs to include in the stats. I won a photography contest all because I was born on Groundhog's Day. I walked in four counties, the north and south parts of one of these counties, and the entirety of another. I walked by channels and seas, all extensions of the Atlantic Ocean. I chose my favorite location for a beach hut, with so many other favorite locations as well. I really loved all the small fishing villages, with their harbours and various types of boats, which took me back in time.

Between my three years, I figured out that I took over 16,300 photos, between both my mobile phone and my camera! About 2,300 from 2016, about 10,000 from 2017, and about 4,000 from 2018. (Good thing for digital these days, instead of the old film days.)

I visited some very small churches, a few churches only powered by candlelight, and so many other churches with their history, architecture, spirituality, where I could say my usual prayers. I never could really identify birds and wildflowers on my own, but appreciated them all nonetheless. My blister theories worked for me fortunately, even though I had a toe nail fall off. I fortunately never encountered any adders or ticks. I decided that I might create three specific photography books from my walks along the SWCP.

It was the people that made my walk all that much more special. I walked with some, both strangers that became friends, new friends, a great friend, and my husband. I felt I had support from those who share a common love of the SWCP. People in the B&Bs were helpful as well. I met authors/writers, artists, and poets. And I learned great words of wisdom from some.

My purple shoes and I experienced a lot together, much of the SWCP walking by myself, and never once did I ever think of giving up. In fact, now that I think about it, I also felt quite safe as a solo woman walking the SWCP. Yes, I felt accomplished, brave, courageous, proud, healthy, and happy!

Scott and I stayed at Mupe Bay for just over two hours and walked back on the SWCP overlooking the seas. One last look of the blue waters, one last smell of the fresh sea air, one last feel of the positive negative ions, one last look at the beauty surrounding me. This time we took the short set of steps that went down to the rocky beach of Lulworth Cove and walked back around the cove on the rocks, filled with more luxury sailing boat yachts, taking an hour to walk from Mupe Bay. There were a lot more people on the rocky beach at this time than this morning enjoying the summer day. We did a four-mile round trip walk today, complete with a few refreshing dips in the water, some napping and sitting quietly on the beach, and some contemplating my walking adventure on England's 630-mile South West Coast Path.

I thought we should walk into one more place that perhaps represented the important fishing industry along the SWCP, so we walked briefly into Cove Fish, a small shack that was selling fresh, local fish "straight off their boat." There was Lulworth Pollack, local scallops, Lulworth lobster, Chesil cold smoked salmon, king prawns, smoked sprats, crab paté, and other fish for sale. Even Samphire was for sale, that salty small skinny green crisp sea vegetable herb that I tried and liked last year at a B&B in Wyke Regis. There were also several photographs on the wall of various fishermen with their fishing boats or other fishing gear, along with a poster of a family history tree of "The Miller Family of Purbeck, Dorset" going back to the 1600s, all the way through the late 1900s, showing ten generations of this fishing family. I figured that some of the photos were of members of this family, and from some research I did found out that, "this family run business has been situated in the picturesque Lulworth Cove for generations." What a great historical record of a fishing family inside this tiny shop, along with seeing all the fresh fish, a final reminder for me of the important fishing industry along the SWCP.

Scott and I stopped in a café for a snack, and later we went out to a nice dinner at a restaurant we ate at last year together, the one we made reservations at this morning, complete with dessert, for my final night along the

SWCP, to celebrate. For dinner I ate the same healthy meal I ate last year, a Super Food Salad with various greens like kale and spinach, quinoa, pumpkin seeds, blueberries, avocado, and a pomegranate dressing. For my final celebration dessert, I had a chocolate torte topped with ice cream (which the ice cream I gave to Scott) and raspberries. Yes, I am still having chocolate and desserts!

As I said, I would write one last Facebook post, and this is what I put on the SWCP Facebook Group pages (with some modifications depending on which group it was posted to):

"Thank you for all the "likes" and comments yesterday as I completed my 630 miles. I mentioned I would write one more post (for now anyway), and it is a longer one. Today on this beautiful summer day, I took my husband and my purple shoes one on more short "repeat" walk today on my last day on the SWCP before we make our way back home tomorrow. Lulworth Cove to Mupe Bay, with lots of sitting time at Mupe Bay, and even a short swim. Over the last several years I have fallen in love with your lovely corner of the world all around the SWCP. My adventure and journey has created so many memories for me, not to mention thousands of photos. I am at a mix of emotions from completing the walk, from pure happiness and excitement of this accomplishment, to sadness that I will miss these 630 miles with all the beautiful scenery when I go home. It has been a journey of ups and downs, both literally and figuratively. I had some challenges with weather last year, my heart racing walking next to cows, and times of feeling lonely. But I walked most of the path by myself, have had great weather as well, and I love walking next to sheep! I've met some great people along the way, including some of you all to walk with, to even meeting a couple of local authors and artists. I had days and days of walking for hours and hours, which is quite calming and meditative. When people ask me my favorite part, I cannot choose one. I tell them that each mile has its own special beauty. I also learned a lot about the history of the SWCP, such as smuggling and mining, and have grown to appreciate important industries, such as fishing and farming. I have loads of experiences and stories that I had every single day of my walking. I've had a few cream teas, too! Of course, I have mentioned that I am writing a book about it all with much detail on scenery, people, thoughts, feelings, history, and much, much more. It will be called "The Arrow Closest To The Acorn – An American Woman's Walking Adventure On England's 630-Mile South West Coast Path," and of course I will let you all know when it is finished. (Might take me several more months as I also have to find a job when I get back home). I want to say a big thank you to everyone who has looked at my photos, commented, and in many ways, being able to share my photos and walks with you all has been a big source of support for me. And a big thank you to Lucy who answered so many questions for me, especially about transportation and other help with my itinerary for these last six weeks. My purple shoes will need a bit of repair if they are to walk with me anymore. And I deserve a great foot massage, too. You will hear from me again, and I will continue to look at all your photos and walks which will bring back the memories for me, but for now, Cheers!"

DAY 41 (DAY 128) STATS: EXTRA WALK OF 4.0 MILES. ABOUT TWO HOURS OF WALKING AND OVER TWO HOURS OF BEACH TIME. PURPLE SHOES, THEN BARE FEET AT THE BEACH. Information on the Cove Fish shop from www.bestofengland.com/cove-fish.

FINAL STATS: 630 SWCP MILES, AND ABOUT 160 EXTRA MILES BETWEEN LAST SUMMER AND THIS SPRING. THIS SPRING'S EXTRA MILES INCLUDES NON-SWCP MILES AND REPEAT MILES. ALL FOR A GRAND TOTAL OF NEARLY 800 MILES OF WALKING!! OF THE 630 SWCP MILES I WALKED ABOUT 420 MILES BY MYSELF, WHICH DOES NOT INCLUDE EXTRA MILES, SO PERHAPS ABOUT 500 MILES TOTAL BY MYSELF! THE EQUIVALENT OF MARK WALLINGTON'S "500 MILE WALKIES." (WELL, NOT EXACTLY…) (I DID NOT TOTAL UP ALL THE HOURS OF WALKING.)

THE FINAL HOURS, BACK HOME, EPILOGUE/REFLECTIONS, AND WHAT'S NEXT (7 MAY 2018 TO BOOK COMPLETION)

"Debby Lee Jagerman-Dungan Walked the South West Coast Path, Britain's Longest National Trail (630 Miles)." – My Completer's Certificate from the South West Coast Path Association.

"South West Coast Path National Trail [Acorn Symbol] Certificate of Completion. Debby Lee Jagerman-Dungan Completed the 630 mile National Trail on May 5, 2018. National Trail Team." – My Completer's Certificate from National Trails UK.

The Final Hours – Monday, 7 May 2018

Upon reading some of the many comments I received on my Facebook posts yesterday, one person reminded me once again, "You were so brave to walk by yourself, it's certainly a journey and a half, well done." Brave! And yes, I guess that is true, it was a journey and a half. Since my adventure was not just about the walking. It was about so much more.

Before Scott and I made our way to Heathrow Airport to fly home, I wanted to take one more final short walk of about a half mile round trip to one final church, the Holy Trinity Church in West Lulworth, a few minutes' walk from The Castle Inn Pub. It was already warm out after breakfast on this record-breaking-heat-Bank-Holiday-Monday in May. It had been like summer the past few days, definitely calm on the Beaufort Wind Scale. On our way to the church, a sign outside our B&B told us, "Twelve days to go till the Royal Wedding." The church was in a lovely setting with green farmland surrounding it. Scott wrote our names in the church book and wrote the word "Peace."

This time as I did one more set of my usual prayers, I did the prayers a bit differently than I have always done. Usually I just sat and said them in a kind of a whisper voice quietly, or just in thought. But this time, with no one inside the church since Scott was outside, I paced up and down the aisle of the church back and forth and said my prayers in a talking-out-loud voice. There were lots of extra thank yous and gratefulness and gratitude for my adventure and journey over the past several years. Gratefulness for keeping me safe and healthy and injury-free, and even mostly blister-free. Gratefulness for the weather, that even with the challenges (gale force winds, strong winds, torrential downpours, rain, excessive heat, fog, thunder, hail, mud), it all still worked out. Gratitude for all the things that worked out positively during my 630-mile adventure. Thankfulness for the safety and health of my family and friends. Thankfulness for the people I have met along the way, from existing friends, to new friends, to every single guardian angel, whether they helped me out in small ways or larger ways, as they were all equally important. Gratefulness to my husband for his companionship, support, and being one of my biggest guardian angels. Gratitude to the rest of my family, especially my Mom, for all their support. Gratitude for my feet and legs. Thankfulness that I have been able to walk (or bike) every single mile. Gratefulness that I was able to walk the majority of the miles by myself, as an American woman on her epic 50th birthday walking adventure. Gratefulness for my making peace with golf courses and cows, and for the horses and sheep and even mountain goats. Gratitude that I have learned so much about this lovely corner of the world that I have fallen in love with. Thankfulness for the oceans and seas and waters for their beauty, and for their negative ions. Gratefulness for the amazing landscape and scenery, the hillsides and headlands, the coves and bays, the beaches and coastline, the wildflowers and trees and shrubbery and nature, and all its amazing beauty that changed with every single mile. Thankfulness for the sounds of the crashing and quiet ocean waves, birds chirping, church bells, and even complete silence. Gratitude for time to meditate and contemplate and just sit. Gratitude for whomever it is, whether a guardian angel above all other guardian angels, or the greater universe in general, or both, that has been watching over me and helping me whenever I needed it, as perhaps that someone was listening to me right at this very moment. Gratefulness to myself for being my own biggest guarding angel, and having the bravery and courage to walk.

I also asked out loud for guidance on the next parts of the gift of my life - the unknown to me now of my next job and career, smoothness for the finishing of writing and publishing of this book, and whatever my next adventures will be. Finally, I still prayed for the world, for peace, love, compassion, and understanding.

I also bought one final cookbook at this church in West Lulworth, "Coast & Country Cooking. 270 Favourite Recipes," a collection of recipes from people living in Dorset, complete with illustrations, "tips and jokes and wisdom." Whether I use this cookbook or not, such as the other cookbooks I have bought I don't know, but I will add this book to the great collection of all my memories from my walk along England's 630-mile South West Coast Path.

Back Home

"The sand may brush off. The salt may wash away. But the memories will last forever." - Unknown

About a week after I returned from England, I thankfully found a job doing something completely different than what I was doing in the past, not related to accounting at all. In fact, they allowed me to work four days a week for a while so that I would have time to finish writing, editing, and publishing this book.

On the 19th of May 2018, I watched the entire elegant Royal Wedding of a British Royal marrying an American actress, Prince Harry, His Royal Highness The Duke of Sussex, to Meghan Markle, Her Royal Highness The Duchess of Sussex. Although I wasn't in England to watch, nor did I watch it live, as it would have been quite early in the morning for me with the time difference, I still felt honored to be able to watch such an historical event on TV. And about five months later in October, the couple announced that they are pregnant and due to give birth in the spring of 2019. Their baby will be seventh in line to the throne, and is yet unnamed.

I also purchased and received two Completer's Certificates in the mail, and proudly hung them by magnets on the side of our refrigerator underneath the map of the SWCP, quite near the living room wall where the five paintings I have of my memories of the SWCP are hanging. See quotes at the beginning of this chapter above for exactly what the certificates say. The image on the National Trails UK Certificate of Completion is of a lighthouse on the coast sitting next to a green hillside on brown rocks. I wonder if it is the Start Point Lighthouse, since that is what this image looks like to me reminding me of the two days that I walked from Lannacombe towards this lighthouse. The image on the SWCP Association Completer's Certificate is of various drawn reminders of the SWCP, including the monument in Minehead, a few directional signposts, possibly the mining ruins of the Wheal Coates Mine that I saw back on the 2nd of July on my way towards Chapel Porth, Smeaton's Tower in Plymouth, a sailboat, some sheep, some cows, a few other random images, and the blue marker at South Haven Point.

I also just had to purchase a few more older SWCP guidebooks because the ones I found in Fowey were so interesting to read and to have. In the 1982 version of "The South West Way" that I had, in its "other books" section, it mentioned a series of three books that they considered, "undoubtedly to date the best collection of books covering the whole path." These are "Coastal Walks. The South-west Peninsula Coast-Path" by Ken Ward and John H.N. Mason, published by Letts Guides. I found them online, and was able to get the first and third books, Minehead to St. Ives, and Plymouth to Poole, in their First Edition form, published in the year 1977. The second book, St. Ives to Plymouth, I was able to get in their Second Edition form. All three booklets are 96 pages, break down the mileage into short three-and-a-half to five-mile sections, have fun hand-drawn maps, brief descriptions of each section, and some history and other information at the end. The first sentence of all three books says, "The South-west Peninsula Coast Path is unique; a walk of 500 miles through some of the finest coastal scenery in Europe." 500! In Europe! More great treasures of my memories of the SWCP.

And on the 24th of October 2018, I had not only finished round three of this book by re-reading the entire book from beginning to end and editing anything necessary, I also finished going through all my miscellaneous random notes, and finished writing this final chapter! However, there are still more things to do…other miscellaneous pages and lists and notes, formatting, deciding on which photos to include, converting interior photos to black and white and organizing them on pages, choosing front and back cover photos, front and back cover designing, and everything else that is required for writing and publishing my book.

Finally, once this book is complete, published, and available for sale, I will write up something for the SWCP Association where people are allowed to write about their experiences after completing the entire SWCP.

Epilogue/Random After Thoughts/Reflections

"The journey of a thousand miles begins with one step." - Lao Tzu

I've had some random after thoughts, reflecting on my 630-mile walking adventure during the months that I have been working on this book.

I've been thinking about the progression of my walking adventure along the SWCP and how while for the most part, I look at my long walk as an "adventure." I think it was also a "journey" as well, especially as it relates to the universe, being taken care of, spirituality, my connection with the Camino de Santiago, and guardian angels. From the beginning I always felt that I would be taken care of by what I call "guardian angels - amazing people, both strangers and friends, who one way or another show up just at the exact right moment in time that I need something, anything, whether big or small, usually when I have not even asked specifically for assistance at the moment, but have needed it anyway." All that is true since I had so many strangers show up to help me out, as well as old friends, new friends, and my husband. I had also realized though that not only are there these types of guardian angels, but that I had been my own biggest guardian angel all along. Being brave and having the courage to walk, and to not walk. To face challenges, and to come to appreciate everything about the SWCP. I had also realized that there is even a guardian angel above all other guardian angels, the greater universe in general, and something or someone greater than me watching over me. At times I didn't think I was on any type of spiritual journey, or even pilgrimage, but perhaps with all this, in some ways, I was.

And yes, it has been a journey and a half. A journey of ups and downs, literally and figuratively, and as Sasha said, "the emotional rollercoaster." With the "down" experiences on my walk including some uncooperative weather, some feelings of loneliness, getting lost, missing miles, and a job loss. And with the "up" experiences including the connection with nature, with the seas, the beaches, the sand, the sky, the beauty, the scenery, the peacefulness, the people, the stories, the history, and everything else. There were the views as well, also both literally and figuratively, of behind me to see where I have been, and ahead of me to see where I shall be going. There was a deeper appreciation and thankfulness and gratitude for everything in my life and all my experiences along all my SWCP walks. And I realized my desire to experience life at a walking pace.

I thought about all the times that I had connections with my SWCP walk and my walk on the Camino de Santiago in Spain, such as in St. Mawes, in Plymouth, St. Michael's Way, The Saints Way, scallop shells and arrows and more, and how really now that I think about it, if it was not for that walk along the Camino Francés that led me to do the walk up the Atlantic coast of Spain of about only twenty miles from Finisterre to Muxía, how I may not have thought about and discovered walking the SWCP at all. It was in that short significant twenty miles in Spain that I fell in love with walking by the seas, waters, and oceans, which led me to falling in love with the SWCP in England.

Even though it may have taken me over the course of three years to complete my SWCP walk, it was worth every single step and every single mile. I realized that it never was about me walking the path in the fastest time possible. Eventually, it did not become about me walking the entire path at once, nor about walking it all by myself. It truly became about exploring and seeing and experiencing and feeling as much as I could along the way.

In the end, I did walk the equivalent elevation gain and loss of climbing the world's tallest mountain, Mount Everest, four times, 115,000 feet of ascent and descent. And then some more, since I ended up walking about 160 miles more in addition to the 630 for a total of about 800 miles. All without being exposed to the elements of snow, ice, crevasses, glaciers, bitter cold, altitude, oxygen tanks, climbing ropes, and ice axes. I must have crossed all 230 bridges, caught 13 ferries, opened and closed 880 gates, and climbed over 436 stiles (one of which was a record-breaking climb due to some cows). I must have passed more than 4,000 Coast Path signs, and went up or down over 30,000 steps, which is "not counting the many climbs and descents where no steps are found."

I recalled back to the 3rd of June last year when I was at the airport setting off on my adventure. I was in my element. I had my inner sense of travel and adventure turned on. My daypacks/rucksacks, hiking boots, camera, hiking poles, hiking pants, many pairs of socks, various shirts and jackets and rain gear, and my purple shoes, all did their job. I took the time and spent the money. My planning and my spreadsheets and utilizing three websites and booking 50 B&Bs last year, and 17 B&Bs this year, all worked out. I completed my epic 50th birthday celebration. I settled the debate of walking alone or with my husband, which turned out to be a combination of both, the love story, plus walking with a few other people, which all was a good combination. Even though I didn't walk the entire path in one go, I still completed all 630 miles on a long-distance walking trail, the longest walking trail in the United Kingdom, and the sixteenth longest hiking trail in the world (not including any in the United States).

I also realized, with the reminder from my husband, that several years ago in my search for books about walking the SWCP written by women walking solo, I had only come across Sasha Harding's book. Now with my book, this is quite possibly the only other one, or one of the very very few, written by women walking solo (even though I also walked with others)! Furthermore, I don't believe that there are any books written by American women walking England's SWCP, whether solo or with others! So am I the first one to write a book about an American woman's walking adventure on England's 630-mile SWCP? Wouldn't that be something if I am! Something to be proud of. I don't have statistics of how many Americans walk the SWCP, whether all at once or over the course of time, and I don't have statistics of how many Americans walk solo or with others, but perhaps compared to the British, I may be one of the few American women to complete the entire SWCP, mostly on my own and with the company of other great people, and to write a book about it!

Back on the 4th of June, I started with a quote, the second quote of this book, "The journey of a thousand miles begins with one step." Back then I said that the journey of 630 miles begins with one step. Now I say that the journey of 800 miles ends with one step, and the gift of my left, and right, life, now begins with one step.

What's Next? Shall I Walk The SWCP Again?

As far as the SWCP goes, what is next for me aside from writing my book? Since I have fallen in love with the SWCP, and fallen in love with being beside the seaside, I know that someday soon, I want to return and walk it all again, hopefully in one go, without missing any miles! I love it that much, especially with reliving it all again as I have been working on this book. In fact, as I was doing my final round of editing for this book, by reading the entire book from beginning to end, I created another spreadsheet called my "SWCP Ideal New Itinerary." It is quite similar to my itinerary last summer actually, but with a few differences.

For example, I would start out by walking from Minehead to Porlock Weir of nine or ten miles on the first day, and take the alternate Coast Path, the lower more seaward "rugged" route next time. I would also walk the entire Tarka Trail instead of bike, and some other days I have increased mileage since I know the terrain. I originally thought about skipping the five miles in the industrial area of Plymouth in my Ideal New Itinerary, but ultimately I decided that when I walk the SWCP again, I want to include this as well in order to complete the entire 630 miles again all in one go. Someone suggested to me that I could perhaps walk the SWCP in the "backwards" direction from Poole to Minehead, but since I am already familiar with the "forwards" direction, know what to expect with the terrain and the possibilities of uncooperative weather, I think I would prefer to walk it forwards again.

This Ideal New Itinerary still has me walking an average of eight or nine miles per day. Again so that I could ideally walk it all in one go, and to not rush my days. To be able to really appreciate my walk again, and to once again explore, see, experience, and feel all that the SWCP has to offer. I still have built in lots of extra/alternate/rest days in case of uncooperative weather. I would also have at least one day where I could collect more fossils and sea glass and pottery. In addition, I am ready to conquer the Undercliffs by myself!

By myself? Or with my husband? Again, that would be the debate. Perhaps a combination of both again though, with this time perhaps he can join me at the beginning, or in other areas that he has not yet been to, and walk what he has not yet walked. I would welcome walking again with Sasha, with old friends, with new friends, and with other people from the SWCP Facebook Groups who love the SWCP.

But still, wouldn't it be epic to say that I really did walk the SWCP all by myself in one go, or mostly by myself, in one go? In fact, perhaps next year in 2019, wouldn't it be something to say that I walked in all in one go as an epic 52nd birthday celebration?

Would I walk in the spring or in the summer of 2019? Maybe I would start out in the spring and end in the middle of summer. Or walk in the entire summer, and hope that next summer would have consistent beautiful warm sunny weather. If I do start in the spring though, maybe it would be around the time that Meghan and Harry have their baby, and I would be in England for that historic event.

Maybe I would also include somehow walking St. Michael's Way, and/or The Saints Way, and/or Lundy Island, and/or the Isles of Scilly along with the 630 miles. I know that I will definitely bring a bathing suit with me next time. Maybe I will get up early in the morning at times to start my walks with the sun rising. I know that I will need to find a new pair (or two) of purple shoes to go along with maybe a new pair of hiking boots and my flip flops. However, I probably would not bring Punxsutawney Phil along next time.

Maybe I could even stay in the "expensive-places-to-stay-someday-along-the-SWCP" list, especially if this book makes me my millions of dollars. Maybe I could incorporate a book signing tour, or promoting a movie, as I walk again. Alternatively, I could stay in budget places like hostels and less expensive B&Bs. Maybe I could stay with old friends and new friends and others who love the SWCP who would kindly offer me a place to stay. Perhaps I would stay in some of my favorite B&Bs again. Or a combination of all of these options. Maybe I could even rent a beach hut for a day, anywhere along the SWCP.

I do know that when I go back to the South West Coast Path, I will walk just for the sake of walking. I will take fewer notes, less pictures, not bring a laptop, and not plan on writing another book. I will just walk and appreciate the South West Coast Path and all that it has to offer. I will walk the path to experience life at a walking pace once more. To once again respect the power of nature, the weather, and the seas. To have more time to hear the crashing waves, and to see the hillsides and headlands and farmland and coves and bays, and to witness each unique mile of an amazing scenery that changes with every mile. To have more time to take walks on long and short beaches, to walk barefoot in the sand, to paddle in the water, and to go for a dip or swim. To have another opportunity to visit beaches that I did not go to before. To have hours to sit on the many beaches that would be my ultimate location for a beach hut, from all those I discovered during the summer last year, to the new places I discovered this spring. To have more time to meditate and contemplate, and to truly value the gift of my left life. And to once again accept what happens with gratefulness, grace, bravery, courage, and strength. Because life certainly does have an amazing way of working itself out.

And don't forget though that in 2020 there would be an additional 2,165 miles I could walk since they are planning on opening up the entire coast of England on the 2,795-mile England Coast Path…

In any case, no matter when and what form I return to the South West Coast Path, as long as it is beside the seaside and I follow the arrow closest to the acorn…

Besides, I have a craving for some more delicious cream tea…

List of Lighthouses/Aids to Navigation along the South West Coast Path

This list includes traditional lighthouses, harbour lights, daymarks, beacons, obelisks, castles, ruins, church towers, chapels, and even a cross and a Huer's Hut, whether currently in use or not, all of which had or continue to serve the extremely important purpose of guiding ships and the people on those ships, along the seas and oceans and waters, in safety. (Note that I tried to keep as an accurate list as I could, but I may have missed a few here and there. I list the name of the structure, its approximate location, and the date that I saw or visited it. Note that a few of these I actually did not see. Finally note that the June, July, and August dates I saw in 2017, and the March and April dates were in 2018, so that I could keep this list in order of walking from Minehead to South Haven Point.) Finally, note that those marked with an asterisk are those currently maintained by Trinity House UK and information about them can be found on their website, trinityhouse.co.uk.

1. Foreland Lighthouse, Lynmouth, June 7*
2. The Little Chapel on the Hill, Ilfracombe, June 10
3. Bull Point Lighthouse, Woolacombe, June 11*
4. Braunton Lighthouse Ruins, Braunton/Saunton Sands, June 13
5. Crow Point Lighthouse, Braunton/Broadsands Beach, March 28
6. Hartland Point Lighthouse, Hartland Quay, June 19*
7. Daymark at Stepper Point, Padstow, June 28
8. Trevose Head Lighthouse, Trevone, June 29 and April 3*
9. St. Eval Church Tower, Mawgan Porth, June 30
10. Huer's Hut, Newquay, April 4
11. Godrevy Lighthouse, Godrevy, July 3*
12. Two Harbour Lights, St. Ives, July 6
13. Pendeen Lighthouse, Pendeen, July 7*
14. Longships LH (seen) and Wolf Rock LH (not seen), Land's End, July 8*
15. Tater Du Lighthouse, Lamorna Cove, July 9*
16. Harbour Light, Newlyn, July 10
17. Harbour Light, Penzance, July 10
18. Lizard Lighthouse, The Lizard, July 13*
19. St. Anthony Lighthouse, Falmouth, July 17*
20. Dodman Cross, Gorran Haven, April 11
21. Harbour Light, Mevagissey, July 21
22. Gribbin Daymark, Fowey, July 23
23. Fowey Lighthouse, Fowey, April 12
24. St. Savior's Chapel, Polruan, April 13
25. Polperro Miniature Lighthouse, Polperro, July 25
26. Harbour Light, Looe, July 25
27. Smeaton's Tower (Eddystone), Plymouth, July 28
28. Breakwater Lighthouse, Plymouth, July 30
29. Wembury Church Tower, Wembury, July 30
30. Start Point Lighthouse, Hallsands, August 4 and April 23*
31. St. Peter's Church Tower, Stoke Fleming, August 5
32. Castle Tea Room, Dartmouth Castle, Dartmouth, August 6
33. Berry Head Lighthouse, Brixham, August 8*
34. Breakwater Light, Brixham, August 8
35. Teignmouth Harbour Lighthouse, Teignmouth, August 12
36. St. Catherine's Chapel, Abbotsbury, August 20
37. The First Lighthouse/Old Higher Lighthouse, Isle of Portland, August 21
38. Portland Bill Lighthouse, Isle of Portland, August 21 and August 22*
39. Trinity House Obelisk, Isle of Portland, August 21
40. The Second Lighthouse/Old Lower Lighthouse, Isle of Portland, August 22
41. Anvil Point Lighthouse, Swanage, August 27*

List of Disclaimers

Note that these are already located throughout the book, but I just wanted to put them into a comprehensive list. I hope I have included them all.

Cows: My disclaimer to you is that please do your own research about walking near cows, because I take no responsibility for your encounters with cows. June 11.

Accommodations and Restaurants/Cafés/Pubs/Tea Rooms: My disclaimer here is that anytime I mention an accommodation by its name, or the proprietors of the accommodation by their names, none of them asked me to mention them. None of them gave me any compensation or any special discounts or anything complimentary or asked me to advertise or anything. I decided to choose which people and what accommodations to include entirely on my own choosing. Although, I did get their permission to use their first names when I decided to include those, or once in a while I changed a name. If I mention the specific name of the accommodation, again it is on my own choosing. This also rings true for any restaurants/cafés/pubs/tea rooms I mention in this book. None of these gave me any compensation or any special discount, nor did they give me anything complimentary to eat in order to mention them, nor did they ask me to advertise them, and I have decided to mention them on my own choosing. June 12.

Blisters: My disclaimer here is that I am not giving any advice about blisters, and if you try any of my theories or actions or advice on anything I have done, I hold no responsibility whatsoever. June 26.

112 or 999 as emergency numbers, etc: My disclaimer here is that I hope this information is accurate, but do not rely upon this only. Please do your own research on this, and I hold no responsibility for anything related to this. July 15.

Arrow Closest To The Acorn: My disclaimer here: I have no responsibility whatsoever if you get lost or turned around or off the path or anything following any of this advice. July 24.

Tides at Lulworth Cove, or for that matter, tides anywhere: My disclaimer here, please check tide tables and make your own knowledgeable decision to walk around the cove (or any beach or anywhere). It is quite possible that since there is the alternate route, that at certain high tides it is not possible to walk around the cove (or any beach or anywhere). May 6.

One Final Disclaimer: I would like to add one final disclaimer at this point in addition to the others I mentioned scattered throughout the book. This book is not a guidebook or booklet, not a suggested itinerary, and not anything official when it comes to things like cows, adders, ticks, blisters, emergency numbers, directions, tides, and information, and all other things I mentioned. I am not responsible for anything, including but not limited to, your safety, getting lost, weather, etc. Nor is this a history book, and I hope all the information from other websites and books is correct. I am also not liable for any personal injury or loss of any kind suffered as a result of reading this book. In the Meantime.

Finally, An Important Note and Acknowledgement: Throughout this book, I quoted some factual information about various things, like about places and history, from the SWCP Association booklets, "Exploring the South West Coast Path: 71 Booklets." I didn't mention exactly which booklet number the quotes were from, and occasionally, instead of saying, "according to the booklet," each time I quote them, please note that when I did not reference any other source for my quotes, the quotes came from these very invaluable booklets. Therefore I thank very much the South West Coast Path Association, and Dave Westcott, the writer of all the booklets, for their use of me quoting from the booklets! June 6.

Bibliography of Books

Mostly in proper bibliographical form, but not in alphabetical order. I believe that most books can be purchased either through the SWCP Association, National Trails UK, an author's website, or on booksellers' websites. I hope I have included them all.

Westcott, Dave and South West Coast Path Association. *Exploring The South West Coast Path: 71 Booklets.* 2015 - 2016.

South West Coast Path Association. *The Complete Guide to the South West Coast Path.* The South West Coast Path Association and Deltor Communications LTD, 2018.

Tarr, Roland. *South West Coast Path: Minehead to Padstow.* London, England: Aurum Press, LTD, 2016. Official National Trail Guide.

Macadam, John. *South West Coast Path: Padstow to Falmouth.* London, England: Aurum Press, LTD, 2013. Official National Trail Guide.

Le Messurier, Brian. *South West Coast Path: Falmouth to Exmouth.* London, England: Aurum Press, LTD, 2015. Official National Trail Guide.

Tarr, Roland. *South West Coast Path: Exmouth to Poole.* London, England: Aurum Press, LTD, 2016. Official National Trail Guide.

Harding, Sasha. *A Brush with the Coast: An artist's search for inspiration along the South West Coast Path.* Great Britain: Sasha Harding and Booths Print, 2015. sashaharding.co.uk.

Harding, Sasha. *A Brush with Anglesey: An artist's continued search for inspiration along Britain's coastline.* Great Britain: Sasha Harding and Booths Print, 2016.

Harding, Sasha. *Plop!* Great Britain: Sasha Harding and Booths Print, 2017.

Wallington, Mark. *500 Mile Walkies.* London, England: Arrow Books Limited, 1986 and 1987.

Watts, Overend. *The Man Who Hated Walking: The South West Coast Path.* Bedford, England: Wymer Pub., 2013.

Haughton, John. *Follow the Acorn: A Very Unofficial Guide to the South West Coast Path: Minehead to Poole.* John Haughton and Publish Nation, 2017.

Livingston, Ruth. *Walking the English Coast: A Beginner's Guide.* Ruth Livingstone and I_AM Self-Publishing, 2016. coastalwalker.co.uk.

Krasner, Helen. *Midges, Maps & Muesli: An Account of a 5,000 Mile Walk Round the Coast of Britain.* Kniveton, England: Garth Publications, 1998 and 2007.

Bunney, Sue. *Love on the Beach.* Great Britain: Pen Press, 2013.

Bunney, Sue. *My Cornish Life.* Sue Bunney, 2015.

Barber, Antonia (Text) and Bayley, Nicola (Illustrations). *The Mousehole Cat.* London, England: Walker Books, LTD, 1990.

Lonely Planet Guidebook. *Walking in Britain: 52 Great Walks.* Multiple authors. Lonely Planet Publications, 2007.

Barrow, Carlotta. *Durlston Bay: And Other Poems from the Jurassic Coast.* Waterside Studio, Swanage.

Tickell, Cripsin. *Mary Anning of Lyme Regis.* Lyme Regis Philpot Museum, 1998.

Garner, Lawrence. *Dry Stone Walls.* Shire Publications Ltd, 1984.

South West Way Association. *The South West Way: A Complete Guide to the Coastal Path: 1982.*

Hunter, W.V. *Cornwall's Coastal Footpath.* Truro, England: Tor Mark Guides/Tor Mark Press.

By me, Jagerman-Dungan, Debby Lee. Windows and Doors Publishing. (Available on Amazon):
- Windows and Doors of the Cotswolds: A Collection of Photographs of the Quintessential Colorful Flowers and Honey-Colored Cotswold Stone in the Land of Market Towns, Wool Churches, and Sheep Hills in England's Countryside.
- Windows and Doors of the Camino de Santiago: A Collection of Photographs from the 775-Kilometer Camino Francés Pilgrimage across Northern Spain-including a few from the Camino Finisterre to Muxía.
- The Porches of Île d'Orléans: Seeing the Island through its Windows and Doors while Walking Chemin Royal.
- To Open and Unlock: A Collection of Photographs of Windows and Doors from Ten Countries.
- Windows of Porvoo: (And a Few Doors).
- Windows and Doors of the Lighthouses of the "Great Lakes Lighthouse Festival": Including Towers, Keepers' Quarters, Fresnel Lenses, Spiral Staircases, Reflections, and Views from 14 Lighthouses in Northeastern Michigan.

Websites of Important Organizations

Not in proper bibliographical form, nor in any particular order. I hope I have included them all.

South West Coast Path Association: southwestcoastpath.org.uk
National Trails UK: nationaltrail.co.uk
Luggage Transfers, LTD: luggagetransfers.co.uk
National Trust: nationaltrust.org.uk
Trinity House UK: trinityhouse.co.uk
Natural England: gov.uk/government/organisations/natural-england
Areas of Outstanding Natural Beauty: gov.uk/guidance/areas-of-outstanding-natural-beauty-aonbs-designation-and-management
RSPB, The Royal Society for the Protection of Birds: rspb.org.uk
Royal National Lifeboat Institution: rnli.org
National Coastwatch Institution: nci.org.uk
HM Coastguard and Maritime and Coastguard Agency: gov.uk/government/organisations/maritime-and-coastguard-agency
SWCP Facebook Group Pages: (1) South West Coast Path (England, UK). Minehead to Poole 630 miles. (2) South West Coast Path.

My "Expensive-Places-to-Stay-Someday-Along-The-SWCP" List

Lighthouse Keepers' Cottages/Holiday Cottages at:
- Foreland Lighthouse (June 7)
- Bull Point Lighthouse (June 11)
- Trevose Head Lighthouse (June 29 and April 3)
- Pendeen Lighthouse (July 7)
- Lizard Lighthouse (July 13)
- St. Anthony Lighthouse (July 17)
- Start Point Lighthouse (August 4 and April 23)
- Anvil Point Lighthouse (August 27)

Information on the above can be found at: trinityhouse.co.uk/lighthouse-cottages

A couple of lighthouses themselves on the Isle of Portland, "The First/Old Higher Lighthouse" and "The Second/Old Lower Lighthouse" (August 21 and 22)

Clavell Tower (August 26)
The House on the Island aka The House in the Sea, Towan Island, Newquay (April 4)
Carswell Farm/Cove Boathouse/Beach Hut – My ultimate location for a beach hut, near Mothecombe (April 20)
Large white house (former coastguard cottages) at Man Sands near Brixham (April 25)

List of Old Guidebooks, Six Paintings, and Old Postcards from "Memories of the SWCP" Photos, page 365

Top Row: "The South West Way" old guidebook; Step-mom's painting of beach of Ringstead Bay; "Cornwall's Coastal Footpath" old guidebook.

Second Row: St. Brannock's Church in Braunton, small artistic print, June 13(not to scale); Two "sea scape" church and lighthouse scenes bought from café/bric-a-brac store in Osmington Mills, August 23.

Third Row: Two paintings from bric-a-brac sale bought in Shaldon of lighthouse and sailboat/river entrance scenes, August 12.

Fourth and Fifth Rows of Old Postcards bought in Weymouth, May 4: Boscastle from the Harbour; Church Cove; The Lizard Lighthouse; Asparagus Island, Kynance Cove; Summer Evening, Mullion Cove, South Cornwall; Early Morning St. Ives. (I have similar photos of all these scenes in my "Harbours, etc.," "Beaches and Coves," and "Lighthouses" sections of my photos.)

"……Oh! I do like to be beside the seaside!……"